MICROECONOMIC THEORY

A SYNTHESIS OF CLASSICAL THEORY AND THE MODERN APPROACH

William Sher

Associate Professor
Department of Economics
Duquesne University

Rudy Pinola

Director
Research and Statistical Services Office
Minnesota Department of Economic Security

NORTH HOLLAND
New York • Oxford

Elsevier North Holland, Inc.
52 Vanderbilt Avenue, New York, New York 10017

Distributors outside the United States and Canada:

Edward Arnold (Publishers), Ltd.
41 Bedford Square, London WC1B 3DQ, England

Library of Congress Cataloging In Publication Data

Sher, William T
    Microeconomic theory: a synthesis of classical theory and the modern approach.

    Bibliography: p.
    Includes index.
    1. Microeconomic. I. Pinola, Rudolph, 1922-   II. Title.
HB172. S53   338.5'01   80-25292
ISBN 0-444-00370-3

Copy Editor   Barry Levine
Desk Editor   John Haber
Design   Edmée Froment
Art Editor   Virginia Kudlak
Art rendered by Vantage Art, Inc.
Cover Design   Paul Agule Design
Production Manager   Joanne Jay
Compositor   Maryland Composition
Printer   Haddon Craftsmen

CONTENTS

Preface   xv

Acknowledgments   xvii

INTRODUCTION   1

    Science and Magic   1
    Usefulness of Scientific Knowledge   3
    Sciences, Social Sciences, Economics, Microeconomics, and Macroeconomics   6
    Theory and Reality   9
    The Methodology of Microeconomics   11
    Relevance of Microeconomics   13
    An Overview of the Book   14

THE THEORY OF THE FIRM: THE ECONOMICS OF PRODUCTION AND COST   21

    Introduction   21
    A Note on Production Theory   24

PRODUCTION WITH ONE VARIABLE INPUT   28

    Introduction   28
    1.1 The Production Function, Schedule, and Curve   29
        1.1.1 The Production Schedule   30
        1.1.2 Average and Marginal Products   30
        1.1.3 The Relationship Between AP and MP   31
        1.1.4 The Law of Diminishing Returns and the Law of Variable Proportions   32
    1.2 The Production Curve   33
        1.2.1 Total Product Curve   33
        1.2.2 The AP and MP Curves   34
    1.3 Graphical Analysis of the Product Curves   35
        1.3.1 The Geometrical Relationship Between TP, AP, and MP   35
        1.3.2 Stages of Production, and Intensive and Extensive Margins   38
    1.4 Production in the Real World: Constant AP and MP   40
    Summary   43

2 PRODUCTION WITH TWO VARIABLE INPUTS: OPTIMAL INPUT COMBINATION AND EFFICIENCY — 45

Introduction — 45
2.1 Production Processes — 46
2.2 Returns to Scale and the Law of Variable Proportions — 48
2.3 Efficient and Inefficient Processes — 50
2.4 Isoquants — 55
2.5 Substitution Between Inputs — 58
    2.5.1 The Marginal Rate of Technical Substitution — 58
    2.5.2 The Decreasing MRTS — 60
2.6 Technical and Economic Efficiency — 63
2.7 Economic Region and Stages of Production — 63
2.8 Returns to Scale and Isoquant Maps — 65
2.9 The AP of the Variable and Fixed Input — 66
2.10 Optimal Combination of Inputs — 67
    2.10.1 Isocost and Input Prices — 68
    2.10.2 Optimal Combination of Inputs for a Given Cost — 71
    2.10.3 Optimal Combination of Inputs for a Given Output — 74
    2.10.4 Limited Number of Processes and the General Case — 76
    2.10.5 The Failure of Tangency and the Corner Solution — 78
2.11 An Increase in Scale and the Expansion Path — 80
2.12 Input Substitution, Price Changes, and Elasticity of Substitution — 82
2.13 Homogeneous and Homothetic Production Functions — 89
Summary — 91
Exercises and Questions for Chapters 1 and 2 on Production Theory — 93

APPENDIX TO CHAPTERS 1 AND 2: A MATHEMATICAL NOTE ON THE THEORY OF PRODUCTION — 95

A1-2.1 Production Function, AP, and MP — 95
A1-2.2 The MRTS, Homotheticity, and Homogeneity — 98
A1-2.3 Diminishing Returns and Returns to Scale — 99
A1-2.4 The Cost Equation, Optimality in Production, and Cramer's Rule — 100
    A1-2.4.1 The Case of the Cobb–Douglas Production Function — 101
        Maximun Output for a Given Cost 101
        Minimum Cost for a Given Output 106
    A1-2.4.2 A General Production Function with Two Inputs — 107
        Maximun Output for a Given Cost 107
        Minimum Cost for a Given Output 109
    A1-2.4.3 The General Case with n Inputs — 111
A1-2.5 The Effect of a Change of Input Price on the Optimal Quantity of Input — 113
A1-2.6 Elasticity of Substitution — 117
A1-2.7 Linear Production Functions, Activities, and Processes — 119

3 THE THEORY OF COST — 122

3.1 Basic Concepts — 122
    Private and Social Costs 122
    Alternative (Opportunity) Cost 123
    Explicit and Implicit Costs 124
    The Concept of Cost in Business and in Economics 124
    The Minimum-Cost Combination as a True Measure of Cost 125
    The Short Run Versus the Long Run 125
    The Cost Function of a Firm 126
3.2 Short-Run Cost Functions — 126
    3.2.1 Total Cost — 126
    3.2.2 Average and Marginal Costs — 129

Contents

3.2.3 The Geometry of Short-Run Cost Curves 134
3.2.4 Cost Curves in Reality: Constant AVC and MC Curves 138
    The Break-Even Chart 140
    Constant AVC for a Given Capacity 141
3.2.5 The Shape of the MC and AC Curves, the Law of Diminishing Returns, and the Law
    of Variable Proportions 143
3.3 The Long-Run Cost Function and the Expansion Path 143
   3.3.1 The Isoquant Map and the Long- and Short-Run TC and AC Curves 144
   3.3.2 Long-Run and Short-Run MC Curves 151
   3.3.3 The Shapes of Long-Run Cost Curves in Theory and in Reality 153
   3.3.4 The Shapes of Long-Run Cost Curves and Returns to Scale 153
3.4 Constant AVC and Long-Run Cost Curves 155
   Summary 162
   Exercises and Questions for Chapter 3 on the Theory of Cost 163

APPENDIX TO CHAPTER 3: A MATHEMATICAL NOTE ON THE THEORY OF COST **165**

A3.1 The Derivation of Short-Run and Long-Run Cost Functions 166
   A3.1.1 The Simple Case of Two Variable Inputs and One Fixed Input 166
     Derivation of a Short-Run Cost Function from the Cobb–Douglas Production Function 168
     Derivation of a Long-Run Cost Function from the Cobb–Douglas Production Function 169
   A3.1.2 AC and MC 171
     Short-Run AC and MC 171
     Long-Run AC and MC 173
   A3.1.3 The Relationship Between AC and MC 174
   A3.1.4 The Derivation of Short-Run and Long-Run Cost Functions in the General Case
     of n Inputs 175
A3.2 The Case of Constant Short-Run AVC and MC 176
A3.3 Constant AVC with Limited Capacity 178

THE THEORY OF CONSUMER BEHAVIOR AND DEMAND **183**

THE THEORY OF CONSUMER BEHAVIOR **185**
4.1 Consumer Preference and the Utility Function 185
4.2 Cardinal Utility and the Law of Diminishing Marginal Utility 186
4.3 The Ordinal Utility Function, Indifference Curves, Indifference Map, Point of Bliss,
   and Marginal Rate of Substitution 188
   4.3.1 Marginal Rate of Substitution 197
4.4 Consumer Income and Input Prices, the Budget Equation, and the Budget Constraint 202
4.5 Changing Income, Commodity Prices, and a Shift of the Budget Constraint 203
4.6 Maximizing Utility Subject to the Budget Constraint: Consumer Equilibrium 204
4.7 Changes in Income, the Definition of Normal and Inferior Goods, and the Income
   Consumption and Engel Curves 209
4.8 Changes in Price, the Price Consumption Curve, and the Derivation
   of a Demand Curve 214
4.9 Substitution and Income Effects, the Slutsky Equation, and Giffen Goods 216
4.10 The Analogy Between Consumption and Production Theories 222
4.11 The Characteristic Approach and the Introduction of New Commodities 226
   Summary 229
   Exercises and Questions for Chapter 4 on the Theory of Consumer Behavior 230

APPENDIX TO CHAPTER 4: A MATHEMATICAL NOTE ON CONSUMER BEHAVIOR **233**
A4.1 The Nature of the Ordinal Utility Function 233
A4.2 The Marginal Rate of Substitution 235

A4.3 Constrained Utility Maximization and the Demand Function   235
A4.4 The Derivation of a Specific Demand Function   237
A4.5 Properties of a Demand Function Derived from a General Utility Function,
        the Slutsky Equation, and Demand Law   239
A4.6 Substitutes and Complements   243
A4.7 The Characteristic Approach to Consumer Theory   245

5 THE THEORY OF DEMAND   **248**

        Introduction   248
5.1   The Market Demand for a Commodity   249
5.2   Elasticities of Demand: Price, Income, and Cross Elasticities   253
5.3   Graphical Measurement of the Price Elasticity of Demand   260
5.4   Determinants of Elasticities   262
5.5   A Class of Constant-Elasticity Demand Curves   263
5.6   Demand and Revenue Behavior: TR, AR, and MR   265
5.7   Graphical Derivation of the MR Curve   269
5.8   MR and Price Elasticity of Demand   271
5.9   The Demand Curve for a Competitive Firm: The Equality of Price and MR   272
5.10 Low Price and High Profit: An Example   273
5.11 Demand in Economic Theory and in Practice   275
        Summary   277
        Exercises and Questions for Chapter 5 on Demand Theory   278

APPENDIX TO CHAPTER 5: A MATHEMATICAL NOTE ON DEMAND   **279**
A5.1 Elasticities of Demand   280
A5.2 The Class of Constant-Elasticity Demand Functions   282
A5.3 Price Elasticity for a Linear Demand Function   283
A5.4 Revenue, Demand, and Price Elasticity of Demand   284

III THE THEORY OF PRICE AND MARKET ORGANIZATION   **287**
        Price Takers   290
        Price Makers   291

6 PRICE DETERMINATION AND THE SUPPLY FUNCTION UNDER
        PERFECT COMPETITION   **293**

        Introduction   293
6.1 Perfect Competition Defined   294
6.2 Time as a Conditional   296
        6.2.1 Definition of Market Period, Short Run, and Long Run   296
        6.2.2 The Industry Supply Curve in the Market Period   297
6.3 Short-Run Analysis of a Typical Firm and the Market   298
        6.3.1 Profit Maximization: The Total Revenue–Total Cost Approach   299
        6.3.2 Profit Maximization: The Marginal Approach   302
        6.3.3 Proof of the Profit-Maximization Conditions   304
        6.3.4 Short-Run Equilibrium and the Supply of the Firm, Break-Even and Shutdown Points 307
        6.3.5 The Short-Run Supply of an Industry   310
        6.3.6 Short-Run Market Equilibrium and the Determination of Market Price   311
        6.3.7 The Existence, Uniqueness, and Stability of Market Equilibrium   313
                Existence 313
                Uniqueness 315
                Stability 316

6.4 Long-Run Analysis of a Typical Firm and Industry   319
    6.4.1 Long-Run Equilibrium of a Typical Firm and Industry   319
    6.4.2 The Long-Run Supply Curve of an Industry—Constant-Cost, Increasing Cost,
          and Decreasing-Cost Industries   323
6.5 Increasing Returns to Scale, Decreasing Long-Run AC, and the Breakdown
    of Perfect Competition   330
6.6 The Break-Even Chart and Perfect Competition   332
    Summary   335
    Exercises and Questions for Chapter 6 on Perfect Competition   336

APPENDIX TO CHAPTER 6: A MATHEMATICAL NOTE ON THE PERFECTLY
COMPETITIVE MARKET   **338**

A6.1 The Short-Run Supply Function of the Firm and Industry   338
A6.2 The Equilibrium of a Perfectly Competitive Market   341
    A6.2.1 The Short-Run Equilibrium of a Perfectly Competitive Market   341
    A6.2.2 The Long-Run Equilibrium of a Perfectly Competitive Market   343
A6.3 The Existence, Uniqueness, and Stability of Market Equilibrium   345
    A6.3.1 The Condition of Existence of Equilibrium   345
    A6.3.2 The Condition of Uniqueness of Equilibrium   345
    A6.3.3 The Condition of Stability of Equilibrium   346
A6.4 The Break-Even Chart and Maximum Profit   348

7 MONOPOLY THEORY AND MARK-UP PRICING   **351**

7.1 Monopoly Theory   351
    7.1.1 Pure Monopoly—An Economic Model   351
    7.1.2 Demand Under Monopoly   353
    7.1.3 Cost of the Monopolist   355
    7.1.4 The Short-Run Equilibrium of a Monopoly   355
        The Total Revenue–Total Cost Approach   355
        The Marginal Revenue–Marginal Cost Approach   357
        Necessary and Sufficient Conditions for Maximum Profit   358
        Profit or Loss in the Short Run   360
    7.1.5 Supply Under Monopoly in the Short Run   361
    7.1.6 Long-Run Equilibrium of a Monopoly   363
    7.1.7 Price Discrimination   366
    7.1.8 Natural Monopoly and Public Regulation   368
7.2 Pricing Models Actually Used by Price Makers—Mark-Up Pricing   371
    7.2.1 A Naive Mark-Up Pricing Model   372
    7.2.2 Average-Cost Mark-Up Pricing   376
        The Pricing Process   377
    7.2.3 Target Profit Pricing   380
    7.2.4 A Comparison of the Three Mark-Up Pricing Models   383
        An Explanatory Comment on the Mark-Up Pricing Models   385
7.3 A Synthesis: Theoretical Equivalence of Mark-Up Pricing Methods and the Monopoly
    Model in Economics   387
    Summary   395
    Exercises and Questions for Chapter 7 on Monopoly Theory and Mark-Up Pricing   397

APPENDIX TO CHAPTER 7: A MATHEMATICAL NOTE ON MONOPOLY THEORY
AND MARK-UP PRICING   **400**

A7.1 The Demand and Revenue Functions of a Monopoly   400
A7.2 Conditions of Maximum Profit   402
A7.3 The Relationship Between MR and e: Its Usefulness and Possible Misunderstanding 409
A7.4 Price Discrimination   410
A7.5 Ceiling Price and Discontinuity of the MR Function of a Monopoly   412
A7.6 Mark-Up Pricing Models   413

A7.7 The Monopoly Model in Economic Theory   415
A7.8 Mathematical Proof of the Theoretical Equivalence Between Mark-Up Pricing
      Models and the Traditional Monopoly Model of Economic Theory   417

8 MONOPOLISTIC COMPETITION   **421**

       Introduction   421
8.1   Assumptions   422
8.2   The Two Demand Curves Facing a Firm Under Monopolistic Competition   424
8.3   Advertising and Quality Variation   427
8.4   The Equilibrium of a Firm in the Short Run Under Price Competition   427
8.5   Constant AVC, Mark-Up Pricing, and Short-Run Equilibrium   432
       8.5.1 Constant AVC and Short-Run Equilibrium   432
       8.5.2 Mark-Up Pricing and Monopolistic Competition   434
8.6   Long-Run Equilibrium of a Firm Under Monopolistic Competition   435
8.7   Increasing Returns to Scale and Long-Run Equilibrium Under
       Monopolistic Competition   438
8.8   Product Differentiation and Long-Run Equilibrium of the Firm   438
8.9   Advertising and Other Sales Expenses   445
8.10   Graphical Presentation and the Simultaneous Solution for Price, Quality,
       and Advertising   446
8.11   Comparison with Perfect Competition and Pure Monopoly   447
       Summary   450
       Exercises and Questions for Chapter 8 on Monopolistic Competition   451

       APPENDIX TO CHAPTER 8: A MATHEMATICAL NOTE ON
       MONOPOLISTIC COMPETITION   **453**
A8.1   The Two Demand Functions for a Firm Under Monopolistic Competition   454
A8.2   Short-Run and Long-Run Equilibrium of the Firm and Market   458
       A8.2.1 Short-Run Equilibrium   458
       A8.2.2 Long-Run Equilibrium   459
A8.3   Quality, Advertising, and Sales Competition   460

9 OLIGOPOLY THEORY   **463**

       Introduction   463
9.1   Assumptions   464
9.2   Duopoly: A Special Case of Oligopoly   466
       9.2.1 The Cournot Model   467
       9.2.2 The Chamberlin Model   470
       9.2.3 The Edgeworth Model   472
9.3   A Few Well-Known Oligopoly Models   476
       9.3.1 The Kinked Demand Curve and Stability of Oligopoly Price   476
       9.3.2 Price Leadership   478
              Dominant Firm Price Leadership   479
              Low-Cost Firm Price Leadership   480
       9.3.3 Cartels and Collusion   481
9.4   Game Theory and Oligopoly Theory   483
       9.4.1 Zero- and Constant-Sum Games: The Maximin–Minimax Principle   483
              The Maximin–Minimax Principle   485
              The Distinction Between Zero-Sum and Constant-Sum Games   487
       9.4.2 The Prisoner's Dilemma and Economic Behavior   488
       9.4.3 Limitations of Game Theory with Respect to Oligopoly   492
       Summary   493
       Exercises and Questions for Chapter 9 on Oligopoly Theory   494

Contents

APPENDIX TO CHAPTER 9: A MATHEMATICAL NOTE ON OLIGOPOLY THEORY **496**
A9.1 Duopoly Models 496
    A9.1.1 The Cournot Model 496
    A9.1.2 The Chamberlin Model 498
    A9.1.3 The Difficulties in Price Competition 500
    A9.1.4 The Stackelberg Leadership–Followership Model 501
A9.2 Elementary Game Theory 503

IV INCOME DISTRIBUTION THEORY AND THE PRICING OF FACTORS OF PRODUCTION

511

10 MARGINAL PRODUCTIVITY THEORY AND THE DEMAND FOR FACTORS OF PRODUCTION

513
    Introduction 513
10.1 Profit Maximization and the Derived Demand for One Variable Productive Factor Under Perfectly Competitive Markets 513
10.2 The Demand for Several Variable Inputs Under Perfectly Competitive Markets 520
10.3 The Demand for One Variable Input Under Imperfect Competition in the Product Market 522
10.4 The Demand for Two or More Variable Inputs Under Imperfect Competition in the Product Market 526
10.5 The Market Demand for Factors of Production 528
10.6 Determinants of Demand for a Productive Factor 530
    10.6.1 Determinants of the Elasticity of Demand for an Input 530
    10.6.2 Determinants of the Location of the Demand Curve for a Productive Factor 532
    Summary 534
    Exercises and Questions for Chapter 10 on the Demand for Factors of Production 535

APPENDIX TO CHAPTER 10: A MATHEMATICAL NOTE ON FACTOR DEMAND **538**
A10.1 The Demand Function of Productive Factors under a Perfectly Competitive Product Market 538
    A10.1.1 The Demand Function of Productive Factors in the One-Variable-Input Case, Including the Special Case of the Cobb–Douglas Production Function 538
    A10.1.2 The Demand Function of Productive Factors in the n-Variable-Input Case, Including the Special Case of the Cobb–Douglas Production Function for Two Inputs 541
A10.2 The Demand Function of Productive Factors Under an Imperfect Product Market, Including the Special Case of a Constant Elasticity of Demand Function and the Cobb–Douglas Production Function 544

11 FACTOR SUPPLY AND FACTOR PRICES

547
    Introduction 547
11.1 The Supply of Labor of an Individual Worker: An Application of Utility Analysis 548
11.2 The Market Supply of Labor and the Determination of the Market Wage Rate Under Perfect Competition 557
11.3 Monopsony and Market Wage Rate 560
11.4 Labor Unions, Collective Bargaining, and Bilateral Monopoly 563
11.5 The Fixed Supply of and Rent on Land 565
11.6 Economic Rent and Quasi-Rent 568

11.7 The Price (Cost) of Captial: A Controversy   570
11.8 Interest as the Cost of Capital Under the Condition of Certainty   572
11.9 Imperfect Capital Markets and Informal Capital Rationing
        by Financial Institutions   574
11.10 Federal Monetary Policy and the Determination of the Market Rate of Interest   575
        Summary   579
        Exercises and Questions for Chapter 11 on Factor Supply and Factor Prices   580

APPENDIX TO CHAPTER 11: A MATHEMATICAL NOTE ON FACTOR SUPPLY
AND FACTOR PRICES   **582**
A11.1 The Supply of Labor   582
A11.2 The Determination of Factor Price (Wage Rate) Under Conditions of Monopoly
         and Monopsony   584
A11.3 Compound Interest and Discounted Present Value of Future Income   588

V GENERAL EQUILIBRIUM AND WELFARE ECONOMICS   **595**

12 GENERAL EQUILIBRIUM IN PERFECTLY COMPETITIVE MARKETS   **597**
        Introduction   597
12.1 Pure Exchange: The Two-Person–Two-Commodity Case; Contract
        and Offer Curves   598
12.2 General Equilibrium in Production: The Two-Input–Two Output Model   609
12.3 The Production Possibility (Transformation) Curve   615
12.4 The Equality of MRPT and MRS: The Condition for General Equilibrium   618
12.5 A Simple Leon Walras General Equilibrium Model of Counting Equations
        and Variables   623
12.6 Input–Output Analysis as a General Equilibrium System   628
12.7 The Iterative Method and the Inverse of the Leontief Matrix   631
        Summary   637
        Exercises and Questions for Chapter 12 on General Equilibrium Analysis   638

APPENDIX TO CHAPTER 12: A MATHEMATICAL NOTE ON GENERAL
EQUILIBRIUM THEORY   **640**
A12.1 The Walras General Equilibrium Model   640
A12.2 The Input–Output Model   648
        A12.2.1 The Production Function, Input Coefficients, and the Technology Matrix   649
        A12.2.2 The Leontief Matrix and the Solution of the System   650

13 WELFARE ECONOMICS   **653**
        Introduction   653
13.1 Cardinal Utility, Ordinal Utility, Interpersonal Comparisons of Utility, and Social
        Economic Welfare   655
13.2 Pareto Superiority, Pareto Optimality, and the Unanimity Principle   658
13.3 Perfectly Competitive Equilibrium and Pareto Optimality   664
13.4 Market Imperfection, Marginal Cost Pricing, and the Theory of Second Best   672
        13.4.1 The Theory of Second Best   675
13.5 External Economies, External Diseconomies, and Public Goods   676
        13.5.1 Strong Externality and Public Goods   679
13.6 Modifications of the Unanimity Principle   681
        Summary   683
        Exercises and Questions for Chapter 13 on Welfare Economics   684

APPENDIX TO CHAPTER 13: A MATHEMATICAL NOTE ON WELFARE ECONOMICS   **686**

A13.1 The Contract Curve Is Pareto Optimal in Pure Exchange   686
A13.2 Pareto Optimality in Production   688
A13.3 Pareto Optimality in General: Production and Exchange   690
A13.4 Perfect Competition and Pareto Optimality   694

VI MICROECONOMICS AND ECONOMIC POLICY **699**

14 APPLICATION OF MICROECONOMIC THEORY TO PUBLIC POLICY ANALYSIS **701**

14.1 Macro- and Microeconomic Analysis of Monetary and Fiscal Policy   701
   14.1.1 Monetary Policy and Mark-Up Stagflation   701
     The Macroeconomic Approach to the Inflation–Unemployment Problem   701
     Monetary Policy and the Mark-Up Pricing Model   706
     Concluding Remarks on Monetary Policy and the Inflation–Unemployment Problem   714
   14.1.2 Fiscal Policy, Inflation, and Unemployment   715
14.2 The Shifting and Incidence of Selected Taxes   721
   14.2.1 The Shifting and Incidence of Sales Taxes Under Perfect and Imperfect Markets   722
   14.2.2 The Shifting and Incidence of the Personal Income Tax   730
   14.2.3 The Shifting and Incidence of the Corporate Income Tax and Mark-Up Pricing   735
   Summary   738
   Exercises and Questions for Chapter 14 on the Application of Microeconomic Theory to Public Policy Analysis   739

References   **741**
Index   **745**

PREFACE

Our purpose in writing this book was to provide students with a rigorous but readable treatment of microeconomic theory that combines the traditional and modern approaches. Rather than clutter up the text with either simplistic applications of theory to the myriad problems of our society or excursions into techniques of analysis that are best left to specialized courses (e.g., linear programming, decision theory, and risk analysis), we have striven to give students a systematic presentation of static microeconomic theory that is technically sound and complete. Although we have avoided the excesses of "window dressing," we have not ignored the relevance of theory to the real world. Thus, we have allocated a considerable amount of space to describing and analyzing the business practice of mark-up pricing and to establishing its equivalence to the traditional theory of monopoly and monopolistic pricing. We have also made extensive use of the empirically observed horizontal average and marginal cost curves in the relevant output range to bring theory into conformity with the real world. We have taken special care to cite the assumptions underlying the development of the various models of market behavior and to explain the relevance of these assumptions in evaluating the predictive power of the model. Finally, Chapter 14 shows how microeconomic theory can be applied to evaluating fiscal and monetary policy and the problems of inflation and unemployment.

Although we have written this book with the nonmathematically oriented student in mind, the extensive mathematical appendixes that appear at the ends of most chapters provide ample sophistication to warrant use of the text in advanced courses or wherever students have a good preparation in mathematics. Overall, the material covered in this text is suitable for use either at the upper undergraduate or first-year graduate level by those majoring in economics, business administration, or public administration. In schools where microeconomic theory is a full-year course, instructors will find that this book provides a good foundation on which to investigate policy issues and special problems in market behavior and performance. Our experience in teaching in Canadian and American schools has reinforced our belief in the value of a text that is complete in its coverage of the basic topics in microeconomics, thus allowing instructors to pick and choose the most relevant issues and problems for further discussion.

Although a rigorous and complete coverage of essential topics is imperative in any good text, they should be presented in a pedagogically sound manner. To facilitate student learning we had two objectives: to build successively on those concepts that are most familiar to students, and to make the text readable by using simple but technically accurate language. To ensure the former, we chose to begin our work with a simple but complete presentation of production theory because students are likely to find the cardinal number system and the concepts of inputs, outputs, and cost more familiar than the ordinal system and the concept of utility. Moreover, once students have progressed through production theory and the maximization of output subject to the constraint of cost, the maximization of utility subject to the constraint of income in consumer theory is easier to understand. Also, the sequence of materials in this book will enable students to develop a better comprehension of and appreciation for the derivation of cost and supply functions on the one hand, and demand and revenue functions on the other hand, before being exposed to the complexities of different market models and, ultimately, the discussion of welfare economics and policy questions.

In classroom use of our materials, we have found that simple but technically correct language allows students to grasp the concepts and theory quicker and better than if they were referred to other resource texts. We have also found that, given careful statements of all the relevant assumptions and complete and detailed explanations of concepts and theorems, students gain a better understanding of theory and its use than if exposed to terse statements or conclusions without adequate explanation. In addition, we have found that liberal use of numerical examples and graphic illustrations has significantly added to student comprehension. Hence, we have made a special effort to employ such examples and illustrations to help clarify important concepts and to prove the validity of basic theorems. Classroom experimentation at Duquesne University has not only reinforced our belief in this approach, but convinced us that students learn complex concepts more quickly and easily with this approach.

ACKNOWLEDGMENTS

It is customary and fitting to give credit to persons who have contributed to the development and preparation of a book or article. In our case, our professional debt extends to so many persons, both living and dead, that a recitation of names would likely be incomplete and inadequate with regard to their respective contributions. Certainly, former university professors, past and current colleagues, and former students have all influenced our thinking, but so too have the innumerable contributors to the economics literature whose brains we have all picked at one time or another. In this respect, we are grateful that as free persons we have had access to the myriad philosophies, opinions, and professional work of others.

On a more immediate basis, we express our appreciation to Kenneth Bowman, Michael Gnat, and John Haber of Elsevier North Holland, Inc., for their interest and assistance in our work. We are particularly grateful to Mr. Bowman for his confidence in the "rightness" of a book which sought to educate rather than entertain.

Finally, we wish to record our appreciation to our wives, Nancy Sher and Lois Pinola, without whose encouragement and understanding this book might not have been written.

SCIENCE AND MAGIC

It has been said that, in the prescientific era, there were two different approaches toward understanding natural phenomena—religion and magic. Although diametrically opposite each other in their approach, religion and magic had essentially the same goal: to unfold the ultimate truth about the universe.

In spite of their differing doctrinal views with regard to humankind's position in the overall scheme of things, all religions are based on a personal faith in the existence of a supreme being or force that guides the behavior of everything. Starting from a fundamental belief in a God or Gods, which need not be proven or justified except by faith, religion provides a cosmic conceptualization of natural phenomena. In such a system, the observation of given natural phenomena is equivalent to witnessing the workings of a supreme being, and the only difference between different religions and denominations lies in their interpretation of such phenomena as it relates to humans and their behavior. Hence, religion provides the basis for developing a set of moral codes and social norms to which humans must subscribe if they are to be in harmony with natural law (or, at least, to avoid the wrath of demons).

In the case of magic, a different approach to understanding natural phenomena developed. Magicians did not believe that everything was prearranged by an omnipotent being. Instead, they saw certain tendencies and relationships in natural phenomena, some of which could easily be observed and understood by everyone. However, since some natural phenomena, such as chemically induced reactions, are not commonly recognized and understood, they could be disguised as being caused by magic.

Religion, science, and magic have a common goal: to explain the occurrence of natural phenomena

Thus, magicians, by virtue of their presumed possession of occult powers, could induce the occurrence of natural phenomena that could not otherwise be "explained." In primitive cultures, this resulted in ceremonials and rituals to induce rain or to cure some malady, whereas in more advanced societies, it meant the ability to use acquired knowledge and talent to entertain audiences with one's mystical powers. Because of their faculty to deduce special relationships from a study of natural phenomena, magicians should receive more credit for scientific inquiry and reasoning than they have been accorded. In advancing their art they certainly can be said to have made discoveries concerning natural phenomena which merit the approval of the scientific community.

Although scientific inquiry and reasoning have a common origin with the spirit and practice of magic, there is a fundamental difference between magicians and scientists, just as between the various denominations within a particular religion. Magicians relied on their knowledge of rare phenomena to generate an aura of mysticism about their work in order to make a living. Thus, magicians did not spread the rare knowledge that they possessed, since secrecy was the key to maintaining its monetary value. On the other hand, modern society developed the entirely different approach of scientists making a living by spreading knowledge through research and teaching. The impetus for this approach was largely the result of public funding and private philanthropy. It is entirely possible that if the public had not supported a scientific research and education system, scientists might also have been forced to keep their understanding of natural phenomena a secret in order to make a living, thereby, limiting the spread of scientific knowledge. This probably would have delayed the industrial and technological development of the modern world by hundreds or even thousands of years.[1] One of the factors that accounts for the widespread difference between the industrialized and developing countries is that the scientific spirit took root years ago in the former, whereas it floundered in the latter. Many reasons have been cited for this uneven development, but none alone provides an entirely satisfactory answer.

---

[1] A good example of the benefits of public-sponsored research is provided by American agriculture. One need only consider the significant increases that have taken place over the past 50 years in agricultural productivity in the United States as a result of federal- and state-supported research and education. These gains in productivity have had far-reaching effects on the whole structure of the American economy by freeing labor to work in industry while still providing American workers and their families with ample food at modest prices. Thus, a ready expansion in the labor supply was made possible even after the massive immigration of the late 1900s had come to a halt. Of course, agricultural research could not have been so successfully employed had not advances in mechanical technology and distribution systems also occurred.

USEFULNESS OF SCIENTIFIC KNOWLEDGE

It is important to note that scientific knowledge, like knowledge possessed by magicians, may not be equally useful to everyone who possesses it. Thus, a competent magician and an outstanding performer may have both learned their trade from the same person, but in the case of the outstanding performer, the knowledge has greater value. It is true that the application of scientific knowledge for productive purposes in real life is undoubtedly more complicated than the application of rare knowledge in magic, but talented individuals are able to apply this knowledge to bring rewards to themselves while often also benefiting others. Since the main topic of this book is economics, one of the social sciences, it might be best to illustrate this point with some examples in economics.

It may have been pointed out in the reader's first course in economics (it will be explained in detail later in this book) that the marginal product curve of a variable input always intersects the associated average product curve at the maximum of the latter, whereas the marginal cost curve always intersects the corresponding average cost curve at the minimum of the latter. This is true under all circumstances, as can be proved mathematically and also explained by common sense (which we shall do later in the book using the batting averages of a baseball player as an example). Although this knowledge may not be useful in everyday life for many students, it can be quite useful for some who may later work in the areas of production, accounting, or finance, provided that they know the true meaning and significance of the phenomena. For those who plan to do more work in economics, this knowledge is certainly important in order to avoid possible mistakes in applying and interpreting basic economic concepts, let alone in the drawing of graphs. To someone else, of course, this knowledge may be of little or no use.

Knowledge of economic concepts and principles is essential to good decision making

Another bit of knowledge that will be highly important to the student of economics is that, provided that the second-order conditions are satisfied, a firm's profit will be maximized under the conditions of perfect competition, monopoly, monopolistic competition, or oligopoly if marginal revenue is equal to marginal cost. This is a truism that cannot be refuted given the assumption of continuous cost and revenue functions and certain regularity conditions of these functions. Most students memorize these conditions for examination purposes, but many do not really understand their true meaning and significance. However, these conditions are based on the assumption of continuous functions, whereas in everyday life people usually encounter discrete cases. It is this sort of discrepancy or difference between theory and everyday experience that often creates confusion in the minds of students. Consequently, the practical value of a theory may remain hidden until the conditions under which it is applicable are fully recognized.

It may be helpful to the reader to point out that the above conditions are logical conclusions that apply when decision making is based on the principle of "always choosing the better alternative among any two possibilities." It can be seen that this simple approach will, by definition, lead to beneficial results and hardly needs any explanation. However, even though the economic concept of marginal analysis is fundamentally based on this disarmingly simple truism, in many instances, after the graphs and mathematics are brought in for a proof of the theorems, students lose sight of the real meaning of the simple truth. Instead, in order to get a good grade in their examinations, they memorize the conclusions without any real attempt at understanding their significance. If this is the case, the learning of economics will neither be beneficial to students in their work and everyday life nor to society in general. On the other hand, if one can, knowingly or unknowingly, apply the simple principle of marginal analysis in business or everyday life, it will inevitably produce beneficial results. We shall cite the true story of a successful businessman to illustrate the significance of the principle of marginal analysis.

Marginal analysis has practical value for those who know how to use it

The businessman started with a little more than $1000, which he eventually turned into millions of dollars worth of real estate by following a principle that is essentially equivalent to marginal analysis. After he made his first million, he wrote a book titled *How to Make a Million in Real Estate in Your Spare Time* (which, incidentally, helped to add even more to his wealth—in a later edition of the book, the word "a" in front of the word "Million" was crossed out and replaced by the word "Three.") This book is no longer on the market, but a copy can be obtained (at a cost of about $500) by attending a seminar conducted by a person designated by the author, the author himself being occupied in his real estate business. The important observation is that the businessman's earnings in real estate are higher than the hundreds of thousands of dollars earned by the seminars. This in itself suggests a proper application of the principle of marginal analysis. What is even more impressive is the fact that the millionaire, who has presumably not taken a course in economics, knows how to apply the principle of marginal analysis in his business operation without being able to identify it as such. For example, in his book he advises his readers (based on his own experience) that in determining how to invest a given amount of savings, the decision maker always compare the net returns from at least two alternatives—(1) improve or repair existing property or (2) purchase a new piece of property—and then choose the alternative that provides the higher return. Although this seems obvious on the basis of common sense, it is surprising that many investors just do not operate in this way. At one extreme are investors who keep buying additional properties while allowing existing ones to run down. At the other extreme are investors who spend all their available resources in improving existing properties to their absolute satisfaction before any additional purchase is considered. In the end, either course of action is contrary to the profit-maximizing behavior that would be indicated by marginal analysis.

It may seem that the above principle has nothing in common with the use of marginal analysis in profit maximization, since the necessary condition for maximum profit, that is, marginal revenue equals marginal cost (MR = MC), appears nowhere in the above arguments. Actually, the rationale of the above approach and that of marginal analysis in profit maximization are identical.

The condition MR = MC that is necessary for profit maximization can be derived by common sense with the use of sequential analysis. For example, imagine that a seller or a producer (under the assumption of zero inventory, a seller and a producer can be identical) can make a choice between two alternatives at each stage: to produce a unit or not to produce a unit. It is obvious that it would be profitable to produce an additional unit if the additional revenue (i.e., the marginal revenue MR) from the unit is greater than the additional cost (i.e., the marginal cost MC). This implies that as long as MR is greater than MC, the current profit cannot be maximum, since producing an additional unit would add to net profit. In other words, if the profit increases with additional production, then the profit for the current level of output cannot be maximum. Conversely, when MC is greater than MR, each additional unit produced results in a reduction in profit. This implies that, under these circumstances, a unit cut in production would result in increased profit or at least reduced loss. In other words, when MC is greater than MR, the total profit decreases for each additional unit in production, and hence the current profit cannot be maximum. Thus, in the continuous case, if the current profit cannot be maximum when MR is greater than MC or when MR is less than MC, then the only other possibility is maximum profit when MR is equal to MC. Hence, by process of elimination we see that profit can be maximum (provided that a maximum exists) only if MR = MC.

The above arguments are based on two simplified assumptions: (1) There is only a single product, that is, there are no joint products; (2) the output quantity, cost, and revenue are continuous variables. In the real world we most often deal with discrete rather than continuous variables, and usually joint products rather than a single product are involved. However, once the true meaning of the economic concept of marginal analysis is understood, the conditions of profit maximization can be applied with minor modifications. The previously discussed case of real estate investment is a good example. It is actually a valid application of the principle of marginal analysis in profit maximization, even though the practitioner may have never realized it.

Although the proper application of the principle of marginal analysis was most likely not the sole factor in the success of the above-mentioned millionaire, it does seem that his clever application of this sound economic principle contributed considerably. This example illustrates two things:

Successful application of economic theory requires more than memorization of textbook versions of basic theorems

1. Economic theory can be helpful in business operations and in everyday life to those who understand the true meaning of the theory, but it will not help those who just memorize the textbook version of the theorems;
2. Many of those successful in business may not have studied economics or know economic theory, but somehow, due to their cleverness or by pure chance, they have consistently made good use of the various principles that are embodied in economic theory.

As we mentioned earlier, a competent magician can be easily trained, but an outstanding performer depends on both training and talent. This is also true in economics as well as in all other sciences. Economic theory can be easily taught to and memorized by an average person, but its successful application in business, in government, in public affairs, or in everyday life requires not only a real understanding of the true meaning of the theory, but also some talent in its use on the part of the individual. Having this in mind, we shall devote more space than other textbooks to the discussion of the assumptions behind each economic theorem and to some commonsense interpretations of the relevant theorems. We do this because the assumptions that underlie a theory impose limitations on its applicability, whereas the commonsense interpretation of a theorem helps the reader to understand the true meaning of the theory. We feel that our approach will help to avoid confusion and misunderstanding and, at the same time, make the application of economic theory in both business operations and everyday life easier.

SCIENCES, SOCIAL SCIENCES, ECONOMICS, MICROECONOMICS, AND MACROECONOMICS

In most discussions on scientific knowledge and inquiry, a distinction is made between the natural sciences and the social sciences. Physics, chemistry, biology, and so on are included in the former, whereas such fields as economics, sociology, and political science are included in the latter. The general impression is often that the natural sciences are the forerunners and the social sciences latecomers in the realm of scientific inquiry and reasoning. It is true that astronomy and physics can be considered as the oldest of all the sciences, but economics can reasonably claim to be the second oldest according to Professor Kenneth E. Boulding (1966). Although physics dates from Newton, economics can be said to date from Adam Smith, whose *The Wealth of Nations,* published in 1776, predates Dalton in chemistry, Darwin in biology, and the disciplines of sociology and psychology, which developed much later. Thus, economics has a relatively long history, predating all the other social sciences and all the natural sciences with the exception of physics. Economics also holds the distinction of being the only social science to date for which a Nobel prize has been awarded annually (since 1969). This indicates the recognition that the economics profession has earned.

Readers have undoubtedly encountered many different definitions of economics. Our own definition is directed more toward providing an introduction to the topics that will be discussed in this book than as a substitute for the others. Therefore, we define economics as a social science that deals with the study of the material well-being of humankind; as such, economics is concerned with the actions of individuals or groups of individuals in the processes of production, exchange, and consumption of goods and services for the purpose of satisfying the unlimited wants of human beings with limited resources. The last part of the above statement is really the key to the study of economics, since if an individual (or a group of individuals, e.g., a nation) possessed unlimited resources, economizing would be unnecessary. Furthermore, if human beings had limited wants that could be easily satisfied, economizing would not be of primary concern. The term *economizing* can be defined in various ways, but its meaning can be most easily illustrated with reference to the economic concept of efficiency in production, that is, the condition of maximum output for a given cost or of minimum cost for a given output. This condition is important when inputs are limited and maximum output is desired. However, when inputs are unlimited due to unlimited resources or more output is not considered desirable due to the limited wants of human beings, the concept of efficiency in production is no longer significant. Under such circumstances, any production process, efficient or inefficient, would be equally good. In the same context, we can state that the study of exchange in economics involves the discovery of the conditions under which increased benefits can be obtained by either all of the participants or at least one participant without reducing the benefits of any others. Again, if there were unlimited resources, everyone could get as much as they wanted, and there would still be some left over. In such a case, the study of exchange would no longer be necessary.

Economizing would be unnecessary if human wants were limited and resources were unlimited

The theory of consumer behavior is also based on the fundamental facts of limited resources and unlimited wants (nonsatiation). If one has unlimited resources, economizing is unimportant.

Thus, the resources of the very rich could, for consumption purposes, be considered virtually unlimited. They could spend a few hundred dollars to stay overnight in a hotel and pay exorbitant prices for many other goods and services without concern for economizing. We can also conceive of a hobo spending money on things other than necessities. In these cases, price does not seem to be a factor (it is certainly not primary), in their decisions on the obtaining of goods. Such behavior can be explained by the phenomenon called the *point of bliss,* as described in Chapter 4. Where we have such a condition, the budget constraint in the theory of consumer behavior is not effective: for the rich due to high income and for the hobo due to a specific preference pattern in limited wants. Therefore, the demand for a commodity which is based on the principle of utility maximization, subject to the constraint of one's budget, is not applicable to them. This demonstrates, at least partially, the significance of the existence of limited resources and unlimited wants in the study of economics and the formulation of economic theory.

In economic theory, two main branches of study have developed: microeconomics and macroeconomics. The former is concerned with a detailed analysis of the behavior of individual economic units, whereas the latter involves an analysis of a total economic system, such as that of a nation. In the case of microeconomics, the explanation of the existence of certain market characteristics is derived through logical deduction. To assist us in our analysis, all economic units are divided into two categories: producers and consumers; however, these two categories are not mutually exclusive. In fact, most, if not all, producers are, at the same time, also consumers. The emphasis is on the economic function that an individual performs in society and not on the person per se. A producer (generally called a firm) is a decision-making unit in production which can consist of either a person or a group of persons (e.g., a corporation). Similarily, a consumer is a decision-making unit that can also consist of a person or a group of persons (e.g., a family). The important thing to remember is that a firm and a consumer are considered as decision-making units in production and consumption, respectively. It is with the behavior of these decision-making units that we shall be concerned in this book.

It should be noted that microeconomics is generally considered as classical economics and macroeconomics a latecomer to the discipline. Although classical economics does not ignore aggregate analysis of the total economic system, its primary concern is the analysis of individual economic units and individual markets. On the other hand, the emphasis of macroeconomics is on the analysis of an economic system as a whole (e.g., that of a nation). A commonly recognized and adequate (but not necessarily perfect) measure for a nation's economic performance is national income, and macroeconomics is often regarded as synonymous with national income analysis. However, this does not mean that macroeconomics does not concern itself with the functioning of individual sectors of the economy.

It should also be remembered that, although microeconomics and macroeconomics are two different approaches for dealing with economic problems, they are generally complementary rather than competitive. In fact, a good knowledge of microeconomics is very helpful in learning macroeconomics.

THEORY AND REALITY

Any scientific theory, whether in the natural or social sciences, is based on certain simplified assumptions from which, by logical deduction, definite conclusions can be derived. These conclusions are usually called theorems. The proof of a theorem is actually a demonstration of the logical consistency between the conclusion and its assumptions. Thus, the applicability of a theory is closely related to its underlying assumptions.

Any economic phenomenon involves numerous relevant variables, some of which are more important than others. In order to make the theory manageable, only a few of the most important variables can be explicitly taken into consideration in the analysis. An economic model that serves as the basis for a theory usually involves only a limited number of variables. This does not, however, imply that these are the only variables involved in the question at hand. It only means that, according to available knowledge and information, the included variables are considered more important and significant and that the omitted variables are either relatively insignificant or tend to cancel out each other and thus can be ignored. It should be understood that certain assumptions concerning the behavior of a model also impose limitations on the applicability of the theory. Therefore, an understanding of the relevant assumptions behind a theory is very important for a true comprehension of the theory and its application to business or everyday life.

A theory cannot be truly realistic with respect to any specific event. If it were, it would lose its essential attribute of generality. On the other hand, a theory cannot be divorced from reality either. If it were, it would be useless. In particular, when theory and reality are in close agreement, it would be a great disservice to the theory if an attempt is made to isolate it from reality or to separate reality from it. A case in point is the concept of marginal analysis as it relates to profit maximization of a firm in economic theory and the mark-up pricing practice of firms in reality. Many economists have realized the consistency between theory and reality in this respect. However, others still refuse to recognize this fact, due to either misunderstanding or confusion. In order

Theory is an abstraction of reality and is based on certain simplifying assumptions from which, by logical deduction, definite conclusions are derived

to clarify the issue, we have devoted an entire section in Chapter 7 to prove formally the theoretical equivalence between marginal analysis in profit maximization in the theory of the firm and mark-up pricing practice of firms in reality.

Obviously, perfect competition and mark-up pricing are inconsistent because firms are price takers under perfect competition. Under perfect competition, firms have no freedom to choose a price other than the one that is determined by market demand and supply. Their only possible choice is the quantity to be produced. On the other hand, a firm operating in imperfect markets, such as monopoly, monopolistic competition, or oligopoly, can choose either price or output quantity, but not both, in order to accomplish its goal (e.g., to maximize profit). Economic analysis of the market starts from the simplest model of perfect competition, where the only meaningful decision variable of the firm as regards profit maximization is the quantity to be produced. When monopoly and other imperfect markets are analyzed, output quantity is still traditionally considered as the decision variable, and there is nothing wrong with this approach. Actually, this approach is simpler than if the price were considered as the decision variable. However, economists should not lose sight of the fact that, in an imperfect market, *either price or output quantity* can legitimately be considered as the decision variable of a firm as regards profit maximization; this is true owing to the definite relationship between output quantity and price, which are linked by the demand function. Once this possible trap is realized, the theoretical consistency between marginal analysis in economic theory and mark-up pricing in the real world of business becomes obvious.

Although perfect competition as an economic model serves as a good starting point in the analysis of market behavior, it should be noted that, more often than not, this admittedly simple and unrealistic model is usually (and unjustifiably) overworked in explaining market situations. For example, the average person, as well as most economists, would refer to rising market prices as a supply and demand phenomenon. In a competitive market, this is precisely the explanation of market price behavior. However, as we shall explain in more detail in Part III, in a system of imperfect markets, the concept of supply as defined in economics is not very meaningful, and it is cost, in conjunction with demand, that determines the equilibrium price. The nature of the supply–demand arguments with respect to their effect on the behavior of market price somehow leaves the important factor—cost—in the dark as a cause of inflation. In reality, as well as in theory, cost is one of the most important determinants of market prices, but because of the indiscriminate application of the unrealistic model of perfect competition, in some instances, the true cause of inflation—rising costs, which result from exogenous factors—is often ignored.

Although older textbooks in intermediate microeconomics usually devote one or two chapters to a discussion of supply and demand models before moving on to the analysis of consumer behavior, production, and cost, they neglect to give adequate warning that the supply function as described is strictly applicable only under perfect competition. Even though the supply curve disappears completely in the chapters dealing with monopoly, monopolistic competition, and oligopoly, the traditional supply and demand model stays with the students, and the importance of cost in the determination of equilibrium price is ignored. Since the imperfect market models are closer to reality, we believe it more beneficial to students (and to economists as well) to put perfect competition in its rightful place in economic analysis as the simplest introductory model and to concentrate on specifying the relationship between imperfect market models and actual business operations. The contents and arrangement of topics in this book reflect this philosophy.

THE METHODOLOGY OF MICROECONOMICS

Microeconomics, just like any other science, is theoretical in nature, and as such it is deductive. Starting from certain basic plausible assumptions, definite conclusions—theorems—are derived by means of logical deduction. A theory consists of (1) assumptions, (2) logical deduction, and (3) conclusions or theorems. In theory, the causal relationship is clear cut. For example, according to economic theory, an increase in demand (a rightward shift of a demand curve) for a given cost or supply will cause the market equilibrium price to rise. On the other hand, a rising price by itself will not result in a shift in the demand for the commodity. This serves to clarify the fallacious statement that "higher demand results in higher market price, which in turn lowers demand, which in turn lowers market price, which in turn raises the demand, which in turn raises the market price, and so on." Once a price change takes place, it will, according to the fallacy, fluctuate up and down without end.

Another example where economic theory has proved very useful is in explaining the causal relationship between the market price of corn and land rent in early England. Because corn was a staple food in England at the time, its price was very important in determining the standard of living. When the price of corn was high, widespread dissatisfaction prevailed. Naturally, politicians blamed the higher price on the high land rent, which, seemingly, was a reasonable argument. However, David Ricardo, one of the outstanding early economists, argued that the higher rent was due to the higher price of corn and not the other way around. Ricardo's arguments seemed to be fallacious, but it turned out that his opponents were demagogues according to economic theory.

As we shall show in Chapter 11, the supply curve of land can be considered vertical (perfectly inelastic). Under these circumstances, the price is essentially determined by demand. In Chapter 10 it will be shown that the demand for productive factors, such as land, is a derived demand, where the market price of the product produced by the factor is an important determinant. These arguments imply that the price of corn determines rent, thus validating Ricardo's arguments.

In theory formulation, deductive reasoning is more fundamental than inductive reasoning

In contrast to the deductive theoretical approach, empirical or statistical studies are inductive in nature. Although the two approaches are complementary, there are indications that deductive theory is more fundamental. In particular, statistical or empirical studies may indicate certain interrelationships, but the direction of a causal relationship—or whether causal relationships exist at all—can only be explained by theory. An example may serve as a good illustration of this point.

As legend goes, storks bring newborn children with them. To our knowledge, there has not been a single serious scientist who has made a theoretical study on this topic. However, it has been said that a curious statistician collected data on the number of childbirths and the number of stork nests in a few Dutch villages; it turned out there was a significant positive correlation between childbirths and storks. Thus, on the basis of a purely empirical study, one might conclude that the legend was proven correct. Without a sound theoretical justification, it is doubtful that any scientist would take the result seriously. This illustrates the importance of theory.

Good theory requires realistic assumptions and sound logic

Good theory is based on realistic assumptions and a sound logical structure. A theory can be logically sound but still make no sense owing to unrealistic assumptions. A professor of one of the authors once got angry in a classroom argument and said, "You can prove that the moon is made of blue cheese if you are willing to make unrealistic assumptions. But the question is: What is the use of such a theory?" This classroom aside indicates that one should not lose sight of the assumptions underlying a theory lest all sorts of nonsensical conclusions be advanced about phenomena.

It is also important to note that a theory cannot be considered firmly established if its logical structure is unsound. An obvious example of such a condition is when the proof of an underlying theorem is false. When this is the case, the resulting theory cannot be accepted as correct. On the other hand, the invalid proof of an underlying theorem cannot by itself be considered an indication that the theory is wrong, since there could exist an alternative valid proof that, once discovered, would make the theory complete and sound. There has been at least one good example in the economics profession where the original proof of a theorem was invalid, but later a valid one was developed. This shows that it is easier to prove a theorem than disprove one, because even if one finds that the proof is invalid, this by itself cannot be taken as an indication that the theorem is wrong. In order to prove that a theorem is wrong, one must logically show that all possible proofs are invalid or that there does not exist a valid proof. This, in general, is not an easy task to accomplish.

A theory that is presented in a textbook is generally expected to be logically sound because it has been examined carefully by many people in the profession. However, more often than not, the assumptions that underlie a theory and govern its applicability are neglected. The result is confusion and misapplication of the theory. Hence, a good understanding of the assumptions underlying a theory is most important. It is for this reason that we have devoted considerable space to stating the assumptions that underlie the theoretical formulations presented in this book.

RELEVANCE OF MICROECONOMICS

Microeconomics is fundamental in economics, both as a pure theory and in its application to such special fields as labor economics, public finance, international trade, and econometrics. It is also very useful in such areas of business administration as accounting, finance, and marketing. In fact, the practical value of microeconomics extends to engineering, medicine, law, and other disciplines. Although economics is not designed to provide a rule of conduct in business operations or economic behavior in everyday life, microeconomic theory can be put to good use more often than one realizes in both business and private life, provided that one knows the true meaning of the theory. We have already mentioned the story of the real estate tycoon who made millions in his spare time using an investment principle that is essentially an application of marginal analysis in profit maximization. Although a proper application of microeconomic principles may not make everyone a millionaire, it can certainly make everyone better off than they would otherwise be. For example, the principle of marginal analysis can be applied to household finance and in the choice of jobs. However, the equality conditions of marginal analysis cannot be taken too seriously, since they can only be fully met in continuous cases. In business, as in everyday life, we deal mostly with discrete cases. Thus, the true spirit of marginal analysis is not in the equality of marginal conditions, but in the choice of the best alternative among any number of possibilities.

As a consumer, one should at least learn from microeconomics that a consumer cannot expect sellers to reduce their prices for the benefit of consumers, since they have neither the obligation nor the inducement to do so. On the other hand, this does not mean that consumers are helpless victims at the mercy of senseless capitalists. On the contrary, capitalists can only make money if they provide the goods and services that consumers desire. Even absolute monopolists cannot always make more profit by simply charging higher prices. The price that maximizes the profit of a monopolist is determined by both demand and cost (but not supply). The relevance of this argument is that consumers, as a whole, are equally powerful as sellers (if not more so) in determining market prices. The implication is that consumers can best take care of their own interests in the marketplace by buying wisely. This seems to be too simple a lesson to be learned from microeconomics, since everyone with any common sense knows it. However, microeconomics provides a greater dimension to our common knowledge and can increase the degree of rationality that we apply to our decisions.

Part I discusses the economics of production and cost

AN OVERVIEW OF THE BOOK

Part I of the book contains a discussion of the economics of production and cost. We begin in Chapter 1 by analyzing the production behavior of a firm with a simple model of one variable input. In Chapter 2 we deal with the case of two variable inputs, which provides more flexibility in production and is closer to reality. If it is assumed that there are only two inputs in production, then no fixed inputs are involved. On the other hand, if it is assumed that more than two inputs are involved, there must be at least one fixed input. Since in production the short run is defined as a situation where some inputs are variable and others fixed, whereas the long run is defined as a situation where all inputs are variable, Chapter 1 is definitely concerned with short-run analysis, whereas Chapter 2 can be concerned with either short- or long-run analysis, depending on the number of inputs involved.

Equilibrium in production is defined as a situation where output is maximized for a given cost or, equivalently, cost is minimized for a given output. Under perfect competition in input markets, a firm faces constant input prices. The locus of equilibrium points in input space as cost changes continuously is defined as the expansion path. When we transfer the information given by the points on an expansion path to a corresponding output cost space, a cost curve is derived. This shows that all points on a cost curve represent the minimum possible cost for a given technology and input prices for each level of output.

Various concepts of cost for both the short and long run are developed in Chapter 3. Certain relationships among total, average, and marginal cost curves are analyzed. The long-run cost curves are derived from the corresponding short-run cost curves, but we also address the modern approach with respect to constant average and marginal cost curves and reconcile these with the traditional smooth U-shaped cost curves.

Part II contains two chapters on the theory of consumer behavior and the related theory of demand. Chapter 4 analyzes consumer behavior by means of utility theory. A brief explanation of the historical and theoretical development of the ordinal utility approach from the cardinal utility approach is offered. Then we illustrate the derivation of indifference maps, which, when combined with the concept of the budget constraint, helps to develop the conditions of consumer equilibrium. A price consumption curve is then represented by the locus of equilibrium points in an indifference map that results when the price of one commodity changes and other factors (income, other prices, and the preference pattern of the consumer) remain constant. Finally, the information from the price consumption curve is transferred to a graph in price–quantity space to derive a demand curve for a consumer.

Part II concerns the theory of consumer and market demand

Using the concepts of substitution and income effects, which correspond to the substitution and income terms in the Slutsky equation, we show that the demand for a normal good is necessarily negatively sloped; this is referred to as the law of demand. However, it is also explained that the demand curve for an inferior good can be positively sloped, in which case the commodity is called a Giffen good; this constitutes the only exception to the demand law. Chapter 4 concludes with a brief discussion of the characteristic approach, rather than the traditional commodity approach, to the analysis of consumer behavior.

In Chapter 5 market demand is derived as a sum of the individual consumer demands for each price. Measures of the characteristics of demand, such as elasticities and related concepts in revenue, are developed and analyzed. A final warning concerning a possible mistake in deriving an empirical demand curve from historical data concludes this chapter and Part II.

Part III brings the results developed in the previous chapters together in order to develop a theoretical formulation of market price determination. However, in all cases profit maximization is assumed to be a firm's goal. We note the essential differences that exist under different market conditions. Thus, firms are price takers under perfect competition, which is the simplest system among all the market models, whereas firms under imperfect markets usually set their prices and let the market determine the quantity. For this reason, they can be called price makers; this category includes firms under monopoly, monopolistic competition, and oligopoly.

Part III combines production theory, cost analysis, and the theory of consumer and market demand in the formulation of price

Chapter 6 discusses the simplest market model of perfect competition; in this case, a firm faces a constant market price, that is, a horizontal straight-line demand curve, as a price taker. We note that the only possible choice that a firm can make as long as it stays in business is the quantity to be produced. Since the first-order (i.e., necessary) condition for profit maximization is MR = MC, then, when price is constant, marginal revenue is equal to price and, therefore, also a constant. Under these circumstances, if marginal cost is a constant, then either MR ≠ MC (unequal constants), or MR = MC throughout and the profit-maximizing quantity is not unique. Hence, the choice of a unique quantity by a firm in order to maximize profit is no longer meaningful. Thus, we show that the commonly experienced constant MC—the modern approach—is inconsistent with perfect competition and that this could be the reason many economists ignore and some even oppose the reality of constant MC. It is shown that a modified constant-MC model, where MC is constant within capacity and rising beyond capacity, is theoretically consistent with perfect competition.

Chapter 7 presents the traditional monopoly model and three mark-up pricing models commonly used by business firms. It is also shown that the mark-up pricing practice of business is theoretically equivalent to traditional marginal analysis in profit maximization under monopoly (i.e., imperfect competition). The equivalence is indicated by an identical choice for the profit-maximizing price under both mark-up pricing and marginal analysis for identical data, that is, for the same demand and cost curves. We explain that the difference in appearance between traditional economic theory and the mark-up pricing practice of business is due to a difference in available information and not a difference in basic theory. Thus, in economic theory, the demand is assumed to be known, whereas, in reality, the demand function or demand curve is not known to the firm. We show that, on the one hand, the theoretical reconciliation between business practice and economic theory brings microeconomic theory closer to market reality without any sacrifice in its theoretical rigor and, on the other hand, provides a theoretical foundation for the construction of econometric models in empirical research to relate price and cost without using the theoretically well-defined but empirically elusive demand function.

Chapter 8 presents the market model under monopolistic competition, which is essentially a long-run theory. In long-run equilibrium, a firm's maximum profit is zero, just like that of a firm under perfect competition. However, the market price is higher than the minimum average cost, which is unlike the situation under perfect competition, where price is equal to the minimum average cost.

The short-run analysis in monopolistic competition is similar to that in monopoly. In short-run equilibrium, the maximum profit of a firm can be either positive, zero, or negative, just like that of a monopolist.

We show that both the mark-up pricing practice of business and the common phenomenon of constant MC are also consistent with marginal analysis in profit maximization under monopolistic competition. Product differentiation under monopolistic competition permits quality and advertising (or other promoting activities) to be treated as choice variables, just as quantity or price is in traditional economic theory. This broadens the scope of economic analysis.

Chapter 9 discusses oligopoly theory. The well-known duopoly model of Cournot is presented first, and then the modified Chamberlin and Edgeworth duopoly models are discussed. Next, the kinked demand curve, price leadership, and cartel oligopoly models are considered. A brief discussion of game theory in connection with oligopoly concludes this chapter.

Part IV, which contains two chapters, deals with the theory of income distribution and factor prices. Factor demand depends on the market for the product for which the factor is used in production. Therefore, the demands for factors of production are referred to as derived demand functions, and the supply of productive factors is not identified to their marginal cost as produced commodities under perfect competition. The essential characteristics of factor markets are different from those of commodity markets. We note that there is a good reason to discuss factor markets separately from commodity markets in order to avoid confusion in applying the theory to real-world problems.

Part IV examines the derivation of the demand for factors of production and a determination of their price

Chapter 10 derives the demand functions for productive factors—labor, land, capital, and entrepreneurship—from the first-order conditions of profit maximization of a firm. The theory develops from simple to more complicated cases: from the simplest—one variable input—to more than one variable input, on the one hand, and from perfect competition in product markets to imperfect markets, on the other. In this respect, there is an essential difference between one-variable-input and more-than-one-variable-input cases. The case of two variable inputs can be considered general, and the simple one-variable-input model is valuable essentially for illustration purposes.

Chapter 11 covers the determination of factor prices. Under perfect competition demand and supply together determine the market price. The supply of labor provided by an individual worker is derived from the indifference map of the worker, income and leisure or, alternatively, income and hours of work being considered as the variables. The market supply is derived from individual supplies by a summation of working hours of all workers for each and every wage rate. We note that economists have long recognized the fact that the labor supply curve may bend back at a higher wage rate. It can be shown graphically that this is consistent with the assumption of utility maximization of a worker and a rational choice between work and income.

One special feature of the land market is that the supply of land can be considered perfectly inelastic—a vertical straight line (i.e., a fixed quantity). An implication of this phenomenon is that the market price is primarily determined by demand (a high demand results in a high market price and a low demand in a low price) and that cost is not a factor in the determination of price. In fact, it is the demand for the factor that determines the compensation that it can obtain in a competitive market, not the interaction between demand and cost as in commodity markets. Thus, rent is primarily determined by demand, and Ricardo's arguments concerning the causal relationship between the price of corn and land rent are consistent with this analysis.

Economists often extend the phenomenon of fixed supply beyond land. In this context, we see that the market price of any commodity (such as an antique or nonreproducible work of art) or service (such as a unique talent in football, baseball, basketball, or boxing) with fixed supply is essentially determined by demand and not cost. Therefore, it is called quasi-rent. For example, if a quarterback earns an annual salary of $300,000 and the best alternative employment other than being a quarterback pays $30,000, then the $270,000 difference is considered as quasi-rent.

We explain that capital theory, under conditions of uncertainty, is still a controversial issue that shall not be formally discussed in order to avoid confusion. Under conditions of certainty and in the absence of risk, the interest rate can be considered as the cost or price of capital. Theoretically, the market rate of interest can be determined by supply (savings) and demand (investment), but, in reality, central banks (the Federal Reserve system in this country) generally manipulate the interest rates based on policy issues that are determined by considerations other than market forces. Furthermore, capital rationing by financial institutions has become the general practice rather than exception. Therefore, the interest rate as a price has (at least partially) lost its allocation function in the capital market. Given such a condition, it seems that a deliberate theoretical development of the interest rate that moves from the time preference of consumers to the supply of capital may not be worth the effort. Consequently, we have omitted this part of capital theory from our discussion.

Part V covers the topics of general equilibrium theory and welfare economics

Part V covers the important and difficult topics of general equilibrium theory and welfare economics. Until now, our theory has been characterized by partial analysis under the assumption of "other things being equal." Although we have introduced the concepts of substitute and complementary goods, when we analyze one market, the interaction between the market under consideration and other related markets is ignored. This is the characteristic of partial analysis. Although the scientific method is consistent with experiments under controlled environments or partial analysis in theory, an economic model that takes all of the markets and relevant variables into consideration simultaneously is considered superior. We show that although the late French economist Leon Walras is considered a pioneer in general equilibrium analysis in microeconomic theory, recent developments in mathematical economics have made major contributions in both the existence and the uniqueness of general equilibrium. However, since advanced mathematics is involved in these developments, we have not discussed them in detail. Instead, we employ graphical analysis to show the logic of general equilibrium analysis. For this purpose, we use the Edgeworth box in both pure exchange and production.

After the simple Walras general equilibrium model is discussed briefly, Chapter 12 concludes with a consideration of the input–output analysis pioneered by the Nobel prize winner Wassily Leontief.

Chapter 13 covers the topic of welfare economics, which is a branch of microeconomics that attempts to develop a theoretical framework to serve as a guide to what ought to be generally called normative economics in contrast to positive economics. We note that although a good scientific theory should not involve individual value judgment, the idea of achieving the greatest welfare for the majority of people in a society in fact does so. The problem is further complicated by the lack of a proper method of measurement of economic welfare for a society as a whole. In technical terms, there does not exist a social welfare function. As an alternative, the concept of Pareto optimality (the unanimity principle) is adopted as the criterion to judge the desirability of social economic alterantives. We argue that although the adoption of the Pareto concept by itself involves value judgment, it can generally be considered as acceptable.

The concept of Pareto optimality is explained and defined; this is essentially an application of the consumer behavior theory developed in Chapter 4. The Edgeworth box is again used as an important tool. The two important theorems in welfare economics concerning the consistency between Pareto optimality and perfect competition are presented. In the conclusion to Chapter 13, some limitations of the Pareto concept are briefly discussed.

The material in Part VI, comprising Chapter 14, the final chapter of our book, contains applications of microeconomic theory to matters of economic policy and the shifting and incidence of sales and income taxes. Some of the sections, such as the one concerned with the treatment of sales tax, are standard in most textbooks, but others cannot be found elsewhere. In particular, the discussion of monetary and fiscal policy is generally covered in macroeconomic textbooks. However, we explain that those discussions in macroeconomics only take the effect of such policy measures on the demand side into consideration, whereas the effect of such policy measures on the cost side are completely ignored. From Part III, we know that the market price and equilibrium quantity of goods and services are determined by both demand and cost and that a theory that ignores the cost side

Part VI looks at the application of microeconomics to policy questions

cannot be complete. In this chapter, we have, by using the theory developed earlier, shown that some of the macroeconomic monetary and fiscal policy measures are theoretically inconclusive if both the demand and cost sides are taken into consideration. We argue that the overwhelming evidence of mark-up pricing practice by business firms cannot be ignored in establishing a practical economic policy. Our theory, which takes mark-up pricing into consideration, may be more helpful. This suggests that microeconomics may be better equipped to provide an answer to the "stagflation" problem of the 1970s than some of the macromodels.

Again, we have given considerable space to the problem of shifting and incidence of taxes because mark-up pricing practice in business and cost behavior under imperfect competition lead to conclusions that differ from the traditional approach. In particular, the shifting of the corporate income tax is closely related to the mark-up pricing practice of business firms. By using one of the mark-up pricing models presented in Chapter 7, more insight is gained into the possible shifting of the personal and corporate income tax.

THE THEORY OF THE FIRM:
THE ECONOMICS OF PRODUCTION AND COST

INTRODUCTION

In economics, a firm is defined as a decision-making unit in production and trading activities (these activities will be defined
later). In general, the notion of a firm corresponds to a proprietorship, partnership, or corporation. However, it could be a division of a conglomerate or a subsidiary of a giant corporation.
The essential point is that a firm is an economic unit that makes
decisions concerning the proper combination and quality of inputs
to be used in producing a given level of output. In a competitive
market, the firm is also a price taker and chooses the quantity
of its output in the short run and its size in the long run.[1] In an
imperfect market, the firm can choose either the quantity (as most
economists assume for the sake of convenience) or, equivalently,
the price (as is done in business practice), but not both.[2] (This
equivalence will be discussed in more detail in Chapter 7.) In
either case, according to theory, the goal is profit maximization;
it is only with respect to available alternatives that the firm operating in a competitive market differs from its counterpart in the
imperfect market.

A firm is also assumed to be impersonal in that, other than the
goal of profit maximization, it does not have any preferences or

---

[1] Perfect competition, which will be precisely defined later, can be thought of as
a condition in which no one firm has dominant control over the market and,
consequently, all firms take the market price as a given datum and set their
production goals or targets so as to maximize profit or returns in the context of
input prices and productivity.

[2] Under imperfect competition, firms have sufficient control over the market to
either adjust production to control price or, through other means, differentiate
their product from those of other firms so as to be able to establish or choose
a price at which profits or revenues can be maximized.

personality. This assumption has been questioned by some economists on the grounds that

1. a firm may be motivated by maximum sales rather than maximum profit;
2. owing to the separation of ownership and management in big corporations, the management of a firm, which actually makes almost all of the decisions, may want security at the expense of profits;
3. a firm may seek technical sophistication or other social goals at the expense of profits; or
4. a firm may have multiple goals instead of just a single goal such as maximum profit.

Although we do not wish to minimize their importance in an analysis of the behavior of the firm, it should be pointed out that the arguments against the traditional assumption of profit maximization as the only goal of the firm in theory are, in all cases, due to misunderstanding. There is an essential difference between economic theory and business practice in that, in order to make the model manageable, economic theory is based on certain very simplified assumptions concerning the environment in which firms operate. For example, economic theory assumes perfect knowledge or perfect information and thus perfect foresight, which, in turn, implies the absence of uncertainty and risk. In reality, the decisions made by a firm primarily involve the future, which is neither certain or known. As a result, the facts may not agree with the goals. This is the old problem of ex ante and ex post. Although the facts may appear to show that rapidly expanding firms and firms with technical sophistication do not necessarily return the highest profits, these fact (if they are facts) cannot be used as proof that profit maximization was not the goal of these firms, and this is obvious if one takes the ex ante and ex post arguments into consideration. The play-safe argument loses ground once the certainty assumption in economic theory is recognized, since in the absence of uncertainty and risk, there is no necessity to play safe.[3]

In reality, a firm may have other goals than maximizing profits. However, to be operable, a scientific model has to be manageable. For this reason (usually the most important factor), among others,

---

[3] It should also be recognized that the assumption of profit maximization includes a minimization of losses and that where risk and uncertainty are introduced, loss minimization is merely another form of profit maximization. Some decision theory merely introduces the notion of conditional profit or loss based on probability and the idea of maximizing expected monetary value, but certain mathematicians have expressed dissatisfaction with this approach. We shall not discuss this approach any further; however, students may wish to refer to advanced texts on decision theory.

profit maximization is singled out for analytical purposes. Thus, the assumption of profit maximization as the only goal of a firm does not deny the existence of other goals, and the multigoal firm can be considered an extension, not a substitution, of the traditional model. Another important reason in favor of the profit-maximization model of the firm is the fact that the theoretical results derived from the model provide rules of behavior for firms, that is, it suggests how a firm should operate if it does want to maximize profits. Even if a firm has other goals, the profit-maximization model may still be useful in showing the alternative costs of other goals, that is, how much profit a firm has to forego in order to accomplish other goals.

The assumption of profit maximization does not rule out other goals, but its rejection would complicate the formulation of a manageable scientific model

Other assumptions that are an integral part of the theory of the firm, but often overlooked, are as follows:

Assumption I.1: Free Disposal. If a firm produces more than it can sell, the merchandise can be thrown away without cost. This assumption may be relevant in specific cases.

Assumption I.2: Divisibility. All inputs and outputs are assumed to be perfectly divisible. This assumption makes it possible for us to apply calculus in the analysis of profit-maximization behavior and to draw smooth, continuous curves for production and cost evaluation. In general, this assumption is not satisfied in reality.

Assumption I.3: Perfect Knowledge. This assumption implies perfect information and the concomitant perfect foresight. Although this assumption is basic to most (if not all) economic models, it is not often mentioned explicitly. Many misunderstandings and false arguments result from the failure to take this assumption into consideration.

Assumption I.4: The Absence of Externalities. This assumption states that costs are pure and exclusive of both external economies and external diseconomies, which are often referred to as spill-over effects. Actually, the former concept, which is symmetric, is more general than the latter, which is asymmetric. For example, an activity in either production or consumption may not only affect others (e.g., the spill-over effects of water and air pollution in production), but itself be affected by the activities of others. In advanced theory, it becomes obvious that the concept of externality is far superior to the concept of spill-over effects. In the theory of production (as in consumer theory), we assume that the output of the firm depends only on its own inputs, not on the inputs of other firms, and that there is no joint product. This is equivalent to the assumption of the absence of externalities. This assumption will be relaxed in the chapters dealing with general equilibrium and welfare economics.

Assumption I.5: Homogeneity of Inputs and Outputs. For simplicity, we assume that labor is homogeneous, that is, any given unit of labor is identical in quality to each other unit. This also applies to capital, land, and the output they produce.

In the traditional standard textbook, production theory (and, for that matter, cost theory and consumer behavior) is implicitly based on the above assumptions, but the implications of these assumptions are only occasionally discussed in advanced treatises.[4] Students, in particular, should be made fully aware both of the assumptions and, as mentioned above, of the fact that there is an essential difference between reality on the one hand, and economic theory on the other, this difference being based on simplified and sometimes unrealistic assumptions. As a result, they would not only learn that the conclusions of economic theory cannot be applied mechanically to everyday life in all cases, but, more importantly, they would also learn that the theory is nevertheless not useless. In fact, they would learn that economic theory is of great help in analyzing and understanding complicated realities as well as in the making of rational decisions, provided that we are aware of its limitations. Realistically, we can only recognize the limitations of the applicability of economic theory if we understand the assumptions that underlie it. Our experiences indicate that many students are not sufficiently exposed to the assumptions and the relevance of their applicability, and that when these are explicitly stated and used in conjunction with different parts of the theory, the level of comprehension is substantially raised.

A NOTE ON PRODUCTION THEORY

In economics, the term production refers to those activities of firms by which inputs are used to produce output. Inputs, in general, involve the productive factors of land, labor, capital and,

---

[4] It seems that many disputes between economists and much of the misunderstanding on the part of students are due to their failure to realize the importance of one or more of the above assumptions. John R. Hicks, an eminent scholar and theorist, in his book *Value and Capital* (1946), said, "Pure economics has a remarkable way of producing rabbits out of a hat—apparently a priori propositions which apparently refer to reality. It is fascinating to try to discover how the rabbits got in, for those of us who do not believe in magic must be convinced that they got in somehow. I have become convinced myself that they get in . . . by the assumption. . . ." Unfortunately, at times, some people have even forgotten the assumptions on which their arguments are based. It is no wonder that we have so many unnecessary disputes among economists. If textbooks fully stressed the important assumptions that underlie economic theory, many unnecessary disputes and misunderstandings could be avoided.

depending on the mode of analysis, entrepreneurship. Raw materials, which are usually the outputs of other firms, may sometimes (but not always) be involved. Output denotes the commodity or service into which the inputs are transformed in the process of their use. The difference between output and input may involve form and the use to which something is put. In the case of an automobile, the finished product can be conceived of as the commodity, yet the tires, steel, and other materials from which a car is made are considered to be inputs by the automaker, whereas they are outputs to their manufacturers. The same commodity may also differ from one location to another; for example, a car in San Francisco is a different commodity than the same car in Detroit. Alternatively, a given commodity can differ as a function of time; for example; a car in September of one year is a different commodity from the same car in November of the previous year.

It follows that in economics, not only activities in agriculture and manufacturing, but also those in transportation, storage, the wholesale and retail trades, and many other services are considered as production. They all involve activities into which inputs are directed to produce a commodity that has exchange value in the market.

This transformation of inputs into a commodity or product is what economists often refer to as the production function. It is nothing more than a general term that refers to the relationship between output and the inputs required to produce that output. This relationship can be equivalently represented or expressed in at least three different ways: numerically, graphically, or in a general mathematical form. In this book, the numerical and graphical methods will be used in the textual narrative; the more sophisticated mathematical techniques will appear only in the appendices. This applies both to production theory, and to all other topics discussed in the text.

Production involves the transformation of inputs into a commodity or product as an output

Although production function is a general term that describes the relationship between output and inputs, a numerical representation of the input–output relationship is often referred to as a production schedule and the graphical representation of this relationship as a production curve. There is a one-to-one correspondence between the former and the latter, that is, corresponding to each production schedule, we have one and only one production curve and vice versa. Since they are equivalent but different ways of showing the same thing, we shall use the representation that is most illustrative and convenient. In addition, since some students are more at ease with numbers, whereas others are more at ease with graphical representations, some important points will be illustrated using both numerical and graphical examples.

This process can be described in a number of ways

Students should recognize that a specific technology gives rise to a specific production schedule, production curve, or production function. In other words, a given production schedule or curve is based on a specific technology, whereas for a different technology, we have a different schedule (or as economists would say, when technology changes, the whole production curve shifts). It is also important to remember that for a given amount or combination of inputs, only the maximum amount of product is considered as the relevant output for a given technology. It follows, therefore, that in the context of our theory, the total product curve is the frontier of the production set. This approach is on solid ground under the assumption that the goal of the firm is profit maximization. Otherwise, there would be no reason why we should only consider the maximum product as output. Oddly enough, while some economists, on the one hand, question the validity of the classical profit-maximization assumption, on the other hand, they still use the maximum output frontier as the total product curve. In this sense, they are logically inconsistent. Thus, although the classical theory of the firm may not seem very realistic, it is, nevertheless, logically consistent from beginning to end, and one has to be very careful before contemplating any modifications to it.

In production theory, inputs can be classified as either fixed or variable. Fixed inputs are those that do not change when output changes. On the other hand, variable inputs must change in order to effect a change in output. The determination as to which inputs are fixed and which are variable is primarily dictated by time and technology, but care must be exercised so as not to be trapped into improper or arbitrary categorization. For example, land might be regarded as fixed, but the mode of its use can make it a variable input when considered in the total realm of economic activity.

Finally, before moving into a discussion of the production process, it is essential that we make the distinction between the concepts of the long run and the short run as used in economics. In production theory, the distinction is not necessarily based on a length of time, although time will largely determine which inputs are fixed and which variable. In the short run, some input(s) are fixed and some are variable, whereas in the long run, all inputs are variable. However, because production processes and technology differ, the short and long runs will differ depending on the product produced.

Chapter 1 deals with the one-variable-input case, which is definitely a short-run analysis. In Chapter 2 we shift to an analysis based on two variable inputs; this chapter can be considered a representation of a long-run model of the production process. The more general n-variable- (e.g., three or more) input case is considered in the Appendix, which can be considered as optional reading (instructors may wish to delete it from their assigned readings). We conclude Part I with a discussion of cost determination in Chapter 3, which builds on materials presented in Chapters 1 and 2. The student should recognize, however, that although our treatment of basic production economics is rigorous and complete, there are many special topics that are an integral part of the theory of production and the firm. These are covered in successively greater depth in the chapters following our discussion of consumer behavior and demand analysis.

PRODUCTION WITH
ONE VARIABLE INPUT

INTRODUCTION

Although, in reality, production processes generally require a wide variety of inputs, it is easier to grasp the essential principles of production and to illustrate the important concepts and relationships between certain entities if we first focus our attention on the simplest model, that is, the case of one variable input (e.g., labor) and one fixed input (e.g., land or capital). Later on, we shall extend our analysis to two variable inputs and, finally, to the general case of n (e.g., three or more) variable inputs.

We begin by assuming that technology is given, land is fixed, and output can only be changed by changing the amount of labor input. This also implies that labor can be combined with land in different proportions to produce various quantities of the product, which can, in principle, be either a physical good (e.g., wheat) or a service (e.g., repair work).

In essence, our model is based on the following specifications:

1. There is only one variable input;
2. there is only one fixed input;
3. the inputs can be combined in various proportions to produce the output in question;
4. the output is a homogeneous product; and
5. technology is given.

This simple model is actually more general than it appears. First of all, the fixed input is fixed only for a given production schedule or curve. It can be changed, but when the fixed input changes, so does the whole schedule or curve.[1] Secondly, the only variable input (which we have denoted labor for illustrative convenience) can be considered a unit comprised of various inputs combined in fixed proportions, such as a worker with a certain amount of tools and equipment using a certain amount of raw material per unit of time. Thus, for example, one unit of labor might consist of one worker with $50 in tools and $100 in materials, in which case two units of labor would include two workers, each with $50 in tools and $100 in materials, and so on. In short, this is what we mean by a unit of labor being a combination of work, tools, and materials in fixed proportions. Similarly, the only fixed input (land or capital) can be considered a unit that consists of a combination of land, capital, and management personnel in fixed proportions.

Any change in the fixed input involves a change in the whole production schedule or curve

1.1 THE PRODUCTION FUNCTION, SCHEDULE, AND CURVE

In economics, production theory is essentially a discussion of the relationships between inputs and output (outputs, in more general cases). Economists usually use the term *production function* to represent this general relationship. The term *function* is a mathematical concept that refers to a relationship between two variables or groups of variables. In mathematics, the ''function'' is a very general and convenient tool for representing the relationships between variables, but it tends to be too abstract for those who do not have an adequate mathematical background. A less abstract and easier to understand but more lengthy way of representing an input–output relationship is by means of a schedule. Corresponding to each schedule, a graphical representation (i.e., a curve) can usually be drawn. Thus, a production function, a schedule, and a curve are different ways of representing the same thing—an input–output relationship. The important advantage of using a schedule or a curve for representing input–output relationships is that they are more specific and the student can readily visualize the transformation. The disadvantage of a schedule is that many numbers and a considerable amount of work are necessary in order to illustrate a point. On the other hand, the disadvantage of a curve is that we cannot draw graphs in more than three dimensions. In fact, it is not easy to draw even three-dimensional graphs to scale. The most commonly used graphs are therefore two dimensional. Thus, the graphical method can only be effectively employed in simple cases not involving more than

---

[1] The perceptive student will recognize, however, that, once the fixed input is allowed to vary, one can, for unique combinations of two or more variable inputs, obtain the same level of output as for some combination of a fixed input and a variable input. This will be made clear later.

three variables. The advantage of using the notion of a production function in mathematical terms is that it can handle the more general case with any number of variables; however, as noted earlier, it has the disadvantage of requiring a greater mathematical sophistication than is normally possessed by students. Consequently, for the convenience of the majority of students, only numerical and graphical methods will be used in the text. Those students who wish to extend their analytical skills can refer to the appendices for the general mathematical methods.

1.1.1 The Production Schedule

A production schedule can be represented in the form of a table that gives the total (maximum) output obtainable from different amounts of the variable input when a specific amount of the fixed input and technology are given. A production schedule is essentially a hypothetical relationship between inputs and output.

As an example, consider the hypothetical case in which corn is produced on 1 acre of land using varying amounts of labor. The fixed input is land, the variable input is person-years of labor time (each unit of labor is defined as a worker equipped with a standard quantity of tools and equipment of standard quality), and the output is bushels of corn. Assume it to be known (recall the assumption of perfect knowledge or information) that, on the same acre of land, by varying the quantity of labor, the total output of corn changes as shown in Table 1.1.

1.1.2 Average and Marginal Products

Columns 3 and 4 in Table 1.1 give the average and marginal products of labor. Since these are important concepts in economics, they need to be precisely defined. The *average product* (AP) of the variable input (in our case labor) is the amount of output produced per unit of the input for each level of the output that is obtained with the corresponding volume of input. In other

TABLE 1.1. Output of Corn (in Bushels) from 1 Acre of Land

Labor	Total output	Average product of labor	Marginal product of labor
0	1		
1	10	10	10
2	24	12	14
3	39	13	15
4	52	13	13
5	60	12	8
6	66	11	6
7	63	9	-3

words, the average product of an input of labor is computed by dividing the total output by the corresponding amount of labor used to produce it. For example, the values in column 3 are computed by dividing the outputs given in column 2 by the corresponding units of labor in column 1.

The *marginal product* (MP) of the variable input is defined, in general, as the ratio of the change in output for a small change in the variable input, all other inputs being held constant. For practical purposes, the MP of the variable input can be considered as the increase in total output attributable to the addition of one unit of the variable input. For example, the values in column 4 are computed by dividing the successive differences in output from column 2 by the corresponding differences in labor from column 1. The MP is sometimes called the increment in output that is obtained from an additional unit of variable input.

1.1.3 The Relationship Between AP and MP

From an examination of columns 3 and 4 of Table 1.1, it is obvious that both AP and MP at first increase, reach a maximum, and then decrease. Furthermore, MP is equal to AP when the latter is at its maximum. The student may ask whether this is simply a matter of coincidence. The answer is no, since there is a definite mathematical relationship between AP and MP. For that matter, as we shall see later, there is actually a definite relationship between any pair of average and marginal entities, such as average and marginal costs or average and marginal revenues. Mathematically, MP is always equal to AP when the latter is at its maximum.[2] In general, whenever MP is greater than AP, the latter will increase. It is important to note that this condition will hold only so long as MP is greater than the AP, regardless of whether MP itself is increasing or decreasing. Many students mistakenly infer that a "greater than" condition means "increasing." When MP is equal to AP, the latter will neither increase nor decrease. On the other hand, when MP is less than AP, the latter will decrease. Thus, MP is always equal to AP at the maximum of the latter.

To illustrate the logic of the aforementioned relationship, and clarify the analysis, we shall use a simple example of batting averages in baseball. If a player has a batting average of three hundred (.300) for 50 games of the season to date, this means (as every schoolchild knows) that the player has gotten three hits out of every 10 times at bat, on the average, for the past 50 games.

There is a definite mathematical relationship between AP and MP or any other pair of average and marginal entities

[2] In the case of cost behavior, however, the marginal cost is generally equal to the average cost when the average cost is at its minimum. There are special cases where cost behavior does not apply, such as when a maximum or minimum does not exist. This will be illustrated later.

If there is a game today, the player's batting average for it is the MP. If the player is lucky and has five hits in 10 times at bat, the batting average for the game (i.e., MP) is .500, which is higher than the overall average the player had before the game. This higher MP will result in the player's average being higher at the end of the game. Thus, whenever MP is greater than AP, the latter will necessarily increase. On the other hand, if the player is unlucky and has a batting average for the game that is less than .300, the overall batting average will be lower at the end of the game. Similarly, if by chance the player's average for the game is exactly .300, then the overall batting average will not be changed at the end of the game.

It is important to understand the logic of the relationship between marginal and average entities because we shall encounter this relationship many times in our discussions. Furthermore, this knowledge may be helpful to those students whose future work will encompass production, accounting, budgeting, or evaluating the behavior of phenomenon in which input–output relationships are involved. For example, many of our tax schemes and social programs can be better analyzed if the relationship between average and marginal products or costs is fully understood.

1.1.4 The Law of Diminishing Returns and the Law of Variable Proportions

As mentioned earlier, one characteristic common to both AP and MP is that they at first increase, reach a maximum, and then decrease. The existence of a decreasing MP has special economic significance. In fact, if the condition of a decreasing MP did not prevail in production, it would not be necessary to study economics. (For that matter, engineering and most scientific research would also probably not be needed.) Imagine, if you will, that the MP of fertilizer always increases for each additional ounce of fertilizer applied to a given plot of earth. This means that each additional application of an ounce of fertilizer will increase the output (e.g., of wheat) even more than the previous ounce, thereby making it possible, if sufficient fertilizer is applied, to raise all of the wheat needed to feed all of the people in the world in a flower pot. If this were true, we would have an abundance of everything, the question of economizing would no longer arise, and the term efficiency would have no practical value.

A decreasing MP has special economic significance

Since a decreasing MP is an inevitable physical phenomenon and, in almost all cases, actual production takes place within the range of decreasing MP, it is one of the most (if not the most) important natural phenomena so far as the study of economics is concerned. This is why economists have treated it as a physical law and called it the *law of diminishing returns* to stress this point. Because of the importance of this physical phenomenon, we shall restate it in its general form.

Definition: Law of Diminishing Returns. As the amount of a variable input is increased, all other inputs being held constant, a point is reached beyond which, for each additional variable input, total output will increase at a decreasing rate. In other words, diminishing return corresponds to decreasing MP. Note that the law of diminishing returns refers to the case where only one input is changed while all other inputs are held constant. A similar but more general concept is the *law of variable proportions*.

Definition: Law of Variable Proportions. If one or more inputs are held constant, proportionate increases in all of the other inputs will at some point lead to a less than proportionate increase in output. In other words, when some inputs are increased proportionately and the remainder held constant, output will increase at a decreasing rate.

In Table 1.1, diminishing returns prevail after the third unit of labor input. The data in this table also demonstrate the law of variable proportions, if labor is considered the combined input of a worker, tools, and equipment. Ultimately, of course, if we kept adding labor to the fixed input (land), we would see that MP becomes negative. Although AP is positive in our example, it could approach zero (but it cannot be negative) when the total output approaches zero. In short, the law of diminishing returns tells us that we cannot keep adding variable inputs to one or more fixed inputs and expect to obtain additional output continuously.

1.2 THE PRODUCTION CURVE

1.2.1 Total Product Curve

The data in columns 1 and 2 of Table 1.1 can be equivalently represented in the form of a graph (see Figure 1.1). In geometry, it is customary to plot the independent variable on the horizontal axis and the dependent variable on the vertical axis. In production, the input (in this case labor, which is denoted L) is the independent variable and is thus plotted on the horizontal axis; the output (in this case corn and denoted Q) is the dependent variable and is thus plotted on the vertical axis. Without the assumption of divisibility, the graph would contain only the eight isolated points 0–G. However, under the assumption of divisibility with respect to both the input labor and the output corn, we can join the successive points by straight-line segments. The result is a curve that shows the relationship between output and labor—the *total product (TP) curve*. It should be noted that the curve at first rises slowly, then rapidly, and then slowly again, until it finally reaches a maximum and starts to decline. This form of curvature represents the behavior of the traditional TP curve, which may not be completely realistic, but nevertheless has val-

The assumption of divisibility is essential to smooth TP, AP, and MP curves

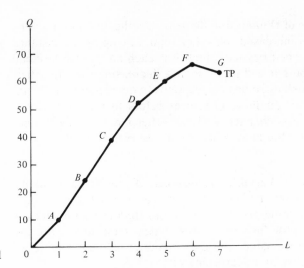

FIGURE 1.1

uable illustrative properties. In the same manner that the behavior of AP and MP is determined from the total output in Table 1.1, so can it be deduced from the behavior of the TP curve in Figure 1.1, albeit not as precisely.

1.2.2 The AP and MP Curves

If we plot the data from column 3 against those from column 1 of Table 1.1 and connect the points by straight-line segments as we did in Figure 1.1, we have the *average product (AP) curve*. Similarly, if we plot the data from column 4 against those from column 1, we obtain the *marginal product (MP) curve*. We have plotted these data in Figure 1.2.

FIGURE 1.2

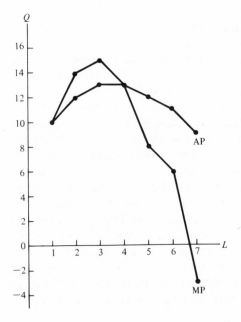

The AP and MP curves clearly exhibit the features of AP and MP which we described earlier; namely, both at first rise (increase), reach a maximum, and then decline (decrease).[3] Furthermore, the MP curve intersects the AP curve at the maximum of the latter. In addition, whereas MP can be either positive, zero, or negative, AP cannot be negative, and a zero AP, although conceivable theoretically, does not have much economic significance.

1.3 GRAPHICAL ANALYSIS OF THE PRODUCT CURVES

Since both AP and MP are defined in terms of TP, the AP and MP curves can be derived from the TP curve. Consequently, certain relationships between the AP and MP curves can be clearly illustrated by the graphical method. Although many economists have observed that the traditional shape of the various product curves is not very realistic, very few authors have pointed out that this approach nevertheless remains extremely valuable as a means of illustrating theory. Once the traditional model is fully understood, other special cases can be easily comprehended, as we shall see later. For this reason, a detailed graphical analysis of the traditional model will serve a useful purpose.

1.3.1 The Geometrical Relationship Between TP, AP, and MP

From the definition of AP, it is obvious that the AP of labor is represented by the slope of a ray drawn from the origin to the point on the TP curve corresponding to the given amount of labor. For example, in Figure 1.3 (for theoretical convenience, we have

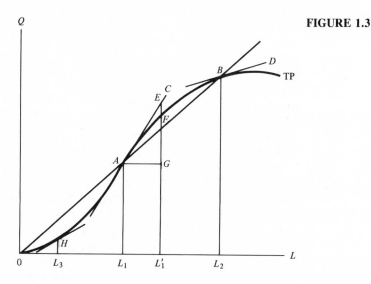

FIGURE 1.3

---

[3] Students may wish to reread Sections 1.1.3 and 1.1.4 to reinforce their understanding of the properties of TP, AP, and MP.

The slopes of rays and tangents to the TP curve provide a basis for determining whether AP and MP are increasing, decreasing, or constant

drawn a smooth TP curve), the AP for labor input L_1 is represented by the slope of $\overline{0A}$. This can be easily shown: For L_1, the output and corresponding labor input are represented by $\overline{L_1A}$ and $\overline{0L_1}$, respectively; by definition, the AP labor for input L_1 is $\overline{L_1A}/\overline{0L_1}$, that is, the slope of $\overline{0A}$. It is also obvious that the APs for labor inputs L_1 and L_2 are identical, since they are both represented by the slope of the same straight line. On the other hand, the MP for labor input L_1 is represented by the slope of $\overline{AC}$, which is tangent to the TP curve at point A, since, by definition, the MP for a given amount of an input is the change in output divided by the corresponding small change in the input. This is precisely represented by the slope of the tangent $\overline{AC}$ in the limit. The concept of the limit can be easily illustrated by assuming an increase in labor input from $\overline{0L_1}$ to $\overline{0L_1'}$, or by $\overline{L_1L_1'} = \overline{AG}$, the corresponding increase in output being represented by $\overline{GF}$. By definition, the MP for $\overline{L_1L_1'}$ is $\overline{GF}/\overline{L_1L_1'} = \overline{GF}/\overline{AG}$, and the slope of $\overline{AC}$ is represented by $\overline{GE}/\overline{AG}$, which is saying the same thing. However, for a small increase in labor input, L_1' approaches L_1 and G approaches A. Consequently, point E approaches point F, and, in the limit, the slope of $\overline{AC}$ is a good approximation of the MP for labor input L_1 for a small change in input. Similarly, the MP for labor input L_2 can be represented by the slope of $\overline{BD}$, which is tangent to the TP curve at point B. In short, a comparison of the slopes of the lines that are drawn tangent to the TP curve will tell us whether MP increases, decreases, or remains the same as we move along the TP curve for increased labor inputs.

Referring to Figure 1.3, we see that since $\overline{AC}$ has a steeper slope than $\overline{0A}$, the MP curve is above the AP curve at labor input L_1. On the other hand, the slope of $\overline{BD}$ is "flatter" (i.e., less steep) than that of $\overline{0B}$, which means that the MP curve is below the AP curve at labor input L_2. Since the MP curve changes from one that is above the AP curve at labor input L_1 to one that is below it at labor input L_2, the MP curve must intersect the AP curve somewhere between L_1 and L_2. It is also clear that the slope of a ray from the origin to the TP curve increases as we move along the TP curve to the right of point A. This means that the AP curve is rising at L_1. On the other hand, the AP curve is declining at L_2. This implies that the AP curve must reach its maximum somewhere between L_1 and L_2.

By the use of geometry, we have shown that the AP curve reaches its maximum between L_1 and L_2, and that the MP curve intersects the AP curve from above between L_1 and L_2. Thus, MP is equal to AP somewhere between L_1 and L_2. The question is whether the MP curve intersects the AP curve at the maximum of the latter. The answer is a definite yes. However, it may be more beneficial to the student if we extend our discussion on the behavior of the MP curve before proving that the AP curve is at its maximum when the MP curve intersects it from above.

It is seen in Figure 1.3. that the tangents $\overline{AC}$ and $\overline{BD}$ are both above the TP curve and that the one to the right ($\overline{BD}$) has a flatter slope. This means that the MP curve (and MP itself) declines as we move to the right of L_1. It can also be seen that the tangent at point H is below the TP curve and that its slope becomes steeper immediately to the right of point H. This means that the MP curve is rising at input level L_3. Since it rises at L_3 and declines at L_1, it follows that the MP curve must reach its maximum between L_3 and L_1. It turns out that the TP curve will have its steepest slope at the point where a tangent crosses TP from below to above, and this point is called the *point of inflection*. Note also that the point of inflection is to the left of L_1, whereas the maximum of the AP curve is to the right of it. This means that MP reaches its maximum before AP.

Figure 1.4 summarizes the above results and provides us with the means of proving that the MP curve intersects the AP curve at the maximum of the latter. The rationale for the proof is as follows:

1. $\overline{OS}$ is tangent to the curve TP at S and therefore represents the MP for input level L_S;
2. $\overline{OS}$ is also a ray from the origin to the TP curve and therefore represents the AP for L_S;
3. hence, MP equals AP immediately above L_S;
4. this means that the MP curve intersects the AP curve at input level L_S;
5. since $\overline{OS}$ is the steepest ray that one can draw from the origin to the TP curve, the AP curve must reach its maximum above L_S; finally,
6. the MP curve intersects the AP curve at the maximum of the latter.

A curve has a zero slope at either a maximum or a minimum.

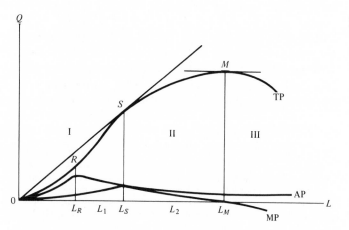

FIGURE 1.4

In Figure 1.4, we see that M is a point at which the curve has a zero slope. Therefore, the TP curve reaches its maximum when L_M labor is used. We can also see that the TP curve has its point of inflection at R; therefore, the MP curve has its maximum at input level L_R then declines, intersecting the AP curve at input level L_S, and finally reaches zero at L_M, where the TP curve is at its maximun.[4] With respect to the AP curve, at first it increases, doing so even after the MP curve has started to decline; it reaches its maximun at input level L_S, where it intersects the declining MP curve, and then starts to decline. Since TP cannot be negative, AP also can never be negative.

From Figure 1.4 it is also clear that as long as the MP curve is above the AP curve (note the important thing is that the MP curve is above the AP curve, not that MP is increasing), the latter will rise. Similarly, as soon as the MP curve goes below the AP curve, the latter starts to decline. However, as long as MP is equal to AP, the AP curve will neither rise nor decline. This means that if the AP curve is flat within a certain range, MP and AP will coincide within this range. We shall encounter this situation later.

1.3.2. Stages of Production, and Intensive and Extensive Margins

As mentioned earlier, one advantage of the traditional model is its rich properties for analytical purposes. Although in covering all of the possibilities in production it must include some that do not have any practical economic significance, the traditional model nevertheless helps us to gain more insight into the physical and technical properties of production. The classification of production into different stages can serve as an example. Economists use the relationships between the TP, AP, and MP curves to classify production into three stages based on the levels of the variable input. Stage I covers the range from zero input to the level of the variable input at which AP is maximum. In other words, stage I corresponds to an increasing AP. Stage II covers the range from maximum AP to zero MP, whereas stage III covers the range of negative MP of the variable input.

Under profit maximization production will never take place in stage III

It is obvious that production would never take place in stage III, since a negative MP means that a producer can get more output by reducing the variable input. Consequently, a producer

---

[4] A moment's reflection with respect to Figure 1.4 will convince the student that TP is maximum when MP is zero. We can appreciate the fact that since MP is some positive value, it adds to TP; however, once MP is zero, nothing is added to TP. Observe that as we proceed to add labor inputs, TP continues to increase until L_M amount of labor is used. At that point, the tangent to the TP curve has a zero slope, meaning that MP is zero and TP is maximum. The student should not infer, however, that TP will always be maximum when MP is zero. We shall explain this point further in a later section.

whose goal was profit maximization would never operate in stage III. Although not as obvious, it is nevertheless true that production should also not take place in stage I. It will be shown in Chapter 2 that stage I of labor corresponds to stage III of some other input and therefore does not result in economical production. For the present, however, common sense will serve to convince us that production should not take place in Stage I, if we assume that the producer, irrespective of the number of workers employed, pays the same wage rate per worker and sells the products for the same price.[5] As proof of this, note that when the AP curve is rising, MP is greater than AP, and that if a producer is hiring less than L_S workers (at L_S, AP is maximum; see Figure 1.4), and still making a profit, then an even larger profit can be made by hiring more workers, since each additional worker will bring in a greater amount of additional revenue than the average worker hired previously. This is true because MP is greater than AP in this range, and the additional revenue that the additional worker brings to the firm is equal to MP multiplied by the price of the output (MP $\times$ P), which is greater than the product of AP $\times$ P. If the latter is greater than the wage rate (and this must be so in order to make a profit), then the additional revenue from the additional worker must be greater than the wage rate; thus, there is a net profit from the additional worker. This argument applies to each and every worker as long as the AP curve is rising. Therefore, a producer who wants to maximize profits will never stop hiring within the range between zero input and L_S. Hence, if the goal is profit maximization, production can only take place in stage II. It should be pointed out that the well-known Cobb–Douglas production function covers stage II only.[6]

The point of zero MP of the variable input L_M is called the *intensive margin,* whereas the point of maximum AP L_S is called the *extensive margin.* The terms intensive margin and extensive margin are used with respect to the fixed rather than the variable input. For example, in agriculture, land is cultivated too intensively when so many workers are used on a given section that the MP labor becomes zero. Similarly, when only a few workers are used on a given section of land, its cultivation is considered extensive, and the border of extensive cultivation is at the point of maximum AP. Hence, the term extensive margin is generally defined as the point of maximum AP of labor with respect to the fixed input (i.e., land) rather than the variable input (i.e., labor). In short, as long as profit maximization is the goal, production will take place between the extensive margin (AP maximum) and intensive margin (MP zero).

Intensive and extensive margins in production are conditions that derive primarily from the fixed input

[5] In technical terms, this is a condition of perfect competition in both input and output markets.

[6] The Cobb–Douglas production function is covered in more detail in the appendix following Chapter 2.

1.4 PRODUCTION IN THE REAL WORLD: CONSTANT AP AND MP

Many economists have come to realize that production in the real world is seldom, if ever, reflected by the smooth bell-shaped AP curves that one often encounters in textbooks. It is very likely that the AP curve will be flat over a considerable range before it begins to gradually decline. Thus, the TP, AP, and MP curves shown in Figure 1.5 (as well as the relationships among them) are more realistic.

In the traditional approach, the reason that the AP at first increases is that there is disproportionately too much fixed input (or, conversely, too little of the variable input), which results in a nonoptimal combination of the inputs. For example, in agriculture, if one person were to cultivate 1000 acres of land without the aid of modern machinery, weeds would likely take over and output would be negligible. If more workers were added, the weeds would be brought under control and it is not only conceivable, but probable, that both the TP and the AP of labor would increase; this is the result of the fact that each additional worker contributes an amount of output that is greater than the

FIGURE 1.5

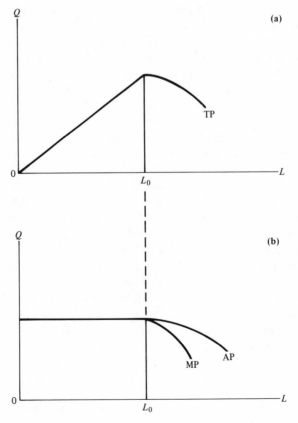

average produced by the previous workers (i.e., MP exceeds AP). However, this phenomenon can only last so long. As more and more workers are hired to cultivate the same thousand acres, sooner or later a point will be reached where the output contributed by an additional worker will not be as great as the average of the previous workers (i.e., MP is less than AP), and, as we have shown earlier, the AP of labor will decrease. This is the rationale behind the traditional bell-shaped AP curve. However, the above arguments are true only when land is not divisible and there is no free disposal. In such a case, one worker is forced to either cultivate all of the thousand acres or leave the land lie idle at a certain cost, it being implicitly assumed that the worker cannot leave part of the thousand acres idle without cost and only cultivate the rest. Under these circumstances, the AP curve will be bell-shaped.

In reality (and by our assumption in the beginning of this chapter), the land is divisible and there is free disposal. Faced with cultivating 1000 acres, the worker has at least two choices: (1) spread the labor thinly over the entire 1000 acres or (2) concentrate the work on a manageable area and let the rest of the land lie idle. In the traditional approach, the bell-shaped AP curve is implicitly based on the assumption that the worker chooses the first alternative. Given the divisibility of land, free disposal, and operating under our assumptions of perfect knowledge and the goal of profit maximization, the proper choice of the worker (or for that matter the manager of the farm) should be the second alternative. If the highest output for one worker can be obtained by cultivating only 50 acres, then if only one worker is available, the choice is to cultivate only 50 acres and let 950 acres lie idle. On the other hand, if two workers are available, 100 acres should be cultivated and the other 900 acres left idle, and so forth. If we further assume homogeneity of land and labor, the AP per worker (note that we are talking about the AP of the variable input—labor—not the AP of the fixed input—land) will be constant up to 20 workers, and the TP curve will be a straight line from the origin to the 20th worker.[7] However, when more than 20 workers are hired to cultivate the thousand acres of land, each additional one will contribute successively less to the output, and MP will become less than AP, with the result that the AP of labor begins to decrease. The range of the decreasing AP of labor is highly relevant for analysis because the number of workers which a firm will hire depends not only on how much revenue an additional worker generates (which is a function of both MP and the price P of the output), but also on the wage rate. If the revenue that an additional worker generates is greater than the wage rate, a

The choice between alternatives in production depends on the assumptions of divisibility, free disposal, perfect knowledge, homogeneity of inputs, and the goal of profit maximization

---

[7] Up to the point where 20 workers are employed MP and AP will coincide.

firm will hire the worker even if the additional output that results is less than the previous average. This is the reason why stage II of the production process is particularly important in economic analysis.

If we were to study manufacturing production, we would discover a situation that is somewhat similar to the case just discussed. It is generally recognized that 100% utilization of plant capacity is the exception rather than the rule. There are many explanations for the underutilization of fixed capacity, one of them being that businesspeople, for various reasons, prefer to have some *reserve capacity* (see, e.g., Andrews, 1949). Under the assumption of homogeneity and divisibility of resources, when workers and raw material are added proportionately to idle machinery, there is no reason to expect that the additional output from an extra worker will be either higher or lower than the output from the original workers. The adding of more shifts will have the same result. For example, if we assumed that a given machine operated by one worker and using a certain amount of raw material can produce an output of 100 units in an 8-hour period, our homogeneity assumption would assure a doubling of the output if the machine were operated by two equally skilled workers in two shifts per day (assuming, of course, that the quantity of all necessary raw materials is also doubled). Alternatively, we might have two machines and two workers producing in one shift what one machine and two workers produce in two shifts. As long as we do not violate the assumption of homogeneity of inputs, AP will be constant and the TP curve will be a straight line in the relevant range.

Some people may argue that land left idle should not be considered a fixed input. This is basically a matter of semantics, but it poses an interesting question in production theory because it is concerned with the problem of the divisibility of inputs and the behavior of outputs. By way of illustration, suppose we start with one fixed and one variable input and assume the fixed input to be present in an uneconomically large proportion so that it results in a lower AP for the variable input than some other combination. Do there exist alternatives that will result in a higher AP? In many cases such alternatives are available. For example, assume that there are 10 machines, all of which are operating, and that with only one worker available to tend them, the maximum output per hour is 10 units. If we now shut off nine of the machines and with the same worker the maximum output per hour rises to 20 units, the question is whether 10 units or 20 units should be considered the output for the fixed input—10 machines—and the variable input—one worker. As we mentioned before, in economics only the maximum possible output is considered the output for a given combination of the inputs and a given technology. In our simple example, we see that for one worker and 10 machines the output is 20 units, not 10 units. Had there been perfect divisibility and homogeneity of inputs, MP and AP would be constant, that is, neither increasing nor decreasing. Hence, an increasing AP can be regarded as the result of indivisibility. For example, it is possible that if a machine needs five workers to operate and only one worker is available, then the machine cannot be operated efficiently, and the output may be less than one-fifth of that when operated by five workers. In reality, it is very likely that with only one worker operating a five-man machine, the machine may not produce at all and hence output will be zero.

An increasing AP is really the result of the indivisibility of inputs

At any rate, for practical or theoretical purposes, the model represented earlier in Figure 1.5(b) may be more useful than the traditional model which is represented by Figure 1.4. It may be useful to point out that the Cobb–Douglas production function, widely used in both theoretical analysis and empirical work, gives rise to only a decreasing AP, particularly in stage II.

Since many authors (see, e.g., Koutsoyiannis, 1975; Lancaster, 1974) have stressed the point that modern microeconomics recognizes the fact that the variable-cost curve is flat over a wide range, we can appreciate the fact that such an observation is rooted in the constancy of the AP of the variable input, which, as we have explained, rests in the divisibility and homogeneity of inputs. Because of its importance in analyzing the real-world production behavior, we shall discuss the case of the constancy of AP in more detail in Chapter 3.

SUMMARY

We have shown that the production function, schedule, and curve are three different methods of expressing the input–output relationship, each having advantages and disadvantages depending on the circumstances. Because schedules and curves can be visualized more easily than functions, they appear to be more specific and concrete. Hence, they are used more often in the beginning and intermediate levels of study in economics. However, at the advanced level, the concept of production function is more useful.

Although, in the real world, we normally deal with a fixed input and more than one variable input for short-run analysis of production, for theoretical convenience and simplicity we have employed the one-variable-input model in this chapter, where we have used the production schedules and graphs for illustrative purposes. We have also emphasized that the production schedule is constructed to show only the maximum amount of output obtainable for a given amount of the variable input, assuming technology and other inputs are fixed. We then showed how this information can be transposed onto a two-dimensional graph with the variable input on the horizontal axis and output on the vertical axis. Both the production schedule and the two-dimensional graph are used to analyze the relationship between changes in total output and the amount of variable input in order to gain an understanding of the concepts of marginal and average product and their significance in the study of the production process.

Based on our analysis of the relationships between total, marginal, and average product, the phenomenon of decreasing marginal product and the law of diminishing returns were explained in the context of the one-variable-input model of production. We also noted the distinction between the law of diminishing returns, which applies to the one-variable-input model, and the law of variable proportions, which is used to describe the phenomenon of decreasing marginal product when there is a proportionate change in more than one variable input, e.g., capital and labor both changing proportionately.

We concluded our discussion of the one-variable-input model by using the graphical method to illustrate the three stages of production and to describe the concepts of extensive and intensive margins in production. It is in the context of our discussion of the three stages of production that we indicate that, although the traditional textbook approach uses smooth, bell-shaped marginal and average product curves to define output behavior over the various stages, empirical evidence indicates that the marginal and average product are constant within a given range, hence challenging the traditional approach. We indicate that the assumptions of divisibility and free disposal provide a sound theoretical justification for the modern approach with regard to the shape of the marginal and average product curves, thus bringing the modern approach closer to reality.

PRODUCTION WITH
TWO VARIABLE INPUTS:
OPTIMAL INPUT COMBINATION AND EFFICIENCY

INTRODUCTION

The main purpose of the one-variable-input case discussed in Chapter 1 was to introduce the fundamental concepts, terminology, and essential relationships that are applicable in production economics and to explain and illustrate the behavior of the various product (output) curves. Although it was not intended to be realistic, we considered it useful in helping the student to understand some fundamental principles of production economics. A more general model, the two-variable-input case, will be analyzed in this chapter.

The two-variable-input model is still a considerable departure from reality because any activity in production usually involves many different kinds and qualities of input such as labor, tools and equipment, and raw material. However, the relationship between output and raw material for a given technology is usually quite rigid and cannot easily be altered. An example of such rigidity is the amount of steel that is used in producing a given size car. Therefore, the question of choice of material does not usually arise. In addition, for analytical purposes in production, buildings or land can usually be treated as a special kind of capital. Therefore, the two-variable-input model, which usually refers to the combination of labor and capital, is more general than it at first appears. Many empirical studies as well as many advanced theoretical analyses are based on such a model.

As we mentioned in Chapter 1, in terms of production, the distinction between the long and the short run is that in the short run a certain input(s) is fixed, whereas in the long run all inputs are variable. If it is assumed that there are only two inputs, the one-variable-input case is a short-run model and the two-variable-input case a long-run model. On the other hand, if it is assumed that there are more than two inputs, the two-variable-input case can be considered a short-run model in that a product is produced by using two variable inputs and one or more fixed inputs. Thus, the two-variable-input model is quite flexible in its representation of different conditions of production.

2.1 PRODUCTION PROCESSES

Economists use the term *production process* (activity) to specify the relationships between the output and inputs, on the one hand, and the specific combination of the inputs used to produce the output, on the other hand. These relationships can be represented by either a schedule (see, e.g., Table 2.1) or a graph consisting of output rays from the origin that correspond to given mixes of the two inputs—labor and capital (see, e.g., Figure 2.1). A suggested formal definition follows.

Definition: Production Process. A relationship between the output and the necessary inputs for a fixed input ratio. It is understood that the output refers to the maximum possible product obtainable from the given inputs.

To provide further clarification and qualification of our definition, two things should be pointed out: (1) Two different input ratios used to produce the same product are considered different production processes and (2) the term production process has a meaning in economics different from that common in industry, where the various steps through which raw materials go in the course of being transformed into a finished product are viewed as the production process. Tables 2.1 and 2.2, as well as Figure 2.1, have been constructed to illustrate the logic of these two limiting qualifications.

Different production processes result from a change in technology

Suppose that two inputs, for example, labor (L) and capital (K), are used in a given combination to produce one output (Q), as shown in Table 2.1. This will be called Production Process 1, and it represents a unique combination of labor and capital to be used to produce output. It should also be remembered that the output obtained for the given capital/labor ratio is determined by tech-

TABLE 2.1. Production Process 1

K	L	Q	Capital/labor ratio
1	2	5	$\frac{1}{2}$
2	4	10	$\frac{1}{2}$
3	6	15	$\frac{1}{2}$
4	8	24	$\frac{1}{2}$
5	10	28	$\frac{1}{2}$

TABLE 2.2. Production Process 2

K	L	Q	Capital/labor ratio
2	1	5	2
4	2	10	2
6	3	15	2
8	4	24	2
10	5	28	2

nology. Therefore, Production Process 1 is unique in that it is conditional on a given technology. Obviously, if we change the technology, we shall have another production process and hence output levels may differ for the same capital/labor ratio. Furthermore, just as a different technology with the same capital/labor ratio may generate a different output schedule, so too may a different capital/labor ratio with the same technology. The important fact to bear in mind is that if homogeneity of inputs prevails throughout the relevant range and technology is given (i.e., fixed), output will increase when inputs increase.

Given the same technology, different production processes result from change in the ratio of inputs

Note that in Production Process 1, the capital/labor ratio is constant, namely, $\frac{1}{2}$ for all output and input levels. In Table 2.2, however, the capital/labor ratio is constant at 2. Different capital/labor ratios distinguish one production process from another, that is, if the capital/labor ratio changes, it can no longer be called the same process. The input–output relationship is implicitly determined by technology. With a different technology, the same quantity and combination of inputs may result in a different quantity of output. As we noted in Chapter 1, a change in technology will shift the product curves. This can be readily perceived from an inspection of Tables 2.1 and 2.2.

Production Processes 1 and 2 can be plotted on a graph, as shown in Figure 2.1. Labor input L is plotted on the horizontal

FIGURE 2.1

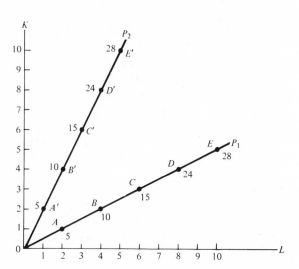

axis, capital K is plotted on the vertical axis, and P_1 and P_2 correspond to Production Processes 1 and 2, respectively. The number adjacent to each point, which corresponds to a given input (labor and capital) combination, represents the output. For example, point A corresponds to the combination of 1 unit of capital and 2 units of labor, which, according to Production Process 1, produces a maximum amount of 5 units of the output. Therefore, we have written the number 5 adjacent to point A, and this simply indicates that, for the given technology, 1 unit of capital combined with 2 units of labor can produce a maximum amount of 5 units of the product. Similarly, 2 units of capital and 4 units of labor can produce 10 units of output and so forth. Note that all of the points on ray $\overline{0P_1}$ have a capital/labor ratio of $\frac{1}{2}$. Similarly, all of the points on ray $\overline{0P_2}$ satisfy the condition of a capital/labor ratio of 2. The important fact to remember in order to understand the graph is that it is a device that uses a two-dimensional scheme to represent a three-dimensional concept (this is similar to a contour map, where the same altitude for various locations is represented by a curve). We shall make intensive use of this technique in this chapter as well as in Chapter 4, The Theory of Consumer Behavior. It is useful for students to familiarize themselves with this type of graph.

2.2 RETURNS TO SCALE AND THE LAW OF VARIABLE PROPORTIONS

The law of variable proportions, as well as the older concept of the law of diminishing returns discussed in Chapter 1, is concerned with short-run phenomena, since at least one input has to be constant while others vary. On the other hand, the concept of *returns to scale* refers to the phenomenon where all inputs are variable. Furthermore, all inputs have to change *proportionately* in order to satisfy the condition of returns to scale. In this sense, returns to scale is essentially a long-run concept.

Returns to scale and diminishing returns are different concepts, but both relate to how output changes with quantity of inputs

It is important to understand that returns to scale and the law of diminishing returns represent entirely different concepts and are not related in any systematic fashion. However, as we shall see later, increasing returns to scale and diminishing returns can occur simultaneously, depending on how we treat our inputs. Moreover, the concept can apply to three possible conditions, namely, constant, decreasing, or increasing returns to scale. Because such a statement may appear confusing and, possibly, inconsistent to the student, we shall define each of these conditions.

Definition: Constant Returns to Scale. If *all inputs* are changed proportionately, output will also change in the same proportion. For example, if all inputs are doubled, then the output will also be doubled; similarly, if all inputs are halved, then the output will also be halved. In general, if all the inputs are multiplied by a given positive number, the output will also be multiplied by the same number. The numerical example of Table 2.1 indicates constant returns to scale for the output range 5–15 units. When capital and labor are doubled from 1 to 2 and from 2 to 4, respectively, output is also doubled from 5 to 10. When capital and labor are further multiplied by 1.5, an increase from 2 to 3 and from 4 to 6, respectively, the output is also multiplied by 1.5, increasing from 10 to 15. A similar condition applies for Production Process 2 (see Table 2.2).

Definition: Decreasing Returns to Scale. If *all inputs* are changed proportionately, output will change less than proportionately. For example, if all inputs are doubled, then output will less than double; similarly, if all inputs are halved, output will decrease by less than one-half. Our numerical examples (see Tables 2.1 and 2.2) indicate decreasing returns to scale in the output range 24–28 units.

Definition: Increasing Returns to Scale. If *all inputs* are changed proportionately, output will change more than proportionately. For example, if all inputs are doubled, output will more than double; similarly, if all inputs are halved, output will decrease by more than one-half. In our numerical examples (see Tables 2.1 and 2.2), increasing returns to scale occur in the output range 15–24.

For the benefit of students who have a better grasp of mathematics, it may be mentioned in passing that the different conditions of returns to scale correspond to the degree of homogeneity of a function. In particular, a production function with homogeneity of degree 1 will result in constant returns to scale; homogeneity of degree <1 will result in decreasing returns to scale; and homogeneity of degree >1 will result in increasing returns to scale. This point will be demonstrated in more detail in Section 2.13 and in the appendix to this chapter.

It is most important for the student to recognize that a production process may show constant returns to scale in one output range and both decreasing and increasing returns in other ranges, as indicated by our numerical example. The direction of processes such as returns to scale, the law of variable proportions, and the law of diminishing returns is determined by the technology and physical conditions that govern the production process. These are taken as data in economic analysis.

In general, constant returns should prevail in most cases because when all inputs are homogeneous and are changed proportionately, it is equivalent, in the case of expansion, to a precise duplication of the input mix of the original production line. Thus, there is no reason why output should not be precisely duplicated. This is true only under the assumption that individual production activities are independent in the sense that a change in the level of one input used will not alter the effectiveness with which another can be used. However, in reality, this assumption may be violated. For example, as the number of production activities in a firm increases, so do both the need for lines of communication and the complexity of planning and coordinating production. For this reason, a change in the quantity of inputs used may result in a change in their quality, which, in turn, may affect the input–output performance, that is, returns to scale as a whole. Thus, decreasing returns to scale can be the result of complications that arise due to changes in the scale of operations.

On the other hand, increasing returns to scale can be the result of certain physical phenomena. For example, the amount of material required to construct a pipeline is directly proportional to its circumference multiplied by its length. On the other hand, the carrying capacity of a pipeline is equal to its cross-sectional area multiplied by the speed at which the fluid moves through it. The circumference of the pipeline is equal to $2\pi r$, whereas its cross-sectional area is equal to πr^2 (π is a constant, approximately equal to 3.1416, and r is the radius of the cross section). If we double the radius of the pipeline (r becomes $2r$), the new circumference is $2\pi(2r) = 2(2\pi r)$ and the new cross-sectional area is $\pi(2r)^2 = 4\pi r^2$. Thus, in this case, a doubling of the input results in a quadrupling of the output (carrying capacity at the same speed), an obvious example of increasing returns to scale.

Unique physical phenomena can result in increasing returns even if the amount of input rises only proportionately

2.3 EFFICIENT AND INEFFICIENT PROCESSES

The concept of efficiency in production can be best understood by first explaining what is meant by an inefficient process and then describing it in detail. We shall use both tabular and graphical methods for illustration.

Definition: Inefficient Process. A production process is considered inefficient if it uses more of at least one input but not less of any others to produce the same quantity of output as another process or combination of processes.

Definition: Efficient Process. A production process that is not inefficient is considered an efficient process. Note that an efficient process as defined here is not unique. In fact, there are usually an infinite number of efficient processes.

The above definition of an inefficient process implies that sometimes such a process can be singled out by pairwise comparison of production processes. However, pairwise comparison of pro-

TABLE 2.3

Process	K	L	Q	Capital/labor ratio
P_1	2	4	10	$\frac{1}{2}$
P_2	4	2	10	2
P_3	3	4	10	$\frac{3}{4}$
P_4	3	3.5	10	$\frac{6}{7}$

cesses is not sufficient. In other words, sometimes a process will indeed be inefficient, but pairwise comparison will not be able to discover it. An example may make this point clear.

The numerical examples of Tables 2.1 and 2.2 are partially reproduced in Table 2.3. In addition, we add two more processes to the illustration.

Since all four processes are assumed to produce the same quantity of output using different combinations of the inputs, we can compare them pairwise in order to discover whether any process is inefficient according to our definition. It is important to point out that the sum of capital and labor for each process is meaningless. For example, the sum of capital and labor in producing 10 units of output is 6 for P_1. This number has no practical meaning because one cannot add two different things, such as 2 oranges and 4 apples. Another way to state this point is that the sum of capital and labor is not independent with respect to our choice of the unit of measure. For example, suppose that the values of L are in units of working days. Then the sum of capital and labor is the same for both P_1 and P_2, namely, 6. On the other hand, if we convert days into hours, for an 8-hour working day the values of L would be 32 and 16 for P_1 and P_2, respectively. Thus, the sum of capital and labor for P_1 and P_2 would now be 34 and 20, respectively. This shows that neither the number 6 nor the numbers 34 and 20 have any practical meaning. The only meaningful comparison that can be made between different processes is to compare capital with capital and labor with labor.

For the reasons elaborated above and from the definition of an inefficient process, it is easily seen that neither P_1 nor P_2 is inefficient according to pairwise comparison, because although P_1 uses more labor than P_2, it also uses less capital. If we compare P_2 and P_3, we reach the same conclusion, that is, neither can be called inefficient. However, when we compare P_1 and P_3, we see that, according to our definition, P_3 is inefficient because it uses the same amount of labor but more capital than P_1. In this case, pairwise comparison has made it possible to determine that P_3 is inefficient, whereas in the case of P_1 versus P_2 we could not make that determination (note that pairwise comparison with P_4 would also show P_3 to be inefficient). However, P_4 is not inefficient when compared separately with either P_1 or P_2. Does this mean that P_1, P_2, and P_4 are all efficient processes? Before arriving at any conclusion, a further test has to be performed.

It can be shown without much difficulty that P_4 is indeed inefficient. An examination of Tables 2.1 and 2.2 reveals that 10 units of output can be produced by using just 3 units of capital and 3 units of labor if one produces 5 units by P_1 and 5 units by P_2. Thus, a combination of P_1 and P_2 can produce the same output as P_4 by using the same amount of capital but less labor. Therefore, P_4 is inefficient according to our definition. Hence, only P_1 and P_2 are efficient processes.

Combining some production processes often enables us to evaluate the efficiency of other production processes

We can arrive at the same conclusion by the graphical method, provided that the graph is accurately drawn. The data of Table 2.3 are plotted in Figure 2.2. The four points P_1, P_2, P_3, and P_4 all represent 10 units of output for their respective combination of inputs. Two points on the same vertical line indicate that the corresponding processes need the same amount of labor to produce the same amount of output. Consequently, a point that is directly above (i.e., on the same vertical line) another point represents an inefficient process because it uses the same amount of labor but more of capital to produce the same amount of output. Thus, since P_3 is directly above P_1, it is an inefficient process. Similarly, if two points that represent the same output are on the same horizontal line, the one to the right corresponds to an inefficient process. Thus, since P_3 is to the right of P_4 on the same horizontal line, it is also an inefficient process. However, P_4 is above and to the left of P_1, whereas P_4 and P_1 are both below and to the right of P_2. Therefore, pairwise comparison does not show whether P_1, P_2, or P_4 is inefficient. However, if we draw a straight line between P_1 and P_2, it is seen that P_4 is above and to the right of the line $\overline{P_1 P_2}$. This indicates that P_4 is inefficient because a proper combination of P_1 and P_2 can be found that produces the same output as P_4 by using less of one input and

Graphical methods may be used for two inputs when the assumptions of divisibility, independence, and homogeneity of inputs are satisfied

FIGURE 2.2

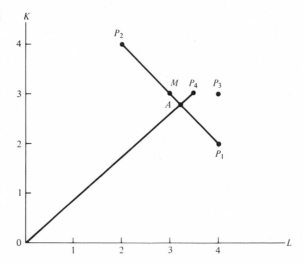

not more of the other. A quick referral to Tables 2.1 and 2.2 will attest to the validity of this observation.

Before we prove the above statement algebraically, it will help the student to gain more insight if we briefly review the assumptions that enable us to draw the line $\overline{P_1 P_2}$.

Assumption 2.1: Divisibility. As mentioned in Chapter 1, if capital and labor are not divisible, only integer units make sense. In that case we can only have three isolated points, and even P_4 will not make sense because it involves a half unit of labor. Only with the assumption of divisibility can we logically draw the line $\overline{P_1 P_2}$.

Assumption 2.2: Independence of Processes. This is the so-called additivity assumption. It simply states that if two processes are simultaneously used to produce a product, the output from one process depends only on the inputs to it, not on the output level of the other process.

Assumption 2.3: Constant Returns to Scale. As defined earlier, this is the condition where output changes proportionately to the change in inputs.

If Assumptions 2.1–2.3 are satisfied, it is possible to produce 10 units (for that matter, any amount) of output with any desired capital/labor ratio between $\frac{1}{2}$ and 2 by a proper combination of the two processes P_1 and P_2. For example, it is possible to determine the combination of P_1 and P_2 that has the same capital/labor ratio, that is, as P_4, $\frac{6}{7}$. This can be done as follows.

Suppose that a proportion $0 \le p \le 1$ of the 10 units is produced by P_1 and the rest by P_2 (a proportion of $0 \le 1 - p \le 1$). Thus, P_1 produces $10p$ units, P_2 produces $(1 - p)10$ units, and the total output produced by the two processes is $10p + (1 - p)10 = 10p + 10 - 10p = 10$ units, the amount desired. Since P_1 needs 2 units of capital and 4 units of labor in order to produce 10 units of output, by the assumption of constant returns to scale it needs $2p$ units of capital and $4p$ units of labor to produce $10p$ units of output. Similarly, P_2 needs $4(1 - p)$ units of capital and $2(1 - p)$ units of labor to produce $10(1 - p)$ units of output. The combined operation needs $2p + 4(1 - p) = 2p + 4 - 4p = 4 - 2p$ units of capital and $4p + 2(1 - p) = 4p + 2 - 2p = 2 + 2p$ units of labor to produce the 10 units of output. Since the desired capital/labor ratio is $\frac{6}{7}$, we set the capital/labor ratio of the combined operation equal to the desired ratio and solve for the unknown p:

$$(4 - 2p)/(2 + 2p) = \tfrac{6}{7} \tag{2.1}$$

which yields $p = \frac{8}{13}$.

This means that if $\frac{8}{13}$ of the 10 units is produced by P_1 and $\frac{5}{13}$ by P_2, the capital/labor ratio of this combined operation will be

$\frac{6}{7}$. This can be verified by computing the capital and labor requirements of the combined operation. The capital and labor needed by P_1 to produce $10 \times \frac{8}{13}$ units of output are $K_1 = 2 \times \frac{8}{13} = \frac{16}{13}$ and $L_1 = 4 \times \frac{8}{13} = \frac{32}{13}$, respectively. For P_2 the corresponding figures are $K_2 = 4 \times \frac{5}{13} = \frac{20}{13}$ and $L_2 = 2 \times \frac{5}{13} = \frac{10}{13}$, respectively. The total amount of capital $K^* = K_1 + K_2$ required for the combined operation is

$$K^* = \tfrac{16}{13} + \tfrac{20}{13} = \tfrac{36}{13} \tag{2.2}$$

and the total labor $L^* = L_1 + L_2$ required is

$$L^* = \tfrac{32}{13} + \tfrac{10}{13} = \tfrac{42}{13} \tag{2.3}$$

Finally,

$$K^*/L^* = (\tfrac{36}{13})/(\tfrac{42}{13}) = \tfrac{6}{7} \tag{2.4}$$

which proves our assertion. Point A in Figure 2.2 represents the combination of processes P_1 and P_2 which produces 10 units of output with a capital/labor ratio of $\frac{6}{7}$, the same as that of P_4. However, the capital requirement of the combined process is $K^* = 2.8$, whereas the labor requirement is $L^* = 3.2$, both of which are less than the corresponding input requirements—3 and 3.5—of P_4. This clearly proves that P_4 is an inefficient process, as we had concluded on the basis of intuitive observation.

The above algebraic method can be formalized so as to enable us to find any point between P_1 and P_2 (i.e., on $\overline{P_1 P_2}$) by finding a proper p. In other words, if the capital/labor ratios of P_1 and P_2 are R_1 and R_2, respectively, then it is possible, provided that Assumptions 2.1–2.3 are satisfied, to combine P_1 and P_2 in such a way that an output with any desired capital/labor ratio R^*, where $R_1 \le R^* \le R_2$ for $R_1 < R_2$, is produced. The proper combination of P_1 and P_2 is specified by the proportion $0 \le p^* \le 1$, that is, the proportion of the output produced by P_1. The following equation can be employed to find the proportion of output produced by P_1 (note that once P_1 is found, P_2 is automatically determined):

$$P^* = (R^*L_2 - K_2)/(K_1 - K_2 - R^*L_1 + R^*L_2)^1 \tag{2.5}$$

---

[1] Equation (2.5) can be derived as follows. Denote the combined capital by K^* and the combined labor by L^*. Then

$$K^* = p^*K_1 + (1 - p^*)K_2$$

$$L^* = p^*L_1 + (1 - p^*)L_2$$

$$K^*/L^* = [p^*K_1 + (1 - p^*)K_2]/[p^*L + (1 - p^*)L_2]$$

Since R^* is the desired capital/labor ratio, we set

$$R^* = K^*/L^*$$

Hence,

$$R^* = [p^*K_1 + (1 - p^*)K_2]/[p^*L_1 + (1 - p^*)L_2] \qquad \text{(continued)}$$

where R^* is the desired capital/labor ratio, K_1 and L_1 are the capital and labor requirements for process P_1, and K_2 and L_2 are the capital and labor requirements for process P_2. Students may wish to test Equation (2.5) and their understanding by using it and the values in Table 2.3 to compute p^* and determine whether it is $\frac{8}{13}$ for $R^* = \frac{6}{7}$.

Equation (2.5) can be used to find any point on a straight line connecting two points on a two-dimensional graph provided that one knows their locations (i.e., the abscissas and ordinates). Referring back to Figure 2.2, we see that when $p^* = 1$, we are at point P_1. As p^* decreases, $1 - p^*$ increases, and we move along the line $\overline{P_1P_2}$ from P_1 toward P_2. At the midpoint M of this line, $p^* = \frac{1}{2}$, but as we move further toward P_2, p^* becomes $< \frac{1}{2}$. Finally, when $p^* = 0$, $1 - p^* = 1$, and we are at point P_2. Mathematicians usually deal with this problem in terms of vectors, but we believe that this algebraic method is easier to understand for most students in intermediate microeconomic theory.

2.4 ISOQUANTS

The straight line connecting P_1 and P_2 in Figure 2.2 represents the same quantity of output for the various combinations of inputs. Economists call this an *isoquant*. The first part of the word, iso, means equal; hence, isoquant means equal quantity. Although in our example the combination of two distinct production processes yielded a straight line, isoquants are more generally characterized by a curve that is convex to the origin. Therefore, a straight-line isoquant represents a special case where only two distinct and independent efficient production processes are available. When there are more than two efficient processes, the corresponding isoquant will generally not be a straight line. An isoquant that takes the form of a smooth curve (which is found in traditional microeconomics textbooks that employ graphical analysis of production with two variable inputs) is another special

An isoquant is a graphical representation of efficient combinations of inputs or production processes

The greater the number of efficient processes the smoother the isoquant

---

In this expression, R^* is the desired K/L ratio. In the above example, $K/L = \frac{6}{7}$, K_1, L_1, K_2, and L_2 are assumed to be known. The only unknown that we have to find is p^*. We have one equation in one unknown, which can be solved. We do this by multiplying both sides by $p^*L_1 + (1 - p^*)L_2$; multiplying out all of the terms, we obtain

$$p^*R^*L_1 + R^*L_2 - p^*R^*L_2 = p^*K_1 + K_2 - p^*K_2$$

By moving all terms containing p^* to the right and all terms not containing p^* to the left, we get

$$R^*L_2 - K_2 = p^*R^*L_2 - p^*R^*L_1 + p^*K_1 - p^*K_2$$

Now factoring out p^* on the right side and moving it to the left side, we obtain

$$p^*(R^*L_2 - R^*L_1 + K_1 - K_2) = R^*L_2 - K_2$$

If we divide both sides by the term in parentheses, the result is Equation (2.5).

TABLE 2.4

Process	K	L	Q	Capital/labor ratio
P_1	2	4	10	$\frac{1}{2}$
P_2	4	2	10	2
P_5	2.5	2.5	10	1

case, where an infinite number of distinct and independent efficient production processes are available. This will become clearer as we proceed with our analysis. For the moment, let us examine the case where three distinct and independent efficient production processes are available.

Suppose that we are given the three processes shown in Table 2.4. A quick inspection indicates that all three processes are efficient, that is, none of them is an inefficient process. The data of Table 2.4 are plotted in Figure 2.3, where the points P_1, P_2 and P_5 represent the same quantity of output for different input combinations. Although the lines $\overline{P_1P_2}$, $\overline{P_1P_5}$, and $\overline{P_2P_5}$, that we have drawn represent an equal quantity of output, all of the points strictly *between* P_1 and P_2 (these endpoints are excluded) no longer correspond to efficient processes because they use more labor and capital than at least one point on either $\overline{P_1P_5}$ or $\overline{P_2P_5}$. This implies that, with process P_5 available, a firm whose goal is profit maximization will not use any combination of P_1 and P_2, since some combination of P_1 and P_5 or P_2 and P_5 will be more efficient. Thus, the curve $\widehat{P_1P_5P_2}$ is now the isoquant. This illustrates an important characteristic of isoquants: Only efficient combinations of inputs are included in isoquants. This condition is often overlooked by students, but, as we shall see later, it is an important condition to remember.

FIGURE 2.3

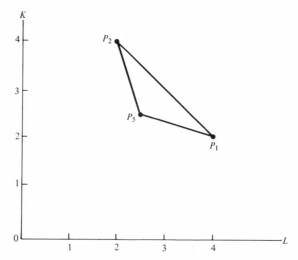

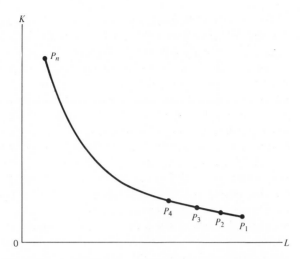

FIGURE 2.4

As the number of distinct and independent efficient production processes increases, the points that represent an equal quantity of output for different input combinations, such as P_1, P_2, and P_5 in Figure 2.3, will become closer and the line segments connecting adjacent points will become shorter; as a result, the isoquant curve will become smoother, as shown in Figure 2.4. In the extreme case, when n approaches infinity, we have an infinite number of efficient processes, and the isoquant becomes a smooth curve. Therefore, we see that the traditional illustration found in many textbooks actually represents the special case of an infinite number of efficient processes.

Another special case is one where only a single efficient process exists. The shape of the isoquant in such a case is shown in Figure 2.5. This case may appear to be too simple to be interesting, but it has more practical value than is often recognized. The well-known input–output analytical model developed by Nobel Prize winner Professor Wassily W. Leontief is actually based on this special case.

FIGURE 2.5

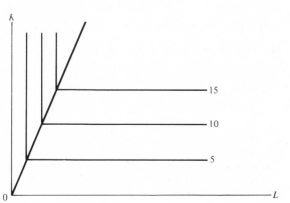

A single, efficient production process may still have practical value, as in input–output analysis

The two extreme cases represented by the isoquants in Figures 2.4 and 2.5 have particular economic significance. First of all, if Figure 2.5 actually represents the technological conditions of production, there is no question of choice in production insofar as the firm is concerned. In this case, the management of a firm is limited to making sure that inputs are combined in the predetermined proportion. There is no need to develop an economic theory regarding the best combination of inputs inasmuch as there is only one capital/labor ratio.[2] Thus, the one-process case, although of great practical value in empirical work, does not have very much analytical value with respect to the theory of the firm. On the other hand, the case where the isoquant is characterized by a smooth curve implies infinite possibilities of substitution between the inputs for a given output, which, in turn, has profound economic significance because it involves innumerable choices in production with concomitant considerations of alternative costs even when input prices are known. This is why the economic problems that a firm (and also society) faces are largely those that deal with evaluating alternative methods of production. It is to the resolution of such problems that economic theory addresses itself.

2.5 SUBSTITUTION BETWEEN INPUTS

Where more than one independent production process is efficient, the rate at which one input can be substituted for another to maintain a constant level of output takes on important practical and theoretical value. The rate of substitution between inputs in the multiple-input case has a meaning and economic significance similar to that of the law of diminishing returns in the one-variable-input case. For this reason it deserves more explanation. We shall employ the concept of the marginal rate of technical substitution (MRTS) to illustrate more fully both the difference between technical and economic efficiency as well as choice in production.

2.5.1 The Marginal Rate of Technical Substitution

Definition: Marginal Rate of Technical Substitution. The rate (represented by the change in capital input divided by the change in labor input) at which one input can be substituted for another in the production process without a change in output.

---

[2] Management must still determine the best level of output to produce, but as a price taker in the product and input markets, the profit-maximization decision is relatively simple.

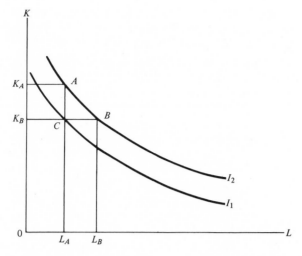

FIGURE 2.6

The essence of this definition of the MRTS is illustrated in Figure 2.6, which shows the various capital–labor combinations that can be used to produce a given amount of output. The isoquants I_1 and I_2 represent, respectively, two different levels of output which can be obtained (produced) by using various combinations of capital and labor.

Consider the isoquant I_2 in Figure 2.6. It tells us that the relevant output (e.g., 10 units) can be produced with $\overline{0L_A}$ units of labor and $\overline{0K_A}$ units of capital; this combination is represented by point A. The same level of output can also be produced by using less capital, say K_B. However, more labor, say L_B, has to be used to compensate for the reduction in capital. This new combination is represented by point B. Thus, in the relevant range, the rate at which labor can be substituted for capital is $(\overline{0K_A} - \overline{0K_B})/(\overline{0L_B} - \overline{0L_A}) = \overline{AC}/\overline{CB}$. In other words, the rate of substitution is the ratio of change in capital input to change in labor input which leaves output unchanged. It is important to note that in production the MRTS is only defined when a movement takes place along a given isoquant.

The above definition implies that the rate of substitution between capital and labor in the range A to B is actually the negative slope of $\overline{AB}$. As point B moves closer to A, the slope of $\overline{AB}$ approaches that of a tangent at point A. For a very small change, the rate of substitution at point A can be approximated by the negative slope of the tangent at that point. This is precisely the mathematical definition of the MRTS. The word "marginal" refers to substitution at the margin (i.e., very small changes), and the word "technical" refers to the fact that the rate of substitution (and, for that matter, the curvature of the isoquants) is determined by technology. Thus, we may write

$$\text{MRTS} = -\Delta K/\Delta L$$

where Δ denotes change. It turns out that the MRTS is also equal to the ratio of the MP of labor to the MP of capital. This can also be shown by the use of Figure 2.6.

Suppose that it takes two steps to move from A to B: first from A to C and then from C to B. The movement from A to C produces a reduction in capital input of $\overline{K_a K_b}$ and a reduction in output of $(I_2 - I_1)$, labor being held constant. The MP of capital has been defined as the change in output divided by the change in capital, all other inputs being held constant. In our case we have

$$\text{MP}_K = (I_2 - I_1)/\overline{K_A K_B}$$

Similarly, a movement from C to B produces an increase in labor of $\overline{L_A L_B}$ and an increase in output of $I_2 - I_1$. Therefore, we have

$$\text{MP}_L = (I_2 - I_1)/\overline{L_A L_B}$$

Since the $I_2 - I_1$ terms cancel out, dividing MP_L by MP_K yields

$$\text{MP}_L/\text{MP}_K = \overline{K_A K_B}/\overline{L_A L_B} = \text{MRTS}$$

This proves our assertion that the MRTS of labor for capital is equal to the ratio of the MP of labor to the MP of capital. Thus, we see that if the MP of labor is double the MP of capital, the MRTS will be 2.0. To illustrate, suppose the MP of labor is 4 and that of capital is 2; then in order to leave output unchanged at, say, 20 units, only 5 units of labor would need to be substituted for 10 units of capital, and $\text{MRTS} = \text{MP}_L/\text{MP}_K = 4/2 = 2.0$.

2.5.2 The Decreasing MRTS

The concept of a decreasing MRTS corresponds to, but is different from, the law of diminishing returns in the one-variable-input case. Whether or not a decreasing MRTS prevails is a technical problem. As with the law of diminishing returns, a decreasing MRTS has important economic significance. Economists try their best to explain why this is so, but they do not really feel obliged to explain the "why" problem, since whether a decreasing, constant, or even increasing MRTS prevails, it is determined by technology, which is taken as data by economists. The job of economists is to explain the economic significance of different MRTS characteristics and how they can be most clearly represented for analytical purposes.

The isoquants in Figure 2.7 have been drawn to indicate the different MRTS characteristics that are determined by technological conditions, which economists take as data. The isoquant in part (a) indicates a decreasing MRTS, that in part (b) an increasing MRTS, that in part (c) a constant MRTS, and that in part (d) a zero MRTS. However, an increasing MRTS, although technologically possible, does not have much economic signifi-

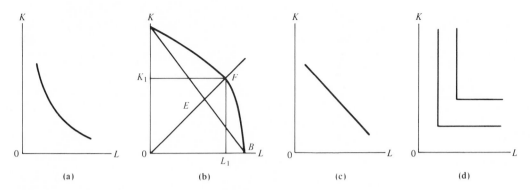

FIGURE 2.7

cance. In part (b), if the curve $\widehat{AB}$ is the isoquant according to technological conditions, then a firm whose goal was profit maximization would never use any process other than A or B (or a combination of them), since processes along the curve $\widehat{AFB}$ would be less efficient than some combination of A and B. The practical isoquant according to *economic* principles is the straight line $\overline{AB}$, which has the same economic significance as part (c). Consequently, for the purpose of economic analysis, only decreasing, constant, and zero MRTS are meaningful. As we mentioned earlier, a zero MRTS does not have economic choice implications, whereas the constant MRTS is also not very interesting with respect to economic choice by a firm. As a result, the most prevalent and interesting case is that of a decreasing MRTS.

What the student should understand is that when we are talking about a decreasing MRTS, it means that as more and more labor is substituted for capital, each additional unit of labor can only be substituted for less and less capital. The reason for this condition is that it becomes more and more difficult to substitute labor for capital, because as more labor is substituted, the MP of labor decreases relative to the MP of capital.[3] As mentioned above, this is similar to, but not the same as, the law of diminishing returns. The student may attempt an explanation of why there must be a decreasing MRTS whenever the law of diminishing returns prevails. However, even in the absence of the law of diminishing returns, a decreasing MRTS may still prevail. Note that the MRTS of labor for capital is defined as $-\Delta K/\Delta L$, which, in turn, is equal to MP_L/MP_K along a given isoquant.

It should be pointed out that the concept of the MRTS is symmetric, that is, with a decreasing MRTS, if capital is substituted

Decreasing MRTS implies decreasing MP of labor relative to capital

---

[3] This does not mean that a decreasing MRTS signifies a higher MP of capital than of labor or that the MP of labor is decreasing. It is only necessary that the ratio MP_L/MP_K become smaller, which simply means that the MP of labor is falling relative to that of capital.

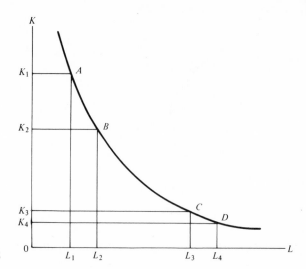

for labor, the MRTS of capital for labor also decreases as long as the MRTS of labor for capital decreases. This is an important observation that can be illustrated with respect to our earlier example involving Figure 2.7.

In Figure 2.8 we show that part (a) of Figure 2.7 indeed corresponds to a decreasing MRTS. If we start from point A and move to point B, $\overline{L_1 L_2}$ labor is substituted for $\overline{K_1 K_2}$ capital in order to keep output constant. However, if we start from point C, where much more labor and less capital is used to produce the same level of output, and move to point D, we find that $\overline{L_3 L_4} = \overline{L_1 L_2}$ labor can only substitute for $\overline{K_3 K_4}$ capital, which is much less than the $\overline{K_1 K_2}$ that we saved as we moved from A to B. Another way of explaining this point is to make use of the fact that the MRTS of labor for capital is defined as the negative slope of the isoquant. It is seen that the slope of the isoquant is steeper at A than at C, which implies that the MRTS of labor for capital decreases as we move from A to C. In fact, for the isoquant shape indicated in Figure 2.8, the absolute value of its slope decreases continuously as we move to the right, which implies a continuously decreasing MRTS. (Some economists use the term "concave from above" or "convex to the origin" to describe a curve of the form shown in Figure 2.8. Similar reasoning would indicate that parts (b), (c), and (d) of Figure 2.7 do in fact show an increasing, constant, and zero MRTS, respectively. As we mentioned earlier, the concept of MRTS is symmetrical. This can be demonstrated with the use of Figure 2.8 by moving back up the isoquant from point D to point A. Note that more capital must be substituted for labor as one moves from B to A than when one moves from D to C.

2.6 TECHNICAL AND ECONOMIC EFFICIENCY

Based on the discussion of increasing MRTS in the last section, it would seem useful to make a distinction between technical and economic efficiency. The curve $\widehat{AB}$ in Figure 2.7(b) might be called the most technically efficient equal-output curve in the sense that technically, for the same output, it is the locus of the minimum amount of one input necessary to produce a given output for a given amount of the other input. For example, with labor input L_1, the minimum capital requirement for the given output is K_1. In this sense, point F is technically efficient. However, with the assumptions of divisibility, independence, and constant returns to scale, F is *not economically efficient*, because point E represents the use of both less labor and less capital for the same output and, in addition, is feasible. This conceptual refinement serves the purpose of filling a gap in the theoretical analysis which is often overlooked. This will become clearer in the next section.

Positively sloped isoquants do not represent economically efficient production processes

2.7 ECONOMIC REGION AND STAGES OF PRODUCTION

Many textbooks and advanced treatises use a graph such as Figure 2.9 to illustrate and define the concept of an economic region based on isoquants that have been defined as efficient (with no distinction between technical and economic efficiency) combinations of inputs for a given output. It is seen that the positively sloped segments of the isoquants are not economically efficient and thus should not be considered as part of them. On the other hand, they could be considered technically efficient as defined in the previous section. Therefore, without the distinction between technical and economic efficiency, Figure 2.9 could further confuse the thoughtful student. Having made this distinction, the isoquants can be considered as technically, but not necessarily economically, efficient equal-output curves. It is in this respect

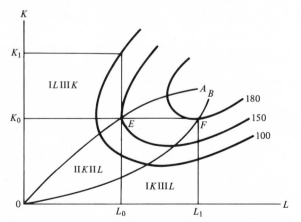

FIGURE 2.9

that we should be able to avoid any ambiguity in the interpretation of isoquants. We shall proceed to make the distinction clearer by means of Figure 2.9.

The curves 100, 150, 180 in Figure 2.9 can be considered technically efficient equal-output curves, each of which has positively sloped segments on both ends. The curve $\widehat{0A}$ is the locus of points where the slope of the equal-output curves is vertical. Similarly $\widehat{0B}$ is the locus of points where the slope of the equal-output curves is horizontal. In other words, the equal-output curves are negatively sloped in the region between $\widehat{0A}$ and $\widehat{0B}$, but positively sloped either above $\widehat{0A}$ or the right of $\widehat{0B}$. It is easy to see that the only economically significant segment of the curves is that between $\widehat{0A}$ and $\widehat{0B}$. This can be illustrated as follows.

With labor input L_0, the maximum output that can be produced is 150 units, provided that K_0 capital is used. On the other hand, with the same labor input and more capital input, $K_1 > K_0$, the output will be reduced to 100 units. Further examination of Figure 2.9 will reinforce our earlier observations with respect to economically efficient production processes. First of all, the input combination $\langle L_0, K_1 \rangle$ will never be used by a firm whose goal is profit maximization because it is possible to produce more output using the same amount of labor but less capital. This is true for all capital–labor combinations represented by points above the curve $\widehat{0A}$. Thus, all points above $\widehat{0A}$ are not economically feasible input combinations. Secondly, the reason that more capital with the same amount of labor will result in less output is that the MP of capital is negative; that is, too much capital is combined with a given amount of labor. This reasoning applies to all points above $\widehat{0A}$. In particular, given the isoquant in Figure 2.9, for all points along $\overline{K_0E}$ the MP of capital is negative. This means that, with a given capital input K_0, if the labor input is less than L_0, the MP of capital will be negative. This indicates that point E corresponds to the maximum AP and the extensive margin of labor. Similarly, for the same capital input K_0, if more labor then L_1 is used, total output begins to decrease (one would move to a lower isoquant), which indicates that the MP of labor becomes negative. For the given capital input K_0, all points to the right of F represent a negative MP of labor, and since point F corresponds to a zero MP for labor, it represents the intensive margin of labor. We see, therefore, that in reference to our earlier discussion, the area above or to the left of $\widehat{0A}$ corresponds to stage I, the area between $\widehat{0A}$ and $\widehat{0B}$ to stage II, and the area to the right or below $\widehat{0B}$ to stage III for labor in production.[4] A similar argument would show that the area below $\widehat{0B}$ corresponds to stage I, the area between

---

[4] Students may wish to refresh their memory by referring back to our discussion in Section 1.3.2 on the different stages of production.

$\widehat{0A}$ and $\widehat{0B}$ to stage II, and the area above $\widehat{0A}$ to stage III for capital in production. Hence, the stages of production are (at least in the two-input cases) symmetric for a fixed and a variable input, and only stage II is an economically feasible region. This also shows that the traditional AP curve of a variable input as illustrated in various textbooks (first rising, reaching a maximum, and then declining) corresponds to backward-bent isoquants. In such cases, we see that only the negatively sloped segments of such isoquants are economically efficient.

2.8 RETURNS TO SCALE AND ISOQUANT MAPS

The concept of returns to scale, which was explained earlier, can also be illustrated by means of isoquant maps. As defined previously, constant returns exist when output changes proportionately to a proportionate change in all inputs. This is illustrated in part (a) of Figure 2.10.

Starting with the production of 10 units of output using 2 units of capital and 1 unit of labor, we observe that output doubles when both capital and labor are doubled and triples when both are tripled. The converse also holds true. If we start with the production of 20 units of output using 4 units of capital and 2 units of labor, output will be halved when both capital and labor are halved.

A doubling of all inputs, assuming a homogeneity of inputs, should result in a doubling of output, but recall Section 2.2

Parts (b) and (c) of Figure 2.10 illustrate increasing and decreasing returns to scale, respectively.

Another approach to studying the isoquants is by an examination of the points $A, B, C, \ldots$ that lie on the same ray from the origin, where $\overline{0A} = \overline{AB} = \overline{BC}$. If the output level at point B is double that at point A, whereas the output level at point C is triple that at A, constant returns prevail, as in part (a) of Figure 2.10. On the other hand, if the output levels at B and C are, respectively, more than double and triple that at A, increasing

FIGURE 2.10

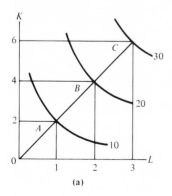
(a)

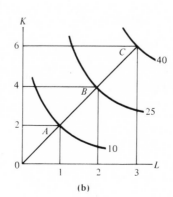
(b)

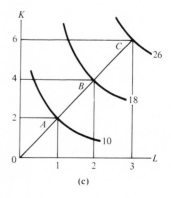
(c)

returns prevail, as in part (b). The student can verify that de-creasing returns to scale prevail in part (c).

Note that the returns to scale condition that prevails is specified by the output–input relationship along a ray extending out from the origin, since it is defined only for the same input ratio and different output levels. It should also be noted that it is possible for a production function to show constant returns to scale only within a certain range of the output, whereas decreasing or in-creasing returns to scale may occur in other output ranges.

2.9 THE AP OF THE VARIABLE AND FIXED INPUT

Production processes are the building blocks of modern economic production theory with respect to the two-variable-input case. The traditional approach is to start with a two-way matrix. Table 2.5, which is based on a production function with two variable inputs and a given technology, is an example of a two-way matrix.

Note that this simple table represents many production pro-cesses. For example, the capital–labor combinations $\langle 1, 2 \rangle$, $\langle 2, 4 \rangle$, and $\langle 3, 6 \rangle$ (this is a vector notation, in which the first number rep-resents capital and the second number labor) and the corre-sponding output figures (values at the intersection of capital and labor) constitute one process, whereas the combinations $\langle 2, 1 \rangle$, $\langle 4, 2 \rangle$, and $\langle 6, 3 \rangle$ and the corresponding output figures represent another process. It is possible that by using this vector notation

TABLE 2.5. Output Matrix

	Labor					
Capital	1	2	3	4	5	6
1	3	6	8	9	10	10
2	6	12	17	21	24	26
3	10	24	39	52	61	66
4	13	30	54	72	85	93
5	15	37	60	80	100	113
6	16	42	66	88	106	120

TABLE 2.6

	TP_L		AP_L		MP_L	
L	$K = 1$	$K = 2$	$K = 1$	$K = 2$	$K = 1$	$K = 2$
1	3	6	3	6	3	6
2	6	12	3	6	3	6
3	8	17	2.7	5.7	2	5
4	9	21	2.2	5.2	1	4
5	10	24	2.0	4.8	1	3
6	10	26	1.7	4.3	0	2

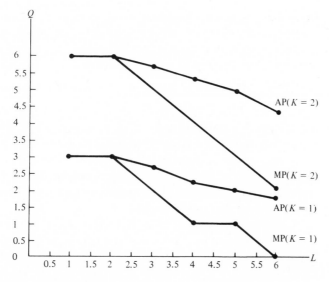

FIGURE 2.11

and the output values, one could construct a three-dimensional surface that graphically illustrates an output (product) surface above a plane on which various capital–labor combinations are plotted. However, one cannot use these numbers on such a three-dimensional surface to demonstrate the meaning and characteristics of isoquants. Therefore, the production process approach is a better pedagogical device. Hence, we use Table 2.5 to illustrate the shift of the TP, AP, and MP curves of labor when the fixed input (in this case capital) changes.

In order to show the shift of the product curves of labor when capital changes, we have constructed Table 2.6 on the basis of the first two rows of Table 2.5. Table 2.6 provides the data for the construction of Figure 2.11. Note that both sets of the AP and MP curves in Figure 2.11 (for $K = 1$ and $K = 2$) show only stage II of production. It is theoretically consistent that both the AP and MP curves shift upward when the fixed input—capital—is increased.

2.10 OPTIMAL COMBINATION OF INPUTS

As mentioned earlier, the definition of an efficient process does not enable us to single out a unique process that can be considered "the efficient process." Instead, we have many (in fact, in the continuous case, an infinite number) efficient processes. This information can be useful to a firm, but, by itself, does not provide sufficient data upon which the firm can base a decision concerning production. Furthermore, the term "optimal combination of inputs" can mean different things to different people. To avoid confusion or ambiguity, we offer the student the following definition.

Definition: Optimal Combination of Inputs. In production, an optimal combination of inputs is that combination of inputs which results in a maximum output for a given cost or, equivalently, the combination of inputs which results in a minimum cost for a given output.[5]

Note that it does not make much sense to talk about maximum output for minimum cost (or vice versa) because, by common sense, minimum cost is zero (negative cost does not make much economic sense as the term is used here), which cannot usually result in positive, let alone maximum, output. It is important to understand the meaning of maximum output for a given cost or minimum cost for a given output.

In production, economic analysis is based on the fundamental idea that a firm makes its production decisions under two sets of constraints: the state of technology, on the one hand, and the input market, on the other hand. As we have noted earlier, our competitive model assumes that the firm is too small to either change the technology in its line of business or to influence the input market. Therefore, it must take the given technology and input prices and try its best to produce the output at a minimum cost. In the previous sections of this chapter we have essentially dealt with only the technological aspect and thus have cautioned the student to observe that although the isoquants convey all the technological information, they provide nothing about costs, which are equally (if not more) important. We shall now turn our attention to the cost side of the analysis.

2.10.1 Isocost and Input Prices

The cost of production (note that we have not used the term cost function, which is reserved for later purposes) is directly related to both the price and the quantity of inputs. We assume a competitive input market, in which input prices are given to the firm. Thus, no matter how much labor or capital it uses, the unit price of each does not change. Suppose that the firm's production budget C, which is the total amount of money available to spend on the inputs, has been determined. This can also be called cost (thus the notation C). Since we assume two inputs only (labor and capital) for the sake of simplicity, C must be spent either on labor, on capital, or on some combination of the two. We shall denote the amount of labor that the firm will hire (a variable) by L and the corresponding price (a constant) by w. By definition,

---

[5] Some textbooks refer to this condition as the least-cost combination for producing a given product. We have no quarrel with such a definition, but feel that ours is clearer and more complete.

the total expenditure on labor is wL, that is, the wage rate multiplied by the quantity of labor. Similarly, the total expenditure on capital is rK, where K and r denote the amount of capital used and the corresponding price, respectively. The easiest way to understand the outlay on capital is to consider the case where the firm rents machinery instead of purchasing it; thus, K would be machine-hours and r the rental per hour. Since the total expenditure on inputs is C, we have, by definition, the following equation:

$$C = wL + rK \qquad (2.6)$$

This is called the *cost equation* (not cost function). In economics, the cost equation represents the relationship between cost and inputs. On the other hand, a *cost function* represents the relationship between cost and output, which will be dealt with in detail in Chapter 3. It is important that the student learn to distinguish between these two terms.

Cost equation versus cost function: a relation of cost and inputs and a relation of cost and output

In cost equation (2.6), C, w, and r are known constants, whereas L and K are variables. Equation (2.6) can be written in the following equivalent form:

$$K = C/r - (w/r)L \qquad (2.7)$$

Expression (2.7) is clearly a linear equation in the two variables K and L. It can be represented by a straight line on a two-dimensional graph, where the horizontal axis is labor and the vertical axis capital. In Figure 2.12, $\overline{AB}$ is such a straight line. In (2.7), C/r is the vertical intersect, and in Figure 2.12, $\overline{0A}$ is equal to C/r—the amount of capital the firm can rent if it spends all of its budget on capital. As a simple numerical example, if the firm budgeted \$10,000 ($C = $10,000$) and the cost of renting capital is \$10 per hour, then the firm can rent 1000 machine-hours if no labor is hired. In this case, $\overline{0A}$ represents 1000 machine-hours.

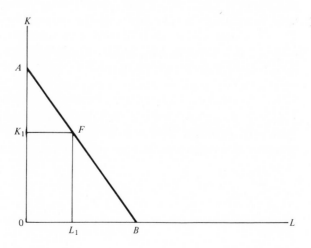

FIGURE 2.12

Similarly, the horizontal intersect $\overline{0B}$ represents the amount of labor (e.g., person-hours) that the firm can buy if all of its budget is spent on labor. Any point between A and B represents a certain combination of labor and capital which the firm can purchase by exhausting its budget. For example, the point F on $\overline{AB}$ denotes that the firm can hire L_1 person-hours and K_1 machine-hours by exhausting its budget (in our case, \$10,000). Thus, $\overline{AB}$ contains all the possible combinations of labor and capital which the firm can purchase with a budget allocation of \$10,000. Any input combination represented by a point to the right of $\overline{AB}$ would cost more than C, whereas any represented by a point within the triangle $\triangle 0AB$ would cost less than C.[6] For this reason, economists call $\overline{AB}$ the *isocost curve* (isocost line).

The slope of an isocost curve represents the negative price ratio between two inputs

Although the firm can afford to buy (here we use the term buy in the general sense, which includes both hire and rent) any combination of labor and capital along the isocost curve $\overline{AB}$, the specific combination that the firm should buy cannot be determined from it alone. In order to answer this question, we need to simultaneously consider the relevant isocost curve and the previously explained isoquants. We shall be examining this problem momentarily. However, before we leave our discussion of the cost equation and isocost curves, it should be pointed out

Under perfect competition it will be a straight line. No matter how much of an input is purchased, unit price will not change

that the slope of the isocost curve $\overline{AB}$ is $-w/r$, the negative price ratio of labor and capital. As we mentioned above, L and K are the variables, whereas C, w, and r represent known constants (parameters). It is important to know how the isocost curve will behave when either one or a combination of the parameters changes.

First of all, when C increases and w and r remain constant, the new isocost curve will shift to the right but remain parallel to the old one. This can be easily illustrated by a simple example. Assume that $w = 1$, $r = 2$, and the original budget $C_0 = 8$; then the corresponding isocost in Figure 2.13 is $\overline{AB}$, since if the total budget is spent on labor, 8 units can be bought (point B), whereas if the total budget is spent on capital, 4 units can be bought (point A). Any other combination of labor and capital which costs exactly C_0 is represented by a point along $\overline{AB}$. Suppose that the total budget is increased to 10 (i.e., $C_1 = 10$). The new isocost curve is $\overline{A'B'}$, since 10 units of labor can be bought if the entire budget is spent on labor (point B') or 5 units of capital can be bought if the entire budget is spent on capital (point A'). This is obviously a parallel shift, which can also be easily shown algebraically. The cost equation for $w = 1$, $r = 2$, and $C_0 = 8$ is

$$K = 4 - \tfrac{1}{2}L \tag{2.8}$$

---

[6] It is important not to regard the area of the triangle $\triangle 0AB$ as being equal to \$10,000.

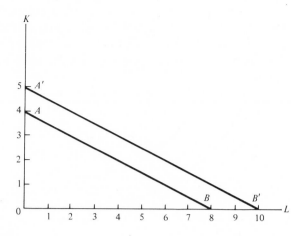

FIGURE 2.13

and the cost equation for $w = 1$, $r = 2$, and $C_1 = 10$ is

$$K = 5 - \tfrac{1}{2}L \qquad (2.9)$$

Comparing (2.8) with (2.9), it is seen that the vertical intercept increased from 4 to 5, but the slope remained the same—a parallel shift.

Students should make sure that they understand the fact that when the wage rate w increases while C and r remain constant, the slope of $\overline{AB}$ will become steeper, that is, point B moves to the left and point A remains where it is. Likewise, when the wage rate w decreases, B moves to the right (point A again not moving). On the other hand, when the price (rental) of capital r increases while C and w remain constant, point A moves down and point B remains where it is. Similarly, when r decreases, point A moves up (point B again not moving). The student may wish to experiment by drawing isocost curves to gain a better feel of how the slope of the line will change as first one and then another change in the input price occurs. Reference to the cost equation will be helpful.

2.10.2 Optimal Combination of Inputs for a Given Cost

We now turn to combining isoquants and isocost curves to show how the firm can determine the optimal combination of inputs for a given cost. Suppose that a firm has a fixed budget C to spend on both labor and capital to produce a given commodity or service. Since we have assumed that the firm operates in a competitive input market, w and r, by implication, will be constant.[7] The firm is assumed to have all of the technical information represented

---

[7] That is to say, the prices of a unit of labor and of a unit of capital will not change regardless of the total amount of each purchased. In short, the firm cannot by itself affect the input prices.

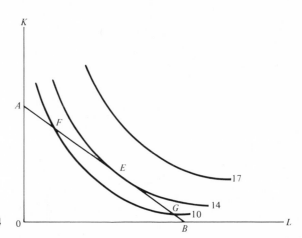

FIGURE 2.14

by the isoquants and the price (cost) information represented by the isocost curves. Hence, the firm must consider the isoquants, on the one hand, and the isocost curves, on the other hand. The only decision the firm can make is to choose a certain input combination (among the infinite many) that will satisfy a certain predetermined criterion. According to our assumed goal of the firm—profit maximization—it will choose that combination of inputs which maximizes output. This is because in operating under perfect competition, the firm can sell all it produces without affecting prices. We shall illustrate the decision process for the case of a fixed budget and given input prices.

Let the fixed budget (cost) C be represented by the isocost curve $\overline{AB}$ in Figure 2.14 and the technological possibilities by the indicated isoquants. Note that the isoquants represent only technically efficient processes (as explained in detail in the previous sections of this chapter). From the figure, it can be seen that 17 units (17 thousand or 17 million if one wishes) of the output are not obtainable because the given budget, when taken in relation to input prices, constrains the firm to or beneath the isocost curve $\overline{AB}$.

If the goal of the firm were not profit maximization, it could choose the input combinations represented by points F and G. At these points, its total budget would be just exhausted and its output level would be 10 units. However, observation tells us that output can be increased without incurring any additional cost by the selection of a better combination of inputs. For example, starting from point F, output can be increased at the same cost by moving down along $\overline{AB}$ until point E is reached. Further downward movement beyond E, however, generates a decrease in output. Similarly, starting from point G, upward movement along $\overline{AB}$ will result in higher output at the same cost until point E is reached. Further upward movement beyond E will result in a lower output. It is obvious that the only input combination resulting in maximum output is given by point E, that is, the production process represented by the ray $\overline{0E}$.

In economics, the point E is called the firm's production *equilibrium*. Equilibrium involves optimality in economics—in this case, an optimal combination of inputs, that is, maximum output for a given cost. From Figure 2.14, it can be observed that the production equilibrium is characterized by the tangency of the isocost curve $\overline{AB}$ to an isoquant (in this case, the 14-unit isoquant). However, if $\overline{AB}$ is not tangent to the 14-unit isoquant (e.g., they intersect at two points), then there must exist another isoquant, representing a higher level of output, such that $\overline{AB}$ and the higher isoquant has at least one point in common with it. If this were so, the 14-unit isoquant would not be the maximum output for the given budget (cost). Therefore, in our illustration, point E must be a point of tangency.

At the point of tangency between two curves, their slopes are equal. As we stated earlier, the slope of the isocost curve is $-w/r$. We have also noted that the slope of the isoquant is, by definition, the change in capital divided by the change in labor, that is $-\Delta K/\Delta L$. However, by definition, MRTS $= -\Delta K/\Delta L$, and, by implication (as shown in section 2.5.1), MRTS $= -\Delta K/\Delta L = MP_L/MP_K$. Thus, the negative slope of the isoquant is MP_L/MP_K, and the negative slope of the isocost is $-(-w/r) = w/r$. At point E (equilibrium), the slopes are equal; hence, point E is characterized by

$$MP_L/MP_K = w/r = MRTS \qquad (2.10)$$

A commonsense explanation of this expression is that the MRTS tells producers the technical opportunity available to them, whereas the price ratio of the inputs tells them the market opportunity that they can exploit. If the two are not equal, producers can improve their position through a recombination of inputs. For example, if MRTS $= 2$ (i.e., if by adding 1 unit of labor, 2 units of capital can be foregone with output remaining the same) and $w/r = 1$ (i.e., the price of labor is equal to the price of capital), the market opportunity available to producers is such that if they forego 2 units of capital, they can add 2 units of labor at the same cost. Under these circumstances, producers can obviously increase their output at the same cost by adding more labor and, at the same time, reducing capital. Thus, when $MP_L/MP_K > w/r$ at point F in Figure 2.14, output can be increased at the same cost by using more labor and less capital. Similarly, if $MP_L/MP_K < w/r$ at point G, output can be increased at the same cost by using more capital and less labor. Consequently, at equilibrium, no further gains in output can be obtained through input substitution at the same budget outlay (cost).

Equation (2.10) can be written in the following equivalent form:

$$MP_L/w = MP_K/r \qquad (2.11)$$

Equilibrium represents an optimal combination of inputs: Output is maximized for a given cost, or cost is minimized for a given output

*Where an isoquant
is tangent to the
isocost curve,
$MP_L/w = MP_K/r$,
equilibrium in
production*

This expression states that equilibrium exists when the ratio of
the MP of labor to the price of labor is equal to the ratio of the
MP of capital to the price of capital. A commonsense interpretation of this expression is that equilibrium exists when the last
dollar spent on labor results in the same additional output as the
last dollar spent on capital. An example will make this clear.

Let us suppose that $MP_L = 10$. This means that 1 additional
unit of labor will result in 10 additional units of output. If $w =$
5, then $10/5 = 2$, which simply states that if one spends \$5 on 1
additional unit of labor and gets 10 additional units of output, the
last dollar spent on labor results in 2 additional units of output.
Now assume that $MP_L/w > MP_K/r$. This says that the last dollar
spent on labor results in more additional output (e.g., 2 units)
than the last dollar spent on capital (e.g., 1 unit). If this is the
case, output is obviously not at a maximum for the given cost,
since if in our earlier illustration producers cut their expenditures
on capital by \$1 (this is possible, taking our divisibility assumption
into consideration), they only lose 1 unit of output, since by
assumption $MP_K/r = 1$. If, at the same time, the producers use
the same dollar to purchase additional labor, their additional output will be 2 units (since $MP_L/w = 2$), and their net gain for the
same cost is $2 - 1 = 1$ unit of output. Therefore, whenever $MP_L/
w > MP_K/r$ (e.g., at point F in Figure 2.14), the output can be
increased at the same cost by adding more labor and reducing
capital. Similarly, if $MP_L/w < MP_K/r$ (e.g., at point G in Figure
2.14), the output can be increased by adding more capital and
reducing labor. Only when $MP_L/w = MP_K/r$ will output be maximum for a given cost.

It is important to understand the reasons why the output will
be maximized for a given cost when (2.10) or (2.11) is satisfied
because it will greatly facilitate one's learning of the theory of
consumer behavior (which we shall discuss later). Students will
realize that there are considerable similarities between production
theory and the theory of consumer behavior. Therefore, we shall
extend our analysis of production theory with respect to the behavior of a firm whose goal is profit maximization under conditions of the competitive model.

2.10.3 Optimal Combination of Inputs for a Given Output

There are circumstances under which a firm is required to produce
a given amount of output. For example, a defense contractor may
have to produce 500 bombers, no more, no less. In such a case,
the profit-maximizer will try to minimize cost for a given level
of output. The student may properly ask whether we have the
same conditions under this approach as we had under that of
maximizing output for a given cost? The answer to this question

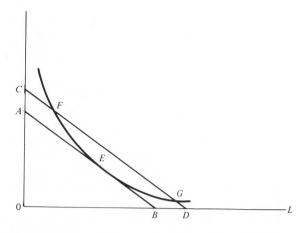

FIGURE 2.15

is yes, under most circumstances, and, in particular, in the case we dealt with in Section 2.10.2.

Let us assume that in Figure 2.15 the output level that the firm must produce is 14 units and that isoquant $\widehat{FEG}$ is a representation of the combination of inputs which generate the required output (14 units). The firm can choose the labor–capital combination represented by the point F or G, which costs C_1 (represented by the isocost curve $\overline{CD}$), which is greater than C_0 (represented by isocost curve $\overline{AB}$). Starting from point F, it is obvious that any labor–capital combination represented by a point along the isoquant and below F will cost the firm less than C_1 for the same output until point E is reached. However, it is clear that the minimum-cost combination will occur at point E, since isocost curve $\overline{AB}$ is the lowest one that is consistent with the isoquant representing 14 units of output. Hence, point F does not represent a minimum-cost combination of the inputs for the given output, and neither does any point above E. Similarly, if we start from point G, costs can be reduced for the same level of output by moving upward along the 14-unit isoquant until, again, point E is reached. Thus, point G and any point between E and G along the isoquant do not represent a minimum-cost input combination. We may conclude that only the input combination represented by point E gives a minimum cost for producing 14 units of output. By comparing Figure 2.15 with Figure 2.14, we see that the condition of minimum cost for a given output is identical with the condition of maximum output for a given cost, that is, the equilibrium condition exists when an isocost curve is tangent to an isoquant.[8] We see, therefore, that the condition for cost minim-

---

[8] As we noted before, an equilibrium condition represents an optimal combination of inputs to the firm whose goal is profit maximization because there can be neither a gain in output, at the same cost, by moving to a different combination of inputs nor a reduction in cost for a given output.

ization with respect to a given output is identical to that of output maximization for a given budget outlay (cost).

2.10.4 Limited Number of Processes and the General Case

The tangency condition, which specifies that MRTS $= w/r$ for an optimal combination of inputs, is an ideal or special case where there are an infinite number of processes, that is, the isoquants are smooth curves. In technical terms, it means that the production function is continuous with continuous first- and second-order derivatives. In reality, however, a firm may face only a limited number of processes, that is the derivatives of the production function may not exist at certain points. As a result, the optimal condition may not be specified by the equality of MRTS and the price ratio of the inputs, and, therefore, inequalities may have to take the place of equality. This is one of the special features of modern microeconomic analysis, and we shall describe it in some depth.

Equal MRTS and input price ratio may not specify optimality if the isoquant is not smooth

Consider the situation shown in Figure 2.16, where there are only the five processes represented by $\overline{0C}$, $\overline{0D}$, $\overline{0E}$, $\overline{0F}$, and $\overline{0G}$. For the given prices of labor and capital w^0 and r^0, respectively, we have an infinite number of parallel isocost curves, $\overline{AB}$ and $\overline{A'B'}$ being only two of them. It can be seen that the minimum-cost input combination for a given output (e.g., 10 units) is represented by the point E, $\langle L_0, K_0 \rangle$. However, at point E, the slope (rather, the negative of the slope) of the isoquant (which is MRTS or $-\Delta K/\Delta L$) is not equal to the negative of the slope of the isocost, w^0/r^0.

FIGURE 2.16

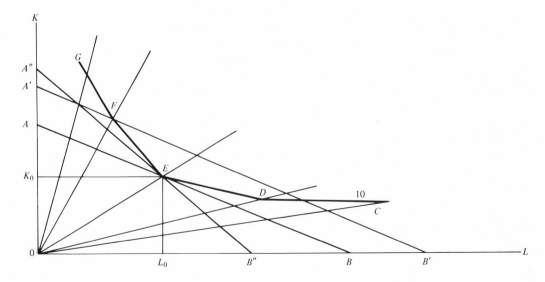

Recall that the slope of an isocost curve is $-w/r$; therefore, the negative of the slope of an isocost curve is $-(-w/r) = w/r$. The slope of the isoquant is $\Delta K/\Delta L$ (where ΔK denotes the change in capital and ΔL the change in labor), and MRTS is defined as the negative of the slope of the isoquants. Thus, we have MRTS = $-\Delta K/\Delta L$. At equilibrium, MRTS = w/r, which means that the slopes of the isocost curve and isoquant at the point of tangency must be the same. This equality of slope indicates the minimum-cost input combination for producing a given level of output.

Referring again to Figure 2.16, we see that to the left of point E the slope of the isoquant is steeper than the slope of the isocost curve; therefore, MRTS $> w^0/r^0$. To the right of point E we have the opposite condition, that is, MRTS $< w^0/r^0$. With w_0, r_0, and cost given, the firm produces 10 units of output with $\overline{0L_0}$ labor and $\overline{0K_0}$ capital because this is the minimum-cost input combination for the given level of output.

Now consider an increase in the wage rate, $w_1 > w_0$, while the price of capital r_0, remains constant. We wish to examine the new minimum-cost combination for producing the same level of output as before. What we have here is a situation where the cost minimization for the same level of output is the objective (see Section 2.10.3). From Figure 2.16 we can see that as the wage rate increases, a new isocost curve must resemble $\overline{A''B''}$ in order for the same level of output to be attained at a minimum cost. Note that the isocost curve $\overline{A''B''}$ has a steeper slope than $\overline{AB}$ because the wage rate has increased while the price of capital has remained constant, leading to a presumed substitution of labor for capital. However, given a steeper slope for the new isocost curve $\overline{A''B''}$, we can observe that it is still flatter than the negative of the slope of the isoquant in the line segment $\overline{EF}$. Consequently, point E will still denote the equilibrium position, which represents the optimal combination of resources for producing 10 units of output.

In the extreme case, if the slope of $\overline{A''B''}$ is the same as the slope of $\overline{EF}$, point E could remain the equilibrium position because, in this case, any point on the line segment $\overline{EF}$ would result in the same cost. However, in this case, equilibrium will not be unique. Similarly, if the slope of $\overline{A''B''}$ is flatter than the slope of $\overline{AB}$. but steeper than that of $\overline{DE}$, point E will represent an equilibrium position. Again, if the slope of $\overline{A''B''}$ is the same as that of $\overline{DE}$, equilibrium will not be unique.

From the above arguments, we may conclude that, in the case of cost minimization for a given level of output, point E will represent an optimal combination of resources as long as the condition

$$\text{MRTS left of } E \geq w_0/r_0 \geq \text{MRTS right of } E \qquad (2.12)$$

holds. This result is equally valid for points C, D, F, and G in Figure 2.16.

Recalling that at equilibirum MRTS = w/r, we see that equilibrium point E in both Figure 2.14 and Figure 2.15 satisfies (2.12) as well as (2.10). It is also clear that the equilibrium condition in Sections 2.10.2 and 2.10.3 is a special case of (2.12). This verifies our statement at the beginning of this section, in which we noted that the traditional smooth-curve model of the isoquant is a special case. Students who are familiar with linear programming should be somewhat acquainted with this model, since it is similar to a simple linear programming problem (which will be discussed in more detail in the appendix to this chapter).

2.10.5 The Failure of Tangency and the Corner Solution

The tangency conditions of optimal input combination in Figures 2.14 and 2.15 are very common. However, there are special cases where the tangency condition may fail. First of all, if a constant MRTS prevails, the isoquants will be straight lines, as shown earlier in Section 2.5.2. In addition, the isocost curve is always a straight line under conditions of the competitive model. Although two straight lines can either intersect or coincide with each other, they cannot have a unique point of tangency. This is illustrated in Figure 2.17.

In part (a), the straight lines labeled 5, 10, and 14 are isoquants with a constant MRTS, and $\overline{AB}$ is the isocost curve, which intersects the 5- and 10-unit isoquants at points F and B, respectively. It is obvious that in this case there can be no tangency of the isocost curve to the isoquants. However, an optimal solution of the maximum-output condition for a given cost exists—point B. This solution results in only one input, which in the present case is labor. Furthermore, since a negative output in our model does not make sense, all optimal solutions (if any exist) must be in the first quadrant (including the axes), and we see that point B is on the border of the feasible region. For this reason, economists refer to this case as a *corner solution* in contrast to an

FIGURE 2.17

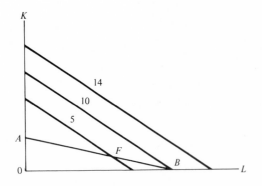
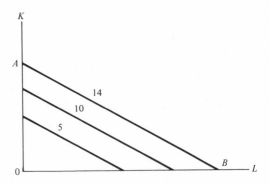

interior solution, such as point *E* in Figures 2.14 and 2.15. In passing, it should be noted that just as the corner solution can limit the input to labor only, one may also have a corner solution that is limited to capital. In summary, it can be appreciated that the corner solution in the two-input case is essentially theoretical, but that in the case of *n* inputs it is a realistic possibility, since all production processes do not use each and every input.

In addition to the situation illustrated in part (a) of Figure 2.17, we also have the possibility of the slope of the isocost curve being the same as that of the isoquants. In such a case, the isocost curve will coincide with one isoquant as, for example, in part (b), where isocost curve $\overline{AB}$ coincides with the 14-unit isoquant. However, the solution is not unique, since one input combination along $\overline{AB}$ is equally as good as any other. In this case, the firm faces an infinite number of input combinations that result in the same cost, admittedly a not very interesting condition so far as decision-making is concerned.

When an isocost curve coincides with an isoquant over some relevant range, no unique combination of inputs is optimal

In the above illustrations we have dealt with the case of a constant MRTS to show why a unique tangency (i.e., an interior solution) is not possible. However, even in the case of a decreasing MRTS, one may still fail to achieve a tangency (interior solution) due to the fact that both labor and capital cannot be negative. As shown in Figure 2.18, it is conceivable that $\overline{AB}$ might be tangent to an isoquant if it was extended below the horizontal axis; however, this would mean a negative capital input at the point of tangency, which does not make economic sense. Meanwhile, we can observe that the isocost curve $\overline{AB}$ reaches the highest isoquant (14 units of output) at point *B* on the horizontal axis. Although there is no tangency, an optimal corner solution exists that results in the exclusive use of the labor input. Thus, when the slope of the isocost curve is flatter than those of the isoquants in the first quadrant, a corner solution will result, and this solution will be optimal. In our case, the price of labor is

FIGURE 2.18

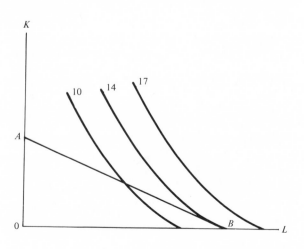

relatively low and that of capital high, thus making it so comparatively expensive to use capital that only labor is employed. Realistically, this can scarcely be regarded as a feasible solution, since in a two-input case such as ours, labor cannot be expected to perform a productive function without the help of some other production factor. Therefore, an interior solution is the more realistic and interesting case. However, it is theoretically possible that in a special situation, such as a primitive economy or the case of Robinson Crusoe, labor could be the only productive factor.

Just as we can have a corner solution for a decreasing MRTS when the price of labor is relatively low, so too may we have a corner solution in the first quadrant if labor is costly and capital relatively inexpensive. It can readily be observed from Figure 2.18 that if the slope of the isocost curve is steeper than those of the isoquants, a corner solution on the vertical axis could result, in which case capital is the only input employed. As we noted earlier, it is unrealistic to assume that one input could perform a production function, albeit theoretically possible.

2.11   AN INCREASE IN SCALE AND THE EXPANSION PATH

As we have shown in Sections 2.10.2 and 2.10.3, the equilibrium of a firm with respect to production or optimal input combination (i.e., maximum output for a given cost or minimum cost for a given output) is characterized by the tangency of an isocost curve to an isoquant in the case of an interior solution. When output expands, however, a firm whose goal is profit maximization will move from one equilibrium point to another, for example, from E to E' in Figure 2.19. Note that E and E' are points of tangency between isocost curves $\overline{AB}$ and $\overline{A'B'}$ and isoquants 10 and 15,

FIGURE 2.19

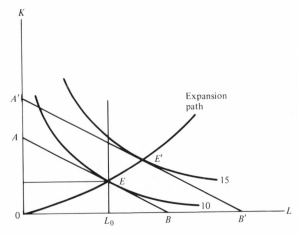

respectively. Furthermore, $\overline{AB}$ is parallel to $\overline{A'B'}$ because the input prices are constant.[9] Suppose the curve $\overparen{0EE'}$ (and also its extension) is the locus of the tangent points between the parallel isocost curves and the isoquants. In such a case, a firm whose goal is profit maximization will travel along this curve when it expands its output or production scale because production efficiency is a necessary condition for profit maximization. For this reason, the curve $\overparen{0EE'}$ is called the *expansion path of production*. We shall now formally define the expansion path.

Definition: Expansion Path. The expansion path is the locus of tangent points between parallel isocost curves and the corresponding isoquants on an isoquant map. The expansion path identifies the optimal combinations of inputs for various levels of output or expenditure. It is also obvious from this definition that all of the isoquants have the same slope along an expansion path.

Some economists define the term *isocline* as the locus of points along which the MRTS is constant. In this case, an expansion path is, in fact, a specific isocline, since at the points of tangency between parallel isocost curves and isoquants, the MRTS is equal to the given price ratio. It is important that students not only remember, but also understand, this condition.

For perfect competition, a budget increase simply means a parallel shift of the isocost curve

Inasmuch as profit-maximizing behavior is assumed under the conditions of the competitive model, we can theoretically assert that a firm will travel along the expansion path. Otherwise, profit cannot be maximized. On the other hand, if a firm's goal is to provide a given amount of employment, it will not travel along the expansion path, but instead travel along a vertical straight line (e.g., $\overline{L_0 E}$ in Figure 2.19) at the specified employment level L_0. Hence, the concept of the expansion path as a description of the firm's rational behavior is only meaningful under the assumption of profit maximization as its goal. There are many similar instances in the theory of the firm where the validity of an assertion is implicitly based on the said assumption. Care must therefore be taken in interpreting the behavior of the firm when one tries to replace this fundamental assumption, because once it is withdrawn, it becomes difficult to define or identify any equilibrium condition or the path along which the firm will move in scheduling its production and use of inputs.

Thus, the points of tangency with successively higher isoquants represent constant MRTS along the expansion path

[9] Under the competitive model, it is assumed that the firm can and will, as a profit maximizer, expand production without influencing the price of inputs or the product. Hence, the budget or isocost curves will move to the right but remain parallel as more inputs are purchased and used to expand output and maximize profits.

2.12 INPUT SUBSTITUTION, PRICE CHANGES, AND ELASTICITY OF SUBSTITUTION

When the price of one input changes while that of the other remains constant, the relative price of the inputs also changes. Common sense tells us that a profit-maximizer will substitute the now cheaper input for the expensive one. This idea can be illustrated by extending the graphical analysis presented in Sections 2.10.2–2.19.

For the purpose of illustration, we assume that the price of labor increases, other things being equal. The "other things" may be looked at in two different ways. First of all, they may include the output, the price of capital, and technology, the latter being represented by the curvature of the isoquants. This is the case that is clear and easy to understand, but few (if any) textbooks have analyzed it. Note that when the wage rate increases while output, the price of capital, and technology remain unchanged, the total cost for the same level of output must necessarily increase, and hence a new equilibrium is established. In the second case, cost, the price of capital, and technology are held constant, but output is allowed to vary. It should be obvious to the student that in such a case output will necessarily decrease.

In partial equilibrium analysis, the approach with which we are dealing here, that is, the "other things being equal" or *ceteris paribus* assumption, is very important. Nevertheless, it is sometimes ignored. The second case above shows that even in the partial analysis, the *ceteris paribus* assumption may not imply that all other things remain the same. In fact, due to the functional relationships that exist between variables (in our case, labor, capital, and some others), an additional factor(s) such as cost, may have to change due to the specified change in the relevant variable. In our example, when the wage rate changed, cost had to change if output was to remain constant. Conversely, if cost were to remain constant, output had to change (decrease, in our case). Recognizing that such conditions exist may eliminate confusion among thoughtful students.

We shall now turn our attention to seeing how, when the wage rate increases, but output, the price of capital, and technology are kept the same, a firm whose goal is profit maximization will substitute capital for labor. In Figure 2.20 we can observe that, for w_0, r_0, and isocost curve $\overline{AB}$, the original equilibrium (i.e., minimum-cost combination of inputs) is $E_0 = \langle L_0 \, K_0 \rangle$. However, when the wage rate increases to $w_1 > w_0$, the price ratio increases so that $w_1/r_0 > w_0/r_0$, the new isocost curve has a steeper slope, and a new tangent point E_1 is established on the same isoquant. In Figure 2.20, E_1 is necessarily above the original point E_0 because of the decreasing MRTS. At the new equilibrium position, less labor and more capital are used.

In economic theory, the above is called the *substitution effect*.

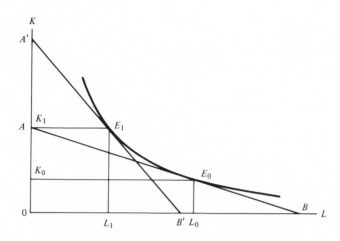

FIGURE 2.20

Note, however, that this requires the total cost for the same level of output to be higher at E_1 than at E_0. This can be illustrated in terms of capital. For isocost curve $\overline{AB}$, the total cost in terms of capital is $r_0 \cdot \overline{0A}$, but for isocost curve $\overline{A'B'}$, the total cost in terms of capital is $r_0 \cdot \overline{0A'}$. Thus, $r_0 \cdot \overline{0A'} > r_0 \cdot \overline{0A}$, since $\overline{0A'} > \overline{0A}$.

The case that we have just described is more relevant in production because the quantity that a firm produces is essentially determined by the market for its output, not by some predetermined level of cost. As long as a firm can make a profit from producing a certain amount of output, cost constraint will not be an absolute condition, since output itself will generate revenue that will more than pay for its cost. (For simplicity, we have ignored a change in the output market.) This situation is fundamentally different from that of a consumer who must deal with a fixed income (which corresponds to the cost of a firm). We shall have more to say on this in Chapter 4. If we have more than two inputs, then the inputs other than the one for which price has changed can be considered a combined input, and, in general, when the price of an input increases, its usage wil be reduced and other inputs substituted in its place to maintain the same level of output.

In the second case, where cost, the price of capital, and technology are held constant, the usage of labor will usually decrease when the wage rate rises; however, in a special case an increase in the amount of labor is theoretically possible, although not likely. These two possibilities are illustrated in parts (a) and (b) of Figure 2.21. In both graphs, the original cost and prices of labor and capital are C_0, w_0, and r_0, respectively. The corresponding isocost curve is $\overline{AB}$, and the equilibrium output is 10 units at point E_0, which implies that $\overline{0L_0}$ labor is being used. When the wage rate increases so that $w_1 > w_0$, the new isocost curve is $\overline{AB'}$, output falls to 8 units, and a new equilibrium point—

If output effect exceeds substitution effect, the amount of labor may increase with its price for a constant price of capital

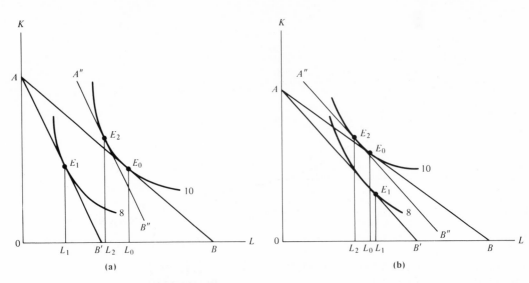

FIGURE 2.21

E_1—with $\overline{0L_1}$ labor is established. The essential difference between parts (a) and (b) is that $\overline{0L_1} < \overline{0L_0}$ in (a) whereas $\overline{0L_1} > \overline{0L_0}$ in (b). In other words, in part (a) less labor is used at the new equilibrium point when the wage rate increases, whereas in part (b) an increase in labor used occurs under the identical conditions of constant cost, fixed price of capital, and given technology. As can be observed and was expected, output decreases in both cases.

The essential difference in the effects shown in parts (a) and (b) of Figure 2.21 can be demonstrated by drawing an imaginary isocost curve $\overline{A''B''}$ parallel to $\overline{AB'}$ but tangent to the 10-unit isoquant at point E_2. From our discussion of the first case, it can be observed that the movement from E_0 to E_2 represents the substitution effect, which is very reliable; that is, a higher price of labor with output, the price of capital, and technology held constant will lead to less labor used at the new equilibrium point. On the other hand, the movement from E_2 to E_1, called the *output effect*, creates the essential difference between parts (a) and (b). In the case of part (a), when output decreases from 10 to 8 units with input prices and technology being held constant, the usage of labor decreases from $\overline{0L_2}$ to $\overline{0L_1}$. This is the normal situation. However, in part (b), the usage of labor increases from $\overline{0L_2}$ to $\overline{0L_1}$. This is a very unusual case and one in which the input (labor, in our case) is called an *inferior factor of production*. We define this as an input of which more will be used when output decreases while input prices and technology are held constant.

In the case of a *normal factor of production*, the output effect reinforces the substitution effect, and an increase in its price will result in less labor used for a given or constant cost. With an

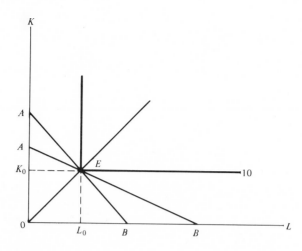

FIGURE 2.22

inferior factor, the output and substitution effects go in opposite directions, making the net result uncertain. Only where the strong negative output effect of an inferior factor outweighs the substitution effect will an increase in the price of the factor lead to more of it being used when cost is constant. A vigorous mathematical presentation of this matter appears in the appendix of this chapter.

It should be noted that the extent to which capital can be substituted for labor for a given change in the wage rate, other things remaining equal, depends on the curvature of the isoquants, which, in turn, is determined by technology. Recall that MRTS is defined as the negative slope of the isoquant, a measure of its curvature. A 10-unit isoquant that exhibits zero MRTS is shown in Figure 2.22. In this special case, capital cannot be substituted for labor regardless of how much the wage rate may increase. As we have explained before, this is the case where labor and capital have to be used in a fixed proportion. As can be observed from the figure, with a wage rate w_0 (represented by isocost curve $\overline{AB}$), E is the equilibrium point for producing 10 units of output. When the wage rate increases so that $w_1 > w_0$ (represented by isocost curve $\overline{A'B'}$), E is still the equilibrium point for 10 units of output. Students may try any other slope of the isocost curve, but E will still be the equilibrium point for 10 units of output, and $\overline{0L_0}$ and $\overline{0K_0}$ amounts of labor and capital, respectively, will be used.

Another extreme case of constant MRTS is shown in Figure 2.23, where $\overline{A''B}$ is a 10-unit isoquant. Let us start with a given set of the prices w_0 and r_0 for labor and capital, respectively; this is represented by the isocost curve $\overline{AB}$. In the figure, B is the corner equilibrium point. When the price of capital decreases to $r_1 < r_0$ and w_0 remains the same, the new isocost curve is $\overline{A'B}$. However, B is still the equilibrium point, and thus no substitution between labor and capital takes place. As a matter of

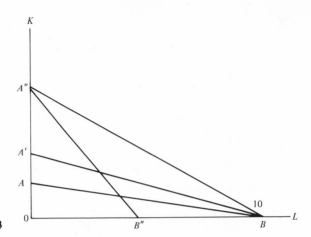

FIGURE 2.23

fact, regardless of how much the price of capital decreases, as long as the price ratio of the inputs is smaller in absolute value than the slope of $\overline{A''B}$, no substitution between the inputs will take place. However, when the wage rate increases to the extent that the ratio of the input prices is greater in absolute value than the slope of the isoquants (such as $\overline{A''B}$), the substitution will be complete; that is, no labor will be used, capital being the only input. The isocost curve $\overline{A''B''}$ represents such a case of a very high wage rate, and, as a result, the new equilibrium point will be A'' instead of B. This is a case of a *none or all condition*. On the other hand, as we mentioned earlier, if the prices of the inputs are such that the slope of the isocost curve is the same as that of the isoquants, then one combination of the inputs will be just as good as another. As a consequence, the problem of choice ceases to be economic and becomes simply one of personal preference or some other criteria.

When the wage rate changes continuously, continuous substitution between labor and capital is possible only in the special case where the isoquants are smooth curves that are strictly convex to the origin. This is the theoretically most interesting case that has been dealt with extensively in the majority of textbooks. In this case, the extent to which labor can be substituted for capital for a given change in the wage rate, the price of capital, technology, and output remaining constant, depends on the curvature of the isoquants. Figure 2.24 has been constructed to illustrate the substitutability between labor and capital under such a condition.

The sensitivity of substitution between capital and labor, other things equal, depends on the isoquant shape

We consider the starting prices of labor and capital to be w_0 and r_0, respectively, and represented by the isocost curve $\overline{AB}$. The two isoquants, one solid and one broken, represent the same amount of output, 10 units in this case. They may represent either the same product produced by two distinct technologies or two different products that can be produced with the same amounts

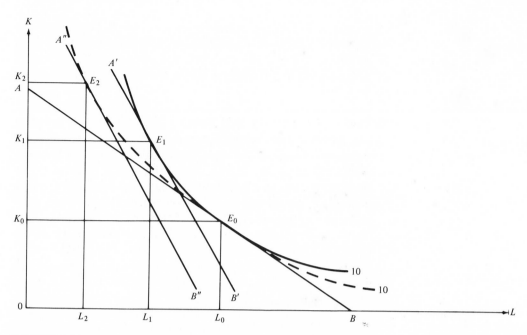

FIGURE 2.24

of labor and capital, that is, $\langle L_0, K_0 \rangle$. Since our intention is to demonstrate the relationship between the substitutability between labor and capital, on the one hand, and technology, on the other hand, it does not make any difference whether the isoquants represent the same or different products.

Suppose that the wage rate increases; the new price ratio of labor and capital is now represented by $\overline{A'B'}$ and $\overline{A''B''}$, which are parallel. With the technology represented by the solid isoquant, the new equilibrium point is E_1, labor input is reduced by $\overline{L_0L_1}$, and, at the same time, capital input is increased by $\overline{K_0K_1}$. On the other hand, with the technology represented by the broken isoquant, for the same price change the new equilibrium point is E_2, labor is reduced by $\overline{L_0L_2} > \overline{L_0L_1}$, and, at the same time, capital is increased by $\overline{K_0K_2} > \overline{K_0K_1}$. In a sense, the substitution between labor and capital is more sensitive in the second case than in the first. It turns out that the slope of the broken isoquant is flatter than that of the solid isoquant in the neighborhood of E_0. Thus, other things being equal, the flatter the slope of an isoquant in the neighborhood of the point of tangency, the easier one input can be substituted for another. Therefore, the curvature of isoquants is a good indication of the ease or difficulty with which one input can be substituted for another. However, there is one defect in the derivative as a measure of curvature, that is, for the same curvature the derivative may show different values if different units of measure are chosen for the variable concerned. We shall use numerical examples to show this point when we deal with the elasticity of demand. A better measure for describing the ease of substitution between two inputs, which is invariant with respect to the choice of units, is the *elasticity of substitution*. We shall first define the term and then explain its meaning.

Definition: Elasticity of Substitution. The elasticity of substitution between two inputs is the ratio of the percentage (proportional) change in the input ratio to the percentage (proportional) change in the MRTS. Since the MRTS is equal to the input price ratio at equilibrium, it can also be defined as the ratio of the percentage (proportional) change in the input ratio to the percentage (proportional) change in the price ratio of the inputs. In short, it measures the relative responsiveness of the input ratio to given proportionate changes in the MRTS of the inputs. In symbols, for the two-input case (labor and capital) the elasticity of substitution σ is

$$\sigma = \frac{[\Delta(K/L)/(K/L)]100}{(\Delta\text{MRTS}/\text{MRTS})100} = \frac{\%\Delta \text{ of input ratio}}{\%\Delta \text{ of MRTS}}$$

$$= \frac{\Delta(K/L)/(K/L)}{\Delta\text{MRTS}/\text{MRTS}} \tag{2.13}$$

$$= \frac{\text{proportional change of input ratio}}{\text{proportional change of MRTS}}$$

As usual, the Greek letter Δ (delta) denotes change. The above steps in our calculation show that the ratio of the *percentage* change in the input ratio to the percentage change in the MRTS is equivalent to the ratio of a *proportional* change in the input ratio to the proportional change in the MRTS because a proportion multiplied by 100 becomes a percentage, and a ratio of two proportions that have been multiplied by 100 in both the numerator and the denominator becomes a ratio of two percentages, since the 100 in the numerator cancels out the 100 in the denominator. Since the MRTS is equal to the input price ratio at equilibrium, and we are only interested in the elasticity of substitution at the equilibrium points, we also have

$$\sigma = \frac{\Delta(K/L)/(K/L)}{\Delta(w/r)/(w/r)} \tag{2.14}$$

Since some authors define the elasticity of substitution in terms of percentage changes, others in terms of proportional changes, and still others in terms of changes in the MRTS or in terms of changes in the input price ratio, students may become confused when referring to different textbooks on price theory or microeconomics. This happens more often with respect to demand elasticities, which will be dealt with in detail in Chapter 5. In order to avoid possible confusion, we have considered it useful to include the alternative definitions here. Using (2.14), the student can readily appreciate why the larger the value of σ, the larger the percentage (proportional) change in the K/L ratio in response to a certain percentage (proportional) change in the w/r ratio. In summary, the elasticity of substitution of inputs provides an indication of the sensitivity of the technical substitution between inputs to a given change in factor prices. Those students who are interested in learning more about the properties of σ should refer to the appendix following this chapter.

2.13 HOMOGENEOUS AND HOMOTHETIC PRODUCTION FUNCTIONS

In keeping with our principle of avoiding the use of mathematics as much as possible in order to enhance the readability of the textual narrative, we have placed most of the mathematical proofs and technical discussions in the appendices. However, some concepts in economics cannot be easily explained without the use of elementary algebra. This section represents one of these instances. Those instructors who wish to skip this section can do so without loss of continuity.

A production function in the one-output, n-input case can be written

$$Q = F(X_1, X_2, ..., X_n) \tag{2.15}$$

where Q is the output, and X_i, $i = 1, 2, ..., n$, the n inputs. A production function can be either homogeneous or not homogeneous. If it is homogeneous, it could theoretically be in any degree from negative infinity to positive infinity. If all the inputs are multiplied by a positive constant c, the output will be multiplied by c^k, and the production function is homogeneous in the degree k. In symbols, if we have

$$c^k Q = F(cX_1, cX_2, ..., cX_n) \tag{2.16}$$

then the production function (2.15) is homogeneous in the degree k.

Theoretically, k could be any number. In production theory, the meaningful range of k is positive, and $k = 1$ has special significance. For convenience, we shall indicate the homogeneous production functions that identify the three different conditions that apply to the input–output relationship; the student should establish the linkage between these conditions in the context of (2.16):

1. A production function that is homogeneous in the degree 1 will exhibit constant returns to scale.

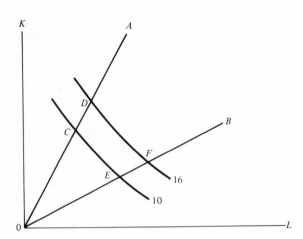

FIGURE 2.25

2. A production function that is homogeneous in degree > 1 will exhibit increasing returns to scale.
3. A production function that is homogeneous in degree < 1 will exhibit decreasing returns to scale.

A special feature of homogeneous production functions, regardless of the degree of homogeneity, is that, on an isoquant map, the MRTS between the two inputs is the same along any ray from the origin. For example, the slopes of the 10-unit and 16-unit isoquants (in fact, infinite other isoquants as well) are the same at point C as at point D and the same at point E as at point F in Figure 2.25. In general, the locus of the same slope of the isoquants is not a straight line for a production function. This is indicated by the non-straight-line expansion path in Figure 2.19, since, by definition, the slopes of all isoquants along an expansion path are the same.

It is obvious that the expansion path of a homogeneous production function is a straight line from the origin. However, the converse is not necessarily true; that is, a production function that results in a straight-line expansion path may not be homogeneous. This needs further explanation, and we now offer a definition for such a production function.

For homogeneous production functions, on isoquant maps MRTS between inputs is the same along a given ray from the origin

Definition: Homothetic Production Function. A homothetic production function has the property that along any ray from the origin of an isoquant map, the MRTS between the inputs is the same. In other words, along any straight line from the origin of the isoquant map, the slopes of all isoquants are identical.

From the above definition, it is seen that homogeneous production functions are special cases of homothetic production functions. When a production function is homothetic or homogeneous, we need only to know the production process employed, regardless of the level of output, in order to determine the MRTS between inputs. This relationship will be of some importance when the topic of income distribution theory is considered.

In concluding this section on production theory, we wish to emphasize its importance because it provides a good foundation for a discussion of cost theory in economics. In fact, the cost function is derived from the equilibrium (optimal) conditions in production. Without a good understanding of this relationship, the true meaning of cost behavior may not be appreciated. This will become more obvious as we proceed with the discussion of cost in Chapter 3.

SUMMARY

This chapter brings the analysis of production closer to reality by introducing the student to the two-variable input model. We further explained that the two-variable input case in production may be considered either with a short-run model (in which two variables and one or more fixed inputs are involved) or, alternatively, with a long-run model (in which case only two inputs, both variable, are involved). Thus, we have a flexible model for the analysis of production.

We introduced the term "production process" and defined it as a fixed input ratio that is used in producing an output. It was then shown that, under the assumptions of divisibility and constant returns to scale, two distinct production processes can be combined to form a third process—or infinitely many different processes (i.e., input ratios). We also explained that an inefficient process is one that, as compared to another process or combination of processes, uses more of one input without any reduction in any of the other inputs to produce the same amount of output. We defined an efficient process as one that is not inefficient, noting, however, that efficient processes are not unique.

To give the student a better understanding of efficient versus inefficient production processes, we used the concept of an isoquant in a two-dimensional graph. We defined an isoquant as a collection of line segments that joint adjacent efficient processes for a given level of output. It was explained that the traditional textbook model of smooth isoquant curves is actually a special case of an infinite number of efficient processes and that, when there are only a finite number of processes available, the isoquants will not be smooth curves. We also gave considerable attention to describing the essential nature of different isoquant curves and to explaining that movement along an isoquant implies substitution between inputs. It was noted that the (negative) slope of an isoquant is defined as the marginal rate of technical substitution (MRTS) and that a decreasing MRTS has special significance in economic analysis even though constant and zero MRTS are technically possible. Finally, we used the map of isoquant curves on a two-dimensional graph to show the meaning of the concept of returns to scale, noting that the distances between various output levels along a ray drawn from the origin of an isoquant map can be employed to determine whether returns to scale occurred as production was increased.

After using the isoquant map to analyze the input–output behavior when two variable inputs are employed, we proceeded to define the optimal combination of inputs in production as that combination resulting in maximum output for a given cost, or equivalently, that combination of inputs which results in a minimum cost for a given output. We explained that this definition is more complete than the traditional one of a minimum-cost combination for producing a given product.

Having brought cost into our analysis for the first time, in order to distinguish between technical and economic efficiency, we introduced the student to the concept of an isocost curve and showed that when no change in the unit price of the inputs is given, irrespective of the amount used, isocosts become straight lines. Moreover, we explained that the isocost line provides complete information of input markets (that is, input prices and costs) needed to help determine the equilibrium condition (maximum output for a given cost or minimum cost for a given output) of a firm. We showed that under the assumption of a decreasing MRTS and smooth isoquants the equilibrium condition is characterized by the tangency of an isoquant and an isocost for an interior solution because it is at this point that the MRTS of the inputs equals the price ratio of the inputs. It was also noted that in the more general case of n inputs the corner solution may be rather common and that the tangency condition is not satisfied.

Finally, a family of isocost lines was used to develop the notion of an expansion path along which a firm would proceed, given the technical production processes as represented by the isoquant map and the behavior of input prices and different budget amounts available to the firm. We defined the expansion path as the locus of equilibrium points for which cost undergoes change. We showed that, if input prices are constant under conditions of perfect competition, although the isocost lines move parallel to each other as the budget changes, the expansion path is not likely to be a straight line. This is due to the tangency conditions, which must be met with different isoquants. The importance of the expansion path in deriving the cost function for the product was emphasized, and the elasticity of substitution of inputs was analyzed in the context of a given technology (i.e., production process as reflected by the shape of the isoquants). We concluded our discussion by noting the distinction between homogeneous and homothetic production functions and their relation to the expansion path for a firm under perfect competition.

EXERCISES AND QUESTIONS FOR CHAPTERS 1 AND 2 ON PRODUCTION THEORY

1. It is said that the marginal product (MP) curve of a variable input always intersects the average product (AP) curve of the input at the maximum of the latter. Do you agree with this statement? In your own words, give an explanation for your answer.

2. For the one-variable-input case, use the graphical method to show the derivation of the MP and AP curves from a total product (TP) curve. Define the underlined terms. A brief explanation should accompany your graphical derivation.

3. It is said that "production will occur only in stage II." First explain what "stage II" means and then indicate whether you agree with that statement. Defend your answer.

4. Explain why economists consider the law of diminishing returns to be so important in the theory of production.

5. Use your own words to explain the meaning of the term "decreasing marginal rate of technical substitution." (It is a good idea to first explain the meaning of MRTS.)

6. Use the graphical method to show the derivation of an *expansion path*. Define this term. An explanation should accompany your graphical derivation.

7. It is said that a firm's output will be maximized for a given cost if the MRTS is equal to the price ratio of the corresponding inputs. Do you agree with the above statement? Defend your answer.

8. Describe what is meant by the terms "increasing returns to scale," "decreasing returns to scale," "constant returns to scale," and the "law of diminishing returns." What are the essential differences, if any, between the law of diminishing returns, on the one hand, and the various concepts of returns to scale, on the other hand. Explain.

9. Suppose that a product requires two inputs for its production. Would it be correct to say that if the prices of the inputs are equal, optimal behavior on the part of producers will dictate that these inputs be used in equal amounts? Explain. Use a graph or graphs to illustrate your explanation.

10. Suppose we have the following four processes for producing commodity X which use K and L in the amounts shown and that the number of units of X produced by each process is as given below when operations are at the unit level; also assume constant returns to scale for each process:

    1. P_1: 2K, 6L $X = 1.5$
    2. P_2: 4K, 4L $X = 1.2$
    3. P_3: 6K, 2L $X = 1.5$
    4. P_4: 4K, 1L $X = 1.0$
        a. Graph each of the processes.
        b. Draw the isoquant for 120 units of output.
        c. Are any of the processes inefficient? If so, which one(s)? Why?

11. The five processes shown in Table E1-2.1 all produce 1 ton of the same product when operated at unit level.

TABLE E1-2.1

	Input required	
Process	Capital (machine-hours)	Labor (person-hours)
P_1	24	2
P_2	20	6
P_3	16	8
P_4	12	24

a. Draw a diagram and plot the points that represent the input combination for the unit level of output for each of the processes.
b. Assuming that the processes can be operated at all levels (including fractions of the unit level) and can be combined without interactions, determine which of these processes is inefficient.
c. Draw in the isoquant for the unit level of production of the good.

APPENDIX TO CHAPTERS 1 AND 2

A MATHEMATICAL NOTE ON THE THEORY OF PRODUCTION

A1-2.1 PRODUCTION FUNCTION, AP, AND MP

If we denote the output by Q and the n inputs by $x_1, x_2, ..., x_n$, a production function can be written

$$Q = f(x_1, x_2, ... x_n)^1 \qquad \text{(A1-2.1)}$$

The MP of input $i = 1, 2, ..., n$ is defined as the partial derivative of the production function with respect to x_i. We denote the MP of x_i by MP_i and the first and second partial derivatives of the production function by

$$f_i \equiv \partial Q / \partial x_i, \qquad f_{ij} \equiv \partial^2 Q / \partial x_j \partial x_i$$

Thus, we have

$$MP_i = f_i, \qquad i = 1, 2, ..., n \qquad \text{(A1-2.2)}$$

Since Q is a function of all the inputs, MP_i is also a function of all the inputs.

The AP of the ith input is defined by dividing the total output Q by the amount of the ith input x_i. Denote the AP of x_i by AP_i; thus,

$$AP_i = Q / x_i \qquad \text{(A1-2.3)}$$

---

[1] It is often overlooked that the production function (A1-2.1) implies the absence of externality (see the Introduction to Part I). Without this assumption, the production function of firm j should be written (assuming that there are m firms in the industry)

$$Q_j = f(x_1^1, x_2^1, ..., x_n^1, ..., x_1^m, x_2^m, ..., x_n^m) \qquad \text{(A1-2.1')}$$

where x_i^j denotes the input i of firm j.

Since Q is a function of all the inputs, AP_i is also a function of all the inputs.

In the text we have shown by commonsense reasoning and a graphical method that the MP curve always intersects the associated AP curve at the maximum of the latter, AP increases when MP is greater than it, and, conversely, AP decreases when MP is less than it. This can be easily shown by partially differentiating AP_i with respect to x_i:

$$\frac{\partial AP_i}{\partial x_i} = \frac{x_i f_i - Q}{x_i^2}$$

$$= \frac{(f_i - Q/x_i)}{x_i} \gtreqless 0 \qquad \text{for} \quad f_i \gtreqless \frac{Q}{x_i}$$

(A1-2.4)

This implies that when MP_i is greater than AP_i, the AP of input i increases. Conversely, when MP_i is less than AP_i, the latter decreases. When $MP_i = AP_i$, AP_i is either maximum or minimum.

In economics, we know that the point of maximum AP_i is meaningful; thus, we conclude that MP_i is equal to AP_i at the maximum of the latter.

The Cobb–Douglas production function with two inputs (e.g., labor L and capital K) is well known:

$$Q = AL^\alpha K^\beta$$

(A1-2.5)

where A, α, and β are constants. It can be easily seen that the MPs of labor and capital are

$$MP_L = \alpha AL^{\alpha-1} K^\beta, \qquad MP_K = \beta AL^\alpha K^{\beta-1}$$

(A1-2.6)

The APs of labor and capital are

$$AP_L = AL^{\alpha-1} K^\beta, \qquad AP_K = AL^\alpha K^{\beta-1}$$

(A1-2.7)

From the above expressions, it is seen that

$$MP_L = \alpha AP_L \qquad \text{or} \qquad MP_L/AP_L = \alpha$$

$$MP_K = \beta AP_K \qquad \text{or} \qquad MP_K/AP_K = \beta$$

(A1-2.8)

Hence, the ratio of the MP of labor (capital) to the AP of labor (capital) is a constant regardless of the level of output and the input ratio. This particular situation is the result of the specific functional relationship (A1-2.5). Since α and β are constants and, in general, do not equal 1, MP cannot be equal to AP for either labor or capital. However, this agrees with (A1-2.4) in that when MP is greater than AP, the latter increases and vice versa. In the case of the Cobb–Douglas production function, AP is either constant, monotonically increasing, or monotonically decreasing; however, for nonconstant AP, neither a maximum nor a minimum exists, and hence, by implication, MP and AP cannot be equal.

We now take the partial derivatives of (A1-2.7):

$$\partial(AP_L)/\partial L = (\alpha - 1)AL^{\alpha-2}K^{\beta} \gtreqless 0 \quad \text{for } \alpha \gtreqless 1 \qquad (A1\text{-}2.9)$$

$$\partial(AP_K)/\partial K = (\beta - 1)AL^{\alpha}K^{\beta-2} \gtreqless 0 \quad \text{for } \beta \gtreqless 1 \qquad (A1\text{-}2.10)$$

Both AP_L and AP_K are constant if $\alpha = \beta = 1$; in this case, MP and AP are equal for all values of L and K. When α, $\beta > 1$, both AP_L and AP_K are monotonically increasing functions, and MP is always greater than AP, which corresponds to stage I. On the other hand, when α, $\beta < 1$, both AP_L and AP_K are monotonically decreasing functions, and MP is always less than AP, which corresponds to stage II. Thus, the most meaningful values for α and β are $0 < \alpha < 1$ and $0 < \beta < 1$.

The Cobb–Douglas production function does not give us the traditional smooth bell-shaped AP and MP curves. The following production function does provide these curves, as well as an isoquant map of the type given in Figure 2.9:

$$Q = AL^2K^2 - BL^3K^3 \qquad (A1\text{-}2.11)$$

where L and K denote labor and capital, respectively, and A and B are constants. We have

$$AP_L = ALK^2 - BL^2K^3, \qquad AP_K = AL^2K - BL^3K^2 \qquad (A1\text{-}2.12)$$

and

$$MP_L = 2ALK^2 - 3BL^2K^3, \qquad MP_K = 2AL^2K - 3BL^3K^2 \qquad (A1\text{-}2.13)$$

With this production function, it can be easily shown that MP is equal to AP at the maximum of the latter for both labor and capital. First of all, in (A1-2.12), we take the partial derivatives of AP_L and AP_K with respect to L and K, respectively, and set them equal to zero:

$$\partial(AP_L)/\partial L = AK^2 - 2BLK^3 = 0,$$
$$\partial(AP_K)/\partial K = AL^2 - 2BL^3K = 0 \qquad (A1\text{-}2.14)$$

We find that AP_L reaches its maximum at $L = A/2BK$, whereas AP_K reaches its maximum at $K = A/2BL$. If we now substitute the labor value $L = A/2BK$ into the expression for AP_L in (A1-2.12), after combining terms we obtain

$$AP_L = A^2K/4B \quad \text{for} \quad L = A/2BK \qquad (A1\text{-}2.15)$$

Similarly, if we substitute the same labor value $L = A/2BK$ into the expression for MP_L in (A1-2.13), after combining terms we obtain

$$MP_L = A^2K/4B \quad \text{for} \quad L = A/2BK \qquad (A1\text{-}2.16)$$

This shows that $MP_L = AP_L$ at the maximum of AP_L. In a similar manner, one can easily show that AP_K reaches its maximum at $K = A/2BL$ and that $AP_K = A^2L/4B = MP_K$ at $K = A/2BL$.

Since a negative output is not meaningful in terms of economic decisions in production, the production function (A1-2.11) has economic significance only within a certain range of input combinations. Either $L > A/BK$ or $K > A/BL$ will result in negative output; thus, for a given amount of capital input $\overline{K}$, labor input cannot be more than $A/B\overline{K}$. Similarly, for a given labor input $\overline{L}$, capital input cannot be more than $A/B\overline{L}$.

From (A1-2.6), (A1-2.7), (A1-2.12), and (A1-2.13), it is seen that AP_L and AP_K for production functions (A1-2.5) and (A1-2.11) are functions of both labor and capital. This indicates that a change in capital (labor) input will result in a shift of both AP_L (AP_K) and MP_L (MP_K), as is demonstrated by the numerical and graphical examples in Section 2.9.

A1-2.2 THE MRTS, HOMOTHETICITY, AND HOMOGENEITY

The MRTS is defined for a movement along an isoquant (i.e., where the change in output is zero). In the two-input case,

$$Q = f(L, K), \qquad dQ = f_L dL + f_K dK = 0 \tag{A1-2.17}$$

and the MRTS is

$$-dK/dL = f_L/f_K \tag{A1-2.18}$$

For the Cobb–Douglas production function, from (A1-2.6) we have

$$MRTS = (\alpha/\beta)(K/L) \tag{A1-2.19}$$

The MRTS of the Cobb–Douglas production function is a function of the input ratio. For a constant capital/labor ratio K/L, that is, along any ray from the origin on an isoquant map, the MRTS is a constant. This is precisely the definition of a homothetic production function. Thus, the Cobb–Douglas production function is homothetic.

The Cobb–Douglas production function is also homogeneous of the degree $\alpha + \beta$. This can be easily shown by multiplying both labor and capital by a positive number t:

$$A(tL)^\alpha(tK)^\beta = At^\alpha L^\alpha t^\beta K^\beta = t^{\alpha+\beta}AL^\alpha K^\beta = t^{\alpha+\beta}Q \tag{A1-2.20}$$

When both inputs are multiplied by t, the output is multiplied by $t^{\alpha+\beta}$. This means precisely that the production function is homogeneous of the degree $\alpha + \beta$.

However, the production function (A1-2.11) is not homogeneous, but homothetic. From (A1-2.13) we have

$$
\begin{aligned}
\text{MRTS} &= \frac{2ALK^2 - 3BL^2K^3}{2AL^2K - 3BL^3K^2} \\
&= \frac{K(2ALK - 3BL^2K^2)}{L(2ALK - 3BL^2K^2)} = \frac{K}{L}
\end{aligned}
\tag{A1-2.21}
$$

Along the same ray from the origin $C = K/L$, where C is a constant, we also have MRTS $= C$. Thus, the production function is homothetic. On the other hand, it can be easily seen that it is not homogeneous. Hence, if a function is homogeneous, it must be homothetic. However, a homothetic function may not be homogeneous, as we have stated in the text.

A1-2.3 DIMINISHING RETURNS AND RETURNS TO SCALE

The law of diminishing returns is synonymous with a decreasing MP; that is,

$$\partial(\text{MP}_i)/\partial x_i = f_{ii} < 0$$

For the Cobb–Douglas production function, from (A1-2.6) we have

$$
\begin{aligned}
\partial(\text{MP}_L)/\partial L &= \alpha(\alpha - 1)AL^{\alpha-2}K^\beta < 0 \qquad \text{for } \alpha < 1 \\
\partial(\text{MP}_K)/\partial K &= \beta(\beta - 1)AL^\alpha K^{\beta-2} < 0 \qquad \text{for } \beta < 1
\end{aligned}
\tag{A1-2.22}
$$

Thus, the law of diminishing returns prevails only when $\alpha, \beta < 1$.

For the production function (A1-2.11), from (A1-2.13) we have

$$
\begin{aligned}
\partial(\text{MP}_L)/\partial L &= 2AK^2 - 6BLK^3 < 0 \qquad \text{for } A/3B\overline{K} < L \\
\partial(\text{MP}_K)/\partial K &= 2AL^2 - 6BL^3K < 0 \qquad \text{for } A/3B\overline{L} < K
\end{aligned}
\tag{A1-2.23}
$$

Thus, for a given capital input $\overline{K}$, when labor input increases, the law of diminishing returns prevails only when labor input is greater than $A/3B\overline{K}$ (a constant). Similarly, for a given labor input $\overline{L}$, when capital input increases, the law of diminishing returns prevails only when capital input is greater than $A/3B\overline{L}$ (a constant).

Diminishing returns and returns to scale are entirely different concepts. The former refers to a decreasing MP, whereas the latter concerns the behavior of a production function when all inputs change proportionately.

Returns to scale:

Proposition A1-2.1. For the general production function (A1-2.1), a constant returns to scale prevails when $f(tx_1, tx_2, ..., tx_n) = tQ$ for $t > 0$; an increasing returns to scale prevails when

$f(tx_1, tx_2, ..., tx_n) > tQ$ for $t > 1$; finally, a decreasing returns to scale prevails when $f(tx_1, tx_2, ..., tx_n) < tQ$ for $t > 1$.

Returns to scale can be most conveniently demonstrated by homogeneous production functions. As a simple example, the Cobb–Douglas production function (A1-2.5) exhibits

constant returns to scale if $\alpha + \beta = 1$

increasing returns to scale if $\alpha + \beta > 1$

decreasing returns to scale if $\alpha + \beta < 1$

As an illustration, suppose that $\alpha + \beta = 2$:

$$A(tL)^\alpha (tK)^\beta = t^{\alpha+\beta} A L^\alpha K^\beta$$
$$= t^2 Q > tQ \qquad \text{for} \quad t > 1 \tag{A1-2.24}$$

On the other hand, if $0 < t < 1$, then $t^2 Q < tQ$. For example, if $t = 0.5$, then $(0.5)^2 Q = 0.25Q < 0.5Q$. This is occasionally overlooked. Thus, for returns to scale purposes, the constant t in the above expression must be > 1.

A1-2.4 THE COST EQUATION, OPTIMALITY IN PRODUCTION, AND CRAMER'S RULE

The characteristics of a production function provide all of the technical information that a firm can obtain. However, technical information alone is not sufficient for a firm to achieve optimal production. In fact, a production function offers a firm an infinite number of alternatives, all of which are efficient in terms of technology. In order to achieve economic optimality, additional information on cost is necessary. Thus, we introduce the following cost equation corresponding to (2.6):

$$C = C_0 + r_1 x_1 + r_2 x_2 + \cdots + r_n x_n$$
$$= C_0 + \sum_{i=1}^{n} r_i x_i \tag{A1-2.25}$$

where C is the total cost, C_0 is the "sunk" or total fixed cost (a constant, which can be zero), and r_i is the price of input x_i, $i = 1, 2, ..., n$. Special attention is called to the fact that expression (A1-2.25) is called a cost equation, not a cost function; the latter term is reserved for later purposes. The student should note that a cost equation is an expression in which cost is a linear function of the *inputs* and their prices, whereas a cost function is an expression in which cost is considered a function of the *output*. We shall discuss the cost function in more detail in Chapter 3.

Optimality in production can be considered in two different but equivalent ways. As a precondition for maximum profit, a firm must maximize output for a given cost or minimize cost for a given output. We have already discussed the general case with n inputs and a general production function; the well-known Cobb–Douglas production function with two inputs will now be used to illustrate all of the essential points.

A1-2.4.1 The Case of the Cobb–Douglas Production Function

Maximum Output for a Given Cost

Mathematically, this case represents a constrained maximization problem. We want to find those values of L and K that will maximize the Cobb–Douglas production function

$$Q = AL^\alpha K^\beta \qquad (A1-2.5)$$

subject to the constraint of a given cost

$$\overline{C} = C_0 + wL + rK \qquad (A1-2.26)$$

where $\overline{C}$ denotes the given (constant) cost, and w and r denote the prices for labor and capital, respectively, which are constants in a competitive input market; in (A1-2.5), L and K are the independent variables, whereas Q is the dependent variable. For the two-input case, there are two different methods of solving the problem. The first is by substitution and the second is by using the Lagrange multiplier. For the purpose of illustration, we shall use both methods.

METHOD 1: SUBSTITUTION. We solve for L in (A1-2.26); thus,

$$L = (\overline{C} - C_0)/w - rK/w \qquad (A1-2.27)$$

Substituting (A1-2.27) into (A1-2.5), we obtain

$$Q = A[(\overline{C} - C_0)/w - rK/w]^\alpha K^\beta \qquad (A1-2.28)$$

Thus, the output Q is a function of only capital K. We can use elementary calculus to find under which conditions Q will be a maximum.

The first-order condition is

$$\frac{dQ}{dK} = \beta A \left(\frac{\overline{C} - C_0}{w} - \frac{r}{w} K \right)^\alpha K^{\beta-1}$$

$$- \frac{\alpha r}{w} A \left(\frac{\overline{C} - C_0}{w} - \frac{r}{w} K \right)^{\alpha-1} K^\beta = 0 \qquad (A1-2.29)$$

and the second-order condition is

$$\frac{d^2Q}{dK^2} = \left[\frac{\beta(\beta-1)}{K^2} - \frac{2\alpha\beta r}{wLK} + \frac{\alpha(\alpha-1)r^2}{w^2L^2} \right] Q < 0 \qquad (A1-2.30)$$

Substituting (A1-2.27) into (A1-2.29), the first-order condition can be written

$$\alpha AL^{\alpha-1}K^{\beta}/w = \beta AL^{\alpha}K^{\beta-1}/r \tag{A1-2.31}$$

that is, precisely Equation (2.11), which defined the tangency between an isoquant and an isocost curve (see point E in Figure 2.14). Equation (A1-2.31) can also be written

$$\beta wL - \alpha rK = 0 \tag{A1-2.31'}$$

Equations (A1-2.31') and (A1-2.26) represent two linear equations in two variables—L and K (remember that α, β, and $\overline{C}$ are constants). Since we are assuming a competitive input market, the firm is a price taker; hence, w and r are also considered constants.

There is a very convenient method for solving a system of linear equations—Cramer's rule. This rule states that the solution for a variable (e.g., x_i) is given by the ratio of two determinants of the coefficients and the constants. For example, assume that we have the three-equation system

$$a_{11}X_1 + a_{12}X_2 + a_{13}X_3 = C_1$$
$$a_{21}X_1 + a_{22}X_2 + a_{23}X_3 = C_2 \tag{A1-2.32}$$
$$a_{31}X_1 + a_{32}X_2 + a_{33}X_3 = C_3$$

We can write

$$A = \begin{vmatrix} a_{11} & a_{21} & a_{13} \\ a_{21} & a_{22} & a_{23} \\ a_{31} & a_{32} & a_{33} \end{vmatrix}, \quad A_1 = \begin{vmatrix} C_1 & a_{12} & a_{13} \\ C_2 & a_{22} & a_{23} \\ C_3 & a_{32} & a_{33} \end{vmatrix}$$
$$A_2 = \begin{vmatrix} a_{11} & C_1 & a_{13} \\ a_{21} & C_2 & a_{23} \\ a_{31} & C_3 & a_{33} \end{vmatrix}, \quad A_3 = \begin{vmatrix} a_{11} & a_{12} & C_1 \\ a_{21} & a_{22} & C_2 \\ a_{31} & a_{32} & C_3 \end{vmatrix} \tag{A1-2.33}$$

where A, A_1, A_2, and A_3 are the determinants. Thus, the solutions for the Xs are

$$X_1 = A_1/A, \quad X_2 = A_2/A, \quad X_3 = A_3/A \tag{A1-2.34}$$

A determinant is a single number computed from a square matrix. Without giving a formal definition, one way to compute the determinant of an $n \times n$ matrix is in terms of the determinants of the $(n - 1) \times (n - 1)$ submatrices, then those of the next lower order $(n - 2) \times (n - 2)$ submatrices, and so on. For example, the first step in computing the determinant of the above 3×3 matrix is

$$A = a_{11}(-1)^{1+1}\begin{vmatrix} a_{22} & a_{23} \\ a_{32} & a_{33} \end{vmatrix} + a_{12}(-1)^{1+2}\begin{vmatrix} a_{21} & a_{23} \\ a_{31} & a_{33} \end{vmatrix}$$
$$+ a_{13}(-1)^{1+3}\begin{vmatrix} a_{21} & a_{22} \\ a_{31} & a_{32} \end{vmatrix}$$

For an $n \times n$ matrix, in the first round, A is the sum of n terms, each of which is the product of an element of a row or a column and the determinant of an $(n - 1) \times (n - 1)$ matrix obtained by striking out the corresponding row and column of the element; furthermore, each term is multiplied by $(-1)^{i+j}$, where i and j are the indices of the element. For example, A is the determinant of a 3×3 matrix; thus, in the first round it is the sum of three terms. If we begin with the elements of the first row, then the first term is the product of a_{11} and the determinant of the submatrix obtained by striking out the first row and first column of the original matrix, that is,

$$a_{11} \begin{vmatrix} a_{22} & a_{23} \\ a_{32} & a_{33} \end{vmatrix}$$

The sign of this term is $(-1)^{1+1}$, that is, positive. The second term is the product of the second element in the first row, a_{12}, and the determinant of the submatrix obtained by striking out the first row and the second column of the original matrix, that is,

$$a_{12} \begin{vmatrix} a_{21} & a_{23} \\ a_{31} & a_{33} \end{vmatrix}$$

The sign of this term is $(-1)^{1+2}$, that is, negative. Similarly, the third term is

$$a_{13} (-1)^{1+3} \begin{vmatrix} a_{21} & a_{22} \\ a_{31} & a_{32} \end{vmatrix}$$

The first term

$$a_{11} \begin{vmatrix} a_{22} & a_{23} \\ a_{32} & a_{33} \end{vmatrix}$$

can be considered the sum of two terms, since

$$\begin{vmatrix} a_{22} & a_{23} \\ a_{32} & a_{33} \end{vmatrix}$$

is the determinant of a 2×2 matrix. Similarly to the above, this sum can be computed as $a_{22}|a_{33}| - a_{23}|a_{32}|$. Since the determinant of a single number is the number itself, we have

$$a_{11} \begin{vmatrix} a_{22} & a_{23} \\ a_{32} & a_{33} \end{vmatrix} = a_{11}(a_{22}a_{33} - a_{23}a_{32})$$

$$= a_{11}a_{22}a_{33} - a_{11}a_{23}a_{32}$$

Thus,

$$A = a_{11}a_{22}a_{33} - a_{11}a_{23}a_{32} - a_{12}a_{21}a_{33}$$

$$+ a_{12}a_{23}a_{31} + a_{13}a_{21}a_{32} - a_{13}a_{22}a_{31}$$

Hence, A is the sum of six terms, each of which is the product of three elements. In general, the determinant of an $n \times n$ matrix is the sum of $n! = n(n - 1)(n - 2)\cdots(n - (n - 1))$ terms (in the above case, $3 \times 2 \times 1$), each of which is the product of n elements with the proper sign. We state without proof that A can be computed no matter which row or column we decide to begin with. For example, we can just as well use the third column instead of the first row:

$$A = a_{13} \begin{vmatrix} a_{21} & a_{22} \\ a_{31} & a_{32} \end{vmatrix} - a_{23} \begin{vmatrix} a_{11} & a_{12} \\ a_{31} & a_{32} \end{vmatrix} + a_{33} \begin{vmatrix} a_{11} & a_{12} \\ a_{21} & a_{22} \end{vmatrix}$$

The student can easily verify that the value of A computed using the elements of the first row is identical with that obtained using the elements of the third column. The student may also try to show that the same result will be obtained using any other row or column by carrying out one more computation. It should be pointed out that the determinant is defined only for square matrices.

With the above knowledge, we can write (A1-2.26) and (A1-2.31′) as follows:

$$wL + rK = (\overline{C} - C_0), \qquad \beta wL - \alpha rK = 0 \tag{A1-2.35}$$

Thus, by using Cramer's rule we have

$$L = \frac{-\alpha r(\overline{C} - C_0)}{-\alpha wr - \beta rw} = \frac{\alpha(\overline{C} - C_0)}{(\alpha + \beta)w}$$

$$\tag{A1-2.36}$$

$$K = \frac{-\beta w(\overline{C} - C_0)}{-(\alpha + \beta)wr} = \frac{\beta(\overline{C} - C_0)}{(\alpha + \beta)r}$$

since

$$\begin{vmatrix} w & r \\ \beta w & -\alpha r \end{vmatrix} = -\alpha rw - \beta rw$$

$$\begin{vmatrix} (\overline{C} - C_0) & r \\ 0 & -\alpha r \end{vmatrix} = -\alpha r(\overline{C} - C_0) \tag{A1-2.37}$$

$$\begin{vmatrix} w & (\overline{C} - C_0) \\ \beta w & 0 \end{vmatrix} = -\beta w(\overline{C} - C_0)$$

Since C_0, α, and β are constants, whereas w and r are considered constants, since they are determined by the competitive input market and are assumed to be known to the firm (a price taker), we find that for a given cost $\overline{C}$, both L and K can be computed. This is the optimal combination of the inputs in the case of maximum output for a given cost (which corresponds to point E in Figure 2.14).

It is seen that $\partial L/\partial C > 0$ and $\partial K/\partial C > 0$. When a firm's total expenditure increases, other things being equal, more of both labor and capital will be employed. We also have that $\partial L/\partial w < 0$ and $\partial K/\partial r < 0$; thus, when the price of one input increases, other things being equal, the quantity in which it is used will decrease.

It is easily seen from (A1-2.30) that the second-order condition for maximum output is satisfied if α, $\beta < 1$, which implies the law of diminishing returns with respect to both labor and capital. Recall that the partial derivatives of MP_L and MP_K in the Cobb–Douglas production function—$\alpha(\alpha - 1)AL^{\alpha-2}K^\beta$ and $\beta(\beta - 1)AL^\alpha K^{\beta-2}$, respectively—can be negative, which indicates that the law of diminishing returns applies only if α, $\beta < 1$. Thus, if the law of diminishing returns prevails for both labor and capital, the second-order condition is satisfied. If a constant returns to scale or a decreasing returns to scale prevails, the second-order condition is again satisfied. The only possible problem is an increasing returns to scale. Even in this case, the second-order condition may still be satisfied, provided that

$$\beta(\beta - 1)/K^2 < -\alpha(\alpha - 1)r^2/w^2L^2 + 2\alpha\beta r/wLK$$

holds. With reasonable values of w, r, L, and K, this inequality may hold even if α, $\beta > 1$. Thus, we can assume that the second-order condition is satisfied under normal conditions for the Cobb–Douglas production function.

METHOD 2: LAGRANGE MULTIPLIER. Instead of using the substitution method, a more convenient and symmetric means of obtaining the conditions for a constrained maximum is the Lagrange multiplier technique. In this approach, the problem is considered as maximizing (A1-2.5) subject to the constraint (A1-2.26). We form the Lagrange function

$$G = AL^\alpha K^\beta + \lambda(\bar{C} - C_0 - wL - rK) \qquad \text{(A1-2.38)}$$

where λ is the Lagrange multiplier for maximum output, given cost. The first-order conditions for a constrained maximum are that the partial derivatives of the Lagrange function are equal to zero:

$$\partial G/\partial L = \alpha AL^{\alpha-1}K^\beta - \lambda w = 0 \qquad \text{(A1-2.39)}$$

$$\partial G/\partial K = \beta AL^\alpha K^{\beta-1} - \lambda r = 0 \qquad \text{(A1-2.40)}$$

$$\partial G/\partial \lambda = \bar{C} - C_0 - wL - rK = 0 \qquad \text{(A1-2.41)}$$

Since the second-order condition is usually satisfied in the case of the Cobb–Douglas production function, we assume that this is indeed the case. The solution of the first-order conditions is the optimal values of L and K.

We use (A1-2.39) and (A1-2.40) to eliminate λ. From (A1-2.39) and (A1-2.40) we have

$$\lambda = \alpha AL^{\alpha-1}K^\beta/w, \qquad \lambda = \beta AL^\alpha K^{\beta-1}/r \qquad \text{(A1-2.42)}$$

Since λ is always equal to λ, we have

$$\alpha AL^{\alpha-1}K^{\beta}/w = \beta AL^{\alpha}K^{\beta-1}/r \qquad \text{(A1-2.43)}$$

This is precisely Equation (2.11), which defined the tangency between an isoquant and an isocost curve. Equation (A1-2.43) can also be written

$$\beta wL - \alpha rK = 0 \qquad \text{(A1-2.44)}$$

The optimal combination of inputs L and K can be obtained by solving the two linear equations (A1-2.41) and (A1-2.44). It is seen that (A1-2.41) and (A1-2.26), as well as (A1-2.31′) and (A1-2.44), are identical. The solution of the first-order conditions (A1-2.39)–(A1-2.41) must be identical to that of Method 1. Thus, the two different methods result in the same solution. However, Method 2 is symmetrical because one does not have to eliminate either of the variables L or K as in Method 1. Furthermore, Method 2 is more convenient in dealing with cases where more than two independent variables are involved.

It should be pointed out that (A1-2.31′) [(A1-2.44)] is actually the equation of the expansion path in Figure 2.19. Equation (A1-2.31′) [(A1-2.44)] can also be written

$$K = (\beta w/\alpha r)L \qquad \text{(A1-2.45)}$$

Since α, β, w, and r are constants, the expansion path of the Cobb–Douglas production function is a straight line. This is to be expected, since, as noted earlier, the Cobb–Douglas production function is homogeneous of degree $\alpha + \beta$, and all homogeneous production functions are homothetic, which implies that the slopes of the isoquants along a ray from the origin are equal. For given prices of the inputs, w and r are constant; hence, all of the isocost curves have the same slope $-w/r$. At tangent points, the isocost curves and the isoquants have the same slope. All of this implies that the expansion path of the Cobb–Douglas production function is a straight line.

Minimum Cost for a Given Output

Mathematically, this case represents a problem of minimizing cost subject to the constraint of a given output. We shall soon discover that the solution is identical to that of the case of maximum output for a given cost. For the Cobb–Douglas production function, the problem is to minimize the cost

$$C = C_0 + wL + rK \qquad \text{(A1-2.46)}$$

subject to the constraint of a given output

$$\bar{Q} = AL^{\alpha}K^{\beta} \qquad \text{(A1-2.47)}$$

$\bar{Q}$ denotes the given (constant) output. As before, A, α, and β are constants, whereas w and r (the prices of L and K, respectively) are considered constant due to the assumption of competitive input markets. In contrast to the previous case, where cost C was a constant and output Q the dependent variable, here L and K are the independent variables, whereas C is the dependent variable. This is the essential difference between the two approaches.

In this case we shall only use Method 2—the Lagrange multiplier technique. We form the Lagrange function

$$H = C_0 + wL + rK + \mu(\overline{Q} - AL^\alpha K^\beta) \tag{A1-2.48}$$

where μ is the Lagrange multiplier for minimum cost, given output. Assume that the second-order condition is satisfied and that the first-order conditions for a constrained minimum are

$$\partial H/\partial L = w - \mu\alpha AL^{\alpha-1}K^\beta = 0 \tag{A1-2.49}$$

$$\partial H/\partial K = r - \mu\beta AL^\alpha K^{\beta-1} = 0 \tag{A1-2.50}$$

$$\partial H/\partial \mu = \overline{Q} - AL^\alpha K^\beta = 0 \tag{A1-2.51}$$

From (A1-2.49) and (A1-2.50) we have

$$1/\mu = \alpha AL^{\alpha-1}K^\beta/w, \qquad 1/\mu = \beta AL^\alpha K^{\beta-1}/r \tag{A1-2.52}$$

Expressions (A1-2.52) imply

$$\alpha AL^{\alpha-1}K^\beta/w = \beta AL^\alpha K^{\beta-1}/r \tag{A1-2.53}$$

Thus, (A1-2.53), (A1-2.43), and (A1-2.31) are identical—the two approaches yield identical optimal conditions. However, (A1-2.53) indicates the tangent point E of Figure 2.15, whereas (A1-2.43) and (A1-2.31) indicate the tangent point E of Figure 2.14.

Equation (A1-2.53) can also be written

$$\beta wL - \alpha rK = 0 \tag{A1-2.54}$$

which is identical to (A1-2.31') and (A1-2.44). Equation (A1-2.54) can also be written

$$K = (\beta w/\alpha r)L \tag{A1-2.55}$$

which is the equation of the expansion path in the case of minimum cost for a given output. Note that (A1-2.45) and (A1-2.55) are identical, which again indicates that the two approaches yield the same result.

Comparing (A1-2.42) with (A1-2.52), it is seen that the Lagrange multiplier in the cost-minimization problem is the reciprocal of the Lagrange multiplier in the output-maximization problem.

A1-2.4.2 A General Production Function with Two Inputs

Maximum Output for a Given Cost

A general production function with two inputs can be written

$$Q = f(x_1, x_2) \tag{A1-2.56}$$

where Q is the output and x_1 and x_2 are the inputs. The cost equation can be written

$$\overline{C} = C_0 + r_1 x_1 + r_2 x_2 \tag{A1-2.57}$$

where r_1 and r_2 are the prices of x_1 and x_2, respectively. The problem is to maximize (A1-2.56) subject to the constraint (A1-2.57). Using the Lagrange multiplier technique, we form the Lagrange function

$$L = f(x_1, x_2) + \lambda(\overline{C} - C_0 - r_1 x_1 - r_2 x_2) \tag{A1-2.58}$$

where λ is the Lagrange multiplier. Since $\overline{C}$, r_1, and r_2 are constants, L is a function of x_1, x_2, and λ. Furthermore, L is identically equal to Q for those values of x_1 and x_2 that satisfy the cost constraint because

$$\overline{C} - C_0 - r_1 x_1 - r_2 x_2 = 0$$

The first-order conditions for maximum L are

$$\partial L/\partial x_1 = f_1 - \lambda r_1 = 0$$

$$\partial L/\partial x_2 = f_2 - \lambda r_2 = 0 \tag{A1-2.59}$$

$$\partial L/\partial \lambda = \overline{C} - C_0 - r_1 x_1 - r_2 x_2 = 0$$

where $f_i = \partial f/\partial x_i$.

Comparing (A1-2.59) with (A1-2.39)–(A1-2.41), it is seen that the latter are special cases of the former, since

$$f_1 = \alpha A L^{\alpha-1} K^\beta, \qquad f_2 = \beta A L^\alpha K^{\beta-1}$$

for the Cobb–Douglas production function, with r_1 and r_2 corresponding to w and r, and x_1 and x_2 corresponding to L and K, respectively.

The first two equations in (A1-2.59) yield

$$f_1/f_2 = r_1/r_2, \quad \text{or} \quad f_1/r_1 = f_2/r_2$$
$$\text{or} \quad \text{MRTS} = r_1/r_2 \tag{A1-2.60}$$

These expressions are identical to (2.10) and (2.11), which signify the tangency between an isoquant and an isocost curve. In the special case of the Cobb–Douglas production function, (A1-2.31) and (A1-2.43) correspond to (A1-2.60).

Equation (A1-2.60) can be written

$$g(x_1, x_2) = f_1 r_2 - f_2 r_1 = 0 \tag{A1-2.61}$$

This is an implicit function that relates the two inputs that satisfy the conditions of maximum output for a given cost, that is, the locus of tangency points on curve $\widehat{0E'}$ in Figure 2.19 (the expansion path of the firm for a given set of input prices).

The second-order condition for a constrained maximum is that the relevant bordered Hessian determinant must be positive:

$$\begin{vmatrix} f_{11} & f_{12} & -r_1 \\ f_{21} & f_{22} & -r_2 \\ -r_1 & -r_2 & 0 \end{vmatrix} > 0 \qquad\qquad \text{(A1-2.62)}$$

Expanding (A1-2.62), we have

$$-f_{11}r_2^2 + 2f_{12}r_1r_2 - f_{22}r_1^2 > 0 \qquad\qquad \text{(A1-2.63)}$$

which implies

$$f_{11}r_2^2 - 2f_{12}r_1r_2 + f_{22}r_1^2 < 0 \qquad\qquad \text{(A1-2.64)}$$

It is generally assumed that $f_{12} = f_{21}$, and this assumption is used in deriving (A1-2.63) from (A1-2.62). It can be easily checked that $f_{12} = f_{21}$ is satisfied for the Cobb–Douglas production function.

It can also be readily checked that the second-order condition for a constrained maximum in the special case of the Cobb–Douglas production function gives

$$f_{11} = \alpha(\alpha - 1)AL^{\alpha-2}K^\beta = \alpha(\alpha - 1)Q/L^2$$

$$f_{22} = \beta(\beta - 1)Q/K^2$$

$$f_{12} = f_{21} = \alpha\beta Q/LK$$

Substituting w for r_1, r for r_2, and the values of the second partial derivatives into (A1-2.64), we have

$$\left[\frac{\alpha(\alpha - 1)r^2}{L^2} - \frac{2\alpha\beta wr}{LK} + \frac{\beta(\beta - 1)w^2}{K^2} \right] Q < 0 \qquad \text{(A1-2.65)}$$

Dividing both sides of (A1-2.65) by w^2 (a positive number), the inequality still holds and is identical with (A1-2.30).

Minimum Cost for a Given Output

This case represents a problem of constrained minimization. In the two-input case, the firm wants to minimize

$$C = C_0 + r_1x_1 + r_2x_2 \qquad\qquad \text{(A1-2.66)}$$

subject to the constraint

$$\overline{Q} = f(x_1, x_2) \qquad\qquad \text{(A1-2.67)}$$

$\overline{Q}$ denotes the given (constant) output. We form the Lagrange function

$$V = C_0 + r_1x_1 + r_2x_2 + \mu[\overline{Q} - f(x_1, x_2)] \qquad \text{(A1-2.68)}$$

where μ is the Lagrange multiplier. It is seen that V is identically equal to C for those values of x_1 and x_2 that satisfy the constraint because

$$\overline{Q} - f(x_1, x_2) = 0$$

The first-order conditions for minimum V are

$$\partial V/\partial x_1 = r_1 - \mu f_1 = 0$$

$$\partial V/\partial x_2 = r_2 - \mu f_2 = 0 \qquad \qquad \text{(A1-2.69)}$$

$$\partial V/\partial \mu = \overline{Q} - f(x_1, x_2) = 0$$

The first two equations in (A1-2.69) yield

$$f_1/f_2 = r_1/r_2 \qquad \text{or} \qquad \text{MRTS} = r_1/r_2 \qquad \text{(A1-2.70)}$$

Thus (A1-2.60) and (A1-2.70) are identical, which indicates that maximizing output for a given cost and minimizing cost for a given output will result in an identical solution. The expansion path for the constrained minimum is also identical with that for the constrained maximum.

The second-order condition is that the relevant bordered Hessian determinant must be negative:

$$\begin{vmatrix} -\mu f_{11} & -\mu f_{12} & -f_1 \\ -\mu f_{21} & -\mu f_{22} & -f_2 \\ -f_1 & -f_2 & 0 \end{vmatrix} < 0 \qquad \text{(A1-2.71)}$$

It can be shown that (A1-2.71) and (A1-2.62) are, in fact, identical. Substituting $-f_1 = r_1/\mu$, and $-f_2 = -r_2/\mu$, after multiplying the first two columns of (A1-2.71) by $-1/\mu$, the third row by $-\mu^2$, and the third column by μ, we have

$$\begin{vmatrix} -\mu f_{11} & -\mu f_{12} & -r_1/\mu \\ -\mu f_{21} & -\mu f_{22} & -r_2/\mu \\ -r_1/\mu & -r_2/\mu & 0 \end{vmatrix} = \mu^2 \begin{vmatrix} f_{11} & f_{12} & -r_1/\mu \\ f_{21} & f_{22} & -r_2/\mu \\ r_1/\mu^2 & r_2/\mu^2 & 0 \end{vmatrix}$$

$$= \frac{-\mu^2}{\mu^2} \begin{vmatrix} f_{11} & f_{12} & -r_1/\mu \\ f_{21} & f_{22} & -r_2/\mu \\ -r_1 & -r_2 & 0 \end{vmatrix} = \frac{-1}{\mu} \begin{vmatrix} f_{11} & f_{12} & -r_1 \\ f_{21} & f_{22} & -r_2 \\ -r_1 & -r_2 & 0 \end{vmatrix} < 0$$

Since

$$1/\mu = f_1/r_1 = f_2/r_2 > 0$$

the second-order condition (A1-2.71) implies

$$\begin{vmatrix} f_{11} & f_{12} & -r_1 \\ f_{21} & f_{22} & -r_2 \\ -r_1 & -r_2 & 0 \end{vmatrix} > 0 \qquad \text{(A1-2.72)}$$

which is the same as (A1-2.62). Thus, the second-order conditions for the two different approaches are also the same.

In (A1-2.71) and (A1-2.72), the mathematical manipulation has used the fact that the multiplication of a row or a column of a determinant by a constant will result in the multiplication of the determinant by the same constant. Thus, if a column or a row is multiplied by a constant, say $-1/\mu$, and the determinant is also multiplied by the reciprocal of the constant, namely, $-\mu$, then the value of the determinant will not change (see Allen, 1959, p. 401).

A1-2.4.3 The General Case with n Inputs

The production function for one output Q with n inputs $x_1, x_2, \ldots, x_n$ can be written

$$Q = f(x_1, x_2, \ldots, x_n) \tag{A1-2.73}$$

It is assumed that the function f has continuous first- and second-order partial derivatives. The cost equation can be written

$$C = C_0 + \sum_{i=1}^{n} x_i r_i$$

or $\tag{A1-2.74}$

$$g(x_1, x_2, \ldots, x_n) = C - C_0 - \sum_{i=1}^{n} x_i r_i = 0$$

For the case of output maximization for a given cost, using the Lagrange multiplier technique, we form the Langrange function

$$L = f(x_1, x_2, \ldots, x_n) + \lambda(\overline{C} - C_0 - \sum_{i=1}^{n} x_i r_i) \tag{A1-2.75}$$

The first-order conditions for maximum L are

$$\partial L/\partial x_i = f_i - \lambda r_i = 0, \qquad i = 1, 2, \ldots, n \tag{A1-2.76}$$

$$\partial L/\partial \lambda = \overline{C} - C_0 - \sum_{i=1}^{n} x_i r_i = 0$$

By eliminating λ, the first n equations in (A1-2.76) yield

$$f_1/r_1 = f_j/r_j, \qquad i, j = 1, 2, \ldots, n \tag{A1-2.77}$$

$n - 1$ independent equations that correspond to (A1-2.60) in the two-input case and (A1-2.31) in the special case of the Cobb–Douglas production function. These $n - 1$ equations constitute the expansion path for the general case.

The second-order condition for a constrained maximum requires that the following bordered Hessian determinants be alternate in sign, starting with plus:

$$\begin{vmatrix} L_{11} & L_{12} & g_1 \\ L_{21} & L_{22} & g_2 \\ g_1 & g_2 & 0 \end{vmatrix} > 0, \qquad \begin{vmatrix} L_{11} & L_{12} & L_{13} & g_1 \\ L_{21} & L_{22} & L_{23} & g_2 \\ L_{31} & L_{32} & L_{33} & g_3 \\ g_1 & g_2 & g_3 & 0 \end{vmatrix} < 0, \qquad \cdots$$

(A1-2.78)

$$(-1)^n \begin{vmatrix} L_{11} & L_{12} & \cdots & L_{1n} & g_1 \\ L_{21} & L_{22} & \cdots & L_{2n} & g_2 \\ & & \vdots & & \\ L_{n1} & L_{n2} & \cdots & L_{nn} & g_n \\ g_1 & g_2 & \cdots & g_n & 0 \end{vmatrix} > 0$$

In our case, since the constraint function is linear, the second partial derivatives of L are identical to the second partial derivatives of f; thus, (A1-2.77) becomes

$$\begin{vmatrix} f_{11} & f_{12} & -r_1 \\ f_{21} & f_{22} & -r_2 \\ -r_1 & -r_2 & 0 \end{vmatrix} > 0, \qquad \begin{vmatrix} f_{11} & f_{12} & f_{13} & -r_1 \\ f_{21} & f_{22} & f_{23} & -r_2 \\ f_{31} & f_{32} & f_{33} & -r_3 \\ -r_1 & -r_2 & -r_3 & 0 \end{vmatrix} < 0, \cdots$$

(A1-2.79)

$$(-1)^n \begin{vmatrix} f_{11} & f_{12} & \cdots & f_{1n} & -r_1 \\ f_{21} & f_{22} & \cdots & f_{2n} & -r_2 \\ & & \vdots & & \\ f_{n1} & f_{n2} & \cdots & f_{nn} & -r_n \\ -r_1 & -r_2 & \cdots & -r_n & 0 \end{vmatrix} > 0$$

The second-order condition is related to the negative-definiteness of a certain quadratic form. Those students who are interested in more detail concerning this point may consult the mathematical appendix in the works by any of the following authors (see the references at the end of this book): Samuelson (1965), Hicks (1946), and Henderson and Quandt (1971).

The $n - 1$ independent equations (A1-2.77) together with the cost equation (A1-2.74) constitute n equations in n variables, x_1, x_2, ..., x_n, which can, in principle, be solved for the xs in terms of the n input prices $r_1, r_2, ..., r_n$ and cost C, corresponding to (A1-2.36) for the special case of the Cobb–Douglas production function:

$$x_1 = h_1(r_1, r_2, ..., r_n, C)$$

$$x_2 = h_2(r_1, r_2, ..., r_n, C)$$

(A1-2.80)

$$\vdots$$

$$x_n = h_n(r_1, r_2, ..., r_n, C)$$

These n expressions indicate the optimal combination of the inputs as functions of the input prices and cost. For the corner solution, set $x_i = 0$ for $x_i \leq 0$ (see Section 2.10.5).

A1-2.5 THE EFFECT OF A CHANGE OF INPUT PRICE ON THE OPTIMAL QUANTITY OF INPUT

The effect of a change in the price of input x_j, other things being equal, on the optimal quantity of input x_i for a given cost is indicated by the partial derivatives of h_i with respect to r_j in (A1-2.80). These partial derivatives can be computed if we know the functions h_i, $i = 1, 2, ..., n$, such as (A1-2.36) for the Cobb–Douglas production function. The expression $\partial L/\partial w < 0$ indicates that when the wage rate goes up, less labor will be used for maximum output at a given cost, whereas $\partial L/\partial r = 0$ indicates that capital price changes will have no effect on the optimal quantity of labor as a result of the specific form of the Cobb–Douglas production function. In general, $\partial L/\partial r$ may not be equal to zero. However, if we do not know the specific form of the function f in (A1-2.73), then we do not know the specific functional forms of h_i in (A1-2.80) either. Under these circumstances, we cannot compute $\partial h_i/\partial r_j$. However, by examination of the first- and second-order conditions of maximum output for a given cost, it may be possible to determine, in general, the sign of the partial derivatives in (A1-2.80).

The quantities of inputs used by an output-maximizing firm for a given cost will always satisfy (A1-2.76), a total of $n + 1$ equations. Changes in the prices of the inputs and cost will normally alter a firm's optimal input combination, but the new input quantities will still satisfy (A1-2.76). If we allow all variables to simultaneously vary (note that C_0 is a constant, not a variable), then working with the differentials rather than the derivatives from (A1-2.76) we obtain

$$f_{11} dx_1 + f_{12} dx_2 + \cdots + f_{1n} dx_n - r_1 d\lambda = \lambda dr_1$$

$$f_{21} dx_1 + f_{22} dx_2 + \cdots + f_{2n} dx_n - r_2 d\lambda = \lambda dr_2$$

$$f_{n1} dx_1 + f_{n2} dx_2 + \cdots + f_{nn} dx_n - r_n d\lambda = \lambda dr_n \qquad \text{(A1-2.81)}$$

$$-r_1 dx_1 - r_2 dx_2 - \cdots - r_n dx_n = -dC$$
$$+ x_1 dr_1 + x_2 dr_2$$
$$+ \cdots + x_n dr_n$$

This is a system of $n + 1$ equations. For our purposes, dx_i, $i = 1, 2, ..., n$, and $d\lambda$ are considered as variables, $n + 1$ in number; f_{ij} and $-r_i$, $i, j = 1, 2, ..., n$, on the left and the terms on the right are regarded as constants.

We denote the determinant of the $(n + 1) \times (n + 1)$ coefficient matrix by D; that is,

$$D \equiv \begin{vmatrix} f_{11} & f_{12} \cdots & f_{1n} & -r_1 \\ f_{21} & f_{22} \cdots & f_{2n} & -r_2 \\ & \vdots & & \\ f_{n1} & f_{n2} \cdots & f_{nn} & -r_n \\ -r_1 & -r_2 \cdots & -r_n & 0 \end{vmatrix} \qquad \text{(A1-2.82)}$$

Next we denote the cofactor of the element of the ith row and the jth column of the coefficient matrix by D_{ij}:

$$D_{ij} \equiv \begin{vmatrix} f_{11} & \cdots & f_{1(j-1)} & f_{1(j+1)} & \cdots & f_{1n} & -r_1 \\ & \vdots & & & & & \vdots \\ f_{(i-1)1} & \cdots & f_{(i-1)(j-1)} & f_{(i-1)(j+1)} & \cdots & f_{(i-1)n} & -r_{(i-1)} \\ f_{(i+1)1} & \cdots & f_{(i+1)(j-1)} & f_{(i+1)(j+1)} & \cdots & f_{(i+1)n} & -r_{(i+1)} \\ & \vdots & & & & & \vdots \\ f_{n1} & \cdots & f_{n(j-1)} & f_{n(j+1)} & \cdots & f_{nn} & -r_n \\ -r_1 & \cdots & -r_{(j-1)} & -r_{(j+1)} & \cdots & -r_n & 0 \end{vmatrix} (-1)^{i+j}$$

$$(A1\text{-}2.83)$$

We obtain D_{ij}—the determinant of an $n \times n$ matrix—by striking out the ith row and the jth column of the original coefficient matrix and attaching the sign $(-1)^{i+j}$ to it. For example,

$$D_{11} = \begin{vmatrix} f_{22} & \cdots & f_{2n} & -r_2 \\ & \vdots & & \\ f_{n2} & \cdots & f_{nn} & -r_n \\ -r_2 & \cdots & -r_n & 0 \end{vmatrix}, \quad D_{12} = - \begin{vmatrix} f_{21} & f_{23} & \cdots & f_{2n} & -r_2 \\ & & \vdots & & \\ f_{n1} & f_{n3} & \cdots & f_{nn} & -r_n \\ -r_1 & -r_3 & \cdots & -r_n & 0 \end{vmatrix}$$

With this compact notation, the solution of (A1-2.81) by Cramer's rule can be written

$$dx_1 = \frac{\lambda \sum_{i=1}^{n} D_{i1} dr_i + D_{(n+1)1}\left(-dC + \sum_{i=1}^{n} x_i dr_i\right)}{D}$$

$$dx_2 = \frac{\lambda \sum_{i=1}^{n} D_{i2} dr_i + D_{(n+1)2}\left(-dC + \sum_{i=1}^{n} x_i dr_i\right)}{D} \qquad (A1\text{-}2.84)$$

$$dx_n = \frac{\lambda \sum_{i=1}^{n} D_{in} dr_i + D_{(n+1)n}\left(-dC + \sum_{i=1}^{n} x_i dr_i\right)}{D}$$

Dividing both sides of (A1-2.84) by dr_1 and assuming that all other input prices and the cost do not change (i.e., $dr_2 = dr_3 = \cdots = dr_n = dC = 0$), we obtain

$$\partial x_1 / \partial r_1 = \lambda D_{11}/D + x_1(D_{(n+1)1}/D)$$

$$\partial x_2 / \partial r_1 = \lambda D_{12}/D + x_1(D_{(n+1)2}/D) \qquad (A1\text{-}2.85)$$

$$\partial x_n / \partial r_1 = \lambda D_{in}/D + x_1(D_{(n+1)n}/D)$$

Expressions (A1-2.85) correspond to the partial derivatives of (A1-2.36) with respect to w and r in the special case of two variable inputs and the Cobb–Douglas production function, as well as to the graphs in Figure 2.21, where it is seen that the output level changes when the price of one input changes for a given cost.

Now consider a price change on an input that is compensated

by a cost change that leaves the output level the same as before. This is particularly significant in production because the output level of a commodity is usually determined by the commodity market and not strictly constrained by cost as cited in the text. Constant output implies [from (A1-2.73)]

$$dQ = f_1 dx_1 + f_2 dx_2 + \cdots + f_n dx_n = 0$$

The first-order conditions (A1-2.76) imply that $f_i/f_j = r_i/r_j$. If we divide through the above expression by $f_j \neq 0$, the result is

$$(f_1/f_j)dx_1 + (f_2/f_j)dx_2 + \cdots + dx_j + \cdots + (f_n/f_j)dx_n = 0$$

Substituting r_i/r_j for f_i/f_j and multiplying through by $r_j \neq 0$, we obtain

$$r_1 dx_1 + r_2 dx_2 + \cdots + r_n dx_n = 0$$

From the last equation of (A1-2.81), it is seen that

$$-dC + x_1 dr_1 + x_2 dr_2 + \cdots + x_n dr_n = -dC + \sum_{i=1}^{n} x_i dr_i = 0$$

From (A1-2.84), we have

$$(\partial x_i/\partial r_j)_{Q = \text{const}} = \lambda D_{ij}/D \qquad\qquad (A1\text{-}2.86)$$

In particular,

$$(\partial x_n/\partial r_n)_{Q = \text{const}} = \lambda D_{nn}/D$$

Since $\lambda = f_i/r_i > 0$, D_{nn} and D have opposite signs by the second-order condition; thus, we have

$$(\partial x_n/\partial r_n)_{Q = \text{const}} = \lambda D_{nn}/D < 0 \qquad\qquad (A1\text{-}2.87)$$

Since the order of the commodities is irrelevant, we can conclude that

$$(\partial x_i/\partial r_i)_{Q = \text{const}} < 0, \qquad i = 1, 2, \ldots, n \qquad (A1\text{-}2.88)$$

When the price of an input increases, output and other prices being constant, less of the input will be used by a firm, which is the same result as in Figure 2.20. In Figure 2.21, this corresponds to the movement from E_0 to E_2 along the same isoquant.

It is to be noted that the sign of $(\partial x_i/\partial r_j)_{Q = \text{const}}$ for $i \neq j$ is generally not known, although for the special case of two inputs, $(\partial x_1/\partial r_2)_{Q = \text{const}}$ is positive (see Figures 2.20 and 2.21). This is obvious, because when one input is reduced, the other input must be increased in order to keep the same level of output (which must occur, since the MP of the inputs is assumed to be positive). When more than two inputs are involved, the reduction of one input may be accompanied by a decrease in one or more of the others. However, at least one input has to be increased in order to keep output constant. In many cases, the result of a simple two-independent-variable model can be generalized to the n-variable case. This is one instance where a three-input model can be considered as a general case, whereas a two-input model cannot. A three-input model and a two-input model are essentially different with respect to substitutability and complementarity. This also indicates that all factors can be simultaneous substitutes, but all cannot be complements. Some authors use the sign of the term $(\partial x_i/\partial r_j)_{Q = \text{const}}$ as the defining factor: x_i and x_j are substitutes if $(\partial x_i/\partial r_j)_{Q = \text{const}} > 0$, complements if $(\partial x_i/\partial r_j)_{Q = \text{const}} < 0$, and independent if $(\partial x_i/\partial r_j)_{Q = \text{const}} = 0$.

It should also be noted that

$$(\partial x_i/\partial r_j)_{Q = \text{const}} = (\partial x_j/\partial r_i)_{Q = \text{const}}$$

This is so because the coefficient matrix is symmetric due to the fact that $f_{ij} = f_{ji}$ and thus $D_{ij} = D_{ji}$.

From (A1-2.84), it is seen that when all input prices are constant $(dr_1 = dr_2 = \cdots = dr_n = 0)$ while cost changes, we have

$$(\partial x_i/\partial C)_{\text{prices} = \text{const}} = -D_{(n+1)i}/D \qquad \text{(A1-2.89)}$$

Taking (A1-2.86) and (A1-2.89) into consideration, (A1-2.85) can be written

$$\partial x_i/\partial r_j = (\partial x_i/\partial r_j)_{Q = \text{const}} - x_j(\partial x_i/\partial C)_{\text{prices} = \text{const}} \qquad \text{(A1-2.90)}$$

The first term on the right side is the substitution term, which corresponds to the movement from E_0 to E_2 in Figure 2.21 (i.e., the *substitution effect*, which is always negative for $i = j$). The second term on the right side is the output or cost term, which corresponds to the movement from E_2 to E_1 (i.e., the *output effect*, as it is commonly called, which can be either positive or negative).

In Section 2.12, we defined the terms normal factor and inferior factor for inputs. We shall now provide a more precise mathematical definition.

Definition: Normal Factor. Input x_i is a normal factor if $(\partial x_i/\partial C)_{\text{prices} = c} > 0$.

Definition: Inferior Factor. Input x_i is an inferior factor if $(\partial x_i/\partial C)_{\text{prices} = c} < 0$.

The term $\partial x_i/\partial r_j$ in (A1-2.90), which is the sum of two terms, indicates the direction of change of the equilibrium quantity of input i when price changes. The first term is always negative for $i = j$, as we have established. However, the second term can be either positive or negative. Thus, the sum can also be either positive or negative. This implies that the equilibrium quantity of input i can either increase or decrease when its price decreases. In the case of a normal factor, $(\partial x_i/\partial C)_{\text{prices} = c} > 0$; taking the negative sign in front of it in (A1-2.90) into consideration, we obtain $\partial x_i/\partial r_i < 0$. Hence, we are sure that the equilibrium quantity of input i will increase when its price decreases. Only the equilibrium quantity of an inferior factor can decrease when its price decreases. Since the occurrence of an inferior factor is very unusual, no further discussion is devoted to this matter.

A1-2.6 ELASTICITY OF SUBSTITUTION

The elasticity of substitution σ is defined in Section 2.12. It can be written

$$\sigma = \frac{d \log(x_2/x_1)}{d \log(f_1/f_2)} = \frac{d(x_2/x_1)(f_1/f_2)}{d(f_1/f_2)(x_2/x_1)} \tag{A1-2.91}$$

Since

$$d(x_2/x_1) = (x_1 dx_2 - x_2 dx_1)/x_1^2$$

we have

$$d\left(\frac{f_1}{f_2}\right) = \frac{\partial(f_1/f_2)}{\partial x_1} dx_1 + \frac{\partial(f_1/f_2)}{\partial x_2} dx_2$$

Along an isoquant, $f_1 dx_1 + f_2 dx_2 = 0$, which implies that $dx_2 = -(f_1/f_2)dx_1$. Substituting the above expressions into (A1-2.91), after some cancellations we obtain

$$\sigma = \frac{f_1^2 x_1 + f_1 f_2 x_2}{f_2 x_1 x_2 [f_1 \partial(f_1/f_2)/\partial x_2 - f_2 \partial(f_1/f_2)/\partial x_1]} \tag{A1-2.92}$$

Since

$$\frac{\partial(f_1/f_2)}{\partial x_2} = \frac{f_{12} f_2 - f_{22} f_1}{f_2^2}$$

and

$$\frac{\partial(f_1/f_2)}{\partial x_1} = \frac{f_{11} f_2 - f_{21} f_1}{f_2^2}$$

by substitution and taking into consideration that $f_{12} = f_{21}$, (A1-2.92) can be simplified to

$$\sigma = \frac{f_1 f_2 (f_1 x_1 + f_2 x_2)}{x_1 x_2 (2 f_{12} f_1 f_2 - f_{22} f_1^2 - f_{11} f_2^2)} \tag{A1-2.93}$$

The second-order condition of maximum output for a given cost requires that

$$- (2 f_{12} f_1 f_2 - f_{22} f_1^2 - f_{11} f_2^2) < 0$$

which implies that

$$2 f_{12} f_1 f_2 - f_{22} f_1^2 - f_{11} f_2^2 > 0$$

Thus, x_1 and x_2 are positive, and f_1 and f_2 are the MPs of x_1 and x_2, respectively (and are also positive). Hence, the elasticity of substitution is positive in the case where the second-order condition is satisfied.

In general, the elasticity of substitution σ is a function of the inputs. However, most of the well-known production functions have the property of a constant elasticity of substitution. For example, the elasticity of substitution for the Cobb–Douglas production function is one. This can be shown by first computing the partial derivatives:

$$f_1 = \alpha A L^{\alpha-1} K^\beta \qquad\qquad = \alpha Q/L$$

$$f_{11} = \alpha(\alpha - 1)AL^{\alpha-2}K^\beta = \alpha(\alpha - 1)Q/L^2$$

$$f_{22} = \beta(\beta - 1)AL^\alpha K^{\beta-2} = \beta(\beta - 1)Q/K^2$$

$$f_2 = \beta A L^\alpha K^{\beta-1} \qquad\qquad = \beta Q/K$$

$$f_{12} = \alpha\beta AL^{\alpha-1}K^{\beta-1} \qquad = \alpha\beta Q/LK$$

$$f_{21} = \alpha\beta AL^{\alpha-1}K^{\beta-1} \qquad = \alpha\beta Q/LK = f_{12}$$

and then substituting:

$$\sigma = \frac{(\alpha Q/L)(\beta Q/K)[(\alpha Q/L)L + (\beta Q/K)K]}{LK[2(\alpha Q/L)(\beta Q/K)(\alpha\beta Q/LK) - (\alpha Q/L)^2\beta(\beta - 1)Q/K^2 - (\beta Q/K)^2\alpha(\alpha - 1)Q/L^2]}$$

$$= \frac{(\alpha\beta Q^2/LK)(\alpha + \beta)Q}{LK[2\alpha^2\beta^2 Q^3/L^2K^2 - \alpha^2\beta(\beta - 1)Q^3/L^2K^2 - \alpha\beta^2(\alpha - 1)Q^3/L^2K^2]}$$

$$= \frac{\alpha + \beta}{2\alpha\beta - \alpha(\beta - 1) - \beta(\alpha - 1)} \qquad\qquad\qquad \text{(A1-2.94)}$$

$$= \frac{\alpha + \beta}{2\alpha\beta - \alpha\beta + \alpha - \alpha\beta + \beta}$$

$$= \frac{\alpha + \beta}{\alpha + \beta}$$

$$= 1$$

It is interesting to point out that the homothetic but not homogenous production function $Q = Ax_1^2 x_2^2 - Bx_1^3 x_2^3$, discussed in Section 2.13, has one thing in common with the Cobb–Douglas production function: The elasticity of substitution for both of them is equal to 1. Since the algebraic proof of the former is a little messy (but nevertheless straightforward), we shall not present it here.

Another well-known production function (of which the Cobb–Douglas production function is a special case) is the constant elasticity of substitution (CES) production function. The CES production function can be written

$$Q = A[\alpha x_1^{-\rho} + (1 - \alpha)x_2^{-\rho}]^{-1/\rho} \tag{A1-2.95}$$

or

$$Q = A[\alpha x_1^{(\sigma-1)/\sigma} + (1 - \alpha)x_2^{(\sigma-1)/\sigma}]^{\sigma/(\sigma-1)} \tag{A1-2.96}$$

where A, α, ρ, and σ are constants: $0 < A$, $0 < \alpha < 1$, $0 < \sigma$, and $\sigma = 1/(1 + \rho)$ or $\rho = (1 - \sigma)/\sigma$. It can be shown that σ is the elasticity of substitution.

All of the above results are for interior solutions, that is, $x_i > 0$, $i = 1, 2, ..., n$. In the case of a corner solution, some xs in (A1-2.80) derived from the first-order conditions (A1-2.76) may be negative or zero. Since negative input does not make much economic sense in our model, we simply set $x_i = 0$ if $h_i(r_1, r_2, ..., r_n, C) < 0$ in (A1-2.80). If the solution is an imaginary or complex number in (A1-2.80) in which case we again have a corner solution, we shall do the same.

A1-2.7 LINEAR PRODUCTION FUNCTIONS, ACTIVITIES, AND PROCESSES

All of the above mathematical models are for production functions that have continuous first- and second-order partial derivatives and for which it is convenient to apply calculus and matrix manipulations. This is, perhaps, why economists traditionally are fond of these models. In reality, there usually are only a limited number of technical possibilities, which we have called processes. In the economic literature, processes are also called activities. Activity analysis is a new approach to dealing with production problems in the general case, for example, n inputs and m outputs. In order to make the model manageable, the production activities (processes) are assumed to represent fixed proportions, that is, linear production functions. Linear programming is the mathematical technique that is used in this case. In the simple case of one output and n inputs with a limited number of available activities (processes), the solution of either the minimum cost for a given output problem or the maximum output for a given cost problem can be found by enumeration of the available activities (processes) without the help of more sophisticated programming techniques. It is also interesting to note that the following simple algebraic manipulations prove that the solutions of both the maximum output for a given cost problem and the minimum cost for a given output problem are identical.

Suppose that we have n inputs and m activities (processes). Activity 1 needs a_{11} of x_1, a_{12} of x_2, ..., a_{1n} of x_n to produce 1 unit of the output. Thus, activity 1 can be represented by a vector:

$$A_1 = \langle a_{11}, a_{12}, ..., a_{1n} \rangle \tag{A1-2.97}$$

Input requirements are uniquely determined for any specific output level of activity 1:

$$x_i = a_{1i}Q, \qquad i = 1, 2, ..., n \tag{A1-2.98}$$

For activities A_2, A_3, ..., A_m we have

$$A_2 = \langle a_{21}, a_{22}, ..., a_{2n} \rangle$$

$$A_3 = \langle a_{31}, a_{32}, ..., a_{3n} \rangle \tag{A1-2.99}$$

$$\vdots$$

$$A_m = \langle a_{m1}, a_{m2}, ..., a_{mn} \rangle$$

When the prices of the inputs are known (e.g., $r_1, r_2, ..., r_n$), the unit cost figures for producing the output by activities 1, 2, ..., m can be computed by the following formulas:

$$c_1 = a_{11}r_1 + a_{12}r_2 + \cdots + a_{1n}r_n$$

$$c_2 = a_{21}r_1 + a_{22}r_2 + \cdots + a_{2n}r_n \tag{A1-2.100}$$

$$\vdots$$

$$c_m = a_{m1}r_1 + a_{m2}r_2 + \cdots + a_{mn}r_n$$

With m activities, we need only m computations. For a given set of input prices $r_1, r_2, ..., r_n$, the smallest unit cost c_j specifies the minimum-cost activity A_j. For a given output $\bar{Q}$, the minimum-cost $C^* = c_j\bar{Q}$ is

$$C^* = (a_{j1}r_1 + a_{j2}r_2 + \cdots + a_{jn}r_n)\bar{Q} = c_j\bar{Q} \tag{A1-2.101}$$

Thus, once the m computations in (A1-2.100) are completed, the c_j gives us the minimum-cost solution A_j for a given level of output. On the other hand, for the same set of the input prices $r_1, r_2, ..., r_n$, the unit cost for the output is still $c_1, c_2, ..., c_m$ in (A1-2.100) for $A_1, A_2, ..., A_m$, respectively. If the total cost $\bar{C}$ is known, then the total output Q_j that can be produced by A_j is $\bar{C}/c_j$. For a given $\bar{C}$, the smallest unit cost c_j will result in the largest output Q^*:

$$Q^* = \bar{C}/c_j \tag{A1-2.102}$$

From (A1-2.101) and (A1-2.102) it is seen that if $\bar{C} = C^*$, then $Q^* = \bar{Q}$ and vice versa; that is, for a given set of input prices, the minimum-unit-cost activity (process) A_j is the solution for both the maximum output for a given cost problem and the minimum cost for a given output problem. This result corresponds to Figure 2.16.

It should be pointed out that the minimum unit cost in (A1-2.100) for a certain set of input prices may not be unique. In this case, any one or combination of the corresponding activities will result in a minimum cost for a given output or a maximum output for a given cost.

When one or more input prices change, it may or may not result in a change of the minimum-unit-cost activity. In Figure 2.16, the two isocost curves AB and $A'B'$ represent two different sets of input prices, but the minimum-cost activity is still the same. However, if the price change results in an isocost curve that has a slope steeper than EF, but flatter than FG, then the minimum-cost activity will shift from E to F. Similarly, if the price change results in an isocost curve that has a slope flatter than DE, but steeper than CE, then the minimum-cost activity will shift from E to D. When there is a change of the minimum-cost activity, input substitution takes place.

These are two essential differences between the traditional continuous production function and the newer activity analysis approach to production theory. The optimal solution of the former is always unique, and input substitution will take place whenever relative price change takes place regardless of how small the change may be. [It is the change in relative price, not in absolute price, of the inputs that matters, because the equilibrium conditions (A1-2.77) are homogeneous of degree zero in the input prices, and thus a proportional change of all the input prices will not have any effect on the optimal solution.] Observed facts tend to confirm that input substitution is not as sensitive as traditional theory predicts. In this sense, activity analysis is more realistic than the traditional approach.

Students who have a better mathematical background might have noticed that our system of equations (A1-2.100) does no more than to single out the extreme points of a convex set (i.e., points C, D, E, F, and G of Figure 2.16) if the isoquant is for 1 unit of output; this is the fundamental principle of linear programming. When the production functions and the cost equation (necessarily) are linear, the question of minimizing cost for a given output is a linear programming problem. However, in our case, since the number of extreme points is usually quite limited, enumeration of all of them will not be a formidable job; hence, computation of the unit cost for all the activities may be a simple and sure way to solve the problem. On the other hand, when more than one output or more than one industry are involved, the problem may become too complex, and thus enumeration of all the extreme points may become very difficult, if not impossible. In such a case, more sophisticated linear programming techniques will help to reduce the required labor. Since linear programming, though very useful in many ways, is not a necessary part of microeconomics, we shall not discuss it in detail, but only mention it casually.

THE THEORY OF COST

3.1 BASIC CONCEPTS

Private and Social Costs

In economics, the cost of producing an item can be considered either from the viewpoint of society as a whole or from the viewpoint of an individual producer or firm. In most cases, these two approaches will yield different results; however, under certain circumstances they will be equivalent. A simple example will serve to illustrate this point.

Suppose that a firm produces 5 million tons of steel per month. To produce this quantity, the firm requires certain amounts of labor (including management personnel), capital, and raw materials, which together cost X dollars according to the going price of the various inputs. If no air control device has been installed, smoke and small particles in the air will accompany the production of steel. As a result, people who reside near the steel mill may incur extra expenses for medical treatment, window washing, car washing, and so forth. Suppose it is known that the total extra expense to all of these residents combined is Y dollars. Hence, the *social cost* of the 5 million tons of steel is $X + Y$ dollars. Since the firm pays for only the labor, capital, and raw materials, the *private cost* (to the firm) of the 5 million tons of steel is X dollars. Since we are assuming $Y > 0$, the social cost $(X + Y)$ is greater than the private cost (X) to the individual producer. On the other hand, if we assume that perfect air control devices are installed, so that the combined extra expense to the neighborhood residents due to steel-producing activities is zero, then the social cost and the private cost to the firm will be identical. However, the additional installation and operation costs for air control will yield a new private cost (X') which may be more or less than $X + Y$. This could have some social implications, but for the moment, we shall not concern ourselves with this fact.

In the above example, air pollution represents what is referred to as an *external diseconomy in production economics*. The significance of the "absence of externality" (see Assumption I.4 in the introduction to Part I) can be easily visualized with respect to social and private costs. With this assumption, social cost and private cost are identical.

In general, when external diseconomies are present, the social cost of producing a commodity will exceed the private cost. On the other hand, when *external economies* prevail, social cost will be less than private cost. In the absence of externalities in production, social cost and private cost will be identical. We shall have more to say on the topic of external diseconomies and economies in Chapter 13 (Welfare Economics), but here (as in all textbooks) the absence of externalities will be assumed; that is, private cost and social cost will be considered identical.

Private and social costs generally differ because of external economics or diseconomies in production

Alternative (Opportunity) Cost

In economics, another way of considering cost is through the concept of *alternative (opportunity)* cost. Up until now, the cost of an item has been expressed in terms of the inputs expended in producing the output; however, it can also be expressed in terms of the amount of another output that could have been produced using the same quantity of inputs employed in producing the original one. For example, with a given amount of labor, capital, and steel, either a certain quantity of steel sheets *or* a certain quantity of steel rods can be produced. If steel sheets are produced, steel rods will have to be foregone, and vice versa. The quantity of steel rods foregone is the alternative (opportunity) cost of producing steel sheets. Conversely, the steel sheets can be considered the alternative (opportuntity) cost of producing steel rods.

To give another example, suppose that with 1 acre of land, one worker, and a certain amount of fertilizer, either 100 bushels of wheat *or* 120 bushels of corn can be produced. The 120 bushels of corn is the alternative (opportunity) cost of the 100 bushels of wheat, whereas the 100 bushels of wheat is the alternative (opportunity) cost of the 120 bushels of corn. Thus, the concept of alternative (opportunity) cost is symmetric. Under certain circumstances, such as international trade, the alternative (opportunity) cost concept is more frequently employed. However, the student should remember that this concept can be equally applied to social as well as private cost. Finally, whereas some economists use the term alternative cost and others use opportunity cost, in either case they are referring to the same thing. For the sake of simplicity, we shall use the term alternative cost in this book, again noting that opportunity cost could just as well be used with no change in meaning.

Explicit and Implicit Costs

Explicit cost and *implicit cost* are two related concepts with respect to private cost. A good example is in the operation of a neighborhood grocery store. In this case, explicit cost would include such items as wages paid to employees (if any) money paid to suppliers for merchandise, and utility payments. If the proprietors (a husband and wife) work in the grocery and, additionally, own the building, they may also invest in the inventory. Assume that both the husband and wife could have each earned $1000 per month somewhere else. Furthermore, let us assume that the building could be leased for $500 per month and that their investment in the grocery could have earned $700 per month if it were invested elsewhere. Hence, the amount 1000 + 1000 + 500 + 700 = $3200 that the husband and wife could have earned otherwise is the implicit cost. In economics, the *total cost* is the sum of the explicit and implicit costs of operating a business.

The Concept of Cost in Business and in Economics

In general, the concept of cost in business is comparable with that in economics. Thus, in much the same manner as in economics, in big corporations with organized accounting systems, such expenses as employee wages, money paid for raw materials, utility payments, and interest payments on borrowed capital comprise the cost. On the other hand, the return (if any) on capital invested by stockholders is treated as profit in business, whereas in economics it is treated as a cost.[1] In economics, not only the normal return on a stockholder's or owner's investment, but also that on borrowed capital is considered as part of a firm's costs. However, due to their nature, economists treat these as implicit costs rather than explicit costs. This implies that part (but not necessarily all) of what is called implicit cost in economics is considered to be profit in business accounting practice and for tax purposes. This difference in concept often produces confusion among students, and, therefore, the reader should note the distinction; this will be of particular importance in Chapter 6, where it will be shown that the profit of a competitive firm in long-run equilibrium is zero. As we shall see, such a conclusion is possible only if normal profits are treated as cost and excess

---

[1] However, it should be noted that the government's treatment of the return on a stockholder's investment for tax purposes is the same as that of business, that is, as profit.

profits as profit. Thus, in economics zero profit means zero excess profit, hence implying that the investment nevertheless yields a positive return. In other words, economics regards a normal return on capital as a necessary cost. It is only a return that is more than necessary for attracting and retaining capital that in economics is termed profit (or, more properly, *economic rent*). This distinction between the concept of cost in economics and that in business accounting practice is important and should definitely be kept in mind. Much nonsensical debate with respect to social and economic policy directly stems from a failure to recognize it. This difference will also have a bearing on the discussions in Chapter 7 concerned with the problems of markup pricing.

The Minimum-Cost Combination as a True Measure of Cost

An implicit assumption underlying the concept of cost in economics which is often overlooked is that only the *minimum cost* for a given technology and given input prices is considered as the cost of a product. For example, if an item can be produced, subject to the prevailing technology and input prices, for a cost of either $50, $60, or $70, then the true measure of its economic cost is $50, not $60 or $70. This is implicit in the derivation of the cost function, as will be discussed in detail later in this chapter.

The Short Run Versus the Long Run

In economics, a distinction is made between short-run and long-run costs. In the short run, some costs, such as the depreciation on a building, are fixed (i.e., they do not vary with the level of output), whereas other costs, such as that of the materials needed to produce the product, do vary with the level of output (and hence are called variable costs). The short-run total cost is the sum of the total fixed cost and the total variable cost. On the other hand, in the long run, there are no fixed costs, that is, all costs are variable. This simply means that, in the long run, every input used in production is capable of being varied, and, therefore, adjustments can be made in the levels of whichever of them are actually employed to produce a product. Hence, we see, that in economics the difference between the short run and the long run is not determined by some tidy demarcation line in time (i.e., 1, 2, 5, or even 10 years), but rather in the context of a condition that permits all inputs to be varied. However, such a condition will involve a shorter period of time in some industries than it will in others. The difference obviously depends on the nature of the inputs used in production and the technology and amount of capital that are used to produce the product.

The difference between the short and long run is due to the existence or nonexistence of fixed costs

The Cost Function of a Firm

For the sake of simplicity, we assume that a firm produces a homogeneous product (no joint products)[2] by using the various inputs that are available to it at going market prices. (In terms of economics, this means that the firm faces competitive input markets.) This assumption enables us to treat the input prices as constants. It is also assumed that technology is given and that the minimum possible cost is considered the cost of a product. This is consistent with the assumption of profit maximization as the primary goal of a firm, to which we have referred earlier. In this chapter, cost is always treated in terms of monetary value.

Definition: Cost Function. The relationship between cost and the corresponding output.

The cost function expresses the relationship between cost and output, which, in turn, depends on the production function and the price of inputs

The above definition should be contrasted to the term *cost equation* (see Chapter 2), which expresses the relationship between cost and the corresponding inputs. The two concepts are related, but distinct. In general, a cost function can be written

$$C = f(Q) \tag{3.1}$$

where Q is the quantity of the output, C is the corresponding total cost (in dollars), and f relates the total cost and the quantity of output. It should be understood that f always assigns the minimum possible value to C that is consistent with prevailing technology. Although the cost function can, in general, be written in the form (3.1), it is implicit that it also contains a certain number of parameters, some of which may have special significance under certain circumstances (e.g., a short-run cost function).

As mentioned above, the distinction between the short- and long-run costs is important in economics. Since the long-run cost function is derived from the associated short-run cost function, we shall discuss the latter first.

3.2 SHORT-RUN COST FUNCTIONS

3.2.1 Total Cost

The short-run total cost is the sum of the total fixed cost and the total variable cost. The total fixed cost is the market value of the fixed input(s), that is, the product of the price and the quantity of the fixed input (in the case of more than one input, the sum

---

[2] A homogeneous product in economics is one such that, for trading purposes, different units have the same properties. Thus, a person on the trading floor of the Chicago Board of Trade will not make any distinction between a bushel of wheat grown by Farmer Brown and one grown by Farmer Smith. The concept of joint products applies when two or more different products are simultaneously produced with the same inputs.

of the products for all fixed inputs) that is used to produce the given product(s). By definition, the total fixed cost is independent of the level of output; that is, the total fixed cost does not change when the level of output changes. On the other hand, the total variable cost is the market value of the minimum quantity of variable input(s), consistent with prevailing technology, required to produce the various quantities of output. Since different quantities of output are associated with different quantities of variable input(s), the total variable cost is a function of the output; that is, when the level of output changes, the total variable cost also changes. The short-run total cost function can be written

$$C = C_0 + V(Q) \tag{3.2}$$

where C is the total cost, C_0 is the total fixed cost, and $V(Q)$ is the total variable cost, which is a function of the output Q. In a sense, (3.2) is a special case of (3.1), since the constant C_0 can be considered a *parameter*, which has special significance in terms of economics. Therefore, among the many possible parameters, C_0 is singled out in the discussion of short-run cost functions. If the constant total fixed cost C_0 is treated as just another parameter (i.e., not singled out), then (3.2) becomes (3.1).

It should be pointed out that the cost function is derived from the associated production function and cost equation under the condition of maximum output for a given cost or minimum cost for a given output (see Chapter 2). We shall demonstrate the derivation of a cost function for the special case of the Cobb–Douglas production function with two variable inputs in the appendix to this chapter. Here, in order to show the close relationship between the cost and production functions without involving mathematics, we shall use the data of Table 1.1 to compute the cost figures. It is assumed that the 1 acre of land is rented at $2000 per year and that the annual payment (wage) per worker is $3000. With prices and quantities given, the computation of cost is as shown in Table 3.1.

In the case of more than one variable input, the total variable

TABLE 3.1

Output	Fixed input	Variable input	Total fixed cost	Total variable cost	Total cost
0	1	0	$2,000	$ 0	$ 2,000
10	1	1	2,000	3,000	5,000
24	1	2	2,000	6,000	8,000
39	1	3	2,000	9,000	11,000
52	1	4	2,000	12,000	14,000
60	1	5	2,000	15,000	17,000
66	1	6	2,000	18,000	20,000

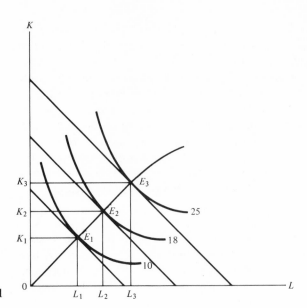

FIGURE 3.1

cost would be computed from points on the expansion path (e.g., see Figure 2.19 for the two-variable-input case). In the case of one fixed input (e.g., land) and two variable inputs (e.g., capital and labor) it has been shown in Chapter 2 that the optimal input combinations for various quantities of output are also indicated by points on the expansion path. Such input combinations are given by curve $0\widehat{E_1E_2}E_3$ in Figure 3.1. We see that in producing 10 units of output, the minimum-cost combination of labor and capital is $L_1 K_1$, whereas for 18 and 25 units of output it is L_2, K_2 and L_3, K_3, respectively.

If we assume that the cost of land is F, the wage rate is w, and the price (better yet, the rental) of capital is r, then the cost figures can be represented by the expressions shown in Table 3.2. Although it is not immediately obvious, a brief examination of Table 3.2 reveals that the cost figure expressions actually represent numbers. Suppose that the total fixed cost $F = \$100$, the wage rate $w = \$5$, and the capital rental $r = \$10$. We can compute the total cost of each output quantity by reading off the quantities of labor and capital from Figure 3.1. For example, if $L_1 = 1$ and $K_1 =$

TABLE 3.2

Output	Total fixed cost	Total variable cost	Total cost
0	F	0	F
10	F	$wL_1 + rK_1$	$F + wL_1 + rK_1$
18	F	$wL_2 + rK_2$	$F + wL_2 + rK_2$
25	F	$wL_3 + rK_3$	$F + wL_3 + rK_3$

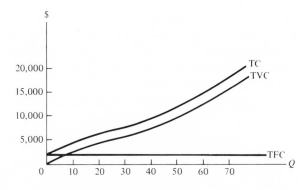

FIGURE 3.2

2, then the total cost for 10 units of output is $F + wL_1 + rK_1 = $100 + $5 + $20 = 125. Assuming $L_2 = 2$ and $K_2 = 3$, the total cost for 18 units of output is $F + wL_2 + rK_2 = $100 + $10 + $30 = 140. The cost for 25 units can be obtained in a similar manner. In principle, we can compute the total cost for any level of output in the above fashion. It is only essential to know the quantities of inputs involved, since we have assumed that prices remain constant.

The cost figures and corresponding quantities of output in Table 3.1 constitute a *cost schedule*. This set of data can also be represented in the form of a graph by plotting the total fixed cost (TFC), the total variable cost (TVC), and the total cost (TC), respectively, versus output Q. Figure 3.2 presents the TFC, TVC, and TC curves that correspond to the data given in Table 3.1. Note that since TFC, by definition, is a constant, the TFC curve is always a horizontal straight line.

The TVC curve always starts at the origin and rises to the right, first at a decreasing rate and then at an increasing rate. On the other hand, the TC curve always starts from the TFC curve at $Q = 0$ and then rises to the right at the same rate as the TVC curve, as indicated by Equation (3.2). It is technically possible for the TC and TVC curves to bend back at the top (see the production schedule of Table 1.1). However, those portions of the TC and TVC curves that bend back do not have practical significance with respect to a firm's decision making and are therefore omitted in discussions on cost. Accordingly, we have not included this possibility in the construction of Table 3.1 and Figure 3.2.

3.2.2 Average and Marginal Costs

The concept of *average cost* (AC)[3] is very appealing to the ordinary businessperson because, in conjunction with price or average

---

[3] Average cost is also referred to as *unit cost*.

revenue, it gives some indication of the *profit margin*. Although AC is not emphasized in profit analysis, it still represents an important economic concept that helps us to understand the cost behavior of a firm.

We can derive AC from TC, which, by definition, is the sum of TFC and TVC. Accordingly, we have the average total cost (ATC), average fixed cost (AFC), and average variable cost (AVC).

Definition: Average Total Cost. Total cost divided by quantity of output:

$$ATC = TC/Q$$

Definition: Average Fixed Cost. Total fixed cost divided by the quantity of output:

$$AFC = TFC/Q$$

Definition: Average Variable Cost. Total variable cost divided by the quantity of output:

$$AVC = TVC/Q$$

From (3.2) we can write

$$TC = TFC + TVC \tag{3.2'}$$

Dividing both sides of (3.2') by the quantity of output Q results in

$$TC/Q = TFC/Q + TVC/Q$$

From the above definitions we have the following relationship:

$$ATC = AFC + AVC \tag{3.3}$$

That is, the average total cost is equal to the sum of the average fixed cost and the average variable cost.

We can use the data in Table 3.1 to illustrate the various average cost concepts and the relationship between them. In Table 3.3, columns 1–4 are directly taken from Table 3.1, whereas columns

TABLE 3.3

Q	TFC	TVC	TC	AFC	AVC	ATC	MC
0	$2,000	$ 0	$ 2,000	—	—	—	$300.00
10	2,000	3,000	5,000	$200.00	$300.00	$500.00	214.29
24	2,000	6,000	8,000	83.33	250.00	333.33	200.00
39	2,000	9,000	11,000	51.28	230.77	282.05	230.77
52	2,000	12,000	14,000	38.46	230.77	269.23	375.00
60	2,000	15,000	17,000	33.33	250.00	283.33	500.00
66	2,000	18,000	20,000	30.30	272.73	303.03	—

5 and 6 are computed by dividing columns 2 and 3, respectively, by column 1. On the other hand, column 7 can be computed in two different but equivalent ways. Using the definition of ATC, column 7 can be computed by dividing column 4 by column 1. Alternatively, using the relationship between ATC, AFC, and AVC in (3.3), column 7 can be computed as the sum of columns 5 and 6. The student can easily check the validity of the above statements by performing a few computations.

The ATC values given in Table 3.3 indicate that our example is not very realistic, since it generally does not cost hundreds of dollars to produce a bushel of corn. The student should understand that it is not necessary for this simple example to be realistic—it is constructed for the sole purpose of illustrating the definitions, relationships, and computational methods of the various cost concepts. However, unrealistic cost figures can be brought closer to real ones through the proper choice of the units of output and price. For example, if the units in column 1 were increased by a factor of 100 and TFC and TVC adjusted downward to reflect more realistic costs, then the ATC of the corn would be only $2–5 per bushel.[4]

As we noted earlier, the average cost is an appealing concept to the ordinary businessperson. However, in the study of the economics of resource use, the concept of marginal cost (MC) has more meaning. Therefore, we shall pay particular attention to the method of its derivation and also its use. The last column of Table 3.3 gives the values of MC, which are computed on the basis of the following definition.

Definition: Marginal Cost. The ratio of the change in total cost to a small change in the level of output:

$$MC = \Delta TC/\Delta Q \tag{3.4}$$

Marginal cost has special meaning because it tells us how total cost changes for a small change in output

As a special case, the marginal cost can be considered the addition to total cost that results from the addition of one unit of output.

As we have already shown, TFC does not change when Q changes. Therefore, the change in TC is equal to the change in TVC. By deduction, we have the following proposition.

---

[4] Thus, if the land cost $1000 per acre and its value was not diminished by normal use, then the only fixed cost involved in producing an annual corn crop would be the interest on capital. At a 10% interest rate, the fixed cost would be $100 per year. This is a more realistic way of considering land purchase cost as a fixed cost, since land, unlike buildings and equipment, is not depreciated for tax or revenue purposes. Where buildings and equipment are an integral part of the farm operations and are used in the growing of the corn, that portion of the total depreciation of buildings and equipment related to their use in corn production, together with a portion of the interest cost, is the fixed cost in the production of corn. Similarly, labor costs are not likely to be of the magnitude shown in Table 3.3, even with a fivefold increase in output.

Proposition 3.1. Marginal cost is equal to the ratio of the change in total variable cost to a small change in the level of output:

$$MC = \Delta TVC / \Delta Q \qquad\qquad (3.4')$$

For practical purposes, marginal cost can be considered the addition to total variable cost that results from the addition of one unit of output.

Hence, on the basis of the above definition of MC, column 8 of Table 3.3 is computed by dividing the successive differences (changes in TC) of column 4 by the corresponding successive differences (changes in Q) of column 1. For example, the change in TC from $2000 to $5000 is $5000 $-$ $2000 $=$ $3000 and the corresponding change in Q is from 0 to 10 or 10 $-$ 0 $=$ 10; thus, the corresponding MC is $3000/10 $=$ $300. In a sense, this $300 is the *average marginal cost* from 0 to 10 units of output. However, in a strict sense, it is neither the MC of the tenth unit nor that of the first unit, second unit, and so on. Similarly, the MC between 10 units and 24 units is ($8000 $-$ $5000)/(24 $-$ 10) $=$ $3000/14 $=$ $214.29. In the real world, we generally encounter the large changes in output assumed in our example (e.g., from 0 to 10 units and from 10 to 24 units). However, the definition of MC is based on the notion of small change. As a compromise, we must be satisfied to use AMC in dealing with large changes. Nevertheless, students should keep in mind that since MC is theoretically defined for a small change in the level of output, it should be interpreted and computed on this basis whenever possible.

Mathematically, expressions (3.4) and (3.4') are equivalent. Since TFC does not change for a change in Q, column 8 can be computed from columns 1 and 4 [using (3.4)]. Furthermore, it is easily seen that column 8 can also be computed from columns 1 and 3 [using (3.4')]. For example, MC from 0 to 10 units of output is ($3000 $-$ 0)/(10 $-$ 0) $=$ $300 and MC from 10 to 24 units of output is ($6000 $-$ $3000)/(24 $-$ 10) $=$ $214.29—the same values we obtained with the use of (3.4). From this example, the student should be convinced that (3.4) and (3.4') are equivalent. The significance of this equivalence has two aspects. First of all, conceptually, MC involves only variable cost, that is, fixed cost does not enter into the determination of MC. Secondly, even if information on TC is not available, MC can still be computed if information on TVC is available.

For the competitive input market, in the case of one variable input, it is easily observed that MC is inversely related with the MP of the variable input; that is, when MP increases, MC decreases, and vice versa. This can be shown by an examination of (3.4'). First of all, in the one-variable-input case, TVC is equal to the product of the price w and quantity L of the variable input, that is, $TVC = wL$. Mathematically, $\Delta TVC = w\Delta L + L\Delta w$;

however, under the assumption of a competitive input market, $\Delta w = 0$ when labor input changes, and hence the above expression becomes

$$\Delta TVC = w\Delta L \tag{3.5}$$

Substituting (3.5) into (3.4'), we obtain

$$MC = \frac{w\Delta L}{\Delta Q} = \frac{w}{\Delta Q/\Delta L} = \frac{w}{MP} \tag{3.6}$$

Recall that the MP of labor has been defined in Section 1.1.2 as the ratio of the change in output to the change in labor. Consequently, since the cost of a unit of labor is w and the change in output from an additional unit of labor is MP, it follows that MC $= w/MP$.

By inspection of columns 6 and 8 of Table 3.3 it can be seen that MC = AVC when the latter is at its minimum. Is this a coincidence? The answer is no. In fact, MC = AVC only at the minimum of the latter, since, presumably, the maximum of AVC does not exist. This also implies that if the minimum of AVC does not exist, then MC will never be equal to AVC. On the other hand, if AVC is a constant, then MC = AVC throughout the output range. The latter implication has important significance in any business application of the economics of production to the firm because empirical studies indicate that AVC is, in many cases, constant within some relevant range. Furthermore, in the minds of businesspeople, AVC is constant because raw material and labor inputs (and their prices) per unit of output are constant.

What has been said about the relationship of MC to AVC does not apply to MC and AFC, since MC is not related to AFC. However, MC is related to ATC by virtue of the relationship of AVC to AC; therefore, whenever MC and AC (i.e., AVC and ATC) are related, MC is equal to AC at the minimum of the latter. A mathematical proof of this phenomenon is presented in the appendix to this chapter. The example of the batting average of a baseball player used in Section 1.1.3 to explain the relationship between AP and MP can also be used to explain the relationship between AC and MC. Students should review Section 1.1.3 if they have any doubt about the relationship between AC and MC.

So far, we have established the following relationships:

MC is always equal to AVC and ATC when the latter are at their minima.

Whenever MC is less than AVC and ATC, the latter will decrease.

Whenever MC is greater than AVC and ATC, the latter will increase.

Whenever MC is equal to AVC and ATC, the latter will remain the same, which implies that MC = AVC when AVC is constant.

The mathematical relationship of MC to AVC and ATC can be summarized in conditional statements

MC and AFC are not related.

Since ATC is the sum of AVC and AFC and AFC decreases when output increases, whereas AVC at first decreases and then increases, it follows that as long as the decrease in AFC exceeds the increase in AVC, ATC will continue to decrease.

At some point in this range, AVC reaches its minimum and starts to increase.

Only when the increase in AVC exceeds the decrease in AFC will ATC start to increase. Hence, AVC reaches its minimum before ATC.

The AC and MC data in Table 3.3 can be plotted in order to show the relationship between the MC and AC curves. However, since the changes in output and cost are relatively large from one input combination to the next (in technical terms, we are dealing with a discrete rather than a continuous change in the variable input), the various cost curves will not be smooth. However, we shall nevertheless use smooth cost curves, which are more convenient for theoretical demonstrations, to illustrate the basic relationships described above. Students may wish to draw the actual AC and MC curves defined by the data in Table 3.3 in order to gain familiarity and facility in interpreting the behavioral relationship between the different cost curves.

3.2.3 The Geometry of Short-Run Cost Curves

From both the definition of AC and MC as well as their relationship to TC, it is obvious that the former can be derived from the latter and vice versa. This can easily be demonstrated by geometrical methods, and (in some cases) the geometry may be very helpful in understanding certain characteristics of cost behavior, such as those of an ever-decreasing AFC.

In terms of geometry, the AFC for any output quantity Q is represented by the slope of a ray from the origin to the corresponding point on the TFC curve. Thus, in part (a) of Figure 3.3, the AFC for Q_1 is the slope of $\overline{0E}$, for Q_2 the slope of $\overline{0F}$, and for Q_3 the slope of $\overline{0G}$. This follows from the definition of AFC. For example, by definition, the AFC for Q_1 is the quotient of TFC (i.e., $\overline{Q_1E}$) divided by output $\overline{0Q_1}$, that is, precisely the slope of $\overline{0E}$. Similarly, the AFC for Q_2 is the quotient of TFC ($\overline{Q_2F}$) divided by output $\overline{0Q_2}$, that is, precisely the slope of $\overline{0F}$. Finally, for the AFC of Q_3, the slope of $\overline{0G}$ is the quotient of $\overline{Q_3G}$ divided by $\overline{0Q_3}$. Since the slope of a ray drawn from the origin to the TFC curve decreases as one moves to the right along the curve (i.e., for increasing Q), the AFC curve declines from left to right. When Q approaches infinity, the slope of the ray approaches zero, which implies that the AFC curve approaches the horizontal

Slopes of rays to TC, TFC, and TVC curves tell whether ATC, AFC, or AVC increases or decreases as output is varied

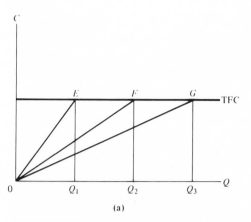

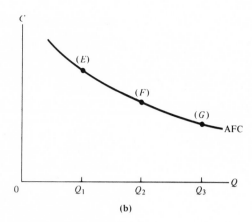

(a)   (b)

FIGURE 3.3

axis. Alternatively, when Q approaches zero, the slope of the ray approaches infinity, which implies that the AFC curve approaches infinity. Thus, the AFC curve will approach the vertical axis when Q becomes very small and the horizontal axis when Q becomes very large, but theoretically never reaches either. In mathematics, the vertical and horizontal axes are called the *asymptotes* of the AFC curve. Part (b) of Figure 3.3 is a representation of the AFC curve as described above. Note that the vertical axes of parts (a) and (b) have different scales; that is, points (E), (F), and (G) in part (b) correspond, respectively, to points E, F, and G in part (a).

For similar reasons to the above, the AVC for each output quantity Q is represented by the slope of a ray from the origin to the corresponding point on the TVC curve. For example, in part (a) of Figure 3.4, the AVC for Q_1 is the slope of $\overline{0E}$, for Q_2

FIGURE 3.4

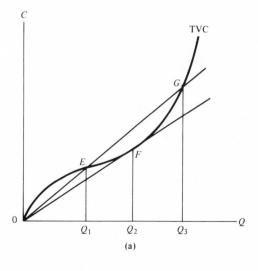

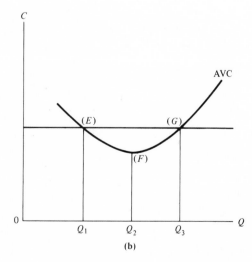

(a)   (b)

the slope of $\overline{0F}$, and for Q_3 the slope of $\overline{0G}$. It should be noted that the slopes of the rays decrease as one moves along the TVC curve from the origin to F, which implies that the corresponding AVC curve declines from the origin to Q_2. However, with movement along the TVC curve to the right of F, the slopes of the rays become steeper, which means that the corresponding AVC curve rises to the right of Q_2. Since (as can easily be seen) of all the rays that can be drawn from the origin to the TVC curve, ray $\overline{0F}$ has the flattest slope, the AVC curve must reach its minimum at Q_2. Furthermore, since E and G lie on the same ray and thus have the same slope from the origin, the AVCs for Q_1 and Q_3 must be equal. All of the above characteristics of the AVC curve are shown in part (b) of 3.4, which represents the transformation of TVC to AVC and, therefore, the behavior of the TVC at given output levels. Points (E), (F), and (G) in part (b) correspond, respectively, to points E, F, and G in part (a).

We have now examined the behavior of the fixed- and variable-cost curves. The same basic logic is applied to examine the behavior of the TC curve. The curves in Figure 3.5 are very similar to those in Figure 3.4 except that, due to the inclusion of TFC, TC starts above the origin. Students should also observe that Q_3 may or may not represent the same quantity in Figures 3.4 and 3.5. However, as we have explained earlier, it is true that ATC reaches its minimum at a higher Q than does AVC. Students should experiment with these cost curves in order to satisfy themselves that the described relationships hold true for the hypothesized cost–output behavior.

We shall now turn our attention to studying the relationships between the MC curve and other cost curves. Here we find that the geometrical relationship between MC and TC or MC and TVC is a little different than those considered above. As noted earlier, AC is defined by the slope of a ray from the origin to the cor-

FIGURE 3.5

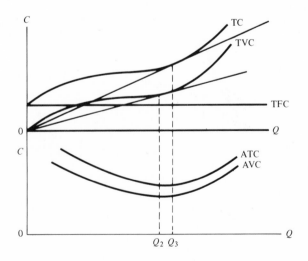

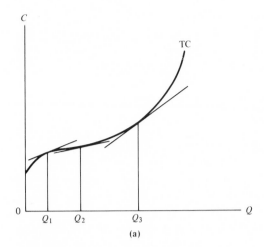

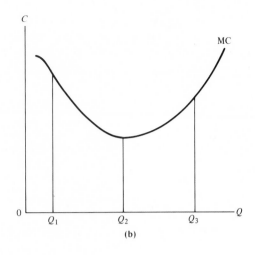

FIGURE 3.6

responding TC curve. However, MC is not represented by the slope of the ray from the origin to the TC and TVC curves. Instead, it is represented by the slope of the tangent to the TC and TVC curves for the designated quantity of output. Since the TC and TVC curves have the same slope for each and every Q, tangents drawn to these curves for the designated outputs will result in identical MC curves. Hence, for illustration purposes we need only use the TC curve.

In part (a) of Figure 3.6, the slope of a tangent to the TC curve becomes flatter as one moves to the right from the vertical axis to the point corresponding to Q_2. This implies a decreasing MC as one moves from the origin to Q_2. On the other hand, after passing Q_2, the slope of a tangent increases as one moves along the TC curve to the right. This implies that MC is increasing. Thus, it is logical to conclude that MC is minimum at Q_2. Another interesting phenomenon is that the tangent at Q_1 is above the TC curve, whereas at Q_3 it is below the TC curve. This means that the tangent must cross the TC curve somewhere (i.e., at the point where it goes from above the TC curve to below it), and the slope of the tangent must change from decreasing to increasing at the same point. In geometry, this point is called the point of inflection, and it is here that the slope of the tangent (and hence, of the TC curve) reaches its minimum. In Figure 3.6, the point on the TC (MC) curve corresponding to Q_2 is the point of inflection. Accordingly, the MC curve declines at Q_1, rises at Q_3, and reaches a minimum at Q_2.

The above geometric development can be used to prove the fact that the MC curve must intersect the AVC curve at the minimum of the latter. Let us examine this proposition with respect to our description of the behavioral relationships between the various cost curves that we have considered thus far.

Slopes of tangents drawn to TC and TVC curves indicate whether MC increases or decreases as output is varied

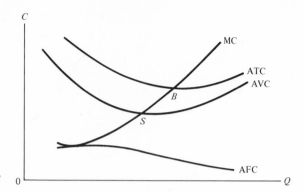

FIGURE 3.7

In Figure 3.4, it has been shown that the ray $\overline{OF}$ is tangent to the TVC curve at Q_2 and that AVC reaches its minimum at Q_2. Since $\overline{OF}$ is tangent to the TVC curve, its slope must also represent MC at Q_2. Hence, since the slope of $\overline{OF}$ represents both MC and AVC at Q_2, MC must be equal to AVC at Q_2, where AVC reaches its minimum. This proves the assertion that has been made; that is, the MC curve intersects the AVC curve at the minimum of the latter. Similar reasoning can be used to prove the fact that MC is equal to ATC at the minimum of the latter.

On the basis of the above arguments, we can draw the traditional graph that shows the characteristics of and relationships between the short-run AC and MC curves. This has been done in Figure 3.7; note that the AFC curve declines to the right and that the MC curve intersects both the AVC curve and the ATC curve at their minima (points S and B, respectively). The vertical distance between the ATC and AVC curves defines the value of the corresponding AFC. In other words, for each and every Q, the height of the ATC curve is the vertical sum of the AFC and AVC curves. This completes our explanation of the behavior of the relevant short-run cost curves based on the input–output relationships that were discussed in Chapters 1 and 2. To refresh their memories, students may wish to reread Chapter 1 and attempt an explanation of the cost behavior that we have described in the context of basic production economics. Such a review and interpretation is invaluable for a full comprehension of the material that follows.

3.2.4 Cost Curves in Reality: Constant AVC and MC Curves

The traditional cost curves discussed in the previous section are commonly used in economic analysis. The traditional forms are very useful for theoretical analysis because they best demonstrate the relationships between the various cost curves as well as all possible characteristics of their behavior. Unfortunately, some students believe that all economists think that cost curves, in

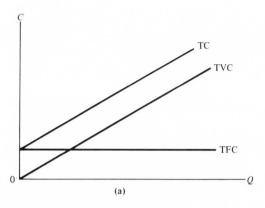
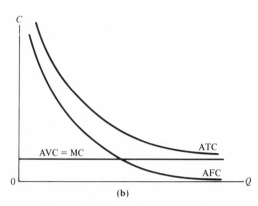

(a)   (b)

FIGURE 3.8

reality, are typically of such a form. As we have mentioned in Section 1.4, the AP and, consequently, MP of a variable input are usually constant within a considerable range and then decrease. This implies constant variable and marginal costs within a certain range. In fact, empirical studies indicate that many (if not all) businesspeople believe that AVC is indeed constant within the relevant range. This mode of cost behavior is also manifested in the case of more than one variable input. It is important to note that such a mode of cost behavior indicates more than just the constant AP and MP of a variable input. In fact, a constant AVC indicates a constant AP for inputs combined in fixed proportions. Hence, four workers with two pieces of machinery will produce twice the output of two workers with one piece of the same type of machinery. However, this should not be confused with the concept of constant returns to scale, which refers to the proportional change of all inputs and involves inputs other than labor and machines. At any rate, there are indications that, in reality, AVC and MC are constant within a considerable range, and this leads to the various forms of the cost curves presented in Figure 3.8.

As we have noted earlier, the TFC curve is always a horizontal line. However, with AVC and MC constant, the TVC and TC curves will be parallel *straight* lines starting from the origin and TFC, respectively, as depicted in part (a) of Figure 3.8 [compare this with the traditional textbook versions given in part (a) of Figures 3.4 and 3.5]. This implies that the AVC and MC curves are represented by the same horizontal straight line, as depicted in part (b). On the other hand, the ATC curve is not a straight line, but instead is an ever-declining curve that approaches but never reaches the constant AVC = MC line as Q increases. This fact can be easily validated by either using the geometric argument of Section 3.2.3 or by examining Equation (3.3) of Section 3.2.2. The shape of the AFC curve in this case is identical to the

When AVC is constant over the relevant range, AC–MC and ATC will be an ever-declining curve approaching, but never reaching AVC

traditional version in Figure 3.7. It is interesting to note that the vertical distance between the ATC and AFC curves defines the AVC curve, which is constant in the case of constant AVC and MC.

The Break-Even Chart

The simple model of the break-even chart has been used by some economists and accountants to assist executives in making decisions. The break-even chart is usually based on a constant variable cost and market price for the product. As a result, both the TC curve and the total revenue (TR) curve are straight lines (see Figure 3.9, in which R denotes revenue). The total cost curve always starts from the TFC, whereas the TR curve starts from the origin. At first, the TC curve is above the TR curve, and the vertical distance between these two lines represents the total loss. The TC and TR curves ultimately intersect at point B, which corresponds to the quantity Q^*. Point B is called the *break-even point*. This implies that, for the given cost and market conditions, the firm will just break even (i.e., zero profit) if it can produce and sell Q^* units of the product. On the other hand, if the firm can sell more than Q^* units of the product, it will earn a positive profit.[5] The vertical distance between the TR and TC curves to the right of Q^* indicates this positive profit.

Break-even charts can help a firm to determine how many units of a particular product it must sell in order to break even. When the market is stable, a firm can usually estimate its sales. Thus, the corresponding profit can be estimated accordingly, and this will help the executives to make decisions. However, the break-even charts must be used with great caution. First of all, AVC

FIGURE 3.9 C, R

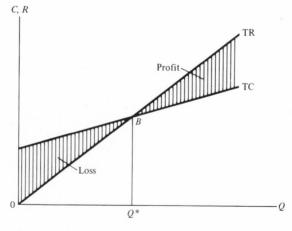

---

[5] Economists and finance theorists conventionally refer to loss as negative profit.

is very likely constant only within the firm's (plant's) present operating (output) capacity, beyond which the AVC will increase perhaps rapidly. Secondly, the market price may change in the near future. For these reasons, the estimated TC and TR curves may be subject to error. However, under the conditions of a stable market and within a given range of operating capacities, the break-even chart is a helpful tool.

Although the break-even chart is a helpful tool that assists firms in making decisions, many economists are skeptical about its usefulness. One of the reasons for this skepticism is that there does not exist a unique profit-maximizing quantity in the model. In this respect, the break-even chart is overly simplified and optimistic, since it implies that if the firm can sell more than Q^*, then the more it sells, the more profit it will realize, without bound. In the long run, it may imply that the optimal size (for profit maximization) is infinite. If this were the case, a perfect competitive market could not exist, and thus the constant-price assumption would break down. In a sense, this simple model is internally inconsistent on purely theoretical grounds. However, this criticism can easily be met by a slight modification of the TR and TC curves. With imperfect competition, the TR curve will no longer be a straight line—its slope will decrease as one moves to the right because price will need to be reduced to sell more. In Chapter 7 we shall show that in this case there exists a quantity that will maximize profit. Another way to meet this criticism is to take into consideration the fact that a firm has a definite operating capacity at a given point in time (basically, the short run). When the capacity of a firm is taken into consideration, the TC curve will no longer be a straight line over its entire range. We shall now discuss in more detail the shape of the TC, AC, and MC curves in this special case.

Constant AVC for a Given Capacity

Part (a) of Figure 3.10 depicts the TC curves and part (b) the AC and MC curves for the special case described above. As we have noted before, the TFC curve is always a horizontal straight line. However, the TVC and TC curves will, in this special case, at first be straight lines from the origin and TFC, respectively, to the capacity quantity Q_0 and then bend upward [as depicted in part (a)], in contrast to both the traditional textbook version of [see part (a) of Figures 3.4 and 3.5] and the simple constant-TVC curve of unlimited capacity [see part (a) of Figure 3.8]. This implies that the AVC curve is at first a horizontal straight line (up to Q_0) and then rises [as depicted in part (b)]. When AVC is constant, MC = AVC, but (as we shall soon explain) MC suddenly becomes greater than AVC when the latter increases as production levels beyond Q_0 are scheduled. As noted earlier, the

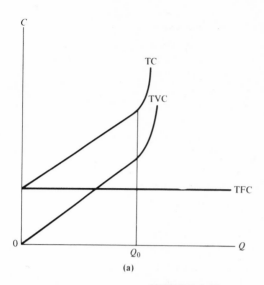

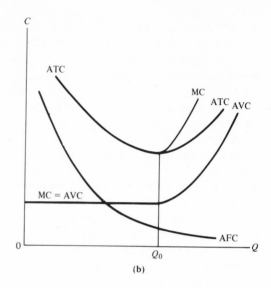

FIGURE 3.10

ATC curve is not a straight line. Students may wish to prove that this property of the ATC curve is valid by either using the geometric argument of Section 3.2.3 or by examining Equation (3.3) of Section 3.2.2.

It should be observed that both the TVC curve and the TC curve (as well as the AVC and ATC curves) have a kink at the same capacity output level Q_0. When the TVC and TC curves have a kink, MC will (for mathematical reasons) be discontinuous at the point at which it occurs. It is interesting to note that the TC curves indicate that both AVC and ATC reach their minima at the same quantity—Q_0 (for other possible cases, see the appendix to this chapter), that is, the output level at which the TC curves have their kinks. This condition is different from the traditional smooth, U-shaped AC curves, where the point of minimum ATC is to the right of the point of minimum AVC. However, the proper relationship between the AC and MC curves still holds in the present case. Due to the fact that AVC is constant up to output level Q_0, MC = AVC at the minimum (which is not unique) of the latter. At Q_0, MC jumps from AVC to ATC (indicated by the TC curve, since one cannot draw a ray from the origin to the TC curve having a slope flatter than that of the one to the TC curve at Q_0) and is equal to ATC at the minimum of the latter.

AVC is often constant up to plant capacity, giving a discontinuity in the MC and a kink in the ATC and AVC curves at production capacity

As we have mentioned previously, empirical studies indicate that in most (if not all) cases AVC and MC are constant within the relevant range and that many (if not all) businesspeople treat AVC and MC as constant in their decisions. It is interesting to note that some accounting textbooks (e.g., see Horngren, 1972), in their theoretical treatment, also consider AVC as constant. Because economists traditionally use the shapes of the various cost curves depicted in Figure 3.7 in their theoretical deliberations, an unnecessary gap is left between economics and reality. By bringing attention to the notion of constant AVC and MC over the relevant range, we have introduced the element of reality into economic theory. We shall have more to say on this condition in Chapters 7–9.

Another difference between economic theory and business practice is that the optimal conditions in most (if not all) neo-classical economic analyses are based on marginal analysis, whereas many business decisions are based on average revenue and cost concepts. However, when AVC is constant, MC = AVC, and in this special case the gap between economic analysis and business practice disappears. Whatever might be said with regard to business practice, economic analysis is probably much more useful in business decisions than most people realize.

3.2.5 The Shape of the MC and AC Curves, the Law of Diminishing Returns, and the Law of Variable Proportions

From Equation (3.6) in Section 3.2.2, it can be seen that the MC and MP of the variable input are inversely related in the one-variable-input case. Only when the law of diminishing returns prevails will MC increase. Similarly, in the case of more than one variable input, MC can increase only when the law of variable proportions prevails. Thus, the shapes of the short-run cost curves in Figure 3.7 are inversely related to those of the product curves of the variable input in Figure 1.4. On the other hand, the shapes of the cost curves in Figure 3.10 correspond to those of the product curves in part (b) of Figure 1.5. In general, cost behavior is closely, and usually inversely, related to the productivity of the inputs. However, the graphs in Figures 1.4 and 1.5, on the one hand, and in Figures 3.7 and 3.10, on the other hand, are of different natures in that the horizontal axes of the former represent the variable input, whereas in the latter they are the output. Furthermore, the vertical axes of the former represent the output, whereas in the latter they are the cost. Hence, a direct comparison of the graphs in Chapter 1 with those in this chapter is not feasible.

3.3 THE LONG-RUN COST FUNCTION AND THE EXPANSION PATH

In economics, the distinction between the short run and the long run is not necessarily based on a length of time, such as one year for the short run and more than one year for the long run. As we have mentioned before, in production economics a distinction is made between the variable and fixed inputs. In the short run, there is some fixed input (or inputs), whereas in the long run, all inputs are variable. Since the cost function is derived from the production function, the market value of the variable inputs constitutes the variable cost, and the market value of the fixed input constitutes fixed cost. Accordingly, in terms of cost, the short run is defined as a period of time that is brief enough to not allow certain costs to be changed. Some expenses, such as those for plant and management personnel, will remain fixed, whereas other costs, such as those for raw materials and direct labor, will change when the level of output changes. On the other hand, in the long run, all costs can be changed. Thus, in the short run, the distinction between variable and fixed costs can be made, whereas in the long run all costs are variable.

In terms of day-to-day business operations, it is the short-run cost that is relevant, since, at any given point in time, plant size and management personnel are given and cannot be changed. However, under certain conditions (e.g., when a new business is initiated or an expansion or contraction of a business takes place), long-run cost becomes relevant. For this reason, some economists refer to the long run as the *planning horizon*. Furthermore, regardless of how one looks at it, the distinction between the long run and the short run not only has theoretical importance, but also practical significance, since it helps us to identify and understand the cost behavior, which, in turn, will facilitate rational decision making.

3.3.1 The Isoquant Map and the Long- and Short-Run TC and AC Curves

An isoquant map theoretically represents all of the technical conditions in production. Since costs are derived from production, cost curves are closely related to the isoquant map—as we have previously shown using Figure 3.1 in conjunction with Table 3.2. In a similar fashion, we can demonstrate the relationship between the short- and long-run cost curves, which will also help students to gain further insight into the relationship between the production and cost functions.

For simplicity in exposition, we assume that there are only two inputs, (e.g., labor L and capital K) and that there are only three possible plant sizes: K_1, K_2, and K_3 each representing a given capital outlay.[6] We first direct attention to part (a) of Figure 3.11, in which $C_1, C_2, ..., C_6$ are parallel isocost curves (lines) and Q_1, $Q_2, ..., Q_6$ are the relevant isoquants.[7] Isoquant Q_1 is tangent to

---

[6] The general case of three or more inputs is treated in the appendix to this chapter. The case of n plant sizes will be treated momentarily.

[7] The isocost curves (lines) are parallel because with input prices given (i.e., they do not vary with the amount purchased), a proportionate increase (decrease) in money outlay will permit a proportionate increase (decrease) in the amount of inputs that can be acquired. Thus, if labor and capital are priced at $1 and $2 per unit, respectively (note that it is not the actual prices but their being given that is important here), then an increase in the money outlay from $10 to $20 will double the amount of inputs that can be purchased.

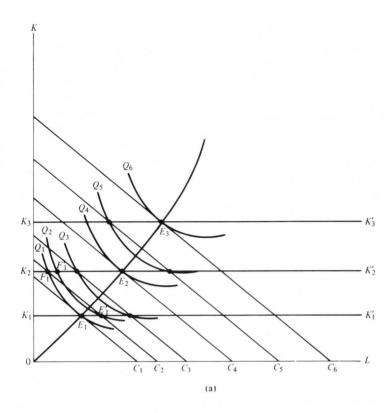

(a)

FIGURE 3.11

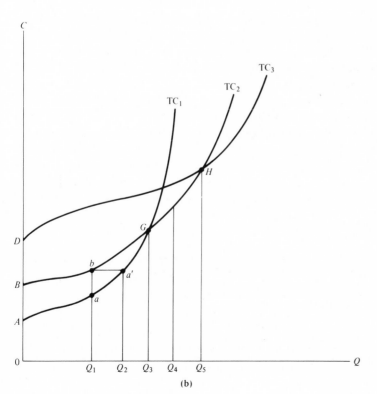

(b)

isocost curve C_1 at E_1, Q_4 to C_4 at E_2, and Q_6 to C_6 at E_3. The three possible plant sizes K_1, K_2, and K_3 each represent a different scale of production or output.[8] If capital were perfectly divisible, then an infinite number of possible plant sizes would be feasible, and the expansion path would be $0\widehat{E_1E_2}E_3$. However, under our assumption of only three plant sizes, production is only possible along either the horizontal straight line $\overline{K_1K_1'}$, $\overline{K_2K_2'}$, or $\overline{K_3K_3'}$ in the short run, and it can only jump from K_1 to K_2 or from K_1 to K_3 in the long run. Let us see how these postulated conditions affect the behavior of the cost curves.

We shall assume that labor is perfectly divisible and that output can be expanded in the short run by adding more labor to a fixed amount of capital. For example, by moving to the right along $\overline{K_1K_1'}$ (small-size plant), $\overline{K_2K_2'}$ (medium-size plant), or $\overline{K_3K_3'}$ (large-size plant), output can be expanded in each case. If we further assume that the prices of labor and capital are w and r, respectively, then TFC for the small-size plant is rK_1, for the medium-size plant rK_2, and for the large-size plant rK_3. This information is plotted on the vertical axis in part (b) of Figure 3.11, where $\overline{0A}$ is the TFC for the small-size plant, $\overline{0B}$ is the TFC for the medium-size plant, and $\overline{0D}$ is the TFC for the large-size plant. With varying amounts of labor employed for each plant size, the TC curve is computed along the lines $\overline{K_1K_1'}$, $\overline{K_2K_2'}$, and $\overline{K_3K_3'}$, respectively, for each plant for changing levels of output.[9] From part (a) it can be seen that isoquant Q_1 intersects $\overline{K_1K_1'}$ and $\overline{K_2K_2'}$ at E_1 and F_1, respectively, which indicates that, in the long run, Q_1 units of output can be produced by either the small- or the medium-size plant. However, F_1 is on a higher isocost curve (C_2) then E_1, which is on isocost curve C_1. Translating this information to part (b), the TC of Q_1 for the small-size plant is Q_1a, which is lower than the TC Q_1b for the medium-size plant. From parts (a) and (b), we observe that the small-size plant is also more efficient for producing output Q_2. This is evident from part (a), where isoquant Q_2 intersects $\overline{K_1K_1'}$ at E_1' and $\overline{K_2K_2'}$ at F_1', which is on a higher isocost curve than E_1'. Similarly, we see that point E_1', in part (a) corresponds to a point a' in part (b), whereas point F_1 in part (a) corresponds to point b in part (b). Since E_1' and F_1 lie on the same isocost curve (C_2), but E_1' cor-

---

[8] The student should recall that each isoquant represents the maximum level of output that can be secured through the use of various combinations of inputs (in our case, capital and labor). Therefore, each isoquant represents a different scale of operation, and the hypothesized plant sizes are consistent not only with this concept, but also with a unique amount of capital which permits the level of output to be achieved at a minimum cost.

[9] Thus, the movement to the right along $\overline{K_1K_1}'$ involves more labor and a move to a higher isocost curve. Since the amount of capital is fixed, a move to a higher isocost curve entails higher variable costs, which are represented in part (b) by the behavior of the TC curves as the output changes.

responds to a higher isoquant (output) than F_1, it follows that the small-size plant $(\overline{K_1K_1'})$ is more efficient for producing output Q_2. This can also be readily observed by comparing the TC curves TC_1 and TC_2 in part (b) for output Q_2, inasmuch as these have been directly derived from part (a). It is obvious that in part (b) both a' and b lie on the same horizontal line.

As we have explained in Chapter 2, we can only draw isocost curves and isoquants if both K and L are perfectly divisible. Although, for simplicity, we have assumed that there are only three plant sizes, an implicit assumption underlying the isocost curves and isoquants is that both K and L are divisible. With this assumption, there are, theoretically, an infinite number of parallel isocost curves between C_1 and C_2. Similarly, there are an infinite number of isoquants between Q_1 and Q_4. As we have shown in Figure 3.11, point F_1 on isoquant Q_1 is on a higher isocost curve than E_1; that is, the cost of producing Q_1 is higher in the medium-size plant than in the small-size plant. On the other hand, it can easily be seen from part (a) that for output Q_4, the small-size plant will produce a higher cost than the medium-size plant.

The short run can be characterized by a given plant that is efficient only for a limited output

In the continuous case, there exists a quantity between Q_1 and Q_4 such that the TC of the output will be the same for small- and medium-size plants; Q_3 is such a quantity. From part (a) of Figure 3.11, we can observe that the points of intersection between Q_3 and $\overline{K_1K_1'}$, on the one hand, and Q_3 and $\overline{K_2K_2'}$, on the other hand, are on the same isocost curve—C_3. Since TC_1 is computed along $\overline{K_1K_1'}$, $TC_1 = C_3$ for Q_3. Similarly, TC_2 is computed along $\overline{K_2K_2'}$, and $TC_2 = C_3$ for Q_3. Therefore, it follows that $TC_1 = TC_2$ for output Q_3 and that the small- and medium-size plants are equally efficient for producing output Q_3. This is further evidenced in part (b) of Figure 3.11 by the intersection of TC_1 and TC_2 at point G for output Q_3. A similar condition exists with respect to the cost behavior of the medium- and large-size plant for output Q_5; that is, the points of intersection of $\overline{K_2K_2'}$ and $\overline{K_3K_3'}$ with Q_5 lie on the same isocost curve—C_5—as shown in part (a). The student should attempt an explanation of why TC_2 is below TC_3 to the left of Q_5, using as a reference part (a) of Figure 3.11.

Given the above information on the cost behavior for various outputs for the specified plant sizes, suppose that we plan to start a business in this industry. If we know that sales during the lifespan of a given plant will not exceed output Q_3, what size plant should we build if we wish to maximize profits by producing the output that minimizes cost? Based on an inspection of part (b) of Figure 3.11, we shall choose the small plant because, of three plant sizes that we have hypothesized, it will result in the lowest cost. On the other hand, if we expect sales to range between Q_3 and Q_5, then the medium-size plant will provide the lowest production costs. Finally, sales greater than Q_5 would

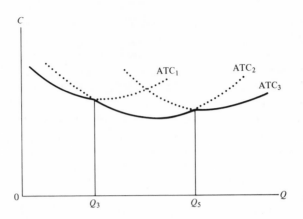

FIGURE 3.12

justify building the large-size plant. Therefore, we can see that only the segment $\widehat{AG}$ of TC_1 is relevant for long-range planning, because once the quantity exceeds Q_3, the small-size plant becomes uneconomical. Similarly, only the segment $\widehat{GH}$ of TC_2 and the segment to the right of H for TC_3 are relevant in the long run. In this special case of only three possible plant sizes, the long-run TC curve becomes $\widehat{AGH}TC_3$, which is composed of the relevant segments of TC_1, TC_2, and TC_3.

So far we have discussed the behavior of TCs in the long run. We shall now illustrate the derivation of long-run AC curves. Recall that AC is defined as the quotient of TC divided by the quantity produced. When $TC_2 > TC_1$ at a given level of output (e.g., Q_1), the corresponding ATC of the medium-size plant (e.g., ATC_2) must be greater than ATC_1. Similarly, when $TC_1 = TC_2$ at a given level of output, $ATC_1 = ATC_2$. In the same manner, the relationship between ATC_2 and ATC_3 is determined by the relationship between TC_2 and TC_3. The ATC curves that correspond to the TC curves in part (b) of Figure 3.11 are shown in Figure 3.12, in which Q_3 corresponds to the Q_3 in part (b) of Figure 3.11. We have already demonstrated in Figure 3.11 that $TC_1 = TC_2$ for output Q_3; therefore the process of derivation of ATC from TC implies that in Figure 3.12 $ATC_1 = ATC_2$ at Q_3.

The same type of relationship applies to the cost curves for output Q_5, that is, for Q_5, $TC_2 = TC_3$ in Figure 3.11, which, by the method described above, implies that $ATC_2 = ATC_3$ in Figure 3.12. Furthermore, we can observe that by connecting the relevant sections of the ATC curves in Figure 3.12, we obtain—in this special case of only three plant sizes—the long-run AC curve, which is shown in the figure by the solid portions of the individual cost curves. It should be noted that, according to the logic of our discussion, the long-run cost is the lowest possible cost for all plant sizes at each and every level of output. This again indicates the importance to our theory of the assumption that the primary goal of a firm is profit maximization, since, given this assumption, the firm will wish to keep cost at a minimum for each level of output.[10] Without this assumption, there is no logical basis for asserting that only the lowest possible cost is the relevant long-run cost to the firm. Furthermore, without this assumption, we would observe that the relevant long-run cost curve would not be well defined.

When the number of plant sizes increases, the number of short-run TC curves that we can draw in part (b) of Figure 3.11 will increase accordingly, and a shorter segment of each short-run TC curve will be relevant to the long-run TC curve. This will also be manifested in the ATC curves of Figure 3.12. In the extreme case, when the fixed cost is considered a continuous variable in the long run, there will be an infinite number of possible plant sizes, with the result that each short-run TC curve will appear as only one point on the long-run TC curve, which will hence become a smooth curve. In summary, we shall have an infinite number of short-run TC curves, each of which will be tangent to the long-run TC curve.

Smooth, long-run TC and AC curves can represent an infinite number of plant sizes, each the most efficient for a given level of output

Mathematically, the long-run TC curve is called the *envelope* of a family of short-run TC curves. One can alternatively consider that the long-run TC is closely related to the expansion path. In the case where only two inputs are involved (e.g., Figure 3.11 for the continuous case), the long-run TC can be read off from the expansion path $0\widehat{E_1E_2}E_3$ of part (a). For example, the long-run TC is C_1 for output Q_1, C_4 for Q_4, and C_6 for Q_6. However, the long-run TC for Q_2 is not C_2 in the continuous case. In fact, it is below (i.e., less than) C_2, as indicated by an implicit isocost curve (line) between C_1 and C_2 (this isocost curve, which is not shown in Figure 3.11, is tangent to isoquant Q_2 at a point on the curve $\widehat{E_1E_2}$). In the continuous case, TC_1 will have only one point on the long-run TC curve, namely, point a in part (b) of Figure 3.11, which corresponds to E_1 in part (a). Thus, each short-run TC is computed from a horizontal straight line (for a given capital input) that has only one point on the long-run TC curve, and this point is determined by the intersection of the horizontal line and the expansion path. This explains the close relationship between TC and the isoquant map, on the one hand, and the expansion

[10] The student should note, however, that minimum cost is a necessary but not sufficient condition for profit maximization. To prove the necessary condition, let us suppose that the firm's goal is not profit maximization, but rather maximum plant size. In this case, only TC_3 and ATC_3 will be the relevant long-run cost curves. However, it can be seen that if the market demand is less than Q_5, and only plant size with TC_3 and ATC_3 is employed, then profits cannot be maximized, since plant sizes with TC_1 and TC_2 would prove superior (i.e., provide lower costs). The same situation exists if either the small- or medium-size plant is selected, in which case either TC_1 or TC_2 becomes the long-run cost curve. Students are left to deduce why these cases would not be profit maximizing.

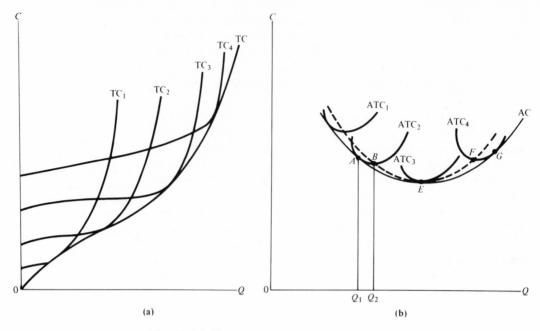

FIGURE 3.13

path and the long-run TC, as well as the short-run and long-run TC curves, on the other hand. Since the above arguments can also be applied to the AC curves, it follows that the long-run AC curve is the envelope of the family of short-run ATC curves. This can be readily observed by reference to Figure 3.13.

A smooth long-run TC curve and a smooth long-run AC curve have been drawn, respectively, in parts (a) and (b) of Figure 3.13. Theoretically, there are an infinite number of short-run TC curves (five of them are drawn), each of which is tangent to the long-run TC curve. Similarly, there are an infinite number of short-run ATC curves (again, only five of them are shown), each of which is tangent to the long-run AC curve. Note that the long-run AC curve does not contain all of the minimum points of the short-run ATC curves. In fact, there is only one point on AC which is *also* the minimum point of a short-run ATC curve—point E in part (b). This is so because the two curves have the same slope at the point of tangency. Observe that the slope of AC is zero when it is at its minimum (i.e., point E) and that ATC_3 is tangent to AC at E. Thus, the slope of ATC_3 is zero at E, which implies that point E is also the minimum of ATC_3. However, note that ATC_2 is tangent to AC at point A, where the slope of AC is negative. Hence, the slope of ATC_2 at the point of tangency is also negative. It is easily seen that the minimum of ATC_2 (i.e., point B) is to the right of and below point A, which further proves that ATC_2 is not at a minimum at the point of tangency to AC.

Length of the segments decreases with increase in the number of plant sizes, tending to points on the long-run AC curve

If B is below A, one may wonder why B is not on the long-run AC curve whereas A is. The reason is simple. Point A corresponds to output quantity Q_1 and point B to Q_2. For output quantity Q_1, Q_1A is the lowest AC obtainable for all possible plant sizes. On the other hand, for output quantity Q_2, there exists another plant size that will result in a lower AC than Q_2B.[11]

It has been said that economists at first intuitively thought that the long-run AC curve should be the locus of the minimum points of the family of short-run ATC curves [e.g., $\widehat{BEF}$ in part (b) of Figure 3.13]. However, an engineering graduate student working for an economist pointed out that the envelope curve is below the locus of all the minimum points except one, which in our case is point E—the minimum point of the envelope curve. Economists have become convinced that it is the envelope curve rather than the locus of the minimum points of the family of short-run ATC curves which should be considered the long run AC. Thus, we should realize that although intuition often helps us to understand reality, it can also mislead us. Scientific methods are more reliable.

Long-run AC is made up of segments of short-run ATC curves, representing efficient plant size for a given level of output

3.3.2 Long-Run and Short-Run MC Curves

Although the long-run TC curve is the envelope of the family of short-run TC curves, and the long-run AC curve is the envelope of the family of short-run ATC curves, the long-run MC curve is not the envelope of the short-run MC curves. Instead, the short-run MC curves always intersect the long-run MC curve at output quantities for which the short-run ATC curves are tangent to the long-run AC curve. To the left of this intersection, any given short-run MC curve is below the long-run MC curve, whereas to the right of the intersection, it lies above the long-run MC curve. This fact can be conveniently explained using Figure 3.14.

In part (a) of Figure 3.14, TC_1 is tangent to TC at output level Q_1. Hence, in part (b), the corresponding ATC curve is tangent to AC at Q_1. By definition, when two curves are tangent at a point, they have the same slope. As we have noted previously, the slope of a TC curve is the corresponding MC at the respective level of output. Considering these two statements together, logic

---

[11] Students should observe that we are not speaking of increasing returns to scale, even though the large-size plant results in lower ACs. In the case of increasing returns to scale, we speak of disproportionate increases in output and decreases in cost that arise as we increase the scale of operations, the same input ratios being applicable irrespective of scale. In other words, the ratios of land, labor, and capital to each other would be the same whatever the scale of operations. In the case under discussion, we have increasing plant sizes, but the labor/capital ratio does not remain the same. In short, the student should recognize that whereas increasing returns to scale will result in decreasing long-run AC, decreasing long-run AC may not imply increasing returns to scale.

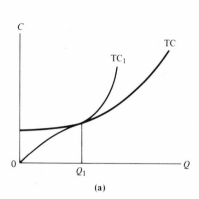

(a)

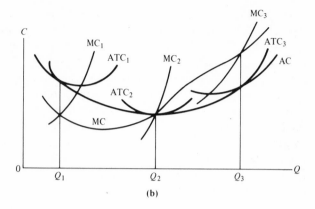

(b)

FIGURE 3.14

tells us that the short-run marginal cost MC_1 is equal to the long-run marginal cost MC at Q_1 [see part (b)]. From part (a), we also observe that TC is below TC_1 to the left of Q_1, where both the long-run and the short-run TC curves are rising; however, at Q_1 TC catches up to TC_1 from below. Therefore, TC must be rising at a faster rate than TC_1. Since the rate of increase of TC is the long-run MC, the rate of increase of TC_1 is the short-run MC, and to the left of Q_1 TC is rising faster than TC_1, it follows that [see part (b)] MC must be above MC_1 to the left of Q_1. To the right of Q_1, we see that TC rises more slowly than TC_1. This implies that MC is below MC_1 to the right of Q_1, as shown in part (b). By the same reasoning, MC intersects MC_2 (MC_3) at Q_2 (Q_3), where ATC_2 (ATC_3) is tangent to AC, MC is above MC_2 (MC_3), to the left of Q_2 (Q_3), and MC is below MC_2 (MC_3) to the right of Q_2 (Q_3). Finally, it should be noted that MC intersects MC_1 at a point below both AC and ATC_1, MC intersects MC_2 on both AC and ATC_2, and MC intersects MC_3 above both AC and ATC_3. These are three typical cases. In general, the long-run MC curve always intersects the short-run MC curves below both the long-run AC curve and the short-run ATC curves to the left of the minimum of AC, whereas the point of intersection is above both the long-run AC curve and the short-run ATC curves to the right of the minimum of AC. At the minimum of AC, the long-run MC, the short-run MC, the long-run AC, and the short-run ATC are all equal. This condition will become especially relevant when we discuss the long-run equilibrium of a competitive firm.

As we have already noted in our discussion of short-run cost behavior, MC is less than AC when AC decreases, equal to AC at the minimum of AC, and greater than AC when AC increases. This condition also applies to the long-run relationship between AC and MC. Students may wish to refresh their memories by referring back to Figures 3.6 and 3.7 as well as the corresponding explanations of the AC and MC relationships. This completes our explanation of the relationship between long-run and short-run costs.

3.3.3 The Shapes of Long-Run Cost Curves in Theory and in Reality

Traditionally, economists consider the smooth U-shaped curves in part (b) of Figure 3.14 as typical for both long-run AC and long-run MC curves. There are good reasons for this, as will become clear when we discuss the long-run equilibrium of price takers or the firm in a competitive market. However, modern microeconomic theory recognizes that the smooth U-shaped AC and MC curves are far from typical. Rather, the L-shaped (flat-bottom) long-run AC curves may be closer to reality. Although the latter may not be consistent with the concept and underlying assumptions of the competitive market, they are consistent with the theory of imperfect competition and the practice of price makers. Since price makers and imperfect markets are more common phenomena, it is important that we adequately discuss the shapes of the cost curves that exist in the real world. There are good reasons (which will be discussed briefly in the Section 3.3.4) to believe that the long-run AC and MC curves are in many cases similar to those that we shall present in Figure 3.17.

3.3.4 The Shapes of Long-Run Cost Curves and Returns to Scale

Figures 3.15–3.17 illustrate some of the long-run and short-run cost curves that conform to real-world production economics. Each figure represents a different condition normally found in business operations.

FIGURE 3.15 The case of increasing and constant returns to scale.

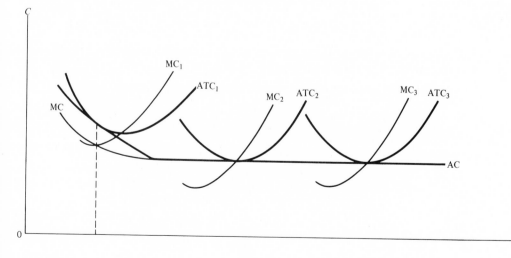

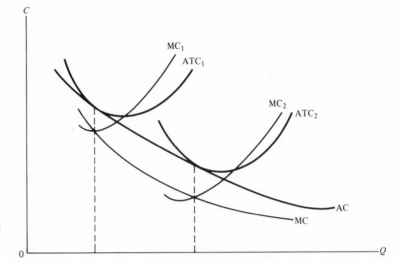

FIGURE 3.16
The case of large-scale industry and increasing returns to scale or natural monopoly.

It should be noted that a horizontal straight-line long-run AC curve is often mentioned in the literature as a possibility. In that case, the long-run AC and MC curves will be identical (see the flat segments of these curves in both Figures 3.15 and 3.17).

Increasing, constant, and decreasing returns to scale, shown in the shape of the long-run AC curve, will prevail over certain stages of production

Although the shapes of the long-run AC and MC curves in Figure 3.14 are similar to the shapes of the short-run AVC and MC curves in Figure 3.7, respectively, the reasons for this similarity differ. As we have explained in Section 3.2.5, the rising short-run MC curve is due to diminishing returns or the operation of the law of variable proportions. On the other hand, the shape of the long-run AC curve is associated with the phenomenon of returns to scale. With increasing returns to scale, the long-run

FIGURE 3.17
A case found in small- and medium-size businesses.

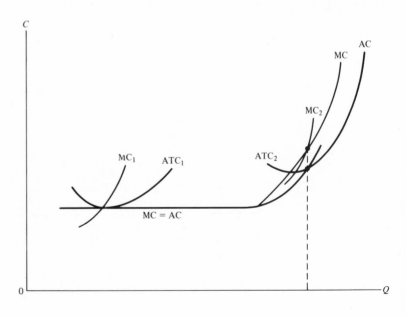

AC decreases as output increases because, by doubling all inputs, output is more than doubled and, under competition, input prices remain constant. This is the case depicted by the long-run AC curve in Figure 3.16. The flat portions of the long-run AC and MC curves in Figures 3.15 and 3.17 depict constant returns to scale, where the long-run AC is constant over the relevant output range. With decreasing returns to scale, the long-run AC increases as output rises, as reflected in Figure 3.17 by the rising portions of the long-run AC and MC curves.

The returns to scale is determined by technology, which is taken as given by economists. It is hard to tell in advance which type of returns to scale is, in general, most likely to apply. In any given industry, it is more likely that constant returns to scale will prevail during certain stages of production, whereas increasing or decreasing returns to scale will prevail during other stages. For different industries, the particular stages will probably be different. For this reason, economists must consider all the possibilities and analyze the implications of each. Because all three types of returns to scale are taken into consideration in part (b) of Figure 3.14, it is probably one of the reasons why those AC and MC curve shapes are normally favored by many economists. However, when evidence shows that certain situations are more likely than others, this should be clearly pointed out so that theory will accord more closely with reality. Section 3.3.3 was included to serve this purpose.

3.4 CONSTANT AVC AND LONG-RUN COST CURVES

Traditionally, the long-run TC curve is considered the envelope of the family of short-run TC curves, the long-run AC curve the envelope of the family of short-run ATC curves, and the corresponding long-run MC curve, although not the envelope of the short-run MC curves, does behave nicely in that it is a smooth U-shaped curve similar to the long-run AC curve, as we have shown above. These long-run cost curves are implicitly based on the assumption of well-behaved, smooth, U-shaped short-run ATC and MC curves. However, as we have mentioned earlier, empirical studies indicate that the short-run AVC and, consequently, the MC are constant within the relevant range. We shall show how this real condition will dictate the shape of long-run cost curves.

Constant AVC in the short run implies a straight-line short-run TC curve starting from the TFC, as shown in Figure 3.18. For the sake of simplicity, we use plant size to represent the fixed cost, and only three plant sizes (1, 2, and 3, where 3 is the largest) are considered feasible. It is immediately obvious that the multiple-plant-size–constant-AVC model is meaningful only if the larger plant results in a lower AVC. Otherwise, the larger plants

The multiple-plant-size–constant-AVC model for long-range planning is meaningful only if the larger plant results in a lower AC. Larger plants cost more (raising fixed cost), so declining AC requires constant AVC

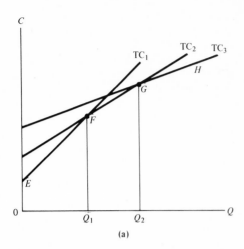

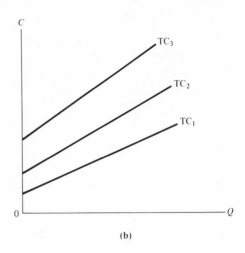

(a)   (b)

FIGURE 3.18

would not be economically feasible, as shown in part (b) of Figure 3.18. In the case where the large plant is not economically feasible or justified because it does not lower the ATC of production, we would have a long-run TC that would be identical to the short-run TC, and, most importantly, there would be no long-run choice problem; this is obviously not a very interesting case. The case shown in part (a) of Figure 3.18 indicates that the long-run TC is given by curve $\widehat{EFGH}$, which is composed of straight-line segments $\overline{EF}$, $\overline{FG}$, and $\overline{GH}$. Each plant size will result in the lowest TC only within a certain range of outputs. Thus, the optimal long-run choice will be plant size 1 if sales will not exceed $\overline{0Q_1}$. However, if sales will range between $\overline{0Q_1}$ and $\overline{0Q_2}$, then the optimal long-run choice will be plant size 2. Alternatively, if sales will exceed $\overline{0Q_2}$, then the optimal long-run choice will be plant size 3. Note that by the assumption of perfect information or perfect knowledge, the decision maker is assumed to be certain of the future market demand. This is often overlooked by many textbooks and thus represents a possible source of confusion.

The AC and MC curves implied in part (a) of Figure 3.18 are plotted in Figure 3.19. With AVC_1 constant, $AVC_1 = MC_1$.[12] Similarly, we also have $AVC_2 = MC_2$ and $AVC_3 = MC_3$ when AVC_2 and AVC_3, respectively, are constant.

From Figure 3.19 we see that the short-run ATC curve corresponding to plant size 1 is asymptotically decreasing, the vertical axis and AVC_1 being the asymptotes. This follows, since the vertical distance between ATC_1 and AVC_1 represents AFC, which

---

[12] We have already noted that a straight-line TC curve starting from TFC implies a constant AVC. We demonstrated earlier (Section 3.2.4) that such a condition also means that $AVC = MC$.

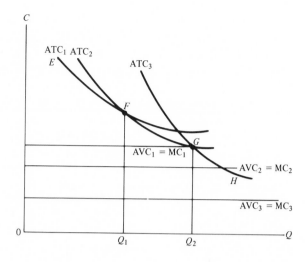

FIGURE 3.19

is an ever-decreasing function of output.[13] The relationships between ATC_2 and AVC_2, on the one hand, and between ATC_3 and AVC_3, on the other hand, are similarly determined. It is obvious that ATC_1 is below ATC_2 within the range of $\overline{0Q}_1$ and above ATC_2 to the right of Q_1. This implies that ATC_1 and ATC_2 intersect at Q_1. Similarly, ATC_2 and ATC_3 intersect at Q_2, as indicated in the graph. For reasons similar to those explained above, the long-run AC curve is $\overbrace{EFGH}$ in Figure 3.19. Note that whereas the long-run TC curve is composed of straight-line segments (see Figure 3.18), the long-run AC curve is not. This is true because, although TVC increases at a constant rate, we have a fixed cost that determines the behavior of the ATC curve. We have already stated that when TVC increases at a constant rate, AVC will be constant and AVC = MC. Therefore, the short-run MC curves are horizontal straight lines. Since they start from different points on the vertical axis and are parallel, they can never intersect. The long-run MC within the range of output $\overline{0Q}_1$ is MC_1, within $\overline{Q_1Q_2}$ it is MC_2, and to the right of Q_2 it is MC_3. It follows that the long-run MC curve, which is composed of horizontal straight-line segments, is discontinuous in the case of a constant short-run AVC.

One important implication of the constant-AVC case with respect to economic theory is that the long-run AC can only be decreasing, never increasing or even constant. This is implied by Figure 3.18. Since part (b) implies only one optimal plant size, the long-run AC curve is identical to one of the short-run asymptotically decreasing ATC curves (in our case, ATC_1) in Figure 3.19. If the short-run TC curves behave like the ones shown in

---

[13] The student is reminded that AVC is constant for each plant size, as has been demonstrated and explained with respect to Figure 3.18, based on which Figure 3.19 has been drawn.

part (a) of Figure 3.18, then the general shape of the corresponding long-run AC curve will be similar to $\widehat{EFGH}$ (see Figure 3.19), that is, a decreasing function of Q. The number of possible plant sizes does not change the general shape of the decreasing long-run AC curve. It will be shown in Chapter 6 that the results deduced here on the basis of the theory of perfect competition will break down under conditions of decreasing long-run AC. The implication with respect to economic theory is that constant AVC is not consistent with perfect competition. However, it is consistent with imperfect market models. In view of the fact that imperfect competition overwhelmingly dominates the real world, the constant-AVC case may be more important than many economists like to believe.

At this time, we state without proof that the long-run TC and AC curves may not be envelopes of the families of the short-run TC and ATC curves, respectively, because the envelope curve of a family of straight-line short-run TC curves may not exist. Mathematically, the straight-line short-run functions do not satisfy the sufficient conditions for the existence of an envelope unless AVC is not a constant in the long run. For a detailed discussion of this point, the student should refer to the appendix at the end of this chapter.

Decreasing long-run AC is unlikely because the constant part of AVC may be greater for a large plant

The above model (i.e., decreasing long-run AC) is based on the assumption that AVC is constant for a given plant size for any quantity of output without an upper limit. In reality, AVC is constant only within a certain output range that is usually limited by plant capacity, which, in turn, is determined by the size of the plant. For a given plant size, AVC is constant up to capacity and increases beyond that. Furthermore, for a given plant size, the constant part of AVC may be either equal to, greater than, or less than that for a larger size plant. According to this criterion, there are three possible cases: (1) AVC is the same for different plant sizes (within their corresponding capacities), (2) AVC is lower for larger plant sizes, and (3) AVC is higher for larger plant sizes. We shall examine the possible shapes of the long-run AC and MC curves for these different cases.

For the sake of simplicity, we again assume that there are only three plant sizes (1, 2, and 3). For case 1, consider part (a) of Figure 3.20, which shows the TC curves. Plant sizes 1, 2, and 3 have capacities of Q_1', Q_2', and Q_3', respectively. The TC curves TC_1, TC_2, and TC_3 are parallel up to their respective capacities. For each plant size, TC increases at a constant rate up to capacity and at a higher rate, beyond it. The long-run TC is $\widehat{ABEFGH}TC_3$. The corresponding AC and MC curves are plotted in part (b), where we see that AVC_1, AVC_2, AVC_3, MC_1, MC_2, and MC_3 coincide up to Q_1', simply being labeled AVC. Curve AVC_1 rises to the right of Q_1', whereas AVC_2 and AVC_3 remain horizontal. Curve ATC_1 declines continuously up to its minimum at Q_1' and then rises. Curve MC_1 is identical to AVC_1 (or, simply, AVC) up

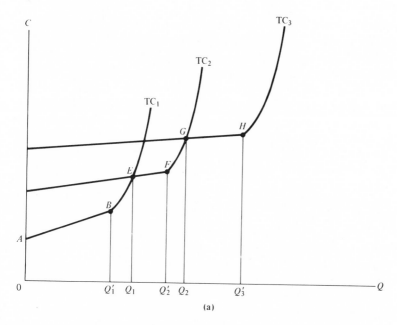

(a)

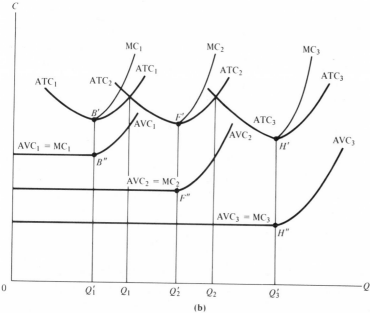

(b)

FIGURE 3.20

to Q_1', at which point it is discontinuous, that is, it jumps from B'' to B' at Q_1'. Furthermore, MC_1 is equal to both AVC_1 and ATC_1 at the minima of the latter, even though the minimum of AVC_1 is not unique. Similarly, AVC_2 is constant up to Q_2' and rises thereafter; ATC_2 declines continuously, reaches its minimum at Q_2', and then increases; and MC_2 is constant up to Q_2', jumps from F'' to F' at Q_2', and is equal to both AVC_2 and ATC_2 at the minima of the latter, even though the minimum of AVC_2

is not unique. Corresponding behavior is observable for AVC_3, ATC_3, and MC_3, respectively. (For a more detailed discussion of these relationships, the student should refer to Section 3.2.4 and Figure 3.10.) In this special case, the long-run AC is $ATC_1B'E'F'G'H'ATC_3$ and the long-run MC is AVC between the origin and Q_1', the part of MC_1 above B' between Q_1' and Q_1, AVC again between Q_1 and Q_2', the part of MC_2 above F' between Q_2' and Q_2, AVC again between Q_2 and Q_3', and the part of MC_3 above H' beyond Q_3'. Both the long-run AC and the long-run MC can increase, then decrease, then increase again, then decrease again, and so forth. In the discrete case, the MC curve is also discontinuous. The number of discontinuities on the long-run MC curve is equal to the number of plant sizes.

In part (b) of Figure 3.20, it appears that point F' can be either below or above both point B' and point H', since if we extend the ray from the origin to point B, point F in part (a) can be either below or above it; similarly, point F can be either below or above the ray $\overline{OH}$. This is significant because if F' is below both B' and H', then the long-run AC curve may have approximately the traditional smooth U-shape in the special case of continuous plant size. On the other hand, if F' is always above B' and, in turn, H' is above F', then the long-run AC curve can only have a positive slope. However, if F' is always below B' and, in turn, H' is below F', then the long-run AC curve can only have a negative slope. These latter two cases have important implications with respect to the analysis of the market which we shall discuss in Part III. Since F' can, theoretically, be either above or below both B' and H', we can conclude that case 1 of the constant-AVC model is consistent with the traditional model of a smooth, U-shaped long-run AC curve and that an optimal firm size can exist in the long-run.

Figure 3.21 depicts case 2 of the constant-AVC model. The capacities for plant sizes 1, 2, and 3 are again Q_1', Q_2', and Q_3', respectively. The slope of the straight-line part of TC_2 is less than that of the straight-line part of TC_1, within their respective capacities; in turn, the slope of the straight-line part of TC_3 is less than that of the straight-line part of TC_2. This implies that AVC_1 is parallel to and above AVC_2 between the origin and Q_1', whereas AVC_2 is parallel to and above AVC_3 between the origin and Q_2'. In part (a), TC_1 intersects TC_2 at Q_1, which implies that in part (b) ATC_1 intersects ATC_2 at Q_1. Similarly, since in part (a) TC_2 intersects TC_3 at Q_2, in part (b) ATC_2 intersects ATC_3 at Q_2. Again, point F' can be either below or above both point B' and point H'. Theoretically, this is again consistent with the traditional model of a smooth, U-shaped long-run AC curve in the special case of continuous plant sizes. This is probably the most realistic case. With a higher TFC (that is, more sophisticated machinery), labor input per unit of output, and so on, or AVC

For an infinite number of plant sizes, the constant-AVC model is consistent with that of a smooth, U-shaped, long-run AC curve

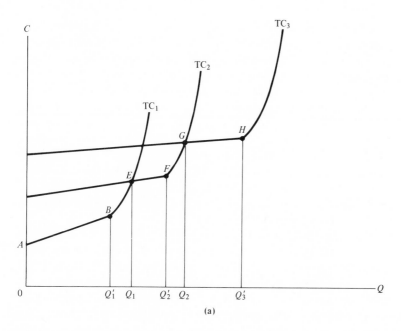

(a)

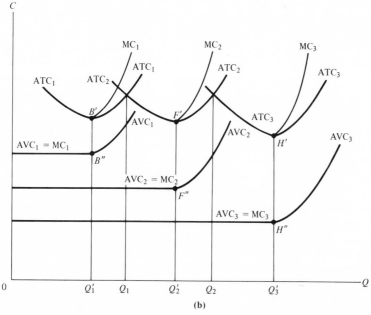

(b)

FIGURE 3.21

should be lower. Otherwise, there is, for example, no reason to use the more sophisticated machinery.

It can easily be demonstrated by a similar graphical method that case 3 of the constant-AVC model is also consistent with the traditional model of a smooth, U-shaped, long-run AC curve in the special case of continuous plant sizes. Thus, the transition from the traditional smooth, U-shaped AVC and MC curves to the constant-AVC–short-run MC model does not require any revision of the theoretical framework so far as long-run analysis is concerned. The addition of the constant-AVC model to the traditional economic short-run analysis only has the effect of enriching it.

Although, as we have explained before, the envelope curves for the families of the short-run TC and AC curves for the constant-AVC model indicated by Figures 3.18 and 3.19 may not exist, the envelope curve for a family of TC curves for constant AVC within the limited range indicated by parts (a) of Figures 3.20 and 3.21 may exist in the special case where fixed cost is a continuous variable. This condition will exist even though the short-run TC curves have kinks at the capacity levels of output for the different size plants. It can easily be seen that each short-run TC curve will have only one point on the long-run TC curve—the point where the kink on the short-run TC curve occurs. Similarly, the envelope of the family of the corresponding short-run ATC curves may also exist, and each short-run ATC curve will have only one point on the long-run AC curve, this point again being where the kink on the short-run ATC curve occurs. This theoretical consistency between the limited-range constant-AVC model and the traditional smooth, U-shaped AVC–short-run MC model may have some significance in pure theory. For practical purposes, however, it is the discrete case that is usually more meaningful.

SUMMARY

In this chapter we have defined and described the relevance of various concepts of cost in the analysis of production. We first explained the difference between those concepts of cost having a general application to the evaluation of production, that is, those that take on meaning in the context of society's valuation of resource use. Thus, the distinctions between private and social costs, explicit and implicit costs, cost in business and cost in economics, and short-run and long-run costs were noted and explained. We then proceeded to define the concepts that are more specifically used in directly analyzing the production of the firm. In this regard, the concepts of total fixed (TFC), total variable (TVC), total (TC), average fixed (AFC), average variable (AVC), and marginal (MC) costs were not only defined, but their relationships to each other were described and illustrated using both numerical and graphical examples.

Inasmuch as the shapes of the various average (ATC, AVC, and AFC) and the marginal (MC) cost curves are closely related to the shapes of the average product (AP) and marginal product (MP) curves, we differentiated between the assumptions that are implicit in the traditional textbook versions of the average and marginal cost curves and those of the revised constant AVC model. We noted that in the traditional textbook version the AP and MP curves are treated as smooth, bell-shaped curves, which implies smooth, U-shaped AVC and MC curves, whereas in the case of the revised constant AVC model the AP and MP are considered constant over the relevant range, thus implying constant AVC and MC curves. It was further noted that many empirical studies indicate that AP and MP are constant up to plant capacity and hence provide support to the revised constant-AVC model. In terms of graphical analysis, this simply means that the ATC curve will now be asymptotically decreasing, the vertical axis and the constant-AVC line being the asymptotes.

Having established the relationship of AP to AVC and of MP to MC, we showed that the phenomenon of rising AVC and MC reflects the condition of diminishing returns and the law of variable proportions in production. Numerical and graphical examples were used to clarify the students' understanding of this relationship and to gain greater insight into the behavior of cost curves under different conditions.

We concluded our discussion on cost with a rigorous explanation of the distinction between the short run and long run in the economics of production and the relationship between short-run and long-run cost curves. It was shown that given the perfect divisibility of the fixed inputs, the long-run AC curve becomes a lower envelope curve of a family of short-run ATC curves because, in the long run, all inputs and costs are variable (fixed costs in the long run are zero). However, we emphasized that students should not regard the long-run AC as the locus of minimum points on the short-run ATC curves or the long-run MC curve as the envelope of the short-run MC curves. Instead, for the traditionally used model of U-shaped AC and MC curves, there is only one point where the long-run AC is equal to the minimum short-run ATC and the long-run MC to the short-run MC, this point being the minimum of the long-run AC. Finally we showed that, rather than being inconsistent with perfect competition, the revised constant-AVC model, in which AVC is constant within plant capacity but rising beyond plant capacity, is consistent with that traditional model with U-shaped long-run AC curves. The revised constant-AVC model therefore gives an added measure of reality to our theory without any loss in theoretical elegance.

EXERCISES AND QUESTIONS FOR CHAPTER 3 ON THE THEORY OF COST

1. In your own words, explain why the MC curve always intersects an AC curve at the minimum of the latter.

2. What do we mean by social cost and private cost? What assumptions are necessary so that the two concepts will be identical? Explain.

3. Explain the relationship between the cost function of a commodity and the corresponding expansion path. Define expansion path.

4. Using the graphical method, show *why* the long-run TC curve of a firm is the envelope of the family of the short-run TC curves. A brief explanation should accompany your graphs.

5. Use the graphical method and common sense to explain why a short-run TC curve is always above the long-run TC curve except at one point.

6. What is the relationship between the long-run and short-run TC and MC curves? Explain.

7. An output is produced by a "constant-returns-to-scale" technology that consists of five processes having the properties shown in Table E3.1.

TABLE E3.1

| | Input required | | |
| | Capital | Labor | Output per period |
Process	(machine-hours)	(person-hours)	(tons)
P_1	7.5	1.0	10
P_2	5.0	2.0	10
P_3	3.75^a	3.0	10
P_4	2.5	5.0	10
P_5	0.0	12.0	10

^{a} Two-digit significance.

Denoting unit input prices by r (dollars per machine-hour) and w (dollars per person-hour), calculate the costs of producing 10 tons of output by each process for each of the following sets of input prices:

i. $r = 2$ $w = 4$
ii. $r = 2$ $w = 2$
iii. $r = 4$ $w = 2$

Which process will be used in each of the cases i, ii, and iii? Why? What is the AC of production in each of the cases i, ii, and iii?

8. Empirical studies indicate that the short-run AVC of a firm in most (if not all) cases is constant. Thus, MC is also constant, and the AVC and MC curves are identical. What is the shape of the long-run AC curve that is implied by this phenomenon? Is this phenomenon consistent with the traditional smooth, U-shaped long-run AC curve? Explain.

9. Constant AVC can reasonably prevail only within the designated levels of plant capacity, beyond which AVC and MC curves will rise. With this modification, what is the implied shape of the long-run AC curve? In particular, could the long-run AC curve be a smooth, U-shaped curve? Explain.

A MATHEMATICAL NOTE ON THE THEORY OF COST

In economics, the term cost function is used to express cost as a function of output. This is in contrast to the term cost equation, which is used to express cost as a function of the inputs and their prices [e.g., Equation (2.6) for the two-input case]. The cost equation is a straightforward linear function of the inputs and their prices. However, the cost function is derived from the optimal conditions in production, that is, maximum output for a given cost or minimum cost for a given output, and thus its properties are determined by the characteristics of the associated production function. In general, the optimal conditions in production yield $n - 1$ independent equations for n variable inputs, as well as the production function and cost equation. Therefore, we have a total of $n + 1$ equations in $n + 2$ variables, that is, n inputs, output, and cost. Note that input prices are considered as parameters, not variables, as a result of the assumption of competitive input markets. If we eliminate the n inputs in the $n + 2$ independent equations and solve for the cost C in terms of the quantity of output Q, the parameters of the production function, and the input prices, we obtain the cost function. It follows that the properties of the cost function essentially depend on the properties of the associated production function, since the cost equation is always linear. This implies that the cost computed from the cost function is the minimum for each and every quantity of output.

Short-run and long-run cost functions are distinguished by the presence and absence, respectively, of fixed cost in the same sense as in the production function. Thus, in the short run we make the distinction between fixed and variable costs, whereas in the long run all costs are variable.

We shall now demonstrate the mathematical procedures in the

derivation of both the short-run and the long-run cost functions. With respect to the short-run cost function, we shall first consider the simple case involving two variable inputs and one fixed input and then the general case involving n variable inputs and m fixed inputs. We shall also consider the simple and general cases for the long-run cost function. A definite cost function can be derived only if the associated production function is precisely given. Thus, in order to give the student some feeling for how an actual cost function can be derived from a given production function, we shall use the well-known Cobb–Douglas production function to derive both a short-run and a long-run cost function in the simple case.

A3.1 THE DERIVATION OF SHORT-RUN AND LONG-RUN COST FUNCTIONS

A3.1.1 The Simple Case of Two Variable Inputs and One Fixed Input

Making use of the results of the appendix to Chapters 1 and 2, we rewrite the production function, cost equation, and expansion path equation [expressions (A1-2.56), (A1-2.57), and (A1-2.61), respectively] as follows:

$$Q = f(x_0, x_1, x_2)$$

$$C = C_0 + r_1 x_1 + r_2 x_2$$

$$g(x_1, x_2) = 0$$

where C_0 is the TFC. If x_0 denotes the fixed input and r_0 the price of x_0, then $C_0 = r_0 x_0$, a constant. We have three equations in four variables: Q, C, x_1, and x_2. (Note that in this context x_0, C_0, r_1, and r_2 are considered constants.) Assume that, by eliminating x_1 and x_2, this system of equations can be reduced to a single expression in which cost is expressed as an explicit function of the quantity of output (plus the fixed cost), the input prices serving as parameters. The short-run total cost function in the two-variable-input case is as follows:

$$C = C_0 + V(Q) \tag{A3.1}$$

where C_0 is the TFC (a constant) and $V(Q)$ is the TVC, which is a function of only the quantity of output, since the input prices that serve as parameters are omitted. Expression (A3.1) corresponds to expression (3.2).

We have already observed that the long-run cost function is the envelope of the family of short-run cost functions and that both the fixed input and the output are considered as variables. In principle, both TFC and TVC are functions of the fixed input

x_0 [see (A3.14)]; thus, (A3.1) can be written in implicit form as follows:

$$G(C, Q, X_0) = C - C_0(X_0) - V(X_0, Q) = 0 \qquad \text{(A3.2)}$$

It is assumed that the first- and second-order partial derivatives of G exist; these are denoted by

$$G_0(C, Q, X_0) = \partial G(C, Q, X_0)/\partial X_0$$

$$G_1(C, Q, X_0) = \partial G(C, Q, X_0)/\partial C$$

$$G_2(C, Q, X_0) = \partial G(C, Q, X_0)/\partial Q$$

$$G_{00}(C, Q, X_0) = \partial^2 G(C, Q, X_0)/\partial X_0^2$$

$$G_{01}(C, Q, X_0) = \partial^2 G(C, Q, X_0)/\partial C \partial X_0$$

$$G_{02}(C, Q, X_0) = \partial^2 G(C, Q, X_0)/\partial Q \partial X_0$$

$$G_{11}(C, Q, X_0) = \partial^2 G(C, Q, X_0)/\partial C^2$$

$$G_{12}(C, Q, X_0) = \partial^2 G(C, Q, X_0)/\partial Q \partial C$$

$$G_{22}(C, Q, X_0) = \partial^2 G(C, Q, X_0)/\partial Q^2$$

We set the partial derivative of (A3.2) with respect to X_0 equal to zero:

$$G_0(C, Q, X_0) = 0 \qquad \text{(A3.3)}$$

and assume that

$$G_{00}(C, Q, X_0) \neq 0$$

$$G_1(C, Q, X_0)G_{20}(C, Q, X_0) \qquad \text{(A3.4)}$$
$$- G_2(C, Q, X_0)G_{10}(C, Q, X_0) \neq 0$$

The first assumption of (A3.4) makes it possible to express X_0 as a function of C and Q in (A3.3). Thus, we have

$$X_0 = g(C, Q) \qquad \text{(A3.5)}$$

Substituting (A3.5) into (A3.2), we obtain the envelope equation:

$$G(C, Q, g(C, Q)) = 0 \qquad \text{(A3.6)}$$

Hence, the fixed input has been eliminated, and the long-run TC is a function of output only.

It should be noted that a linear short-run TC function, such as

$$C = F + vQ \qquad \text{(A3.1')}$$

where F and v are constants, may not satisfy conditions (A3.4) because the second-order direct and cross partial derivatives of the linear cost function are all equal to zero. As a result, the envelope of a family of linear short-run TC functions may not exist. However, if the constants F and v are functions of the fixed input [see (A3.14)], an envelope of the family of linear short-run TC functions may exist provided that certain conditions are satisfied.

Derivation of a Short-Run Cost Function from the Cobb–Douglas Production Function

The Cobb–Douglas production function with three inputs (e.g., labor L, capital K, and plant size S, a fixed input) can be written

$$Q = AL^{\alpha}K^{\beta}S^{\gamma} \qquad (A3.7)$$

Since A and γ are constant, and S is also constant in the short run, we may write $B = AS^{\gamma}$. We then have

$$Q = BL^{\alpha}K^{\beta} \qquad (A3.8)$$

which is identical to (A1-2.5) except for the different notation in the constant.

If we denote the prices of L, K, and S by w, r, and v, respectively, and take $C_0 = vS$, we obtain the cost equation

$$C = C_0 + wL + rK \qquad (A3.9)$$

which is identical to (A1-2.26).

The corresponding expansion path (i.e., the implicit function g) introduced in Section A3.1.1 is represented by expression (A1-2.31), which is reproduced here as

$$\beta wL - \alpha rK = 0 \qquad (A3.10)$$

Equation (3.9) can also be written in the form

$$wL + rK = C - C_0 \qquad (A3.9')$$

Using Cramer's rule and solving for L and K in terms of α, β, C, w, and r, from (A3.10) and (A3.9) we obtain

$$L = \alpha(C - C_0)/(\alpha + \beta)w \qquad (A3.11)$$

$$K = \beta(C - C_0)/(\alpha + \beta)r \qquad (A3.12)$$

Substituting (A3.11) and (A3.12) into (A3.8), after some algebraic manipulation we obtain the short-run cost function:

$$C = C_0 + (\alpha + \beta)(B\alpha^{\alpha}\beta^{\beta})^{-1/(\alpha+\beta)}(w^{\alpha}r^{\beta})^{1/(\alpha+\beta)}Q^{1/(\alpha+\beta)} \qquad (A3.13)$$

Comparing (A3.13) and (A3.1), we see that C_0 is the TFC in both cases; however, the second term on the right side of (A3.13), which is the TVC and thus corresponds to $V(Q)$ in (A3.1), involves not only Q, but also the production-function parameters B, α, and β as well as the input prices w and r (which, as we mentioned above, also serve as parameters).

By definition, $B = AS^{\gamma}$ and $C_0 = vS$. Substituting these values into (A3.13), the short-run cost function that is derived from the

Cobb–Douglas production with the one fixed input S and the two variable inputs L and K is

$$C = vS + (\alpha + \beta)(AS^\gamma\alpha^\alpha\beta^\beta)^{-1/(\alpha+\beta)}(w^\alpha r^\beta)^{1/(\alpha+\beta)}Q^{1/(\alpha+\beta)}$$

(A3.14)

Various derivations of the short-run TC function from the Cobb–Douglas production function for the two-input case have appeared in many microeconomics textbooks. In particular, for the special case $\alpha + \beta = 1$, the student can refer to page 85 of Henderson and Quandt (1971). However, a mistake in the derivation of the short-run TC function has occasionally occurred. One example of this can be found in Koutsoyiannis (1975, p. 99). That particular expression is correct *only* in the special case $\alpha + \beta = 1$, the problem being that, in the general case, he made use of the expression (in our notation)

$$(\alpha/\beta)^{\beta/(\alpha+\beta)} + (\beta/\alpha)^{\alpha/(\alpha+\beta)} = [(\alpha/\beta)^\beta + (\beta/\alpha)^\alpha]^{1/(\alpha+\beta)}$$

In fact, the above equality holds only in the special case $\alpha + \beta = 1$, that is, it does not hold in the general case $\alpha + \beta \neq 1$. Consequently, his expression is incorrect.

Derivation of a Long-Run Cost Function from the Cobb–Douglas Production Function

For the three-input case in the short run, one input (plant size) is considered fixed and two inputs (labor and capital) are considered variable. The short-run TC function derived from the Cobb–Douglas production function is given by (A3.14), where S (plant size) is constant. The first term on the right side of (A3.14) is the TFC, whereas the second term is the TVC. It is interesting to note that both TFC *and* TVC are functions of the plant size S. The fact that TVC is also dependent on S is often overlooked. In general, the short-run TC function is written in the form (A3.1), which does not exclude the possibility that the fixed input will enter TVC as a parameter. However, some economists nevertheless infer that only TFC depends on the fixed input. The cost function (A3.14) shows that both TFC and TVC are dependent on the fixed input. Fortunately, this fact has been realized by some economists [see, e.g., page 76 of Henderson and Quandt (1971)].

As mentioned before, the long-run TC function is the envelope of the family of short-run TC functions, that is, it touches each and intersects none. The mathematical procedure for the derivation of the envelope equation is defined in general terms by (A3.2)–(A3.6). In the special case ($\alpha + \beta = 1$), the cost function (A3.14) can be written in implicit form as

$$G(C, S, Q) = C - vS - (\alpha + \beta)(AS^\gamma\alpha^\alpha\beta^\beta)^{-1/(\alpha+\beta)}$$
$$\times (w^\alpha r^\beta)^{1/(\alpha+\beta)}Q^{1/(\alpha+\beta)} = 0$$

(A3.15)

Setting the partial derivative with respect to S equal to zero, we obtain

$$-v + \gamma(A\alpha^\alpha\beta^\beta)^{-1/(\alpha+\beta)}(w^\alpha r^\beta)^{1/(\alpha+\beta)}S^{-(\alpha+\beta+\gamma)/(\alpha+\beta)}Q^{1/(\alpha+\beta)} = 0$$

(A3.16)

which corresponds to (A3.3). It can be seen that the first condition in (A3.4) is satisfied, and we can solve (A3.16) for S:

$$S = (A\alpha^\alpha\beta^\beta)^{-1/(\alpha+\beta+\gamma)}(w^\alpha r^\beta)^{1/(\alpha+\beta+\gamma)}Q^{1/(\alpha+\beta+\gamma)}(\gamma/v)^{(\alpha+\beta)/(\alpha+\beta+\gamma)}$$

(A3.17)

which corresponds to (A3.5).

Substituting (A3.17) into (A3.14), after considerable algebraic manipulation we obtain the long-run TC function:

$$C = (\alpha + \beta + \gamma)(A\alpha^\alpha\beta^\beta\gamma^\gamma)^{-1/(\alpha+\beta+\gamma)}(w^\alpha r^\beta v^\gamma)^{1/(\alpha+\beta+\gamma)}Q^{1/(\alpha+\beta+\gamma)}$$

(A3.18)

Logically, we should also be able to derive the long-run TC function directly from the production function and a cost equation, as in (A3.2), where all inputs are considered variables. Moreover, the long-run TC functions derived by the two different methods should be identical. Hence, this procedure can also be used as a check for possible mistakes.

The second approach (i.e., using the production function and cost equation) involves the maximization of (A3.7) subject to the constraint

$$C = wL + rK + vS$$

(A3.19)

The first-order conditions for the constrained maximum (the expansion path equation) are

$$\beta wL - \alpha rK = 0, \qquad \gamma rK - \beta vS = 0$$

(A3.20)

Note that in the three-variable-input case the expansion path is composed of two equations. In general, the expansion path is composed of $n - 1$ equations in the n-variable-input case. We shall consider this case shortly.

One way to derive the cost function involves using Cramer's rule to solve the three linear equations (A3.19) and (A3.20) for L, K, and S, and substituting the values obtained into (A3.7). The solutions of the linear equations can be obtained in a straightforward manner:

$$L = \alpha C/w(\alpha + \beta + \gamma)$$

$$K = \beta C/r(\alpha + \beta + \gamma)$$

(A3.21)

$$S = \gamma C/v(\alpha + \beta + \gamma)$$

Substituting (A3.21) into (A3.7), after some algebraic manipulation we obtain the long-run TC function:

$$C = (\alpha + \beta + \gamma)(A\alpha^\alpha\beta^\beta\gamma^\gamma)^{-1/(\alpha+\beta+\gamma)}(w^\alpha r^\beta v^\gamma)^{1/(\alpha+\beta+\gamma)}Q^{1/(\alpha+\beta+\gamma)}$$

(A3.22)

which is identical to the long-run cost function (A3.18) that was derived from the envelope approach.

It is interesting to point out that the algebra is much more troublesome in the first approach than in the second. The reason for this may be that the second approach is symmetric (i.e., all inputs are treated symmetrically), whereas the first approach is not (i.e., the fixed input is treated as a parameter in the derivation of the short-run cost function). It is only in the derivation of the envelope equation that the fixed input is treated as a variable, the other inputs having been eliminated. At any rate, the two different approaches produce the same result. Although in economic theory the first approach is the traditional way to derive the long-run cost function, in practice, the second may actually be easier in most cases.

A3.1.2 AC and MC

Short-Run AC and MC

The short-run TC function (A3.14) derived from the Cobb–Douglas production function implies that

$$AFC = vS/Q$$

(A3.23)

that is, AFC is a decreasing function of Q, since both v and S (and hence the product vS) are constants. Furthermore, AVC is given by

$$AVC = (\alpha + \beta)(AS^\gamma\alpha^\alpha\beta^\beta)^{-1/(\alpha+\beta)}(w^\alpha r^\beta)^{1/(\alpha+\beta)}Q^{(1-\alpha-\beta)/(\alpha+\beta)}$$

(A3.24)

and will be either a constant (if $\alpha + \beta = 1$), a decreasing function of Q (if $\alpha + \beta > 1$), or an increasing function of Q (if $\alpha + \beta < 1$). It is impossible to tell in advance how AVC will behave. Since α and β are determined by technology, the behavior of AVC depends on technological conditions.

As mentioned previously, ATC = AFC + AVC, that is,

$$ATC = vS/Q + (\alpha + \beta)(AS^\gamma\alpha^\alpha\beta^\beta)^{-1/(\alpha+\beta)}$$
$$\times (w^\alpha r^\beta)^{1/(\alpha+\beta)}Q^{(1-\alpha-\beta)/(\alpha+\beta)}$$

(A3.25)

and will be a decreasing function of Q if $\alpha + \beta > 1$, since in this case both the first and the second terms on the right side of

(A3.25) are decreasing functions of Q, and the sum of two decreasing functions is also a decreasing function.

In the case $\alpha + \beta = 1$, the second term on the right side of (A3.25), that is, the term

$$(\alpha + \beta)(AS^{\gamma}\alpha^{\alpha}\beta^{\beta})^{-1/(\alpha+\beta)}(w^{\alpha}r^{\beta})^{1/(\alpha+\beta)}Q^{(1-\alpha-\beta)/(\alpha+\beta)}$$

is a constant. However, the first term on the right, vS/Q, is a decreasing function of Q. Therefore, ATC will be a decreasing function of Q. In this case, we can say something more about the behavior of ATC: It is an asymptotically decreasing function, the vertical axis and the constant-AVC curve being the asymptotes. This also implies that the long-run AC is a decreasing function of Q. We shall have more to say later concerning this point.

It is only in the case $\alpha + \beta < 1$ that the short-run ATC will at first decrease, reach a minimum, and then begin to increase. For simplicity in notation, write the constant in (A3.25) as

$$k = (\alpha + \beta)(AS^{\gamma}\alpha^{\alpha}\beta^{\beta})^{-1/(\alpha+\beta)}(w^{\alpha}r^{\beta})^{1/(\alpha+\beta)}$$

We then have

$$\frac{d(\text{ATC})}{dQ} = \frac{-vS}{Q^2} + \left(\frac{1 - \alpha - \beta}{\alpha + \beta}\right) kQ^{(1-\alpha-\beta)/(\alpha+\beta)-1} \qquad \text{(A3.26)}$$

Setting the above expression equal to zero and solving for Q (we denote this Q by Q^*), we obtain

$$Q^* = [(\alpha + \beta)vS/k(1 - \alpha - \beta)]^{(\alpha+\beta)} \qquad \text{(A3.27)}$$

The short-run ATC curve reaches its minimum at Q^*; to the left of Q^*, ATC is a decreasing function of Q, whereas to the right of Q^*, it is an increasing function of Q. It is easily seen that Q^* is positive, since $(1 - \alpha - \beta) > 0$ for $\alpha + \beta < 1$ and all other terms on the right side of (A3.27) are positive. It is also interesting to note that Q^* is an increasing function of the plant size S for a given v, since

$$\frac{\partial Q^*}{\partial S} = (\alpha + \beta) \left[\frac{(\alpha + \beta)v}{k(1 - \alpha - \beta)}\right]^{\alpha+\beta} S^{(\alpha+\beta-1)} > 0 \qquad \text{(A3.28)}$$

for $\alpha + \beta < 1$. Thus, the larger the plant size, the larger the quantity of output at which ATC reaches its minimum.

The short-run MC of the cost function (A3.14) is

$$\text{MC} = [k/(\alpha + \beta)]Q^{1/(\alpha+\beta)-1} \qquad \text{(A3.29)}$$

which is a constant if $\alpha + \beta = 1$, a decreasing function of Q if $\alpha + \beta > 1$, and an increasing function of Q if $\alpha + \beta < 1$, since

$$\frac{\partial(\text{MC})}{\partial Q} = \left(\frac{1}{\alpha + \beta} - 1\right)\left(\frac{k}{\alpha + \beta}\right)Q^{1/(\alpha+\beta)-2} \gtrless 0 \qquad \text{(A3.30)}$$

for $\alpha + \beta \gtrless 1$.

In summary, the short-run MC can be either a constant, a decreasing function of Q, or an increasing function of Q for a cost function derived from the Cobb–Douglas production function. However, it cannot be decreasing within a certain output range and constant or increasing within a different range. In other words, the Cobb–Douglas production function does not offer us the traditional smooth, U-shaped MC curves. This implies, as was shown in the previous subsection, that the corresponding short-run AVC is not the traditional textbook version of a smooth, U-shaped curve.

Long-Run AC and MC

The long-run AC and MC functions derived from the Cobb–Douglas production function can be computed from the long-run TC function (A3.18) or (A3.22).

For simplicity of notation, we denote the collection of constant terms in (A3.18) and (A3.22) by k^*, that is,

$$k^* = (\alpha + \beta + \gamma)(A\alpha^\alpha\beta^\beta\gamma^\gamma)^{-1/(\alpha+\beta+\gamma)} \tag{A3.31}$$
$$\times (w^\alpha r^\beta v^\gamma)^{1/(\alpha+\beta+\gamma)}$$

The long-run AC is given by

$$AC = k^*Q^{1/(\alpha+\beta+\gamma)-1} \tag{A3.32}$$

Hence, AC is a constant for $\alpha + \beta + \gamma = 1$, a decreasing function of Q for $\alpha + \beta + \gamma > 1$, and an increasing function of Q for $\alpha + \beta + \gamma < 1$, since

$$d(AC)/dQ = [1/(\alpha + \beta + \gamma) - 1]k^*Q^{1/(\alpha+\beta+\gamma)-2} \gtrless 0 \tag{A3.33}$$

for $\alpha + \beta + \gamma \gtrless 1$.

The long-run MC can similarly be computed from (A3.18) or (A3.22). We have

$$MC = [1/(\alpha + \beta + \gamma)]k^*Q^{1/(\alpha+\beta+\gamma)-1} \tag{A3.34}$$

As in the AC case, MC is a constant for $\alpha + \beta + \gamma = 1$, a decreasing function of Q for $\alpha + \beta + \gamma > 1$, and an increasing function of Q for $\alpha + \beta + \gamma < 1$, since

$$d(MC)/dQ = [(1 - \alpha - \beta - \gamma)/(\alpha + \beta + \gamma)^2]$$
$$\times k^*Q^{1/(\alpha+\beta+\gamma)-2} \gtrless 0 \tag{A3.35}$$

for $\alpha + \beta + \gamma \gtrless 1$.

As shown earlier in this section, the long-run AC and MC curves derived from the Cobb–Douglas production function can be either constant, a decreasing function of Q, or an increasing function of Q. However, neither of them can be a decreasing function within a certain output range, reach a minimum, and then become an increasing function. In other words, neither the long-run nor the short-run AC and MC cost curves derived from the Cobb–Douglas production function have the traditional text-book version of the smooth, U-shaped curve.

It is interesting to note that the Cobb–Douglas production function is homogeneous of the degree $\alpha + \beta + \gamma$. Recall that a homogeneous production function exhibits constant returns to scale if it is homogeneous of the degree 1, increasing returns to scale if it is homogeneous of the degree > 1, and decreasing returns to scale if it is homogeneous of the degree < 1. Therefore, in production, constant returns to scale corresponds to constant long-run AC and MC, in which case we also have AC = MC. This is clearly shown in our example, since from (A3.32) and (A3.34) we have

$$AC = k^* = MC \qquad \text{for} \quad \alpha + \beta + \gamma = 1$$

On the other hand, with increasing returns to scale in production, both the long-run AC and the long-run MC are decreasing functions of Q, and MC < AC. In our example, from (A3.32) and (A3.34) we have

$$AC = k^* Q^{1/(\alpha+\beta+\gamma)-1} > [1/(\alpha + \beta + \gamma)]k^* Q^{1/(\alpha+\beta+\gamma)-1} = MC$$

for $\alpha + \beta \gamma > 1$.

Similarly, for the case of decreasing returns to scale in production, both the long-run AC and the long-run MC will be increasing functions of Q, and MC > AC.

A3.1.3 The Relationship Between AC and MC

The assertion has been made in the text that the MC curve always intersects the AC curve at the minimum of the latter. This can be easily proven by differentiating AC. Since, by definition, AC $= C/Q$, AC is at its minimum if

$$\frac{d(C/Q)}{dQ} = \frac{(QdC/dQ - C)}{Q^2} = 0$$

This implies that

$$QdC/dQ - C = 0$$

and

$$C = QdC/dQ$$

Dividing both sides by Q, we obtain

$$C/Q = dC/dQ$$

However, the left and right sides are precisely AC and MC, respectively. This proves that AC = MC at the minimum of AC.

A3.1.4 The Derivation of Short-Run and Long-Run Cost Functions in the General Case of n Inputs

Assume that an output Q can be produced by n inputs x_1, x_2, ..., x_n. In the short run, some of the inputs can be fixed and others variable. Since in the short run the fixed inputs are combined in fixed proportions, they can be considered as one combined fixed input. Thus, if the first m inputs are fixed, then

$$x_1 = \sum_{i=1}^{m} w_i x_i.$$

Hence, x_2, x_3, ..., x_n can be treated as $n - 1$ variable inputs. Let us denote the prices of the n inputs by P_1, P_2, ..., P_n, respectively. We can write the production function, which is assumed to possess first- and second-order continuous partial derivatives, and the cost equation, respectively, as follows:

$$Q = f(x_1, x_2, ..., x_n) \tag{A3.36}$$

$$C = \sum_{i=1}^{n} P_i x_i \tag{A3.37}$$

Since X_1 is a constant in the short run, we can treat it as a parameter, omit it in writing the production function, and write $C_0 = P_1 x_1 = \text{const}$. Then (A3.36) and (A3.37) can be rewritten

$$Q = f(x_2, x_3, ..., x_n) \tag{A3.38}$$

$$C = C_0 + \sum_{i=2}^{n} P_i x_i \tag{A3.39}$$

In order to maximize (A3.38) subject to the constraint (A3.39), we must form the Lagrange function

$$L = f(x_2, x_3, ..., x_n) + \lambda \left(C - C_0 - \sum_{i=2}^{n} P_i x_i \right) \tag{A3.40}$$

where λ is the Lagrange multiplier. The first-order conditions of constrained maximum are

$$\partial L / \partial x_n = f_i - \lambda P_i = 0, \qquad i = 2, 3, ..., n \tag{A3.41}$$

where

$$f_i = \partial f(x_2, x_3, ..., x_n) / \partial x_i, \qquad i = 2, 3, ..., n \tag{A3.42}$$

In (A3.41), we have $n - 1$ equations that, by eliminating λ, yield $n - 2$ independent equations of the form

$$f_i / P_i = f_j / P_j, \qquad i \neq j, \qquad i, j = 2, 3, ..., n \tag{A3.43}$$

The $n - 2$ independent equations in (A3.43) constitute the expansion path in the $(n - 1)$-variable-input case.

We have a total of n equations in (A3.38), (A3.39), and (A3.43) and a total of $n + 1$ variables, namely, Q, C, and $n - 1$ xs. This system of n equations and $n + 1$ variables can, in principle, be used to eliminate any $n - 1$ variables in order to express one of the remaining variables as a function of the other remaining variable. For our purposes, we eliminate the $n - 1$ xs and express cost C as a function of output Q. We have the short-run cost function

$$C = C_0 + V(Q) \tag{A3.44}$$

where the constant C_0 is the TFC and $V(Q)$, a function of output Q, is the TVC.

The derivation of the long-run cost function from the family of short-run cost functions in the general n-input case is identical to that in the case of two variable inputs and one fixed input. In general, both C_0 and $V(Q)$ are functions of the fixed input x_1 [see (A3.14)]. If the partial derivative of (A3.44) with respect to x_1 is set equal to zero, then it, together with (A3.44) itself, can be used to eliminate x_1. The result is the envelope equation of the family of short-run cost functions in (A3.44), and this envelope equation yields the long-run cost function. This can always be done, provided that the sufficient (but not necessary) conditions of (A3.4) are satisfied.

It is interesting to point out that the long-run cost function can also be derived (in most cases probably more easily) directly from the production function and cost equation by treating all the x_i, $i = 1, 2, \ldots, n$ as variables [instead of using (A3.38) and (A3.39) to derive (A3.44), from which we then derive the envelope equation]. However, the direct approach to deriving the long-run cost function will result in n equations in the system of equations (A3.41). Consequently, the system of equations (A3.43)—the expansion path—will also be increased to $n - 1$ instead of the previous $n - 2$ equations. These $n - 1$ equations, together with the production function and cost equation, constitute $n + 1$ equations in $n + 2$ variables, namely, Q, C, and n xs. Eliminating the n inputs (i.e., the xs) by using the $n + 1$ equations, and expressing C as a function of Q, the long-run cost function can be obtained. The advantage of the direct approach is that it is symmetric in the sense that all inputs are treated equally. As a result of this symmetry, the direct approach may actually be easier. Our own experience in deriving a long-run cost function from the Cobb–Douglas production function provides some evidence to support this point.

A3.2 THE CASE OF CONSTANT SHORT-RUN AVC AND MC

A short-run cost function with constant AVC and MC can be written

$$C = F + vQ \tag{A3.45}$$

where F is the TFC and v is the AVC. Two short-run cost functions associated with two different plant sizes can be written

$$C_1 = F_1 + v_1 Q \tag{A3.46}$$

$$C_2 = F_2 + v_2 Q \tag{A3.47}$$

If C_1 is associated with a small plant and C_2 with a large plant, then $F_1 < F_2$, since the large plant must be associated with a higher fixed cost. If the AVC of the large plant is higher than the AVC of the small plant, then C_2 would never be considered an economically feasible cost function, since

$$C_1 = F_1 + v_1 Q < F_2 + v_2 Q = C_2 \tag{A3.48}$$

for all Q if $F_2 > F_1$ and $v_2 > v_1$; that is, a firm whose goal was profit maximization would consider only the lowest cost among all possible costs as the cost function. Hence, for $F_2 > F_1$, both C_1 and C_2 can be considered as cost functions for different output levels if and only if $v_2 < v_1$. In this case, we can determine the output ranges for $C_1 > C_2$ and for $C_1 < C_2$. From (A3.46) and (A3.47) we have

$$C_1 = F_1 + v_1 Q \leq F_2 + v_2 Q = C_2$$

which implies that $C_1 \leq C_2$ for all $Q \leq Q_1$, where

$$Q_1 = (F_2 - F_1)/(v_1 - v_2) \tag{A3.49}$$

This value corresponds to the Q_1 in Figure 3.18. Once we know TFC and AVC for the two different plant sizes, we can use (A3.49) to determine the output range within which $C_1 < C_2$. Formula (A3.49) also implies that when $Q > Q_1$, $C_1 > C_2$.

Similarly, if we have

$$C_3 = F_3 + v_3 Q \tag{A3.50}$$

where $F_3 > F_2$ and $v_3 < v_2$, then

$$C_2 = F_2 + v_2 Q \leq F_3 + v_3 Q = C_3$$

only if

$$Q \leq Q_2 = (F_3 - F_2)/(v_2 - v_3) \tag{A3.51}$$

This also implies that $C_3 < C_2$ for $Q > Q_2$. The Q_2 here corresponds to the Q_2 in Figure 3.18.

Both the short-run AVC and the short-run MC are equal to v (i.e., the constant AVC), as can be easily seen from (A3.45). The ATC is given by

$$\text{ATC} = v + F/Q$$

and is an asymptotically decreasing function of Q, the asymptotes being the vertical axis and the curve of the constant AVC v, as we have drawn in Figure 3.19.

In the discrete case, the long-run TC is composed of C_1 for $0 \leq Q \leq Q_1$, C_2 for $Q_1 \leq Q \leq Q_2$, and C_3 for $Q > Q_2$, as shown in Figure 3.18. Similarly for AC, as shown in Figure 3.19, the long-run MC is discontinuous and composed of disconnected horizontal straight lines.

In the continuous case, if both F and v are functions of the fixed input [see (A3.14) for $\alpha + \beta = 1$], it is possible that the long-run TC, AC, and MC curves can be smooth and continuous, provided the short-run cost function satisfies the sufficient conditions (A3.4) for the envelope equation. Since (A3.4) contains sufficient but not necessary conditions, then even if it is not satisfied, continuous and smooth long-run TC, AC, and MC curves may still exist; however, they may not be derivable.

A3.3 CONSTANT AVC WITH LIMITED CAPACITY

A mathematical model in which AVC is constant within a certain output range and increasing beyond it can be specified by the following cost function:

$$C = C_0 + vQ \qquad \text{for} \quad Q \leq Q_c$$

$$C = C_0 + V(Q) \qquad \text{for} \quad Q \geq Q_c \tag{A3.52}$$

$$V'(Q) > 0 \qquad \text{and} \qquad V''(Q) > 0$$

where C_0 and v are constants, $V(Q)$ is the TVC function beyond capacity, and Q_c is the capacity output level. From cost function (A3.52), it is easily seen that

$$\text{AVC} = \text{MC} = v \qquad \text{for} \quad Q \leq Q_c \tag{A3.53}$$

For $Q \geq Q_c$, MC is positive, since, by definition,

$$\text{MC} = C'(Q) = V'(Q) > 0$$

because C_0 is a constant. Furthermore, MC is an increasing function of Q, since

$$d(\text{MC})/dQ = V''(Q) > 0$$

The MC curve is discontinuous if $v \neq V'(Q)$ at Q_c. It is continuous only if $v = V'(Q)$ at Q_c. Since $V(Q)$ can be any function as long as $V'(Q)$, $V''(Q) > 0$, the fact that $v = V'(Q)$ at Q_c can be only coincidental.

The ATC for cost function (A3.52) is given by

$$\text{ATC} = v + C_0/Q \qquad \text{for} \quad Q \leq Q_c$$

$$\text{ATC} = C_0/Q + V(Q)/Q \qquad \text{for} \quad Q \geq Q_c \tag{A3.54}$$

Hence, ATC is a decreasing function of Q for $Q \leq Q_c$ because

$$d(\text{ATC})/dQ = -C_0/Q^2 < 0 \qquad \text{for} \quad Q \leq Q_c \tag{A3.55}$$

However, for $Q \geq Q_c$, ATC can be either a decreasing or an increasing function of Q, since

$$d(\text{ATC})/dQ = [V'(Q) - \text{ATC}]/Q \gtrless 0 \tag{A3.56}$$

for $V'(Q) \gtrless \text{ATC}$ and $Q \geq Q_c$.

In general, the relationship between MC and ATC can be represented by the following expression:

$$\frac{d(\text{ATC})}{dQ} = \frac{C'(Q) - C(Q)/Q}{Q} \tag{A3.57}$$

$$= \frac{\text{MC} - \text{ATC}}{Q} \gtrless 0 \quad \text{for} \quad \text{MC} \gtrless \text{ATC}$$

For $Q \leq Q_c$, MC < ATC, since MC = AVC = $v < v + C_0/Q$ = ATC, and ATC is a decreasing function of Q, as shown by (A3.55). This is in agreement with (A3.57). However, the relationship between MC and ATC for $Q \geq Q_c$ and, consequently, at Q_c is determined by the TVC function $V(Q)$. There are three possibilities as far as the behavior of MC and ATC and the relationship between them are concerned.

CASE 1

If $V'(Q) = \text{ATC}$ at Q_c, then the MC curve is discontinuous at this point. The MC curve is below the ATC curve between the origin and Q_c, jumps to it at Q_c, and then goes above it to the right of Q_c. By the definition of the cost function (A3.52), the ATC curve is always continuous, but it may have a kink at Q_c. This is a very special case in which ATC = $[C_0 + V(Q)]/Q$ reaches its minimum at Q_c. This situation is illustrated in Figure A3.1.

FIGURE A3.1

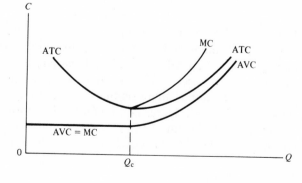

CASE 2

If $V'(Q) > $ ATC at Q_c, then the MC curve is discontinuous at this point. The MC curve is below the ATC curve between the origin and Q_c, jumps above it at Q_c, and then stays above it to the right of Q_c. In this case, the MC curve is either below or above—but never intersects—the ATC curve. Note that this situation seems to contradict our previous assertion that the MC curve always intersects the ATC curve at the minimum of the latter. In fact, there is no contradiction at all. The above assertion says that *if* the MC curve intersects the ATC curve, then the intersection must be at the minimum of the latter; however, it does not say that the MC curve *always* intersects the ATC curve. This is a case in which the TC curve is not smooth; consequently, the MC curve is discontinuous and does not intersect the ATC curve at all. In a purely mathematical sense, the MC curve still intersects the ATC curve at the minimum of the latter if both curves, corresponding to $C = C_0 + V(Q)$, are extended to the left of Q_c. The MC and ATC curves do not intersect in our case because of our restriction on the cost function $C = C_0 + V(Q)$ in the range $Q \geq Q_c$. Without this restriction, the picture would have been different. Case 2 is illustrated in Figure A3.2.

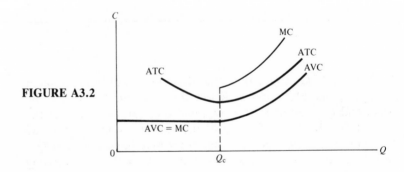

FIGURE A3.2

CASE 3

If $V'(Q) < $ ATC at Q_c, then ATC is a decreasing function of Q at Q_c and continues to be a decreasing function up to the quantity (say Q^*) at which MC = ATC; thereafter, it is an increasing function of Q. Since MC is an increasing function of Q to the right of Q_c [by our assumption that $V''(Q) > 0$], Q^* always exists. Although ATC is a decreasing function of Q both to the left and to the right of Q_c, the ATC curve may still have a kink at Q_c. In this case, the MC curve will intersect the ATC curve at the minimum of the latter. The MC curve can be either discontinuous (more likely) or continuous (only by coincidence) at Q_c. If the MC curve is discontinuous, then its rising portion, which starts at Q_c, can (theoretically) be initially either below or above the constant-AVC curve. However, it would make more economic sense for the rising portion of the MC curve to be initially above the constant-AVC curve at Q_c. The situation for case 3 is illustrated in Figure A3.3.

FIGURE A3.3

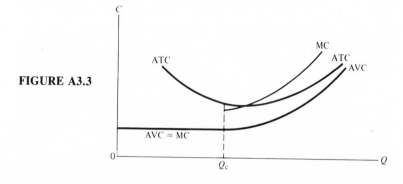

THE THEORY OF
CONSUMER BEHAVIOR AND DEMAND

A market is essentially composed of buyers and sellers of commodities and services. In reality, a seller may not be a producer; for example, people who sell their houses, cars, or some other property in their possession are not producers. However, sellers of this type represent only a small portion of all sellers. For simplicity in analysis, we shall assume that all sellers are producers. As we have noted earlier, in economics, a producing unit is called a firm. The theory of the firm, which was described in Part I, contains the theory of production and the theory of cost. It is an analysis of the essential characteristics and behavior of sellers. However, sellers represent only one "arm" of a market. Hence, in order to have a good understanding of the market, we shall now turn our attention to an analysis of the characteristics of the other arm—buyers.

A buyer may not be the *ultimate* consumer. Thus, some producers are buyers of productive factors and raw materials. However, directly or indirectly, the ultimate purpose of all production is consumption. Therefore, markets for consumer goods have special significance in economic analysis, and for this reason economic theory devotes most of its attention to these markets and related aspects of consumption. On the other hand, the markets for such productive factors as labor, capital, and land are treated separately under the heading of *income distribution*, since special features apply to them.

Since consumers are the ultimate buyers of the chain of produced commodities and services, a sound understanding of consumer behavior is important in order to understand the buyer side of the market. Hence, the theory of consumer behavior provides a useful and convenient starting point for the study of *market demand*. It should be noted that economists use the concept of market demand, which describes the relationship between market price and the quantity that buyers are willing and able to buy, to characterize the aggregate activities of all the buyers in the marketplace. In short, *aggregate demand* is the totality of all buyers' demands; however, in order to gain an insight on market demand, it is necessary to start with consumer demand. Therefore, in Part II, we shall begin with an intensive analysis of consumer behavior and conclude with a discussion of the theory of market demand.

THE THEORY OF CONSUMER BEHAVIOR

4.1 CONSUMER PREFERENCE AND THE UTILITY FUNCTION

The behavior of a consumer in the marketplace (i.e., what choice a consumer makes) is influenced by numerous factors, among which individual preference and purchasing power are singled out by economists as the two most important. Whether this is the most desirable approach is open to question, but it should be noted that almost all economists knowingly or unknowingly accept it as the basis for an analysis of market demand. In this respect, our emphasis follows tradition.

Casual observation will show that different people have different preference patterns. For example, some people like to lie on the beach to get a suntan and never get wet, whereas others prefer to stay in the water most of the time; however, the majority will intermittently play in the water and lie on the beach (each person in a different combination). On the other hand, some people would rather wander on the beach and pick up shells, each selecting different sizes, colors, and shapes. Note that so far cost has not been a factor in our example, the differences in individual behavior being reflective of pure differences in preference. In the marketplace, preference is a necessary but not sufficient condition for effective action because purchases involve payments that have to be supported by purchasing power.

Individual preference is conceivably the most important determinant of a consumer's market behavior. However, an individual's preference is subjective. Although economists are not responsible for explaining *why* individual preference patterns differ (this is left to psychologists and/or sociologists), *how* to represent and/or measure a consumer's preference must be set-

Individual preference is the most important determinant of consumer behavior

tled before they can incorporate it into a theory of consumer behavior.

The problem of consumer preference representation has long been settled without much controversy via the concept of a *utility function*, which is very similar in our mode of treatment to the production function of Chapters 1 and 2. Thus, the relationship between the amount of commodities and/or services that an individual consumes and the satisfaction (*utility*) derived from them can be likened to the relationship between inputs and output in production. In mathematical form, a utility function can be written

$$U = U(X_1, X_2, ..., X_n) \qquad (4.1)$$

The utility function expresses the relationship between consumption and satisfaction from consumption of a commodity

where $X_1, X_2, ..., X_n$ are the quantities of the n commodities that the individual consumes. The U on the left side of (4.1) denotes some kind of measure or index of utility that the individual derives from consuming the commodities. On the other hand, the U on the right side is a functional notation that relates the quantities of the commodities that the individual consumes to the utility derived from them. This functional relationship, which is determined by the individual's preference pattern, is usually different for each individual. However, the infinite number of different functional relationships that exist for different individuals do have certain properties in common. These common properties are the main concern of economists, since they permit us to develop demand schedules for commodities.

4.2 CARDINAL UTILITY AND THE LAW OF DIMINISHING MARGINAL UTILITY

The development of a measure of consumer preference and the concept of the measurability itself has a long history. In the early stage of development of economic theory, 19th century economists W. Stanley Jevons, Leon Walras, and later Alfred Marshall assumed that utility (satisfaction) was measurable and that the unit of measure—just like such physical measures as weight in terms of pounds, length in terms of feet, and temperature in terms of degrees—could be defined as a *util*. This cardinal measure of utility (satisfaction) was very convenient and easy to understand. For example, if one were able to tell that for a given consumer the utility of an orange was 10 utils and that of an apple was 5 utils, then one could state that an orange would offer this consumer twice the satisfaction of an apple. Moreover, this could also be taken to imply that the consumer would be willing to pay twice as much money for an orange than for an apple.

To further facilitate analysis, economists developed the concept of *marginal utility* (MU).

TABLE 4.1

Quantity of drink (glasses)	Total utility (utils)	Marginal utility (utils)
0	0	0
1	10	10
2	16	6
3	20	4
4	22	2
5	22	0

Definition: Marginal Utility. The change in utility for a small change in one commodity provided that the consumption of all other commodities is kept constant. In symbols, this can be expressed

$$MU_1 = \Delta U/\Delta X_1 \quad \text{for} \quad X_2, X_3, ..., X_n = \text{const} \quad (4.2)$$

where MU_1 denotes the MU of X_1 and Δ denotes change.

To illustrate the applicability of the MU concept to an individual's demand for a commodity, we can consider one's thirst after a game of touch football. The first glass of a soft drink (e.g., Coca Cola®) will offer a great deal of satisfaction, the second glass will again offer quite a bit of satisfaction but less than the first, the third glass will still be satisfying but less so than the second, and so on. Suppose that we are told that the satisfaction the consumer derives from drinking Coca Cola®, in terms of utils, is as given in Table 4.1.

The total satisfaction (utility) that the consumer derives from consuming more of the soft drink increases (column 2), but the additional satisfaction (utility) from each additional glass decreases (column 3). The phenomenon indicated by column 3 was designated by early economists as the *law of diminishing marginal utility*.

Definition: Law of Diminishing Marginal Utility. The phenomenon in which the additional satisfaction (utility) derived from the consumption of an additional quantity of a commodity decreases.

It should be pointed out that for certain commodities MU may at first increase and then decrease. Furthermore, in some special cases, MU may be constant over a given range of commodity consumption. For example, many economists consider the MU of money to be approximately constant over a broad range. Thus, diminishing MU is a phenomenon that may prevail under certain—but not all—circumstances. However, diminishing MU

The marginal utility for some commodities may be constant

usually prevails after a sufficient amount of a commodity is consumed.[1]

The concept of diminishing MU, if realistic, is very useful in predicting a consumer's market behavior. For example, if it were known that to certain consumers the MU of money is constant at 20 utils per dollar and that the price of a Coke® is 20¢ per glass (which is worth 4 utils to them), then consumers whose preference (in terms of utils) is indicated by Table 4.1 would not buy more than three glasses of Coke® if they were utility maximizers, since they would gain less satisfaction (utility) from a purchase of the fourth glass than they would lose; that is, the gain in utility from the fourth glass of Coke® is 2 utils, whereas the loss in utility from a surrender of 20¢ is 4 utils. It should be emphasized that an assumption of the constant MU of money is essential in the above arguments. Otherwise, the situation would be more complicated.

4.3 THE ORDINAL UTILITY FUNCTION, INDIFFERENCE CURVES, INDIFFERENCE MAP, POINT OF BLISS, AND MARGINAL RATE OF SUBSTITUTION

The concept of cardinal utility (i.e., that satisfaction can be measured by the number of utils) and the law of diminishing MU have been very useful in the development of the economic theory of consumer demand. Consequently, they have dominated discussions on consumer behavior and demand in economics for an extended period of time. However, economists have come to realize that the assumptions underlying the cardinal utility theory are very restrictive. Thus, it is doubtful that any consumer can precisely tell how many units of satisfaction (utility)—be they expressed in utils or something else—he or she can derive from consuming a unit (i.e., a small quantity) of a commodity, which is what the cardinal utility theory requires. If only a few consumers can satisfy the underlying assumptions of the cardinal utility theory, then the applicability of a beautiful, logically consistent economic theory based on cardinal utility would be quite limited in the real world. It is important for students to understand that cardinal utility is not a false theory—it is just that the un-

---

[1] It should also be noted that we are dealing with a given time constraint. Consuming four cans of a soft drink in 1 hour will obviously produce a different MU schedule than the consumption of the same amount of the soft drink over a period of 24 hours, 10 days, or 1 year. Thus, MU is conditional not only with respect to the amount consumed or purchased, but also with respect to the time frame over which the consumption occurs. To a large degree, the constant MU that exists for money is due to its attribute as a store of value. However, even in the case of money, it may evidence diminishing MU to some people. It should also be noted that consumption and purchase are identical under the assumption of zero inventory.

derlying assumptions are very restrictive. In order to successfully develop a theory based on cardinal utility, the merits as well as the limitations of the theory must be known. Recall the argument mentioned in the introductory chapter, in which the professor pointed out that if one were willing to make unrealistic assumptions, one could prove the moon to be made of blue cheese. From a scientific viewpoint, then, the assumptions underlying a theory set the limitations on its applicability. This is not only true in economics, but also in every other area of scientific study. Moreover, the principle of *Occam's razor* states that if two theories essentially lead to the same conclusion, the superior theory is the one that involves less-restrictive assumptions. Therefore, it should be recognized that the underlying assumptions must always be clear and explicit in order to avoid the confusion that could develop when addressing the theory to real-world phenomena or problems. The fact that the real world simply does not accord with the assumptions underlying the theory does not invalidate it. Thus, it follows that the cardinal utility theory cannot be considered false just because the assumption of cardinal measurement of utility is not possible in the real world.

Cardinal utility theory requires highly restrictive assumptions

The theory of ordinal utility was developed and expanded in this century. Economists who have made important contributions in this area include Eugene Slutsky, John R. Hicks, Kenneth Arrow, Gerald Debreu, Leonid Hurwicz, and Tjalling Koopmans (Arrow, Hicks, and Koopmans have been awarded the Nobel Prize). Although the theory of ordinal utility requires less-restrictive assumptions than the theory of cardinal utility, all of the important characteristics of consumer behavior and demand can still be derived.

The essential difference between the theories of ordinal and cardinal utility is that cardinal utility theory requires individual consumers to be able to tell precisely what amount of satisfaction they derive from consuming a small amount (e.g., one unit) of a commodity, whereas ordinal utility theory requires only that the consumer be able to distinguish which of two different commodities provides greater satisfaction when consumed. In other words, cardinal utility theory holds that the relative magnitude of the measure of satisfaction utility is important (i.e., if an orange yields 6 utils and an apple 3 utils, then the orange offers twice the satisfaction to the consumer than does the apple). On the other hand, the ordinal approach does not attach any significance to the relation between the absolute magnitude of consumer satisfaction derived from an orange and that derived from an apple. The fact that a consumer prefers an orange to an apple is all the information required by ordinal utility theory. How much more the consumer prefers the orange to the apple is irrelevant. The implication is that whereas most consumers are very likely to be able to tell, without ambiguity, that they prefer the orange to the

Preferred ordering is essential in ordinal utility theory

apple, it is not likely that many of them can tell precisely how much more satisfaction is derived. Thus, ordinal utility theory is less restrictive than cardinal utility theory.

Although it requires less-restrictive assumptions, ordinal utility theory still requires seemingly innocent, but nevertheless important, assumptions concerning consumer behavior.

Assumption 4.1: Complete Ordering. A consumer must be able to order (i.e., rank) all possible alternatives, each of which may involve a certain number of commodities and/or services (i.e., *bundles* of commodities and/or services), by the *"preferred"* and *"indifferent"* relationships; that is, for any two bundles A and B, individual consumers must be able to state one and only one of the following: they prefer A to B, they prefer B to A, or they are indifferent between A and B (however, they cannot say that they do not know). Note that indifference between A and B is not the same as "I don't know." The concept of indifference involves precision in evaluating commodities. If a consumer is indifferent between two bundles of commodities, this means that he or she derives *exactly the same* level of satisfaction from each. We shall explain this in further detail momentarily.

Assumption 4.2: Transitivity of the "Preferred" and "Indifferent" Relationships. If A is preferred to B, and B is indifferent to C, then A must be preferred to C. Similarly, if A is preferred (indifferent) to B, and B is preferred (indifferent) to C, then A is preferred (indifferent) to C.

Assumption 4.2 implies that if A is indifferent to B, B indifferent to C, C to D, ..., Y to Z, then A must be indifferent to Z, *regardless* of how many bundles we have between A and Z. This consequence of Assumption 4.2 can create problems. For example, a brilliant student once raised a question concerning the transitivity of the "indifferent" relationship based on the following situation. If a meeting was scheduled for 2 P.M. and for some reason it had to be delayed by 1 minute, then if someone asked me if I would be indifferent between 2 P.M. and 1 minute after 2 P.M. I would say yes. Similarly, if I was asked whether I would be indifferent between 1 minute after 2 P.M. and 2 minutes after 2 P.M. I would also say yes. Following this pattern minute by minute, the last alternative could be 6 P.M., 10 P.M., or even 4 A.M. the next morning. However, if someone asked me whether I would be indifferent between 2 P.M. and 6 P.M., I would say no, that is, the assumption of the transitivity of the "indifferent" relationship would be violated.

The preceding example illustrates two important points. First of all, the "indifferent" relationship represents a precise concept, that is, the alternatives are placed at *precisely the same* level of utility (satisfaction) in the consumer's preference field. In commonsense terms, indifference is not the same as "I don't mind." In the above example, "indifferent between 1 minute after 2 P.M. and 2 P.M." usually means that "I don't mind" if the meeting is delayed by only 1 minute. However, if one were to ask you whether you preferred to have a meeting on time or 1 minute later, you would most likely answer that you preferred the meeting to be held on time rather than delayed. Secondly, although the transitivity assumption seems reasonable and innocent, it does impose a considerable restriction on a consumer's rational behavior. Even the "preferred" relationship may manifest circularity under very usual circumstances. For example, if you have three friends, say *A*, *B*, and *C*, and are asked whom you like better, you might say that you like *A* better than *B* and *B* better than *C*. Hence, from Assumption 4.2, it would be implied that you like *A* better than *C*. However, if *B* is left out of the picture, you might say that you like *C* better than *A*.[2] Because the different characteristics possessed by *A*, *B*, and *C* are noncomparable, there cannot exist a common scale, particularly in a person's mind, to measure them. Thus, circularity may sometimes occur in an individual's preference ordering, hence causing the assumption of the transitivity of the "preferred" relationship to be violated. This is particularly common with respect to preference ordering for a group of people. We shall have more to say on this point in Chapter 13 (Welfare Economics). For the present, students should always keep in mind that the transitivity assumption may not be as innocent as it appears.

Preferred relationships may manifest circularity under some circumstances

Assumption 4.3: Nonsatiation or Greed. A consumer always prefers to have more of a commodity than less of it. We shall have more to say on this assumption later.

---

[2] Such a condition can easily develop in boy–girl relationships (i.e., a boy prefers girl *A* over girl *B*, and girl *B* over girl *C*, but if girl *B* is taken out of the picture, he prefers girl *C* over girl *A*). The staff of a large office was questioned to see how they would react to the following example. Assume that the boy is considering marriage and has a choice of three girls: Girl *A* has lots of money but is ugly, girl *B* is very good-looking but has no money, and girl *C* is reasonably good-looking and has a small farm in Wyoming. *If* the boy's first (but not only) concern is to live comfortably, he chooses *A* over *B*; but if *C* has only a moderate amount of money, he may prefer *B* over *C*, since *B* is very good-looking. However, if *B* is taken out of the picture by someone else, then the boy *might* well say that he prefers *C* over *A*. The women in the office said the boy would marry *A*, make *B* his mistress, and rent the farm from *C*. Interesting?? Yes! However, this perfect solution is not relevant to our problem, since we are only considering the rank of the girls in the boy's preference scale. In reality, he may not be able to get any of them. This distinction is very important because preference is a necessary but not sufficient condition for choice. In the marketplace, preference can be transformed into choice only when it is combined with ability to pay (i.e., income is a factor).

Assumption 4.4: The Absence of Lexicographic Ordering. Suppose that there are only the two commodities X and Y and that varying combinations of X and Y appear in different bundles. Let us say that the consumer prefers a bundle with more X regardless of the amount of Y. However, if two bundles contain the same amount of X, then and only then will the consumer prefer the one with more Y. In other words, the consumer looks at X first, and only when two bundles contain the same amount of X will Y become relevant; otherwise, the amount of Y is irrelevant. This is very much like the process involved in picking the "right" word from a list of synonyms, as in a dictionary or lexicon; hence the name.

Assumption 4.5: The Absence of Externalities. There are no external economics or external diseconomies involved in the consumption of the commodity. Some economists refer to this as the independence or "the consumer is selfish" assumption. It means that the satisfaction (utility) that a consumer derives from consuming a commodity depends only on the quantity that he or she consumes, regardless of what others may consume. For example, this assumption will be violated if the satisfaction that you as a consumer derive from an old car is lower when your neighbor gets a new car than it would be if your neighbor did not get a new car.[3]

Given Assumptions 4.1–4.5, a consumer's preference according to ordinal utility theory can be represented by a utility function of the form (4.1), which is reproduced here for convenience:

$$U = U(X_1, X_2, ..., X_n) \tag{4.1}$$

The absence of externalities simplifies formulation of a utility function

However, the interpretation and characteristics of the utility function are quite different in terms of ordinal utility than in terms of cardinal utility. Any order-preserving function can serve as an ordinal utility function, that is, if a bundle $(X_1^*, X_2^*, ..., X_n^*)$ is preferred to another bundle $(X_1, X_2, ..., X_n)$, then any function that assigns a larger number to U^* than to U can serve as an

---

[3] Assumptions 4.4 and 4.5 are usually not mentioned in most textbooks. However, they are very important on theoretical grounds. If a consumer's preference is characterized by lexicographic ordering, then theoretically we do not have enough numbers to represent his or her preference. (For further details on this point, the interested reader can consult Debreu, 1954.) The absence of externalities is implied by the utility function that economists usually employ, in which the utility that a consumer derives is considered a function of the quantity of the commodities that he or she consumes, not of that consumed by others. However, in the presence of externalities, the utility derived by one consumer, in general, must also be considered a function of the quantity of the commodities consumed by all other consumers. In this case, the utility function will be much more complicated [see (4.1')].

ordinal utility function. Furthermore, any monotonic transformation of this function can also serve as an ordinal utility function. Thus, an ordinal utility function may not be unique.

The utility function (4.1) implies the absence of externality. Otherwise, it must be written

$$U_1 = U_1(X_1^1, X_2^1, ..., X_n^1, ..., X_1^m, X_2^m, ..., X_n^m) \qquad (4.1')$$

where X_i^j is the amount of commodity i, $i = 1, 2, ..., n$, consumed by individual j, $j = 1, 2, ..., m$. Thus, the utility function will be much more complicated when externality is introduced. This point is often overlooked in many textbooks. We note it here in order to alert the student to limitations that are inherent when externalities are not included in a utility function.

The utility function can be represented equally as well in the form of graphs. In fact, some characteristics of the utility function can be more easily illustrated by graphical methods than by those of mathematics. However, a major disadvantage of graphical methods is that the number of commodities which can be taken into account is severely limited. Since graphs cannot be drawn in more than three dimensions (and even three-dimensional graphs are not easy to draw), we must be satisfied with two-dimensional graphs, which means that, at most we can only consider two commodities. However, this approach is actually more useful than it at first appears, since when we deal with a group of commodities, we can always single out one as our target and treat all the others as a combined commodity.

Two important concepts in the graphical analysis of consumer behavior are the *indifference curve* and the related *indifference map*. To facilitate comprehension of the graphical analysis, we offer the following definitions of these two concepts.

Definition: Indifference Curve. The locus of all bundles of commodities and/or services which offer the same utility (satisfaction) to a consumer.

Definition: Indifference Map. A collection of indifference curves showing different levels of utility obtained from different bundles or commodities and/or services.

Before drawing indifference curves, it is necessary to recognize the important characteristics or conditions that are applicable to them. First of all, we must know or understand whether the indifference curve has a positive or negative slope. In Figure 4.1, X and Y are two commodities; we start with the bundle of commodities A and see which bundles the consumer may be indifferent to with respect to A. In order to determine which bundles may be indifferent to A, we first eliminate those bundles that cannot be indifferent to it. For this purpose, we draw vertical and

An indifference curve represents combinations of commodities that yield the same amount of satisfaction

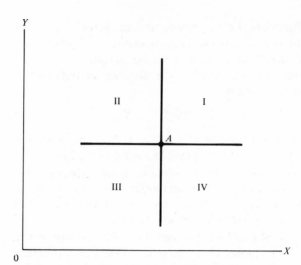

FIGURE 4.1   0

horizontal straight lines that go through A. These two perpendicular straight lines divide the nonnegative commodity space
into four quadrants, the origin being A. Any bundle in quadrant
I, including those represented by points on the lines, must be
preferred to A by Assumption 4.3 (nonsatiation). By the same
assumption, A will be preferred to any bundle in quadrant III
(again including those represented by points on the lines). It follows that an indifference curve cannot have a positive slope if
neither X nor Y produces disutility (i.e., has negative utility).[4] On
the other hand, any bundle within quadrant II (but not including
those on the lines) contains more of Y but less of X than bundle
A. Therefore, it could be preferred to A, indifferent to A, or less
preferred than A. In general, it is impossible to tell which relation
will hold without reference to a specific individual. The important
point to bear in mind is that any bundle in quadrant II *could* be
indifferent to A with respect to *some* consumer. This is also true
for any bundle within quadrant IV. Thus, due to Assumption
4.3, an indifference curve that goes through A must extend into
quadrants II and IV. This implies that an indifference curve must
have a negative slope when both X and Y are considered as goods.
On the other hand, if one is a good and the other is a bad (e.g.,
income and work, respectively), then an indifference curve will
have a positive slope. The latter situation will be discussed in
Chapter 11.

Theorem 4.1: Indifference Curves Cannot Intersect. *A second char-*
  acteristic of indifference curves can be expressed as a theorem.

---

[4] By Assumption 4.3, it is clearly seen that the indifference curve containing
bundle A as a point cannot extend into quadrant I or III.

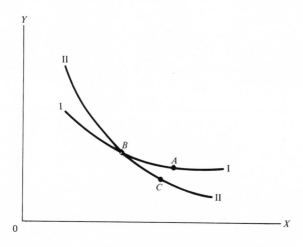

FIGURE 4.2

The proof of Theorem 4.1 is accomplished by developing a contradiction. Let us assume that two indifference curves do intersect. Consider Figure 4.2, in which it is assumed that indifference curves I and II intersect at point B. Arbitrarily choosing point A on indifference curve I and point C on indifference curve II, we can see the following from Figure 4.2:

A is indifferent to B by the definition of an indifference curve.

B is indifferent to C by the definition of an indifference curve.

A is indifferent to C by transitivity.

Since A contains more of both X and Y than C, A must be preferred to C by Assumption 4.3. However, by Assumption 4.1, A cannot be simultaneously indifferent to C and preferred to C. This completes our proof of the theorem.

Note that the relative locations of points A and C are essential to the proof. Once point A is picked, point C must be chosen in such a way that it is not to the right or above A, since otherwise the theorem could never be proven. Furthermore, one cannot argue that the bundles on indifference curve II must be preferred to the bundles on indifference curve I (or vice versa), since, as can be seen from Figure 4.2, this argument is false. Finally, it should be noted that although indifference curves cannot intersect, it does not follow that indifference curves are parallel. It is true that straight lines must be parallel if they do not intersect, but this does not apply to curves. As a simple example, consider Figure 4.3, in which AA' and BB' cannot be considered parallel and yet never intersect.

Indifference curves need not be parallel

Another characteristic of indifference curves is that all possible bundles of commodities can be represented by appropriate indifference curves on an indifference map.

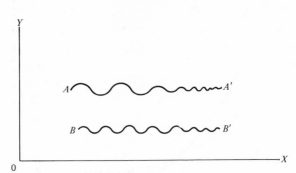

FIGURE 4.3

The assumptions concerning consumer behavior and the characteristics of indifference curves can be summarized as follows:

Assumptions:
4.1. Complete ordering of all alternatives.
4.2. Transitivity of both "indifferent" and "preferred" relationships.
4.3. Nonsatiation.
4.4. The absence of lexicographic ordering of preference.
4.5. The absence of externalities.

Characteristics:
1. Indifference curves for commodities have a negative slope.
2. Indifference curves cannot intersect.
3. There is one indifference curve that passes through each bundle of commodities.

The assumption of nonsatiation rules out the existence of a "point of bliss"

It is worthy of mention that an indifference map may quite reasonably take the form shown in Figure 4.4, where the bundle *B* (the bull's-eye) offers the highest utility to the consumer. Economists call the bundle *B* the *point of bliss*. However, it should be recognized that, by Assumption 4.3, a point of bliss cannot exist.

FIGURE 4.4

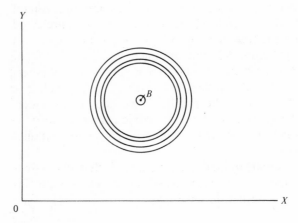

It should also be pointed out that a consumer's preference is not related to the prices of the commodities concerned. Some authors make an additional assumption—the absence of a money illusion—in order to account for this point. Since the utility function and indifference curves are designed to represent consumer preference without considering income and commodity prices, the absence of a money illusion is a built-in part of utility theory. Therefore, we do not single it out as an additional assumption. It is understood that a consumer's preference is independent of his or her income and market prices. This is quite reasonable, since regardless of how rich or poor the buyer, and whatever the prices, a Cadillac® is likely to be preferred to a Pinto®. Thus, it is essential to distinguish between preference and choice in the market, as mentioned in footnote 2. We shall return to this point later.

4.3.1 Marginal Rate of Substitution

In the modern theory of consumer behavior, a cardinal measure of utility (satisfaction) is not assumed. Therefore, the concept of marginal utility (MU) has no place in the modern theory. Although an absolute measure of utility is not stressed, a relative measure is important. The marginal rate of substitution (MRS) is employed for this purpose. Thus, stress is placed on substitution between commodities rather than on the absolute subjective utility that a consumer derives from different commodities. Before describing its application, we shall first offer a definition of the MRS in the context of two commodities, which also provides a basis for its extension to bundles of commodities.

Definition: Marginal Rate of Substitution of X for Y. The ratio of the amount of Y that a consumer is willing to give up to the resulting small gain in X, a constant level of satisfaction being maintained. In symbols, we have

$$\text{MRS} = -\Delta Y/\Delta X, \qquad U = \text{const}$$

Again, Δ denotes change. The negative sign on the right side of the expression for MRS serves to make it positive. Since either ΔX or ΔY is positive, the other must be negative, and hence $\Delta Y/\Delta X$ is always negative. Therefore, the introduction of the negative sign on the right side of the expression makes MRS positive.

It is important to note that MRS is only defined along a given indifference curve. One can not talk about MRS when a change in both X and Y involves a jump from one indifference curve to another. For example, let us first consider Figure 4.5, in which the MRS of X for Y when the consumer holds the bundle $A = \{X_0, Y_0\}$ is $-\overline{Y_0Y_1}/\overline{X_0X_1}$, $\overline{Y_0Y_1}$ being the change in Y (negative

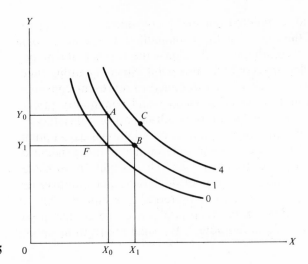

FIGURE 4.5

due to a decrease of Y from Y_0 to Y_1) and $\overline{X_0 X_1}$ being the change in X (positive due to an increase in X from X_0 to X_1). Thus, $\overline{Y_0 Y_1}/\overline{X_0 X_1} < 0$ and $-\overline{Y_0 Y_1}/\overline{X_0 X_1} > 0$. However, the MRS between X and Y is not defined if the two bundles A and C are involved. Obviously, ΔY and ΔX are well defined if a movement from A to C takes place. However, the ratio of these two changes cannot be called the MRS because the MRS is only defined along a given indifference curve. In other words, a leap from A to C puts the consumer on a different level of satisfaction and, therefore, violates our definition of MRS.

In geometry, $\overline{AF}/\overline{FB}$ is considered the slope of the straight line $\overline{AB}$, which is different from that of the tangent to indifference curve 1 at point A. However, when the change in X is very small, X_1 approaches X_0; hence, B approaches A, and the slope of $\overline{AB}$ approaches the slope of the tangent at A. The slope of a tangent is a good approximation of the slope of the curve at a point. It follows that the MRS at a point can actually be defined as the negative slope of the indifference curve that passes through the point.

Since indifference curves are usually not straight lines, the MRS along a given indifference curve usually varies from one point to another. Observation tells us that the indifference curves in Figure 4.5 indicate decreasing MRS. Thus, as we move along an indifference curve to the right, the absolute value of its slope decreases. In commonsense terms, we see that the consumer is willing to give up less and less of Y for the same amount of X when he or she has more of X and, at the same time, less of Y. In other words, the relative utility of X compared with Y to the consumer decreases as he or she consumes more of X and, at the same time, less of Y. This is further demonstrated in Figure 4.6. When the consumer has the bundle A with X_0 of X and Y_0 of Y, he or she is willing to give up $\overline{Y_0 Y_1}$ of Y for a gain $\overline{X_0 X_1}$ of X.

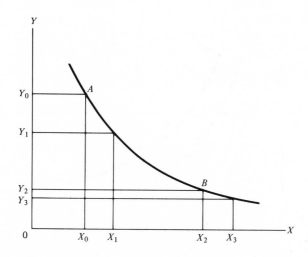

FIGURE 4.6

However, when the consumer has bundle B with X_2 of X (which is more than X_0 of X) and Y_2 of Y (which is less than Y_0 of Y), he or she is only willing to give up $\overline{Y_2Y_3}$ of Y (which is less than $\overline{Y_0Y_1}$ of Y) for the same gain in X ($\overline{X_2X_3} = \overline{X_0X_1}$). To put it another way, the consumer was willing to sacrifice less of Y for the same gain in X when his or her holding of X had increased from X_0 to X_2. This situation indicates that the relative utility from two commodities gained by consumers depends on the relative amount of the commodities they have in their possession. Consumers gain relatively more utility from a commodity of which they have relatively less and vice versa. This can also be explained by using the old MU concept.

Although MU by itself has no meaning in modern ordinal utility theory, the ratio of the MUs of two commodities is meaningful in the new theory, and we see that the MRS between two commodities is precisely the ratio of their MUs. In fact, the MRS was originally defined to take the place of MU in modern theory (see Hicks, 1946). It can be easily shown that our definition of MRS is equivalent to the MU ratio.

Consider Figure 4.7, in which, for the purpose of demonstration, the MRS at A can be approximated by $-\overline{Y_0Y_1}/\overline{X_0X_1}$. The movement from A to B can be considered as taking place in two steps: first from A to C and then from C to B. The movement from A to C produces a decrease in utility from 2 to 1 due to a decrease in Y from Y_0 to Y_1, X being held constant. The ratio of the change in utility divided by the change in Y (i.e., $\Delta U/\Delta Y$), X being held constant, is precisely the definition of the MU of Y (i.e., MU_Y) in the old approach. Thus, we have $MU_Y = (1 - 2)/\overline{Y_0Y_1}$. Similarly, from C to B we have $MU_X = (2 - 1)/\overline{X_0X_1}$. Hence,

$$\frac{MU_X}{MU_Y} = \frac{1/\overline{X_0X_1}}{-1/\overline{Y_0Y_1}} = -\frac{\overline{Y_0Y_1}}{\overline{X_0X_1}} = MRS \qquad (4.3)$$

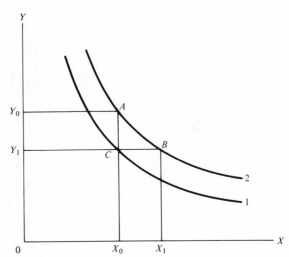

FIGURE 4.7   0

Note that the actual numerical values attached to the two indifference curves are irrelevant as long as they preserve the ordering
of the consumer's preference. This is true because the two differences in utility levels represented by MU_X and MU_Y are identical except for their opposite signs; thus, they cancel each other
out in (4.3). This explains why MU is meaningless whereas MU
ratios are meaningful in ordinal utility theory.

Decreasing MRS is the most common case, but constant, zero,
and even increasing MRS cannot be ruled out altogether. In fact,
there are possible cases where a decreasing MRS would not prevail. For example, it is not unreasonable that the MRS between
The slope of an
indifference curve
tells us whether
MRS is increasing,
decreasing, or
constant
two commodities, such as natural gas and electricity for cooking
purposes, might be constant for some consumer. If the MRS is
constant, the two commodities are called *perfect substitutes*, and
the indifference curves are straight lines. There also exist some
cases where one commodity cannot be substituted for another;
for example, a right shoe cannot be substituted for a left shoe on
a normal person. Consequently, a normal person will derive the
same level of utility from a bundle of two right shoes and one left
shoe as from a bundle of one right shoe and one left shoe. In this
case, we would expect to find that the MRS between right and
left shoes is zero, and *each* indifference curve would hence consist of two perpendicular straight lines. Finally, in some special
cases (e.g., money to a miser), it may happen that the more of
a commodity one has, the more one desires. In this case, the
indifference curves are concave toward the origin (i.e., the opposite of those in Figure 4.7). Parts (a)–(c) of Figure 4.8, obtained
by graphical analysis, show the indifference curves for the cases
of constant, zero, and increasing MRS, respectively. It should
be noted that although X and Y in part (a) are called perfect

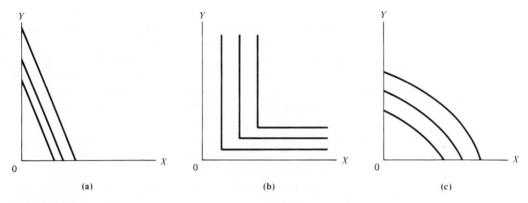

FIGURE 4.8

substitutes, the slope of the indifference curves may not be equal
to one. When we say that X and Y are perfect substitutes, it does
not mean that 1 unit of X will offer the same utility as 1 unit of
Y. It only means that if 1 unit of X offers the same utility as $\frac{1}{2}$
unit of Y when the consumer has 100 units of both X and Y, then
1 unit of X will still offer the same utility as $\frac{1}{2}$ unit of Y when he
or she has 300 units of X and 0 units of Y. Thus, the MRS is not
a function of the quantities of X and Y, but rather is constant for
any amounts of X and Y that the consumer possesses.

Finally, it should be pointed out that the shape of the difference curves (and, therefore, the behavior of MRS) represents the
preference pattern of the relevant consumer. In other words, the
consumer's preference is the sole determinant of the shape of the
indifference curves once the characteristics of the commodities
are given. Theoretically, we cannot rule out any of the four possible modes of MRS behavior (or any of the corresponding
indifference curve shapes); however, a decreasing MRS is the
most common case.

Comparing the shapes of the indifference curves with those of
the isoquants discussed in Chapter 2, students will undoubtedly
notice the similarities in their construction. However, there are
a few essential differences between isoquants and indifference
curves that should be mentioned. First of all, the numerical values
attached to isoquants are cardinal, that is, the absolute magnitude
of each value has an essential meaning. Thus, an isoquant labeled
6 represents three times the output of an isoquant labeled 2. On
the other hand, the numerical values attached to indifference
curves are meaningful only in terms of order, not in terms of
absolute magnitude. Secondly, as we have explained in Chapter
2, isoquants cannot (subject to certain assumptions) take the
shape of the indifference curves shown in part (c) of Figure 4.8.
In consumer behavior theory, the shape of the indifference curves
given in part (c) cannot be ruled out.

4.4 CONSUMER INCOME AND INPUT PRICES, THE BUDGET EQUATION, AND THE BUDGET CONSTRAINT

Consumer preference analysis alone does not determine a specific choice in the marketplace. A commodity or a bundle of commodities is bought not only because it is preferred, but also because a consumer has the means to pay for it. The consumer's income and the relative prices of the commodities, together with consumer preference, determine which specific bundle of commodities is chosen. Economists use the budget equation to bring consumer income and prices into the theory.

In developing the budget equation and budget constraint, we start by assuming that the consumer at any moment or over a given period of time has a certain amount of money to spend—*income M*—and that he or she faces a competitive market, that is, commodity prices are determined by the market. In the case of the latter condition, we are simply saying that the consumer cannot bargain with the seller as regards price. However, the consumer can buy as many units as he or she wishes at the market price P of the commodity. In general, if there are n commodities X_i, $i = 1, 2, ..., n$, respectively, in the market, then the amount of a consumer's income spent on X_i is $P_i X_i$. Since that part of a consumer's income which is not spent is saved, and savings can be considered a commodity, the total amount spent must be equal to the income of the consumer. From this information we can write the budget equation as follows:

Given a competitive market, the budget constraint is a straight line with negative slope only when income is fixed

$$M = P_1 X_1 + P_2 X_2 + \cdots + P_n X_n \tag{4.4}$$

For the purpose of graphical presentation, it is assumed that there are only the two commodities X and Y, in which case the budget equation can be written

$$M = P_X X + P_Y Y \tag{4.5}$$

The above expression can be equivalently written in the following form:

$$Y = M/P_Y - (P_X/P_Y)X \tag{4.6}$$

As explained above, M, P_X, and P_Y are constants (i.e., parameters) in expression (4.6), whereas X and Y are the variables. In the $X-Y$ space, budget equation (4.6) can be represented by a straight line, M/P_Y being the vertical intercept and $-P_X/P_Y$ the slope. Since both P_X and P_Y must be positive (they could theoretically be zero if the commodities were free goods, but for our purposes this case is not of interest and, therefore, we rule it out), the straight line must have a negative slope. Assume that $\overline{AB}$ in Figure 4.9 represents such a budget constraint. Then $\overline{0A} = M/P_Y$, which is the amount of Y that the consumer can buy if all of his or her money is spent on Y. Similarly, the horizontal

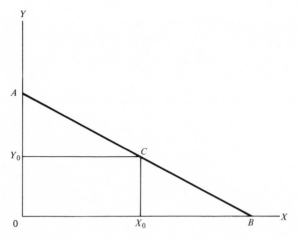

FIGURE 4.9

intercept $\overline{0B}$ is equal to M/P_X, which is the amount of X that the consumer can purchase if all of his or her money is spent on X. Any other point on $\overline{AB}$, for example, $C = \{X_0, Y_0\}$, represents a bundle of X and Y which costs the consumer precisely the same amount of money as $\overline{0A}$ of Y or $\overline{0B}$ of X. Thus, all bundles on $\overline{AB}$ cost the same amount of money, say M^0, for the given prices of X and Y. Any bundle inside the triangle $\triangle 0AB$ costs less than M^0, whereas any bundle to the right and above $\overline{AB}$ costs more than M^0. Under our simplified assumption that a consumer has a given income to spend on X and/or Y, his or her choice is limited to a bundle on $\overline{AB}$. For this reason, economists usually call $\overline{AB}$ the *budget constraint (budget line)*.

4.5 CHANGING INCOME, COMMODITY PRICES, AND A SHIFT OF THE BUDGET CONSTRAINT

It should be noted that for a given set of parameters M^0, P_X^0, and P_Y^0, there is a unique budget constraint. When any one or a combination of the parameters change, the budget constraint will shift. For example, an increase of income with prices remaining constant, will result in a parallel shift of the budget constraint, to the right. Part (a) of Figure 4.10 shows that $\overline{A'B'}$ represents a higher income than the budget constraint $\overline{AB}$. In part (b), the shift of the budget constraint from $\overline{AB}$ to $\overline{AB'}$ indicates a decrease in P_X for M^0 and P_Y^0 constant. The case in part (b) can be easily understood by noting that if all of the consumer's income is spent on Y, then he or she can buy the same amount of Y as before, since M^0 and P_Y^0 do not change. Therefore, M^0/P_Y^0 does not change, and point A will not move. However, P_X has decreased (e.g., from P_X^0 to P_X^1; thus, $M^0/P_X^0 < M^0/P_X^1$ for $P_X^0 > P_X^1$). Since $\overline{0B} = M^0/P_X^0$ and $\overline{0B'} = M^0/P_X^1$, it follows that point B' will be to the right of point B. Moreover, since two

An increase or decrease in income involves a parallel shift in the budget line

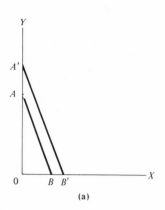
(a)

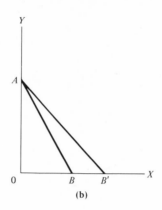
(b)

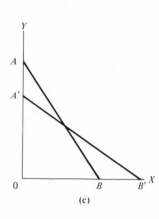
(c)

FIGURE 4.10

points determine a straight line, when P_X decreases the new budget constraint is $\overline{AB'}$. The shift of the budget constraint from $\overline{AB}$ to $\overline{A'B'}$ in part (c) indicates a simultaneous increase of P_Y and decrease of P_X. It is important for students to understand how and why the budget constraint will behave when one or a combination of the parameters changes. The graphs in Figure 4.10 represent only three of the many possibilities. Students will gain more insight into the budget constraint if they try drawing similar graphs that indicate possible changes of one or more of the parameters.

4.6 MAXIMIZING UTILITY SUBJECT TO THE BUDGET CONSTRAINT: CONSUMER EQUILIBRIUM

With the tools of the indifference map and budget constraint that we have developed to represent consumer preference, consumer income, and market conditions, we are ready to deal with the theoretical problem of consumer choice in the marketplace. The assumptions underlying our individual consumer choice model are as follows:

1. The consumer has a given income that is spent on two commodities.
2. The consumer faces given market prices.
3. The consumer's behavior satisfies Assumptions 4.1–4.5.
4. The consumer's behavior satisfies certain regularity conditions, so that the corresponding indifference curves are smooth.
5. The consumer is a utility (satisfaction) maximizer.
6. The commodities are perfectly divisible.

Assumptions 1, 2, and 6 enable us to draw a budget constraint (budget line) instead of just a few isolated points. Assumptions 3, 4, and 6 enable us to draw an indifference map for the consumer

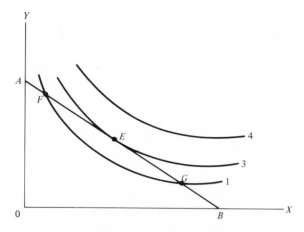

FIGURE 4.11

in which the indifference curves have no kinks or discontinuities. Assumption (5) enables us to derive a unique solution for the problem.

In Figure 4.11, AB is the budget constraint, whereas indifference curves 1, 3, and 4 are only three of the infinite number possible for the consumer. The consumer is both free to and can afford to buy any bundle of commodities along $\overline{AB}$. If the consumer bought bundle F, then, as indicated by indifference curve 1, all of his or her income would be spent and satisfaction level 1 would be obtained. Similarly, the consumer might spend all of his or her income for bundle G, thus obtaining the same level of satisfaction. The consumer could also buy either bundle A or B, but this would give a level of satisfaction lower than 1, since A and B are on lower indifference curves than F and G. By inspection, we can see that the consumer would prefer to be on indifference curve 4; however, this is obviously beyond the consumer's means. From the graph, it can be seen that E is the bundle on $\overline{AB}$ which is on the highest indifference curve, namely, indifference curve 3, that is within the consumer's means. Point E is characterized by the tangency of the budget constraint $\overline{AB}$ and indifference curve 3, that is, $\overline{AB}$ touches indifference curve 3 at one point but does not intersect it at any point. If there did exist a point of intersection, then $\overline{AB}$ would have at least one point on an indifference curve higher than indifference curve 3. From our graph, we can conclude that the consumer's satisfaction (utility) will be maximized with a purchase of bundle E of the two commodities.

The point of maximum consumer satisfaction for a given income represents *consumer equilibrium*. It should be noted that in economics the term equilibrium implies optimality. It usually involves either a maximum or minimum condition, depending on the particular phenomenon being studied. In the present case, consumer equilibrium denotes maximum satisfaction for a given

Consumer equilibrium represents maximum satisfaction for a given income

income. Later on, we shall encounter the equilibrium of a firm, which is characterized by maximum profit.[5]

It is a well-known fact in geometry that two curves have the same slope at the point of tangency. Recall that the MRS is defined as the negative slope of the indifference curve at a given point, which, by implication, is also equal to the MU ratio [see Equation (4.3)]. Furthermore, the slope of the budget constraint is $-P_X/P_Y$. Therefore, we can express the condition of consumer equilibrium as

$$\text{MRS} = \text{MU}_X/\text{MU}_Y = P_X/P_Y \qquad (4.7)$$

Admittedly, this is a mathematical property; however, it also has a commonsense interpretation. The MRS represents the subjective view of the consumer as regards the substitutability between commodities X and Y. For example, if MRS $= \text{MU}_X/\text{MU}_Y = 2$, then, at the margin, the consumer can derive twice the satisfaction from 1 unit of X than from 1 unit of Y; thus, the consumer is *willing* to give up 2 units of Y for 1 unit of X. Moreover, in doing so, the consumer's level of satisfaction will not change. The price ratio in (4.7) indicates the market opportunity that the consumer has the privilege to enjoy. For example, if the price ratio is equal to one, then $P_X = P_Y$, and for each unit of Y the consumer gives up in the market, 1 unit of X can be obtained in return, no change in expenditure being required. If this were the case, the consumer could obviously gain more satisfaction, without an increase in expenditure, by simply purchasing more of X and, at the same time, less of Y. In this case, the satisfaction gained would exceed the satisfaction lost at the prevailing MRS. This indicates that if the status quo is such that MRS is greater than the price ratio, then the consumer's satisfaction is not maximum for the given income, since a higher satisfaction can be achieved with the same expenditure by substituting X for Y. In terms of Figure 4.11, if the consumer has bundle F, then he or she can move to a higher indifference curve for the same ex-

Consumer equilibrium requires MRS for commodities to be equal to their price ratios

penditure by moving to the right along the budget constraint AB. With a decreasing MRS and a constant price ratio, when the consumer substitutes X for Y, MRS decreases; thus, the gap between MRS and the price ratio narrows. There is a tendency for the two to approach equality, which represents the condition of consumer equilibrium, that is, the point at which satisfaction is maximized. This is why a decreasing MRS is important to our theory: to satisfy, mathematically, the second-order (i.e., sufficient) condition for utility maximization. We shall deal with this

---

[5] As we shall see later on, in economic analysis a maximum-profit condition is synonymous with minimum loss. Thus, a firm that suffers a loss in the short run will experience a minimum loss when it operates subject to the condition MC = MR.

condition in more detail in the appendix at the end of this chapter. Meanwhile, the student should recognize that with an increasing or constant MRS, the more substitution that takes place, the larger will be the gap between MRS and the price ratio. It will end at a point where only one commodity will be purchased in the two-commodity case. We shall illustrate these possibilities later.

In the opposite case, that is, if MRS is less than the price ratio, the consumer will be at a point below E (say G) in Figure 4.11. It is evident that the consumer can derive more satisfaction without a change in expenditure by substituting Y for X, that is, moving upward along the budget constraint $\overline{AB}$. This indicates that the consumer's satisfaction for the given income is not maximum at point G.

A third possibility is that MRS is equal to the price ratio, which means that the consumer's subjective view concerning the substitutability between X and Y is completely in agreement with the market opportunities. There is nothing that the consumer can do to improve his or her level of satisfaction without an increase in expenditure. This case is represented by point E in Figure 4.11, which proves the graphical result that a consumer's satisfaction will be maximized when MRS is equal to the price ratio.

As we have indicated above, the tangency condition for consumer equilibrium is valid only in an ideal situation. Without getting too involved, it can be graphically demonstrated that the tangency condition signifies consumer equilibrium only for an *interior solution* under a condition of decreasing MRS. Consider the graphs in Figure 4.12. Part (a) represents the case of an increasing MRS. The tangency point F obviously results in minimum rather than maximum satisfaction. This is the case in which, mathematically, the second-order condition of constrained utility maximization is violated. As a result, the tangency condition generates minimum rather than maximum satisfaction. The graph shows that an optional solution still exists, that is, bundle B results in maximum satisfaction for the consumer. This is usually referred

FIGURE 4.12

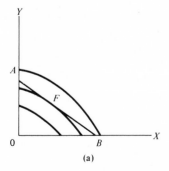
(a)

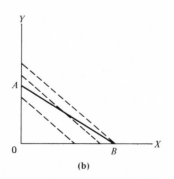
(b)

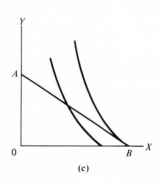
(c)

to as a *corner solution*, in contrast to the interior solution, which is referred to as a utility maximizing bundle inside the first quadrant rather than on one of the axes.

Part (b) of Figure 4.12 shows the case of a constant MRS, the dashed lines represent indifference curves. Here the result is a corner solution, except in the special case when the budget constraint and the indifference curves have the same slope. In the latter case, any bundle on the budget constraint is just as good as any other, that is, there is no question of choice. This is obviously not a very interesting case in theory.

In part (c) we have a decreasing MRS, but MRS is greater in absolute value than the price ratio P_X/P_Y everywhere along the budget constraint $\overline{AB}$. It is conceivable that an extension of $\overline{AB}$ below the horizontal axis might be tangent to some indifference curve in the fourth quadrant, but a point in the fourth quadrant represents a negative amount of Y and, realistically, a consumer cannot consume a negative amount of a commodity. Hence, a point of tangency, if it exists, does not have much economic meaning in the context of our model. In this special case, the tangency solution fails. However, a corner solution is still meaningful. This is the case where the relative price of Y is too high in relation to the consumer's preference. Therefore, the consumer ends up spending all of his or her income on X. This is quite meaningful in the general case of n commodities, since no one buys each and every commodity in the market. Consequently, we obtain a corner solution of some sort.

Tangency of a budget line to an indifference curve establishes equality between MRS and the price ratio

In order to demonstrate the significance of our assumption that the consumer's behavior satisfies certain regularity conditions, so that the corresponding indifference curves are smooth, consider Figure 4.13. At point E, the budget constraint $\overline{AB}$ touches indifference curve 1, but MRS is not equal to the price ratio. In fact, MRS at E varies, depending on in which direction one

FIGURE 4.13

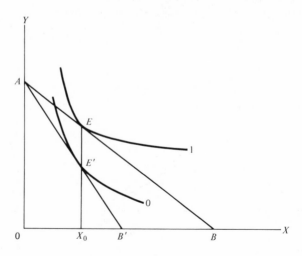

moves; that is, the MRS of X for Y for an increase of X is different than that for a decrease of X. Although consumer equilibrium makes good sense, the condition of the equality of MRS to the price ratio fails in this case.[6]

It is important to understand that the tangency condition (4.7) for consumer equilibrium is only the first-order condition in terms of mathematics. The second-order condition—a decreasing MRS— is of equal (if not greater) importance. The latter condition rules out the cases indicated by parts (a) and (b) of Figure 4.12, whereas the regularity assumption rules out the possibility indicated by Figure 4.13. The case indicated by part (c) of Figure 4.12 results when the implicit constraints (i.e., $X \geq 0$ and $Y \geq 0$) are ignored (as often occurs).

4.7 CHANGES IN INCOME, THE DEFINITION OF NORMAL AND INFERIOR GOODS, AND THE INCOME CONSUMPTION AND ENGEL CURVES

As shown in Section 4.6, given the consumer's income and pref- erence pattern, as well as the prices of the commodities, his or her satisfaction will be maximum if the budget constraint is tan- gent to an indifference curve, provided that the second-order condition is satisfied. Since income and the prices are treated as parameters, if any one or a combination of the parameters changes, then the point of tangency and, accordingly, the equi- librium quantity of the commodities will also change. In order to analyze the unambiguous effects of a change in one parameter, scientific method dictates that only one parameter at a time be allowed to change, the others remaining constant. We shall now analyze the effects of a change in the consumer's income, the consumer's preference and commodity prices being held con- stant, on the equilibrium quantity of the commodities purchased.

Consider Figure 4.14. Given the consumer's income M^0 and the prices of commodities X and Y, $\overline{AB}$ is the budget constraint. The equilibrium bundle is $E_0 = [X_0, Y_0]$. If the consumer's income increases to $M^1 > M^0$, the budget constraint shifts to $\overline{A'B'}$, which is paralleled to $\overline{AB}$. The original bundle no longer maximizes the consumer's satisfaction. The graph shows that only $E_1 = [X_1, Y_1]$ will result in maximum satisfaction for income level M^1. Thus, the consumer buys more of both X and Y with the higher income, which is the usual case. However, there is a special case where an increase in a consumer's income may result in less of a com-

---

[6] The implication of this case is that two different budget constraints such as $\overline{AB}$ and $\overline{AB'}$ may be tangent to different indifference curves at the same vertical straight line. In such a case, the demand curve for X will not be single-valued; that is, the demand curve will be a vertical straight line at X_0 for a certain price range.

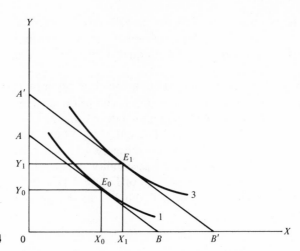

FIGURE 4.14

modity being purchased at <u>equilibrium</u>. For example, in Figure 4.15 it is seen that although $\overline{A'B'}$ represents a higher income, the equilibrium bundle $E_1 = [X_1, Y_1]$ contains less of X than bundle $E_0 = [X_0, Y_0]$. In this special case, X is called an *inferior good*. To distinguish between these two cases, we can define normal and inferior goods according to the following criteria.

Definition: Normal Good. A commodity that a consumer will buy more of with a higher income and less of with a lower income at equilibrium, given constant prices and a constant preference pattern.

Definition: Inferior Good. A commodity that a consumer will buy less of with a higher income and more of with a lower income at equilibrium, given constant prices and a constant preference pattern.

FIGURE 4.15

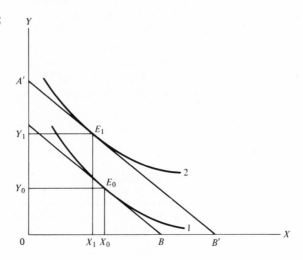

Normal goods are most common, whereas inferior goods represent a special case. However, examples of inferior goods are not hard to find. In the United States, a low-income family may consume a considerable amount of hamburger per week. When income increases, more steak or a better quality beef will be consumed, given the same capacity of food intake, whereas less hamburger will be consumed. Thus, hamburger is an inferior good, whereas steak is a normal good.

The following true story will shed more light on the above example. A young gas station attendant was once asked why he preferred evening work. His response was that he was "moonlighting." The reason for his taking the second job was that he wanted to feed his young son steak a couple of times a week, which he could not afford without "moonlighting." In the absence of "moonlighting," he could only afford hamburger every day. For this family, a higher consumption of steak due to the higher income would undoubtedly result in a lower purchase of hamburger. Hamburger, to this family, is obviously an inferior good.

Hamburger may be an inferior good in the United States, but it is quite possibly a normal good in a poor country where all kinds of meat are scarce. This indicates that a commodity may be a normal good within a certain range of income and an inferior good within another range. It is also possible that a commodity may be a normal good for some consumers, but an inferior good for others in the same income bracket. In other words, whether a commodity is a normal good or an inferior good depends on the preference pattern of the consumer.

We can further note that when there are only two commodities, if one is an inferior good, then the other must be a normal good. This is shown in Figure 4.15, in which we can observe that X is an inferior good and Y is a normal good. One can also explain this in terms of common sense. Thus, suppose that the consumer purchases a bundle of commodities $[X_0, Y_0]$. When the consumer's income increases, he or she can purchase more of Y and the same amount of X as before. Since the consumer's entire income is spent, if less is spent on X (the inferior good), then more must be spent on Y (the normal good), inasmuch as less spending on one commodity must lead to more spending on the other. However, two commodities can both be normal goods simultaneously.

All goods cannot be inferior goods, but all goods can be normal goods

The above two-commodity case can be generalized to the general n-commodity case as follows: All n commodities can simultaneously be normal goods, but all n commodities cannot simultaneously be inferior goods. There must be at least one normal good in a group of n commodities. It is possible (but not likely) that $n - 1$ of the n commodities are inferior goods and only one a normal good. Usually, there are more normal goods than inferior goods (if any) in a group of commodities. The term "normal good" has its commonsense connotation.

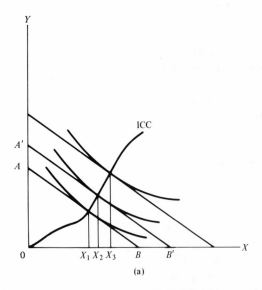 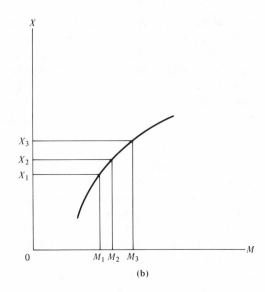

(a)   (b)

FIGURE 4.16

When income changes little by little, each corresponding budget constraint will be tangent to one and only one indifference curve. When income is considered a continuous variable, there are an infinite number of possible parallel budget constraints and an infinite number of corresponding points of tangency. The locus of the points of tangency forms a curve that represents the equilibrium bundles for a consumer at various levels of income. This curve is called the *income consumption curve* (ICC) and is shown in part (a) of Figure 4.16. The ICC can be defined as follows.

Definition: Income Consumption Curve. The locus of equilibrium points for all possible levels of income with constant prices and a given consumer preference pattern.

From an ICC, we can derive an *Engel curve*, which stresses the relationship between the income level and the quantity of a commodity purchased, while ignoring the information on the quantity of the other commodity purchased. The curve is named in honor of a 19th century German statistican, Christian Lorenz Ernst Engel, who first developed it. The Engel curve in part (b) of Figure 4.16 is derived from the ICC in part (a). Income level M_1 in part (b) corresponds to the budget constraint $\overline{AB}$. With budget constraint $\overline{AB}$, the consumer buys X_1 of X at equilibrium, which is indicated by the point $[M_1, X_1]$ in part (b). Income level M_2 corresponds to budget constraint $\overline{A'B'}$, and X_2 is the same for both graphs. Corresponding to each point on the ICC of part (a), there is one and only one point in part (b). Consequently, we have a unique curve that relates quantities of X

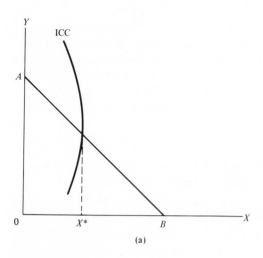

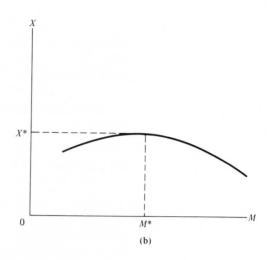

FIGURE 4.17

purchased to different income levels. This functional relationship between the quantity of a commodity purchased and the income level is called an Engel curve.

It is easy to see that the shape of an Engel curve is closely related to that of the corresponding ICC. In part (a) of Figure 4.16, the ICC has a positive slope throughout its range, this also being true for the corresponding Engel curve in part (b). This is the case where both X and Y are normal goods. On the other hand, if either X or Y is an inferior good, then the ICC will have a negative slope in the range where one commodity is an inferior good; the corresponding Engel curve will also have a negative slope in the same range. This is illustrated in part (a) of Figure 4.17, where the ICC has a positive slope for an income level lower than some M^* represented by budget constraint $\overline{AB}$ and a negative slope beyond income level M^*. This shows that X is a normal good for an income level less than M^* and an inferior good for an income level greater than M^*. The corresponding Engel curve for X also has a positive slope for an income level less than M^* and a negative slope for an income level greater than M^*, as is shown in part (b) of Figure 4.17. It is easy to see that part (a) implies that Y is a normal good at all levels of income and that the corresponding Engel curve for Y will have a positive slope over its entire range.

To enhance their understanding of the ICC, students should attempt an explanation of why it will have a positive slope close to the origin and then bend downward if Y is a normal good at low levels of income and an inferior good at high levels of income, whereas it will bend leftward when X is an inferior good. It should be noted that when an ICC has a positive slope, it means that both commodities are normal goods. However, when one of the

The slope of an ICC curve indicates whether a commodity is an inferior or normal good

commodities is an inferior good (remember that both commodities cannot simultaneously be inferior goods in the two-commodity case), the ICC will have a negative slope. The negative slope of an ICC may indicate that either X or Y, but not both, is an inferior good. In order to determine whether X or Y is an inferior good, one must first examine the budget constraints and indifference curves.

4.8 CHANGES IN PRICE, THE PRICE CONSUMPTION CURVE, AND THE DERIVATION OF A DEMAND CURVE

A change in the price of one commodity, given the prices of all other commodities, the consumer's income, and the consumer's preference pattern, will result in a change of the equilibrium quantity of the commodities. In the two-commodity case, the changes can be shown on a graph. Consider Figure 4.18. With a given income M^0 and prices P_X^0 and P_Y^0 of X and Y, respectively, we have the budget constraint $\overline{AB}$ and the bundle $E_0 = [X_0, Y_0]$, which results in a maximum consumer satisfaction at utility level 1. When the price of X decreases to $P_X^1 < P_X^0$, income and P_Y being constant, the budget constraint shifts to $\overline{AB'}$. The consumer is no longer satisfied with the bundle E_0 because the decrease in the price of X makes it possible to move to a higher indifference curve and a different bundle of commodities. The highest indifference curve that the consumer can attain with the new budget constraint is indifference curve 3; thus, we have bundle $E_1 = [X_1, Y_1]$, which results in a new equilibrium. We can observe that when the price of X decreases, other things being equal (the student should consider which other things are equal), the quan-

The PCC curve provides a validation of the basic demand law

FIGURE 4.18

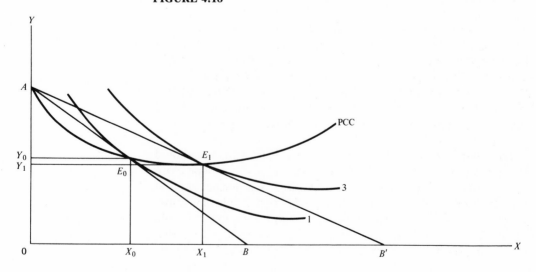

tity of X demanded increases. This is precisely the *demand law* that is stated in many economics textbooks.

The student should recognize that when the price of X increases, other things being equal, the budget constraint will rotate around point A and move back toward the origin. A new equilibrium and a different bundle of goods will result from the price change. If we assume that the price of X changes little by little, other things being equal, the budget constraint will rotate around the point A continuously. The higher (lower) the price of X, the steeper (flatter) the slope of the budget constraint. Each budget constraint will be tangent to one indifference curve. The locus of the points of tangency form the *price consumption curve* (PCC). To avoid confusion, the PCC should be distinguished from the ICC. The ICC starts from the origin, which is due to the fact that with zero income none of the commodities can be bought. On the other hand, the PCC will start from point A, the reason being that a vertical budget constraint implies an infinite price of X for a positive P_Y. Thus, if finite, all of the consumer's income can only be spent on Y, that is, bundle A. It is also obvious that with income fixed, the PCC cannot go above A on the vertical axis.

The information in the PCC of Figure 4.18 can be transferred to another graph, where the horizontal axis is the quantity of X and the vertical axis is the price of X, in order to show the functional relationship between quantity purchased and the price of a commodity. Such a graph is given in Figure 4.19, where P_X^0 is the price of X corresponding to the budget constraint $\overline{AB}$ in Figure 4.18. The equilibrium quantities X_0 in the two graphs are identical. The point $[X_0, P_X^0]$, labeled (E_0) in Figure 4.19, corresponds to, but is not exactly the same as, point E_0 in Figure 4.18, since we lose the information on Y in the former. Similarly, the point $[X_1, P_X^1]$, labeled (E_1) in Figure 4.19, corresponds to E_1 in Figure 4.18. To each and every point on the PCC in Figure

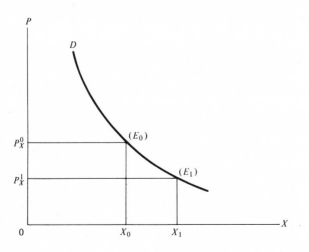

FIGURE 4.19

4.18, there corresponds one and only one point on the curve (as we have drawn it) in Figure 4.19. (In some special cases, the curves may not represent a one-to-one relationship.) The curve that we have derived in Figure 4.19 from the PCC is precisely the *demand curve* for the commodity X. We shall define these two curves as follows.

Definition: Price Consumption Curve. The locus of equilibrium points in the commodity space when the price of one commodity changes continuously while consumer income and all other prices are held constant for a given consumer preference pattern.

Definition: Demand Curve. The curve for a commodity and a specific consumer that shows the equilibrium quantities bought by the consumer at various market prices while consumer income and all other prices are held constant for a given consumer preference pattern.

Attention is called to the fact that the above definitions explicitly specify the "other things" in the phrase "other things being equal", that is, consumer income, consumer preference, and the prices of all other commodities. Secondly, a demand curve (or, more generally, a *demand function*) shows the relationship between the quantity purchased and the market price of a commodity. Furthermore, the quantities along a demand curve are *specifically* the equilibrium quantities. This means that the quantities along a demand curve will maximize a consumer's satisfaction for the corresponding prices. It is often overlooked that the demand curve involves consumer optimality, not just any relationship between price and quantity. In short, it is consistent with our assumption that the consumer is a utility (satisfaction) maximizer.

4.9 SUBSTITUTION AND INCOME EFFECTS, THE SLUTSKY EQUATION, AND GIFFEN GOODS

In Section 4.8, from an indifference map we derived a demand curve that had a negative slope and was consistent with the demand law. This is the most common condition that prevails in the market. However, there are exceptions to the demand law, which are referred to as the *Giffen paradox* by some people and *Giffen goods* by others. A Giffen good must be an inferior good, but not all inferior goods are Giffen goods. In order to explain this point, we must introduce into our discussion the Slutsky equation and the related concepts of substitution and income effects.

The *Slutsky equation* is an important part of the modern theory of consumer behavior. The equation is a pure mathematical

A Giffen good is an inferior good, but not all inferior goods are Giffen goods

expression derived from the first-order conditions of constrained utility maximization of a consumer. The second-order conditions imply certain properties of individual terms in the equation. Unfortunately, both the mathematics in the derivation of the equation and the analysis of the properties of the equation are quite involved. This is perhaps one of the reasons that whereas the original Slutsky article, "On the Theory of the Budget of the Consumer," was published in the Italian journal *Giornale degli Economisti* in July 1915, it was completely ignored by economists outside of Italy until the mid 1930s. The British mathematician R. G. D. Allen first introduced Slutsky's work to the English-speaking world in 1936 in an article entitled "Professor Slutsky's Theory of Consumer's Choice" that was published in *Review of Economic Studies*. It was the exposition and interpretation of the Slutsky equation by Nobel Prize winner J. R. Hicks, a British economist, in his celebrated book *Value and Capital,* first published in 1939, in terms of the substitution and income effects that made the Slutsky theory popular. We shall consider the mathematical aspects of the Slutsky equation in the appendix to this chapter; here our attention will be focused on the graphical exposition and interpretation, albeit imprecise, of the Slutsky theory (which may properly be called the Slutsky–Hicks theory of consumer choice).

The Slutsky–Hicks theory is a refinement of traditional demand theory in that when the price of one commodity changes (e.g., decreases), consumer income and all other prices being constant, there are two effects that take place in the process. First of all, this commodity is now relatively cheaper than all the other commodities, which will lead the consumer to substitute it in place of the others. This effect, which will result in more of the cheaper commodity being purchased in equilibrium, is called the *substitution effect*. At the same time, however, a second condition is manifested, that is, the consumer's real income increases due to the decrease in the price of the commodity. Since, by assumption, the consumer's income is constant, it follows that when the price of a commodity decreases, the purchasing power of the income increases. This can be considered an increase in real income. A change in real income will usually cause a change in the consumer's purchases of commodities at equilibrium. We may rightfully ask whether the increase in income will cause the consumer to buy more or less of the commodity whose price has gone down. From Section 4.8, we know that the answer to this question is conditional. If the commodity is a normal good, an increase in income will result in more of the commodity being purchased. On the other hand, if the commodity is an inferior good, less will be purchased. As we shall see, it is the *income effect* that creates some uncertainty concerning the validity of demand law. It is also the income effect that provides a theoretical explanation of

A decrease in the price of a commodity produces both substitution and income effects

the exception to the demand law, that is, a Giffen good. Prior to the Slutsky–Hicks refinement of the effect of a change in the price of a commodity, other things being equal, into substitution and income effects, the phenomenon of a positively sloped demand curve could not be explained by economic theory. For many years, it was referred to as the Giffen paradox. It is no longer a paradox, and can be explained in theory by means of the income effect.

For graphical exposition, we assume that there are only two commodities X and Y. We shall first consider the case where X is a normal good, the case where X is an inferior good but not a Giffen good, and, finally, the case where X is a Giffen good. In each case, our analysis will be based on a decrease in the price of X, other things remaining equal.

Consider Figure 4.20, where consumer income M^0 and the prices P_X^0, and P_Y^0 of X and Y, respectively, are given. As before, we have the original budget constraint $\overline{AB}$. For a given consumer preference pattern, we have a set of the indifference curves, of which only two (labeled 1 and 3) are drawn. We can observe that the budget constraint $\overline{AB}$ is tangent to indifference curve 1 at E_0 and that the consumer will buy X_0 of X at price P_X^0. When the price of X decreases from P_X^0 to P_X^1, other things being equal, the budget constraint shifts to $\overline{AB'}$. The consumer is no longer satisfied with the bundle E_0 because he or she can move to a higher indifference curve. The new equilibrium bundle is now E_1. Thus, the consumer buys more of X (given by the quantity $\overline{X_0X_1}$) due to a decrease in its price. The quantity $\overline{X_0X_1}$ can be decomposed into two parts. First of all, consider what bundle would be purchased if the consumer were not allowed to move to a higher indifference curve, that is, if confined to indifference curve 1. If the consumer were an expenditure minimizer, a condition being assumed, the bundle E_0 would not be purchased at the new price P_X^1 and constant P_Y^0. With the new price ratio, the bundle that minimizes expenditure on indifference curve 1 is E',

FIGURE 4.20
X is a normal good.

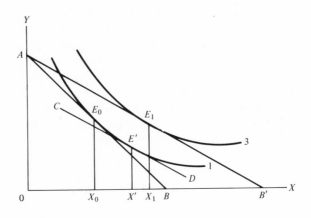

which is a point of tangency between indifference curve 1 and an imaginary budget constraint $\overline{CD}$ that is parallel to the new budget constraint $\overline{AB'}$ (i.e., $\overline{CD} \parallel \overline{AB'}$). A movement along a given indifference curve is interpreted as keeping the consumer's real income constant. The change in the purchased quantity of X is solely caused by a change in the relative prices due to a decrease in P_X while P_Y remains constant. This is the Slutsky–Hicks substitution effect. Students can convince themselves that the bundle E_0 costs more than E' for P_X^1 and P_Y^0 by drawing a budget constraint parallel to $\overline{CD}$ that passes through point E_0. Such a budget constraint will clearly be above $\overline{CD}$ and, therefore, represent a higher consumer outlay.

Having shown that movements along indifference curve 1 leaves the consumer's real income unchanged and that E' is a point on this curve, it follows that the jump from E' to E_1 represents an increase in income, prices being constant. This is the Slutsky–Hicks income effect. In short, $\overline{X_0 X'}$ represents the substitution effect and $\overline{X' X_1}$ the income effect of a fall in the price of X. The algebraic sum of the substitution effect and the income effect is called the total effect. In terms of Figure 4.20 we have

$\overline{X_0 X'}$	substitution effect
$\overline{X' X_1}$	income effect
$\overline{X_0 X_1} = \overline{X_0 X'} + \overline{X' X_1}$	total effect

Our graphical illustration shows that X is a normal good. In this case, the substitution and income effects operate in the same direction, one reinforcing the other. A decrease in the price of X results in an increase in the quantity of X purchased by the consumer at equilibrium. The demand curve has an unambiguous negative slope. Thus, the demand law prevails for all normal goods.

Let us now examine the case in Figure 4.21, where the notation is identical to that of Figure 4.20, but the results differ. In this case, the substitution effect is represented by $\overline{X_0 X'}$, the income effect by $\overline{X' X_1}$, and the total effect by $\overline{X_0 X_1}$. Here X is an inferior good. Whereas the income effect reinforced the substitution effect in Figure 4.20, the income effect partially cancels the substitution effect in Figure 4.21 due to the fact that the two effects operate in opposite directions. In Figure 4.21, we can see that with a decrease in the price of X, the substitution effect results in more of X being purchased by the consumer at equilibrium for an inferior good, but the income effect results in less of X being purchased. Thus, since the negative income effect of an inferior good (but not a Giffen good) only partially cancels the substitution effect (as shown in Figure 4.21), the demand law still holds.

In Figure 4.22, the substitution effect is still represented by $\overline{X_0 X'}$. A decrease in the price of X results in an increase in the

The income effect may either reinforce or cancel out the substitution effect

220

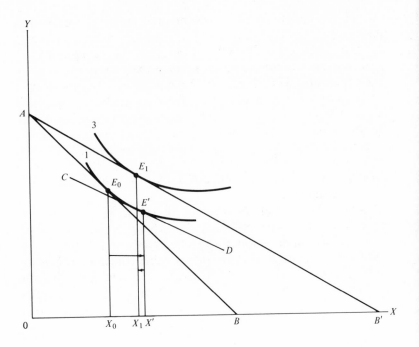

FIGURE 4.21
X is an inferior good, but not a Giffen good.

FIGURE 4.22
X is a Giffen good.

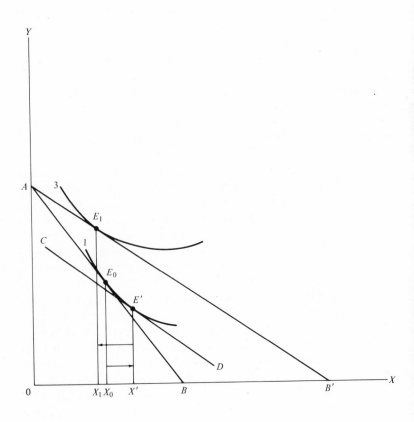

purchased quantity of X at equilibrium due to the substitution effect alone. This is similar to the previous two cases, which is not surprising, since we have already noted that the substitution effect is very reliable. However, the income effect $\overline{X'X_1}$ is negative; that is, an increase in income results in a decrease in the purchased quantity of X. Thus, as in Figure 4.21, X is an inferior good. The essential difference between Figures 4.21 and 4.22 is that whereas the negative income effect only partially cancels the substitution effect in the former, the strong negative income effect more than offsets the substitution effect in the latter. It is in the latter case that the demand law is violated and the demand curve for X is positively sloped. In this case, X is called a Giffen good. Thus, a Giffen good must be an inferior good, and only those inferior goods whose negative income effects have a larger absolute value than their substitution effects become Giffen goods. Hence, not all inferior goods are Giffen goods, which is precisely the assertion that we made in the beginning of this section.

From the above explanation, we can see that inferior goods are not very common and that a Giffen good is even more rare. The Slutsky equation (see the appendix to this chapter) indicates that an inferior good becomes a Giffen good not only when the income effect is negative, but also when the quantity of the inferior good purchased by the consumer is relatively large, since the income term in the Slutsky equation is the product of the quantity and rate of change. The refinement represented by the Slutsky–Hicks theory enables us to explain the logical possibility of the existence of Giffen goods; however, in reality, a Giffen good has seldom been observed.

It should be pointed out that whereas a new product will sometimes not sell at a low price, sales will increase considerably when the price is higher. However, it cannot automatically be concluded that in this case the commodity is a Giffen good. The reason for this caveat is that a Giffen good is defined as a commodity that a consumer will buy more of at a higher price (for a given consumer preference pattern). In other words, a Giffen good is defined under the assumption that the preference of a consumer is independent of the price of the commodity. However, consumers, due to a lack of information, sometimes judge the quality of a commodity by its price. This may result in more of the commodity being purchased at a higher price and less being purchased at a lower price. This is a case where consumer preference is not independent of the price of the commodity, which violates one of the implicit assumptions for a Giffen good. Thus, in such a situation, the commodity is not a Giffen good. This point has occasionally been overlooked. Therefore, we caution students against categorizing a commodity as a Giffen good simply because of the fact that more of it is sold at a higher price.

4.10 THE ANALOGY BETWEEN CONSUMPTION AND PRODUCTION THEORIES

There are more similarities than differences between the theory of consumer behavior and the theory of production. In terms of logical structure and the processes of deduction or mathematics, they are almost identical except for differences in the interpretation of the relevant variables and the fact that a production function is based on cardinal measurement, whereas in modern theory the utility function is based on ordering.

The comparison of the two theories can be carried out both in terms of graphs and in terms of mathematical expressions. For example, it can be observed that parts (a) and (b) of Figure 4.23 are almost identical in appearance, although their interpretations are different. The axes in part (a) represent inputs, whereas in part (b) they represent commodities. The curves in part (a) are isoquants, which indicate quantities of output, and the numerical values attached to the isoquants are cardinal. On the other hand, in part (b) the indifference curves indicate levels of satisfaction, the attached numerical values only having significance as regards ordering, that is, their absolute magnitudes have no meaning here. For example, the values 4 and 8 attached to the isoquants in part (a) indicate not only that isoquant 8 represents more output than isoquant 4, but also that it represents exactly twice the output of isoquant 4. However, the same values attached to the indifference curves in part (b) indicate only that indifference curve 8 represents a higher level of satisfaction than indifference curve 4. There is no implication that indifference curve 8 represents twice the satisfaction of indifference curve 4. As a matter of fact, we would do equally well if we had used the values 1, 2, and 3 for indifference curves 4, 8, and 9, respectively. Another difference is that the shape of the isoquants is essentially determined by technology, whereas that of the indifference curves is determined by the preference pattern of the consumer. Equations (4.8a) and (4.8b) are production and utility functions, respectively. They

Production and utility functions are mathematically similar, but their interpretations differ

FIGURE 4.23 (a) Isoquant map; (b) indifference map.

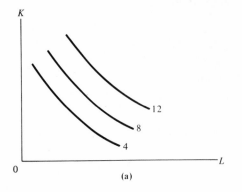

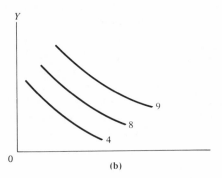

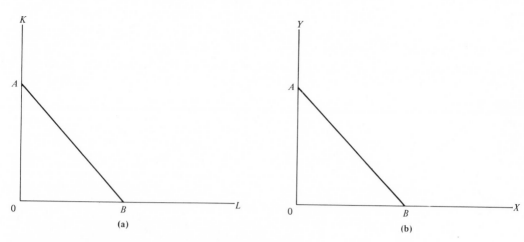

FIGURE 4.24 (a) Isocost curve; (b) budget constraint.

could be written identically, but their interpretations are different just as for the graphs. The ordinal characteristic of the utility function is indicated by the fact that if any cardinal function can represent a consumer's preference, then any monotonic transformation of the function can serve the same purpose. We shall have more to say on this point in the appendix to this chapter.

Production	Consumption	
(a) $Q = f(L, K)$	(b) $U = U(X, Y)$	(4.8)
(a) $C = wL + rK$	(b) $M = P_X X + P_Y Y$	(4.9)
(a) MRTS $= -dK/dL$	(b) MRS $= -dY/dX$	(4.10)
$= \text{MP}_L/\text{MP}_K$	$= \text{MU}_X/\text{MU}_Y$	
$= w/r$	$= P_X/P_Y$	

The graphs in Figure 4.24 are also identical in appearance, that is; they are negatively sloped straight lines. However, the line in part (a) indicates equal-cost combinations of the inputs and is called an isocost curve, the slope of which is determined by the input-price ratio. The line in part (b) indicates an equal expenditure for different bundles of commodities. For a fixed expenditure or income (expenditure and income are identical when saving is zero), and given the prices of the commodities, all available bundles are represented by this line, which is called the budget constraint. The slope of the budget constraint is determined by the price ratio of the commodities. The corresponding equations—(4.9a) and (4.9b)—are both linear. In (4.9a), L and K are the variables and C, w, and r are the parameters, whereas X and Y are the variables and M, P_X, and P_Y are the parameters in (4.9b).

Parts (a) and (b) of Figure 4.25 both indicate that equilibrium (more properly, interior equilibrium) is characterized by the tangency of a straight line and a curve. Although the mathematical properties are identical in both cases, the interpretations are dif-

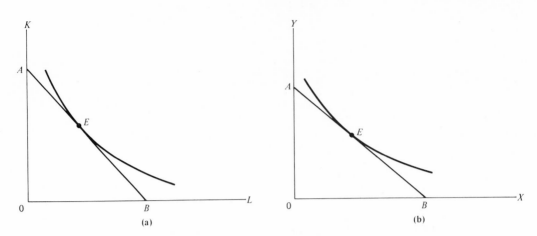

FIGURE 4.25 (a) Firm equilibrium; (b) consumer equilibrium.

Tangency conditions in production and consumer demand theory imply optimality

ferent, as indicated by the corresponding expressions in (4.10a) and (4.10b). The tangency of part (a) indicates the condition MRTS = w/r, which characterizes the maximum output that can be secured for a given cost or the minimum cost for a given output of a firm. The tangency of part (b) indicates the condition MRS = P_X/P_Y, which signifies maximum satisfaction for a given income (expenditure) or minimum expenditure for a given level of consumer satisfaction. Both cases are called equilibrium, which indicates that in economics equilibrium implies optimality. Again note the use of the qualifier word "or," which tells us that equilibrium indicates that one or the other of two conditions is satisfied. In production, these conditions are maximum output for a given cost or minimum cost for a given output. The same is true for consumer equilibrium, except that we deal with satisfaction and income (expenditure).

Part (a) of Figure 4.26 shows the locus of equilibrium points

FIGURE 4.26

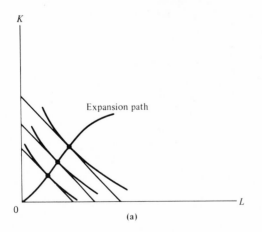
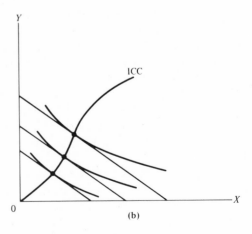

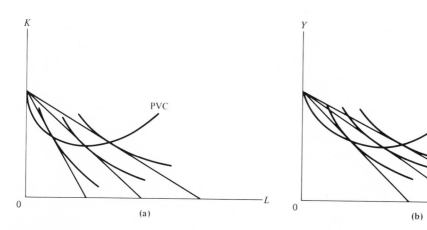

FIGURE 4.27

when cost changes but input prices remain constant, whereas part (b) gives the locus of equilibria when income (expenditure) changes but commodity prices remain constant. The former is called the expansion path, which is most important in production theory because the cost function is derived from it. The latter is called the income consumption curve (ICC), from which an Engel curve can be derived.

Parts (a) and (b) of Figure 4.27 show the locus of equilibrium points for a firm and a consumer, respectively, when one parameter undergoes change (in our case, a change in the price of labor and in the price of commodity X, respectively), all other parameters remaining constant. The locus of equilibrium points in part (b), which is called the price consumption curve (PCC), is one of the most important concepts in consumption theory because the demand curve of a commodity (in this case X) is derived from the corresponding PCC. Theoretically, in part (a) there is a curve that corresponds to the PCC in part (b). However, this *price variation curve* (PVC), which is the locus of equilibrium points when the price of labor changes, does not have much theoretical importance; that is, no theoretical development is based on it. In particular, the demand curve for labor is not derived from it, since the PVC is the locus of equilibrium points for a given cost, whereas the demand for labor by a firm is based on maximum profit, not necessarily on a given cost. We shall have more to say on this point in Chapter 10, which is concerned with income distribution theory. It should be pointed out that all of the points on the loci in Figures 4.26 and 4.27 satisfy either expression (4.10a) or (4.10b).

The above comparisons indicate that production theory and the theory of consumer behavior are indeed technically equivalent, the differences being in their interpretations and the implications that flow from each. A student who has mastered the fundamental principles in production theory will not find it too difficult to understand the theory of consumer behavior, notwithstanding the unfamiliar concept of an ordinal utility function which appears in the modern theory.

4.11 THE CHARACTERISTIC APPROACH AND THE INTRODUCTION OF NEW COMMODITIES

The traditional approach to the analysis of consumer behavior which we have presented up to this point involves treating commodities as the objects of choice. Professor Kelvin Lancaster argues that people buy commodities for certain characteristics they embody and not for the commodities per se. For example, beef can be considered a commodity with such characteristics as taste, calories, and protein. Pork is a commodity that also possesses the characteristics of calories and protein, but in different proportions than beef, and the taste of pork differs from that of beef. Calories and protein are homogeneous characteristics, and there exists an objective measure for their quantities. However, taste is a different story; that is, there does not exist an objective measure for taste. This suggests the difficulties inherent in the characteristic approach. Nevertheless, the characteristic approach to the analysis of consumer behavior does have its merits

The characteristic approach to consumer behavior provides a basis for evaluating new product markets

compared with the traditional commodity approach. In particular, the traditional approach considers the commodities in the market as given, and there is no way to analyze whether a new commodity can be introduced into the market. The characteristic approach provides a theoretical framework to analyze the marketability of a new commodity, provided that it possesses the same measurable characteristics as some commodities already in the market, but in different proportions. We shall use a simple example to illustrate the main ideas of the approach (for more details, see Lancaster, 1960).

The essential difference between the traditional and the characteristic approaches is in the reformulation of the budget constraint as the analysis is transformed from commodity space to characteristic space. The shapes of the indifference curves are similar in both cases, but the budget constraint may be different when more than two commodities are taken into consideration. This will become obvious later.

Suppose that there are two commodities X and Y, both of which possess the two characteristics C and P (for calories and protein), but in different proportions. Let 1 unit of X contain 1 unit of C and 10 units of P, and 1 unit of Y contain 10 units of C and 1 unit of P. Assume that a consumer has a budget of $20 and that the prices of X and Y are both $1 per unit. If all of the consumer's money is spent on X, then he or she gets 20 units of C and 200 units of P. On the other hand, if the $20 is spent on Y, then the

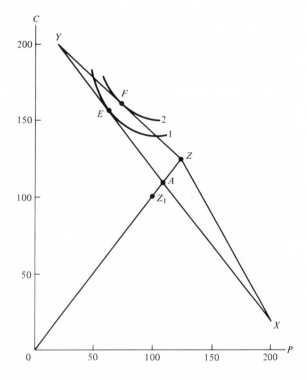

FIGURE 4.28

consumer gets 200 units of C and 20 units of P. If part of the consumer's money is spent on X and the remainder on Y, then different combinations of C and P can be obtained. This is shown in Figure 4.28, where the horizontal and vertical axes represent the characteristics P and C, respectively, rather than the traditional commodities. The points X and Y show the combinations of characteristics P and C that the consumer can get if the \$20 is spent only on X or Y, respectively. It can be shown that all possible combinations of P and C that the consumer can obtain by spending the \$20 on both X and Y are on the straight line $\overline{XY}$. (For a mathematical proof of this statement, see Section A4.7 in the appendix at the end of this chapter.) The straight line $\overline{XY}$ in the characteristic space corresponds to the budget constraint in the traditional approach.

The indifference curves for a consumer in characteristic space have a shape similar to that of the corresponding curves in commodity space. Consumer equilibrium is attained at a point of tangency between an indifference curve and $\overline{XY}$, that is, point E in Figure 4.28. If $\overline{XY}$ is tangent to the highest indifference curve at either X or Y, then we have a corner solution, that is, the consumer buys only one of the two commodities. Since E is between X and Y, equilibrium is attained by purchasing a combination of X and Y.

Now suppose that a third commodity Z, also having charac-

Characteristics must be well defined (or measurable) before one can use the characteristics approach

teristics C and P, is produced. Let 1 unit of Z contain 5 units of C and 5 units of P. This does not tell us whether Z will be chosen by the consumer, since we do not know its price. Thus, the marketability of Z not only depends on its content of C and P, but also on its price. Suppose that the price of Z is also $1 per unit. Then the consumer can get 100 units of C and 100 units of P by spending the $20 on Z; this is represented by point Z_1 in Figure 4.28. The consumer will never buy Z at this price because 110 units of C and 110 units P (point A) can be obtained with the same amount of money by purchasing 10 units of X and 10 units of Y. Since all consumers face the same prices, point Z_1 is dominated by point A. Given these prices and rational consumers, the firm that introduces Z will not find any buyers in the market at the price of $1 per unit.

Suppose that the price of Z is reduced to 80¢ per unit. A consumer with $20 can now buy 25 units of Z to obtain 125 units of C and 125 units of P; this is represented by point Z in Figure 4.28. The cost of point A is the same as that of point Z, but the latter offers more of both C and P. Therefore, Z will be preferred to A by any rational consumer, that is, Z dominates A. For similar reasons, any point between A and Y is dominated by at least one point on line $\overline{YZ}$, and any point between A and X is dominated by at least one point on line $\overline{XZ}$. Thus, the possible combinations of C and P that the consumer can obtain with $20 are extended from the straight line $\overline{XY}$ to the curve $\widehat{XZY}$. In Figure 4.28, point E no longer represents consumer equilibrium because the consumer can now move to a higher indifference curve (i.e., a higher level of satisfaction) with the same budget. The graph shows that point F is the new equilibrium and that the consumer's satisfaction is raised from 1 to 2 with the introduction of the new commodity. In this case, the consumer switches from a combination of X and Y to a combination of Y and Z. Thus, the introduction of Z reduces the market for commodity X. It should be noted that since consumers' tastes are different, some may switch from a combination of X and Y to a combination of X and Z. In either case, the consumer's satisfaction can increase with the introduction of Z.

In the case of corner solutions, a consumer's equilibrium can occur at either X or Y before and after the introduction of Z. The satisfaction of such a consumer will not be influenced by the introduction of the new commodity Z.

If consumer tastes are diverse, then once any new commodity is introduced and actually sold in the market, some consumer's satisfaction will be at a higher level. However, no consumer will have a lower level of satisfaction.[7] Although the introduction of

---

[7] It should be remembered that consumer satisfaction is here considered only in terms of the amount of C and P that can be obtained for a given expenditure on the commodities.

a new commodity will usually reduce the market share of an existing one but not eliminate it, in some special cases a new commodity may completely eliminate old ones from the market. For example, students may wish to convince themselves that if the price of Z goes below 50¢ per unit, whereas X and Y cannot be profitably marketed below $1 per unit, then Z will take over, X and Y disappearing from the market. In this case, all consumers who have consumed X and/or Y will be better off due to the new product, since for the same expenditure they can obtain more C and P through purchases of Z than of either X or Y.

As mentioned above, the problem in the characteristic approach is defining and (sometimes) measuring characteristics. However, it does create an unexplored frontier in the analysis of the marketability of new commodities. Thus, it merits some discussion, especially in the area of managerial economics.

SUMMARY

In this chapter we have shown that individual preference and purchasing power are the two important determinants of both consumer behavior and the demand for goods and services. We noted that, whereas in the early stages of the development of the theory of consumer behavior the notions of a cardinal utility function and marginal utility (MU) were used to represent consumer preference, utility cannot actually be measured and so the concepts of ordinal utility and marginal rate of substitution (MRS) were adopted to maintain analytical rigor. We explained that, although the concept of MU is no longer meaningful, it is still implicit in the concept of the MRS, which is nothing more than the ratio of the MUs of two commodities as represented by the slope of an indifference curve at a given point.

We have shown that the concept of ordinal utility can be effectively employed by use of a map of indifference curves and isocosts to analyze consumer behavior and the demand for a commodity. With the behavior assumptions of complete ordering, transitivity, nonsatiation, the absence of externalities concerning consumers, and the absence of lexicographic ordering, we demonstrated that indifference curves possess the following features: (1) They are negatively sloped, (2) they do not intersect, and (3) a given bundle of goods can be on one and only one indifference curve. It was further explained that feature (2) does not imply that indifference curves are parallel, and that under the assumption of nonsatiation a "point of bliss" does not exist. Moreover, we noted that while the concepts of indifference curves and MRS in demand theory are similar to those of isoquants and MRTS in production theory, there are some important exceptions. Thus, a decreasing MRS, like a decreasing MRTS, is very common in both cases, and MRS in consumption can be either zero or increasing. However, whereas isoquants in production represent measured values (e.g., 10, 20, 30, etc. units of output), indifference curves in consumption represent only ordinal ordering.

In describing the condition for consumer equilibrium, we indicated that it is analogous to that for a firm in production theory; that is, the tangency between the budget line and an indifference curve for a consumer can be compared to the tangency between the isocost and an isoquant for a firm. Thus, using the assumptions of perfect divisibility of commodities and regularity of consumer preference (meaning that consumers behave rationally), we noted that the tangency condition guarantees maximum utility for a given income or, alternatively, a minimum expenditure for a given level of satisfaction if MRS is decreasing. This condition is essentially the same as that applying to the maximization of output for a given budget or to the minimumizing of cost for a given output in production (that is, the requirement that isoquant and isocost be tangent when MRTS is decreasing yields an equilibrium condition). We also noted in the case of consumer equilibrium that the tangency condition establishes the equality between MRS and the price ratio of the commodities. However, we emphasized that when MRS is zero, constant, or increasing, or when a corner solution under decreasing MRS exists, the tangency condition is no longer met.

We concluded our discussion on consumer behavior by observing that the locus of equilibrium points given by the tangency solution as income increases constitutes an income consumption curve, and the locus of such points when the price of one commodity changes, other things remaining equal, provides us with a price consumption curve. We showed that in the latter case the demand curve of a consumer can be directly derived, although Slutsky (and later Hicks) has demonstrated that the demand curve represents both income and substitution effects as the price of a commodity undergoes change. Finally, we explained that a commodity can be called a normal good (with demand curve having negative slope) if the income effect is positive and a Giffen or inferior good (positively sloped demand curve) if the income effect is negative, but that not all inferior goods have a demand curve with positive slope. The characteristic approach in the analysis of consumer behavior concludes this chapter.

EXERCISES AND QUESTIONS FOR CHAPTER 4 ON THE THEORY OF CONSUMER BEHAVIOR

1. What are the assumptions that a consumer's behavior must satisfy in order that an indifference map can be constructed? Explain.

2. What does the term decreasing *marginal rate of substitution* mean? First define the italicized term and then explain its qualified nature or form.

3. Draw indifference maps that show the following characteristics and explain why each of your graphs possesses that characteristic:

   a. Decreasing MRS.
   b. Increasing MRS.
   c. Constant MRS.

4. What does the "point of bliss" mean in an indifference map? What assumption can we make so that a point of bliss may not exist? Explain.

5. What are the conditions under which a consumer will be at equilibrium? Use your own words or a numerical example to explain why this is so. Are there exceptions? Explain.

6. How can an ICC be derived? What is the relationship between an ICC and an Engel curve? Use graphs to help explain your answers.

7. Explain the relationship between the PCC and the demand curve for a commodity.

8. For a two-commodity case, use the graphical method to show how the demand for X behaves when the price Y decreases. A brief explanation in words should accompany your graphical presentation.

9. What is the difference between a normal good and an inferior good? Use graphs to facilitate your explanation.

10. How is it possible that the demand curve for a commodity can be positively sloped (i.e. a higher price accompanied by a higher quantity demanded)? Is the demand curve of an inferior good necessarily positively sloped? Give your answers in terms of income effects and substitution effects.

11. Use the graphical method to derive an ICC and a PCC. Explain the difference between these two curves.

12. What factors can cause a shift of a consumer's demand curve? Use the graphical method to show how a demand curve will shift when one of the factors has been changed in a specific manner or form.

13. Define the following in your own words:

    a. Giffen paradox
    b. Inferior good

14. Draw graphs and explain the following in terms of substitution and income effects:

    a. The commodity concerned is an inferior good, but not subject to the Giffen paradox.
    b. The prevalence of a Giffen paradox.

15. Suppose that a consumer has a given amount of income and tries to maximize his or her satisfaction. Give the conditions under which the utility will be maximized. Why? If there are only two commodities, will the consumer always buy both of them? Explain.

16. It is said that two indifference curves cannot intersect. Do you agree with the above statement? Use graphs and a verbal explanation to justify your answer.

17. Using the graphical method, derive a demand curve for a commodity where the consumer's preference is represented by straight-line indifference curves. A written explanation is necessary.

18. Using the graphical method, show how the demand for X behaves when income increases. A brief explanation should accompany your graphical presentation.

19. Compare a consumer's equilibrium and a firm's equilibrium under conditions of a competitive market. What are the similarities and differences? Explain.

20. A college student who is studying for final exams has only 6 hours of study time remaining and wants to get as high a total score as possible in three subjects: economics, mathematics, and statistics. How should the student's time be allocated if the relationships shown in Table E4.1 between study time and test grade for each subject are assumed to hold? Explain the derivation of your answer.

TABLE E4.1

Economics		Mathematics		Statistics	
Hours	Grade	Hours	Grade	Hours	Grade
0	30	0	40	0	70
1	44	1	52	1	80
2	65	2	62	2	88
3	75	3	70	3	90
4	83	4	77	4	91
5	88	5	83	5	92
6	90	6	88	6	93

A MATHEMATICAL NOTE
ON CONSUMER BEHAVIOR

A4.1 THE NATURE OF THE ORDINAL UTILITY FUNCTION

The mathematical formulation and tools of the theory of consumer behavior are very similar (and, in many cases, identical) to those of production theory. Thus, in the following we shall omit some of the details that have already been discussed in the appendix to Chapter 2. Students should review the appendix to Chapter 2 in order to gain a better perspective on the materials that will be presented here.

The utility function of a consumer subject to Assumption 4.5 (absence of externalities) can be written

$$U = U(X_1, X_2, ..., X_n) \tag{A4.1}$$

where X_i, $i = 1, 2, ..., n$, are the n commodities that the consumer may consume. This is a general mathematical expression for representing a consumer's preference, that is, it serves the same purpose as the indifference map in the graphical method. The properties of the utility function are determined by the consumer's preference pattern. In general, it is assumed that any order-preserving function can serve as a utility function, provided that it possesses continuous and finite first- and second-order partial derivatives with respect to all of its variables. For the sake of convenience, we offer the following notation to define the utility function with respect to the commodities consumed:

$$U_i = \partial U/\partial X_i, \qquad i = 1, 2, ..., n$$
$$U_{ij} = \partial^2 U/\partial X_i \partial X_i, \qquad i, j = 1, 2, ..., n \tag{A4.2}$$

Assumption 4.3 (nonsatiation) implies that

$$U_i > 0, \qquad i = 1, 2, ..., n \tag{A4.3}$$

Furthermore, the second-order cross partial derivatives are assumed to be symmetric; that is,

$$U_{ij} = U_{ji}, \qquad\qquad i, j = 1, 2, \dots, n \qquad (A4.4)$$

The latter assumption is not very restrictive, since it is satisfied by most functions if the cross partial derivatives exist. As a professor once remarked to one of the authors on this point, "it takes some ingenuity to construct a function whose cross partials are not symmetric." Consideration of this statement should convince the student that the assumption of symmetry is indeed not very restrictive and can easily be satisfied.

In the case of cardinal utility, U_i is called the marginal utility (MU) of commodity i. In the case of ordinal utility, the utility function is not unique. Any order-preserving function can also serve as a utility function. Furthermore, any monotonic transformation[1] of an order-preserving function can also serve as a utility function. For this reason, the values of the partial derivatives of an ordinal utility function are also not unique. However, the ratios of the partial derivatives are not affected by the transformation. For example, if the utility function (A4.1) is an order-preserving function, a simple linear transformation such as

$$V = A + aU, \qquad a > 0 \qquad (A4.5)$$

can also serve as a utility function, since whenever $U^{**} > U^*$, we also have $V^{**} > V^*$. (Note that if $a < 0$, then the linear transformation will no longer be monotonic.) It is easily seen that the MU of a commodity computed using (A4.5) is different from that computed using (A4.1) except in the special case where $a = 1$, since

$$\partial V/\partial X_i = a\partial U/\partial X_i \gtrless \partial U/\partial X_i \qquad \text{for} \quad a \gtrless 1 \qquad (A4.6)$$

As a result, the MU concept is not useful within the confines of ordinal utility theory. On the other hand, the ratios of the partial derivatives will not be affected by the transformation. For example,

$$\frac{\partial V/\partial X_i}{\partial V/\partial X_j} = \frac{a\partial U/\partial X_i}{a\partial U/\partial X_j} = \frac{\partial U/\partial X_i}{\partial U/\partial X_j}, \qquad i, j = 1, 2, \dots, n \qquad (A4.7)$$

This result is not only valid for the linear transformation, but also for any monotonic transformation. Thus, let

$$V = T(U) \qquad (A4.8)$$

Since, by the process of deduction, V is a function of X_1, X_2,

---

[1] A function $T(U)$ is defined as a monotonic transformation of U if $T(U^{**}) > T(U^*)$ whenever $U^{**} > U^*$. Thus, it is an order-preserving transformation.

$\ldots, X_n$, we have

$$\frac{\partial V/\partial X_i}{\partial V/\partial X_j} = \frac{T'\partial U/\partial X_i}{T'\partial U/\partial X_j} = \frac{\partial U/\partial X_i}{\partial U/\partial X_j} \tag{A4.9}$$

for all $i, j = 1, 2, \ldots, n$.

A4.2 THE MARGINAL RATE OF SUBSTITUTION

Since the ratios of the partial derivatives of an ordinal utility function are invariant with respect to a monotonic transformation, they can take the place of MU. In this way, we obtain what is called the marginal rate of substitution (MRS) [see Hicks (1946, p. 20) for the formulation of the MRS]. The MRS of X_j for X_i can be defined as the quantity of X_j that would just compensate the consumer for the loss of a marginal unit of X_i provided that the quantity of all other commodities and the consumer's level of satisfaction are constant. This definition of MRS turns out to be mathematically equivalent to the ratio of two MUs. This can be shown by taking the derivative of the utility function (A4.1):

$$dU = U_1 dX_1 + U_2 dX_2 + \cdots + U_n dX_n \tag{A4.10}$$

Since MRS is defined only when $dU = 0$, (A4.10) can be written

$$-U_i dX_i = U_1 dX_1 + U_2 dX_2 + \cdots$$
$$+ U_j dX_j + \cdots + U_n dX_n \tag{A4.11}$$

Dividing both sides by $U_i dX_j$ and setting $dX_h = 0$, $h \neq i, j$, we have

$$\text{MRS} = -\partial X_i/\partial X_j = U_j/U_i \tag{A4.12}$$

It is important to note that MRS is defined subject to the conditions that (1) the changes in X_i and X_j do not result in any change in utility (that is, movement along a given indifference curve is involved), and (2) only X_i and X_j change, all other commodities remaining constant.

A4.3 CONSTRAINED UTILITY MAXIMIZATION AND THE DEMAND FUNCTION

By the nonsatiation assumption of (A4.3), the utility function (A4.1) may not have an absolute maximum. However, consumers are always constrained by the finite amount of money available to them, that is, income M. Furthermore, consumers are also given the prices $P_1, P_2, \ldots, P_n$ of the n commodities. Since all of the consumers' income is spent on the n commodities, we have the budget equation

$$M = P_1 X_1 + P_2 X_2 + \cdots + P_n X_n = \sum_{i=1}^{n} P_i X_i \tag{A4.13}$$

The assumption that all of a consumer's income must be spent is not restrictive in the general n-commodity case, since savings can be properly considered a commodity.

The mathematical problem is to maximize (A4.1) subject to the constraint (A4.13). To do this we employ the Lagrange multiplier method. We construct the Lagrange function

$$L = U(X_1, X_2, ..., X_n) + \lambda(M - \sum P_i X_i) \tag{A4.14}$$

where λ is the Lagrange multiplier (a positive constant).

The first-order conditions of a constrained maximum are

$$\partial L / \partial X_i = U_i - \lambda P_i = 0, \quad i = 1, 2, ..., n$$
$$\partial L / \partial \lambda = M - \sum P_i X_i = 0 \tag{A4.15}$$

The second-order conditions are that the bordered Hessian determinants (see the appendix at the end of Chapter 2 concerning the determinant of a matrix) must alternate in sign:

$$\begin{vmatrix} U_{11} & U_{12} & -P_1 \\ U_{21} & U_{22} & -P_2 \\ -P_1 & -P_2 & 0 \end{vmatrix} > 0$$

$$\begin{vmatrix} U_{11} & U_{12} & U_{13} & -P_1 \\ U_{21} & U_{22} & U_{23} & -P_2 \\ U_{31} & U_{32} & U_{33} & -P_3 \\ -P_1 & -P_2 & -P_3 & 0 \end{vmatrix} < 0$$

$$\vdots \tag{A4.16}$$

$$(-1)^n \begin{vmatrix} U_{11} & U_{12} & \cdots & U_{1n} & -P_1 \\ U_{21} & U_{22} & \cdots & U_{2n} & -P_2 \\ & & \vdots & & \\ U_{n1} & U_{n2} & \cdots & U_{nn} & -P_n \\ -P_1 & -P_2 & \cdots & -P_n & 0 \end{vmatrix} > 0$$

If the second-order conditions are satisfied, then the solution of the first-order conditions (A4.15) yields the n demand functions for the commodities. In general, the demand for any commodity is a function of the n prices and the consumer's income. The properties of the demand function for any commodity depend on the properties of the utility function. If the utility function is not specified, then an explicit demand function cannot be derived. However, due to the properties of the famous Slutsky equation, there are certain general statements that can be made concerning the demand function even without a specific utility function.

By eliminating λ, the first system of n equations in (A4.15) yields $n - 1$ independent equations of the form

$$U_i / U_j = P_i / P_j, \quad i, j = 1, 2, ..., n \tag{A4.17}$$

Equation (A4.17) corresponds to the condition of tangency between an indifference curve and a budget constraint. The left side is the MRS between X_i and X_j (which represents the subjective view of the consumer) and the right side is the price ratio (which represents the market opportunities available to the consumer).

The $n - 1$ equations in (A4.17), together with the second equation in (A4.15), which is precisely the budget constraint, constitute n equations in the n variables X_1, X_2, ..., X_n. In general, we can solve this system on n equations in terms of the $n + 1$ parameters P_1, P_2, ..., P_n and M. Thus, the solution of this system of n equations can be written

$$X_1 = D_1(P_1, P_2, ..., P_n, M)$$

$$X_2 = D_2(P_1, P_2, ..., P_n, M) \qquad\qquad (A4.18)$$

$$\vdots$$

$$X_n = D_n(P_1, P_2, ..., P_n, M)$$

These are the demand functions for the n commodities.

From the system of equations (A4.17), and given the budget equation, it is obvious that the demand functions must have the property of homogeneity of the degree zero in all of the prices and income; that is, if all of the prices and income are multiplied by a constant, then the demand functions for all of the n commodities will not be altered. This can be verified by the following reasoning. The n demand functions are the solutions of the $n - 1$ equations in (A4.17) and the budget equation. If we multiply all of the prices and income by the constant a, from (A4.17) we obtain

$$U_i/U_j = aP_i/aP_j = P_i/P_j, \qquad i, j = 1, 2, ..., n, \qquad (A4.17')$$

which is identical to (A4.17). The situation with the budget equation is similar. If we multiply all of the prices and income by the constant a, from (A4.13) we obtain

$$aM = aP_1X_1 + aP_2X_2 + \cdots + aP_nX_n \qquad\qquad (A4.13')$$

which is identical to (A4.13), since the a on the left cancels out those on the right. The solution of the system of equations (A4.17') and (A4.13') must be identical to that derived from (A4.17) and (A4.13). This proves our assertion.

Other properties of a demand function derived from the utility maximization assumption will be shown after we derive the Slutsky equation. However, we shall first derive the demand function from a specific utility function in order to demonstrate the practical meaning of the above generalities.

A4.4 THE DERIVATION OF A SPECIFIC DEMAND FUNCTION

Let us consider a simple example. If there are only the three commodities X_1, X_2, and X_3, then the utility function is as follows:

$$U = \ln X_1X_2X_3 \qquad\qquad (A4.19)$$

With income M and the prices P_1, P_2, and P_3, respectively, the budget equation is

$$M = P_1X_1 + P_2X_2 + P_3X_3 \qquad (A4.20)$$

The Lagrange function is

$$L = \ln X_1X_2X_3 + \lambda(M - P_1X_1 - P_2X_2 - P_3X_3) \qquad (A4.21)$$

The first-order conditions are

$$\partial L/\partial X_1 = X_2X_3/X_1X_2X_3 - \lambda P_1 = 0$$
$$\partial L/\partial X_2 = X_1X_3/X_1X_2X_3 - \lambda P_2 = 0$$
$$\partial L/\partial X_3 = X_1X_2/X_1X_2X_3 - \lambda P_3 = 0 \qquad (A4.22)$$
$$\partial L/\partial \lambda = M - P_1X_1 - P_2X_2 - P_3X_3 = 0$$

Eliminating λ, (A4.22) yields the following three equations:

$$P_1X_1 - P_2X_2 \qquad\quad = 0$$
$$P_2X_2 - P_3X_3 = 0 \qquad (A4.23)$$
$$P_1X_1 + P_2X_2 + P_3X_3 = M$$

Using Cramer's rule to solve for the Xs, we obtain

$$X_1 = M/3P_1$$
$$X_2 = M/3P_2 \qquad (A4.24)$$
$$X_3 = M/3P_3$$

These are the demand functions for X_1, X_2, and X_3, respectively, and they have certain desirable properties. First of all, they obey the demand law, that is, they have a negative slope in the price–quantity graph. We have

$$\partial X_i/\partial P_i = -M/3P_i^2 < 0, \qquad i = 1, 2, 3 \qquad (A4.25)$$

All of the commodities are normal goods, since

$$\partial X_i/\partial M = 1/3P_i > 0, \qquad i = 1, 2, 3 \qquad (A4.26)$$

On the other hand, the demand for X_i is a function of income M and only its own price P_i; it is not a function of the other prices. In general, the demand for a commodity should be a function of income and all prices. This special case, indicating that the commodities are independents rather than substitutes or complements, is the result of the specific properties of the utility function.

Some students may wish to compare the close similarities of our demand functions with those of Henderson and Quandt (1971). Although our utility function is different from theirs, the derived demand functions would be identical if the number of commodities were the same. The reason for this is simple: Our utility function is a monotonic transformation of theirs. This also indicates that ordinal utility can accomplish the same job as cardinal utility insofar as the demand function is concerned. Since ordinal utility theory requires less restrictive assumptions than cardinal utility theory, the former is considered superior. In the rules of the scientific game, this is called the principle of *Occam's razor,* which states that the superior theory of two that give rise to essentially the same consequences is the one that involves the less restrictive assumptions.

A4.5 PROPERTIES OF A DEMAND FUNCTION DERIVED FROM A GENERAL UTILITY FUNCTION, THE SLUTSKY EQUATION, AND DEMAND LAW

Expressions (A4.25) and (A4.26) indicate the properties of the demand functions (A4.24) which can be derived only when the specific utility function (A4.19) is known. Hence, the following question arises: Is it possible to derive certain properties of the demand functions without knowing the specific utility function? In other words, can we derive certain properties of the demand functions if the utility function is only specified in the general form (A4.1) with the known properties (A4.3) and (A4.4)? The answer is yes. A major contribution to pure economic theory in this respect was made by the mathematician Eugene Slutsky (1952) in an article originally published in the Italian journal *Giornale degli Economisti* in July 1915. The famous Slutsky equation, which corresponds to expressions (A4.25) and (A4.26), is the basis of the modern mathematical theory of consumer behavior.

The properties of the Slutsky equation are derived from the conditions of constrained utility maximization of a consumer. Purchases by a rational consumer will always satisfy the conditions (A4.15), that is, although changes in prices and income will, in general, alter the quantities of the various commodities purchased by a consumer, the new quantities, based on the new prices and income, will still satisfy the conditions (A4.15). The effect of the price and income changes on the consumer's purchases can be derived through total differentiation of (A4.15) by allowing all variables to vary simultaneously as follows:

$$U_{11} dX_1 + U_{12} dX_2 + \cdots + U_{1n} dX_n - P_1 d\lambda$$
$$= \lambda dP_1$$
$$U_{21} dX_1 + U_{22} dX_2 + \cdots + U_{2n} dX_n - P_2 d\lambda$$
$$= \lambda dP_2$$
$$\vdots$$
$$U_{n1} dX_1 + U_{n2} dX_2 + \cdots + U_{nn} dX_n - P_n d\lambda \qquad \text{(A4.27)}$$
$$= \lambda dP_n$$
$$-P_1 dX_1 - P_2 dX_2 - \cdots - P_n dX_n - 0 d\lambda$$
$$= -dM + X_1 dP_1 + \cdots + X_n dP_n$$

We have a total of $n + 1$ equations. For our purposes, we consider $dX_1, dX_2, \ldots, dX_n$ and $d\lambda$ as the $n + 1$ unknowns and all other terms, such as $U_{ij}, dP_i, dM, P_i,$ and $X_i, i, j = 1, 2, \ldots, n$, as constants. For convenience in notation, we denote the determinant of the coefficient matrix by D:

$$
D = \begin{vmatrix}
U_{11} & U_{12} & \cdots & U_{1n} & -P_1 \\
U_{21} & U_{22} & \cdots & U_{2n} & -P_2 \\
& & \vdots & & \\
U_{n1} & U_{n2} & \cdots & U_{nn} & -P_n \\
-P_1 & -P_2 & \cdots & -P_n & 0
\end{vmatrix}
\tag{A4.28}
$$

Note the similarity between (A4.28) and the last expression in (A4.16). The properties in (A4.16) will be used later.

The coefficient matrix (A4.28) is an $(n + 1) \times (n + 1)$ matrix. If we strike out the ith row and jth column of the matrix, we have an $n \times n$ matrix, the determinant of which is called the *minor* of the i, j element of the original matrix. If the minor is multiplied by $(-1)^{i+j}$, then this determinant is called the *cofactor* of the element. We denote the cofactor of U_{ij} by D_{ij}; for example,

$$
D_{11} = \begin{vmatrix}
U_{22} & \cdots & U_{2n} & -P_2 \\
U_{32} & \cdots & U_{3n} & -P_3 \\
& \vdots & & \\
U_{n2} & \cdots & U_{nn} & -P_n \\
-P_2 & \cdots & -P_n & 0
\end{vmatrix} (-1)^2
$$

$$
D_{12} = \begin{vmatrix}
U_{21} & U_{23} & \cdots & U_{2n} & -P_2 \\
U_{31} & U_{33} & \cdots & U_{3n} & -P_3 \\
& & \vdots & & \\
U_{n1} & U_{n3} & \cdots & U_{nn} & -P_n \\
-P_1 & -P_3 & \cdots & -P_n & 0
\end{vmatrix} (-1)^3
\tag{A4.29}
$$

Using this notation, by Cramer's rule (see the appendix at the end of Chapter 2) we have

$$
dX_1 = \left[\lambda \left(\sum_{i=1}^{n} D_{i1} dP_i \right) + D_{n+1,1} \left(-dM + \sum_{i=1}^{n} X_i dP_i \right) \right] \Big/ D
$$

$$
dX_2 = \left[\lambda \left(\sum_{i=1}^{n} D_{i2} dP_i \right) + D_{n+1,2} \left(-dM + \sum_{i=1}^{n} X_i dP_i \right) \right] \Big/ D
$$

$$
\vdots
$$

$$
dX_n = \left[\lambda \left(\sum_{i=1}^{n} D_{in} dP_i \right) + D_{n+1,n} \left(-dM + \sum_{i=1}^{n} X_i dP_i \right) \right] \Big/ D
$$

$$
\tag{A4.30}
$$

Dividing both sides of the ith equation by dP_j, and assuming that income and all other prices do not change, that is, $dM = dP_i$

$= 0$, $i \neq j$, we obtain

$$\frac{\partial X_i}{\partial P_j} = \frac{\lambda D_{ji}}{D} + X_j \frac{D_{n+1,i}}{D} \qquad (A4.31)$$

For example, when P_1 changes but income and all other prices remain constant, from the first equation we obtain

$$\frac{\partial X_1}{\partial P_1} = \frac{\lambda D_{11}}{D} + X_1 \frac{D_{n+1,1}}{D} \qquad (A4.32)$$

This expression, in fact, gives us the slope (rather, the inverse of the slope) of the demand curve for commodity 1 in the traditional quantity–price two-dimensional graph.

The rate of change in the quantity of commodity i when income changes, all prices being constant, is

$$\partial X_i / \partial M = -D_{n+1,i}/D \qquad (A4.33)$$

Changes in commodity prices will result in changes in the consumer's level of satisfaction because a new equilibrium lies on a different indifference curve (see, e.g., Figure 4.18). Consider a situation in which a price change is compensated for by an income change that leaves the consumer's level of satisfaction unchanged, that is, $dU = 0$. From (A4.10), we have

$$U_1 dX_1 + U_2 dX_2 + \cdots + U_n dX_n = 0$$

Since in equilibrium $U_i/U_j = P_i/P_j$, we also have

$$P_1 dX_1 + P_2 dX_2 + \cdots + P_n dX_n = 0$$

Finally, from the last equation of (A4.27),

$$-dM + X_1 dP_1 + X_2 dP_2 + \cdots + X_n dP_n = 0$$

This implies

$$\left(\frac{\partial X_i}{\partial P_j}\right)_{U = \text{const}} = \frac{\lambda D_{ji}}{D} \equiv S_{ji} \qquad (A4.34)$$

For later convenience, we write this term in the form of S_{ji}. Taking (A4.33) and (A4.34) into consideration, (A4.31) can be written

$$\frac{\partial X_i}{\partial P_j} = \left(\frac{\partial X_i}{\partial P_j}\right)_{U = \text{const}} - X_j \left(\frac{\partial X_i}{\partial M}\right)_{\text{prices} = \text{const}} \qquad (A4.35)$$

This is the famous Slutsky equation. For $i = j$, $\partial X_i/\partial P_i$ is the slope of the demand curve plotted on a graph with price as the horizontal axis and quantity as the vertical axis. Economists traditionally draw graphs for demand curves in such a way that quantity is on the horizontal axis and price on the vertical axis. In this case, the slope of the demand curve for commodity i is

$\partial P_i / \partial X_i$ rather than $\partial X_i / \partial P_i$. Some students occasionally become confused with respect to this. However, a little caution will help to avoid possible mistakes.

The first term on the right side of (A4.35) is the substitution term, which corresponds to the substitution effect in the graphical representation. This is only a correspondence, since the former is a rate and the latter an absolute value. The second term on the right side of (A4.35) is the income term, which corresponds to the income effect. Again, the mathematically and graphically measured effects are not identical, the latter being only an interpretation of the former. The sum of these two terms corresponds to the total effect.

The sign of the Slutsky equation gives the sign of the slope of the demand curve of commodity i when $i = j$. Note that the slope of the demand curve in a traditional graph is $\partial P_i / \partial X_i$, that is, the inverse of the slope of the Slutsky equation. Since $\partial X_i / \partial P_i$ is the sum of two terms, we have to examine the sign of each of them in order to know the sign of the sum.

It is easy to see that the substitution term is always negative when the price of the commodity changes:

$$S_{ii} < 0 \qquad\qquad\qquad (A4.36)$$

This follows from the fact that $\lambda > 0$ due to the assumption in (A4.3), the first-order conditions (A4.15), and $P_i > 0$. Furthermore, D_{ii} and D always have opposite signs, which follows from the second-order conditions (A4.16). This is obvious when $i = n$. Since each and every commodity can be considered the nth commodity, $D_{ii}/D < 0$, $i = 1, 2, ..., n$. Thus, (A4.36) follows.

The substitution term is also symmetric for commodities i and j; that is,

$$S_{ij} = S_{ji} \qquad\qquad\qquad (A4.37)$$

This is a result of assumption (A4.4). Due to this assumption, the matrix of the determinant D_{ij} is symmetric; hence, $D_{ij} = D_{ji}$ and (A4.37) follows.

From expression (A4.33), the sign of the income term cannot be determined. Theoretically, the demand curve of a commodity can have either a positive or a negative slope. However, in the case of a normal good (for the definition of a normal good, see Section 4.7), $\partial X_i / \partial M > 0$. Taking the negative sign in front of the income term in the Slutsky equation into consideration, the sign of the equation is unambiguous. We may conclude that

$$\partial X_i / \partial P_i < 0 \qquad \text{for normal good } i \qquad (A4.38)$$

The demand law holds for all normal goods; that is, the demand curve for all normal goods has a negative slope.

In the case of an inferior good, the sign of the Slutsky equation is indeterminant. Since the income term is the product of the quantity of the commodity demanded and the partial derivative with respect to income, if X_i is small, it is unlikely that the income term will outweigh the substitution term. Even if X_i is an inferior good, its demand curve will still likely have a negative slope. It is only in the special case where X_i is relatively large that the Slutsky equation can be positive, that is, the case of a Giffen good. This is why a Giffen good is quite rare: It not only has to be an inferior good, but the negative income effect also has to be quite strong.

Slutsky's contribution to the theory of consumer behavior is in the decomposition of the effect of a change in price on the change of demand into two parts: the substitution and income effects. This refinement has considerable theoretical significance in the analysis of consumer behavior. It shows the cause of the unusual case of a Giffen good (which for a long time was called the Giffen Paradox). On the other hand, it also destroyed the theoretical foundation of the long held "demand law," that is, the negatively sloped demand curve. As we have shown, the substitution term for a commodity undergoing price change is always negative and theoretically very reliable. Many economists derive the demand curve of a consumer for a commodity from the substitution effect alone, ignoring the income effect (often called the *compensated demand*). Such a demand curve always has a negative slope for normal goods, inferior goods, and even a Giffen good, as well as some other theoretical advantages. However, since it can hardly be observed in the market, its practical value is reduced. Thus, we did not derive it in the text.

A4.6 SUBSTITUTES AND COMPLEMENTS

Although we have shown that the substitution term of a commodity whose price undergoes change is negative in (A4.36), the substitution term of a commodity when the price of another commodity changes (i.e., S_{ji}) can be either positive or negative. Economists use the sign of this substitution term to define commodities i and j as being either *substitutes* or *complements*.

By common sense, when the price of beef goes up while the price of pork remains constant, the latter becomes relatively cheaper, and consumers will buy more pork with the same real income. Thus, $S_{ji} > 0$, and pork and beef are called *substitutes*. On the other hand, when the price of eggs goes down, other prices being constant, consumers buy more eggs, and since bacon goes together with eggs, the consumption of bacon will also rise. In this case, $S_{ji} < 0$, and bacon and eggs are called *complements*. Having shown that the substitution term is symmetric, it follows that if commodity i is substituted for commodity j, then j must also be substituted for i. This is also true for complements. The significance of the substitution term can be summarized as follows: Commodities i and j are *net substitutes* if $S_{ji} > 0$; they are *net complements* if $S_{ji} < 0$; and they are *independents* if $S_{ji} = 0$.

Before the appearance of the Slutsky equation, economists used the terms substitutes and complements on the basis of the direction of the shifts in demand for commodity i when the price of commodity j changed. This is shown by the sign of the Slutsky equation (the total effect) rather than the substitution term alone. These are now called *gross substitutes* and *gross complements*.

Definition: Gross Substitute. Commodity i is called a *gross substitute* for commodity j if the demand curve for i shifts to the right when the price of commodity j increases, all other prices, income, and preferences being held constant (i.e., if $\partial X_i / \partial P_j > 0$).

Definition: Gross Complement. Commodity i is called a *gross complement* for commodity j if the demand curve for i shifts to the left when the price of j increases, other things being equal (i.e., if $\partial X_i / \partial P_j < 0$).

It is also possible that a change in the price of commodity j may have no effect on the demand curve for commodity i. If $\partial X_i / \partial P_j = 0$, we say that i is *independent* of j. It should also be observed that since the cross price elasticity of demand for commodity i with respect to a change in the price of commodity j is defined as the partial derivative of the demand for i with respect to the price of j multiplied by the price of j and divided by the quantity of i, and since P_j and X_i are positive, then E_{ij} and $\partial X_i / \partial P_j$ will always have the same sign. The above definition is equivalent to the following commonly used criteria for categorizing commodities as substitutes, complements, and independents:

Commodities i and j are gross substitutes if $E_{ij} > 0$.
Commodities i and j are gross complements if $E_{ij} < 0$.
Commodities i and j are independents if $E_{ij} = 0$.

From the above definition, we can easily prove the following theorem.

Theorem A4.1. *All n commodities can be net substitutes for each other, but not all n commodities can be net complements for each other.*

This theorem can be proved by an expansion of the determinant D in (A4.28) by alien cofactors. Thus, we have

$$\sum_{i=1}^{M} P_i D_{ij} = \sum_{i=1}^{M} P_j D_{ij} = 0 \qquad (A4.39)$$

Students can verify this result by referring to textbooks that present matrix operations (see, e.g., Allen, 1959, p. 401).

From (A4.39), by substitution we have

$$\sum_{i=1}^{M} P_i S_{ij} = \sum_{j=1}^{n} P_j S_{ji} = 0 \tag{A4.40}$$

Since $P_i > 0$, $S_{ii} < 0$, and $S_{jj} < 0$, we must have at least one $S_{ij} > 0$ for $i \neq j$, that is, there must be at least one pair of commodities that are substitutes. It is theoretically possible that all of the other $n - 1$ commodities are substitutes of commodity i because, for $S_{ii} < 0$ and $S_{ij} > 0$ for all $j \neq i$, (A4.40) may hold. This proves our theorem.

One implication of our theorem is that the graphical representation of two commodities can only show the case where X and Y are substitutes. It is impossible in the two-commodity case to show that they are complements. Economic theory is usually illustrated by two-dimensional graphs and then generalized to n-dimensional cases. For the most part, this approach is theoretically valid. However, in dealing with substitutes and complements, we find that the two-commodity case is indeed a special case, whereas the three-commodity case can be considered general.

A4.7 THE CHARACTERISTIC APPROACH TO CONSUMER THEORY

The utility function can generally be formulated in terms of characteristics in much the same manner as for commodities. Traditionally, the arguments of the utility function are in terms of commodities, such as in (A4.1). If the analysis of consumer behavior is in terms of characteristics rather than commodities, the arguments of the utility function have to be formed with respect to the characteristics. If there are n characteristics, then the utility function can be written

$$U = U(C_1, C_2, ..., C_n) \tag{A4.41}$$

where C_i, $i = 1, 2, ..., n$, denote the characteristics. The properties of this utility function will be similar to those of the utility function (A4.1). For demand analysis, the budget equation must be transformed from commodity space to the corresponding characteristic space, which for the two-commodity and two-characteristic case is a simple matter. Suppose that a unit of X contains a_{11} units of characteristic 1 and a_{12} units of characteristic 2, the corresponding figures for Y being a_{21} and a_{22}. We have

$$a_{11}X + a_{21}Y = C_1 \tag{A4.42}$$

$$a_{12}X + a_{22}Y = C_2 \tag{A4.43}$$

Equation (A4.42) says that X units of commodity X and Y units of commodity Y will result in C_1 units of characteristic 1. Similarly, (A4.43) says that the same amounts of X and Y will result in C_2 units of characteristic 2. The corresponding figures in the text are $a_{11} = 10$, $a_{12} = 1$, $a_{21} = 1$, and $a_{22} = 10$ for $P =$ characteristic 1 and $C =$ characteristic 2. For $X = 15$ and $Y = 5$, we obtain

$$C_1 = 10 \times 15 + 1 \times 5 = 155$$

$$C_2 = 1 \times 15 + 10 \times 5 = 65$$

For different combinations of X and Y, different values of C_1 and C_2 will be derived. For example, for $X = 10$ and $Y = 10$, we obtain $C_1 = 110$ and $C_2 = 110$. The important thing is that for any given pair of X and Y, we have one and only one corresponding pair of C_1 and C_2. There is a one-to-one correspondence, and a unique transformation from X–Y space to C_1–C_2 space exists.

Solving (A4.42) and (A4.43) for X and Y by using Cramer's rule, we obtain

$$X = [a_{22}/(a_{11}a_{22} - a_{12}a_{21})]C_1 - [a_{21}/(a_{11}a_{22} - a_{12}a_{21})]C_2$$

$$\text{(A4.44)}$$

$$Y = [-a_{12}/(a_{11}a_{22} - a_{12}a_{21})]C_1 + [a_{11}/(a_{11}a_{22} - a_{12}a_{21})]C_2$$

$$\text{(A4.45)}$$

The budget constraint in X–Y space is

$$M = XP_X + YP_Y \qquad \text{(A4.46)}$$

The transformation is accomplished by substituting (A4.44) and (A4.45) into (A4.46). We have the budget constraint in C_1–C_2 space given by

$$M = \frac{a_{22}P_X - a_{12}P_Y}{a_{11}a_{22} - a_{12}a_{21}} C_1 + \frac{a_{11}P_Y - a_{21}P_X}{a_{11}a_{22} - a_{12}a_{21}} C_2 \qquad \text{(A4.47)}$$

In (A4.46), M, P_X, and P_Y are considered parameters, whereas X and Y are the variables. In X–Y space, the budget constraint can be equivalently written

$$Y = M/P_Y - (P_X/P_Y)X \qquad \text{(A4.48)}$$

which is obviously a negatively sloped straight line because M/P_Y and P_X/P_Y are constants and $P_X/P_Y > 0$.

In (A4.47), M, P_X, P_Y, a_{11}, a_{12}, a_{21}, and a_{22} are constants, whereas C_1 and C_2 are the variables. The budget constraint in C_1–C_2 space can be equivalently written

$$C_2 = \frac{a_{11}a_{22} - a_{12}a_{21}}{a_{11}P_Y - a_{21}P_X} M - \frac{a_{22}P_X - a_{12}P_Y}{a_{11}P_Y - a_{21}P_X} C_1 \qquad \text{(A4.49)}$$

Since both

$$\frac{(a_{11}a_{22} - a_{12}a_{21})M}{a_{11}P_Y - a_{21}P_X} \quad \text{and} \quad \frac{a_{22}P_X - a_{12}P_Y}{a_{11}P_Y - a_{21}P_X}$$

are constants, the budget constraint in C_1–C_2 space is also a straight line. This proves the assertion that we made in Section 4.11.

The numerical example in the text implies that the budget constraint in X–Y space is

$$Y = 20 - X \tag{A4.50}$$

On the other hand, the budget constraint in C_1–C_2 space is

$$C_2 = 220 - C_1 \tag{A4.51}$$

It is also interesting to note that both the pair $X = 15$, $Y = 5$ and the pair $X = 10$, $Y = 10$ satisfy the budget constraint (A4.50). The corresponding pairs in terms of characteristics (i.e., $C_1 = 155$, $C_2 = 65$ and $C_1 = 110$, $C_2 = 110$) computed from (A4.42) and (A4.43) satisfy the budget constraint (A4.51). These numbers give some intuitive feeling that the budget constraints (A4.48) and (A4.49) do correspond to each other.

THE THEORY OF DEMAND

INTRODUCTION

One of the primary goals in the analysis of consumer behavior is to gain more insight into the demand for a commodity. In Section 4.8 of Chapter 4, we derived the demand curve for a commodity from the price consumption curve (PCC), which is the locus of consumer equilibrium and hence contains the point of maximum satisfaction (utility) for a given income when the price of a commodity changes (all other things being equal). Two important points concerning the demand curve and the PCC should be noted. First of all, each point on a demand curve represents maximum consumer satisfaction for the given price–quantity relationship. Thus, a demand curve specifies the optimal choices of the consumer at various prices. In this respect, each price–quantity relationship is unique, that is, it cannot be satisfied by just any price–quantity combination. This is why we can predict that a rational consumer will always buy the quantity specified by his or her demand curve. This important point is often completely overlooked. Secondly, the graphical derivation of the PCC explicitly defines what "other things" remain constant. In the two-dimensional (i.e., two-commodity) case, they are consumer income, price of the other commodity, and consumer preference. The two-commodity case can be generalized to the N-dimensional (N-commodity) case by extending the number of these constants from 3 to $N + 1$, namely, income, preference, and the other $N - 1$ prices. Usually, in a first course in microeconomics, students are forced to accept this statement on faith, since they have not yet been exposed to the theoretical tools that are necessary in order to understand its true meaning and validity.

The individual's demand curve represents optimal price–quantity combinations for the consumer

To avoid confusion, it should be pointed out that the demand curve derived in Chapter 4 is that of a single consumer. However, it is the *market demand curve* (the demand of *all* consumers, not just one) that is of primary concern to business, since it specifies the revenue that one can expect to obtain by selling a given quantity of commodity. In this chapter, we shall show that since the market demand curve is always equivalent to the average revenue (AR) curve, in the absence of price discrimination, the total revenue (TR) curve can be derived from the AR curve and, in turn, the marginal revenue (MR) curve can be derived from the TR curve.[1] We shall derive the market demand for a commodity from the individual consumer demands, discuss the various characteristics of market demand, and explore the relationship between revenue and demand.

5.1 MARKET DEMAND FOR A COMMODITY

The market demand curve for a commodity is the *horizontal* sum of the individual consumer demand curves for the commodity, that is, the quantity demanded in the market at each price is the sum of the quantities demanded by all consumers at that price. This approach is valid only under Assumption 4.5 (absence of externality). For example, if instead of keeping an old car for several more years as originally intended, a person buys a new car because a neighbor has purchased one, then externality is not absent. Hence, the demand of one consumer is not independent of those of other consumers, and the market demand would not be the sum of the individual consumer demands because the interdependence of demands indicates that the demand of one consumer is not only a function of price, but also of the quantity purchased by other consumers. In such a case, the interactions between consumer demands would have to be taken into consideration, which would make analysis more complicated. Thus, Assumption 4.5 is carried over into our immediate discussion and we are on solid theoretical ground in summing the individual consumer demands in order to derive the market demand.

To illustrate the derivation of the market demand, let us assume

---

[1] The student should be careful to distinguish between the two types of demand curve that may confront the individual seller. If the seller is a monopolist (i.e., has exclusive control over the market), the market demand curve is relevant for the purpose of planning. However, if the seller operates under conditions of perfect competition, the market price (as distinct from the market demand curve) is the relevant demand information since, by definition, this seller provides such a small part of the total product in the market that he or she can sell any amount at the market price. In the real world, a wheat farmer is the closest to a seller in a competitive market. A wheat farmer, say, takes the market price as a datum and markets accordingly. Hence, this farmer's demand curve is a horizontal straight line.

TABLE 5.1

P	Q_A	Q_B	Q_C	Q
$6	0	0	0	0
5	1	0	0	1
4	2	1	0	3
3	3	2	1	6
2	4	3	2	9
1	5	4	3	12

that there exist only the three consumers A, B, and C with demands Q_A, Q_B, and Q_C, respectively, as shown in Table 5.1. For each and every price, we add up the corresponding quantities demanded by each of the individuals, which yields the last column in Table 5.1. When the price is $5, A buys 1 unit, and the quantity demanded by the whole market is 1 unit, as shown in the last column. On the other hand, when the price is reduced to $4, A buys 2 units and B buys 1 unit; as a result, the quantity demanded by the whole market is 3 units. Similarly, if the market price is $3, the quantity demanded by the whole market is 6 units (3 + 2 + 1).

The data of Table 5.1 are plotted in Figure 5.1, where D_A, D_B, and D_C are the demand curves for A, B, and C, respectively. The market demand curve D is the horizontal sum of the three individual consumer demand curves. It is interesting to note that the slope of the market demand curve is flatter than those of the individual consumer demand curves. Furthermore, even though all three individual consumer demand curves are straight lines, the market demand curve is not a straight line. This is contrary to mathematical theory, which states that the sum of linear func-

The slope of the market demand curve is always flatter than that of the individual's demand curve

FIGURE 5.1

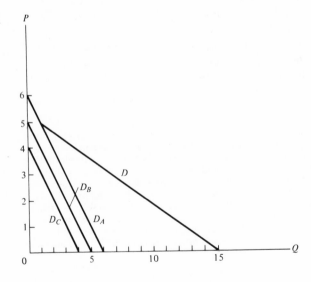

tions must be linear. The reason for this phenomenon is that the quantity demanded cannot be negative. As a result, the relevant price range for C's demand is between \$4 and \$0, whereas those for B and A are between \$5 and \$0 and \$6 and \$0, respectively. This is one instance in economic theory where valid mathematical operations may result in a paradoxical conclusion if sufficient care is not taken concerning some implicit constraints on the variables. This problem is more mathematical than economic,[2] and most students would probably not be hurt by ignoring it.

If there are more than three consumers, as is usually the case, the market (aggregate) demand is derived by adding up the quantities demanded by all of the consumers for each and every price. In terms of graphs, the market demand curve is the horizontal

---

[2] This can be demonstrated by reference to the data in Table 5.1, where the demand schedules for A, B, and C are based on the following demand functions, respectively:

$$Q_A = 6 - P \quad \text{for} \quad P \le 6$$

$$Q_B = 5 - P \quad \text{for} \quad P \le 5$$

$$Q_C = 4 - P \quad \text{for} \quad P \le 4$$

In general, the aggregate demand function for the commodity is written

$$Q = Q_A + Q_B + Q_C$$

However, this is not correct due to the implicit constraints that are applicable to each individual's demand function. For example, if we were simply summing up the demand functions, we would have

$$Q = Q_A + Q_B + Q_C$$
$$= 6 - P + 5 - P + 4 - P$$
$$= 15 - 3P = 3(5 - P)$$

Thus, if the market price is \$6, the quantity demanded will be $Q = 15 - (3 \times 6) = 15 - 18 = -3$. This certainly does not make economic sense, since people cannot buy a negative amount. The reason for this ridiculous result is ignorance of the constraints for Q_B and Q_C. The proper mathematical expression for the aggregate demand function is as follows:

$$Q = Q_A = 6 - P \qquad\qquad\qquad \text{for } 5 \le P \le 6$$

$$Q = Q_A + Q_B = 6 - P + 5 - P = 11 - 2P \qquad\qquad \text{for } 4 \le P \le 5$$

$$Q = Q_A + Q_B + Q_C = 6 - P + 5 - P + 4 - P = 3(5 - P) \quad \text{for } P \le 4$$

Hence, the aggregate demand function is not the simple algebraic sum of the individual demand functions. Rather, the constraints on the price range for each and every individual demand function must be taken into consideration. Otherwise, the algebraic sum of the individual demand functions may not be the true aggregate demand function for the market. Mathematical operations in economics usually involve more than simple manipulations; therefore, caution should be exercised with respect to the proper restriction of the variables.

Without the above restrictions, the aggregate demand function according to mathematical methods alone is $Q = 3(5 - P)$, which certainly does not agree with the last column of Table 5.1. According to this demand function, $Q = 0$ for $P = 5$, but in the table, $Q = 1$ for $P = 5$. Furthermore, $Q = -3$ for $P = 6$ according to the demand function, but the table shows that $Q = 0$ for $P = 6$.

(rather than the vertical) sum of the individual consumer demand curves. We again note that proper caution must be exercised with respect to the restrictions on the price values as they apply to each and every individual demand function.

In Chapter 4 we showed that the demand curve for a normal good definitely has a negative slope. In fact, even for an inferior good, the demand curve is likely to have a negative slope. Only in the special case where the negative income effect is very strong and the quantity of the inferior good consumed by the consumer is quite large may the demand curve have a positive slope. This is the case of a Giffen good, which is rarely encountered for an individual consumer. Furthermore, a commodity may be a Giffen good within different price ranges for different consumers. It is also possible for a commodity that is a Giffen good for some consumers to not be one for others. The Slutsky equation shows that whether or not a commodity is a Giffen good to a consumer depends on the consumer's preference pattern. This observation has significance because although a commodity may be a Giffen good to certain consumers within a given price range, the market demand curve can still be negatively sloped if the same commodity is not a Giffen good to many other consumers. (This can easily be shown by using simple linear demand functions selected such that whereas some have a positive slope and others a negative slope, their sum has a negative slope.) Thus, the phenomenon of a Giffen good in the market is likely to be a rare occurrence.

The market occurrence of a Giffen good is rare

Students should be alerted to the fact that a market phenomenon in which consumers purchase more of a commodity at a higher price and less of it at a lower price may not by itself confirm the occurrence of a Giffen good. People sometimes judge quality by price, or a high-priced commodity may raise the social status of the user. In either case, the consumer's preference has become a function of market price. This is inconsistent with the basic condition of the Slutsky equation, which is derived from the consumer's utility function (which, in turn, depends on the quantity— not the price—of a commodity). Since even some outstanding economists have occasionally made this mistake in interpretation, students should be particularly observant of these distinctions.

Summarizing the above arguments, we can conclude that the market demand for commodity i is a function of all prices, consumer income, consumer preference, and the number of consumers, since each individual consumer's demand is a function of these factors. The sum obviously depends on the number of individual demands to be added. If we denote the prices by P_1, P_2, P_3, ..., P_n, income by M, and the number of consumers (i.e., the *population*) by N, then the market demand function for commodity i can, in general be written

$$Q_i = D_i(P_1, P_2, ..., P_i, ..., P_n, M, N) \tag{5.1}$$

Note that consumer preference, which determines the characteristics (i.e., form) of the demand function D, is not given in
(5.1) as a variable. It is not proper to include a variable that
represents consumer preference in (5.1), although some economists do.

Since only two variables can be handled easily in a graphical
representation, the demand for Q_i is defined as the price–quantity
relationship of commodity i only, other things being equal. In
effect, we are assuming that P for all other commodities, as well
as M and N are held constant. This is a special case that can be
written

$$Q_i = D_i(\overline{P}_i, \overline{P}_2, ..., P_i, ..., \overline{P}_n, \overline{M}, \overline{N}) = D_i(P_i) \tag{5.2}$$

where a bar indicates that the corresponding quantity is constant.

5.2 ELASTICITIES OF DEMAND: PRICE, INCOME, AND CROSS ELASTICITIES

The curvature or slope of a demand curve indicates the responsiveness of consumers to a change in market price. This information is very important to business because revenue behavior
is closely related to the response of consumers to changes in
price. Although the derivative is usually employed as a measure
of curvature, there is a major drawback in using it as a measure
of consumer responsiveness because its value depends on the
units of measure selected for both price and quantity. For example, the data in Table 5.1 show that when the market price is
reduced to $4 from $5, the quantity purchased by consumers will
increase from 1 to 3 units; thus, the ratio of the change in quantity
demanded to the change in price is $-2/1$ (since the change in
price is negative and the change in quantity is positive, the ratio
is negative). Suppose that in the above ratio the quantity is measured in pounds and the price is measured in dollars. If the measure
of quantity is changed to ounces but price is still measured in
dollars, the ratio will be $-32/1$. Thus, although they measure the
same changes, the two ratios are quite different. Alternatively,
it is easy to see that if the measure of quantity remains the same
but the measure of price changes from dollars to cents, the ratio
will also change. In technical terms, we say that the derivative
of the demand curve is not independent with respect to choice
of units. However, *elasticity* is a measure that is invariant with
respect to the choice of units. In order to give the student a better
feel for the concept of elasticity as it is used in demand analysis,
we shall first define it in reference to different attributes of demand and then demonstrate its derivation in each case.

*Elasticity must be
invariant with
respect to choice
of units of
measurement*

Definition: Price Elasticity of Demand. The ratio of a percentage
change in demand to the percentage change in price, other

things being equal (equivalently, the ratio of the proportional change in demand to the proportional change in price, other things being equal).

Definition: Income Elasticity of Demand. The ratio of a percentage (proportional) change in demand to the percentage (proportional) change in income, other things being equal.

Definition: Cross Elasticity of Demand for Commodity X with Respect to the Price of Commodity Y. The percentage (proportional) change in the demand for X to the percentage (proportional) change in the price of Y, other things being equal.

In symbols, if Δ denotes change, the price elasticity of demand E can be written

$$E = -\frac{(\Delta Q/Q)100}{(\Delta P/P)100} = -\frac{\Delta Q/Q}{\Delta P/P} = -\frac{\Delta Q}{\Delta P} \times \frac{P}{Q} \tag{5.3}$$

The first expression to the right of E is the ratio of a percentage change in demand to the percentage change in price whereas, the second expression is the ratio of a proportional change in demand to the proportional change in price. The equal sign between them holds because the 100 in the denominator cancels out the 100 in the numerator. This shows the equivalence between the percentage changes and proportional changes referred to above. The last expression represents the form in which economists usually write price elasticities. The negative sign is added to indicate that we are dealing with a negatively sloped demand curve. The term $\Delta Q/\Delta P$ is the inverse of the slope of the usual demand curve (the slope of the usual demand curve is $\Delta P/\Delta Q$, since P is plotted on the vertical axis and Q on the horizontal axis), which is usually negative. Since demand curves usually have a negative slope, without the negative sign, E would usually be negative. Since students feel more comfortable working with positive numbers, a negative sign is usually added for the sake of convenience. It should be noted that some economists do not add the negative sign; hence, students must be alert to this possible inconsistency when studying economic literature.

It should be noted that the "other things being equal" condition is essential for computing elasticity. The phrase "other things being equal" in the definition of price elasticity implies that price elasticity is not defined when either the price and income or two prices change simultaneously. The price elasticity of a commodity can only be computed when a change in its own price is accompanied by a change in the quantity purchased, all other things remaining constant. In mathematical terms, this means that the partial (rather than total) derivative must be used in place of $\Delta Q/\Delta P$. This is sometimes overlooked.

Partial rather than total derivative is used to measure elasticity

The income elasticity of demand E_M and cross elasticity of demand E_c can be written

$$E_M = (\Delta Q/\Delta M)(M/Q) \tag{5.4}$$

$$E_c = (\Delta Q_i/\Delta P_j)(P_j/Q_i) \tag{5.5}$$

In (5.5), Q_i and P_j denote the quantity of commodity i and the price of commodity j, respectively. Note that no negative sign is added to either (5.4) or (5.5). Mathematically, partial derivatives would be used in both (5.4) and (5.5).

The invariant property with respect to the choice of a unit of elasticity can be demonstrated by using the same numerical example that was employed at the beginning of this section. As before, suppose that we initially have a price of $5 and a quantity of 1 pound and that when the price is reduced to $4 the quantity purchased rises to 3 pounds. With this condition, we have price elasticity $E = -(2/-1)(5/1) = 10$ if the measure of quantity is pounds. If we change the measure of quantity from pounds to ounces, the price elasticity of demand is $E = -(32/-1)(5/16) = 10$, which is the same as before.

Students who test the effect of changing the unit of price measurement from dollars to cents will find that the price elasticity will still be the same. This should reinforce the point that we made earlier with respect to the use of the slope of the demand curve to measure the effect of a change in price.

The property that elasticity is invariant with respect to the choice of a unit of measurement can be proved in general by using the definitions of elasticity that we presented earlier. Since the change of a unit of measure usually involves multiplication by a constant (e.g., a change from pounds to ounces is carried out by multiplying the pound figures by 16 and a change from dollars to cents is carried out by multiplying the dollar figures by 100), the constants in the numerator and denominator cancel each other out. For example, consider a simultaneous change in the units of measure of both quantity and price such that Q is multiplied by a and P by b; from (5.3) we have

$$E = \frac{-\Delta Qa}{\Delta Pb}\frac{Pb}{Qa} = \frac{-\Delta Q \cdot P}{\Delta P \cdot Q}$$

which shows that, in general, elasticity is invariant with respect to the choice of a unit of measure.

Some alert students may have noticed a problem when we computed the price elasticity for the case in which price was reduced from $5 to $4 and at the same time demand increased from 1 to 3 units. We used the price–quantity pair $\langle 5, 1 \rangle$ as the P and Q in expression (5.3). There is no reason why we could not have used the price–quantity pair $\langle 4, 3 \rangle$ in computing the price elasticity. However, had we done so, the price elasticity would have been $\frac{2}{3}$, which is smaller than 10. This raises an interesting

TABLE 5.2

P	ΔP	Q	ΔQ	E_1	E_2	E
$5	—	1	—	—		
4	−1	3	2	10	$\frac{8}{3}$	$\frac{9}{2}$
3	−1	6	3	4	$\frac{3}{2}$	$\frac{7}{3}$
2	−1	9	3	$\frac{3}{2}$	$\frac{2}{3}$	1
1	−1	12	3	$\frac{2}{3}$	$\frac{1}{4}$	$\frac{3}{7}$

question: Which is the correct figure for the price elasticity? If we did not have a good answer to this question, it is obvious that the concept would not be very meaningful. The answer to this question rests on the discrepancy between the theoretical definition and market reality. In the theory, the three elasticities of demand are defined with respect to very small changes in both variables. When this is the case, the problem of choice between the two price–quantity pairs disappears because, regardless of which pair one uses, there is no essential difference in the value of price elasticity. For example, if the price change were from $5.00 to $4.99 and the quantity change from 1 to 1.02 units, a choice of the pair ⟨5, 1⟩ would not be essentially different from a choice of the pair ⟨4.99, 1.02⟩. In order to show the effects of choosing different price–quantity pairs, Table 5.2 has been prepared. The values in column E_1 are the price elasticities computed by using the upper price–quantity pairs, whereas those in column E_2 are obtained by using the lower pairs, for each corresponding change of price and quantity.

The values in column E_1 are at least twice as large as the corresponding values in column E_2, and one is more than three times greater. Nevertheless, the values in both column E_1 and column E_2 can be taken as the price elasticities for the various intervals. However, these values cannot be considered meaningful for either theoretical or practical purposes, since they are the result of relatively large changes in both price and quantity. In reality, statistical data usually show changes of comparable magnitude. As a compromise, when the changes in price and quantity are relatively large, (and hence a choice between two price–quantity pairs may make an essential difference in the obtained value of the price elasticity), the averages of the two prices and the two quantities are used in place of P and Q. Thus, the formula for the price elasticity—(5.3)—is modified to

$$E = -\frac{\Delta Q}{\Delta P} \times \frac{(P_1 + P_2)/2}{(Q_1 + Q_2)/2} \tag{5.6}$$

Expression (5.6) as now written shows the rationale behind the modified formula for the price elasticity of demand. In practice,

Theoretical rigor requires changes in variables to be small in measuring elasticity

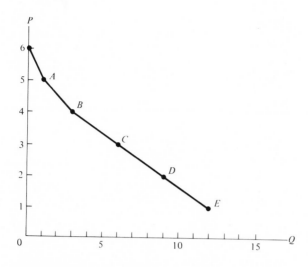

FIGURE 5.2

the following equivalent form is more convenient to use, since the 2s in the numerator and denominator of (5.6) cancel out:

$$E = - \frac{\Delta Q}{\Delta P} \times \frac{P_1 + P_2}{Q_1 + Q_2} \qquad (5.7)$$

In Table 5.2, the values in column E were computed with the use of modified formula (5.7). It should be noted that each value in column E is between the two corresponding values in columns E_1 and E_2.

The data of Table 5.2 are interpreted graphically in Figure 5.2. The number 10 in column E_1 of Table 5.2 is the price elasticity at point A for a movement from A to B along the demand curve in Figure 5.2, whereas the number $\frac{8}{3}$ in column E_2 of Table 5.2 is the price elasticity at point B for a movement along the demand curve from A to B in Figure 5.2. These are the two extremes. The number $\frac{9}{2}$ in column E of Table 5.2 is the price elasticity at the midpoint between A and B, and it is obvious that this value is more representative than either of the two end points for the range between A and B. This is the justification of the compromise formula.

Examining our problem of the price elasticity of demand a bit further, we note that the number 4 in column E_1 of Table 5.2 is the price elasticity at point B for a movement from B to C along the demand curve, $\frac{3}{2}$ is the price elasticity at point C, and $\frac{7}{3}$ is the price elasticity at the midpoint between B and C. This chain of reasoning points out the distinction between precision in theory and compromise in practice to which we referred earlier.

Observant students should have no doubt noticed the fact that the price elasticity increases continuously as one moves upward along a straight-line demand curve. This is a mathematical property that can be easily observed from the definition of E. For a

The slope of the demand curve is not synonymous with price elasticity

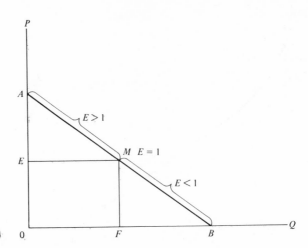

FIGURE 5.3

straight-line demand curve, the slope $\Delta P/\Delta Q$ ($\Delta Q/\Delta P$) is constant. When an upward movement along the demand curve takes place, P increases, simultaneously Q decreases, and consequently, the value of E will necessarily increase. For a straight-line demand curve as shown in Figure 5.3, it is easy to see that the price elasticity at point B is zero, since $P = 0$ at B and thus $E = -(\Delta Q/\Delta P)(P/Q) = 0$ for finite values of Q and $\Delta Q/\Delta P$. Similarly, the price elasticity at point A is infinite because $Q = 0$ at A, and zero divided into any finite number is infinity.

The price elasticity at midpoint M is unitary. This assertion can be proven as follows. The slope of the demand curve $\overline{AB}$ is $\overline{A0}/\overline{0B} = \overline{MF}/\overline{FB}$; thus, $\Delta Q/\Delta P = \overline{FB}/\overline{MF}$. However, for point M, $P = \overline{E0} = \overline{MF}$ and $Q = \overline{0F} = \overline{FB}$. By substitution, at point M,

$$E = (\overline{FB}/\overline{MF})(\overline{MF}/\overline{FB}) = 1$$

For the sake of simplicity, we have ignored the signs in the above derivation. It can be checked that the sign for E is correct according to our definition.

As we have explained above, the price elasticity increases continuously when moving upward along a straight-line demand curve. Thus, combining the above results, we can conclude that in Figure 5.3, $E < 1$ between B and M and $E > 1$ between M and A, M being the midpoint of the demand curve. As we shall show later, the concept of price elasticity of demand has important implications with respect to decision-making and policy analysis. Furthermore, we shall observe that a value of "1" for the price elasticity has significance because it permits us to quickly and conveniently evaluate the effects of a price change on revenue. For this reason, we provide the following definition for distinguishing between the different types of price elasticity.

Definition: Elastic, Unitary Elastic, and Inelastic Demand. The demand is said to be elastic if $E > 1$, unitary elastic if $E = 1$, and inelastic if $E < 1$.

Whereas price elasticity of demand pertains to a *movement* along a demand curve, the income and cross elasticities of demand are related to a *shift* in the demand curve. The income elasticity of a commodity can be either positive or negative. If it is positive, an increase in income will shift the demand curve to the right, and the commodity is called a normal good. On the other hand, a negative income elasticity indicates a leftward shift of the demand curve when income increases, this corresponding to an inferior good as defined in Section 4.7 of Chapter 4. It is possible that the demand for a commodity may show positive income elasticity within a certain range with respect to price and income and negative income elasticity in a different range.

The cross elasticity of demand between X and Y can also be either positive or negative. Economists use the sign of the cross elasticity to classify whether commodities are substitutes, complements, or independents. For the sake of convenience, we offer a further qualification to the definition of gross substitute, gross complement, and independent given in Section A4.6 of the appendix to Chapter 4.

Definition: Gross Substitute, Gross Complement, and Independent. Commodity X is a gross substitute for commodity Y if the cross elasticity of Y with respect to the price of X is positive; X is a gross complement of Y if the cross elasticity of Y is negative; and X is independent of Y if the cross elasticity of Y is zero.

Note that the determination of whether two commodities are net substitutes or net complements is similarly based on the sign of the cross substitution term in the Slutsky equation.

In most cases, if X is a substitute for Y, then Y, in turn, is also a substitute for X. Essentially the same reasoning applies for complements or independent pairs of commodities. However, the concepts of substitutes, complements, and independents between pairs of commodities are not symmetric. In other words, X may be a substitute for Y, but Y may not be a substitute for X. Similarly, X may be a complement of Y, but Y may not be a complement of X. This also applies to independent relationships. Theoretically, it is possible for X to be a substitute for Y, while, at the same time, Y is a complement of X. Examples of the last case are not easy to come by. On the other hand, it is not too hard to find examples that show the asymmetry of the concepts. There is little doubt that if the price of beef (in particular, steak) goes

Symmetry of cross elasticities between two commodities is not likely

down and people's incomes and other prices remain constant, the demand for steak sauce will tend to shift to the right (i.e., increase). In this case, the cross elasticity of demand of steak sauce with respect to the price of steak is negative; hence, steak sauce is a complement of steak. However, if the price of steak sauce slightly increases, it can hardly be expected to produce a shift in the demand curve for steak. Thus, steak may not be a complement of steak sauce.

Even in the usual case, if X is a substitute for Y (which, in turn, is a likely substitute for X), the cross elasticity of X with respect to the price of Y is unlikely to be equal to the cross elasticity of Y with respect to the price of X.

5.3 GRAPHICAL MEASUREMENT OF THE PRICE ELASTICITY OF DEMAND

Price elasticity of demand is by far the most important of the various concepts of elasticity that we have discussed. Since graphical analysis is often an important tool in economics, we may ask the following question: Is there a simple way to figure out the price elasticity of a commodity from its demand curve? The answer is yes, as we shall now prove.

Consider the straight-line demand curve $\overline{EF}$ in Figure 5.4. Let us suppose that we want to find the price elasticity of the commodity at point A (initial price P_0 and quantity Q_0) of the demand curve. When the price is reduced to P_1, the quantity is accordingly increased to Q_1. Substituting these price and quantity values into elasticity formula (5.3) (for the graphical method, we may ignore the signs and note that $\Delta P = \overline{P_0 P_1}$ and $\Delta Q = \overline{Q_0 Q_1}$), we obtain

$$E = (\overline{Q_0 Q_1}/\overline{P_0 P_1})(\overline{0P_0}/\overline{0Q_0})$$

FIGURE 5.4

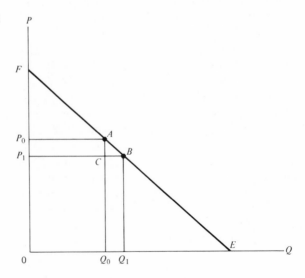

In the graph, $\overline{Q_0Q_1} = \overline{CB}$ and $\overline{P_0P_1} = \overline{AC}$. Since $\triangle ABC$ and $\triangle AEQ_0$ are similar triangles, their corresponding sides are proportional. Therefore, we have

$$\overline{Q_0E}/\overline{AQ_0} = \overline{CB}/\overline{AC} = \overline{Q_0Q_1}/\overline{P_0P_1}$$

Since it is obvious that $\overline{0P_0} = \overline{AQ_0}$, we hence obtain

$$\overline{Q_0Q_1}/\overline{P_0P_1} = \overline{Q_0E}/\overline{0P_0}$$

By substitution we have

$$E = (\overline{Q_0E}/\overline{0P_0})(\overline{0P_0}/\overline{0Q_0}) = \overline{Q_0E}/\overline{0Q_0}$$

Since $\overline{0F} \parallel \overline{Q_0A}$, we have

$$\overline{Q_0E}/\overline{0Q_0} = \overline{AE}/\overline{FA}$$

(In geometry, there is a theorem which states that parallel straight lines cut other parallel straight lines in equal proportions.) Thus, we finally obtain

$$E = \overline{AE}/\overline{FA}$$

Hence, the price elasticity at a point on a straight-line demand curve is equal to the lower segment divided by the upper segment. In such a case, the student can quickly observe that the price elasticity increases as one moves from point E to point F on the demand curve in Figure 5.4. This is also in agreement with our earlier observation that price elasticity is infinite when $Q = 0$ and $P > 0$.

Although demand curves are not usually straight lines, the above result can be applied to any demand curve. Consider the demand curve D in Figure 5.5. The price elasticity at point A can be measured by the ratio $\overline{AE}/\overline{FA}$, where $\overline{EF}$ is tangent to demand curve D at point A and intersects the horizontal and vertical axes at points E and F, respectively. With this result, the price elasticity at any point on a demand curve can easily be figured out using just a ruler.

FIGURE 5.5

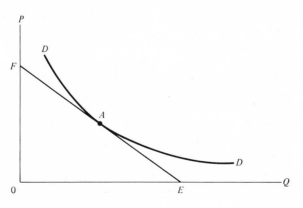

5.4 DETERMINANTS OF ELASTICITIES

Elasticities are measures of the responsiveness of demand to changes in the underlying factors (e.g., price or income) that determine it. The derivation of individual demand curves in Chapter 4 clearly shows that the shape of the demand curve is essentially determined by consumer preference. Thus, consumer preference should logically be an important determinant of elasticity. However, market demand is the sum of the individual consumer demands, and people have diverse preference patterns that are obscured by the process of summation. Hence, economists traditionally ignore consumer preference in their discussion of the determinants of elasticities. Instead, attention is focused on the characteristics of commodities.

Consumer preference, good substitutes, and time are important determinants of price elasticity

As noted previously, price elasticity of demand is by far the most important of the various concepts of elasticity that we have discussed. It is generally recognized that the more and better the substitutes for a specific commodity, the greater will be its price elasticity. Commonsense reasoning can show the truth of this statement. If there are good substitutes for a commodity, and the price of the commodity increases while the prices of its substitutes remain constant, then consumers will select one of the substitutes; consequently, the percentage change in quantity demanded tends to be large. A related observation is that the finer the classification of commodities (which results in more and better substitutes for a given commodity), the greater the elasticity. For example, the demand for beef is highly price elastic because there exist such ready substitutes as pork, chicken, lamb, and fish. However, we find that the overall demand for meat is less elastic because of the lack of close substitutes.

It is said that the greater the number of possible uses for a commodity, the higher its price elasticity. Another factor often mentioned is the importance of a commodity in the consumer's budget. If consumers usually spend a very small proportion of their income on a commodity, the price elasticity of the commodity is likely to be very low. For example, salt is a commodity for which the number of possible uses is few, and people spend a very small proportion of their income on it. Hence, common sense tells us that the amount of salt consumed by people depends essentially on preference and has little relation to its price.

It is often mentioned that the length of time under consideration is related to price elasticity. In general, demand is likely to be more price elastic (less inelastic) over a longer period of time, that is, the longer the period of time, the easier it is for consumers and firms to substitute one commodity for another. For example, if the price of natural gas increases, but the prices of electricity and other fuels remain constant, then the consumption of natural gas in the month immediately after the price change will probably decrease very little. On the other hand, over a period of years, the consumption of gas will most likely decrease to a much greater extent due to the fact that many people will switch from gas to electricity or other fuels for cooking, heating, and so forth (especially in new houses).

Students must be very careful in applying the above arguments in the real world. The above example is based on the important assumption that only the price of gas has risen. In reality, the prices of related commodities are not independent of the price of gas, especially over a long period of time. Thus, the interaction between markets can modify the result. However, the *tendency* will most likely hold, that is, the longer the period, the higher the price elasticity of a commodity.

5.5 A CLASS OF CONSTANT-ELASTICITY DEMAND CURVES[3]

As we have shown in Section 5.4, the price elasticity of demand varies as one moves from a given point to another on a straight-line demand curve. Although this is true in most cases, there is a class of demand curves for which the price elasticity is the same at all points, that is, *constant-elasticity demand curves.*

Unitary-elasticity demand curves are a special case of constant-elasticity demand curves. Unitary elasticity means that when price is reduced, for example, by 1%, the quantity demanded will increase by 1%. Since total revenue TR is, by definition, the product of price and quantity, if one variable is reduced by 1% while the other is increased by 1%, then the decrease and increase will cancel each other out and leave TR unchanged. For example, if the original price and quantity are P_0 and Q_0, respectively, then $TR_0 = P_0 Q_0$.

Suppose that price is reduced by 1%. Thus, we now have the new price $P_1 = P_0/1.01$. When the quantity is increased by 1%, the new quantity is $Q_1 = 1.01 Q_0$. Hence, as a result we obtain

$$TR_1 = P_1 Q_1 = (P_0/1.01)1.01 Q_0 = P_0 Q_0 = TR_0$$

In Figure 5.6, D_1 is a demand curve with unitary elasticity. At price P_0, the quantity demanded is Q_0, and $TR_0 = P_0 Q_0$ is represented by the rectangle $0P_0 A Q_0$. At price P_1, the quantity demanded is Q_1, and $TR_1 = P_1 Q_1$ is represented by the rectangle $0P_1 B Q_1$, which has the same area as rectangle $0P_0 A Q_0$. The price elasticity at point A is the same as that at point B, namely, $E = 1$. In fact, the price elasticity is $E = 1$ at each and every point on the curve.

It should be pointed out that a demand curve with unitary elasticity is not unique; that is, there can exist an infinite number of unitary-elasticity demand curves for a commodity, two of

Unitary-elasticity demand curves are constant-elasticity demand curves, but the reverse is not always true

---

[3] This section can be skipped without discontinuity.

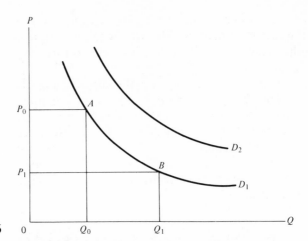

FIGURE 5.6

which are shown in Figure 5.6. The demand curve D_2 that is to the right of D_1 represents a higher TR. In fact, each point on D_2 represents a higher TR than any point on D_1. This can easily be seen by writing out the formula for the family of unitary-elasticity demand curves as

$$Q = AP^{-1} \quad \text{or} \quad PQ = A \tag{5.8}$$

where A is a constant. It will be shown in the appendix to this chapter that (5.8) fully describes the family of unitary-elasticity demand functions. These are one-parameter (namely, A) functions, which also represent the TR along the demand curve. If A_1 denotes the parameter for D_1 and A_2 that for D_2, then $A_2 > A_1$. Corresponding to each A, we have one and only one demand curve similar to D_1 and D_2. In the continuous case, there are an infinite number of As in price–commodity space.

It should be noted that the class of constant-elasticity demand curves represents two-parameter functions that can be written

$$Q = AP^{-a} \tag{5.9}$$

where both A and a are constants. It is also important to note that only when both A and a are constants will (5.9) fully describe the class of constant-elasticity demand functions. Some economists write the constant-elasticity demand function as

$$Q = AP^{-E} \tag{5.10}$$

which is mathematically incorrect. The paradox is that in (5.9), the constant a is the price elasticity, whereas in (5.10), the price elasticity E (which is, in general, a function of Q and thus P) is not the price elasticity at all. A mathematical demonstration based on this paradox will be presented in the appendix to this chapter. It will also be shown that the constant a in (5.9) is indeed the price elasticity.

As a final note on constant elasticity of demand, it should be pointed out that in the special case where $a = 1$ (5.9) becomes (5.8). Thus, unitary-elasticity demand functions are a special case of the class of constant-elasticity demand functions.

We shall now proceed to a discussion of the relationship between demand and revenue in their more general application to decision making by the firm. The student should recognize that for more than one demand curve to exist for a commodity, we must be talking about either individual consumer demand curves or the variation that exists with respect to a market demand curve as a result of changes in incomes and/or the prices of the other commodities.

5.6 DEMAND AND REVENUE BEHAVIOR: TR, AR, AND MR

The importance of demand as far as firms or sellers are concerned lies in the close relationship between demand and the receipts (i.e., revenue) that they can obtain from the sales of their products. For analytical convenience, we shall define the three interrelated terms TR, AR, and MR as follows.

Definition: Total Revenue. The product of price and quantity:

$$TR = PQ \tag{5.11}$$

Definition: Average Revenue. The quotient of total revenue divided by quantity:

$$AR = TR/Q = P \tag{5.12}$$

By implication, P is always equal to AR in the absence of price discrimination.

Definition: Marginal Revenue. The change in total revenue due to a small change in quantity:

$$MR = \Delta TR/\Delta Q \tag{5.13}$$

For practical purposes, MR can be considered as the additional revenue that results from one additional unit of sales.

We shall use Table 5.3 to illustrate the derivation of each of the above-defined measures of revenue and the relationships among them. The first two columns contain the price and quantity values, that is, the demand schedule. Notice that the price is constant, which indicates a horizontal demand curve. Column 3 gives TR (the product of columns 1 and 2), whereas column 4 gives AR (computed by dividing column 3 by column 2). It is interesting to note that columns 1 and 4 are identical except when $Q = 0$, in which case AR is not defined. Is this a coincidence? The answer

Under perfect competition, price to the seller is constant or given, and hence

P = AR = MR

TABLE 5.3

P	Q	TR	AR	MR
$2	0	0	—	—
2	1	2	2	2
2	2	4	2	2
2	3	6	2	2
2	4	8	2	2
2	5	10	2	2

is no. As we indicated in the definition, AR is always equal to price in the absence of price discrimination. Column 5 gives MR, which is computed by dividing the successive differences of column 3 by the corresponding differences of column 2. (The student should recall our discussion of the relationships between TP, AP, and MP in Chapters 1 and 2, as well as the description of the relationship between TC, AC, and MC in Chapter 3.) It turns out that column 4 and 5 are also identical. Is this always the case? The answer is no. This only occurs in the special case where price (and, therefore, AR), is constant. When AR is constant, MR = AR. This is the same relationship that we explained first in connection with AP and MP and then in connection with AC and MC. In terms of our familiar graphical analysis, we can see that when the demand curve is a horizontal straight line, it is the same as the AR and MR curves. This relationship will take on special importance in Chapter 6 when we deal with the competitive market.

The data of Table 5.3 are plotted in Figure 5.7, where the demand curve, the AR curve, and the MR curve comprise the same horizontal straight line. The TR curve is a straight line starting from the origin and rising by a fixed amount for each additional unit of the commodity sold.

If the demand curve has a negative slope, MR will no longer be equal to AR, since, to sell more, price must be reduced, and the change in TR will not equal price, but instead will be a function

FIGURE 5.7

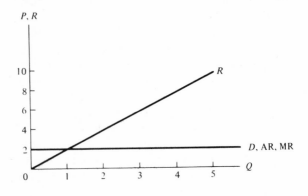

TABLE 5.4

P	Q	TR	AR	MR
$6	0	0	—	—
5	1	5	5	5
4	3	12	4	3.5
3	6	18	3	2
2	9	18	2	0
1	12	12	1	−2

of price and quantity. In this case, MR will be less than or equal to AR. Furthermore, the TR curve will no longer be a straight line, since MR is actually the slope of the corresponding TR curve.

We shall now demonstrate the impact of a negatively sloped demand curve on the relationships between TR, AR, and MR. Consider Table 5.4, the first two columns of which are taken from Table 5.1. Note that the MR values in column 5 are no longer the same as the AR values in column 4 (except when 1 unit of the commodity is sold).

The reason that MR is less than the price except when the first unit is sold is simple: More units can be sold only at a lower price, and the reduction in price must be applied to all units, not just the additional unit. Therefore, the MR for the additional unit(s) is equal to the price minus the loss in revenue attributable to the previous units. For example, in Table 5.4, the price of the second and third units is $4. However, the price of the first unit must be reduced from $5 to $4 in order to sell the additional units. Hence, the loss in revenue attributable to the first unit must be shared by the second and third units, that is, $0.5 each. This means that the additional revenue from the second or third unit is $4 − $0.5 = $3.5.

The preceding example also illustrates that the MR for the third unit in Table 5.4 is actually the average of the MRs for the second and third units. If we had more accurate information concerning the demand for our commodity, the MR for the third unit would have been lower than $3.5, whereas the MR for the second unit would have been higher than $3.5; however, the average MR would be $3.5.

It is important that students always keep in mind that whereas in theory MR is defined for a small change in quantity (much smaller than 1 unit), in reality, unit or multiple unit changes often occur. For this reason, the MR computed by using formula (5.13) is actually the average MR within the range of the change in quantity. In practice, these estimates are sufficient for learning purposes or making decisions.

The data of Table 5.4 are plotted in Figure 5.8. Note that the

A positive, negative, or zero MR indicates if TR is increasing, decreasing, or at maximum

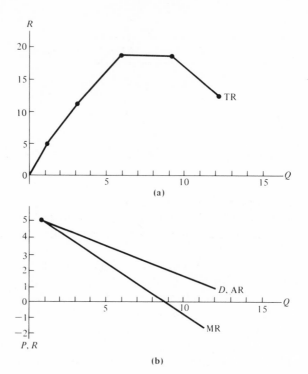

FIGURE 5.8

vertical scale of part (a) is different from that of part (b). This is in accord with the data of Table 5.4 and the fact that TR is shown in part (a), whereas, price, AR, and MR are shown in part (b). However, the horizontal scales are the same for both graphs. The usual MR–AR relationship is shown in part (b): MR is less than or equal to AR, since the AR curve has a negative slope. In this discrete case, AR = MR at $Q = 1$ and $P = \$5$. In a continuous case, the two are equal at a quantity infinitesimally close to zero. It is also seen that TR increases when MR is positive, reaches a maximum at the Q for which MR = 0, and decreases when MR is negative.[4] These are general mathematical relationships that hold between total, average, and marginal curves under all circumstances. In this discrete case, TR is maximum for more than one value of Q, and MR = 0 for only one value of Q. In a continuous case, MR would be equal to zero for all Q such that TR is maximum. As we explained earlier, the given values are actually estimates of the average MR within certain ranges rather than accurate MR values at the indicated points.

---

[4] Since, by definition, MR is the change in TR resulting from the sale of an additional unit of commodity, and since from Table 5.4 we see that TR remains the same as the quantity sold increases from 6 to 9 units, it follows that when MR is zero, TR reaches its maximum.

5.7 GRAPHICAL DERIVATION OF THE MR CURVE

In economics, one is often given a demand curve without the corresponding numerical figures. Hence, we must ask if there exists a simple way to derive the MR curve from a demand curve. The answer is yes. For the sake of simplicity, we begin with a straight-line demand curve and then proceed to show how the MR can be derived from a general demand curve.

Consider Figure 5.9, in which AD is the demand curve. Let us determine the MR for any quantity Q.

We first state without proof that in the case of a straight-line demand curve the MR curve is also a straight line that starts from the same point on the vertical axis. (This statement will be proven in the appendix to this chapter.) Suppose that AM is the MR curve that corresponds to demand curve AD; then the MR for Q_1 is $\overline{Q_1 M}$. The question is how to find a simple way to determine the point M.

With the given demand curve, the corresponding price for Q_1 is P_1, and TR $= PQ$ is given by the rectangle of $0P_1BQ_1$. On the other hand, the TR for Q_1 can also be represented by the area underneath the MR curve up to Q_1, that is, $0ACMQ_1$. (Mathematically oriented students will recognize the truth of this statement based on the fact that TR is the integral of the MR function.) These two areas have the area $0P_1CMQ_1$ in common. Thus, the areas of the triangles $\triangle ACP_1$ and $\triangle BMC$ must be equal. Furthermore, $\triangle ACP_1$ and $\triangle BMC$ are similar triangles, since angle ACP_1 equals angle BCM and angles AP_1C and CBM are both right angles. Since similar triangles with the same area are congruent, the corresponding sides being equal to each other, we have $\overline{AP_1} = \overline{BM}$.

The above results offer us a simple way of determining the point M for a straight-line demand curve. For any quantity Q_1, draw a vertical straight line from Q_1 which intersects the demand curve at point B. Next draw a horizontal straight line from B

FIGURE 5.9

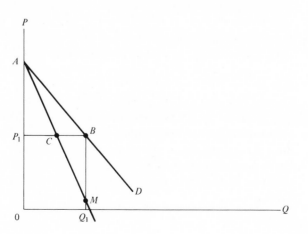

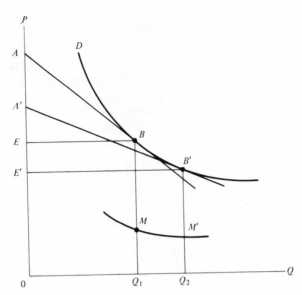

FIGURE 5.10   0

which intersects the vertical axis at point P_1, and mark BM in such a way that $\overline{BM} = \overline{AP_1}$. The distance $\overline{Q_1 M}$ is the MR for Q_1, and the straight line $\overline{AM}$ is the MR curve. Note that if the point M is below the horizontal axis at a given Q, then the MR for this Q is negative.

Another simple way of finding the MR curve in the case of a straight-line demand curve is to draw a horizontal straight line from any point (such as B) on the demand curve. Then find the point C such that $\overline{P_1 C} = \overline{BC}$. The straight line $\overline{AC}$ is the MR curve.

The MR curve corresponding to a demand curve that is not a straight line can be similarly derived. Since the MR curve is usually not a straight line, many points have to be derived in order to obtain a reasonably accurate MR curve.

Consider Figure 5.10, in which D is the demand curve. In order to derive the MR for Q_1, draw a vertical straight line from Q_1 which intersects D at B. Next draw AB, which is tangent to D at point B and intersects the vertical axis at point A. Then draw the horizontal straight line from B which intersects the vertical axis at E, and mark $\overline{BM}$ on $\overline{BQ_1}$ (or an extension of it) such that $\overline{BM} = \overline{AE}$. Distance $\overline{Q_1 M}$ is the MR for Q_1. Similarly, for Q_2 we can mark $\overline{B'M'}$ on $\overline{B'Q_2}$ (or an extension of it) such that $\overline{B'M'} = \overline{A'E'}$; the distance $\overline{Q_2 M'}$ is the MR for Q_2. After establishing a reasonable number of points such as M and M', draw a curve (such as $\widehat{MM'}$) through these points; this is the MR curve that corresponds to the demand curve. The more points (such as M and M') one derives, the more accurate will be the MR curve.

5.8 MR AND PRICE ELASTICITY OF DEMAND

There is a mathematical relationship between MR and the price elasticity of demand which has many uses. In particular, it is very useful for markup pricing in the special case of constant AVC (this will be discussed in more detail in Chapters 7–9, which are concerned with imperfect markets). This relationship is written

$$MR = P(1 - 1/E) \qquad (5.14)$$

where MR is marginal revenue, P is price, and E is the price elasticity of demand. Relationship (5.14) can easily be derived by the methods of calculus, which will be illustrated in the appendix to this chapter. However, it can also be derived by the graphical method, which is presented here. We shall derive (5.14) for the simple case of a straight-line demand curve. However, the result holds for any demand curve.

Consider Figure 5.11, in which AD is the demand curve. From Section 5.7, we know that $\overline{AP_1} = \overline{BM}$ and that $\overline{Q_1M}$ is the MR for Q_1. From Section 5.3, we also know that the price elasticity of Q_1 is $E = \overline{BD}/\overline{AB}$. Since $\triangle ABP_1$ and $\triangle BDQ_1$ are similar triangles, their corresponding sides are proportional; thus,

$$\overline{AP_1}/\overline{BP_1} = \overline{BQ_1}/\overline{DQ_1}$$

Hence,

$$\overline{AP_1} = \overline{BP_1}(\overline{BQ_1}/\overline{DQ_1})$$

Since $\overline{AP_1} = \overline{BM}$, by substitution we obtain

$$\overline{BM} = \overline{BP_1}(\overline{BQ_1}/\overline{DQ_1}) = \overline{BQ_1}(\overline{BP_1}/\overline{DQ_1})$$

MR is positive when E > 1, negative when E < 1, and constant when E = 1

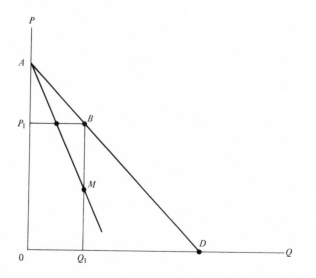

FIGURE 5.11

However, the MR for Q_1 is

$$\overline{Q_1M} = \overline{BQ_1} - \overline{BM}$$

and by substitution we obtain

$$MR = \overline{BQ_1} - \overline{BQ_1}(\overline{BP_1}/\overline{DQ_1}) = \overline{BQ_1}(1 - \overline{BP_1}/\overline{DQ_1})$$

Since $\overline{BP_1} = \overline{0Q_1}$, we have

$$\overline{0Q_1}/\overline{DQ_1} = \overline{AB}/\overline{BD} = 1/E$$

and $\overline{BQ_1}$ is equal to the price of Q_1. By substitution, we obtain (5.14).

The above proof is important for a producer or a firm because it shows the close relationship between the price elasticity of demand and the additional revenue that one can obtain from selling an additional unit of the commodity. Using (5.14) in conjunction with cost information, one can determine the profit-maximizing quantity or price. We shall have more to say on the relationship between MR and price elasticity in Chapters 7–9. It should be pointed out that (5.14) is useful only for monopolists. In the case of a competitive firm, the situation is rather simple, and the above complicated proof of the MR–price elasticity relationship is not necessary. We shall now turn our attention to the case of a competitive firm.

5.9   THE DEMAND CURVE FOR A COMPETITIVE FIRM: THE EQUALITY OF PRICE AND MR

Except for the special case of a Giffen good, the demand curve of a commodity is, in general, negatively sloped. However, this demand curve is for the market as a whole or for an industry, not for a firm under competition. In the case of a monopoly, the demand of the industry is also the demand of the firm, since, by definition, the firm is the industry under monopoly. In the following pages, we shall focus our attention on the firm's position in the industry under different market conditions and show how the demand and MR curves affect the profitability of operation.

As one learns in the study of economic principles, the market price is determined by the intersection of the supply and demand curves of the industry; this is illustrated in part (a) of Figure 5.12. Since the competitive firm is very small relative to the entire industry, it is a price taker and can sell as many units as it wishes at the market price P_0. This implies that the competitive firm's demand curve is a horizontal straight line, for example, d in part (b) of Figure 5.12. This demand curve is considered perfectly elastic because its price elasticity is infinite.

We have already shown that price and MR are equal for a horizontal demand curve. This is the familiar average–marginal

P

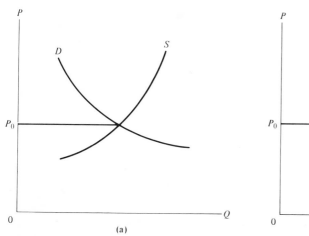

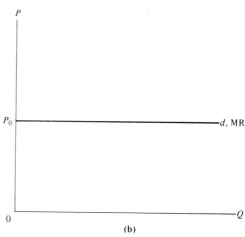

(a)

(b)

FIGURE 5.12

relationship that was explained in detail in Chapter 1 with respect
to AP and MP using the batting average of a baseball player as
an example. Since the price is always the AR, we can look to
Equation (5.14) for proof that MR $=$ P, since as E approaches
infinity, $1/E$ approaches zero. Thus, $1 - 1/E$ approaches 1 and,
consequently MR $=$ P. Hence, in the special case of perfect
competition, the firm's MR is the market price.

The implication of the above result is that a truly competitive
firm does not need market research because its demand and,
consequently, its price elasticity of demand are known. Therefore, no purpose will be served by market research. However,
for an imperfect competitor (e.g., a monopolist), the shape of the
demand curve and, consequently, the price elasticity of demand
are, in general, not known. In this case, market research can
provide some information on demand and price elasticity, which,
in turn, can help an imperfect competitor make decisions that
will result in higher profits. It should be pointed out that higher
profits for the producer may not necessarily come at the expense
of consumers. In some special cases, higher profits for producers
and increased benefits for consumers can occur simultaneously.
In short, this is not a *zero-sum* game.[5] The following example will
help to explain this point.

*Only firms under
imperfect
competition need
to know the price
elasticity of
demand*

5.10 LOW PRICE AND HIGH PROFIT: AN EXAMPLE

The considerable reduction in the price of phonograph records in
the 1940s is often used as an example that illustrates the relation
between a high price elasticity of demand, lower price, and higher

[5] A zero-sum game is one in which the gain of one person or group is exactly
equal to the loss of another person or group.

profit. Starting in the late 1930s, a few record dealers and producers (e.g., Columbia Records) performed experiments which
showed that the price elasticity of demand for musical records
was quite high. The MC of records was relatively low because
the largest part of the cost was fixed. This was a case in which
economic theory would suggest the existence of the possibility
that a lower price might result in higher total profits due to a large
increase in the quantity sold. Although unit profit might be lower,
total profit would be higher because the larger sales volume would
more than balance the lower unit profit.

Led by Columbia Records, the price of records was reduced
in some cases by 80%. As a result, the total expenditure on records rose greatly. Since the increase in cost was very slight, total
profits for the record industry also increased.

The above is a classic example where higher profit for the
producers did not come at the expense of consumers. Of course,
we are assuming that a lower price is, other things being equal,
beneficial to consumers. As our illustration shows, a higher profit
for producers and greater benefits to consumers are not necessarily competitive; in fact, under certain circumstances they can
be complementary. This implies that poor management (and con-
sequent low profits) of big business firms may do more harm to
consumers than the higher profits obtained by well-managed
firms. We shall discuss this concept in more detail in Chapter 7.

It should be pointed out that the above result is based on the
important assumption that the demand function is elastic. On the
other hand, if the demand function were inelastic, a reduction in
price would result in a lower TR. Similarly, if the demand were
unitary elastic, TR would not change when the price was either
reduced or raised. Since we are talking about a movement along
a negatively sloped demand curve, a reduction in price is accompanied by an increase in quantity, and hence, the price–revenue
relationship can equivalently be stated as a quantity–revenue
relationship. Furthermore, since TR and MR are functionally related, the price–revenue (quantity–revenue) relationship can
equivalently be stated either in terms of TR or in terms of MR.
The relationships between price elasticity and revenue are summarized in Table 5.5.

TABLE 5.5. Relationships Between Price (Quantity) Elasticity and Revenue

		Elastic demand $E > 1$	Unitary demand $E = 1$	Inelastic demand $E < 1$
MR		Positive	Zero	Negative
TR	Price rises (quantity falls)	Falls	No change	Rises
	Price falls (quantity rises)	Rises	No change	Falls

5.11   DEMAND IN ECONOMIC THEORY AND IN PRACTICE

Chapters 4 and 5 have been devoted to the theory of demand. It is no exaggeration to say that demand analysis is an essential part of the analysis of market behavior. In Chapter 7 (as well as in Chapters 8 and 9), it will be shown that the concept of demand is much more important than that of supply in the study of imperfect markets. The example in Section 5.10 concerning the record industry also shows that the shape of the demand curve is very important to a firm's pricing policy and profit position. It is no wonder that many big firms devote considerable resources to market research, which essentially is an attempt to gain more information on demand. Moreover, it should be emphasized that whereas demand is a well-defined and clear-cut concept in theory, it is not something that is easily estimated for an industry or firm in practice. *Econometrics* is a special field in economics which deals with this problem; however, it is still far from providing tested and practical applications for industrial use. This problem will not be discussed in detail, since to do so would require a larger volume than this book; however, it will help the student if we point out a common mistake that can easily be made.

If a firm has well-kept records on the volume sold and price of its product for many years, it is tempting to use simple statistical methods to estimate the demand for its product on the basis of these data. For example, assume that such a set of data is shown in Figure 5.13, in which each point is a price–quantity pair for a specific year.

If the records contain information for the years 1950–1977, there will be a total of 28 points or paired observations. A well-known statistical technique often used to fit a curve to a scatter diagram[6] is the method of least squares. Using this technique in

Improper measure of demand leads to ridiculous conclusions

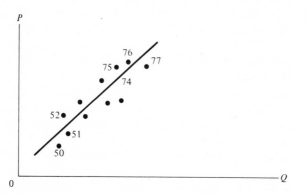

FIGURE 5.13

---

[6] Students who have had a course in statistics will recognize that Figure 5.13 is a scatter diagram.

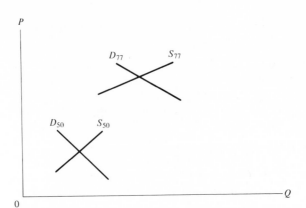

FIGURE 5.14

Figure 5.13, we might obtain the indicated positively sloped line. If this were the demand curve, the correct pricing policy suggestion would involve drastically raising the price of the product. This, of course, if carried out, would probably be disastrous to the firm or industry. The alert students may have already sensed that something is wrong. In fact, as we have already concluded, only the demand curve for a Giffen good can have a positive slope. If one is sure that the commodity involved is not a Giffen good, but the statistical data result in a positively sloped demand curve, then something must have gone wrong.

Actually, the straight line obtained by applying the least squares method to the points in Figure 5.13 is neither the demand nor the supply curve. This can be easily seen in Figure 5.14, in which just two points from Figure 5.13 are reproduced. We may assume that the market can best be analyzed in terms of both supply and demand conditions. In such a case, each observed point can be regarded as an equilibrium point, that is, the intersection of the supply and demand curves for that year. Taken in this context, what the scatter diagram shows is a series of equilibrium points, and we can see that the least squares method yields neither the demand nor the supply curve. In fact, it is meaningless. In econometrics, this is referred to as the *identification problem*; that is, the fitted curve can be identified as neither the demand nor the supply curve. It could be anything or nothing.

The above example is designed to warn students that whereas the well-defined theoretical concept of demand is essential to economic analysis, it is not something that is easily estimated for a firm or industry in practice. The conceptual clarification is very important as regards understanding the relationship between economic theory under imperfect competition and the general business practice of markup pricing. This topic will be discussed in more detail in Chapters 7–9.

SUMMARY

In this chapter we have shown that, given the assumption of the absence of externalities, the market demand curve for a commodity is the sum of the individual consumer demand curves for that commodity. We explained that although, in general, the demand for a commodity is a function of all prices, consumer income, and the consumer preference, we may simplify our analysis by assuming quantities other than price to be constant, thereby making the demand for a commodity a function of price only. This enabled us to formulate the concept of a demand curve (function) and to use it for evaluating the sensitivity of demand to changes in the price of the commodity. We defined this sensitivity of demand to price change as the price elasticity of demand and illustrated several methods for its calculation, noting the problems involved with each method. We also explained that, while the price elasticity of demand is closely related to the slope of the demand curve, they are entirely different concepts. Thus, for example, a straight-line demand curve, which has a constant slope, does not have constant elasticity even if the relative steepness of the slope is a general representation of the relative price elasticity of demand.

In addition to the concept of price elasticity, we defined and explained the relevance of income elasticity and cross elasticity in economic analysis. As with price elasticity, it was explained that elasticity is a term used to describe the sensitivity of the demand for a commodity to changes in the underlying parameters, i.e., income and the prices of other commodities. In the case of cross elasticity, we noted that two commodities could be classified as gross substitutes, complements, or independents depending on whether their cross elasticities were positive, negative, or zero. All three concepts of elasticity were shown to have significance in demand analysis, and examples were used to clarify the distinctions among them.

We concluded our discussion on demand elasticities by showing that demand and, hence, the revenue that a firm receives from the sale of its output, is closely related to the price elasticity of demand. Since average revenue (AR) is equal to total revenue (R) divided by quantity(Q), we explained that, in the absence of price discrimination, the demand curve is also the average revenue curve and, therefore, price elasticity could be used to evaluate the effect on average revenue due to a change in the price of the commodity. Additionally, we showed that since the marginal revenue (MR) curve can be derived from the demand (or what is the same thing, from the AR curve in the absence of price discrimination), MR is also related to the price elasticity of demand for the product. Finally, although we noted the importance of demand analysis in economics and business, we alerted the student to the difficult problem of specifying a demand curve or demand function from price–quantity data that are available in the real world.

EXERCISES AND QUESTIONS FOR CHAPTER 5 ON DEMAND THEORY

1. What are the conditions that can result in a shift of a demand curve? Explain how they work.

2. What can you say about the price elasticity at certain points on a demand curve of a commodity which is a straight line? *Justify* your answer.

3. What is the difference between income elasticity and price elasticity? Is any knowledge of the elasticities helpful to a monopolist? Why?

4. Under what conditions will two commodities X and Y be substitutes? Complements? Explain.

5. Use the graphical method to derive the MR curve when the demand curve is a straight line. Prove that your method is correct.

6. Does a firm under perfect competition need to worry about the price elasticity of demand for its product? Explain.

7. The *law of demand* states that larger quantities of any commodity will be purchased at low prices than at high prices. Suppose that the average price of steel in a country rose from $400 per ton to $450 per ton over the period 1973 to 1978, while the total amount of steel purchased rose from 100 million tons to 120 million tons. Does this indicate that the law of demand does not hold? Explain.

8. Why are market researchers interested in the elasticity of demand? Does a firm under perfect competition need market research? Defend your position.

A MATHEMATICAL NOTE ON DEMAND

The market demand for a commodity is derived from the individual consumer demands for the commodity. Under Assumption 4.5 (absence of externality) with respect to consumption, the summation of the individual consumer demands can be considered the market (aggregate) demand for the commodity. The utility function that we used in Chapter 4 to derive a consumer's demand schedule implies the absence of externality, since the utility of the ith consumer is a function of the quantity consumed by i alone, that is, it is not a function of the quantity consumed by $j \neq i$. When externality exists with respect to consumption, the utility of the ith consumer is, in general, a function of the quantities of the various commodities consumed by i as well as the quantities consumed by other consumers. For this reason, we are justified in taking the sum of the individual consumer demands as the market (aggregate) demand for the commodity.

In Chapter 4, it was shown that an individual consumer's demand for a commodity is derived from the solution of the first-order conditions of consumer equilibrium, provided that the second-order conditions are satisfied. Since the first-order conditions involve the prices of all the commodities and the consumer's income, the individual consumer's demand for a commodity is a function of all the prices and his or her income. If there are n commodities and m consumers, then the jth consumer's demand for the ith commodity can be written

$$Q_{ij} = D_{ij}(P_1, P_2, ..., P_n, M_j), \quad \begin{aligned} i &= 1, 2, ..., n \\ j &= 1, 2, ..., m \end{aligned} \tag{A5.1}$$

There are a total of mn individual consumer demand functions.

The market (aggregate) demand for a commodity i is the sum of Q_{ij} over the m consumers, taking into consideration the proper constraints (if any) on the individual demand functions. Mathematically, this can be expressed as follows:

$$Q_i = \sum_{j=1}^{m} D_{ij}(P_1, P_2, ..., P_n, M_j)$$

$$= D_i(P_1, P_2, ..., P_n, M, N) \qquad (A5.2)$$

where M denotes the total income of all consumers and N is the number of consumers, that is, m.

It should be understood that D_i not only depends on the level of M, but also on its distribution among the individual consumers. It is conceivable that for the same total income, the demand function for commodity i could be different for different distributions of this income (e.g., the more unequal the distribution of income, the higher the demand for luxuries). Thus, D_i is not only specified for a give M, but also for a given distribution of M.

With n commodities, the demand for any single one is a function of $n + 2$ independent variables, that is, n prices, total income M, and the number of consumers N. However, since only two-dimensional graphs can easily be drawn, economists use the "other things being equal" approach: All prices other than that of the given commodity, total income, and the number of consumers are assumed constant. In such a case, (A5.2) becomes

$$Q_i = D_i(\overline{P}_1, \overline{P}_2, ..., P_i, ..., \overline{P}_n, \overline{M}, \overline{N}) = D_i(P_i) \qquad (A5.3)$$

where the barred quantities denote constants.

The demand function (A5.3) characterizes partial analysis of a market, that is, it ignores the interaction between markets. In general, demand functions should be written in the form (A5.2) so that they will fully express the conditions under which the demand for a commodity is being quantified.

A5.1 ELASTICITIES OF DEMAND

The mathematical expressions for the elasticities of demand are straightforward. If we denote the price elasticity of commodity i by E_{ii}, the cross elasticity of commodity i with respect to the price of commodity j by E_{ij}, and income elasticity by E_M, we obtain the following equations:

$$E_{ii} = -(\partial Q_i/\partial P_i)(P_i/Q_i) \qquad (A5.4)$$

$$E_{ij} = (\partial Q_i/\partial P_j)(P_j/Q_i) \qquad (A5.5)$$

$$E_M = (\partial Q_i/\partial M)(M/Q_i) \qquad (A5.6)$$

It is important to note that the elasticities are defined in terms of the partial derivatives of the demand function (A5.2). In empirical work, when elasticities are computed, one has to make sure that only one independent variable has changed at a time. For example, if two prices have changed simultaneously, neither price nor cross elasticity can be legitimately computed without a proper statistical adjustment of the data. In the real world, statistical data often involve simultaneous changes of more than one independent variable; hence, proper care must be exercised in order to avoid errors.

In calculating the price elasticity of demand, a negative sign is added to the right side of (A5.4). Most economists do this in order to make the direct price elasticity positive, since demand law implies that the partial derivative is negative except in the special case of a Giffen good. However, some economists do not bother to add the negative sign. In this case, the direct price elasticity of demand will usually be negative. In the case of cross elasticity, there is no negative sign added to the right side of (A5.5), since E_{ij} can be either positive, negative, or zero. In fact, the sign of E_{ij} is used to define whether commodities i and j are gross substitutes, gross complements, or independents (as distinguished from the similar definition of net substitutes, net complements, or independents in terms of the cross substitution term in the Slutsky equation). Specifically, we can state the following:

1. Commodity i is a gross substitute for commodity j if $E_{ij} > 0$ and vice versa (i.e., commodity j is a gross substitute for commodity i if $E_{ji} > 0$).
2. Commodity i is a gross complement for commodity j if $E_{ij} < 0$ and vice versa.
3. Commodity i is independent of commodity j if $E_{ij} = 0$ and vice versa.

Although the above statements are symmetric, the values of E_{ij} are not, that is, in general, $E_{ij} \neq E_{ji}$. Furthermore, it is possible that $E_{ij} > 0$ while either $E_{ji} < 0$ or $E_{ji} = 0$. In other words, although commodity i is a substitute for commodity j, commodity j can be a complement for commodity i. There are real cases that illustrate the above asymmetric characteristics. For example, as stated in the text, steak sauce is certainly a complement for steak, but steak can hardly be considered a complement for steak sauce. Although the demand for steak sauce may shift when the price of steak changes, a change in the price of steak sauce can hardly be expected to have any effect on the demand for steak.

The income elasticity of demand can theoretically be either positive, negative, or even zero. If $E_M > 0$ for commodity i, then it is a normal good, whereas if $E_M < 0$ for commodity i, it is an inferior good. Economists have not given a name to a commodity whose income elasticity is zero.

It should be noted that both normal goods and inferior goods are for the most part defined with respect to the income term in the Slutsky equation and not with respect to the income elasticity of demand. However, the Slutsky equation relates only to a specific individual consumer's demand, not to the market (aggregate) demand. Since a commodity can be an inferior good for one consumer and a normal good for another, it is meaningful to define a good as being normal or inferior in the aggregate in terms of income elasticity.

A5.2 THE CLASS OF CONSTANT-ELASTICITY DEMAND FUNCTIONS

In the simple case of the demand for a commodity being a function of its price, other things being equal, the class of constant-elasticity demand functions can be written

$$Q = AP^{-a} \tag{A5.7}$$

where both A and a are constants. It can be easily shown that a is the constant elasticity. Since

$$dQ/dP = -aAP^{-a-1} = -aAP^{-a}/P = -aQ/P \tag{A5.8}$$

by substitution,

$$E = -(dQ/dP)(P/Q) = -(-aQ/P)(P/Q) = a \tag{A5.9}$$

It is important to note that only when the exponent a in (A5.7) is a constant does it represent the price elasticity of demand. If the exponent a in (A5.7) is not a constant, for example, if it is a function of Q, then it will no longer be the price elasticity of demand. However, some economists write

$$Q = AP^{-E} \tag{A5.10}$$

where E denotes the direct price elasticity, and they consider (A5.10) a constant-elasticity demand function. This is incorrect; that is, (A5.7) represents the class of constant-elasticity demand functions and (A5.10) does not. This is because that the direct price elasticity E is a function of quantity Q. When this is the case, the exponent E is not even the direct price elasticity. This can be easily shown if we write (A5.10) in the noncommital form

$$Q = AP^{-U(Q)} \tag{A5.11}$$

where U is a function of Q, which, in turn, is a function of P. Differentiation of (A5.11) with respect to P gives

$$dQ/dP = -UQP^{-1} - \ln PQ(dU/dQ)(dQ/dP)$$

Solving for dQ/dP, we have

$$\frac{dQ}{dP} = -\frac{UQ}{P[1 + \ln PQ(dU/dQ)]}$$

Multiplying both sides by $-P/Q$ gives

$$-\frac{dQ}{dP} \times \frac{P}{Q} = \frac{U}{1 + \ln PQ(dU/dQ)}$$

Since, by definition, the left side of the above expression is the direct price elasticity of demand E, we have

$$E = \frac{U}{1 + \ln PQ(dU/dQ)} \tag{A5.12}$$

Hence, E can be either greater than or less than U—the exponent in (A5.11)—depending on whether $\ln P$ and/or dU/dQ are negative or positive. It is only in the special case where U is a constant (and, consequently, $dU/dQ = 0$) that E will be equal to U. This proves our assertion. Hence, the class of constant-elasticity demand functions can only be legitimately written in the form (A5.7), that is, not in the form (A5.10).

The class of constant-elasticity demand functions in the general case of n commodities can be written in a similar fashion; that is, the demand for commodity i can be written

$$Q_i = A_i \prod_{j=1}^{n} P_j^{a_{ij}} M^{a_i} \tag{A5.13}$$

where A_i, a_{ij}, and a_i are constants. In (A5.13), a_{ii} is the direct price elasticity, a_{ij}, $i \neq j$, is the cross elasticity with respect to the price of commodity j, and a_i is the income elasticity. Equation (A5.13) can also be written

$$\log Q_i = \log A_i + \sum_{j=1}^{n} a_{ij} \log P_j + a_i \log M \tag{A5.13'}$$

Thus, a constant-elasticity demand function must be log linear in prices and income. This type of demand function is worth knowing because it is often used in empirical work for the simple reason that the least-squares method of statistics can be directly applied to it in order to estimate the elasticities.

A5.3 PRICE ELASTICITY FOR A LINEAR DEMAND FUNCTION

In Section 5.2, it was shown by the graphical method that price elasticity is unitary at the midpoint, inelastic below the midpoint, and elastic above the midpoint of a straight-line demand curve. This result can be proven mathematically with even less difficulty.

A linear demand function can be written

$$Q = a - bP \tag{A5.14}$$

where a and b are positive constants. The demand curve in Figure 5.3 is actually the inverse of (A5.14), that is,

$$P = a/b - (1/b)Q \tag{A5.14'}$$

The horizontal intercept of Figure 5.3, $\overline{0B}$, is a, and the vertical intercept, $\overline{0A}$, is a/b. From (A5.14) we also have

$$dQ/dP = -b$$

Since

$$E = -\frac{dQP}{dPQ} = \frac{b[a/b - (1/b)Q]}{Q} = \frac{a}{Q} - 1 \qquad (A5.15)$$

then at the midpoint of the demand curve, $P = a/2b$. From (A5.14), the corresponding Q is $a/2$. Substituting this value of Q into (A5.15), we obtain

$$E = 2a/a - 1 = 1 \qquad (A5.16)$$

This proves that price elasticity is unitary at the midpoint of a straight-line demand curve.

Below the midpoint of the demand curve, $P < a/2b$ and, consequently, $Q > a/2$. This implies that $a/Q < 2$. Substituting this value into (A5.15), we derive

$$E < 1 \qquad (A5.17)$$

for points below the midpoint of the demand curve. At the point on the horizontal axis, $Q = a$, and from (A5.15) we obtain

$$E = 0 \qquad (A5.18)$$

Similarly, for points above the midpoint of the demand curve, $P > a/2b$, which corresponds to $Q < a/2$. This implies that $a/Q > 2$. Substituting this value into (A5.15), we obtain

$$E > 1 \qquad (A5.19)$$

for points above the midpoint of the demand curve. At the point on the vertical axis, $Q = 0$ and $a/Q \to \infty$; therefore,

$$E \to \infty \qquad (A5.20)$$

at the intersection of the demand curve and the vertical axis.

A5.4 REVENUE, DEMAND, AND PRICE ELASTICITY OF DEMAND

By definition, the total revenue TR is equal to the product of quantity Q and price P, that is,

$$\text{TR} = QP(Q) \qquad (A5.21)$$

It is important to remember that revenue is really just a function of the quantity—not of both quantity and price—since price itself is a function of quantity. The notation $P(Q)$ in (A5.21) indicates that the price P is a function of the quantity along the demand curve. Thus, P and Q are not two independent variables, but are functionally related by the demand function. If one variable is known, the other is automatically determined. For example, with linear demand function (A5.14) and its inverse (A5.14′), the TR function is

$$\text{TR} = QP = Q[a/b - (1/b)Q] = (a/b)Q - (1/b)Q^2 \qquad (A5.22)$$

For constant-elasticity demand function (A5.7), the corresponding inverse is

$$P = A^{1/a}Q^{-1/a} \qquad (A5.7′)$$

Thus, the TR function is

$$\text{TR} = QP = QA^{1/a}Q^{-1/a} = A^{1/a}Q^{1-1/a} \qquad (A5.23)$$

Marginal revenue MR is defined as the derivative of the TR function,

$$\text{MR} = d\,\text{TR}/dQ = P + Q\,dP/dQ \qquad (A5.24)$$

When the demand curve has a negative slope, $dP/dQ < 0$, and hence

$$\text{MR} < P \qquad \text{for} \quad Q > 0 \qquad (A5.25)$$

for a negatively sloped demand curve. In the special case of perfect competition, the firm is a price taker and the demand curve is a horizontal straight line, that is, P is a constant; thus, $dP/dQ = 0$ and

$$\text{MR} = P \qquad (A5.26)$$

This proves the assertion of the equality of price and MR made in Section 5.9.

The relationship between MR and price elasticity that was derived by the graphical method in Section 5.8 can easily be derived from (A5.24). Multiplying the second term on the right side of (A5.24) by $1 = P/P$, we obtain

$$\text{MR} = P + P(Q\,dP/dQP) = P(1 - 1/E) \qquad (A5.27)$$

since

$$\frac{Q\,dP}{dQP} = \frac{1}{(dQ/dP)(P/Q)} = -1/E$$

In the special case of a linear demand function, from (A5.22) we have

$$\text{MR} = a/b - (2/b)Q \qquad (A5.28)$$

This shows that MR is a linear function of the quantity Q for a linear demand function, a fact that we have used in the text without proof. Comparing equations (A5.28) and (A5.14′), it is seen that the demand and MR curves have the same vertical intersect, since they both contain the same constant—a/b. It is also obvious that the slope of the MR curve is twice as steep as that of the demand curve, since the slope of the demand curve is $-1/b$, whereas that of the corresponding MR curve is $-2/b$, which is twice the absolute value of the former.

The MR for the constant-elasticity demand function can be computed from equation (A5.23) with the use of (A5.24):

$$\text{MR} = (1 - 1/a)A^{1/a}Q^{-1/a} \qquad\qquad (A5.29)$$

From (A5.29) we can see that MR is positive only if $a > 1$. Since a is the constant elasticity and firms will never expand output to where MR is negative, it follows that only in the case where $a > 1$ will constant elasticity have value to business. In fact, this remark applies to any demand function, that is, a rational firm will never operate at the range of its demand where it is inelastic. From (A5.27), MR < 0 for $E < 1$. This implies that TR will increase when quantity is reduced. Moreover, reduced quantity also means reduced cost. A combination of added revenue and reduced cost will definitely increase profit. Thus, if a firm is operating under a condition of inelastic demand, its profits cannot be maximum. Profits can be increased by raising the price and, consequently, reducing the quantity. It should be pointed out that this argument applies only to an imperfect (e.g., monopolistic) market. A competitive firm faces a perfectly elastic demand, is a price taker, and has no freedom of choice as regards price.

THE THEORY OF
PRICE AND MARKET ORGANIZATION

Part I dealt with the economics of production and cost. The fundamental assumption underlying our theory was that a firm faces a given technology and input prices, and that its choice criterion is the combination of inputs which will maximize output for a given cost or, alternatively, minimize cost for a given output. In Part II we dealt with the problems of consumer choice and consumer demand. Our theory was based on the assumption of a consumer with a given income facing known market prices for different commodities. In order to maximize the satisfaction (utility) derived, a consumer chooses some unique combination of commodities which is in accordance with his or her preference pattern. In both Parts I and II, market prices were assumed to be given; that is, we did not yet consider the important question of price determination. It is to this question that we now turn our discussion. It is important to understand that the preceding chapters have been directed to laying the foundation for the proper treatment of this economic problem. Otherwise, the coverage of this important topic would be quite superficial.

People on the street, as well as many economists, are accustomed to saying that "Market price is determined by supply and demand." Some economists even jokingly make the statement, "Teach a parrot to say 'supply and demand,' and you have an economist." Although the concepts of supply and demand are of equal importance in perfectly competitive markets, they are not in imperfectly competitive (e.g., monopolistic) markets. In these cases, the concepts of cost (rather than supply) and demand are more general to the analysis of market price. This is sometimes overlooked by economists. We shall examine this distinction in emphasis in more concrete terms in Chapters 7–9.

In economics, the term *market* has a special meaning.

Definition: Market. A market is a theoretical construct with specific characteristics in which a single price for a commodity or service is established and buyers and sellers carry out their economic transactions.

Based on certain characteristics, economists classify the numerous varieties of market into four categories: perfect competition, monopoly, monopolistic competition, and oligopoly. Each of these *economic models* is based on a set of specific assumptions. This will become apparent when we consider each model individually.

The concept of *industry* is related (by construction) to that of market. In general, an industry can be defined as "a collection of firms producing a homogeneous product." However, we shall see that under certain circumstances a collection of firms producing close substitutes, but not a homogeneous product, can also be considered an industry. Chapter 8 will provide a more-detailed discussion of this point.

In economic analysis, it is important to make the distinction between the different *market structures* that have been categorized as perfect competition, monopoly, monopolistic competition, and oligopoly. The characteristics of price and quantity, as well as how price and quantity are determined in an industry and/or firm, can be quite different under each of the four market structures. In particular, a firm under perfect competition is a *price taker*, and its only choice involves the quantity to produce in order to accomplish its goal. On the other hand, a firm under monopoly, monopolistic competition, or oligopoly can choose either price or quantity (but not both) as the criterion for determining production policy. In practice, almost all firms of the latter three categories choose price as the criterion and let the market determine the quantity that they can sell. In theory, for the sake of convenience, economists usually consider quantity instead of price to be the criterion chosen by a firm. In fact, the two different approaches are theoretically equivalent for a given demand under monopoly, monopolistic competition, and oligopoly. However, in the real world, a perfectly competitive firm is unique in this respect. Thus, in order to stress this point, we single out firms in a perfectly competitive market as *price takers*, whereas firms under the other three market structures are considered *price makers*.

Under perfect competition firms are price takers

In everyday life, almost all sellers set their prices. This indicates that perfect competition is not a close approximation of everyday life. However, many economic textbooks have devoted a disproportionate amount of space to perfect competition as compared to the other market structures. A few authors even draw conclusions (sometimes explicitly and sometimes implicitly) concerning reality based on the perfectly competitive model. This lack of understanding of the true meaning and usefulness of perfect competition as an economic model inevitably results in confusion.

Perfect competition is the simplest of the four economic models. It is comparatively easy to understand, even though it is based on a more "heroic" set of assumptions than the other models. Once the perfect competition model is fully understood, it is somewhat easier to understand the other, more sophisticated models. For this reason, the model of perfect competition is an important and useful tool in the study of complex economic systems. Although some of the conclusions based exclusively on the model of perfect competition may be far from reality, it nevertheless enables us to gain a better perspective on what might be regarded as an ideal system in order to more forcefully analyze and evaluate the market structures that are usually found in the real world.

The model of perfect competition provides a good pedagogical introduction to price determination

In order to avoid confusion and facilitate their understanding of market analysis, students should recall some basic points from Parts I and II. First of all, in Part I it was clearly indicated that the cost of production for a firm is determined by technology, input prices, and the firm's behavior, that is, it does not depend on consumer choice. Secondly, in Part II it was shown that the demand of individual consumers is determined by their preference patterns and incomes, which are not at all affected by the producer's behavior. Taken together, these two observations imply that cost and demand are determined by separate, independent factors. In other words, a change in demand will not change the cost of production and vice versa.

The student should also appreciate the fact that here we are essentially dealing with partial analysis, that is, we analyze one industry at a time and there is no interaction between industries. Moreover, this means that the "other things being equal" assumption prevails regardless of whether or not we mention it explicitly. For example, if the demand for a commodity changes as a result of either a change in consumer income or a change in preference pattern, then the market price and purchased quantity of the commodity will change for a given cost, but the market prices and purchased quantities of all other commodities will remain constant. This implies two things. First of all, the factor that causes a change in the demand for the product of a given industry does not cause any change in the demand for or cost of the products of all other industries. Secondly, the changes in the market price and purchased quantity of the given commodity do not affect the demand for or cost (and, consequently, market price or purchased quantity) of the product (commodity) of any other industry. This is not very realistic, but it is scientific in terms of the logic of the model; therefore, it helps us understand a complex situation by focusing attention on the effects of a change of one factor at a time. Thus, partial analysis as used here serves the same purpose as a controlled experiment in the physical sciences. In short, partial analysis may not be very realistic, but it is very important in economic theory.

Before proceeding to a detailed discussion of perfect competition, we wish to note two fundamental assumptions that are common to all four economic models: (1) The goal of a firm is to maximize profit (as stated in Part I) and (2) there is an absence of government intervention (however, the effects of government interference on the market will be analyzed in the case of a monopoly).

PRICE TAKERS

Sellers in a perfectly competitive market are price takers; that is, they can sell any quantity they wish at the market price without affecting the price of the commodity. Thus, it is not necessary for these sellers to reduce their price below the market price. Moreover, they will be unable to sell a single unit if their asking price is above the market price. In some ways the stock market is a reflection of this situation. Thus, if one owns a few hundred shares of the common stock of a corporation which is traded on the stock exchange, he or she can sell any amount of this stock at the market price in a trading day. It is not necessary that one reduce the price of the stock below the market price in order to sell it. On the other hand, one will be unable to sell a single share in the stock exchange at a price higher than the market price. In this sense, a small stockholder is a price taker in the stock market and is faced with the same market condition as a firm under perfect competition.

Under perfect competition a firm can sell all it wants to without affecting price

An opposite condition exists if one owns a substantial amount of the common stock of a corporation. In this case, if one tries to sell an amount of shares which is considerably above that sold on an average trading day, the market price may be suppressed by this action. Under such circumstances, one is no longer a price taker.

There are fundamental differences with respect to market operation and strategy in the above two cases. Therefore, economists have constructed different economic models for the analysis of different situations in order to focus attention on the special features that are applicable under different circumstances.

Although certain similarities exist between perfect competition in economics and the operation of the stock exchange, the stock market is not perfectly competitive in the strict sense. Perfect competition is an economic model that satisfies certain very restrictive assumptions. Therefore, it is important to understand the meaning and implications of these assumptions in order to understand the usefulness and limitations of a given model. For this reason, in Chapter 6 we shall first discuss the assumptions on which the model of perfect competition is based and then proceed to examine the processes by which price and output are determined in the market in both the short run and the long run. We shall also have more to say on the behavior of the firm in its role as a profit maximizer and how the firm's individual actions are conditioned by the market.

PRICE MAKERS

In contrast to the model of perfect competition, where business firms are price takers, the market models of imperfect competition, that is, pure monopoly, monopolistic competition, and oligopoly (of which duopoly is a special case), emphasize the role of the producer as a price maker. These are the cases that we encounter in everyday life. When we go to a store, we observe that the price for each and every commodity has been set by the seller, and as consumers we can buy almost any quantity we wish at the given price. Although we are more familiar with price makers than price takers, and with the myriad variation of market practices that we face each day, we are not usually able to offer a systematic theory or explanation for the diversity of practices that abound. Economic models, which are generalizations of reality, cannot be expected to explain every detail or variation of actual business practice. On the other hand, they do provide a basis for explaining the more-salient features that are relevant to decision making in modern business.

The fact that economic models are not mirror images of reality is a result of the simplified assumptions we must make when building them. These assumptions allow us to keep our models manageable and thus deduce the behavioral relationships that exist between given variables. However, not all of our assumptions will be satisfied in the real world. Thus, although business practice may sometimes appear to contradict economic theory, the contradiction disappears once the assumptions underlying the economic models are taken into consideration. An obvious example of such an apparent contradiction, which we shall be discussing in Chapter 7, is that of traditional monopoly theory versus mark-up pricing as actually practiced by the majority of business firms.

Assumptions that underlie economic models enable us to generalize about the real world

Economists usually refer to the existence of price makers as a representation of imperfect markets in that firms possess certain market power. The fact that firms can set the prices of their products is an indication of market power; otherwise, they would be price takers. In this context, the size of a firm is not the sole determinant of market power. Thus, the corner grocery store as well as a supermarket chain, or the "big three" auto makers as well as the small manufacturers, all possess varying degrees of market power. At times, the corner grocery store may exert more market power than a supermarket. To facilitate analysis and evaluation, economists classify all price makers, small and large alike, into three types of market practice—monopoly, monopolistic competition, and oligopoly—depending on the market power and certain other relevant characteristics exhibited by particular firms. In theory, each economic model is based on certain assumptions that characterize the model. In this respect, the distinction between various models is clear cut. However, in reality, a firm may be classified into one category according to certain criteria, but its decision process may be better approximated by a different model. From the student's point of view, it is important first to understand the reasoning, the logical structure, and the implication of the underlying assumptions. Then and only then can one apply the theory to everyday life.

PRICE DETERMINATION
AND THE SUPPLY FUNCTION
UNDER PERFECT COMPETITION

INTRODUCTION

As we mentioned in the introduction to Part III, the concept of supply is meaningful under perfect competition. It will be shown that the supply function of a firm is closely related to its marginal cost (MC), which is a logical conclusion of our model. In order to show the significance of this observation, it is necessary to have a clear idea of the nature of the perfectly competitive model and the assumptions that govern the operation of firms under perfect competition.

In the social as well as natural sciences, a model is based on certain clearly stated assumptions. The less restrictive the assumptions, the better the model. The anecdote cited in the introduction to Part I concerning how one can prove that the moon is made of blue cheese if unrealistic assumptions are made also applies here. This is why, in scientific theory, the principle of "Occam's Razor" (eliminating all unnecessary assumptions) is generally observed. On the other hand, very restrictive assumptions are sometimes needed in order to make a model logically consistent. Under these circumstances, the omission of certain necessary assumptions does not make the model better or more realistic. On the contrary, it may result in a model that is no longer logically self-contained. This will become more evident as we proceed with our definition of perfect competition and the use of the model for analyzing price and output determination in the market. Later in this chapter we shall have more to say on the attempt of some economists to modify the perfectly competitive model in order to meet some of the criticisms of it.

6.1. PERFECT COMPETITION DEFINED

In economic theory, perfect competition is a model that is based on four assumptions.

Assumption 6.1: Homogeneous Product. There is a homogeneous product for which a market exists. All units of the product are identical in all respects and there is no advantage for a buyer to choose between sellers. The market is completely impersonal with regard to each unit of product irrespective of the sellers.

Consumer preference dictates whether a commodity is homogeneous

The common stock of a corporation has the characteristics of a homogeneous product in that one share is precisely the same as another regardless of who the sellers are. If one wishes to order 100 shares of a given stock, there is no distinction made between sellers, and the only consideration is the market price, which is the same to all buyers. In this sense, a stock exchange contains many markets, since by our definition the stocks of each corporation constitute a market. A similar condition exists in the commodity market, where a given grade of wheat, barley, or oats represents a homogeneous product and buyers do not distinguish between sellers.

Many commodities (in particular, brand-name manufactured goods) do not satisfy Assumption 6.1. For example, two shirts with the same brand name but different colors are not identical. Moreover, two shirts of the same color and style which are made of the same material and by the same worker are not identical if they carry different brand names. Since one brand name may offer more prestige than the other, some people may be willing to pay more for it. Thus, what is important is not whether one unit of a commodity is *actually* different from another unit, but whether consumers *think* that they are different. For this reason, manufactured products seldom satisfy the requirements of a perfectly competitive market.

Assumption 6.2: Free Entry and Exit. All sellers and buyers have complete freedom of entry and exit in the market.

Freedom of entry and exit in the market is not only enjoyed by sellers, but also by buyers. In a perfectly competitive market, there is no legal, social, or financial restriction that would prevent one from participating as a seller. There is no patent that grants a monopoly right to a seller in a perfectly competitive market. Social taboo is absent. The fact that even financial difficulties do not bar the average person from participating as a seller rules out industries that require a great deal of initial investment as being perfectly competitive. In a perfectly competitive industry, one does not need a large amount of capital to start a business; hence, entry is open to many. Similarly, in a perfectly competitive market there is freedom of entry and exit for buyers. Any market that involves high-pressure sales or imposes restrictions that discriminate between buyers (e.g., electric utility rates) cannot be perfectly competitive.

Assumption 6.3: Many Small Sellers and Buyers. All buyers and sellers must be quite small relative to the size of the market. In other words, the amount of a commodity that a seller may offer or that a buyer may want to purchase must be negligible in the market.

For example, if the number of outstanding shares of common stock of a corporation is one million, and 10,000 shares are traded in an average business day, then someone who owns 100 shares can be considered a small stockholder. On the other hand, if a mutual fund, trust, or institution owns 100,000 shares of the stock, it cannot be considered a small stockholder. The important thing here is that both sellers and buyers must be small in the sense that whatever amount a trader wants to buy or sell must not have any perceptible effect on the market price. This implies that both buyers and sellers in a perfectly competitive market are price takers.

Assumption 6.4: Perfect Information or Knowledge. Sellers and buyers have perfect information or knowledge concerning the market.

Sellers and buyers are not only assumed to know what is currently going on in the market, but also what is going to happen tomorrow, the day after tomorrow, and so forth. This is the most unrealistic of the assumptions of the perfectly competitive model, but it is a necessary one. If we did not make this assumption, uncertainty and risk would be involved, and this would make the model more complicated. The importance and necessity of Assumption 6.4 can be better illustrated by assuming its absence. In this case, just as in reality, sellers would not know the precise costs of their commodities nor the market prices, which means that there would be no way for them to decide what amounts to sell in order to maximize their profits. Even if they were to know the costs and prices today, but not those of tomorrow, uncertainty would be involved. Therefore, the quantities that maximize their profits today may turn out to be unsatisfactory after tomorrow's prices are known. With respect to buyers, without Assumption 6.4, demand will not have the precise meaning developed in Part II. A model that does not include Assumption 6.4 must have a mechanism to deal with the problems of uncertainty and risk.

The assumption of perfect information simplifies analysis

Some economists attempt to make the model of perfect competition more realistic in appearance by eliminating Assumption 6.4 and calling the model one of *pure competition*. It may appear that pure competition is a better model than perfect competition according to the principle of "Occam's Razor." However, without Assumption 6.4, and without a mechanism to deal with the problems of uncertainty and risk, the model is incomplete or logically inconsistent and, therefore, cannot be any better than a logically consistent albeit unrealistic model.

Although Assumption 6.4 results in the model of perfect competition being far from realistic, since neither sellers nor buyers have such information or knowledge of the market, any seller or buyer must have some information or knowledge about the market, however imperfect it may be. Furthermore, market information can be improved at a cost. Obviously, the cost of perfect information, if possible at all, would be very high. In this sense, Assumption 6.4 implies that market information is free of cost and that perfect information is feasible. In reality, market information is not free and perfect information may not be possible. This imposes certain limitations on the application of the model of perfect competition with respect to analyzing market behavior. In order to avoid confusion, students must understand the full implications of Assumption 6.4.

Although not always stated explicitly, as a general rule, Assumption 6.4 actually underlies almost all economic theory. Without this assumption, economists are not on solid ground when they draw a cost curve for a firm, and it is more difficult to justify the meaning of a demand curve for an industry. It will be shown in Chapter 7 that the most difficult problem a business firm encounters in decision making in the real world is the lack of knowledge of the demand for its product. As a result, firms must have some kind of "rule of thumb" on which to base their decisions.

In theory, if we do not make Assumption 6.4, then we cannot draw demand and cost curves with certainty. If this were the case, economic theory would certainly take a quite different form, if it could be developed at all. Thus, although Assumption 6.4 is unrealistic, it is necessary for economic theory. We cannot safely eliminate Assumption 6.4 without changing the whole structure of economic theory; however, once we attempt to apply economic theory in the real world, the limitations that result from Assumption 6.4 must be taken into consideration.

6.2 TIME AS A CONDITIONAL

6.2.1 Definition of Market Period, Short Run, and Long Run

We have already discussed the meaning of the short run and long run in economics with respect to production and cost. It was noted that in economics the short run and long run are not determined strictly in terms of a length of time, such as 1, 2, or 3 years. In production, the short run is defined as a period of time such that some inputs are variable and others are fixed, whereas in the long run all inputs are variable. In terms of cost, we distinguish between fixed and variable costs in the short run, whereas all costs are variable in the long run.

In a discussion of price determination in the market, economists traditionally consider it significant to distinguish between the market period, the short run, and the long run, which in this case are defined as follows.

Definition: Market Period. A period of time which is so short that the output of each firm and the number of firms in an industry are fixed.

Definition: Short Run. A period of time during which a firm's plant is fixed, but output can be changed by increasing or decreasing the use of variable inputs. For an industry, the number of firms is constant in the short run.

Definition: Long Run. A period of time such that plant size can be adjusted according to cost and market conditions. In the limit, a firm can liquidate its business entirely if market conditions are unfavorable. On the other hand, new firms may enter the industry if the market is favorable. Thus for an industry, the number of firms is variable in the long run.

6.2.2 The Industry Supply Curve in the Market Period

Traditionally, economists consider the industry supply curve in the market period a vertical straight line. The reasons for this condition are as follows. Since the quantity of the commodity is, by definition, fixed for each firm in the market period, the supply curve of each firm is a vertical straight line. Inasmuch as the industry supply curve is the horizontal sum of the supply curves of all firms, it must also be a vertical straight line. Under these circumstances, the market price is determined solely by demand. This is illustrated in Figure 6.1. If the demand is D_1, the market

A strictly vertical straight-line market supply curve is not logically supportable

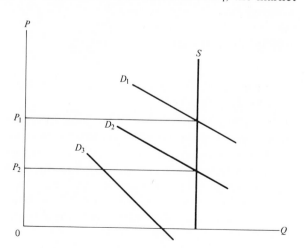

FIGURE 6.1

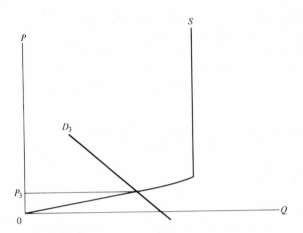

FIGURE 6.2

price is P_1, whereas if the demand is D_2, the market price is P_2. Supply alone determines the quantity. However, many textbooks never consider the possibility or probability of demand being D_3. Given such a condition, what would the market price be? If the industry supply curve were strictly a vertical straight line, could the market price be negative with a demand of D_3? In order to avoid this dilemma, we suggest that the industry supply curve in the market period should be modified to the shape shown in Figure 6.2.

The supply curve has a positive slope at very low prices because, even though the quantity of a commodity in the market period is fixed for a firm, the quantity that a firm is willing to sell at certain prices may not be fixed. In particular, if the market price is very low, some firms may not be willing to sell all their product in the current period. Instead, they will keep some inventory in anticipation of a price adjustment. Even if the commodity is perishable, under the usual but seldom mentioned assumption of free disposal (Assumption I.1—things can be thrown away without cost), whatever the demand, the market price of a commodity can never be negative. Our modified industry supply curve in the market period is not only more theoretically satisfactory, but also more reasonable.

6.3 SHORT-RUN ANALYSIS OF A TYPICAL FIRM AND THE MARKET

In Part I, it was shown that in the short run in production, some inputs are fixed and others are variable. As a result, there is a distinction between fixed and variable costs for a firm. As we have previously noted, in the short run, the number of firms in an industry is fixed, whereas in the long run, not only are all inputs and, consequently, costs for a firm variable, but, moreover, the number of firms in an industry is variable. In the market, producers face, on the one hand, a given cost function that is determined by technology and the input (e.g., labor) market and, on the other hand, a given revenue function that is determined by demand. Producers choose a level of production that will accomplish their goal, which is generally assumed to be profit maximization. Hence, students should appreciate that there are essential differences between short-run analysis and long-run analysis with respect to the market behavior of a firm. Theoretically, long-run analysis is most relevant in a stationary state. In a changing world, the long run is meaningful only in the sense of a planning period. We shall see that short-run analysis is more important to a study of a firm's market behavior, whereas long-run analysis is more important to the study of the theory of capital investment.

Under Assumption 6.1 (homogeneity), the cost functions of all firms in the same industry must be identical, since product homogeneity implies homogeneous inputs. Therefore, it makes sense to talk about a typical firm. All theoretical results derived for a typical firm can be applied to every other firm in an industry. For the sake of simplicity, it is further assumed that inventory is zero or constant; hence, the quantity produced is the same as the quantity sold.

Product homogeneity implies homogeneous inputs and identical cost functions for all firms in the industry

A firm under perfect competition is a price taker due to Assumptions 6.1-6.4 (see Section 6.1), in particular, Assumptions 6.1 and 6.3. In facing a given market price, a firm can only adjust the quantity to be produced and sold. Although its plant size is fixed in the short run, a firm can adjust its output by increasing or decreasing the use of variable inputs. Since the number of firms in an industry is fixed in the short run, when a typical firm adjusts its production level, the quantity of product in the industry will be adjusted accordingly, because all other firms are assumed to follow suit. For a given cost, a firm's adjustment in the quantity produced for various possible market prices (and based on the principle of profit maximization) will yield the supply curve of the firm, from which the supply curve of the industry can be derived.

6.3.1 Profit Maximization: The Total Revenue– Total Cost Approach

In order to give a clear picture of the profit-maximizing output choice, we shall use both numerical examples and the corresponding graphs to illustrate the logic of the total revenue–total cost (TR–TC) approach. Since profit is defined as the difference between TR and TC, the easiest way to demonstrate the relationship between profit and output is by comparing TR and TC for each and every quantity produced. Consider Table 6.1, in which column Q shows the quantity produced, column TR_1 shows

TABLE 6.1

Q	TR_1	TFC	TVC	TC	π_1	TR_2	π_2
1	$ 6	$10	$ 5	$15	$ −9	$ 4	$− 11
2	12	10	9	19	−7	8	− 11
3	18	10	10	20	−2	12	− 8
4	24	10	13	23	1	16	− 7
5	30	10	17	27	3	20	− 7
6	36	10	23	33	3	24	− 9
7	42	10	30	40	2	28	− 12
8	48	10	39	49	−1	32	− 17
9	54	10	49	59	−5	36	− 23
10	60	10	60	70	− 10	40	− 30

the corresponding total revenue when the price is $6 per unit, column TFC is the total fixed cost, column TVC is the total variable cost, column TC is the total cost (i.e., the sum of columns TFC and TVC), column π_1 is the profit for the given level of output, column TR_2 is the total revenue when the market price is $4 per unit, and column π_2 is the corresponding profit for the same cost data.

Given a market price of $6 per unit, it can be seen that the maximum profit occurs when the output is either 6 or 5 units. Hence, the quantity that maximizes profit is not unique. This is due to the fact that we have used discrete data in the hypothetical example. If continuous data had been used the output level that maximized profit would have been unique. At any rate, if the firm produces 6 units (where MR = MC) at a market price of $6 per unit, it will obtain a maximum profit of $3. On the other hand, if the market price were $4 per unit, the total revenue would be as shown in column TR_2, and the corresponding profit figures for the same cost data would be as given in column π_2. Unfortunately, the profit is negative for all quantities produced. The minimum loss is $7 and occurs at either 5 or 4 units of output. Since the minimum loss of $7 is less than the TFC of $10 (which cannot be recovered anyway), the firm's loss will be minimized if it produces 5 units of output (where MR = MC). In economics, the criterion of profit maximization covers both the case of maximum profit and the case of minimum loss. In other words, the output level that minimizes loss is also considered to be the quantity that maximizes profit (provided that a positive profit is impossible for all quantities).

A firm's loss is minimized if negative profit is less than TFC

The data in Table 6.1 cover two cases: positive maximum profit and negative maximum profit with a positive output. However, still another possibility exists: If the price is too low, the loss may be more than the TFC for any positive quantity produced. Since to do nothing is always a feasible alternative, the firm will shut down under these circumstances. It can be easily seen that if the

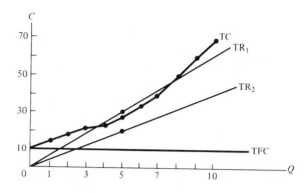

FIGURE 6.3

market price is reduced to $3 per unit, then zero output will result in a minimum loss (i.e., maximum profit).

The data in Table 6.1 can be presented graphically. In Figure 6.3, the TFC curve is a horizontal straight line. Therefore, we observe that the TC curve starts from the TFC curve, rising first at a decreasing rate and then at an increasing rate. The total revenue curve TR_1 is for a market price of $6 per unit, whereas TR_2 is the total revenue curve for a market price of $4 per unit. It should be noted that the TR curve is always a straight line for a perfectly competitive firm because the market price is a constant. In short, the slope of the TR curve depends on the market price, being steeper for a higher price and flatter for a lower price. In Chapter 7, it will be shown that TR for a monopolistic firm is not, in general, a straight line. In Figure 6.3, the vertical distance between the TR and TC curves indicates the profit. At any Q, if the TR curve is above the TC curve, then the vertical distance measures a positive profit. Alternatively, if the TC curve is above the TR curve, then the vertical distance measures a negative profit. For example, when the market price is $6 per unit, the TR_1 is above the TC curve for $Q = 4$–7 units of output. Hence, the firm can make a profit if it produces any quantity from 4 to 7 units. However, the largest distance between TR_1 and the TC curve in this range is at 6 (5) units of output. Thus, 6 (5) units of output will result in maximum profit. On the other hand, the TC curve is above TR_1 for $Q \le 3$ and $Q \ge 8$. This indicates a negative profit for the corresponding range of output.

When the market price is $4 per unit, the total revenue curve TR_2 is below the TC curve everywhere. In this case, the vertical distance between the TC curve and TR_2 indicates the extent of the loss. Under these circumstances, the firm has to compare the minimum loss to TFC for all positive Qs. If the minimum loss for a positive Q is less than TFC, then this Q is considered the profit-maximizing quantity, and the firm will continue to produce this Q, since it is covering all variable costs and part of the fixed costs. Otherwise, the best output choice would be zero, that is, a shutdown of the plant. In our example, the vertical distance between the TC curve and TR$_2$ is $7 for 5 (4) units of Q. This is the minimum loss that the firm would experience, since losses would be higher at any other output. However, even if the firm sustains a loss at output $Q = 4$ or 5, it will not shut down, since all variable costs and some of the fixed costs are covered. Thus $Q = 4$ or 5 is the output that maximizes profit.

The TR–TC approach to profit maximization is straightforward and easily understood. However, it does not lead to an important analytical result. Using geometry, it can be shown that the vertical distance between the TR and TC curves is largest (or smallest) when their slopes are the same. In economics, this corresponds to marginal analysis, which we shall now consider.

6.3.2 Profit Maximization: The Marginal Approach

We have previously defined the terms marginal product (MP), marginal cost (MC), and marginal revenue (MR). These are important analytical concepts, and students should make sure that they understand their true meaning. Hence, it is recommended that students review Chapters 1, 3, and 5 before proceeding.

It has already been pointed out that MR and MC are important concepts in economic analysis; however, it will soon become obvious that the average variable cost (AVC) is also relevant to the analysis of the short-run behavior of a firm. In Chapter 5, we explained that the market price is equal to the MR of a firm under perfect competition. Hence, using the data in Table 6.1, we can construct Table 6.2. Since Tables 6.1 and 6.2 are based on the same set of data, the profit figures for the various output quantities at a given market price are identical. For example, for a market price of $6 per unit, the profit is $1 when $Q = 4$ and $3 when $Q = 6$, whereas for a market price of $4 per unit, the profit is -7 for $Q = 5$ and -9 for $Q = 6$. Both tables also indicate that the profit is a maximum for $Q = 6$ or 5 when the price is $6 per

TABLE 6.2

Q	$P_1 = MR_1$	MC	π_1	$P_2 = MR_2$	π_2	AVC
0	—	—	-10	—	-10	—
1	6	5	-9	4	-11	5
2	6	4	-7	4	-11	4.5
3	6	1	-2	4	-8	3.3
4	6	3	1	4	-7	3.25
5	6	4	3	4	-7	3.4
6	6	6	3	4	-9	3.8
7	6	7	2	4	-12	4.3
8	6	9	-1	4	-17	4.9
9	6	10	-5	4	-23	5.4
10	6	11	-10	4	-30	6.0

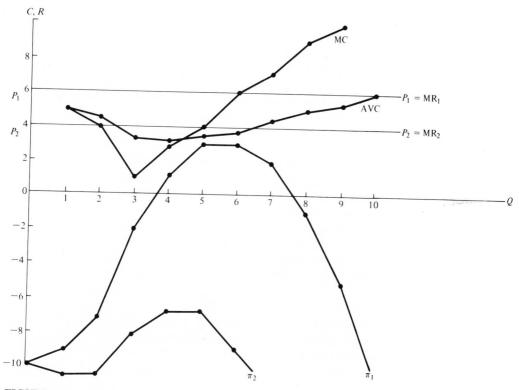

FIGURE 6.4

unit and for $Q = 5$ or 4 when the price is $4 per unit. In the former case, profit is positive, whereas in the latter case it is negative. However, there is a peculiar phenomenon in Table 6.2: in both cases, the price or MR is equal to MC at maximum profit. Is this just by chance? The answer is no. It turns out that this phenomenon has considerable theoretical importance, which will be proved by logic later in the text and by mathematical means in the appendix to this chapter.

The data in Table 6.2 are plotted in Figure 6.4, where the horizontal straight lines for $P_1 = 6$ and $P_2 = 4$ are the MR curves for these two prices, respectively, MC is the marginal cost curve, AVC is the average variable cost curve, and π_1 and π_2 are the profit curves for P_1 and P_2, respectively. It can be seen that when MR = MC, the profit curves reach their maximum values for both P_1 and P_2. The graph also shows that $P_2 = $ MC at two points: $Q = 2$ and $Q = 5$. Furthermore, π_2 reaches a local minimum at $Q = 2$ and a maximum at $Q = 5$. The student should observe the behavior of MC, which is decreasing at $Q = 2$ and increasing at $Q = 5$. This is very significant. It will be proved mathematically in the appendix that, under perfect competition, a firm's profit will be maximized when (1) MR = MC and (2) MC is increasing; these are respectively referred to as the first-order (necessary)

Both first- and second-order conditions must be met for profit maximization

and second-order (sufficient) conditions for profit maximization. Only when both conditions are satisfied will the profit be maximum. Mathematically, condition 1 signifies either maximum or minimum profit, whereas conditions 1 and 2 together ensure maximum profit. The combination of condition 1 and a decreasing MC (e.g., at $Q = 2$ in Figure 6.4) is indicative of minimum profit. This must always be kept in mind in order to avoid confusion.

6.3.3 Proof of the Profit-Maximization Conditions

The proof of the profit-maximization conditions can easily be understood if one looks at the matter in terms of sequential decision making. For example, in deciding whether it is profitable to produce the first unit, one compares the additional revenue MR brought in with the additional cost MC. If MR > MC, the first unit by itself is profitable to produce. The second unit and so on will be examined in a similar manner. Even if the first unit shows MR < MC, one should not conclude that production can never be profitable; that is, the second and third units should be sequentially examined. If the gap between MR and MC narrows— or at least does not widen—more units should be examined until one obtains MR > MC. Even then, the results of producing one more unit must be examined. If the additional unit shows MR < MC, then the last unit for which MR ≥ MC is the quantity that maximizes profit. However, this is not the end of the process. Further study is needed.

At the stage where MR ≥ MC, the total profit should be examined. If the total profit is positive, the last unit that satisfies the condition MR ≥ MC will result in maximum profit. On the other hand, if the total profit is negative, one more comparison has to be made. If the negative profit is less than TFC, the last unit that satisfies the condition MR ≥ MC is the best choice. However, if TFC is less than the smallest loss for a positive output, then zero quantity or shutdown (i.e., of the plant) will be the best choice. The reason that the above process will result in maximum profit or minimum loss can be easily shown by using our simple example. Before proceeding, students might find it beneficial to refer to Table 6.2 in order to reinforce their understanding of the marginal principle that is involved in the behavior of the total profit curves in Figure 6.4.

In the case where $P_1 = \$6$, both the values in Table 6.2 and the curves in Figure 6.4 show that the first unit of output generates revenue of $6 and only costs $5; that is, MR > MC.

The first unit by itself brings in a net profit of $1; thus, the first unit should be produced. Similarly, the second unit by itself brings in a net profit of $2, the third unit a net profit of $5, and so on. Until the fifth unit of production, each additional unit brings in a net profit. Therefore, five units should be produced. The sixth unit by itself does not bring in a profit nor does it result in a loss. In this case, the firm is *indifferent* as to whether or not to produce the sixth unit. (As mentioned above, this is due to the fact that our numerical example is discrete; in a continuous case, this ambiguity would disappear.) At any rate, examination of the seventh unit shows that it generates an additional revenue of $6, whereas the additional cost of producing it is $7. Thus, if the seventh unit is produced, the total profit will be lowered. This is shown in Figure 6.4 by the fact that π_1 declines to the right of the sixth unit. From Figure 6.4 it can also be seen that MC $= P_1$ = MR$_1$ at $Q = 6$. For any increase in production above 6 units, the additional cost exceeds the additional revenue, and hence profit will decrease. Conversely, the revenue brought in by producing any unit below the total of 6 is greater than its cost. Therefore, any cut in production to less than 6 units will cause a reduction in profit. In other words, when MR = MC at $Q = 6$, profit will be maximized, and any change in the level of output will cause profit to be reduced. Again, the student should note the peculiar result of 6 (5) being equally profitable. As we have noted this is due to the discrete data.

In the case where $P_2 = 4, the loss that results from producing the second unit by itself is zero. However, the loss that results from producing the first unit by itself is $1. Hence, the loss incurred by producing an additional unit is decreasing, and thus the profit brought in by the next unit must be examined. It is seen that the third unit by itself results in a net profit of $3, whereas the fourth unit adds $1 to the total profit. Hence, the profit from the fifth unit must be examined. We find that the fifth unit by itself results in a zero profit.

As in the case of our first illustration (i.e., $P_1 = 6), here we again have a borderline condition due to the discrete nature of the data. However, there is an essential difference between this case and the previous one. The first case exhibited a positive net profit when MR = MC, whereas the present case shows a negative profit. In the previous case, we can conclude that profit is maximum when MR = MC, provided that MC is increasing. In the present case, one more step is necessary, that is, the total loss at that Q where MR = MC must be compared with the TFC. In our case, the total loss at $Q = 5$, where MR = MC, is $7, which is less than the TFC of $10. We may conclude that 5 units is the best choice, that is, production of this quantity will result in maximum profit (minimum loss).

As we pointed out during our discussion of the TR–TC approach (Section 6.3.1), if the market price is $3 per unit, an output of $Q = 0$ (i.e., a plant shutdown) is the best choice. The marginal approach will lead to the same conclusion. As an exercise, stu-

TR–TC and the marginal approach yield the same conclusions respecting profit-maximizing outputs

dents should try to derive this conclusion by using the reasoning process described above.

As we have mentioned previously, MR = MC at both $Q = 2$ and $Q = 5$ when $P_2 = \$4$ per unit. We have also concluded that profit is maximum (minimum loss in this case) at $Q = 5$. When $Q = 2$, we can observe that the total profit curve reaches a local minimum in the sense that profit increases (loss decreases) as we move to either the right or the left. As we have explained earlier, the third unit by itself results in a net profit of \$3; and therefore, as we move from the second unit to the third unit, profit must increase (loss must decrease) by \$3. Hence, profit will increase (loss will decrease) when more than 2 units are produced. Similarly, since the first unit by itself results in a net loss of \$1, it follows that if the first unit were not produced, profit would again increase (loss decrease). This implies that the profit must be a minimum (or the loss a maximum) at $Q = 2$. Further elaboration on this point will prove beneficial.

An examination of Figure 6.4 shows that the MC curve is declining at $Q = 2$. A small increase in quantity above 2 units generates an amount of additional revenue which exceeds the additional cost of production. Consequently, a small increase in quantity will result in greater profit (less loss). On the other hand, for a small decrease in quantity, the reduction in cost is greater than the cut in revenue. Therefore, a decrease in output will also result in an increase in profit (decrease in loss). Thus, either an increase or a decrease in output from $Q = 2$ will result in an increase in profit (decrease in loss). This indicates that profit must be a minimum (loss a maximum) at $Q = 2$.

The above results can be stated as the following theorem.

Theorem 6.1. *(1) Profit will be maximum if (a) MR = MC and (b) MC is increasing. (2) Profit will be a local minimum if (a) MR = MC and (b) MC is decreasing.*

The preceding discussion would seem to indicate that the marginal approach is more troublesome than the TR–TC approach. Actually, the marginal approach is more convenient. Once the rationale is fully understood, there is no need to examine the profitability of each and every unit. The only thing one has to do is determine the quantity at which MR = MC and MC is increasing. If the total profit is positive at this quantity, no further work is needed—this quantity is the profit-maximizing output. If the total profit is negative, a comparison between this loss and the total fixed cost is all that is needed. Furthermore, the use of marginal analysis in examining the firm's profit-maximizing position leads to a quick and convenient identification of the firm's supply curve, which is, indeed, a remarkable accomplishment. Section 6.3.4 deals with this topic.

6.3.4 Short-Run Equilibrium and the Supply of the Firm, Break-Even and Shutdown Points

In economics, the term *equilibrium* not only implies the lack of a tendency for change under given external conditions, but also indicates that certain optimal conditions are being met. For example, at a given market price and cost, a firm's best choice with respect to production is to produce the quantity that maximizes profit. Once this decision is made, there is no tendency for the firm to change its level of output unless either price, cost, or both change. In this case, that is, when the firm has chosen its profit-maximizing level of output, we say that the firm is at equilibrium because there is no reason for it to change its output, since it is in the best position possible under the circumstances. Thus, equilibrium and optimality are closely related, if not synonymous. We can define equilibrium with respect to the production condition of a firm as follows:

Definition: Equilibrium. A firm is said to be in equilibrium if the quantity of the commodity that it produces maximizes its profit for a given cost and market price.

In economics, the term *supply* has special meaning. The supply schedule or curve of a firm describes the relationship between the price of a commodity and the quantity of that commodity which the firm is willing to sell. For each market price, there is usually a unique quantity that a firm is willing to sell. It is this unique price–quantity relationship that economists usually call the *supply of a firm*. This leads us to the following definition.

Definition: Supply of a Firm. The functional relationship between the market price and the quantity of the commodity which the firm is willing to sell.

This price–quantity relationship is usually called a *supply function*. It may also be represented by a numerical schedule or a curve. The terms *supply function, supply schedule,* and *supply curve* denote different methods of representing the same price–quantity relationship. Each approach has its advantages and disadvantages. We shall use all of them on different occasions.

Having given the above definitions, and recalling the assumption that profit maximization is the primary goal of a firm, we are now ready to derive the supply curve of a firm. It turns out that the short-run supply curve of a firm is identical to certain portions of the MC curve.

For our present purposes, we need the MC, AVC, and ATC curves. For the sake of illustration, we have drawn the typical smooth, U-shaped cost curves in part (a) of Figure 6.5. We can

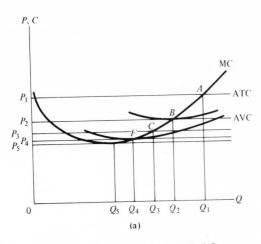

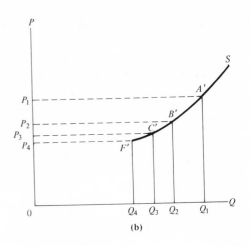

(a)　　　　　　　　　　　(b)

FIGURE 6.5

see that if the market price is P_1, then the conditions for profit maximization (as stated in Section 6.3.2 and proved in Section 6.3.3) will lead to an output level of Q_1, at which point the profit will be maximized. We can also observe that even though there are two points which satisfy the condition MR = MC, only point A satisfies the second-order condition. Furthermore, since P_1 > ATC at Q_1, the average and, consequently, total profits are positive. Hence, A is the point of the firm's equilibrium output for P_1 and, according to our definition of supply, lies on the firm's supply curve. Similarly, we can see that when the price is P_2, Q_2 is the output level that maximizes profit, since MR = MC and the second-order condition is again satisfied. In this case, price is equal to ATC, which implies that TR = TC (i.e., zero profit). Although the net profit is zero, the full amount of the fixed cost is covered, which is water under the bridge, so to speak, in the short run. The student should remember that since fixed costs represent an investment that has already been made, all that the firm really must do in order to remain in business in the short run is cover its variable costs.

With the new quantity–price pair (Q_2, P_2), the point B in part (a) of Figure 6.5 becomes the firm's new equilibrium position. Therefore, we say that B is on the firm's short-run supply curve. Point B also represents the minimum of the ATC curve, which is called the *break-even point*. This is understandable, since when the price is equal to ATC at equilibrium, TR = TC (there is no profit or loss), and the firm is just breaking even.

When the price is P_3, Q_3 is the output level that satisfies both the first- and second-order conditions of profit maximization. However, in this case the profit of the firm is negative, since P_3 < ATC at Q_3. On the other hand, P_3 > AVC, which implies that if Q_3 is produced, the revenue per unit (i.e., price) covers AVC and part of the fixed cost. In other words, if Q_3 is produced, the total loss is less than TFC in the short run. If we compare zero output with Q_3, we can see that the minimum-loss (maximum-profit) quantity is Q_3. Taking all the above information into consideration, we can establish that Q_3 is the equilibrium quantity of output for P_3. Hence, point C is on the firm's supply curve.

When the price is P_4, Q_4 is the output that satisfies both the first- and second-order conditions of profit maximization. It can be observed from part (a) of Figure 6.5 that P_4 = AVC at Q_4. This implies that the firm's TR is just equal to TVC if Q_4 is produced for a price of P_4, and, therefore, the firm's total loss is equal to TFC. Under these circumstances, the firm is indifferent between producing Q_4 or a plant shutdown. Thus, point F can be either considered or not considered a point on the firm's supply curve. This is not important, since, theoretically, a point has neither length nor width. The important thing to remember is that when the market price goes below P_4 to, for example, P_5, even though Q_5 satisfies both the first- and second-order conditions of profit maximization, P_5 < AVC at Q_5 and any other Q. Under these circumstances, the price is not sufficient to cover AVC, and any level of output other than zero will result in a loss that is greater than TFC. Hence, a zero level of output rather than Q_5 is the equilibrium quantity of production. This implies that when the price is below the minimum AVC, a profit-maximizing firm will shut down. For this reason, the point of minimum AVC—F in part (a) of Figure 6.5—is called the *shutdown point*.

Profit-maximizing firms will shut down when price falls below AVC

The points A', B', C', and F' in part (b) of Figure 6.5 correspond to points A, B, C, and F in part (a). As we have explained previously, these points indicate the quantities that a profit-maximizing firm is willing to produce and sell for the corresponding prices. According to our definition of supply, these are all relevant points on the supply curve of the firm. If we plot all of the points of the rising MC curve which are above the point F of part (a) in part (b), we obtain the relevant supply curve (labeled S) of the firm. Note that the rising portion of the MC curve which is below the AVC curve is not part of the supply curve because profit-maximization behavior dictates that the firm will shut down when the price is below the minimum AVC.

Although the above arguments are based on the traditional smooth, U-shaped AC and MC curves, the resulting conclusion can also be applied to the more realistic case where AVC is constant over a certain range of output and then increases (see Figure 3.10). Our final result can be stated as the following proposition.

Proposition 6.1. The short-run supply curve of a firm under perfect competition is precisely the rising portion of its MC curve which is above the minimum AVC. If the market price is lower than the minimum AVC, then a profit-maximizing firm will shut down rather than produce any output.

Our observed result is remarkable in that the firm's short-run supply curve can be conveniently identified by its MC curve. Once the MC and AVC curves are known, the firm's supply curve is also known. Furthermore, since only the rising portion of the MC curve comprises the firm's supply curve, the latter must have a positive slope. Unfortunately, this significant result is only true for a firm under perfect competition. It will be shown in Chapters 7–9 that the rising portion of the MC curve cannot be identified as the supply curve if the firm operates under imperfectly competitive markets.

6.3.5. The Short-Run Supply of an Industry

The supply of an industry is, by definition, the sum of the supplies of all its individual firms. Accordingly, the industry supply curve can be derived by a horizontal summation of the supply curves of all firms in the industry. However, this is strictly true only under the following assumption.

Assumption 6.5: Independence of the Production Costs of a Firm. The production costs of a firm are a function of its own output only, not of the quantities produced by other firms or the output of the industry as a whole.

Independence of production costs implies changing industry output will not shift firms' MC curves

Assumption 6.5 is reasonable for an industry that does not use specialized labor or other special resources, and where the industry is relatively small compared with the economy as a whole. Under these circumstances, the industry can be considered a small buyer in perfectly competitive resource markets. Therefore, the expansion or contraction of the output of the industry will not have an affect on the price of the resources, and the production costs of a firm in the industry will be independent of both the output levels of other firms in the industry and the output of the industry as a whole. Were this not so, an expansion of industry output and the use of more inputs would cause input prices to be bid up, which, in turn, would shift the cost curves upward. (It has been shown in Chapter 3 that, in general, cost is an increasing function of input prices.)

Since the firm's supply curve and the rising portion of its MC curve which lies above the minimum AVC are identical, it follows that an upward shift of the MC curve resulting from an increase of the total output of the industry implies an upward shift of the firm's supply curve. In this case, the firm's MC curve and, accordingly, its supply curve) will be a function of the industry output. Under these circumstances, the derivation of the industry supply curve from the supply curves of the individual firms is

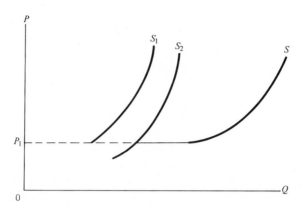

FIGURE 6.6

more complicated. However, the mathematical procedure for deriving the industry supply curve under such conditions is still straightforward and will be presented in the appendix to this chapter.

Thus, under Assumption 6.5, the industry's supply curve is simply the horizontal sum of the supply curves of the individual firms in the industry. For the purpose of illustration, suppose that we have an industry consisting of only two firms in a given perfectly competitive market and that the firms have the supply curves S_1 and S_2 shown in Figure 6.6. Then the supply curve for the industry[1] will be the horizontal sum of S_1 and S_2, labeled S in the graph. Note that, in accordance with our discussion of Figure 6.5, S and S_2 are identical for prices below P_1 because S_1 is zero for prices less than P_1. For prices greater than P_1, the horizontal distance between the vertical axis and S_1 is equal to that between S_2 and S. Since both S_1 and S_2 have a positive slope, S necessarily has a positive slope. Hence, under Assumption 6.5, we can make the assertion that the industry supply curve in a perfectly competitive market has a positive slope.

It should be pointed out that the industry supply curve may not have a positive slope in the absence of Assumption 6.5; that is, the industry supply curve may have a negative slope if the production costs of a firm are not independent of the outputs of other firms or of the total industry output. This will be explained in the appendix to this chapter.

6.3.6 Short-Run Market Equilibrium and the Determination of Market Price

Up until now we have assumed that firms in a perfectly competitive market face a given market price and that they try to maximize their profits by choosing the most profitable output in

---

[1] In the present context, industry supply curve and market supply curve are used interchangeably. This is true only as long as inventories of the product are zero or constant. The student should consider the rationale of this statement.

accordance with production costs and the market price. We have not explained how the market price is determined. On the basis of our derivation of the supply curve in Section 6.3.5 and the explanation of market demand presented in Chapter 5, we are now ready to discuss the theoretical determination of market price.

In partial analysis we deal with one industry (i.e., market) at a time, assuming that other things (including other markets) remain the same. The market price is determined by the interaction of buyers and sellers. In economics, all of the relevant market information concerning buyers is summarily embodied in the demand curve, whereas the information concerning sellers in a perfectly competitive market is embodied in the supply curve. In Chapter 7 we shall show that the supply curve is not very meaningful under the conditions of monopoly (and other imperfect markets), which is often ignored in many textbooks. Thus, whereas the determination of market price in a competitive market is closely related to both the demand for and the supply of a commodity, in an imperfect market it is determined by the cost (rather than supply) and demand. The latter condition will be explained in Chapters 7–9.

Demand and supply curves embody all relevant market information for price determination

Economists are fond of the term *equilibrium price*, which is generally referred to as the market price that will prevail in the absence of any external disturbances. Some economists simply define the equilibrium price as the market price at which the quantity of a commodity demanded and the quantity supplied are equal. It is often overlooked that, in economics, equilibrium implies more than the mere lack of change. It also implies certain conditions of optimality. This will become clear shortly.

From Chapter 5 we know that, in general, the market demand curve for a commodity has a negative slope, the exception being for the very unusual case of a Giffen good. Furthermore, from Section 6.3.5 (using the rule by which supply curves are added), we know that the market supply curve of a commodity has a positive slope. Therefore, we can construct the demand and supply curves shown in Figure 6.7, the resultant equilibrium price $\overline{P}$ and equilibrium quantity $\overline{Q}$ being given by the intersection of these two curves.

From Figure 6.7 it can be seen that P satisfies the above-mentioned condition of demand being equal to supply. However, there is something else that can be shown. From Chapters 4 and 5 we know that consumer satisfaction is maximized if the consumer purchases the quantity indicated by his or her demand curve for a given price, since the demand curve is derived from the conditions that are consonant with the maximum satisfaction of each consumer. To put it another way, the market demand curve is the horizontal sum of the individual consumer demand curves. Thus, for a given price, the corresponding quantity on the market

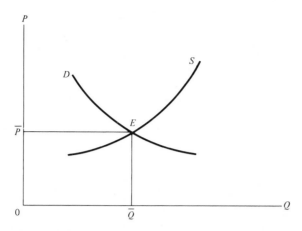

FIGURE 6.7

demand curve will result in maximum satisfaction for all consumers in the market. Similarly, the firm's supply is derived from the conditions of profit maximization, which implies that, for a given price, the corresponding quantity on the supply curve will maximize the profit for all firms in the market that are producing the given product. In Figure 6.7, at equilibrium price $\bar{P}$, the point E is on both the demand curve and the supply curve; that is, the quantity demanded is equal to the quantity supplied. Hence, the satisfaction of all consumers and the profits of all firms are maximized. The above explanation yields the following proposition:

Proposition 6.2. A perfectly competitive market is in equilibrium if and only if (1) there is only one price in the market, (2) quantity demanded is equal to quantity supplied, (3) the satisfaction of all consumers in the market is maximized, and (4) the profits of all firms in the industry are maximized.

6.3.7 The Existence, Uniqueness, and Stability of Market Equilibrium

Many textbooks (in particular, those at the intermediate level) fail to discuss the important simplifying assumption of the existence, uniqueness, and stability of market equilibrium. Unfortunately, to implicitly assume that a unique and stable equilibrium exists without a single word of explanation leaves something to be desired. We shall use simple examples to demonstrate the significance of each of these concepts.

Existence

Theoretically, market equilibrium may not exist at a positive price and/or a positive quantity. Figure 6.8 illustrates two possibilities. In part (a), the supply curve is above the demand curve in the first quadrant. Mathematically, it is conceivable that if both the curves were extended to the left of the vertical axis, they might intersect at a point in the second quadrant. However, this would indicate a negative quantity being produced and sold, which does not make economic sense. This case, in which equilibrium does not exist at a positive quantity, can be conceived of as one where the MC of production is too high relative to the demand price. (Remember that in a competitive market the firm's supply curve is the rising portion of the MC curve which lies above the minimum AVC.) What we have in this case is a commodity that is technically feasible but not economically marketable. For example, although it is technically feasible to produce a pure-gold lunchbox or a pure-gold automobile, we do not see these commodities in the market. On the other hand, although a rare occurrence, occasionally silver- or gold-plated automobiles are produced (in fact, a gold-plated automobile was recently manufactured for a rich Arab businessman). At any rate, these commodities, which are only occasionally traded, cannot constitute a perfectly competitive market, since there are too few buyers. As another example, we might consider the once sizeable markets for work horses and buggies. Due to a decrease in the demand for them, trading in these commodities has now almost disappeared. The above represent only a few examples of the markets depicted by part (a) of Figure 6.8.

A commodity may be technically feasible but not economically marketable

On the other hand, there are some very useful items so plentiful in nature that the MC of production for a very large quantity is zero under normal circumstances. If demand is not very high, people are able to secure as much of this type of commodity as they need from natural sources. As a result, the commodity does not command a positive price. This is usually called a *free good,* air being an obvious example. Although air is very useful, it is free because it naturally exists in great abundance. Alternatively,

FIGURE 6.8

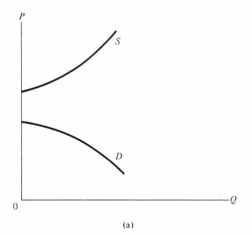

(a)

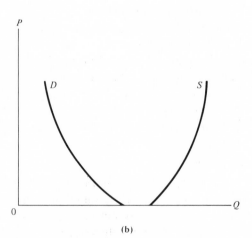

(b)

there are commodities that were free at one time, but have ceased to be so because of changes in the environment. In many areas of the United States water is such a commodity. It is still free in the wilderness, but in our cities it commands a positive price. Part (b) of Figure 6.8 represents a free good because, given the existing demand schedule (curve), no cost is involved in providing the commodity to meet user requirements.

The above examples show that market equilibrium may exist under certain circumstances, but not exist under others. In a fast-changing society, the discussion of the existence of market equilibrium cannot be safely omitted because the conditions that once assured its existence may at another time preclude it.

Uniqueness

When equilibrium does exist in a competitive market, another troublesome situation may occur: There may be more than one equilibrium. Figure 6.9 shows two of many possibilities that can exist or develop.

Part (a) shows that the demand curve has a negative slope throughout its range. However, the supply curve has a positive slope at lower prices and a negative slope at higher prices. According to our definition, points A and B both indicate market equilibrium. The trouble with this situation is that it is theoretically inconclusive whether the market will settle at a price of P_1 or P_2 for a given demand and supply combination.

Some economists have found evidence that the labor supply curve in certain labor markets is "backward bending." This is reasonable, because when the wage rate is low, the standard of living is low, and hence a higher wage rate will attract people to work longer hours and/or induce more people to engage in pro-

Unique equilibrium may not be possible with a "backward bending" labor supply curve

FIGURE 6.9

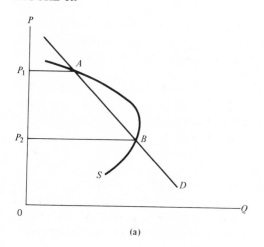

(a)

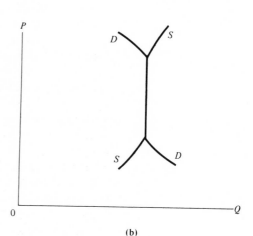

(b)

ductive activities. Thus, a higher wage rate will result in a larger quantity of labor being supplied at the lower range of wage rates. However, once the wage rate is high, the standard of living is also high, and leisure, as a normal good, becomes more precious as the wage rate goes up. Since the number of hours in a day or a week is fixed, if the worker decides to have more leisure, the hours of work must automatically be reduced. This explains the rationale behind the supply curve of labor bending back at a higher wage rate, which may result in more than one equilibrium price and quantity. We shall present a more-detailed explanation of this point in Chapter 10.

Part (b) of Figure 6.9 depicts a case in which the demand and supply curves have vertical segments that coincide with each other. In this case, the equilibrium quantity is unique, but the equilibrium price is not.

Parts (a) and (b) of Figure 6.9 show some of the possible cases in which the equilibrium price and/or quantity may not be unique. In advanced economic theory, uniqueness of equilibrium is an important topic that deserves careful treatment. For our purposes, an awareness that under unusual circumstances market equilibrium may not be unique is sufficient.

Stability

Another theoretical problem in the discussion of market equilibrium is that of its stability. In advanced economic theory, the distinction is made between *dynamic* and *static* stability. In static analysis, it is well known that a competitive market with a negatively sloped demand curve and a positively sloped supply curve is stable if equilibrium does exist. However, in the case of dynamic analysis (such as the *Cobweb model*), the same market may not be stable. Since the discussions in this book essentially involve static stability, we shall forego any further discussion of dynamic stability.

The theoretical importance of stability is that even if market equilibrium does exist, there is no guarantee that it will be attained. For example, we may assume that the market behavior of buyers and sellers is such that buyers tend to bid up the market price if the quantity demanded exceeds the quantity supplied at a given price. On the other hand, sellers tend to lower their prices if the quantity supplied exceeds the quantity demanded. A market with a negatively sloped demand curve and a positively sloped supply curve will be stable if equilibrium exists. This can be demonstrated using Figure 6.10.

Given a market price of P_0, the quantity demanded is equal to the quantity supplied at Q_0. Everyone in the market is happy and there is no tendency to change, that is, equilibrium will remain stable as long as there is no external disturbance. On the other

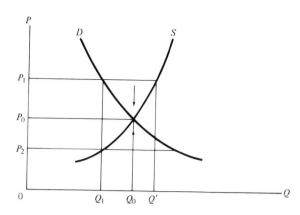

FIGURE 6.10

hand, if the market price is currently at P_1, the quantity supplied Q' exceeds the quantity demanded Q_1. According to our assumption of profit-maximation behavior, sellers will cut production, lower their prices, and the market price will approach the equilibrium price, which is indicated by the arrow pointing downward. Similarly, if the market price is currently at P_2, the quantity demanded exceeds the quantity supplied. As a result, buyers will bid up the market price, which will again approach the equilibrium price. Thus, we can see that if market price is at equilibrium, it will remain at that level. On the other hand, if the market price is either higher or lower than the equilibrium price, there is a tendency for the market price to move toward equilibrium. In economics, this is called *stable equilibrium*.

Figure 6.11, which is a reproduction of the upper portion of part (a) of Figure 6.9, provides us with a different set of circumstances. If the market price is initially P_0, the quantity demanded and the quantity supplied are equal. In the absence of an external disturbance, equilibrium will be maintained and price will remain at P_0. On the other hand, if the initial market price is above the equilibrium price (e.g., P_1), and there is no reason to believe that this could not happen, the quantity demanded exceeds the quan-

FIGURE 6.11

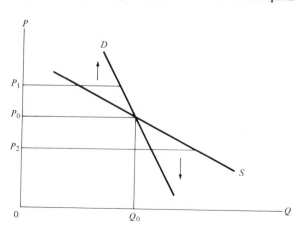

tity supplied. According to our behavior assumption, buyers will bid up the market price, which will move away from the equilibrium price P_0. Conversely, if the market price is initially below the equilibrium price (e.g., P_2), the quantity supplied exceeds the quantity demanded. As a result, the market price will move downward, again away from the equilibrium price. Since P_1 is any starting price above equilibrium, whereas P_2 is any starting price below equilibrium, the tendency is to move away from the equilibrium price regardless of whether the starting price is above or below equilibrium. Only in the special case where the starting price happens to be at the equilibrium price will the market stay at equilibrium in the absence of an external disturbance. It is clear that this is a case of *unstable equilibrium*.

Unstable equilibrium engenders movement away from the equilibrium price

Another possibility is the case of *semistable equilibrium*, that is, stable in one direction but unstable in another. Such a condition is illustrated by Figure 6.12, in which the supply curve is tangent to the demand curve at point E. The quantity demanded exceeds the quantity supplied at a market price either above or below the equilibrium price P_0. By the same reasoning used above, it can be shown that the market price will go up at any price either below or above P_0, rising to the equilibrium price P_0 if the market price starts below P_0 and moving further away from equilibrium if the market price starts above P_0. Therefore, we have stable equilibrium at market prices below P_0 and an unstable market when prices are above P_0. In short, we have semistable equilibrium.

The significance of stability of equilibrium is that it allows a competitive market to survive any external disturbance, no matter how violent it might be. In other words, there exists a built-in internal adjustment mechanism for a stable market which will enable the market to attain equilibrium after any external disturbance. This is an exceedingly important observation and condition, since, theoretically, there is no need for government interference in times of either inflation or high unemployment in

FIGURE 6.12

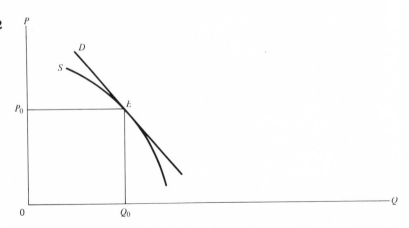

a stable market. On the other hand, government interference is necessary in order to restore equilibrium after a disturbance in a semistable market. Thus, the condition of stability of market equilibrium may have important policy implications. Some economists argue that the less government interference in the economic activities of the private sector the better. However, this argument is theoretically justified only under the assumption of stable equilibrium. Otherwise, without governmental interference a competitive market could break down under the pressure of either inflation or deflation.

Stable equilibrium may justify rejection of government intervention in the market

6.4 LONG-RUN ANALYSIS OF A TYPICAL FIRM AND INDUSTRY

6.4.1 Long-Run Equilibrium of a Typical Firm and Industry

The long-run analysis of a firm in the market and of an industry involves a consideration of market demand and long-run cost behavior. It also involves a consideration of the conditions under which firms and an industry are in equilibrium. For example, a typical firm and industry can be in long-run equilibrium if and only if they are also in short-run equilibrium. However, the converse is not necessarily true, that is, a typical firm and industry may be in short-run equilibrium but not in long-run equilibrium. Furthermore, a typical firm may be in short- and long-run equilibrium, even if the industry that it is part of is not in long-run equilibrium. When all firms in the industry are in long-run equilibrium, then and only then can we have long-run equilibrium of the industry. Thus, as we shall see, market demand and both short- and long-run cost functions are involved in long-run analysis, with the firm and industry making a series of adjustments.

Long-run adjustments of a firm are essentially changes in the size or scale of operations, whereas those of an industry basically involve changes in the number of firms. For a given demand, once all firms have adjusted to an optimal size and the industry has the optimal number of firms, then long-run equilibrium of the industry will prevail. The term *optimal* in this connection does not necessarily mean large. By optimum conditions we mean the size that yields maximum profits. Hence, a medium-size plant may be more profitable than a large-size plant. In order to illustrate our arguments, consider Figure 6.13. In part (a), the initial demand and supply conditions for the industry determine the market price P_0. In part (b), MC and AC are the long-run marginal and average cost curves, respectively, for a typical firm, whereas MC_1, ATC_1, MC_2, ATC_2, MC_3, and ATC_3 are the short-run marginal and average total cost curves, respectively, for three different plant sizes. Suppose that the firm faces the market price P_0 and that it operates plant size 1. In this case, the short-run profit maximizing (or rather loss-minimizing) quantity of output is Q_1. This quantity certainly does not represent long-run equi-

In economics, a large firm is not necessarily one of optimal size

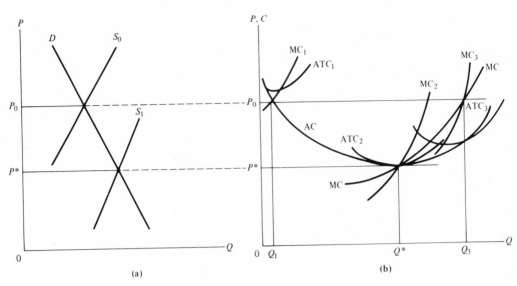

FIGURE 6.13 (a) Industry; (b) firm.

librium, since as we can see, the firm can expand its plant to size 3 and make a positive profit by producing Q_3. Note that at Q_3 both the long-run and the short-run MC are equal to MR, that is, the market price P_0. Thus, for the given market price, the firm's optimal plant size is 3, and the short-run and long-run profit-maximizing quantity is Q_3. Also note that for the given market price P_0, plant size 2 is not optimal, since total profit would not be as large. Students should reinforce their understanding of this statement by examining the profit-maximizing output for plant size 2 and comparing it with that for plant size 3.

The essential point to be understood here is that a firm's long-run profit will be maximized only if the market price or MR is equal to its long-run MC. This equality determines the optimal plant size for the given price. It may seem that Q^*, the quantity corresponding to the lowest long-run AC, should result in maximum profit. Although Q^* does result in the highest profit per unit, the *total* profit at Q^* for P_0 is less than at Q_3. In fact, for a market price P_0, only Q_3 and plant size 3 can result in the highest total profit. The reason behind this result is precisely the first- and second-order conditions for maximum profit of a firm, which have been explained in detail in Sections 6.3.2 and 6.3.3. Although these sections were concerned with short-run analysis, the rationale applies equally well to long-run analysis. Hence, a firm's long-run profit can be maximum only if the firm adjusts its plant size such that the market price or MR is equal its long-run MC. Since short-run maximum profit is a necessary condition for long-run profit maximization, the profit of the firm is maximum in the long run if and only if the market price or MR is equal to both the short-run and the long-run MC. As can be seen, this occurs at Q_3 in the graph for P_0.

Since a competitive firm is, by assumption, very small relative to the industry, the expansion of a single firm will not have a perceptible effect on the market price. Therefore, a single firm's long-run adjustment will end at plant size 3 for market price P_0. The typical firm is in both short-run and long-run equilibrium. However, the industry is not in long-run equilibrium because our typical firm is making a positive profit. Recall that in economics cost also includes a normal profit; thus, positive profit means excess profit. When this occurs, new firms will be attracted into the industry, output will increase, and P_0 cannot remain the long-run equilibrium price for the industry. Moreover, although we have assumed that the typical firm is the only one that has adjusted its plant size, in our model (as we have explained earlier), all firms are identical, and hence all firms will make similar adjustments. Remembering that the short-run industry supply curve is the horizontal sum of the supply curves of the individual firms (which, in turn, are the rising portions of the MC curves above the minimum AVC), we therefore see that when all firms expand their size, their supply curves and, consequently, the industry supply curve shift to the right. In summary, we see that for the given demand, with new firms attracted into the industry and all existing firms expanding output, the industry supply curve will shift to the right and market price will go down. This is another reason that P_0 cannot be the long-run equilibrium market price.

A firm may be in long-run equilibrium while the industry is not

The above example proves our assertion that a typical firm may be in long-run equilibrium while the industry is not. It also implies that a market price as P_0, which is higher than P^* (equal to the minimum long-run AC), cannot be the long-run market equilibrium price because, at a price higher than P^*, there exists a plant size that would permit firms to make a positive excess profit in the long run. When such a condition exists, new firms will be attracted into the industry, and, as a result, the number of firms in the industry tends to increase. Consequently, the industry cannot be in long-run equilibrium. Similarly, if the market price is below P^*, no firm can make a normal profit for any plant size, and an exit of firms will take place, causing the industry supply curve in part (a) of Figure 6.13 to shift to the left. Thus, the industry also cannot be in long-run equilibrium if the market price is below P^*. If the market cannot be in long-run equilibrium at a price either above or below P^*, it can only be in long-run equilibrium at P^*. This result can be proved in an alternative way.

Consider Figure 6.14, in which part (a) shows the demand and short-run supply curves of the industry, the short-run equilibrium price being P^*. Part (b) shows the cost and revenue curves of a typical firm; MC and AC are the long-run marginal and average

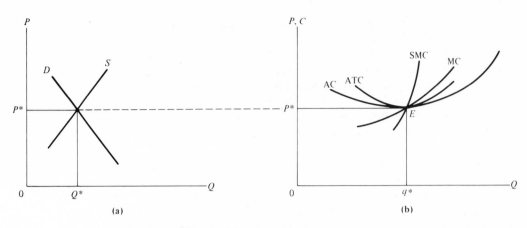

FIGURE 6.14 (a) Industry; (b) firm.

cost curves, respectively, whereas SMC and ATC are the corresponding short-run cost curves for a plant of given size. It is understood that although the vertical scales of both graphs are identical, the quantity (horizontal) scales differ. At the market price P^*, the optimal plant size and output for the firm is that which results in a minimum long-run AC. With this size, the short-run and long-run profit-maximizing quantity is q^*, which satisfies the profit-maximizing conditions, that is, MR = MC with MC increasing. The next condition that we have to examine is whether the *industry* is in short-run and long-run equilibrium. The industry is certainly in short-run equilibrium at P^* because demand is equal to the short-run supply at this price. Further examination shows that the industry is also in long-run equilibrium if no excess profits are earned or losses sustained by the firms in the industry.

Long-run equilibrium involves zero excess profits for firms in the industry

For a given demand curve, the market price changes only if the market supply curve shifts. For a given technology and input prices, a shift of the market supply curve can only be the result of one or both of the following two phenomena: (1) Firms adjust their sizes simultaneously, in which case the supply curve shifts to the right (left) when size expands (contracts), and (2) the number of firms in the industry changes, in which case the supply curve shifts to the right when more firms come into the industry and to the left when existing firms go out of business. In the absence of either of these two conditions, the market price will remain stable, and long-run equilibrium of the market prevails.

We have concluded that if the market price is equal to the minimum long-run AC, the typical firm will be in both long-run and short-run equilibrium when it produces that output quantity at minimum short-run and long-run ACs. Hence, there is no incentive for the firm to adjust its size. Since all firms are assumed identical, no firm will adjust its size at P^* and q^* in part (b) of Figure 6.14, and the industry supply curve will not shift because of size adjustments by firms. It is also seen in the same graph that the maximum (excess) profit for the typical firm is zero with optimal plant size when the market price is P^*. Therefore, there is no incentive for new firms to enter into nor for existing firms to exit from the industry. This means that the industry is in long-run equilibrium. We can consider the following proposition to be proven:

Proposition 6.3. In a perfectly competitive market, the identical firms and the industry will be in long-run equilibrium if and only if the market price is equal to the minimum long-run AC of the typical firm.

Proposition 6.3 implies that the following conditions exist for a typical firm in long-run equilibrium:

$$P = MC = SMC = ATC = AC$$

where P denotes market price, MC and SMC denote the long-run and short-run marginal costs, and ATC and AC denote the short-run and long-run average total costs, respectively. The only point that satisfies the above conditions is the minimum long-run AC. Proposition 6.3 also implies that the firm's excess profit in long-run equilibrium is zero, that is, that the firm is earning normal profits, no more, no less.

6.4.2 The Long-Run Supply Curve of an Industry—Constant-Cost, Increasing-Cost, and Decreasing-Cost Industries

The long-run supply curve of a firm can be defined as the rising portion of the long-run MC curve which is above the minimum long-run AC. However, the long-run supply curve of an industry cannot be defined as the horizontal sum of the supply curves of its individual firms because the number of firms in an industry is the essential variable in the long run. Theoretically, the long-run industry supply curve depends on the cost behavior of the firms when the number of firms in an industry undergoes change. Before we derive the long-run supply curve of an industry, we shall define the following cost conditions for an industry.

Definition: Constant-Cost Industry. An industry for which the cost function of a firm is independent of the number of firms in the industry. In other words, when the number of firms in the industry changes, the cost curves of the existing firms will not shift.

Definition: Increasing-Cost Industry. An industry for which the cost curves of existing firms will shift upward (downward) when the number of firms in the industry increases (decreases).

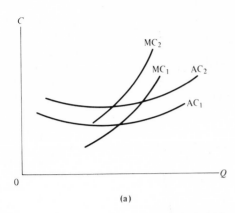
(a)

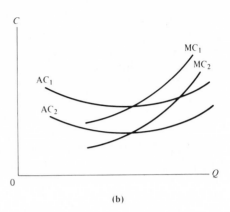
(b)

FIGURE 6.15

Definition: Decreasing-Cost Industry. An industry for which the cost curves of existing firms will shift downward (upward) when the number of firms in the industry increases (decreases).

The above definitions can be illustrated graphically. (For the sake of simplicity, we shall draw only long-run MC and AC curves in each case.) Consider part (a) of Figure 6.15, in which MC_1 and AC_1 are the long-run cost curves of a typical firm for a given number of firms (say 1000) in the industry, whereas MC_2 and AC_2 are the cost curves for a typical firm when there are a larger number of firms (say 1200) in the industry. What we have is a case of an increasing-cost industry, since the cost curve of the existing firm has risen as the number of firms in the industry has increased. On the other hand, part (b) illustrates the case of a decreasing-cost industry. For a constant-cost industry, MC_1 and MC_2, as well as AC_1 and AC_2, would coincide.

We can define the long-run supply of an industry as follows.

Definition: Long-Run Supply of an Industry. The price–quantity relationship after the industry, and all firms in the industry, have adjusted their long-run equilibrium positions to meet various demand conditions.

Given the above definition and our discussion of constant-, increasing-, and decreasing-cost industries, we can state the following proposition.

Proposition 6.4. The long-run industry supply curve is a horizontal straight line for a constant-cost industry, positively sloped for an increasing-cost industry, and negatively sloped for a decreasing-cost industry.

We shall now proceed to prove Proposition 6.4 by means of

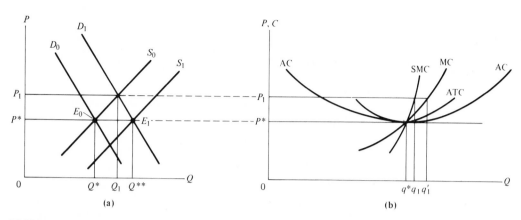

FIGURE 6.16 (a) Industry; (b) firm.

graphical analysis. Let us first examine the case of the constant-cost industry. Consider Figure 6.16, in which part (a) depicts the industry demand and supply conditions, whereas part (b) depicts the short-run and long-run cost behavior of the typical firm.

Given the industry's demand curve D_0 and short-run supply curve S_0, the market is in short-run equilibrium at the price P^* and quantity Q^*. At the same time, part (b) shows that all firms in the industry are in both short-run and long-run equilibrium at the quantity q^*, since at that output level each firm's profit is maximized. It is obvious that at price P^* it would be unprofitable for the firms to produce either less or more than quantity q^*, since this would involve a cost that was higher than the price. Furthermore, no entry into or exit from the industry will take place because the excess profit of existing firms is zero. Therefore, the industry will be in long-run equilibrium.

Suppose that the demand curve becomes D_1. In this case the market will move to short-run equilibrium at a new price P_1 and quantity Q_1. The increase in the market quantity of the product from Q^* to Q_1 in part (a) is the result of an expansion in production by existing firms along their short-run MC curve (SMC) from q^* to q_1, as shown in part (b). It would be tempting to argue that firms should also expand their size, thereby causing the typical firm's output to increase to q_1' along the long-run MC curve. However, this argument is not valid because P_1, which is not the long-run industry equilibrium price, cannot last. Why should this be? As we have noted before, given perfect knowledge, there is no reason for a rational firm to adjust its size because it knows that excess profits will be short-lived and that price will eventually come down.

From Figure 6.16, we see that firms are currently making short-run excess profits at market price P_1, which will attract new firms into the industry. As new firms enter into the industry, the short-

*Excess short-run
profits are not
sustainable*

run industry supply curve will shift to the right. How far the industry supply curve will shift depends entirely on the change in the number of firms, since (as stated above) the existing firms, with perfect information, will not change their size while the industry is making its adjustments. The industry can only attain its new long-run equilibrium if enough new firms are established so that the short-run industry supply curve shifts to S_1 and the original equilibrium price P^* is restored. As long as the short-run industry supply curve is to the left of S_1, the market price will be above P^* for D_1, and all existing firms will make short-run positive excess profit. Hence, new firms will continue to enter into the industry, and thus the industry cannot be in long-run equilibrium. On the other hand, if too many firms enter the industry, and the short-run industry supply curve shifts to the right of S_1, the market price will be below P^* for D_1, and all firms will suffer short-run negative profit, even at their optimal size. Therefore, an exit of existing firms will take place. Consequently, the industry cannot be in long-run equilibrium at a market price other than P^*.

The above arguments apply to any shift of the demand curve to the right. Similarly, the arguments can also be applied to any shift of the demand curve to the left. The locus of the long-run industry equilibrium points, such as E_0 and E_1, for shifts in demand constitute a horizontal straight line, which according to our definition is precisely the long-run industry supply curve. This proves the first part of Proposition 6.4. It should be remembered that for the locus of long-run industry equilibrium points to be on a horizontal straight line, AC and MC must not change as firms enter into and exit from the industry.

Figure 6.17 can be used to prove the second part of Proposition

FIGURE 6.17 (a) Industry; (b) firm.

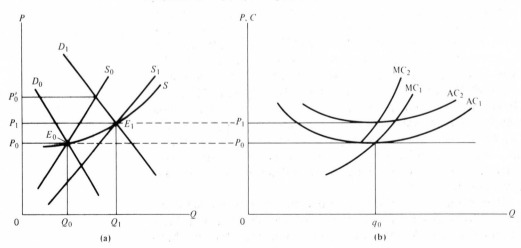

6.4. For the sake of simplicity, we have omitted the short-run cost curves in part (b); that is, all of the cost curves are for the long run. Suppose that the original demand and short-run supply curves for the industry are D_0 and S_0, respectively. Thus, the short-run equilibrium price is P_0. For the given number of firms, it turns out that P_0 is equal to the minimum long-run average cost of a typical firm AC_1. Since we are dealing with an increasing-cost industry, the firm's cost curve depends on the number of firms in the industry. For a given number of firms in the industry, we have a given set of long-run AC and MC curves for the firm (AC_1 and MC_1 are such cost curves for a typical firm when the market price is P_0). Under these circumstances, the typical firm as well as all other identical firms are in both short-run and long-run equilibrium. Since existing firms are making a normal profit, no exit from the industry takes place. Furthermore, since excess profit is zero for existing firms, new firms do not enter into the industry. Thus, the industry is also in long-run equilibrium.

An increasing-cost industry implies an upward shift in the firm's MC curve

Let us suppose that the demand curve becomes D_1, in which case the short-run market price will increase to P_0', a movement along the short-run industry supply curve S_0. This cannot be a long-run equilibrium condition for the industry because existing firms will make positive excess profit at price P_0'. New firms will be attracted to the industry, and since this is an increasing-cost industry, the cost curves of the typical firm will shift upward when the entry of new firms takes place. This is depicted in part (b) of Figure 6.17, in which AC_2 and MC_2 are the long-run average and marginal cost curves of a typical firm for an increased number of firms in the industry. It is important to note that the long-run MC and, therefore, the short-run MC for the optimal plant size of the firm have shifted to the left. This by itself has the effect of shifting the short-run industry supply curve to the left. However, the entry of new firms has the effect of shifting the short-run industry supply curve to the right.

When two such opposite forces take place simultaneously, theoretically we are not sure whether the short-run industry supply curve will shift to the right or to the left. If the combined result of the two opposite forces shifted the short-run industry supply curve to the left, given demand curve D_1, the net effect of the entry of new firms would push the market price above P_0', which, in turn, would result in excess profits for all firms, that is, the new firms as well as the old. This would lead to more new firms entering into the industry, which would push the industry supply curve further up. In such a case, an increase in demand would generate a force that would continuously push the price of the commodity up. This kind of market, although theoretically possible, cannot be observed, that is, has little practical significance. Furthermore, when new firms and new plants are established, more resources must have been shifted to the industry; thus, the capacity of the industry must increase as a result of the entry of new firms. This implies that the short-run supply curve of the industry must shift to the right when entry takes place even in an increasing-cost industry. For this reason, we shall assume that the net effect of the entry of new firms is to shift the short-run industry supply curve to the right (from S_0 to S_1), as shown in part (a) of Figure 6.17.

Entry of new firms causes the industry supply curve to shift to the right

From the above analysis, it can be seen that when demand increases, the short-run equilibrium price goes up immediately, a movement along the short-run supply curve of the industry. When the entry of new firms takes place, the short-run industry supply curve shifts to the right and the short-run equilibrium price goes down along the given demand curve. As long as the established firms make an excess profit, new firms will continuously enter into the industry. As more firms are established, the short-run and long-run cost curves of established firms go up contin-

As more firms enter cost curves shift upward in an increasing-cost industry

uously. Some economists argue that it is conceivable that too many firms may enter the industry, thus resulting in "*overshoot*,"[2] and that the excess profit of established firms may become negative, which will result in an exit of firms. Hence, the short-run equilibrium price may fluctuate around the long run equilibrium price. However, this cannot be true in our model because of Assumption 6.4 (perfect information or knowledge). Therefore, we may conclude that new firms will continuously enter into the industry and, at the same time, that the short-run and long-run cost curves of established firms will continuously shift upward until the short-run industry supply curve shifts to S_1 and a short-run market price P_1 for the given demand D_1 is established. For the given number of firms in the industry corresponding to S_1, the long-run cost curves for the typical firm (and all other identical firms) are AC_2 and MC_2, where P_1 is just equal to the minimum of AC_2. Then and only then can we have long-run equilibrium for the industry as well as for all firms in the industry.

From Figure 6.17, we can see that the new equilibrium quantity Q_1 for the industry is definitely larger than the original quantity Q_0. The new equilibrium quantity for the typical firms can be either larger or smaller than the original quantity. This will depend on the nature of the shift of the long-run cost curves, which is determined by technology and input market conditions. The new long-run equilibrium price must be higher than the original price due to the upward shift of the long-run AC of the firm. In part (a) of Figure 6.17 we see that E_0 is the original point of long-run equilibrium, whereas E_1 is the new equilibrium point of the industry. According to our analysis, E_1 must be to the right of and

---

[2] In this case "overshoot" simply means industry production in excess of that warranted by demand at the given price.

above E_0. The above arguments apply to any increase in demand. If demand increases continuously, the adjustment of the firms and the industry will generate an infinite number of such long-run equilibrium points as E_1, each corresponding to a given demand. (The reverse would occur for a decrease in demand, in which case point E_1 would be to the left of and below E_0.) The locus of these equilibrium points constitutes a positively sloped curve (S in Figure 6.17), which, by our definition, is precisely the long-run supply curve of an increasing-cost industry. This proves the second part of Proposition 6.4.

The proof of Proposition 6.4 for a decreasing-cost industry is similar to the proof given above. Students should try to carry out the proof in order to test their understanding of the behavior of long-run cost and supply curves.

The reasons for the existence of constant, increasing, or decreasing cost for various industries are usually based on the input market conditions. It is usually argued that if an industry is relatively small in the economy and does not require specialized inputs, then the industry is a small buyer in the input market and, therefore, input prices will be constant when the industry expands. As a result, it is assumed that a constant-cost industry will prevail. It should be pointed out that this argument is true only under Assumption 6.5 (an absence of external economies or diseconomies). In a somewhat similar manner, it is generally noted that when an industry is relatively large in the economy or uses specialized inputs, it faces a positively sloped supply curve in the input market. The entry of new firms results in a shift of demand for inputs to the right, thus producing higher input prices, which, in turn, cause the cost curves of existing firms to shift upward. There is another reason that the cost of existing firms may increase when new firms enter the industry: external diseconomy. For example, when more firms are established, the existing firms may have to spend more on air and/or water pollution control, thus creating higher production costs.

External economies (diseconomies) may be the cause of decreasing (increasing) cost industries

A decreasing-cost industry may be due to external economies in the industry (external to the firms but internal to the industry) and/or a negatively sloped long-run supply curve in the input market. Some economists, such as Henderson and Quandt (1971), define an external economy as the phenomenon where an expansion of industry output lowers the cost of each firm in the industry. According to this definition, whenever external economics prevail, the costs of existing firms go down when the industry expands (i.e., new firms enter the industry). Whenever the supply curves of input markets are negatively sloped, an increase in the demand for inputs will result in lower input prices.

Some economists argue that a decreasing-cost industry is inconsistent with perfect competition. This contention is not correct and results from confusing the decreasing-cost industry with the

decreasing long-run AC of the firm. Perfect competition may
prevail for a decreasing-cost industry if the long-run AC of the
firm is not decreasing. Still, the long-run supply curve of the
industry can be negatively sloped. With a negatively sloped supply curve, an equilibrium of the market may not only exist, but
may also be unique. Furthermore, the equilibrium may also be
stable provided that the demand curve is negatively sloped and
flatter than the supply curve, as indicated in Section 6.3.7. Thus,
there is no inconsistency between a decreasing-cost industry and
perfect competition. However, if economies of scale exist, thus
decreasing the long-run AC of the firm, perfect competition will
break down. We shall discuss this condition in Section 6.5.

A decreasing long-run AC for firms is not necessary for a decreasing-cost industry

6.5 INCREASING RETURNS TO SCALE, DECREASING LONG-RUN AC, AND THE BREAKDOWN OF PERFECT COMPETITION

As has been shown in Chapter 3, increasing returns to scale
implies a decreasing long-run AC for the firm under the assumption of a competitive market for production. When this is the
case, there does not exist a minimum long-run AC for a typical
firm. As has been shown in Section 6.4.1, a typical firm in a
perfectly competitive market will be in long-run equilibrium only
if the market price is equal to the firm's short- and long-run MCs
as well as the minimum short- and long-run ACs. When there
does not exist a minimum long-run AC, these conditions can
never be met. Thus, long-run equilibrium cannot exist for the
firm. As a result, long-run equilibrium also cannot exist for the
industry, since the existence of long-run equilibrium for the firm
is a necessary condition for the existence of long-run equilibrium
for the industry.

The breakdown of the perfectly competitive model under increasing returns to scale can be better understood by reference
to Figure 6.18, in which AC is the long-run average cost curve.
It can be observed that for any market price above zero (e.g.,
P_0), the firm will make more profit the larger its size in a perfectly
competitive market. Therefore, the optimal size of the firm is

FIGURE 6.18

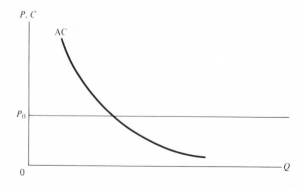

infinite. Since the market cannot be infinitely large, there cannot be more than one firm in the industry in the long run. Since, by definition, a perfectly competitive market can exist only if there are many small sellers, we see that perfect competition cannot exist in an industry where increasing returns to scale prevail.

Increasing returns to scale is not, however, the only instance for which decreasing long-run AC occurs. As we have shown in Chapter 3 (in particular, Figures 3.19 and 3.20), constant AVC may also imply decreasing long-run AC. This model probably more accurately depicts public utilities, which are commonly referred to as a *natural monopoly*. Unfortunately, many economists and textbooks use public utilities to illustrate increasing returns to scale and decreasing long-run AC. Actually, this is a misinterpretation of increasing returns to scale. Although it is true that large producers with more capital investment (e.g., larger and more-sophisticated machinery and other facilities) may secure a lower AC for a larger quantity of production, this is, in many cases, the result of lower AVC and not increasing returns to scale. Let us examine this issue in more depth.

In the public utility sector we may find that larger electric generators require more labor and fuel to operate; however, due to a larger quantity of output, the average labor and fuel costs per kilowatt-hour of electricity may be lower as a result of the lower average input of labor and fuel. Although the TFC may be quite high, the AFC for a large output may not be high. The combined effect of lower variable and fixed costs per unit of output is a lower ATC. Note that the input ratio (in particular, the capital/labor ratio) is usually different for large and small producers in the same industry. Recall that, by definition, increasing returns to scale involves the same input ratio as one moves from small-scale to large-scale production methods. In reality, many large-scale production systems are usually more capital intensive (i.e., have a higher capital/labor ratio) than small systems. Thus, the concept of returns to scale cannot theoretically be applied to these cases. However, the constant-AVC model can be used to illustrate this situation.

Decreasing long-run AC is not necessarily due to increasing returns to scale

Constant AVC, when combined with the situation in which a large plant size results in lower AVC (the case depicted by Figure 3.19), is not consistent with perfect competition. Empirical studies indicate that AVC is indeed constant in the relevant range, which is inconsistent with the well-established competitive model. It is probably for this reason that many economists have not taken the constant-AVC model seriously. To put it another way, the constant-AVC case flies in the face of the established competitive model, which has caused many economists to dismiss it. As we have shown in Chapter 3, a modified constant-AVC model, in which AVC is constant only within the given plant capacity and increases beyond that capacity, is consistent not only with a decreasing long-run AC, but also with the traditional smooth, U-shaped MC and AC curves. Thus, there are different constant-AVC models, not just one. It is a more-flexible model than appears at first sight.

What we have shown is that whereas increasing returns to scale implies decreasing long-run AC, decreasing long-run AC is not confined to the case of increasing returns to scale. Sometimes (perhaps in most cases in real production) large plant size is more capital intensive, and hence the capital/labor ratio is different for large and small sizes. When this is the case, the lower AC for a large-size plant cannot be referred to as the result of increasing returns to scale. In short, what we have pointed out is the confusion between decreasing long-run AC due to increasing returns to scale, which is predicated on a fixed input ratio, and decreasing long-run AC attributable to constant or decreasing AVC in which input ratios differ as plant size undergoes change.

Perfect competition is compatible with a decreasing cost industry but not increasing returns to scale

In the above analysis, we have indicated that perfect competition breaks down whenever decreasing long-run AC for a typical firm prevails. Although perfect competition and increasing returns to scale are inconsistent, the breakdown of perfect competition is not confined to the case of increasing returns to scale. However, it is important to point out that perfect competition may prevail in a decreasing-cost industry, although the breakdown of perfect competition will take place sooner or later under the condition of decreasing long-run AC for the firm. This distinction should be understood in order to avoid possible confusion.

6.6 THE BREAK-EVEN CHART AND PERFECT COMPETITION

In Section 3.2.4 of Chapter 3, we explained the nature and use of a break-even chart. We also briefly mentioned that the widely used, simple chart represented by Figure 3.9 is internally inconsistent in theory. With the knowledge that we have accumulated, we can now say more about this situation. The straight-line TR curve implies perfect competition, whereas the straight-line TC curve implies constant AVC. If the short-run TC curves were like those depicted by part (b) of Figure 3.18, then the long-run AC curve for the firm would also be the short-run ATC curve shown in part (b) of Figure 3.8. In this case, the firm's optimal production would be either zero or infinity in the long run. If the market price was equal to or lower than AVC, the firm would have to close down in the long run. However, if the market price was above AVC, the profit-maximizing quantity would be infinite. On the other hand, if the short-run TC curves were like those in part (a) of Figure 3.18, then the long-run AC would be decreasing. In either case, perfect competition could not exist in the long run.

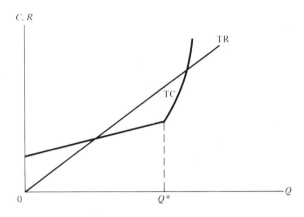

FIGURE 6.19

Hence, the break-even chart of Figure 3.9 based on perfect competition is obviously internally inconsistent.

Although the simple break-even chart is inconsistent with perfect competition, a slightly modified constant-AVC model can be consistent with perfect competition in both the short run and the long run. Assume that the AVC is constant up to capacity but increases beyond capacity as in Figure 6.19, in which TR is the total revenue curve for a competitive firm and TC is the total cost curve, characterized by constant AVC up to capacity Q^* and increasing AVC beyond that. When TC increases rapidly to the right of Q^* (as shown in Figure 6.19), the capacity quantity Q^* is the short-run profit-maximizing quantity for the given plant size. In the long run, the optimal plant size is that which results in a minimum long-run AC. Since Figures 3.20 and 3.21 show that this modified constant-AVC model is consistent with the traditional smooth, U-shaped long-run AC curve, all of the conclusions derived from the traditional analysis of the competitive market apply to it. Consequently, there is no inconsistency between constant AVC per se and perfect competition once the short-run limited-capacity factor is taken into consideration.

Figure 6.19 depicts only one possibility. Casual observation indicates that many producers do occasionally operate on overtime, which can be interpreted as operating beyond capacity. Does this mean that these firms are not profit maximizers? Basing the answer to this question on Figure 6.19 can be misleading. The answer depends on the rate of increase in variable cost after capacity is reached. For illustrative purposes, consider Figure 6.20, in which, as in Figure 6.19, TR and TC are the total revenue and total cost curves, respectively, whereas Q^* is the capacity quantity. The difference between this figure and Figure 6.19 is that the rate of increase of TC is lower. In particular, the slope of the TC curve immediately to the right of Q^* is still flatter than the slope of the TR curve even though the slope of the TC curve

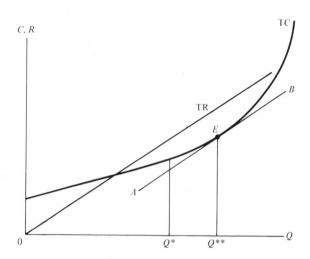

FIGURE 6.20   0

increases further to the right. Under these circumstances, Q^* is no longer the profit-maximizing quantity. The graphical example in Figure 6.3 together with the marginal analysis of Section 3.3 of Chapter 3 can be applied here. Assume that in Figure 6.20, $\overline{AB}$ is parallel to TR and tangent to TC at E. It is obvious that Q^{**}, not Q^*, is the short-run profit-maximizing quantity because MR = MC at Q^{**}. The analysis is identical to the traditional model. Thus, the model of constant-AVC with limited capacity can be reconciled with the traditional model of smooth, U-shaped AC and MC curves, and the break-even chart can be used in maximum-profit analysis even for firms in a competitive market, provided that the market (price) is relatively stable and that the incremental cost information beyond capacity is accurate.

A constant-AVC model with limited capacity is consistent with traditional theory

The above result is consistent with production theory as developed earlier. It was shown in Chapters 1 and 2 that production can only take place in stage II for a rational producer, where both the AP (average product) and MP (marginal product) of the variable input are decreasing. Decreasing AP of the variable input implies increasing AVC. In this sense, with traditional economic analysis in production, both cost and market behavior are more relevant under circumstances where over-capacity operation prevails. When there is underutilization of capacity, the traditional model may not be relevant. It has been said that the classical theory is valid only under conditions of full employment. The above analysis indicates that there may be some truth in this statement. Empirical studies show that producers ordinarily prefer to have certain excess capacity. This implies that the traditional analysis is only meaningful in times of prosperity. That is why John M. Keynes called his book *The General Theory of Employment, Interest, and Money*. However, as we have shown, the modified constant-AVC model seems to be able to deal with both prosperity and less-than-prosperity economic conditions.

SUMMARY

In this chapter we analyzed the profit-maximizing behavior of firms and the market determination of price in the context of the model of perfect competition. We noted that the model of perfect competition is based on four important assumptions: (1) a homogeneous product, (2) free entry and exit of firms, (3) many small sellers and buyers, and (4) perfect information. The nature and relevance of these assumptions were discussed at length in order to avoid any misunderstanding concerning the economic environment within which the model is to be evaluated.

After describing the nature and applicability of the four assumptions on which the model of perfect competition is based, we proceeded to analyze the behavior of the firm as a profit maximizer in three different time frames (market period, short run, and long run) to see how the element of time affects market supply and price. We began by defining the market period as one in which the output and the size and number of firms all are fixed. It was shown that under such conditions the supply curve of the firm (and the industry) is traditionally considered as a vertical straight line on a two-dimensional graph, but that, in reality, the supply curve could, without loss of rigor, be reasonably modified to include a positive slope in the lower price range. We explained that, in the market period as traditionally defined, cost has little or nothing to do with the market price of the commodity and that demand is all important.

We next defined the short run as a period in which firms can change their output but the size and number of firms in the industry are fixed. It was shown that, since the price of the commodity is given to the firm under perfect competition, the firm will seek to maximize its profits by adjusting output to where marginal revenue (MR) is equal to marginal cost (MC), provided MC is rising.

We also defined this condition as the short-run equilibrium position of the firm, since any departure from it would lead to less profit or greater losses. We emphasized, however, that in short-run equilibrium (where MR = MC and MC is rising) a firm can be earning either positive, zero, or negative profits, but that even in the event of loss the firm can continue to operate so long as it covers its variable costs. Given the latter condition, we demonstrated that the segment of the MC curve which lies above the average variable cost (AVC) becomes the relevant short-run supply curve of the firm and that, with the absence of externalities, the market supply curve for a commodity becomes the horizontal sum of the supply curves of firms in the industry. Market price and the equilibrium output in the short run were then shown to be simultaneously determined by the intersection of the market demand and supply curves which, by our definition of equilibrium, also implied maximum profits (or minimum losses) for the firm and maximum satisfaction for consumers. However, it was shown that market equilibrium may not be unique or stable since it depends on the shapes of the demand and supply curves.

We concluded our discussion by first defining the long run as a period in which output and the size and number of firms in the industry all vary and then analyzing the type of adjustments that yield the long-run supply curve of the firm and the industry. The profit-maximization condition of the firm in long-run equilibrium was again described as one in which MR is equal to MC with MC rising, but in contrast to short-run equilibrium, positive and negative profits can no longer exist. Moreover, since profit in the long-run is zero, it means that price will be equal to long-run and short-run AC and MC at the minimum of AC for the firm. We then showed that the shape of the long-run market supply curve depends on the cost behavior of the firms as the number of firms in the industry undergoes change and that a constant-cost industry is one in which the cost curves of the firms are independent of the number of firms in the industry. Conversely, an increasing- (decreasing-) cost industry was described as one in which the cost curves of existing firms shift upward (downward) as the number of firms in the industry increases. Finally, we noted that a decreasing long-run AC for a firm is inconsistent with perfect competition since the firm's optimal size under such a condition would not exist. Hence, the commonly used break-even chart of constant AVC (as described in Chapter 3) is internally inconsistent and must be modified to incorporate AVC that rises as production exceeds plant capacity.

**EXERCISES AND QUESTIONS FOR CHAPTER 6
ON PERFECT COMPETITION**

1. What are the conditions under which the profit of a competitive firm will be maximized? Why?

2. "My firm is now operating at a loss and the short-run MC is increasing. If market price rises a little, I will not increase output, because if I did, MC would go up and I'll just be taking a greater loss on a higher volume." Is this reasoning correct? Why or why not? Clearly state the assumption(s) that you are making with respect to your answer.

3. What is the short-run supply curve of a firm under perfect competition? Is there any relationship between the short-run supply curve of a firm and its cost curves? Defend your answer.

4. Some people argue the following: "According to the 'law of supply,' the higher the price, the more of any product that will be offered for sale. Mass production and technological progress result in a higher supply and much lower prices than previously. We may conclude that the 'law of supply' is wrong, at least for these cases."

Do you agree with the conclusion reached in the quotation? Why or why not?

5. What do we mean by equilibrium of a market? stable equilibrium? unstable equilibrium? What are the relationships between static stability and dynamic stability? Explain.

6. What are the conditions for short-run and long-run equilibrium of a firm under perfect competition? Is it possible for a competitive firm at equilibrium to have excess profit (more than normal) in the short-run and in the long-run? Why or why not? Use graphs to illustrate your answers.

7. Most textbooks consider the supply curve of an industry in the market period as a vertical straight line. Do you agree with this observation? Defend your answer. You may use a simple example to illustrate your point.

8. "An increase in supply will almost certainly lower the price and increase the quantity of a commodity bought and sold."
   a. Under what very special circumstances would an increase in supply result in no fall in price?
   b. Under what equally special circumstances would the increase in supply result in no increase in the quantity bought and sold? What would then happen to price?

9. Do external effects (external economies or external diseconomies) such as air pollution and water pollution have any relationship to an industry's supply curve? Defend your answer.

10. Under the impact of stricter antipollution standards, new car prices may increase. Explain what will happen to used-car prices, to rates for renting cars, and to gasoline prices under these circumstances. Use a graph(s) to illustrate the logic of your explanation.

11. The market demand and supply functions for a commodity are given by the following formulas:

    $$Q_D(P) = 100 - 10P$$

    $$Q_S(P) = 50 + 10P$$

    a. Graph the supply and demand curves and identify the equilibrium price and quantity.
    b. Calculate the elasticity of demand and the elasticity of supply at the equilibrium price.

12. Empirical studies indicate that in most (if not all) cases, the short-run AVC of a firm is constant. Is this phenomenon consistent with the model of perfect competition? Why? A modified version of the constant AVC-model says that it is constant within the capacity range but increases beyond capacity. Does this modification reconcile the phenomenon of constant AVC and the economic model of perfect competition? Explain.

APPENDIX TO CHAPTER 6

A MATHEMATICAL NOTE ON THE PERFECTLY COMPETITIVE MARKET

A6.1 THE SHORT-RUN SUPPLY FUNCTION OF THE FIRM AND INDUSTRY

In the short run, the total cost of production to a firm is the sum of the total fixed costs and the total variable costs. In symbols, the total cost function of a firm can be written

$$C = F + V(Q) \tag{A6.1}$$

where C is the total cost, F is the total fixed cost (TFC), and $V(Q)$ is the total variable cost (TVC), which is a function of the level of output Q. The total revenue R of a firm is, by definition, equal to the price multipled by the quantity:

$$R = PQ \tag{A6.2}$$

The profit π of a firm is, by definition, equal to the difference between total revenue and total cost:

$$\pi = R - C = PQ - F - V(Q) \tag{A6.3}$$

The first-order condition for profit maximization of a firm is

$$d\pi/dQ = dR/dQ - dC/dQ = 0 \tag{A6.4}$$

where dR/dQ is the MR, which is equal to price P in the special case of a perfectly competitive market, and dC/dQ is the MC. Thus, the first-order (necessary) condition for profit maximization of a firm requires that

$$MR = MC \tag{A6.5}$$

which is identical to condition 1 for profit maximization of a firm as given in Section 6.3.2.

The second-order (sufficient) condition for profit maximization of a firm requires that

$$d^2\pi/dQ^2 = d^2R/dQ^2 - d^2C/dQ^2 < 0 \tag{A6.6}$$

Since the price P is constant for a perfectly competitive firm, $d^2R/dQ^2 = 0$. (For a firm in an imperfect market, this term, in general, is not zero. We shall discuss the case of an imperfect market in Chapters 7–9.) Since d^2C/dQ^2 is the slope of the MC function, and taking the negative sign in front of this term in (A6.6) into consideration, the second-order condition implies increasing MC. This is identical to condition 2 for profit maximization of a firm as given in Section 6.3.2. Thus, we have mathematically proved the first- (necessary) and second-order (sufficient) conditions for profit maximization of a firm given in the text.

Since the firm is assumed to always produce the quantity that will maximize its profit, and since the MR is identical to the market price P for a perfectly competitive firm, it follows from (A6.5) that the quantity a firm will produce always satisfies the expression

$$P = dC/dQ \tag{A6.7}$$

Since the cost is a function of Q, its derivative is also, in general, a function of Q. Equation (A6.7) involves two variables: P and Q. If we solve for Q in terms of P (assuming that an explicit expression can be derived), we obtain

$$Q = S(P) \tag{A6.8}$$

that is, the quantity of a commodity which a firm is willing to produce and sell is a function of the market price. However, a firm is willing to produce a product only if the market price is above (or at least equal to) the minimum AVC. Therefore, the short-run supply function of a firm becomes

$$Q = S(P) \quad \text{for} \quad P \geq \min \text{AVC}$$
$$Q = 0 \quad \text{for} \quad P < \min \text{AVC} \tag{A6.9}$$

Since AVC is nonnegative, the supply function of a firm is meaningful only for nonnegative prices. Due to the second-order (sufficient) condition for profit maximization of a firm, the supply function (i.e., curve) must have a positive slope.

Under Assumption 6.1 (homogeneity of product and inputs) and Assumption 6.4 (perfect knowledge or information), the cost functions of all firms must be identical. In addition, since firms also face an identical market price, the supply functions of all firms must also be identical. If there are n firms in the market and each firm's supply is denoted

$$Q_i = S_i(P) \quad \text{for} \quad P \geq \min \text{AVC}$$
$$Q_i = 0 \quad \text{for} \quad P < \min \text{AVC} \tag{A6.10}$$

then

$$Q = nQ_i = nS_i(P) \qquad \text{for} \quad P \geq \text{min AVC}$$

$$Q = 0 \qquad\qquad\qquad \text{for} \quad P < \text{min AVC} \tag{A6.11}$$

Since the individual firm's supply function has a positive slope, the industry supply function must also have a positive slope, albeit less steep than that of the individual firm.

The above derivation of the supply function can be illustrated by the following simple example. Assume that the total cost function of a typical firm is

$$C = 10 + 6Q - 2Q^2 + \tfrac{1}{3}Q^3 \tag{A6.12}$$

where TFC $= 10$ and

$$\text{TVC} = 6Q - 2Q^2 + \tfrac{1}{3}Q^3 \tag{A6.13}$$

The MC is the derivative of either (A6.12) or (A6.13) with respect to Q, that is,

$$\text{MC} = 6 - 4Q + Q^2 = 2 + (Q - 2)^2 \tag{A6.14}$$

Equating MC to the market price P, we obtain

$$2 + (Q - 2)^2 = P \qquad \text{or} \qquad (Q - 2)^2 = P - 2$$

which yields

$$Q = 2 \pm (P - 2)^{1/2} \qquad \text{for} \quad P \geq 2 \tag{A6.15}$$

When $P < 2$, the right side of (A6.15) involves a complex or imaginary number that does not have much meaning insofar as the quantity of output is concerned. Therefore, we only consider function (A6.15) for $P \geq 2$. Function (A6.15) has two branches for $P > 2$. However, the branch $Q = 2 - (P - 2)^{1/2}$ has a negative slope, which violates the second-order condition for profit maximization of a firm. Thus, this branch is disregarded for our purposes.

As we have explained in the text, producers will only produce and sell their products if the market price is higher (or at least equal to) the minimum AVC. When we divide (A6.13) by Q we obtain

$$\text{AVC} = 6 - 2Q + \tfrac{1}{3}Q^2 \tag{A6.16}$$

The minimum value of AVC can be located by setting the derivative with respect to Q equal to zero and solving for Q:

$$d\text{AVC}/dQ = -2 + \tfrac{2}{3}Q = 0 \tag{A6.17}$$

which yields

$$Q = 3 \tag{A6.18}$$

This indicates that AVC reaches its minimum at $Q = 3$. Substituting $Q = 3$ into (A6.16), we obtain the minimum AVC:

$$\min \text{AVC} = 6 - 6 + \tfrac{1}{3}3^2 = 3 \tag{A6.19}$$

The above results imply that the firm's supply function for the given cost function (A6.12) is

$$Q_S = 2 + (P - 2)^{1/2} \quad \text{for} \quad P \geq 3$$
$$Q_S = 0 \qquad\qquad\quad \text{for} \quad P < 3 \tag{A6.20}$$

For n identical firms, the industry supply function is

$$Q_S^* = 2n + n(P - 2)^{1/2} \quad \text{for} \quad P \geq 3$$
$$Q_S^* = 0 \qquad\qquad\qquad\quad \text{for} \quad P < 3 \tag{A6.21}$$

It can be seen that the slope of the individual firm's supply function is

$$dQ_S/dP = (P - 2)^{-1/2}/2 > 0 \quad \text{for} \quad P \geq 3 \tag{A6.22}$$

and that the slope of the industry supply function is

$$dQ_S^*/dP = n(P - 2)^{-1/2}/2 > 0 \quad \text{for} \quad P \geq 3 \tag{A6.23}$$

The slopes of the individual firm's and industry supply functions are both positive.

A6.2 THE EQUILIBRIUM OF A PERFECTLY COMPETITIVE MARKET

A6.2.1 The Short-Run Equilibrium of a Perfectly Competitive Market

In Chapter 5 we derived the demand function for a commodity from an individual consumer's demand, which, in turn, is derived from the consumer's utility function and budget constraint. The demand function for a commodity can be written

$$Q_D = D(P) \tag{A6.24}$$

A market is in equilibrium if the quantity demanded is equal to the quantity supplied for a given price. We can write the industry supply function (A6.11) in a comparable form to the demand function (A6.24), that is,

$$Q_S = S(P) \tag{A6.25}$$

In equilibrium,

$$Q_D = Q_S \quad \text{or} \quad D(P) = S(P) \tag{A6.26}$$

We have one equation in one variable (i.e., P), which can, in general, be solved. We denote the solution of (A6.26) by P^*, which is the equilibrium price. Substituting price P^* into either (A6.24) or (A6.25) yields the equilibrium quantity

$$Q^* = D(P^*) = S(P^*) \tag{A6.27}$$

The above equality holds, since P^* satisfies (A6.26).

The above arguments, as do all textbooks in general, assume that (A6.26) can be solved explicitly for P, which is not always true. In any case, the solution of (A6.26) may not be an easy matter. For example, assume that we have supply function (A6.21). For the sake of simplicity, let the demand be linear, so that we have

$$Q_D = A - aP, \qquad A, a > 0 \tag{A6.28}$$

At equilibrium, demand equals supply. Thus, equating (A6.21) and (A6.28), we obtain

$$A - aP = 2n + n(P - 2)^{1/2} \qquad \text{for} \quad P \geq 3$$

The solution for P in the above expression is

$$P^* = [(n^2 - 2an + 2Aa) \pm (n^3 - 4an^2 + 4An$$
$$- 20a^2n + 8Aa^2)^{1/2}n^{1/2}]/2a^2 \qquad \text{for} \quad P \geq 3 \tag{A6.29}$$

The equilibrium quantity can be found by substituting (A6.29) into (A6.28):

$$Q^* = A - [(n^2 - 2an + 2Aa) \pm (n^3 - 4an^2$$
$$+ 4Aan - 20a^2n + 8Aa^2)^{1/2}n^{1/2}]/2a \tag{A6.30}$$

The sole purpose of the above exercise is to show that the solution of (A6.27) for P^* may not be a simple matter and that in some cases an explicit solution may not be feasible. From the simple cost function (A6.12), we derived the industry supply function (A6.21), which is also simple enough. However, when we use this simple supply function and a linear demand (which is the simplest meaningful function that can be used), the expressions for the equilibrium price P^* and quantity Q^* become rather lengthy. Since both (A6.29) and (A6.30) involve square roots on the right sides, this imposes certain restrictions on the values of A and a in order that $P^* \geq 3$ and $Q^* \geq 0$. When more complicated demand and supply functions are involved, the mathematical skills required to solve (A6.27) and to analyze the restrictions on the parameters can be considerable. This is why economists usually employ linear demand and supply functions for illustrative purposes: The mathematical operations are rather simple. Suppose that we have the demand function (A6.28) and a linear supply such as

$$Q_S = B + bP, \qquad b > 0 \tag{A6.31}$$

The equilibrium price is

$$P^* = (A - B)/(a + b) \qquad\qquad (A6.32)$$

Since A, a, and b are, by assumption, positive, it follows that if B is positive, then as long as $A > B$, the equilibrium price will be positive. However, if B is positive and *greater* than A, then the market price will, according to (A6.32), be negative, which does not make much economic sense. This is the case indicated by part (b) of Figure 6.8 (i.e., the case of what is usually called a free good). A free good, such as air, commands a zero price. Thus, even in the simple case of linear demand and supply functions, the mathematical expression for an equilibrium price— (A6.32)—is not, strictly speaking, correct. The proper expression for market price in this simple case is

$$P^* = (A - B)/(a + b) \qquad \text{for} \quad A > B$$
$$P^* = 0 \qquad\qquad\qquad \text{otherwise} \qquad\qquad (A6.33)$$

Substituting (A6.33) into either the demand function (A6.28) or the supply function (A6.31), we obtain the proper expression for the equilibrium quantity:

$$Q^* = (Ab + Ba)/(a + b) \qquad \text{for} \quad Ab + Ba > 0$$
$$Q^* = 0 \qquad\qquad\qquad\qquad \text{otherwise} \qquad\qquad (A6.34)$$

It can be seen that if the condition $Ab + Ba > 0$ is not satisfied, then it must be due to the fact that $B < 0$. In this case, we have the condition indicated by part (a) of Figure 6.8.

This simple example indicates that mathematical expressions in economics usually require certain restrictions on the values of the parameters or properties of the functions involved. Proper caution must be exercised concerning the necessary restrictions on mathematical expressions in economics; otherwise, false inferences or wrong conclusions can result. There are examples in economic literature where valid mathematical operations resulted in invalid theorems due to a failure by the authors to take the necessary restrictions or constraints into consideration. One of the authors has collected a few examples that are available on request.

A6.2.2 The Long-Run Equilibrium of a Perfectly Competitive Market

In the short run, an industry has a given number of firms; that is, n is a constant. In the long run, the number of firms is a variable that is part of the solution of the system. In order to show the special features of long-run equilibrium and its solution, we first rewrite the demand function (A6.24):

$$Q_D = D(P) \tag{A6.24}$$

However, the industry supply function for the special case of n identical firms is written in a slightly different, but equivalent, form:

$$Q_S = nS_i(P) \tag{A6.25'}$$

where $Q_i = S_i(P)$ is the typical firm's supply function.

An industry is in long-run equilibrium only if the aggregate demand equals the aggregate supply, that is, only if

$$Q_D = Q_S = nS_i(P) \tag{A6.35}$$

In addition to the equality of demand and supply, long-run equilibrium of the industry requires that profit equal zero for each firm. Hence,

$$\pi_i = PQ_i - C_i(Q_i) = 0 \tag{A6.36}$$

where π_i denotes the profit, Q_i the quantity, and C_i the long-run total cost function for firm i. The last expression implies that $P = AC$ for each and every firm. Furthermore, the first-order condition for profit maximization of a firm requires that

$$P = MC$$

The above conditions hence imply that

$$AC = MC \tag{A6.37}$$

The above five equations involve the five variables Q_D, Q_S, Q_i, P, and n. The system can, in general, be solved. The procedure is to first solve for Q_i from (A6.37). The solution of Q_i will be in terms of the parameters of the total cost function. We then solve for P from (A6.36). The quantities Q_D and Q_S can be computed from (A6.24) and (A6.25'), respectively. Finally, the number of firms n can be computed from (A6.35). All the Qs, P, and n will be in terms of the parameters of the cost and demand functions. For example, if the long-run total cost function of a typical firm and the demand function for the industry are

$$C_i = b_1 Q_i + b_2 Q_i^2 + b_3 Q_i^3 \tag{A6.38}$$

$$Q_D = A - aP \tag{A6.39}$$

then the AC and MC functions are, respectively,

$$AC = b_1 + b_2 Q_i + b_3 Q_i^2 \tag{A6.40}$$

$$MC = b_1 + 2b_2 Q_i + 3b_3 Q_i^2 \tag{A6.41}$$

Using (A6.37), we have

$$Q_i^* = -b_2/2b_3 \qquad \text{for} \qquad b_2 < 0, \quad b_3 > 0,$$
$$\text{or} \qquad b_2 > 0, \quad b_3 < 0 \qquad\qquad (A6.42)$$

Substituting (A6.42) into either (A6.40) or (A6.41), and using (A6.36) or the first-order condition for profit maximization of a firm, the market price P^* is

$$P^* = b_1 - b_2^2/4b_3 \qquad\qquad (A6.43)$$

Substituting P^* into the linear demand function (A6.39), we obtain the aggregate equilibrium quantity

$$Q^* = A - a(b_1 - b_2^2/4b_3) \qquad\qquad (A6.44)$$

Using (A6.35) and the fact that $S_i = Q_i^*$ in (A6.42), we obtain the number of firms

$$n = 2ab_1b_3/b_2 - 2Ab_3/b_2 - ab_2/2 \qquad\qquad (A6.45)$$

Thus, once we know the long-run cost function of the firm and the market demand function, the equilibrium quantity of each firm, the market price, the number of firms, and the aggregate quantity can be computed.

A6.3 THE EXISTENCE, UNIQUENESS, AND STABILITY OF MARKET EQUILIBRIUM

A6.3.1 The Condition of Existence of Equilibrium

In Section A6.2, to a certain extent, we were discussing the existence problem of market equilibrium when we talked about restrictions on the values of the parameters of the demand and supply functions. Since the market price and quantity must be nonnegative in order to make economic sense, a formal statement of the existence problem is that equilibrium in a market exists if

1. a solution of Equation (A6.26) exists,
2. the value of the solution P^* is real and nonnegative, and
3. the value of Q^* from (A6.27) is real and nonnegative.

A6.3.2 The Condition of Uniqueness of Equilibrium

One example in Section A6.2 indicated that the solution of (A6.26) could result in multiple values for P^* in (A6.29) and for Q^* in (A6.30). This is a case where the market equilibrium is not unique. Other possible examples of nonunique market equilibrium would be a case where the solution P^* is unique but Q^* is multivalued and vice versa. Whenever either the solution P^* or the quantity

Q^* (or both) has more than one nonnegative value, then the market equilibrium is considered nonunique. Hence, the equilibrium of a market is unique only if

1. equilibrium exists, and
2. there is only one value for both P^* and Q^*.

A6.3.3 The Condition of Stability of Equilibrium

In advanced economic theory, there are essential differences between dynamic and static stability. Since our discussions are concerned with static analysis, we shall not discuss dynamic stability. Static analysis considers only the tendency of change when the market is not at equilibrium, not the time path of the adjustment process. Conditions of stability are derived from assumptions about the market behavior of buyers and sellers. The Walrasian assumption, by the French economist Leon Walras, states that buyers tend to raise their bids if the quantity demanded exceeds the quantity supplied, whereas sellers tend to lower their prices if the converse is true. It is more convenient to state the stability conditions in terms of excess demand rather than with the usual demand and supply functions. The excess demand function $E(P)$ is defined as the difference between the demand and supply:

$$E(P) = D(P) - S(P) \tag{A6.46}$$

If the Walrasian assumption is correct, a market is stable if a price rise diminishes excess demand, that is, if

$$dE(P)/dP = dD(P)/dP - dS(P)/dP < 0 \tag{A6.47}$$

The English economist Alfred Marshall has made a slightly different assumption concerning market behavior. As a result, under certain circumstances, a market may be stable under the Walrasian assumption, but unstable under the Marshallian assumption (and vice versa). For the usual case, where the demand function is negatively sloped and the supply function is positively sloped, the market will be stable in both the Walrasian and the Marshallian sense. On the other hand, if both the demand function and the supply function are positively or negatively sloped, then if it is Walrasian stable, it will be Marshallian unstable (and vice versa). This clearly shows that the concept of stability is not absolute, but relative to the appropriate assumption concerning market behavior.

The Marshallian assumption states that producers tend to raise their output when the price that the buyers are willing to pay exceeds the price that sellers are willing to accept. When this is the case, producers realize that buyers are offering a price higher than necessary for the commodity to be profitably produced.

Therefore, their profit can be increased by increasing the quantity supplied and vice versa. This idea can be put in mathematical form if we assume that the inverse functions of both the demand and the supply exist. Thus, the inverse functions of demand and supply can be respectively written

$$P_D = D^{-1}(Q) \quad \text{and} \quad P_S = S^{-1}(Q) \tag{A6.48}$$

The usual demand and supply curves that economists draw are actually based on these inverse functions, not the demand and supply functions (A6.24) and (A6.25). In terms of these inverse functions, the excess demand price can be defined as

$$G(Q) = D^{-1}(Q) - S^{-1}(Q) \tag{A6.49}$$

The market is stable according to the Marshallian assumption if an increase in quantity reduces the excess demand price; that is,

$$dG(Q)/dQ = dD^{-1}(Q)/dQ - dS^{-1}(Q)/dQ < 0 \tag{A6.50}$$

In almost all calculus textbooks, there is an inverse function rule which says that the derivative of an inverse function has the same sign as the derivative of the original function, provided that both are single-valued functions. From this, it can easily be seen that both (A6.47) and (A6.50) are satisfied; thus, the equilibrium is stable in both the Walrasian and the Marshallian sense if the demand function has a negative slope; that is, $dD(P)/dP < 0$ and $dD^{-1}(Q)/dQ < 0$, and the supply function has a positive slope, that is, $dS(P)/dP > 0$ and $dS^{-1}(Q)/dQ > 0$. On the other hand, if both the demand and the supply function have either a positive or a negative slope, then the equilibrium (if it exists) will be Marshallian unstable if it is Walrasian stable and vice versa. This can be shown by dividing both sides of (A6.50) by $dD^{-1}(Q)/dQ \cdot dS^{-1}(Q)/dQ$ (a positive number) to obtain

$$\frac{1}{dS^{-1}(Q)/dQ} - \frac{1}{dD^{-1}(Q)/dQ} < 0 \tag{A6.51}$$

The inverse function rule also says that

$$\frac{dD(P)}{dP} = \frac{1}{dD^{-1}(Q)/dQ} \quad \text{and} \quad \frac{dS(P)}{dP} = \frac{1}{dS^{-1}(Q)/dQ} \tag{A6.52}$$

Substituting these values into (A6.51), we obtain

$$dS(P)/dP - dD(P)/dP < 0 \tag{A6.53}$$

The Walrasian stability condition (A6.47) and condition (A6.53), which is the equivalent of the Marshallian stability condition, cannot be fulfilled simultaneously. If an equilibrium is stable in the Walrasian sense, it cannot be stable in the Marshallian sense (and vice versa). In short, the stability of a market depends not only on the properties of the demand and supply functions, but also on the assumed behavior of the participants.

In economics, as well as in many other scientific fields, conditions of stability are considered an important part of the theoretical framework. On the other hand, unstable equilibrium has little practical importance. If unstable equilibrium exists at all, it can hardly be observed in reality. If a perfectly balanced egg can stand on its end, it can be considered as unstable equilibrium. Presumably, it can stand on one end forever in the absence of an external disturbance. However, once disturbed, it can never restore its precarious position by itself. In a changing world, what are the chances of actually observing such a precarious equilibrium in reality? It is probably quite realistic to assume that market equilibrium is indeed stable once the implication of stability is understood.

A6.4 THE BREAK-EVEN CHART AND MAXIMUM PROFIT

In Chapter 3, we explained the break-even chart, which is often used by business in market analysis. In Section 6.6, we also explained the inconsistency between the simple break-even chart and perfect competition. However, with a slight modification of the total cost function, the break-even chart technique can be reconciled with perfect competition. We shall demonstrate this argument with the use of simple mathematics.

As we have explained earlier, the simple break-even chart implies perfect competition and constant AVC. The total revenue and cost functions can be respectively written

$$R = PQ \qquad\qquad\qquad\qquad (A6.54)$$

$$C = F + VQ \qquad\qquad\qquad (A6.55)$$

where R, C, P, and Q denote total revenue, total cost, market price, and quantity of output, respectively, F denotes the total fixed cost (TFC), and V denotes the average variable cost (AVC). Under perfect competition, the price P is constant to a firm; F and V are constants and known to the firm. The solution for the break-even quantity Q_b is obtained by setting $R = C$ and solving for Q, which yields

$$Q_b = F/(P - V) \qquad\qquad\qquad (A6.56)$$

The break-even quantity is positive if and only if the price is greater than AVC. When price is equal to AVC, the quantity is not defined. This is the case where the total revenue and cost curves are two parallel lines. Since they will never intersect, no solution exists.

Using (A6.56), the break-even quantity can easily be computed for a given price, TFC, and AVC. It is easily seen that for a given cost, the higher the price, the smaller the quantity required in order to break even. On the other hand, for a given market price, the higher the TFC F or the AVC V (or both), the higher the quantity required in order to break even. All of these observations agree with common sense. This may be one of the reasons that the break-even chart is often used by business. However, this simple model is certainly inconsistent with perfect competition. First of all, the first-order condition for profit maximization of a firm is that MR = MC. In this special case, MR = P and MC = V. Hence, the first-order condition requires that

$$P = V \qquad\qquad\qquad\qquad (A6.57)$$

However, since both P and V are constants, there is no way that a firm can equate them if they are not equal. On the other hand, if (A6.57) does hold, then (A6.56) shows that the break-even quantity does not exist. It is also obvious that the second-order condition for profit maximization of a firm is not satisfied in this case. Thus, this simple model is inconsistent with perfect competition.

A modified constant-AVC model such as

$$C = F + VQ \qquad \text{for} \quad Q \le Q_0$$

$$C = F + V(Q) \qquad \text{for} \quad Q > Q_0 \qquad\qquad (A6.58)$$

$$dV(Q)/dQ > 0 \qquad \text{and} \qquad d^2V(Q)/dQ^2 > 0$$

where Q_0 is the capacity quantity and $V(Q)$ is the TVC function, can be consistent with perfect competition. In this case, the profit-maximizing quantity Q^* will be the solution of the expression

$$P - dC/dQ = 0 \qquad\qquad\qquad\qquad (A6.59)$$

In view of the restrictions on the TVC function in (A6.58), the market price must be positive and the second-order condition satisfied. As an example, suppose that the cost function is

$$C = F + VQ \qquad\qquad \text{for} \quad Q \le Q_0$$

$$C = F + aQ + bQ^2 \qquad \text{for} \quad Q > Q_0 \qquad (A6.60)$$

$$V, F, a, b > 0$$

Since we know that the cost function for $Q \le Q_0$ is inconsistent with perfect competition, the solution must be for $Q > Q_0$. In this special case, the expression corresponding to (A6.59) is

$$P - a - 2bQ = 0 \qquad\qquad\qquad\qquad (A6.61)$$

which yields the profit-maximizing quantity

$$Q^* = (P - a)/2b \qquad\qquad\qquad\qquad (A6.62)$$

Since the second-order condition

$$-d^2C/dQ^2 = -2b < 0 \qquad\qquad\qquad (A6.63)$$

is also satisfied, the solution (A6.62) is indeed the profit-maximizing quantity. This verifies our statement in the text that, in a perfectly competitive market, a firm's profit-maximizing quantity is always greater than its short-run capacity if the AVC is constant within its capacity.

MONOPOLY THEORY
AND MARK-UP PRICING

7.1 MONOPOLY THEORY

Pure monopoly is an economic model which, like perfect competition, has probably never existed in a strict sense, especially as defined in theory. On the other hand, the economic model of monopoly may approximate the activities and decision processes of many business firms that are not classified as pure monopoly in theory. Economic theory can only provide general guidance toward a better understanding of economic activities. Therefore, a mechanical application of theory to everyday life is hardly practical, if ever possible. Only those who understand the true meaning as well as the limitations of economic theory can best benefit from it.

In this chapter, we first present the traditional monopoly theory, after which we describe a few pricing models that are actually used by firms in practice. We then proceed to bring economic theory and business practice together in a synthesis to show their theoretical equivalence.

7.1.1 Pure Monopoly—An Economic Model

Pure monopoly, like perfect competition, is an economic model that is based on four fundamental assumptions:

Assumption 7.1: Homogeneous Product or Differentiated Products. However, there is no close substitute for the commodity or commodities that a monopolist sells.

Assumption 7.2: No Free Entry. This may result from various causes, such as patent laws that prohibit others from producing or imitating a product under patent (an obvious example is the Polaroid camera), control over the source of raw material [Aluminum Company of America (Alcoa) before World War II, for example], technical conditions that require very high initital costs but generate decreasing average unit cost over an output range that is large compared with market demand [examples being the so-called natural monopolies, e.g., public utilities (gas, electric, and water)], and the extent of market power possessed by the seller (e.g., a corner grocery may possess as much market power as a supermarket).

Assumption 7.3: One Seller, but Many Small Buyers.

Assumption 7.4: Perfect Information or Knowledge. This is available to the buyer and seller free of cost.

As mentioned previously, although Assumptions 7.1–7.4 are sometimes not in accord with reality, they are nevertheless essential to economic theory. This is particularly true of Assumption 7.4, which in the present case refers to the monopoly's complete knowledge of market demand conditions and costs. The importance of Assumption 7.4 can be better illustrated by imagining a situation in which it is absent. Without such assumed knowledge, it would be impossible to construct demand and cost schedules or draw demand and cost curves. In such a case, monopolists would have no idea as to the shape or position of their revenue and cost schedules (curves), and the economist would be in no better position to produce them. It is obvious that if economists could not draw the demand and cost curves, then the study of economics would be quite different. From a logical standpoint, those who proceed to draw demand and cost curves, on the one hand, while ignoring or even refuting Assumption 7.4, on the other hand, are being inconsistent.

Perfect information is essential for developing reliable demand and cost functions

In comparing the fundamental assumptions of pure monopoly with those of perfect competition, we can see that the essential modifications apply to Assumptions 7.2 and 7.3 relative to the corresponding Assumptions 6.2 and 6.3. The modification of Assumption 7.1 relative to Assumption 6.1 is not essential, whereas Assumption 7.4 is not relative to Assumption 6.4. The assumption of one seller, that is, Assumption 7.3, is the special feature of monopoly. However, the basis for this assumption is contained in Assumption 7.2, which is indeed essential for the model.

The public usually associates a monopoly with big companies, regarding small firms as victims of large monopolistic enterprises. However, as we mentioned in Assumption 7.2, the existence of monopoly depends not only on cost conditions, but also on the extent of the market. An obvious example is the small general store in an isolated small town, where the closest other town is 200 miles away (such as may be the case in Montana or Wyoming).

The general store may be quite small, but it enjoys monopoly power because it is impractical to drive 200 miles to buy a loaf of bread or a gallon of milk.

7.1.2 Demand Under Monopoly

The essential difference between a monopoly and a perfectly competitive firm is the nature of the demand schedule that each faces. This is important to remember, because the shapes of the cost curves for a monopoly are assumed to be similar to those of the curves for a perfectly competitive firm. In Chapter 6, it was demonstrated that the demand curve facing a perfectly competitive firm is a horizontal straight line, whereas that for the entire industry usually has a negative slope. Since under monopoly the firm is the industry, it follows that the demand curve for the firm is negatively sloped. This has special significance when we consider the profit-maximizing output level of the monopolist in comparison with that of the perfectly competitive firm. Therefore, we shall briefly discuss some of the essential conditions that apply when we introduce the negatively sloping demand curve into our analysis.

When the demand curve is a horizontal straight line, the average revenue (AR) or, equivalently, the price (P) is equal to the marginal revenue (MR). On the other hand, when the demand curve is negatively sloped, the demand curve is always the AR curve (in the absence of price discrimination), but the corresponding MR curve will be identical to or below the demand curve. From our earlier discussion (Chapters 3 and 6), remember that when an average curve is stationary, the corresponding marginal curve is identical to it, but when the average curve declines, the marginal curve is below it. This condition, which holds for both revenue and cost curves, makes the monopoly model a bit more complicated than the perfectly competitive model of Chapter 6. We shall illustrate the behavioral relationship between the price, total revenue (TR), AR, and MR that face the monopolist with a negatively sloped demand curve. Consider the hypothetical data given in Table 7.1. The market demand for the product is indicated

With a negatively sloped demand curve, AR ≠ MR for the monopolist

TABLE 7.1

Q	P	TR	AR	MR
3	$10.00	$ 30.00	$10.00	—
8	8.00	64.00	8.00	$6.80
15	7.40	111.00	7.40	6.71
21	7.00	147.00	7.00	6.00
26	6.75	175.50	6.75	5.70
30	6.55	196.50	6.55	5.25
33	6.20	204.60	6.20	2.70
35	6.00	210.00	6.00	2.70

by the first two columns, TR (the product of price and quantity) is given in column 3, AR, which is the same as price, is shown in column 4, and MR is shown in column 5.

Recall that TR is defined as the product of quantity and price, whereas MR is the change in TR divided by the change in quantity or, in the special discrete case, the additional TR attributable to one unit of additional sales. Theoretically, MR is defined for a small change in quantity, but in many cases the change may be quite large, as the data in Table 7.1 show. Consequently, the computed MR is actually the average MR over the corresponding quantity range. For example, the average MR for the 4th–8th units is

$$\text{MR} = \Delta\text{TR}/\Delta Q = 34/5 = 6.8$$

which is considered the MR of the 8th unit of the commodity. If we had more-detailed information, the MR for the 8th unit would be different from this figure. Thus, the figures can only be considered as approximations to the true MR.

The data of Table 7.1 have been plotted in Figure 7.1 in order to show the relationship between the AR and MR curves. Looking at Table 7.1 and Figure 7.1, it becomes readily apparent that the monopolist faces a different revenue profile than does the firm under perfect competition. Because the monopolist is the industry, the market will absorb a larger output only if price is reduced. Under perfect competition, we saw that the individual firm could sell any amount of its output without affecting market price; hence, the firm had only to concern itself with the cost of production. In the case of a monopoly, the firm must concern itself with both the demand (revenue) and cost behavior. As we shall observe later, the price elasticity of demand becomes a critical item in determining the level of output and market price for the product under monopoly.

FIGURE 7.1

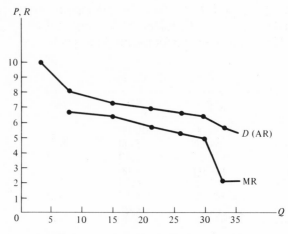

TABLE 7.2

Q	TFC	TVC	TC	MC
0	$50.00	$ 0	$ 50.00	—
3	50.00	11.00	61.00	$ 3.67
8	50.00	24.00	74.00	2.60
15	50.00	39.00	89.00	2.14
21	50.00	56.00	106.00	2.83
26	50.00	75.00	125.00	3.80
30	50.00	96.00	146.00	5.25
33	50.00	119.00	169.00	7.67
35	50.00	144.00	194.00	12.50

7.1.3 Cost of the Monopolist

Traditionally, the shapes of the various short-run cost curves of a monopoly and of a perfectly competitive firm are considered to be similar. There are good reasons for this assumption, one of which is theoretical convenience. Inasmuch as we have already discussed cost behavior at some length in Chapter 3, we shall simply provide the cost data necessary for illustrating the conditions of equilibrium. Students may wish to refer to this earlier chapter on plant size, output, and cost behavior in order to reinforce their understanding.

Hypothetical cost data for the monopolist are given in Table 7.2: the various quantities Q of the commodity produced; the total fixed cost (TFC), which, by definition, is a constant; the total variable cost (TVC) at each level of output; the total cost (TC), which is the sum of TFC and TVC for each level of output; and the marginal cost (MC). Since we have encountered similar cost curves before, we shall defer plotting them on a graph until later.

7.1.4 Short-Run Equilibrium of a Monopoly

The Total Revenue–Total Cost Approach

Since we are assuming that monopolists are unregulated and free to pursue their goal, that is, profit maximization, they will choose the output or the corresponding price—but not both (some textbooks use the wording "output and price," which is conceptually incorrect, as will become clear later in this chapter)—at which the difference between TR and TC (which is defined as profit) is largest. If we combine the relevant data from Tables 7.1 and 7.2 to form Table 7.3, it becomes obvious that our hypothetical monopolist will choose an output of either 26 or 30 units, which will, according to the demand schedule (i.e., Table 7.1), result in a price of either $6.75 or $6.55, respectively. Equivalently, the monopolist can choose a price of either $6.75 or $6.55, which

TABLE 7.3

Q	TR	TC	Total profit
3	$ 30.00	$ 61.00	$ -31.00
8	64.00	74.00	-10.00
15	111.00	89.00	22.00
21	147.00	106.00	41.00
26	175.50	125.00	50.50
30	196.50	146.00	50.50
33	204.60	169.00	35.60
35	210.00	194.00	16.00

The monopolist may choose either price or output, but not both, as the decision variable

will, according to the demand schedule (Table 7.1), result in a quantity sold of either 26 or 30 units, respectively. Note that if the monopolist chooses the quantity of 26 units, the market will determine the price of $6.75. Having chosen the level of output to be sold, the monopolist has no freedom to choose the price, since this is functionally determined by market demand. Alternatively, if the monopolist chooses a selling price, the quantity that can be marketed is functionally determined by the demand, that is, there is no longer any freedom to choose the quantity. This condition is often overlooked by many economists, who state that the monopolist can choose both the output and price level. As a result of such statements, many students become confused. It seems that some obvious misunderstanding about general business practice in mark-up pricing in economic theory is due to the confusion over the monopolist's freedom of choice. If the goal is profit maximization, the monopolist's freedom of choice is restricted to *either* price *or* quantity, but not both. We shall have more to say on this topic later in this chapter.

Table 7.3 shows that the highest possible total profit which our monopolist can make ($50.50) occurs at either a quantity of 26 or 30 units. The same information can be obtained graphically. In Figure 7.2, the distance between the TR and TC curves represents the total profit or total loss. When the TR curve is above

FIGURE 7.2

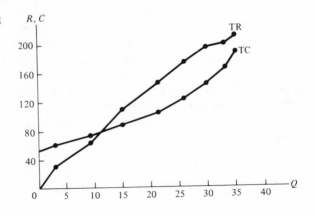

the TC curve, the profit is positive, whereas when the TR curve is below the TC curve, the profit is negative. The largest distance between these two curves occurs when the TR curve is above the TC curve at either 26 or 30 units. This indicates that the highest profit occurs at either 26 or 30 units of output (sales), which is the same result as obtained in Table 7.3.[1]

This example results in equal profit at both 26 and 30 units of output. In economics, this is referred to as a solution that is not unique. The trouble with this kind of situation is that we cannot make a definite assertion as to what quantity the monopolist will produce and put on the market. Some authors, such as Lancaster (1974), make an additional assumption.

Assumption 7.5. If more than one quantity results in the same maximum profit, the producer will always produce and sell the larger quantity.

Based on Assumption 7.5, we can assert that the monopolist will produce and sell 30 units.

The Marginal Revenue–Marginal Cost Approach

Neoclassical economics is generally referred to as the marginal analysis approach. The reason for this reference is that many key arguments in neoclassical economics are based on marginal concepts. The profit-maximization problem of the monopolist can be equivalently or better answered in terms of the MR and MC instead of the TR and TC. Table 7.4 combines the MC, MR, and profit information from Tables 7.1–7.3. It is seen that MR is equal to MC at 30 units of output and that at this level profit is also at a maximum.

The marginal approach results in a unique solution that is in agreement with Assumption 7.5; that is, the larger quantity will

TABLE 7.4

Q	MC	MR	Total profit
3	$ 3.67	—	$ − 31.00
8	2.60	$6.80	− 10.00
15	2.14	6.71	22.00
21	2.83	6.00	41.00
26	3.80	5.70	50.50
30	5.25	5.25	50.50
33	7.67	2.70	35.60
35	12.50	2.70	16.00

[1] For the sake of simplicity, we have used the terms output and sales to mean the same thing when discussing the monopolist's profit-maximizing decision. This presumes zero inventory.

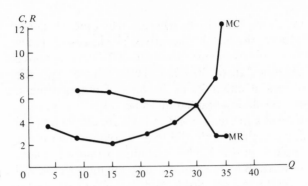

FIGURE 7.3

be produced if more than one quantity results in the same maximum profit. Figure 7.3 shows that the same result can be derived by graphical analysis. At 30 units of output, and only at 30 units of the output, MR is equal to MC. Although Figure 7.3 does not show the maximum profit as clearly as Figure 7.2, we can employ commonsense reasoning to prove that profit is indeed maximized when MR = MC. From Figure 7.3, it is seen that for any level of output less than 30 units, MR > MC; hence, any additional unit of output up to 30 units brings in more additional revenue than it costs. Thus, if production stops short of 30 units, profit cannot be a maximum because each additional unit can still bring in an additional profit. Conversely, for any output level greater than 30 units, MC > MR, which means that any additional units cost the monopolist more than they add to the TR. When this is the case, profit can obviously be increased by cutting output back to 30 units. Therefore, if profit cannot be at a maximum either above or below 30 units of output, it must be at a maximum when output is at 30 units. This proves our assertion that profit will be maximum when MR = MC. A rigorous mathematical proof of this assertion is presented in the appendix to this chapter.

Necessary and Sufficient Conditions for Maximum Profit

For increasing MC, the condition for profit-maximization is the same under monopoly and perfect competition

The condition MR = MC is a necessary but not sufficient condition for maximum profit. As in the case of the perfectly competitive firm, MR = MC may result in either maximum or minimum profit. Recall that profit will be maximized for a perfectly competitive firm if MR = MC and MC is increasing. In the monopoly case, we have similar but more complicated conditions for maximum profit to exist. Finally, we can write them as follows:

Necessary

$$MR = MC \tag{7.1}$$

Sufficient

$$MC \ increasing \tag{7.2a}$$

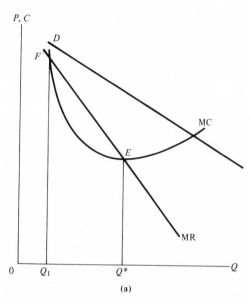

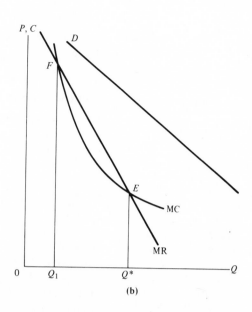

FIGURE 7.4

or

MC constant   (7.2b)

or

MC decreasing, but slower than MR.   (7.2c)

In other words, the profit of a monopoly will be maximized if MR = MC and MC is increasing, that is, the same conditions as for a perfectly competitive firm. However, due to the negatively sloped demand curve and the negatively sloped MR curve facing a monopoly, MC may not be increasing at the point of intersection between the MC and MR curves. In order to satisfy the maximum-profit condition, it is only necessary that MC decrease more slowly than MR. Figure 7.4 has been constructed to provide a visual demonstration of these two points. In part (a), MR = MC at both point E and point F. However, at F, both the MC curve and the MR curve are declining; however, since the MC curve is declining faster than the MR curve, output Q_1 will result in minimum profit or maximum loss. At point E, MR = MC, and the MC curve is rising whereas the MR curve is declining; there-fore, conditions (7.1) and (7.2a) are satisfied, and output Q^* results in maximum profit. In part (b), not only does MR = MC, but the MC curve is also declining at both point E and point F. However, the MC curve declines faster than the MR curve at F, but slower at E. Since conditions (7.1) and (7.2b) are satisfied only at E, output Q^* results in maximum profit, whereas output Q_1 gen-erates minimum profit. A commonsense proof, such as offered in the preceding section on the MR–MC approach, can be used to explain why Q^* results in maximum profit whereas Q_1 yields minimum profit. Students may wish to refer to that section and test their understanding of this important condition.

Profit or Loss in the Short Run

It should be pointed out once more that in the context of economic theory maximum profit does not imply positive profit. In economics, maximum profit is synonymous with minimum loss. Like a perfectly competitive firm, a monopolist can make either positive, zero, or even negative profit in short-run equilibrium. Also like the perfectly competitive firm, a monopolist does not have control over demand and must adjust output in response to the market demand for the product. An obvious example of this is the situation in a Communist country. Although the government-run business has almost absolute monopolistic power, it still cannot set a very high price and at the same time expect to sell a large amount of the commodity. Even under Communism, consumers can still refuse to buy a commodity if the price is too high. This further demonstrates our previous statement that a monopolist can only determine either quantity or price, but not both. Even a monopoly cannot freely set both its price and its quantity at any level if it wants to maximize profit. It is constrained by the market for its product (i.e., demand), on the one hand, and the input market and technology (i.e., cost), on the other hand. Under certain circumstances, a monopoly may be forced to take a loss in the short run, provided that the loss is less than the TFC. In this respect, it is not different from the perfectly competitive firm.

> *Like the perfectly competitive firm, a monopolist must adjust output in response to market demand*

Although Figures 7.3 and 7.4 identify the profit-maximizing output in each case, they do not indicate whether the profit is positive, zero, or negative. Since the price and AR curves are the same, we need the ATC curve in our diagrams in order to determine whether positive, zero, or negative profits are generated. To illustrate these different circumstances, parts (a)–(c) of Figure 7.5 have been drawn to show positive, zero, and negative profit, respectively. In all three cases, quantity Q^* results in maximum profit [it can be checked that conditions (7.1) and (7.2c) are satisfied in all three cases]. In part (a), by definition, TR = $\overline{0Q^*} \times \overline{0P^*}$, that is, the product of price and quantity, which is represented geometrically by the area of the rectangle $0P^*AQ^*$. On the other hand, TC = $\overline{BQ^*} \times \overline{0Q^*}$, that is, the product of ATC and quantity, which is respresented geometrically by the area of the rectangle $0CBQ^*$. Profit π is defined as the difference between TR and TC, that is, $\pi =$ TR $-$ TC, which in part (a) is represented geometrically by the area of the rectangle $ABCP^*$. Since, in this case, TR $>$ TC, the profit is positive. For similar reasons, in part (b) the profit is zero because TR $=$ TC, whereas in part (c) the profit is negative because TR $-$ TC < 0.

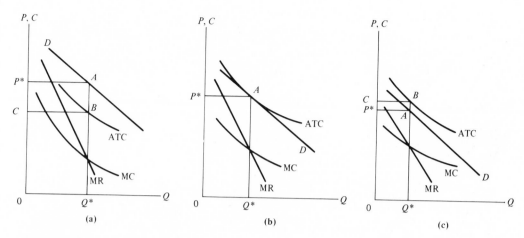

FIGURE 7.5

As in the case of a perfectly competitive firm in the short run, a monopoly's short-run loss must be less than the TFC. In other words, in order to keep the monopoly in business, at equilibrium, the price must be greater than or at least equal to the AVC. However, whereas the shutdown point for a perfectly competitive firm is the minimum AVC, in the case of a monopoly the minimum AVC is not the shutdown point. In fact, there is no such thing as a single shutdown point under monopoly. The factor determining whether a monopoly will shut down or stay in business is whether the price is equal to the AVC at the profit-maximizing output level. When the price is less than the AVC at this level, the monopoly will shut down; otherwise, it will stay in business even if it does not cover all its fixed costs in the short run. For example, in part (c) of Figure 7.5, we assume that the AVC for Q^* is less than $\overline{Q^*A}$ or the price P^*. Should the AVC exceed $\overline{Q^*A}$ for output Q^*, then Q^* would no longer be the equilibrium quantity. Instead, zero would be the equilibrium output, that is, a shutdown in operations.

7.1.5 Supply Under Monopoly in the Short Run

As we have shown in Chapter 6, the short-run supply curve of a perfectly competitive firm is the rising portion of its MC curve which lies above the minimum AVC. For a monopoly, it is an entirely different story. To say the least, supply under monopoly does not have the same meaning as under perfect competition. The supply function of a firm, as defined by economists, is the relationship between the market price and the quantity that a firm is able and willing to sell, other things being equal. The term "other things being equal" here includes technology and input prices, which implies that the cost curves of the firm are given. Under these circumstances and the assumption of profit max-

Under monopoly there is no single or unique supply curve

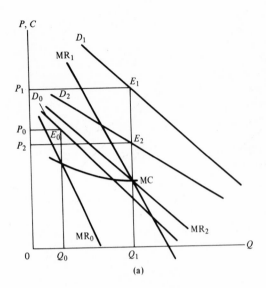

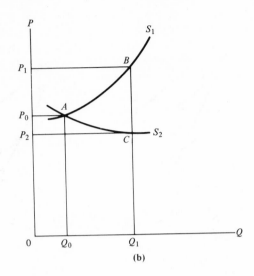

FIGURE 7.6

imization as the goal of a firm, a relevant portion of the MC curve comprises the short-run supply curve of a perfectly competitive firm regardless of how demand shifts. However, for a given set of cost curves, the price–quantity relationship that a monopoly is able and willing to supply depends on the pattern of shifts in demand. For this reason, there exist an infinite number of supply curves for a monopoly for a given set of cost curves. This can be demonstrated by referring to Figure 7.6.

In part (a), MC is the given marginal cost curve of the monopoly. Suppose that the initial demand is D_0 and that the associated marginal revenue is MR_0. The profit-maximizing output is Q_0 and the market price is P_0. The point $\langle Q_0, P_0 \rangle$ is plotted in part (b) as point A. Next, suppose that the demand shifts to D_1 with marginal revenue MR_1. The new equilibrium output is Q_1 and the corresponding market price is P_1. The point $\langle Q_1, P_1 \rangle$ is plotted in part (b) as point B. A curve connecting E_0 and E_1 can be the locus of the profit-maximizing quantity–price pairs generated by a particular pattern of demand shifts. The corresponding curve in part (b), labeled S_1, can be regarded as a monopoly supply curve for the particular pattern of demand shifts. However, with a different pattern of demand shifts, a different supply curve would have been generated. For example, if demand had shifted to D_2 instead of D_1, the quantity supplied would still be Q_1, since MR_2 intersects MC at the same point as MR_1 intersects MC. However, the market price would be $P_2 < P_1$, and the associated point in part (b) would be C. The supply curve based on this specific shift of demand would be S_2, which is significantly different from S_1. In fact, S_1 is positively sloped and S_2 negatively sloped. Thus, with a negatively sloped MC curve, the slope of the corresponding supply curve (if it can be called a supply curve at all) can be either positive or negative. As a matter of fact, it could be horizontal. The shapes of the curves in part (b) essentially depend on the pattern of the shifts of demand. This kind of curve does not agree with the true meaning of a supply curve in economics, where supply should be independent from demand.

For the reasons given above, economists might be better off disregarding the concept of a supply function in the analysis of a monopoly. For that matter, they might disregard the concept of a supply function with respect to all imperfect markets. It is the joint behavior of demand and cost—not supply—which is essential to the theory of imperfect markets.

7.1.6 Long-Run Equilibrium of a Monopoly

In general, long-run equilibrium must also imply short-run equilibrium. However, short-run equilibrium does not necessarily imply long-run equilibrium. Thus, the long-run adjustment that usually results in a change in plant size changes one short-run equilibrium to another, still in accord with long-run equilibrium.

A monopoly is marked by the absence of competitors. Consequently, in contrast to the firm under perfect competition, for which long-run economic (excess) profit is necessarily zero, a monopoly may earn long-run economic profit. However, the economic profit of a monopoly, as well as that of a perfectly competitive firm, cannot be negative in the long run. Theoretically, a monopoly can earn either positive or zero economic profit, but zero economic profit can only be coincidental. By the nature of its condition, it is more likely that a monopoly will earn a positive economic profit in long-run equilibrium.

Unlike the perfectly competitive firm, the monopolist can earn a positive profit in the long run

As we have concluded earlier in this chapter, a monopoly can earn either positive, zero, or negative economic profit in the short run. If a monopoly incurs a short-run negative economic profit or loss, it will be forced to look for other, more-profitable uses for its resources. One possibility is that its existing plant size is not optimal and that it can earn positive or at least zero economic profit if its plant size is altered appropriately. If this is the case, these alterations will be made and the monopoly will remain in business. On the other hand, if there does not exist a plant size that will enable the monopoly to avoid negative economic profit or loss in the long run, it will leave the industry. We shall now illustrate the long-run adjustment process, starting with negative short-run profit.

Consider Figure 7.7, in which AC and MC are the long-run average and marginal cost curves, whereas D and MR are the demand and marginal revenue curves. The original plant size of

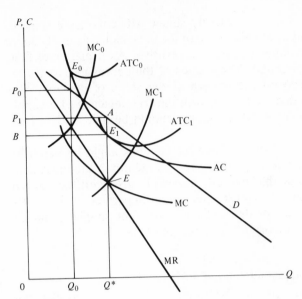

FIGURE 7.7

the monopoly is indicated by ATC_0 and MC_0.[2] With the given demand and the associated MR and MC curves, the quantity–price pair $\langle Q_0, P_0 \rangle$ results in a short-run, maximum-profit, equilibrium condition of the monopoly. From Figure 7.7, it can be seen that due to the small plant size, short-run maximum profit is negative because the AC $(\overline{Q_0 E_0})$ is greater than the price P_0. However, there are plant sizes that will result in long-run positive economic profit, as indicated by the range where AC is below D, which is also the average revenue curve. Among the infinite number of plant sizes that could result in positive economic profit, the one that results in maximum long-run positive profit is characterized by the intersection of the long-run marginal cost curve MC and the marginal revenue curve MR at point E, with quantity Q^* of the commodity being produced. Since long-run equilibrium must also imply short-run equilibrium, the short-run marginal cost curve corresponding to the optimal plant size, MC_1, must also intersect the marginal revenue curve, MR at point E. In short, the long-run optimal plant size that maximizes long-run profit is represented by ATC_1 and MC_1, which, as we have noted, denote a unique short-run condition for profit maximization when given the demand and associated MR curves. With quantity Q^*, the economic profit is positive because price P_1 is greater than the AC $(\overline{Q^* E_1})$. The resultant total economic profit to the monopoly is represented by the area of the rectangle $P_1 A E_1 B$.

An interesting phenomenon often overlooked in the graphical

---

[2] This combination of an ATC curve and the corresponding MC curve, as well as subsequent combinations, can be conceived of as a series of short-run cost curves, each representing a different plant size and scale of operation.

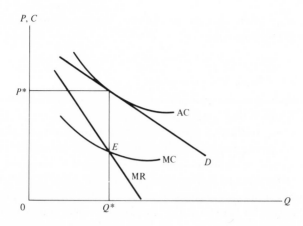

FIGURE 7.8

analysis is that the long-run adjustment of a monopoly from a negative economic profit condition in the short run to a positive economic profit condition in the long run (in fact, another short-run equilibrium) is not necessarily at the expense of consumers. This suggests that, in real life, mismanagement of a monopoly may do more harm to consumers than the higher profits of well-managed monopolistic firms. In making such a statement, we do not imply an advocacy of monopoly, but only point out a theoretical possibility that may deserve empirical research.

Consumer welfare and long-run monopoly profits are not necessarily incompatible

We have illustrated the long-run adjustment from a negative economic profit position to a positive economic profit position. The long-run adjustment that starts from a positive or zero economic profit short-run equilibrium is very similar to the above case. Students may wish to try drawing similar graphs in order to test their understanding of the adjustment process.

We have mentioned above that a monopoly in long-run equilibrium may earn either positive or zero economic profit. It should be pointed out, however, that if the demand and cost conditions are such that a monopoly can only earn zero economic profit in the long run, it must be impossible to earn a positive economic profit in the short run, since the status quo is always available to the monopoly in the long run. Hence, the long-run adjustment process that leads to zero long-run economic profit must start from a short-run position where economic profit is negative or zero. In the latter case, no adjustment is necessary. The case of zero economic profit in long-run equilibrium is illustrated in Figure 7.8.

In summary, the long-run maximum-profit position of a monopoly is identified by the intersection of the long-run MC curve and the MR curve, provided that MC is actually increasing or else decreasing more slowly than MR at the point of intersection. A monopoly can earn either a positive or a zero economic profit in long-run equilibrium, but logic tells us that it will not continue to operate at negative economic profit. As we noted earlier, it is more likely that the monopolist will earn positive economic profit in the long run.

7.1.7 Price Discrimination

Price discrimination occurs when a homogeneous product is sold at more than one price in the same place and at the same time. Two conditions are necessary for price discrimination. First of all, there must be identifiable, distinct markets; that is, the customers in different markets can easily be identified, and the price elasticities of demand are not the same for the different markets. Secondly, the commodity or service under consideration cannot easily be transferred. The former condition is obvious, since a monopoly cannot practice price discrimination if it does not face distinct groups of customers, whereas price discrimination would not benefit the monopoly if the demands or price elasticities of demand were the same for the different markets. The second condition is necessary because it would hardly be practical to sell a product at $1 per unit to one group of individuals and at $2 per unit to another group if the product could be transferred without cost from the first group to the second group. If this were the case, either a profit-motivated secondary market or nonprofit-motivated transfer (or both) would eliminate the higher-priced market.

As an example of price discrimination, consider that in certain cities some movie houses charge a lower price to students. The student demand is different from the nonstudent demand due to differences in taste and income. Furthermore, since students must present identification cards, nonstudents cannot obtain student tickets. All conditions for price discrimination are satisfied. Note that we are dealing with a homogeneous product because every customer—students as well as nonstudents—has equal access to any vacant seat in the theater, irrespective of the type of ticket they hold.

The degree of price discrimination depends on the divisibility of consumers into separate markets

Theoretically, a monopoly can charge each customer a different price according to individual demand. This is the so-called *discrimination of the first degree*. *Second-degree price discrimination* refers to the case where a monopoly charges different prices to many different groups of customers, but not to the extent that each customer is charged a different price. When all customers can be classified into two groups and each group is charged a different price, we have *third-degree price discrimination*, which we shall illustrate by means of Figure 7.9.

In Figure 7.9, the demand for one market is given by curve D_1 and that for the other market by curve D_2. The associated marginal revenue curves are MR_1 and MR_2. The aggregate demand (curve D) of the two markets is the horizontal sum of curves D_1 and D_2 (recall the derivation of the market demand curve from individual consumer demand curves in Chapter 5); MR, the mar-

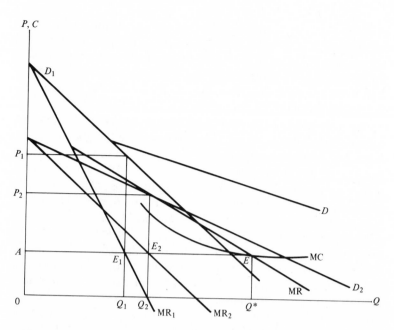

FIGURE 7.9

ginal revenue curve associated with the aggregate market demand, is the horizontal sum of MR_1 and MR_2; and MC is the
marginal cost curve for the monopoly. Since we are assuming a
homogeneous product, the MC is the same whether the product
is sold in market 1, market 2, or both. Hence, we have only one
MC curve for the monopoly. The monopoly's profit will be maximized when MR = MC, that is, at point E.[3] Thus, the profit-
maximizing output is Q^*. However, to be effective and maximize
profits, a monopoly that practices price discrimination not only
must equate its MC to its aggregate MR, but also must equate its
MC to the MRs of all its markets, so that $MC = MR_1 = MR_2$.
This can be explained by common sense.

Profit-maximization with price discrimination requires that MR in each market be equal

The reason that the profit of the monopoly will be maximized
when $MC = MR_1 = MR_2$ is simply an extension of the arguments
given in our discussion of the MR–MC approach (Section 7.1.4);
there is no need to repeat it here. The reason that $MR_1 = MR_2$
signifies maximum profit can also be explained by common sense.
Suppose that $MR_1 \neq MR_2$, for example, $MR_1 = \$2$ and MR_2
$= \$1$. This means that the monopoly can get $2 from selling one
additional unit in market 1 as opposed to $1 from selling one
additional unit in market 2. This also means that if the monopoly
cuts one unit in market 2, it loses $1 in revenue, but if it turns
around and sells this unit in market 1, it gains $2 in revenue. This

---

[3] It can be checked in this case that the second-order condition for profit maximization is also satisfied.

combined action results in the same number of units sold, but a net gain of $2 - 1 = \$1$. Obviously, the profit of a monopoly is not maximum when $MR_1 > MR_2$. A similar argument will show that a monopoly's profit cannot be maximum when $MR_2 > MR_1$. Thus, $MR_1 = MR_2$ is a necessary condition for the earning of a maximum profit by the monopoly.

The allocation of the profit-maximizing output Q^* to the two separate markets can easily be explained once the above reasoning is fully understood. In Figure 7.9, it can be seen that only Q_1 and Q_2 satisfy the condition $MC = MR_1 = MR_2$, where $\overline{Q^*E} = \overline{Q_1E_1} = \overline{Q_2E_2}$. From the construction of MR, we have $\overline{AE} = \overline{AE_1} + \overline{AE_2}$, which in turn implies $\overline{0Q^*} = \overline{0Q_1} + \overline{0Q_2}$. Hence, if the monopoly allocates Q_1 and Q_2 of the product in market 1 and market 2, respectively, it will sell precisely the profit-maximizing quantity Q^*, and its profit will be maximized. When this allocation of output (product) to the two markets is made, the demand curves D_1 and D_2 will determine the prices P_1 and P_2 in markets 1 and 2, respectively. We observe that the price in market 1 is higher than that in market 2. We state the following without proof: It is always true that the market with a higher price elasticity of demand will have a lower price and vice versa. (A rigorous mathematical proof of this statement will be given in the appendix to this chapter.)

7.1.8 Natural Monopoly and Public Regulation

When increasing returns to scale or constant AVC prevails in production, the long-run AC will decrease. In this case, the industry is called a *natural monopoly*. Under these circumstances, forced competition is neither practical nor beneficial to consumers, since the breaking up of the monopoly into smaller units would simply raise costs by preventing the cost reductions inherent on the basis of size. Therefore, public regulation is a compromise method of dealing with this situation. However, there are theoretical and practical problems in regulating price under monopoly.

The natural monopoly situation is illustrated in Figure 7.10, in which AC and MC are the average and marginal cost curves, respectively, D is the demand curve, and MR is the associated marginal revenue curve. Without regulation, Q_1 is the profit-maximizing output of the monopolist and the demand, in turn, determines the market price P_1. The monopoly earns a positive economic profit represented by the area of the rectangle $ABCP_1$. It has been shown that in advanced economic theory it is the quantity–price pair $\langle Q_3, P_3 \rangle$ that will provide maximum economic welfare to society as a whole. In other words, a regulatory agency should set a price P_3 in order to maximize economic welfare. However, this will create a problem because at P_3 consumers will buy Q_3, whereas with this quantity AC is $\overline{GQ_3}$, which is greater than the price P_3 or AR. This will result in a total negative

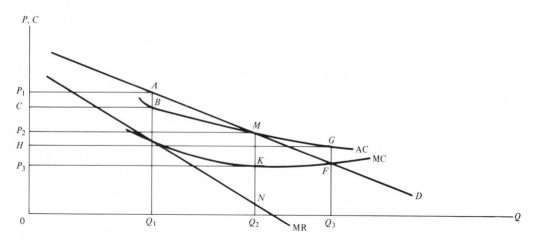

FIGURE 7.10

economic profit, represented by the area of the rectangle $FGHP_3$.
Since we are talking about the long run (i.e., increasing returns
to scale), the monopoly will not stay in business. If the commodity
or service is desirable, the only way to keep the monopoly in
business is to provide a public subsidy in the amount of $FGHP_3$.
The political problems associated with subsidizing a monopoly
and the difficulties associated with the determination of demand
and MC behavior have led, in practice, to *average cost pricing*
in the public utility field. In Figure 7.10, such a compromise price
is P_2, which is determined by the intersection of the demand or
AR curve and the long-run AC curve.

*Marginal cost
pricing, though
theoretically
sound, may not be
administratively
practical*

   If we are perceptive, we see that regulation, in fact, changes
the shapes of the effective demand and MR curves of the monopoly. Without regulation, the demand curve is the straight line
D, whereas the associated MR curve is the straight line MR. With
a regulated ceiling price P_2, the monopoly is free to charge a
lower (but not higher) price, and the effective demand curve
becomes P_2MD. Consequently, the associated MR curve now
consists of the two disconnected line segments $\overline{P_2M}$ and the segment of MR to the right of Q_2, that is, $\overline{NMR}$. The reason for the
discontinuity of the MR curve is that price discrimination is not
allowed. As long as the monopoly charges the ceiling price, it,
like the perfectly competitive firm, finds its demand curve horizontal, and MR = AR = P_2. At P_2, it can sell Q_2 according to
the demand curve. However, if it wants to sell more than Q_2, it
has to lower the price below P_2. Since no price discrimination
is allowed, the lower price is not only applied to the additional
unit, but also to all Q_2 units. As a result, the MR curve will
manifest a drastic drop at Q_2, resulting in its discontinuity at this
quantity. The implication of this situation is that, in Figure 7.10,
MC falls in the gap of MR between M and N. In a sense, the
first-order condition for maximum profit of a monopoly is satisfied

at Q_2 and the corresponding price P_2. There is no incentive for the monopoly to reduce its price below P_2 as long as MC is between M and N. On the other hand, should MC fall below N, the regulated price would no longer be effective. Profit maximization would call for higher quantity than Q_2 and, consequently, a lower price than P_2.

It is interesting to point out that in the case where a price ceiling is combined with first-degree price discrimination, the market could potentially be extended to Q_3, and hence the price would be as high as P_2 for the majority of consumers, but as low as P_3 for some others. The profit of the monopoly would also be increased from zero to positive (represented by the area of the triangle $\triangle FKM$) because, with first-degree price discrimination, the MR curve $\overparen{P_2MD}$ will no longer be discontinuous. On the surface it seems that some people would be better off and no one worse off if we moved from a uniform price system to some form of price discrimination. On this basis alone, regulation combined with price discrimination might result in higher economic welfare for society as a whole. Although such a possibility would seem to exist on theoretical grounds, in practice, however, the difficulties (mentioned above) associated both with the determination of demand and with deciding how to carry out price discrimination may render the theoretically superior possibility impractical. Furthermore, the above arguments are valid only under the assumption that those who pay a higher price such as P_2 are not unhappy when someone else pays a lower price such as P_3, that is, Assumption 4.5—the absence of externality. The final observation on this problem is that public utility pricing to maximize economic welfare is not conclusive. However, it may deserve more research, and some thoughtful students may want to give it some consideration.

Public regulation under conditions of constant AVC can also be illustrated graphically. Consider Figure 7.11, in which D is the demand curve and MR is the associated marginal revenue curve.

Given constant AVC, MC pricing always results in a loss to the monopolist

Suppose that the monopoly has already chosen its optimal plant size. The straight line AVC = MC is the monopoly's constant average variable cost (and marginal cost) curve. As was shown in Chapter 3, the average total cost (ATC) is an asymptotically decreasing function, and AVC is the asymptote. Without public regulation, the profit-maximizing quantity is Q_1, or, equivalently, the profit-maximizing price is P_1. On the other hand, the social welfare maximizing price according to MC pricing is P_3, and the corresponding quantity is Q_3. Since ATC is always above AVC, and in this special case AVC = MC, MC pricing always results in a loss to the monopolist. If a government subsidy to monopolists is politically impractical, a compromise alternative is that of AC pricing, which will result in a market price of P_2. This result is very similar to the traditional, U-shaped AC and MC curves as shown in Figure 7.10. Thus, the analysis of public reg-

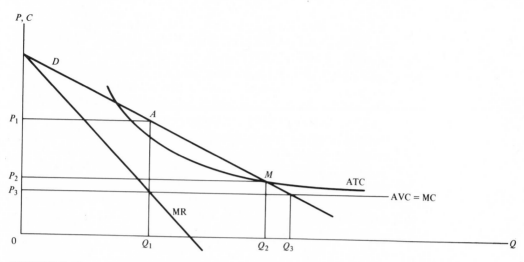

FIGURE 7.11

ulation in natural monopoly can be carried out without difficulty under conditions of constant AVC and MC.

7.2 PRICING MODELS ACTUALLY USED BY PRICE MAKERS— MARK-UP PRICING

As we mentioned earlier, based on certain criteria, a firm can be classified as fitting one of several economic models. Whether a firm should be properly classified as a monopoly or an oligopoly depends on the criteria employed. In reality, very few cases (if any) satisfy the pure monopoly assumption of only one firm (i.e., Assumption 7.3). On the other hand, many firms act as a monopoly according to the profit-maximization assumption of economic modeling. The essential difference between monopoly and oligopoly in economic theory is that the decision criteria of a monopoly take only the cost and demand information of the monopoly into consideration, not the possible reactions of its competitors, since, by definition, a meaningful competitor does not exist. Under perfect competition, the criteria have a similar characteristic because there are so many small competitors that the reaction of each is negligible and can be ignored for practical purposes. Under oligopoly, however, the story is entirely different. In this case, a competitor's reaction to the decision of the firm is significant and must be taken into consideration. Therefore, an essential feature of the oligopoly model is the reaction of competitors and how to incorporate this feature into the decision rules for analyzing price and output behavior and its impact on society.

Under monopoly the reaction of competitors need not be considered in setting price

Let us consider the nature of the oligopoly problem. Suppose that a firm is trying to determine the price at which to sell its commodity. Obviously, there are many internal and external factors to be taken into consideration. The most important external (to the firm, not the industry) factors are customer behavior and possible competitor behavior. In economics, all factors concerning cost are contained in the *cost function*, all relevant information concerning customer behavior is contained in the *demand function*, and all relevant information associated with competitor behavior is contained in the *reaction function*. The analysis of the profit-maximization conditions of the firm under the perfectly competitive model of Chapter 6 and under the pure monopoly model of the first part of this chapter took into consideration only cost and customer (or market) demand and ignored the reaction of competitors. As we noted above, under perfect competition, the existence of many small competitors and the negligible reaction of each made it practical to ignore the reaction of competitors. Under monopoly, our definition of one seller made this consideration unnecessary. For this reason, if a firm is a price maker rather than a price taker, and its price-setting rule does not explicitly take competitor reaction into consideration, then the firm can be considered a monopoly for analytical purposes even if it is not the only firm in the industry.[4] It is in this light of ignoring competitor reaction that we examine the following mark-up pricing models within the construct of monopoly.

7.2.1 A Naive Mark-Up Pricing Model

Many firms, especially those in the retail trade, use a very simple mark-up method to set their prices. The selling price of a commodity is usually determined by a certain percentage mark-up on the wholesale price paid by the retailer. The mark-up, which is usually referred to as the *profit margin* by businesspeople, actually includes fixed and capital costs. The difference in the treatment of cost in economics and in business stems from a conceptual difference in defining profit (see Chapter 3). In economics, cost includes a normal return to capital, whereas in business accounting, the return to capital [at least the return to that part of capital which is provided by the owner(s), such as stock] is not considered as cost, but is rather considered as profit. In economics, a normal return to capital is that return which is necessary to retain capital in the enterprise or industry. Economic (or excess) profit is that return which is more then necessary to retain capital in the industry. On the other hand, gross profit in business includes (at least partly) capital cost and sometimes some other

---

[4] Although the oligopoly model will not be discussed until Chapter 9, we thought it would be useful to provide the student with the basic distinction between monopoly, perfect competition, and oligopoly in order to appreciate and understand better the discussion on mark-up pricing that follows. Otherwise, we felt that students might confuse mark-up pricing with oligopoly.

fixed costs. However, since capital cost is part of the fixed cost in the short run, and the conditions of profit maximization are essentially based on variable and marginal cost, the conceptual difference between economics and business will not materially affect our analysis.[5]

Because the practice is most generally employed in the retail trade, the naive mark-up model offers us a good point of departure for beginning a fairly extensive description and analysis of mark-up pricing.

The naive mark-up pricing model can be written

$$P = av \tag{7.3}$$

where P is the price, v is the AVC (in many cases, the wholesale price), and $a > 1$ is called the *mark-up parameter*.

In many cases, the AVC is constant as we have argued in Chapter 3. However, it is not essential that v should be constant. Even if v is a decreasing function or an increasing function of the quantity of the commodity produced or sold, the naive mark-up pricing method can be carried out provided that the quantity is known.

Mark-up pricing does not assure profit

The determination of the mark-up parameter a is a complicated matter both in practice and in theory. It may require considerable research in order to answer the following question: What factors determine the magnitude of a? The models that we shall deal with later in this chapter offer some hint on the answer to this question. For our present purposes, we may consider a as subjectively determined.

Note that the mark-up pricing based on (7.3) can, at most, determine the profit per unit. It does not give the total profit, which is the most important figure of interest to the business-person.

In order to calculate the total profit, two more pieces of information are needed: the TFC and the quantity to be sold. If we denote the TFC by F and the quantity to be sold by Q^*, then the total revenue R and total cost C are[6]

$$R = PQ^* = avQ^* \tag{7.4}$$

$$C = F + vQ^* \tag{7.5}$$

---

[5] In the long run, there are no fixed costs because all inputs can be varied; hence, returns to capital cannot be considered as comprised of two separate parts, that is, one to cover fixed costs and one to cover capital invested by the owners of the enterprise. In the short run, whether we treat the profit as the businessperson does or as the economist does is really immaterial, since profit maximization is based on the behavior of MC on the one hand, and MR on the other hand. Once profit is maximized, the returns to capital and the coverage of fixed costs will also be maximized.

[6] Note use of R and C, as opposed to TR and TC, to facilitate mathematical manipulation here and elsewhere.

By definition, the total profit π is[7]

$$\pi = R - C = (a - 1)Q^*v - F \gtreqless 0 \qquad (7.6)$$

$$\text{for} \quad Q^* \gtreqless F/(a - 1)v \quad \text{and} \quad a \neq 1$$

Even though there is a positive mark-up on AVC (in business jargon, a positive profit margin), the actual profit to the firm could be either positive, zero, or negative due to the fixed or overhead cost and the uncertainty of quantity, which is as yet unknown.

In (7.6), F and v are usually known to the firm, whereas a—the mark-up parameter—is determined by the firm. It may seem that the firm can always make a positive profit if a sufficiently high a is chosen. However, we are dealing with a monopoly; that is, the firm is the industry and is faced with a negatively sloped demand curve. Since a negatively sloped demand curve implies that Q^* is a decreasing function of a, that is, the higher the mark-up on price the less quantity will be sold, it follows that a cannot be independently chosen. Therefore, the monopolist or price maker must have some idea of the relationship between a and Q. This can be demonstrated by a simple linear demand function:

$$P = B - bQ \qquad (7.7)$$

where P is the price, Q is the quantity demanded, and B and b are positive constants. Equating the P in (7.7) and the P in (7.3), we obtain

$$av = B - bQ \qquad (7.8)$$

which yields

$$Q = B/b - (v/b)a \qquad (7.9)$$

Since both b and v are positive, Q is obviously a decreasing function of a; that is, when a increases, Q necessarily decreases. For this reason, if the demand function is known, under certain conditions a can be chosen such that the profit shown in (7.6) can be maximized.

The trouble with business decisions in reality is that the demand function is not known. Consequently, the mark-up parameter a is, in practice, chosen by some kind of rule of thumb or trial and error. This is perhaps why many economists consider this kind of business practice as "rule of thumb" without much theoretical importance, whereas some even consider it as contrary to the profit-maximization rule of economic theory. (We shall have more to say about this later.) However, this is the simplest mark-up pricing model. It is simple almost to the extent of naiveté. However, its advantage is precisely in its simplicity, that is, it is easy

---

[7] For decreasing or increasing AVC, v in the above expressions should be written v^*, which denotes the AVC at Q^*. Thus, constant AVC is not essential in mark-up pricing.

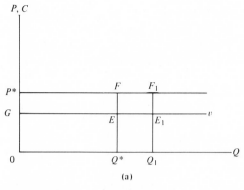
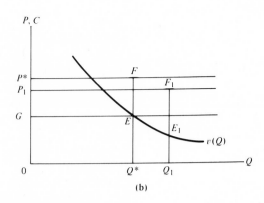

FIGURE 7.12

to carry out. As a result, most (if not all) small-scale businesses use this kind of pricing technique. If the price is profit maximizing, it will only be so by rare coincidence.

Naive mark-up pricing can also be illustrated graphically, as shown in Figure 7.12. In part (a), we have the case of a firm with constant AVC. The mark-up parameter is $a = \overline{0P^*}/\overline{0G} > 1$. In the case of the firm with decreasing AVC [part (b)], for a given mark-up parameter, the mark-up price will depend on the quantity sold. For Q^*

$$a = \overline{Q^*F}/\overline{Q^*E} > 1 \qquad \text{and} \qquad P^* = av^*$$

where $v^* = \overline{Q^*E}$. For Q_1,

$$a = \overline{Q_1F_1}/\overline{Q_1E_1} = \overline{Q^*F}/\overline{Q^*E} \qquad \text{and } P_1 = av_1$$

With decreasing AVC, given a mark-up parameter, the mark-up price depends on the quantity sold

where $v_1 = \overline{Q_1E_1}$. Let $\overline{Q_1F_1} = k\overline{Q^*F}$; then $\overline{Q_1E_1} = k\overline{Q^*E}$, since $\overline{Q_1F_1}/\overline{Q_1E_1} = \overline{Q^*F}/\overline{Q^*E}$ implies

$$\overline{Q_1F_1} \times \overline{Q^*E} = \overline{Q_1E_1} \times \overline{Q^*F}$$

By substitution, we have

$$k\overline{Q^*F} \times \overline{Q^*E} = \overline{Q_1E} \times \overline{Q^*F}$$

and $\overline{Q^*F}$ on both sides cancel out. The mark-up on AVC for quantity Q^* is $\overline{EF}$, whereas for Q_1 it is $\overline{E_1F_1}$. Since

$$\overline{E_1F_1} = \overline{Q_1F_1} - \overline{Q_1E_1} = k\overline{Q^*F} - k\overline{Q^*E} = k\overline{EF}, \quad k < 1$$

the absolute mark-up on AVC is proportionally less when quantity increases with decreasing AVC and a constant mark-up parameter. This results in a proportional decrease in price, since

$$P_1 = av_1 = a\overline{Q_1E_1} = ak\overline{Q^*E} = kav^* = kP^*$$

Students may use a parallel argument to illustrate that the mark-up price will increase proportionally with the increase in AVC when quantity increases in the case of increasing AVC. Similarly, the mark-up price will be a constant for constant AVC regardless of the quantity.

The above argument is based on the implicit assumption that the mark-up parameter a is independent of the quantity Q. If a is a function of Q, then entirely different results will be derived. More empirical research on business behavior is required in order to identify whether a is a function of Q and, if so, in what way.

In both part (a) and part (b) of Figure 7.12, the TVC is given by rectangle $0Q^*EG$, the TFC and profit are given by rectangle $GEFP^*$, and the TR is given by rectangle $0Q^*FP^*$ for P^* and Q^*. The profit can be either positive or negative, depending on the TFC.

7.2.2 Average Cost Mark-Up Pricing

In Section 7.2.1, the price was derived by a simple mark-up on the AVC. In that model, the mark-up included not only possible profit, but also fixed cost. The important consideration is the proper choice of the mark-up parameter. Once the mark-up parameter is determined, the clerical staff can carry out the actual pricing work. Furthermore, when market conditions change, the mark-up parameter can easily be changed. Therefore, it is a simple and very flexible way to set a price in practice. When a firm sells various items of nonstandard merchandise, and each item constitutes a very small proportion of the total business of the firm (such as in the retail trade), the allocation of overhead or fixed cost to the various items can be quite difficult, if not impossible. Therefore, the naive mark-up pricing model of Section 7.2.1 is a practical way to do business. This is perhaps why many, if not all, firms in the retail trade actually use the naive mark-up pricing method.

On the other hand, there are cases where each item produced by a firm is different from every other item and the revenue from each item is a significant proportion of the total income of the firm for an entire year. This would be the case for electric generators produced and sold by Westinghouse. Each generator is different in some way from every other generator, and each generator may cost millions of dollars. Under these circumstances, the proper allocation of overhead or fixed cost to each item produced becomes essential because the failure of any item to cover its proper share of overhead cost can mean the difference between a positive or negative profit for the year. The essential difference between the naive pricing model of Section 7.2.1 and the model of this section is that the former is based on a mark-up on the AVC, whereas the latter is based on the ATC in the accounting sense, that is, ATC excluding a return to equity capital. This latter pricing model is actually used by certain divisions of Westinghouse. In describing the AC mark-up pricing model we shall

AC mark-up pricing implies knowledge of product overhead costs

attempt to preserve the usage of terms as traditionally employed by Westinghouse and other users of this method. However, where there is an essential difference between business practice and economic theory, we shall offer a brief explanatory note in order to avoid any confusion that might result from differences in terminology. We shall first describe the terms used in AC mark-up pricing, followed by an outline of the process by which price is actually determined. We then conclude our discussion with a brief analysis of the model, comparing it to the naive model with respect to some of the more salient features of each.

Definition: Direct Costs. Costs that, theoretically, will occur only if a job is undertaken. These usually include material, factory labor, engineering, and other factory-related costs. Direct costs are sometimes referred to as the *base cost* or *variable costs*.

Definition: Overhead Costs. All costs other than direct costs. Overhead costs are sometimes referred to as *semivariable* or *fixed cost*. Total cost (TC) = Direct Cost (VC) + Overhead (FC), and ATC = AVC + AFC, where ATC, AVC, and AFC denote average total, average variable, and average fixed cost, respectively. Note that a normal return to capital, which is considered as part of cost in economics, is not included in the cost computation here; rather, it is considered a part of profit. As we said earlier, this distinction, although important in economic logic, is not such as to pose a problem in the application and use of AC mark-up pricing.

Definition: Income Before/After Taxes. Net income (profit) before taxes IBT = SB − TC, where SB is sales billed (customer price). Since corporate income tax is 48%, income after taxes IAT = $0.52 \times$ IBT (52% of IBT).

The zero profit multiplier (ZPM = TC/VC) is usually computed by using the previous year's cost figures for a division, a department, or a product line. Thus, in computing the ZPM, TC and VC are the total cost and total variable cost, respectively, for Q units. However, the ZPM can be used to compute the total cost for individual items because

Use of ZPM for total cost estimation assumes prior knowledge of VC and TC behavior

$$ZPM = \frac{TC}{VC} = \frac{ATC \times Q}{AVC \times Q} = \frac{ATC}{AVC}$$

The Pricing Process

Step 1. Compute the direct or variable cost.
Step 2. Compute the total cost for one unit of the product (e.g., a generator) by using the established ZPM:

$$ATC = ZPM \times AVC \qquad (7.10)$$

Step 3. Determine the profit rate $0 < r < 1$ that the market will bear. (In economic theory, r is a function of demand.)

Step 4. Computed income or profit after taxes on the basis of sales billed:

$$IAT = r \times SB$$

By the definition of IAT, we have

$$IBT = r \times SB/0.52 \quad \text{or} \quad IBT \approx 2r \times SB$$

Step 5. The price P or sales billed is

$$P \text{ or } SB = ATC/(1 - 2r), \quad r \neq \tfrac{1}{2} \tag{7.11}$$

Formula (7.11) is derived by the following algebraic manipulations. By the definition of IBT, we have

$$SB = ATC + IBT$$

Taking step 4 into consideration, by substitution we have

$$SB = ATC + 2r \times SB$$

The result of step 5 follows directly from this expression. The ATC in (7.11) excludes a normal return to capital, which is incorporated in ATC in economic theory.

Thus, SB is the price and $1/(1 - 2r)$ is the mark-up factor on AC. From the definition of ZPM, we have the following expression:

$$ATC = ZPM \times AVC \tag{7.12}$$

By substitution, (7.11) can also be written

$$P \text{ or } SB = [ZPM/(1 - 2r)]AVC \tag{7.13}$$

Comparing (7.13) with (7.3), it is obvious that the mark-up parameter a of the naive pricing model becomes $ZPM/(1 - 2r)$ in the more-sophisticated model actually used by such giant business firms as Westinghouse; moreover, $ZPM/(1 - 2r) > 1$, since $ZPM > 1$ and $1/(1 - 2r) > 1$.

In the simplified case where the corporate income tax is zero, IBT and IAT will be identical; hence, (7.13) becomes

$$P \text{ or } SB = [ZPM/(1 - r)] AVC \tag{7.13'}$$

Thus, the mark-up parameter a of the naive model corresponds to $ZPM/(1 - r) > 1$, since $ZPM > 1$ and $1/(1 - r) > 1$.

In terms of ZPM and r the mark-up parameter a in the naive model is actually more sensitive to the magnitude of ZPM than the rate of profit r. Table 7.5 illustrates some aspects of this relationship. With a naive mark-up parameter $a = 2.25$, the rate of profit r after taxes is 10% when ZPM = 1.8, but less than 6% when ZPM = 2 and 17% when ZPM = 1.5. [The value of r when ZPM = 2 and $a = 2.25$ is not shown in Table 7.5; students may

TABLE 7.5

r	0.06	0.08	0.10	0.17
		ZPM $= 2$		
a	2.27	2.38	2.50	3.03
		ZPM $= 1.8$		
a	2.04	2.14	2.25	2.73
		ZPM $= 1.5$		
a	1.70	1.79	1.88	2.25

wish to calculate it for themselves by using the formula $a = $ ZPM/$(1 - 2r)$.] It can be easily checked that when $a = 2.25$ and ZPM $= 1.5, r = 0.17$. Since a lower ZPM implies lower overhead cost, the values in Table 7.5 show that overhead cost is more important to the rate of profit than a higher mark-up. Efficient management can reduce overhead cost and, therefore, efficiency in management may be more important to the rate of profit than a higher mark-up.

Given the mark-up parameter, a lower ZPM implies a higher profit rate

A graphical illustration of AC mark-up pricing in the case of zero corporate income tax is given in Figure 7.13, where $\overline{Q}$ is the quantity, rectangle *DEFH* represents fixed cost, and rectangle $0\overline{Q}ED$ represents the TVC (all for the previous year). Thus the zero profit multiplier is

$$\text{ZPM} = \frac{0\overline{Q}FH}{0\overline{Q}ED} = \frac{0\overline{Q} \times \overline{Q}F}{0\overline{Q} \times \overline{Q}E} = \frac{\overline{Q}F}{\overline{Q}E}$$

or

$$\text{ZPM} = \text{TC/TVC} = \text{ATC}_1/\text{AVC}$$

(ATC$_1$ denoting the average total cost excluding the return to equity capital, that is, the average cost as employed in accounting

FIGURE 7.13

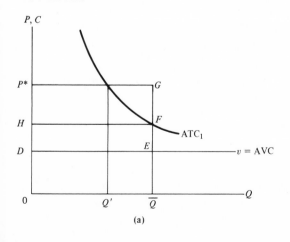

(a)

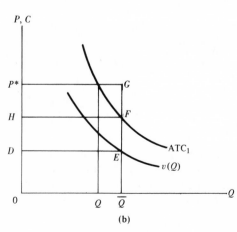

(b)

rather than in economics), and

$$1/(1 - r) = \overline{\overline{QG}}/\overline{\overline{QF}}$$

from (7.13'),

$$P^* = (\overline{\overline{QF}}/\overline{\overline{QE}})(\overline{\overline{QG}}/\overline{\overline{QF}})(\overline{\overline{QE}}) = \overline{\overline{QG}}$$

In Figure 7.13, total profit (including the return to equity capital) is represented by rectangle FGP^*H. The profit is positive for the given ZPM, r, and $\overline{Q}$. However, $\overline{Q}$ is the previous year's sales. It can easily be observed that if the current year's sales are less than Q_x for the same cost conditions as in the previous year and the given ZPM and r, then the actual profit will be negative.

7.2.3 Target Profit Pricing

Another well-documented pricing method actually used by such giant business firms as General Motors is the so-called *target profit method*, which is very convenient when TFC and AVC figures are readily available. However, this method involves more subjective elements than the two models described previously.

In the naive pricing model, only the mark-up parameter a involves subjective judgment. In the AC mark-up pricing model, only the profit rate r involves subjective judgment, since the ZPM can be computed from objective data. On the other hand, the target profit method requires both profit and quantity to be subjectively determined in order to compute the price. The following notation is used in the target profit method:

P: Price of the commodity

Q: Quantity of the commodity

C: Total cost, equal to the TFC plus the TVC. Note that total cost here refers to the total cost for Q units of the commodity, not one unit, excluding a return to equity capital.

π: Profit, including a normal return to capital in the context of business practice rather than economic terminology

R: Total revenue

F: Total fixed cost, this excluding a return to equity capital

V: Total variable cost

v: Average variable cost

Target-profit pricing assumes that the demand function is known

In planning its mark-up price, a firm usually has reliable information on F and v. It is vaguely known that P and Q are inversely related, but the precise relationship is usually unknown. This information is not sufficient to determine either price, quantity, or profit. This can be easily seen from the following equations, where profit, by definition, is equal to total revenue minus total cost:

$$\pi = R - C \tag{7.14}$$

and

$$R = PQ \tag{7.15}$$

$$C = F + V = F + vQ \tag{7.16}$$

Substituting (7.15) and (7.16) into (7.14), we obtain

$$\pi = PQ - \bar{F} - \bar{v}Q \tag{7.17}$$

where the bars over F and v indicate that they are known. Hence, we have one equation in three unknowns: π, P, and Q. From elementary algebra, we know that there does not exist a definite solution when one equation involves three unknowns. In other words, we cannot compute either π, P, or Q without knowing any two of them. On the other hand, if we know any two of them, the other one is automatically determined. In economics, we solve this dilemma by assuming that we know the demand function; thus, once Q is known, so is P (and vice versa). Since, in economics, we assume that the firm seeks to maximize its profits, the first-order condition for profit maximization reduces the problem to one equation in one variable, which enables us to solve for the one remaining unknown: quantity. Thus, in general, a solution is possible. We shall have more to say on this point later.

In practice, a price maker sets its price and allows the buyers to determine the quantity to be purchased. As we mentioned above, a firm cannot determine the price without knowing the quantity and the profit. Therefore, a producer has two alternatives from which to choose: (1) arbitrarily determine a price or (2) arbitrarily or subjectively determine a quantity and total profit. Many firms, such as General Motors, choose the second alternative. The profit level that they choose is called the *target profit*, and (by convention) the quantity that they choose is usually 70–80% of capacity. We shall now describe the mechanics of this procedure along with some of the problems involved in its use.

We denote the target profit by π^* and the chosen quantity by Q^*; then the price can be computed by rearranging (7.17). In the case of constant AVC we have

$$P^* = \bar{v} + \bar{F}/Q^* + \pi^*/Q^* \tag{7.18a}$$

whereas in the case of decreasing or increasing AVC we obtain

$$P^* = v^* + \bar{F}/Q^* + \pi^*/Q^* \tag{7.18b}$$

where v^* denotes the AVC at Q^*.

Although the actual market price P^* is set by the price maker based on accounting information for $\bar{v}$ and $\bar{F}$ and the subjectively determined target profit π^* and quantity Q^*, the actual profit and quantity sold might be quite different from π^* and Q^*, respectively. The target profit π^* is usually positive, but actual profit may be negative. It is interesting to examine the conditions under which actual profit will be negative.

We denote the target profit and actual profit by π^* and π, respectively, and the target and actual sales by Q^* and Q, respectively. By substituting (7.18a) into (7.17), for the constant AVC case we obtain

$$\pi = Q(\bar{v} + \bar{F}/Q^* + \pi^*/Q^*) - \bar{F} - \bar{v}Q \qquad (7.19)$$

which yields

$$\pi = \left(\frac{Q}{Q^*} - 1\right)\bar{F} + \frac{Q}{Q^*}\pi^* \qquad (7.20)$$

Expression (7.20) shows that as long as actual sales are higher than target sales, actual profit will be higher than target profit. Negative profit is possible only if $Q/Q^* < 1$ (i.e., only if actual sales are less than target sales) because Q, Q^*, $\bar{F}$, and π^* are presumably positive. When $Q < Q^*$, the actual profit depends on the relative magnitudes of Q and Q^*, on the one hand, and $\bar{F}$ and π^*, on the other hand. This can be shown by letting π^* be a fraction g of $\bar{F}$, that is,

$$\pi^* = g\bar{F}, \qquad 1 \geq g > 0 \qquad (7.21)$$

Substituting (7.21) into (7.20) and rearranging the terms, we obtain

$$\pi = (Q/Q^* + gQ/Q^* - 1)\,\bar{F} \qquad (7.22)$$

Since $\bar{F} > 0$, profit π can be negative only if the term in parentheses on the right side of (7.22) is negative, that is,

$$Q/Q^* + gQ/Q^* - 1 < 0 \qquad (7.23)$$

which yields

$$Q < Q^*/(1 + g) \qquad (7.24)$$

A few values of g and the corresponding relative values of Q and Q^* which will result in a negative actual profit are listed in Table 7.6. These figures show that if the target profit is equal to the TFC, then the actual profit will be negative only if actual sales fall below half of target sales. On the other hand, if the target profit is only one-tenth of the TFC, and actual sales fall short of

TABLE 7.6

g	Relative values of Q and Q^*
1	$Q < Q^*/2$
$\frac{1}{2}$	$Q < 2Q^*/3$
$\frac{1}{10}$	$Q < 10Q^*/11$

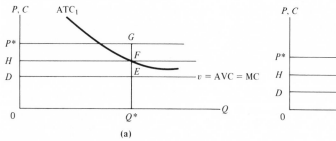

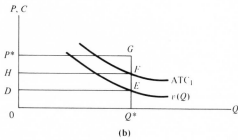

(a)   (b)

FIGURE 7.14

ten-elevenths of target sales, then the actual profit will become
negative. This indicates that when the TFC is relatively high
compared to the target profit, a relatively small deviation of actual
sales from target sales will result in an actual loss rather than a
profit.

A graphical illustration of target profit mark-up pricing from
the constant-AVC case is shown in part (a) of Figure 7.14. The
TVC is represented by rectangle $0Q^*ED$, the AVC by $\overline{Q^*E}$, the
TFC (excluding a return to equity capital) by rectangle $DEFH$,
the AFC by $\overline{EF}$, the target profit (including a return to equity
capital) by rectangle FGP^*H, and average profit by $\overline{FG}$. According to (7.18a), the mark-up price is

$$P^* = \overline{Q^*E} + \overline{EF} + \overline{FG} = \overline{Q^*G}$$

When AVC is not a constant, as in part (b) of Figure 7.14, the
AVC that corresponds to Q^* (which we denote by v^*) is $\overline{Q^*E}$.
According to (7.18b), the mark-up price is

$$P^* = \overline{Q^*E} + \overline{EF} + \overline{FG} = \overline{Q^*G}$$

All other aspects of part (b) of Figure 7.14 are similar to those
of part (a). The curves ATC_1 in Figure 7.14 represent the average
total cost excluding a return to equity capital, which is different
from the concept of average total cost in economics, where a
return to equity capital is included.

7.2.4 A Comparison of the Three Mark-Up Pricing Models

In order to facilitate a comparison of the three mark-up pricing
models that we have described, we shall use the following unified
notation:

P: Price

v: Average variable cost

C_0: Average fixed cost (excluding return to equity capital)

C_1: Average profit (including return to equity capital)

The equation for the naive mark-up pricing model, $P = av$ [Equation (7.3)], which we described earlier, can also be written

$$P = v + m_1 v \qquad\qquad (7.25)$$

where $m_1 = a - 1$ and $m_1 > 0$, since a, which is the mark-up parameter, is greater than one (i.e., $a > 1$).

The equations for the AC mark-up pricing model [Equations (7.13) and (7.13')] can be rewritten

$$P = v + m_2 v \qquad\qquad (7.26)$$

where $m_2 = ZPM/(1 - 2r) - 1$ for a 50% corporate income tax and $m_2 = ZPM/(1 - r) - 1$ for a zero tax (ZPM is the zero profit multiplier and r is the rate of profit on sales). Since $ZPM > 1$ and $1/(1 - r) > 1$, $ZPM/(1 - r) > 1$ and $ZPM/(1 - 2r) > 1$. Equation (7.26) can also be written

$$P = v + m_1' v + m_2' v \qquad\qquad (7.26')$$

where $m_1' = F/V$ and $m_2' = b(1 + F/V)$, F and V denoting the TFC and TVC of the previous year. This makes the constant b as follows:

$$b = 1/(1 - r) - 1 > 0$$

for the zero corporate income tax case, and

$$b = 1/(1 - 2r) - 1 > 0$$

for the 50% corporate income tax case, since $1/(1 - r) > 1$ and $1/(1 - 2r) > 1$.

The above expressions can easily be derived by using (7.13), (7.13'), and the definition of ZPM. For the zero tax case, (7.13') can be rewritten

$$P = v(1 + F/V)/(1 - r) = v(1 + F/V)(1 + b)$$
$$= v[1 + F/V + b(1 + F/V)]$$

We can see that (7.26') follows by substitution. In a sense, $m_1' v$ is the estimated AFC and $m_2' v$ the profit. A similar derivation for the 50% corporate income tax can be carried out by first changing the r to $2r$ in the expression $1/(1 - r)$ and then changing the corresponding definition of b from $1/(1 - r) - 1 > 0$ to $1/(1 - 2r) - 1 > 0$.

The equations for the target profit mark-up pricing model [Equations (7.18a) and (7.18b)] can be rewritten

$$P = v + C_0 + C_1 \qquad\qquad (7.27)$$

It can be seen that all of the above expressions [i.e., (7.25)–(7.27)] in fact represent a mark-up on AVC. In the special case where $AVC = \text{const}$, $MC = AVC$ (see Chapter 3), and the mark-ups are actually on MC.

An Explanatory Comment on the Mark-Up Pricing Models

It was argued in Chapter 3 that empirical studies show the AVC usually to be constant within the relevant range. Consequently, from a practical viewpoint the special case of constant AVC may be more interesting than the other cases.

It appears that the three mark-up pricing models are quite different with respect to their degree of sophistication. Actually, they have more fundamental similarities than differences.

First of all, all three models are essentially cost oriented, as indicated by the obvious absence of demand and revenue curves in Figures 7.12–7.14. Although demand is not ignored, it is taken into consideration only by way of subjective judgment rather than through an objective criterion that explicitly describes the demand and MR curves.

Second, AVC and a subjective judgment about market demand play a major role in all three models. In the special case of constant AVC, where MC = AVC, MC plays a major role in actual business pricing by implication because, as mentioned above, empirical studies indicate that AVC is constant within the relevant range in most (if not all) cases. Thus, MC plays a very important part in business decision making. Since business accounting records do not explicitly show the MC and MR figures, many economists assume that business decisions are not based on marginal concepts as developed in economic theory. In the context of our analysis, such a belief seems unwarranted and probably in error.

Third, for all three models, the payment to borrowed capital (interest) is considered as cost, but a return (if any) to equity capital is considered as profit. This is different from economic theory, where *all* returns to capital, borrowed as well as equity, are treated as cost. This is one of the basic differences between economic theory and business practice, regardless of whether or not a firm practices mark-up pricing.

Fourth, the mark-up pricing models that we have described are quite flexible theoretically in that they can be considered as applicable pricing methods not only by a monopoly, but also by oligopolistic firms. Through the proper modification, which involves the mark-up parameter a, the rate of profit r, and the target profit π^* and quantity Q^* in the naive, AC, and target profit mark-up pricing models, respectively, considerable flexibility is available to the firm in establishing a price for its products. When these parameters are treated only as functions of firm-related factors (such as general market conditions and possible customer reaction to the price), but not in the context of the possible reaction of competitors, we are dealing essentially with monopoly pricing models. However, if the parameters are also considered to be functions of the reaction of competitors (such as will be described in Chapter 9, Oligopoly Theory), then these pricing methods become oligopoly pricing models. Since little is known about the firm's behavior with respect to the actual determination

Different mark-up pricing models provide flexibility to business in pricing its products

of these parameters (different firms may use different criteria), all of the above three models can be considered either monopoly or oligopoly models.

Fifth, none of the above three models is geared to the maximization of profit as is found in economic theory.

Finally, although intended profit, including a return to equity capital, is likely positive in all three models, the actual profit may be either positive or negative due to the uncertainties in the quantity actually sold.

The essential differences between the above three pricing models rest in the treatment of fixed cost, profit, and quantity sold or produced. The mark-up on AVC in the naive pricing model, $(a - 1)v$, includes AFC, a return to equity capital, and a possible profit. Since the AFC and unit profit depend on the quantity, which is not explicitly taken into consideration, in some cases it is questionable whether the projected profit can be positive or negative. Although this pricing model seems to be so naive as to preclude its use by a rational firm, it is actually employed by many retailers (in particular, small ones) on the basis of cost considerations. Since the allocation of fixed cost is not easily determined as a result of the uncertainties in the quantity that will be sold, when a firm sells many different items (e.g., a general store in a small town), the work of allocating fixed cost to each and every item becomes quite costly, if not impossible. Furthermore, the accuracy of the allocated fixed cost can never be ensured due to the uncertainty in the quantity that will be sold. It is for these reasons that the naive mark-up model becomes an attractive method for practical pricing.

The three features that distinguish the AC and target profit mark-up pricing models from the naive mark-up pricing model are the allocation of fixed cost, the concept of a subjectively determined profit, and the treatment of the quantity to be sold. These three elements are not independent of each other. For

The most common mark-up models differ in their treatment of fixed costs and demand

example, without quantity being known or given, the AFC cannot be computed. The allocation of fixed cost makes the two alternative models more refined than the naive pricing model in that the mark-up on AVC is partitioned into two parts: AFC and profit, including a return to equity capital. On the other hand, the differences between the AC and target profit mark-up pricing models rest in the methods of allocating fixed cost and determining profit and quantity.

The ZPM method of the AC mark-up pricing model implies that the allocation of fixed cost and the related quantity are based on historical data, that is, the previous year's figures. Thus, they are objectively determined. On the other hand, the allocation of fixed cost in the target profit model depends on the subjectively determined quantity, which is normally 70–80% of capacity. As a result, the latter involves more subjective judgment than the former.

The rate of profit r in the AC mark-up pricing model is subjectively determined on the basis of "what the market will bear." Demand enters into the picture through a consideration of r. In this case, the only comment that economists can make is that r is a function of demand, nothing more. In the target profit mark-up pricing model, both the target profit and the target quantity are subjectively determined. In such a case, economists would say that the firm actually considers the demand to be perfectly inelastic (i.e., the demand curve is a vertical straight line at the target quantity Q^*). Thus, to economists it appears that the target profit mark-up pricing model is the only one that explicitly incorporates the concept of a demand function. This may be one of the reasons for economists being suspicious about mark-up pricing in practice, in spite of the fact that it is widely used. Economists traditionally consider demand to be at least as important as cost in a firm's attempt to maximize profits or attain some other objective.

7.3 A SYNTHESIS: THEORETICAL EQUIVALENCE OF MARK-UP PRICING METHODS AND THE MONOPOLY MODEL IN ECONOMICS

As we have mentioned before, the difference between mark-up pricing in practice and the monopoly model in economic theory may be more apparent than real. In this section, we shall show that, under the same set of assumptions, mark-up pricing in practice and the profit optimization goal of price makers (except under oligopoly) in economic theory are, in fact, equivalent.

To a great extent, the failure to comprehend the consistency (or the lack of it) between economic theory under imperfect competition and mark-up pricing in practice is the result of a lack of understanding of the importance of the assumptions that underlie economic theory. This is particularly applicable to the assumptions of perfect information or knowledge with respect to demand (Assumption 7.4) and profit maximization as the goal of the firm. In mathematical terms, these two assumptions impose two restrictions on the model, which results in a determinate system that would not otherwise obtain. This can be shown by counting the number of equations and the number of unknowns, as we shall now demonstrate.

Consistency between theory and practice depends on the assumptions made

There are four variables (i.e., unknowns), that determine a firm's decision: cost, revenue, price, and quantity. These unknowns are not necessarily independent. In economic theory, the assumption of perfect information or knowledge (Assumption 7.4) enables us to write the cost and demand functions:

$$C = g(Q) \quad \text{cost function} \tag{7.28}$$

$$Q = D(P) \quad \text{demand function} \tag{7.29}$$

By definition, revenue is related to price and quantity as follows:

$$R = PQ \tag{7.30}$$

Thus, we have a system of three equations in four unknowns (C, R, P, and Q), which, in principle, cannot be solved. However, the assumption of profit maximization as the goal of a firm requires that MR = MC, that is, that

$$MR(Q) = MC(Q) \tag{7.31}$$

This imposes a further restriction on the model. The Qs in parentheses indicate that both MR and MC are functions of Q. We now have a system of four equations in four unknowns, which, in principle, can be solved.

REMARK: One may wish to consider MR and MC as additional unknowns, which would give a total of six unknowns. This alternative approach does not create any difficulty, since two additional relations, such as MR = dR/dQ and MC = dC/dQ, can also be added. These two equations, together with (7.28)–(7.31), constitute a system of six equations in six unknowns, which is again determinate.

   In practice, a firm still faces the same four unknowns, but it has reliable information only on cost. Thus, we only have (7.28) and (7.30), that is, a system of two equations. Since a system of two equations in four unknowns cannot be solved without introducing further restrictions, in order to solve this indeterminate system some arbitrary restrictions must be imposed. As we observed earlier, the different mark-up pricing models are actually distinguished by the imposition of different restrictions on the indeterminate system in order to obtain a definite solution.

   In economic theory, the above four-equation system, which includes the expressions for TC and TR, is most convenient. However, in practice, the information most readily available to a firm concerns the AVC and TFC. Since the quantity is, in general, not known, and the TVC is, by definition, the product of quantity and AVC, the TVC and TC are not known. Hence, it is more convenient and rational for a firm to base its decisions on the most reliable information, that is, on the AVC. In spite of all the differences in appearance, we can prove the following theorem.

Theorem 7.1. *The various mark-up pricing models and the monopoly model are essentially equivalent from a theoretical point of view.*

Before demonstrating the proof of Theorem 7.1, we offer the following definition.

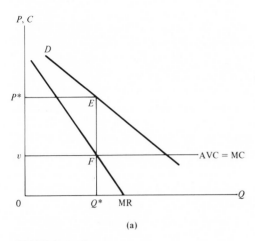

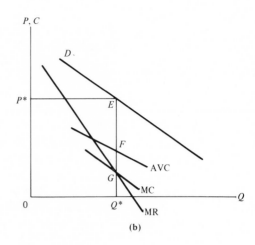

FIGURE 7.15

Definition: Theoretical Equivalency of Economic Models. Two
models that appear to be different are, in fact, considered theoretically equivalent if they yield the same solution under the
same set of assumptions and with the same set of data.

By the assumption of perfect information or knowledge in
economic theory (Assumption 7.4), we can draw a demand curve
and the associated MR and MC curves of Figure 7.15. For the
sake of simplicity, we assume a straight-line demand curve,
which, in turn, implies a straight-line MR curve. Also for the sake
of simplicity, we assume a straight-line MC curve. For the purpose of illustration, we present two cases: constant MC and declining MC.

> *Given perfect
> information, mark-
> up pricing models
> are consistent with
> profit-maximization
> models*

Consider Figure 7.15. According to the theory developed in
Section 7.1, Q^* is the profit-maximizing output in both cases.
Together with the presumably known demand D, Q^* will determine the profit-maximizing price P^*. This is the conclusion that
we arrive at from the application of economic theory.

In practice, if a firm that is assumed to be a profit maximizer
has all the information indicated by Figure 7.15 (i.e., AVC, MC,
D, and hence MR), then in both cases the mark-up price will be
P^* and the mark-up parameter will be

$$a = \overline{Q^*E}/\overline{Q^*F} > 1$$

because only P^* will result in maximum profit. It can easily be
shown that the mark-up parameter a, as computed above, will
result in a profit-maximizing price because

$$P^* = av = \frac{\overline{Q^*E}}{\overline{Q^*F}} \times \overline{Q^*F} = \overline{Q^*E}$$

Algebraically, the naive mark-up pricing model can be expressed by a very convenient and easy-to-understand formula in the special case where both the AVC and the price elasticity of demand are constant. In this case, the AVC $\bar{v}$ is equal to the MC; that is, $\bar{v}$ = MC.[8] Remembering the well-known equation for MR that utilizes price and the price elasticity of demand, we have

$$MR = P(1 - 1/e) \tag{7.32}$$

Since the first-order condition for profit maximization is that MR = MC, we can write

$$P(1 - 1/e) = \bar{v} \tag{7.33}$$

Taking into consideration that

$$1/(1 - 1/e) = 1 + 1/(e - 1)$$

(7.33) yields

$$P = \bar{v}[1 + 1/(e - 1)] \tag{7.34}$$

Thus, we have the mark-up parameter

$$a = 1 + 1/(e - 1)$$

The mark-up on AVC is

$$\bar{v}/(e - 1) > 0$$

since MC is usually positive and at equilibrium MR = MC. Hence, MR must be positive, which [from (7.32)] implies that e > 1 and $1/(e - 1) > 0$. It should be noted that in Chapter 5 the price elasticity of demand has been defined as being positive for negatively sloped demand curves.

Many intermediate microeconomic textbooks have used this or similar expressions to demonstrate the consistency between marginal analysis in economic theory and mark-up pricing. Although the form of this approach (proof) should be considered as a step forward in the development of economic theory, it occasionally leads to the misconception that mark-up pricing is consistent with economic theory only in the special case of constant AVC and price elasticity of demand. However, the consistency or the equivalence between mark-up pricing and marginal analysis in imperfect markets is really quite general. A mathematical demonstration of this point will be presented in the appendix to this chapter. For the present, a simple example based on linear demand and AVC functions should prove sufficient to demonstrate the general consistency of the equivalence.

Constant AVC is not essential for equivalency between mark-up pricing and marginal analysis

Let us assume the following linear demand function:

$$P = B - bQ \tag{7.35}$$

---

[8] As noted in (7.18a) and (7.18b), the symbols $\bar{v}$ and v^* distinguish constant average variable cost from increasing (decreasing) average variable cost.

where B and b are constants. Then TR is given by

$$R = QP = BQ - bQ^2 \tag{7.36}$$

whereas MR is given by

$$MR = B - 2bQ \tag{7.37}$$

Let us further assume the linear AVC function to be

$$v = C + cQ \tag{7.38}$$

where C and c are constants. Then TVC can be written

$$TVC = Qv = CQ + cQ^2 \tag{7.39}$$

whereas TC can be written

$$TC = F + TVC = F + CQ + cQ^2 \tag{7.40}$$

where F—the TFC—is a constant. the TC function implies that the MC function is

$$MC = C + 2cQ \tag{7.41}$$

If we equate MR in (7.37) and MC in (7.41) and solve for Q, the equilibrium quantity is

$$Q^* = (B - C)/2(b + c) \tag{7.42}$$

Thus, the profit-maximizing quantity is a function of both the demand function (indicated by B and b) and the AVC function (indicated by C and c). In the special case of constant AVC, $c = 0$ in (7.38) and hence $v = C$. If we denote this constant AVC by $\bar{v}$, then (7.42) becomes

$$Q^* = (B - \bar{v})/2b \tag{7.43}$$

It can easily be checked that this expression is correct for the special case of constant AVC by equating $\bar{v} = MC$ to MR in (7.37) and solving for Q.

In practice, a firm sets the price of its merchandise, not the quantity sold. Theoretically, it should not be difficult for a firm to change from quantity to price as its decision variable, since the demand that links the two is assumed to be known and single-valued [as in (7.35)]. By substituting (7.43) and (7.42) into (7.35), the profit-maximizing price P^* is

$$P^* = (\bar{v} + B)/2 = \bar{v} + (B - \bar{v})/2$$

or $\tag{7.44}$

$$P^* = v^* + (B - C)/2$$

where $v^* = C + cQ^*$. Expression (7.44) implies that the mark-up parameter a is

$$a = 1 + (B - \bar{v})/2\bar{v} \quad \text{or} \quad a = 1 + (B - C)/2v^* \tag{7.45}$$

It can be seen that the profit-maximizing mark-up parameter depends on both the demand (indicated by B) and the AVC (indicated by $\bar{v}$ or v^*). Thus, the higher the demand (i.e., the larger B), the higher the mark-up for a given cost. Alternatively, the higher the cost (i.e., the larger $\bar{v}$ or v^*), the lower the mark-up for a given demand and $(B - C) > 0$. This agrees with common sense.

The above illustrative example shows that the naive mark-up pricing method used by business firms in practice and the traditional monopoly model of economic theory will result in an identical solution under the same set of assumptions and with the same set of cost and revenue data. According to our definition of the theoretical equivalency of economic models, we have the following theorem.

Theorem 7.2. *The naive mark-up pricing method used by business firms in practice is theoretically equivalent to the traditional monopoly model of economic theory.*

When compared with the naive mark-up pricing model, the AC and target profit mark-up pricing methods represent the result of refinements on the allocation of fixed cost, on the one hand, and on the estimation of profit, on the other hand. Moreover, it is the methods used to allocate fixed cost and estimate profit which constitute the essential difference between the two refined models. However, all three models are theoretically equivalent under the assumption of perfect information or knowledge (Assumption 7.4). This can easily be shown by the graphical method.

Figure 7.16 is essentially a reproduction of Figure 7.13 except that a demand D and the associated MR and MC curves are added; ATC_1, which excludes a return to equity capital, represents the businessperson's concept of average total cost, whereas

Equivalency of the naive, AC, and target profit pricing models is assured with perfect information

FIGURE 7.16

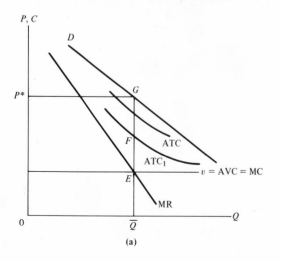

(a)

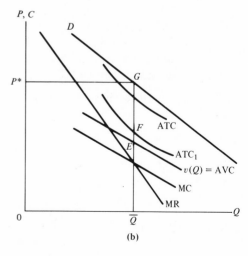

(b)

ATC, which includes a return to equity capital, represents the concept of average total cost in the context of economic theory. Without the D and MR curves, $\overline{Q}$ and ZPM (i.e., the line segment $\overline{EF}$), are determined by the previous year's output and cost data, whereas the rate of profit r is given by the line segment $\overline{FG}$ as determined by the subjective judgment of the management of a firm. However, with the demand D and the associated MR and MC curves known, it is no longer necessary to use last year's data to determine $\overline{Q}$ and $\overline{EF}$. Furthermore, subjective judgment is no longer needed to determine $\overline{FG}$. Under the assumption of profit maximization, we see that the solution based on MR = MC yields the profit-maximizing quantity $\overline{Q}$ [i.e., Q^* in (7.42) and (7.43)], which, in turn, determines $\overline{EF}$, $\overline{FG}$, and, consequently, the profit-maximizing price P^* [equation (7.44)]. Thus, with the dual assumption of perfect information or knowledge (Assumption 7.4) and profit maximization as the goal of the firm, the previous year's data and subjective judgment are no longer needed in order to derive the profit-maximizing price P^*, which is the price that "the market will bear."

Students have no doubt realized that Figure 7.16 precisely represents the traditional monopoly model of Section 7.1, except that ATC_1 is defined as the average total cost excluding a return to equity capital, whereas ATC conforms to the concept of average total cost in the context of economic theory. This proves that the AC mark-up pricing model will result in the same equilibrium solution as the monopoly model of economic theory under the same set of assumptions and with the same set of cost and revenue data. According to our definition of the theoretical equivalency of economic models, we have the following theorem.

Theorem 7.3. *The AC mark-up pricing method used by business firms in practice is theoretically equivalent to the traditional monopoly model of economic theory.*

Figure 7.17 is essentially a reproduction of Figure 7.14, except that the now presumably known demand D and the associated MR and MC curves are added; ATC_1, which excludes a return to equity capital, represents the businessperson's concept of average total cost, whereas ATC, which includes a return to equity capital, represents the concept of average total cost in the context of economic theory.

As an exercise, students may wish to use an argument parallel to that used for the AC mark-up pricing method in order to prove that the target profit mark-up pricing method is theoretically equivalent to the traditional monopoly model under the same set of assumptions and with the same set of cost and revenue data. In other words, under the assumptions of perfect information or knowledge (Assumption 7.4) and profit maximization as the goal of the firm, the subjectively determined target profit and target

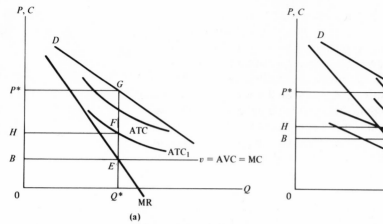
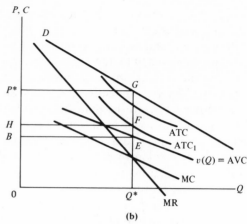

(a)   (b)

FIGURE 7.17

sales (i.e., target quantity) will be automatically determined by the values of the solution to the system [(7.35)–(7.45)]. As a result, the mark-up price will maximize the profit, and the target profit will be the maximum profit. This proves the following theorem.

Theorem 7.4. *The target profit mark-up pricing method used by business firms in practice is theoretically equivalent to the traditional monopoly model of economic theory.*

Theorems 7.2–7.4 show that the various mark-up pricing models are theoretically equivalent to the traditional monopoly model of economic theory under the same set of assumptions and with the same set of data. Thus, we have proven Theorem 7.1. This theoretical development does more than merely prove the theoretical equivalence between economic theory and business practice; it may also bridge the gap between the theory of the firm and the realities of business practice.

Experience has shown that many students find it difficult to relate the marginal analysis of a firm with actual business operations. They feel that textbooks always contend that a firm must determine the quantity of merchandise to be produced or sold in order to maximize profit, whereas in everyday life most firms (with very few exceptions) set their prices rather than their output or sales level and let the buyers determine the quantity to be purchased. For this reason, these students consider economic theory to be far removed from reality. Actually, although it is not always made clear to students, in economic theory it is implied that under imperfect competition, either the quantity or the price (but not both) can be treated as the decision variable. We hope that the preceding discussions and examples serve to eliminate some of the misunderstanding and hence make this point clear.

The conclusions of marginal analysis in economics are truisms that cannot be refuted. The basic problem is their applicability to the solution of real-life problems. Insofar as business firms are concerned, demand is never precisely known and, in fact, is usually subject to considerable uncertainty. As a result, the MR curve is never really known with certainty. Under such circumstances, a strictly marginal calculation is neither feasible nor beneficial. On the other hand, economic theory can certainly provide useful guidance for business decisions. It is in this light that the synthesis or reconciliation between the various mark-up pricing methods used in practice and traditional economic theory can be considered as a useful contribution.

Strict application of marginal analysis requires precise information

It should be pointed out that the proof of Theorem 7.1 (the equivalence between the various mark-up pricing models and the monopoly model of economic theory) does not make the various mark-up pricing methods either more or less useful. As long as the demand is not known, subjective judgment will play an important role in mark-up pricing. Moreover, as long as subjective judgment plays an essential role, mark-up pricing cannot be considered a scientific method. As a result, although they use the same mark-up pricing method under essentially the same circumstances, some businesspeople may be very successful while others fail. Thus, our synthesis does not seem to be very helpful. On the other hand, it does serve to point out the problems in mark-up pricing. We have seen that information concerning demand is the key to better decision making. Thus, the more accurate the information concerning demand, the less subjective judgment necessary and the closer the target profit will be to the maximum possible profit.

In the real world, information on cost and demand is not free. There is a trade-off between expenditures on information gathering and the gain in possible higher profit that may be obtained from better information. It is the existence of this trade-off which in some cases may make the naive mark-up pricing method actually superior to the more-refined methods. Conversely, as a result of advances in econometric methods, more economic research may result in a profit that is high enough to more than offset the additional cost it entails. These are theoretical possibilities that deserve more study. Ambitious students may wish to direct their research toward this topic and thereby possibly contribute significantly to the application of economic theory to business decision making.

SUMMARY

In this chapter we described and evaluated the economic model of monopoly, not only as a logically consistent and valid construct but also as one which can be adapted to the business practice of mark-up pricing without loss of theoretical vigor. We noted that, in contrast to the model of perfect competition, monopoly involves only one seller and a lack of free entry into the industry. However, the assumptions of perfect information and a homogeneous product were retained in our analysis of pure monopoly, although they were subsequently relaxed when we introduced the concepts of price discrimination and mark-up pricing.

In describing the profit-maximizing behavior of the monopolist, we observed that, unlike the firm under perfect competition, the monopolistic seller faces a demand curve of negative slope, which also means that the MR curve has a negative slope. Because of the special features of the demand and MR curves, we emphasized that while the first-order condition for profit-maximization still requires MR = MC, the second-order condition is no longer limited to MC rising. Instead, it can be satisfied when MC is constant, or even when MC is declining but at a slower rate than the decline in MR.

Both the short-run and long-run conditions of monopoly were then examined, and it was noted that, whereas in long-run equilibrium the firm under perfect competition makes zero profit, the monopolist may still enjoy positive profit. Also, it was explained that, if its market can be subdivided and the price elasticities of the submarkets differ, a monopoly may further increase its profit by practicing price discrimination.

It was shown that, because the significance of a decreasing long-run AC with respect to the incidence of natural monopoly results in the development of public utilities as a means of regulating monopolistic pricing practices, although marginal cost (MC) pricing can maximize economic welfare for society as a whole, it may call for a subsidy to the monopolist, which, in turn, creates political problems that can negate the effectiveness or benefits of MC pricing. Consequently, we argued that MC pricing does not automatically offer the tidy solution to natural monopoly (as in the case of public utilities) that many economists have come to accept.

Finally, we demonstrated that, in the real world, because of the lack of reliable information on the demand for the product, the monopolist, unlike the firm under perfect competition, is faced with the problem of setting a price before sales actually take place. Given this lack of information on demand on the one hand, and fairly reliable cost information on the other, the monopolist is forced to set prices, taking cost into consideration, on a subjective evaluation of demand. This means that price is essentially based on cost, a practice which is generally known as mark-up pricing in business. We described three mark-up pricing models used by different types of businesses: the naive, the average cost, and the target profit price models. It was shown that the naive mark-up model is generally used by retailers because of its simplicity and the lack of reliable cost data by retailers, whereas the more sophisticated average cost and target profit pricing models are used by large firms, such as Westinghouse and General Motors, who have better information systems. We concluded our discussion of mark-up pricing models by demonstrating that the monopoly model in theory, and the practice of mark-up pricing in business, are equivalent since, given identical information, they result in the same price and quantity in equilibrium. Thus, we concluded that the mark-up pricing model brings economic theory closer to reality without compromising theoretical rigor.

EXERCISES AND QUESTIONS FOR CHAPTER 7 ON MONOPOLY THEORY AND MARK-UP PRICING

1. What are the conditions under which the short-run profit of a monopoly will be maximized? Why? What are the differences between this case and that of a perfectly competitive firm? Explain.

2. What are the conditions under which the long-run profit of a monopoly will be maximized? Why? What are the differences between this case and that of a perfectly competitive firm? Explain.

3. Describe the supply function of a monopoly. How does it differ from that under perfect competition?

4. Compare the short-run and long-run equilibrium conditions of a perfectly competitive firm and a monopoly.

5. Under what circumstances may a monopolist charge different prices for the same commodity in different submarkets? Give your explanation in terms of a graphical exposition.

6. Is mark-up pricing, which is generally practiced by business firms, consistent with the marginal analysis of profit maximization in economic theory? Defend your answer.

7. The owners of a tract of land in the Gateway Center of downtown Pittsburgh say that they are perfectly free to set their price at any level whatsoever because the supply of that particular kind of land is perfectly inelastic. Are they correct? Explain. (Clearly state the assumptions that are implicit in your answer.)

8. You operate a roadside stand selling roses for 40¢ each. The roses cost you 20¢ each. Almost all of your sales are on Sunday. It is now Sunday afternoon, and because of bad weather it appears certain that purchasers will take less roses than you had anticipated. Your estimate of the demand schedule for the rest of Sunday is shown in Table E7.1.

TABLE E7.1

Price (¢)	Sales
60	40
50	50
40	70
30	100
20	160
15	175
10	200

You expect that tomorrow sales will be zero. Since you have no storage facilities, any roses not sold today will spoil. You have 200 roses on hand right now. Your aim is to maximize profit. What price are you going to charge? Why? Explain. [Explicitly state the assumption(s) that you are making.]

9. Assume it to be known with certainty that a monopolist faces the following demand and cost functions:

$$Q = 100 - P, \qquad C = 50 - 20Q + Q^2 \qquad \text{for} \quad Q \geq 20$$

a. Compute the profit-maximizing quantity Q^*. (This is the solution for the monopoly problem according to traditional monopoly theory.)
b. Compute the profit-maximizing mark-up price P^*. What is the mark-up on MC?
c. Compute the quantity corresponding to the mark-up price P^* determined in part b.
d. Is the quantity determined in part c identical to the quantity determined in part a? Does this indicate the theoretical equivalence between marginal analysis in monopoly theory and mark-up pricing in business practice? Explain.

10. Assume it to be known with certainty that a monopolist faces the following cost function:

$$C = 50 - 20Q + Q^2 \qquad \text{for} \quad 20 \leq Q \leq 100$$

The monopolist does not know the demand for the product, but only that the productive capacity is 100 units (i.e., the current plant size is such that if it produces 100 units or less, the cost will be represented by the above cost function; however, when more than 100 units are produced, cost will rise very rapidly). The monopolist has to set the price of the product.
a. If you were in charge of marketing, with the responsibility of setting the price, what would be your recommendation to top management with respect to the price to set? Do you need more information in order to compute a price? Explain.
b. If you knew the demand function, how would you compute the price? Explain.

11. Assume that each additional unit produced costs your firm $10 (this could be labor and raw material costs for a producer or the wholesale price for a retailer). Your overhead cost, excluding a return to your own capital, is $1000. The only information available concerning demand is that in the last four years your firm sold 500, 600, 400, and 500 units, respectively. You have to set a price for your commodity. How would you go about establishing a price for the product? Compare the pricing method with the marginal analysis of profit maximization in traditional microeconomic theory.

12. Why do some economists consider mark-up pricing practice to be inconsistent with the assumption of profit maximization as the goal of the firm in economic theory? Explain (use graphs).

13. What are the special features of long-run equilibrium of a firm under

monopoly? How do they compare with those of a perfectly competitive firm in long-run equilibrium? Explain.

14. Empirical studies indicate that in most (if not all) cases, the short-run AVC is constant. Is this phenomenon consistent with the marginal analysis of profit maximization of a monopolistic firm? Explain.

APPENDIX TO CHAPTER 7

A MATHEMATICAL NOTE
ON MONOPOLY THEORY
AND MARK-UP PRICING

A7.1 THE DEMAND AND REVENUE FUNCTIONS OF A MONOPOLY

The essential difference between a perfectly competitive firm and a monopoly rests in the demand function that they face. In general, the demand function facing the ith industry can be written

$$Q_i = D_i(P_1, P_2, ..., P_i, ..., P_n, Y) \tag{A7.1}$$

where Q_i denotes the quantity of commodity i, D_i denotes the demand function for commodity i, P_i, $i = 1, 2, ..., n$, denotes the prices of commodity i, and Y denotes the income. In partial analysis, it is assumed that the effect of a change in P_i (and, consequently, in Q_i) on P_j, $j \neq i$, and Y is negligible and can be ignored. As a result, P_j, $j \neq i$, and Y are considered to be constant for D_i. Hence, (A7.1) can be written

$$Q_i = D_i(P_i) \tag{A7.2}$$

This is a good approximation when industry i is a small part of the economy as a whole. When we deal with a specific industry, we omit the subscript i, and the demand function is usually written

$$Q = D(P) \tag{A7.3}$$

It is usually assumed that D has the following two properties:

$$dQ/dP < 0 \quad \text{for an industry} \tag{A7.4a}$$

$$\exists D^{-1}, \quad P = D^{-1}(Q),$$

$$D \text{ and } D^{-1} \text{ are single-valued} \tag{A7.4b}$$

That is, the inverse function D^{-1} of D exists, and both D and D^{-1} are single-valued functions.

Whereas an industry's demand curve has a negative slope, a perfectly competitive firm faces a horizontal demand curve; that is, the demand function facing a perfectly competitive firm has the following property:

$dP/dQ = 0$ for a perfectly competitive firm   (A7.5)

Due to this special feature, the marginal revenue is equal to the price for a perfectly competitive firm:

$P = \text{MR}$ for a perfectly competitive firm   (A7.6)

In the case of a monopoly, we have a different story. Since, by definition, there is only one firm in a monopolistic industry, the firm's demand is the industry's demand. The demand function for a monopoly has the following properties:

$dQ/dP < 0$ and $dP/dQ < 0$ for a monopoly (A7.7)

Since the demand curve for a monopoly is negatively sloped, the MR will be less than the average revenue (AR) or price (P). In order to show this, we first define total revenue R as

$R = PQ$ (A7.8)

The MR is defined as the derivative of the R function with respect to quantity (not with respect to price). Since according to (A7.4b) price is a function of the quantity, we have

$\text{MR} = dR/dQ = P + Q\,dP/dQ$ for a monopoly   (A7.9)

It can be seen that (A7.6), which is for a perfectly competitive firm, represents a special case of (A7.9); that is, when $dP/dQ = 0$ as per (A7.5), (A7.9) becomes (A7.6). From (A7.9) it is seen that

$\text{MR} = P + Q\,dP/dQ < P$ for $P, Q > 0$ and $dP/dQ < 0$

(A7.10)

Recall that the price elasticity of demand e is defined as

$e = -(dQ/dP)P/Q$ (A7.11)

Multiplying the second term on the right side of (A7.9) by $P/P = 1$ and factoring out the P, we obtain

$\text{MR} = P[1 + (dP/dQ)Q/P]$

which can be written

$\text{MR} = P\{1 + 1/[(dQ/dP)P/Q]\}$

Substituting (A7.11) into the above expression, we obtain

$\text{MR} = P(1 - 1/e)$ (A7.12)

Expression (A7.12), which relates MR, on the one hand, to the price and price elasticity of demand, on the other hand, is often seen in textbooks. The advantage of this expression is that it clearly shows the relationship between MR and the price elasticity of demand. In fact, since price is positive, (A7.12) clearly shows that

$$\text{MR} \gtrless 0 \quad \text{for} \quad e \gtrless 1 \tag{A7.13}$$

Recall that demand is considered as elastic if $e > 1$, inelastic if $e < 1$, and of unitary elasticity when $e = 1$. When demand is elastic, additional sales due to a reduction in price will result in additional revenue. On the other hand, when the demand is inelastic, additional sales due to a reduction in price will result in a reduction of TR. The TR will not change when quantity (and thus price) changes if the demand elasticity is unitary. This knowledge is certainly valuable to a monopolist.

A7.2 CONDITIONS OF MAXIMUM PROFIT

Profit is defined as the difference between TR and TC, which is considered a function of the output. Thus, we have

$$C = F + V(Q) \tag{A7.14}$$

Where F is the TFC, which can, of course, be zero, and $V(Q)$ is the TVC, which is a function of Q. It should also be noted that (A7.14) is the cost *function* (as distinguished from the cost *equation*, where cost is considered a function of the inputs).

Let us denote the total profit by π. By definition,

$$\pi(Q) = R(Q) - C(Q) = QP - F - V(Q) \tag{A7.15}$$

The first-order condition for profit maximization is

$$d\pi(Q)/dQ = P(Q) + QdP/dQ - dV(Q)/dQ = 0 \tag{A7.16}$$

Since

$$\text{MC} = dC(Q)/dQ = dV(Q)/dQ \tag{A7.17}$$

(A7.16) implies

$$\text{MR} = \text{MC} \tag{A7.18}$$

which is precisely the necessary condition for profit maximization (i.e., condition (7.1) in the text).

The second-order condition for profit maximization requires that

$$d^2\pi(Q)/dQ^2 = d^2R(Q)/dQ^2 - d^2C(Q)/dQ^2 < 0 \tag{A7.19}$$

or

$$d^2R(Q)/dQ^2 < d^2C(Q)/dQ^2 \tag{A7.20}$$

For maximum profit, the slope of the MC curve must be greater than that of the MR curve at their point of intersection. Although the slope of the MR curve cannot mathematically be negative, it is usually negatively sloped in the neighborhood of equilibrium. For this reason, when the MC curve is rising at its point of intersection with the MR curve, (A7.20)—which is identical to the second-order condition for profit maximization of a firm under perfect competition—is satisfied. However, the MR curve of a monopoly is usually declining; therefore, the MC curve may not have to rise. If both the MR curve and MC are declining at their point of intersection, the second-order condition for profit maximization is satisfied if the MC curve declines more slowly than the MR curve; in this case, (A7.19) is satisfied. This proves the validity of the sufficient condition for profit maximization (7.2a) or (7.2b).

In order to illustrate the above results, we shall use two simple, specific demand functions and two simple, specific MC functions to compute the equilibrium quantity and price.

CASE 1: LINEAR DEMAND FUNCTIONS

A linear demand function can be written

$$Q = A/B - (1/B)P \tag{A7.21}$$

where A and B are positive constants. The inverse of (A7.21) is

$$P = A - BQ \tag{A7.22}$$

The TR function is

$$R = PQ = AQ - BQ^2 \tag{A7.23}$$

The MR function is

$$MR = dR/dQ = A - 2BQ \tag{A7.24}$$

Case 1A: Constant MC
The MC function in the case of constant MC can be written

$$MC = C \tag{A7.25}$$

where C is a constant. This implies that

$$TC = C_0 + CQ \quad \text{and} \quad MC = AVC$$

where C_0 is some constant.

The first-order condition for profit maximization requires that $MR = MC$. By substitution, we obtain

$$A - 2BQ = C \tag{A7.26}$$

Thus, the quantity Q^* that will maximize profit for the given demand and cost functions is

$$Q^* = (A - C)/2B \qquad\qquad\qquad\text{(A7.27)}$$

Hence, once the demand function (specified here by A and B) and the cost function (specified here by C) are known, the quantity that maximizes profit can be computed by using (A7.27). Economists usually consider the quantity Q to be the decision variable, and (A7.27) gives the equilibrium solution in this case. However, the equilibrium solution can be equivalently stated in terms of price instead of quantity. Since the demand is assumed to be known [this must be the case; otherwise, (A7.27) cannot be derived in the first place], we substitute (A7.27) into (A7.22), and the profit-maximizing price P^* is

$$P^* = (A + C)/2 \qquad\qquad\qquad\text{(A7.28)}$$

Therefore, theoretically, it does not make any difference whether quantity Q or price P is considered as the decision variable, since a single-valued demand function that relates these two variables is assumed to be known.

It is easily seen that the second-order condition for profit maximization is satisfied because

$$d^2R/dQ^2 = -2B < 0 = d^2C/dQ^2 \qquad\qquad\text{(A7.29)}$$

Equation (A7.28) implies that, in the case of constant MC (and thus constant AVC), when MC (and thus AVC) increases (decreases), the profit-maximizing price should only increase (decrease) by one-half the amount of the increase (decrease) of MC (and thus AVC), regardless of the slope (except horizontal) of the demand, because from (A7.28)

$$\partial P/\partial C = \tfrac{1}{2} \qquad\qquad\qquad\text{(A7.30)}$$

This result may have some important implications during periods of inflation. As we have argued in Chapter 3, AVC is, in reality, usually constant within the relevant range, and this implies constant MC. A linear demand function can be considered to be a good approximation for nonlinear functions over a short interval. In such a case, given (A7.30), we would observe that as AVC increases, MC also increases, but the profit-maximizing price should only increase by one-half of the increase in cost. However, common sense tells us that when cost increases, price should increase by at least the amount of increase in AVC. In this respect, business pricing practice is probably guided by common sense rather than the result of the above analysis. In this case cost inflation may be unnecessarily high even from the profit-maximizing standpoint of business. There may be room for further study with respect to this matter.

Case 1B: Linear MC
The linear MC function can be written

$$MC = C_1 + C_2 Q \qquad (A7.31)$$

where C_1 and C_2 are constants; C_2 can be either positive or negative, depending on whether the MC curve is positively or negatively sloped. This MC function implies the following TC function:

$$TC = C_0 + C_1 Q + \tfrac{1}{2} C_2 Q^2 \qquad (A7.32)$$

where C_0 is an arbitrary constant.

As before, the first-order condition for profit maximization requires that MR = MC. Equating (A7.24) and (A7.31), we obtain

$$A - 2BQ = C_1 + C_2 Q \qquad (A7.33)$$

which yields the profit-maximizing quantity Q^*. Thus,

$$Q^* = (A - C_1)/(2B + C_2) \qquad (A7.34)$$

and the corresponding profit-maximizing price P^* is

$$P^* = (AB + AC_2 + BC_1)/(2B + C_2) \qquad (A7.35)$$

The second-order condition for profit maximization requires that

$$-2B < C_2 \qquad (A7.36)$$

Since, by assumption, B is positive, if $C_2 > 0$, then the second-order condition is satisfied. On the other hand, even if C_2 is negative, the second-order condition is still satisfied, provided the absolute value of C_2 is less than $2B$; that is, the MC curve declines more slowly than the MR curve, which was noted as sufficient condition (7.2c) in the text.

A shift of the MC curve in the linear case is a change in C_1, which can be considered a change in MC. The effect of a change in MC on the profit-maximizing price is indicated by the partial derivative of (A7.35) with respect to C_1 (other parameters being constant):

$$\frac{\partial P^*}{\partial C_1} = \frac{B}{2B + C_2} = \frac{1}{2 + C_2/B} \qquad (A7.37)$$

It can easily be seen that (A7.30) is a special case of (A7.37): When MC is constant, $C_2 = 0$, and (A7.37) and (A7.30) are identical. With linear demand and linear MC curves, the effect of a shift of the MC curve on the profit-maximizing price depends on the ratio of the slopes of the demand and MC curves. Furthermore, it makes a big difference whether the MC curve has a positive or negative slope. If the MC curve has a negative slope, then $C_2 < 0$. For a given demand, the steeper the slope of the MC curve, the larger the effect of a given shift in MC on the profit-maximizing price. It may seem that when the absolute value of C_2 is greater than $2B$, (A7.37) will be negative. This would imply that an increase in MC results in a decrease in the profit-maximizing price, which is contrary to common sense. Further examination indicates that this is the case in which the second-order condition for profit maximization is violated. Thus, if $C_2 < 0$, then a restriction on C_2 must be imposed on (A7.37), namely, $|C_2| < 2B$. When C_2 is positive, the MC curve has a positive slope. For a given demand, the steeper the slope of the MC curve, the smaller the effect of a given shift in MC on the profit-maximizing price. Equation (A7.22) indicates that B is the slope of the inverse demand function. Since C_2 is the numerator and B the denominator of one of the terms on the right side of (A7.37), the effect of the slope of the inverse demand function (curve) on the profit-maximizing price for a given shift in the MC curve will be just the opposite to that of the slope of the MC curve.

    Comparing (A7.30) and (A7.37), it is interesting to note that (A7.30) does not involve the slope of the demand function, whereas (A7.37) involves the slopes of both the demand and the MC curve. Since empirical studies indicate that MC is usually constant within the relevant range, this result may have important implications with respect to cost–price inflation, i.e., price inflation attributable to rising costs.

CASE 2: CONSTANT PRICE ELASTICITY DEMAND FUNCTIONS

The class of constant price elasticity demand functions can be written

$$Q = AP^{-B} \tag{A7.38}$$

where A and B are positive constants. It is easily seen that the constant B is the price elasticity. We have

$$dQ/dP = -BAP^{-B-1} = -BQ/P \tag{A7.39}$$

The price elasticity of demand e is defined as

$$e = -(dQ/dP)P/Q \tag{A7.11}$$

By substitution,

$$e = -(-BQ/P)P/Q = B \tag{A7.40}$$

It should be noted that the constant price elasticity demand function is not linear and that the linear function has variable price elasticity along the demand curve.

When $B = 1$, we have unitary elastic demand; in this case, (A7.38) can be written

$$QP = A \tag{A7.38'}$$

Since, by definition, QP is the TR, we have a special case: The TR is constant and the MR is zero as one moves along a unitary elastic demand curve. If this were the case, then regardless of what price a monopoly charges, its TR would be the same. This kind of demand function cannot be realistic. If it were, the monopolist would charge a price so high that the quantity and hence the cost would be infinitesimally small, since the cost-minimizing quantity and the profit-maximizing quantity are identical for constant TR.

The inverse of function (A7.38) is

$$P = A^{1/B}Q^{-1/B} \tag{A7.41}$$

The total revenue R is

$$R = PQ = A^{1/B}Q^{1-1/B} \tag{A7.42}$$

The MR is

$$MR = (1 - 1/B)A^{1/B}Q^{-1/B} \tag{A7.43}$$

Case 2A: Constant MC

With the MC function (A7.25), the first-order condition for profit maximization requires that

$$C = (1 - 1/B)A^{1/B}Q^{-1/B} \tag{A7.44}$$

The solution for the profit-maximizing quantity $Q*$ is

$$Q* = (1 - 1/B)^B A C^{-B} \tag{A7.45}$$

Substituting (A7.45) into (A7.41), the profit-maximizing price $P*$ is

$$P* = C/(1 - 1/B) = [1 + 1/(B - 1)]C \tag{A7.46}$$

It can be seen that the profit-maximizing price is a function of MC and the price elasticity of demand; it is not related to the constant A in the demand function. This is obviously different from the linear demand function case.

From (A7.45) and (A7.46), it can be observed that when demand is inelastic, $B < 1$. In this case, both the profit-maximizing quantity and the profit-maximizing price will be negative, which does not make economic sense. Similarly, with unitary elastic demand, the profit-maximizing quantity will be zero, and the monopoly will go out of business. Thus, only an elastic demand is consistent with monopoly for a constant elasticity demand function.

The effect of a change in MC on the profit-maximizing price is indicated by the partial derivative of (A7.46) with respect to C:

$$\partial P^*/\partial C = 1/(1 - 1/B) = 1 + 1/(B - 1) \tag{A7.47}$$

The higher the price elasticity (the larger B), the smaller the effect of a given change in MC on the profit-maximizing price and vice versa. In the extreme case, when the elasticity B approaches infinity, $\partial P^*/\partial C = 1$, that is, the change in the profit-maximizing price will be the same as the change in cost. When B is close to 1, $\partial P^*/\partial C$ can be very large, so that when MC increases a little, the profit-maximizing price will increase by a large amount in this special case. If we compare this result with that of Case 1A—a linear demand function—it becomes obvious that the behavior of the profit-maximizing price when cost changes depends on the shape of the demand function. Without knowing the demand function, generalization could be misleading.

Case 2B: Linear MC
In the case of a linear (rather than constant) MC and a constant elasticity demand function, the derivation of an explicit expression for P^* in terms of the parameters of the cost and demand functions (including the constant elasticity) is not easy, if at all possible. However, the effect of a change in the MC on the profit-maximizing price can be indicated by computing the partial derivative of P^* with respect to C_1 from the equilibrium condition MC = MR. Equating the linear MC function (A7.31) and the MR function (A7.43) for constant elasticity demand, we obtain

$$C_1 + C_2 Q = (1 - 1/B) A^{1/B} Q^{-1/B} \tag{A7.48}$$

Substituting (A7.38) and (A7.41) into (A7.48), we obtain

$$C_1 + C_2 A P^{-B} = (1 - 1/B) P \tag{A7.49}$$

If we take the total derivative on both sides, assuming that all other changes besides those in P and C are zero, we obtain the following partial derivative:

$$\partial P/\partial C_1 = 1/[ABC_2 P^{-(1+B)} - 1/B + 1] \tag{A7.50}$$

Expression (A7.50) is much more complicated than the previous ones [e.g., (A7.30), (A7.37), and (A7.47)] because it not only involves the parameters of cost, the demand functions, and the constant elasticity, but also the price. However, it can be easily shown that (A7.50) is positive for $C_2 > 0$. Since (A7.50) will be positive if

$$ABC_2 P^{-(1+B)} - 1/B + 1 > 0$$

the above holds because it is equivalent to

$$AB^2 C_2 P^{-(1+B)} + B > 1 \quad \text{for} \quad C_2 > 0 \tag{A7.51}$$

Expression (A7.51) always holds, since A, B, and P are positive and $B > 1$ for MR > 0 [see (A7.43)].

When $C_2 < 0$, $\partial P/\partial C_1 > 0$ stills holds as long as the second-order condition for profit maximization is satisfied. This can be easily checked by differentiating (A7.43), substituting (A7.38) into the resulting expression, and then comparing the result with C_2, which is the derivative of MC with respect to Q.

A7.3 THE RELATIONSHIP BETWEEN MR AND e: ITS USEFULNESS AND POSSIBLE MISUNDERSTANDING

The well-known relationship between MR and the price elasticity of demand e is shown in (A7.12). This relationship can be useful in solving for the profit-maximizing price in the special case of constant MC and constant price elasticity (e.g., Case 2A in Section 7.2.2). The first-order condition for profit maximization requires that MR = MC. Thus, we equate (A7.12) and (A7.25):

$$P(1 - 1/e) = C \qquad (A7.52)$$

This yields

$$P^* = C/(1 - 1/e) \qquad (A7.53)$$

which is identical to (A7.46) if we take into consideration that B is the constant price elasticity. Since, by assumption, both C and e are constants, P^* can be computed using (A7.53). Moreover, since the derivation of (A7.53) is much easier than that of (A7.46), this may seem to be an easier way to solve for P*. It would be tempting to use (A7.12) and the first-order condition for profit maximization MR = MC to obtain such an expression as

$$P = MC/(1 - 1/e) \qquad (A7.54)$$

Hence, the difficulty encountered in Case 2B of Section 7.2.2 would seem no longer to exist: An explicit expression for the profit-maximizing price can be derived using (A7.54). However, this is not a solution even if e is a constant. For example, in Case 2B, if we substitute the linear MC function (A7.31) and the constant price elasticity B into (A7.54), we obtain

$$P = (C_1 + C_2 Q)/(1 - 1/B) \qquad (A7.55)$$

This is not a solution, since the right side involves the variable Q. In order to obtain a solution for P^*, we must eliminate Q by using the demand function. However, if (A7.38) is substituted into (A7.55), we obtain (A7.49), with which we have encountered difficulty in deriving an explicit expression for P^* in terms of the parameters and B.

The point here is that an expression such as (A7.54) can only be considered an implicit function of Q in general, because P is generally a function of Q. The price elasticity e, by virtue of the demand function, and, similarly, MC are also functions of Q, except in the special case where both MC and e are constant. In order to avoid possible misunderstanding, (A7.54) should be written

$$G(Q) = P(Q) - MC(Q)/[1 - 1/e(Q)] = 0 \qquad (A7.56)$$

Mathematically, expression (A7.56) is identical to the first-order condition for profit maximization direct from the condition MR = MC, namely,

$$G(Q) = MR(Q) - MC(Q) = 0 \qquad (A7.57)$$

Certain statements found in some microeconomics textbooks indicate that there are economists who misunderstand expressions similar to (A7.54). Thus, the above clarification seems to be necessary. We shall have more to say concerning this point in Sections A7.6 and A7.7 on mark-up pricing.

A7.4 PRICE DISCRIMINATION

As we have mentioned, price discrimination is feasible only when a monopoly faces different demand functions for different groups of consumers and a homogeneous product. For the sake of simplicity, we shall only deal with the case of third-degree price discrimination, that is, two distinct demand functions. Let us denote the quantity and price for market 1 by Q_1 and P_1, respectively, whereas Q_2 and P_2 are those for market 2. We denote the total quantity by Q. By definition, we have

$$Q = Q_1 + Q_2 \qquad (A7.58)$$

The demand and inverse demand functions are

$$Q_1 = D_1(P_1) \quad \text{and} \quad P_1 = D_1^{-1}(Q_1) \qquad (A7.59)$$

and

$$Q_2 = D_2(P_2) \quad \text{and} \quad P_2 = D_2^{-1}(Q_2) \qquad (A7.60)$$

Since the product is homogeneous, the monopoly faces only one cost function:

$$C = F + f(Q) = F + f(Q_1 + Q_2) \qquad (A7.61)$$

Let us denote the TR in markets 1 and 2, respectively, by R_1 and R_2; thus,

$$R_1 = P_1(Q_1)Q_1 \qquad (A7.62)$$

and

$$R_2 = P_2(Q_2)Q_2 \qquad (A7.63)$$

The total profit π is

$$\pi = R_1(Q_1) + R_2(Q_2) - C \tag{A7.64}$$

The first-order condition for profit maximization yields the equilibrium solution, provided that the second-order condition is satisfied. The first-order conditions are

$$\frac{\partial \pi}{\partial Q_1} = \frac{dR_1(Q_1)}{dQ_1} - \frac{dC}{dQ}\frac{\partial Q}{\partial Q_1} = 0$$

$$\frac{\partial \pi}{\partial Q_2} = \frac{dR_2(Q_2)}{dQ_2} - \frac{dC}{dQ}\frac{\partial Q}{\partial Q_2} = 0 \tag{A7.65}$$

Since

$$\frac{\partial Q}{\partial Q_1} = \frac{\partial Q}{\partial Q_2} = 1$$

from (A7.58), we have

$$\frac{dR_1(Q_1)}{dQ_1} = \frac{dC}{dQ} = \frac{dR_2(Q_2)}{dQ_2} \tag{A7.66}$$

which implies that

$$MR_1 = MR_2 \tag{A7.67}$$

If MR_1 were not equal to MR_2, the monopoly could increase its TR without affecting TC by shifting sales from the low-MR market to the high one, thus increasing total profit. The equality of the MRs does not imply the equality of the prices in the two markets. Let us denote the prices and the price elasticities of demand in the two markets by P_1, P_2, e_1, and e_2, respectively. Then from (A7.12) and (A7.67) we obtain

$$P_1(1 - 1/e_1) = P_2(1 - 1/e_2)$$

or

$$P_1/P_2 = (1 - 1/e_2)/(1 - 1/e_1) \tag{A7.68}$$

Price will be lower in the market with the higher price elasticity of demand. This proves the statement that was made at the end of Section 7.1.7. The prices will be equal only if the price elasticities of demand are equal, since, in this case, price discrimination will not be beneficial to the monopoly. This justifies the first condition for price discrimination as stated in the beginning of Section 7.1.7.

The second-order conditions for profit maximization are

$$d^2R_1/dQ_1^2 - d^2C/dQ^2 < 0, \qquad d^2R_2/dQ_2^2 - d^2C/dQ^2 < 0$$

$$(d^2R_1/dQ_1^2 - d^2C/dQ^2)(d^2R_2/dQ_2^2 - d^2C/dQ^2) - (d^2C/dQ^2)^2 > 0$$

$$\tag{A7.69}$$

The first two inequalities are identical to (A7.19), which implies that for a monopoly to obtain a maximum profit, each market must separately satisfy the second-order condition for profit maximization. However, price discrimination sets still an additional requirement, which is indicated by the last inequality. In terms of Figure 7.9, the first two inequalities are concerned with the second-order conditions for profit maximization at points E_1 and E_2, whereas the last inequality is concerned with the second-order condition for profit maximization at point E. The profit of a price-discriminating monopoly will be maximized only if the second-order condition for profit maximization is satisfied at all relevant points. Since all of the marginal revenue curves—MR_1, MR_2, and MR—necessarily have a negative slope, whenever the MC curve is rising at the point of intersection with MR, the second-order condition is satisfied. In addition, since the slope of MR is flatter than those of MR_1 and MR_2, whenever the second-order condition is satisified at E, it must also be satisfied at E_1 and E_2.

A7.5 CEILING PRICE AND DISCONTINUITY OF THE MR FUNCTION OF A MONOPOLY

In Section 7.1.8, we stated without proof that the MR function (curve) of a monopoly is discontinuous at the quantity where the regulated price intersects the demand under the ceiling price system (i.e., the monopoly is free to charge a lower—but not a higher—price than the regulated one). We shall now prove that the gap between the regulated price and the MR is positive and that the magnitude of the gap depends on the quantity and the slope of the demand function at the given quantity.

As we have shown in (A7.9), the MR for a monopoly is given by

$$MR = P + QdP/dQ \qquad (A7.9)$$

at any quantity Q. The price P is the same as AR, the slope of the inverse demand function (dP/dQ) is negative for a monopoly and Q is positive; thus,

$$MR = AR + QdP/dQ < AR \qquad (A7.70)$$

for any quantity Q other than $Q = 0$.

The monopoly can sell as many units of the product as it wishes (up to the demand) at the regulated ceiling price $\bar{P}$. Therefore, the monopoly, just as a perfectly competitive firm, faces a horizontal demand curve, the slope of which is zero. As we have shown in Chapter 6, MR = AR under these circumstances. Thus,

$$MR = AR = \bar{P} \qquad (A7.71)$$

as long as the monopoly sells its product at the ceiling price. The maximum quantity Q_2 (corresponding to Q_2 in Figure 7.10) that a monopoly can sell at $\bar{P}$ is determined by the demand function:

$$Q_2 = D(\bar{P}) \tag{A7.72}$$

If the monopoly wishes to sell a quantity greater than Q_2, it can only do so by reducing the price below $\bar{P}$. If this is the case, the ceiling price will no longer be effective, and the MR of the monopoly will be represented by (A7.70). Thus, there are two MR values at Q_2: $\bar{P}$, which is the regulated ceiling price according to (A7.71) and corresponding to $\overline{Q_2 M}$ in Figure 7.10, and the MR according to the demand of the monopoly without regulation [(A7.70)], which corresponds to $\overline{Q_2 N}$ in Figure 7.10. From (A7.70), it can be seen that the latter is less than the former as long as Q_2 is positive. The gap between these two MRs at Q_2 is $-Q_2 dP/dQ > 0$, since $Q_2 > 0$ and $dP/dQ < 0$. The magnitude of the gap depends on both the quantity Q_2 and the slope of the demand function at Q_2 because it is the product of these two terms. This completes the proof of the assertion that we made in the beginning of this section.

A7.6 MARK-UP PRICING MODELS

Mathematically, the mark-up pricing models that we have discussed are quite simple and straightforward. Consequently, there is no need to repeat the algebra. However, the following summary notations will help students further their understanding of the various models:

P: Price

Q: Quantity

V: Total variable cost

F: Total fixed cost

R: Total revenue $R = PQ$

C: Total cost $C = F + V$

c: Average total cost $c = C/Q$

v: Average variable cost $v = V/Q$

π: Total profit

r: Rate of profit on sales $r = \pi/R$

a: Mark-up parameter

ZPM: Zero profit multiplier $\text{ZPM} = (F + V)/V = 1 + F/V$

The naive mark-up pricing model (model 1) can be written

$$P = av \tag{A7.73}$$

TABLE A7.1

Model	Decision variable	Terms the firm knows	Terms subjectively determined
1	P	v	a
2	P	v and ZPM	r
3	P	v and F	π and Q

The AC mark-up pricing model (model 2) can be written

$$P = [\text{ZPM}/(1 - r)]v \tag{A7.74}$$

The target (overbarred) profit mark-up pricing model (model 3) can be written

$$P = v + (F + \overline{\pi})/\overline{Q} = [1 + (F + \pi)/V]v \tag{A7.75}$$

Table A7.1 summarizes the special features of the three models.

In spite of the differences between the above three mark-up pricing models with respect to sophistication and practical implications in business applications, they are, in fact, equivalent in terms of accounting. Thus, it can be shown that

$$a = \text{ZPM}/(1 - r) = 1 + (F + \pi)/V \tag{A7.76}$$

By definition,

$$\pi = R - C = PQ - (F + V)$$

Thus,

$$PQ = F + V + \pi$$

or

$$P = v + (F + \pi)/Q \tag{A7.77}$$

Expression (A7.77) is an identity that holds for any of the three mark-up pricing models. For the naive model, we have (A7.73). In accounting,

$$av = v + (F + \pi)/Q$$

Dividing both sides of the above expression by v and taking into consideration that $V = vQ$, we obtain

$$a = 1 + (F + \pi)/V \tag{A7.78}$$

For the AC mark-up model, we have (A7.74). Equating (A7.74) and (A7.77), after some manipulation we can obtain

$$\text{ZPM}/(1 - r) = 1 + (F + \pi)/V \tag{A7.79}$$

For model 3, the multiplier on AVC in (A7.75) is identical to the right sides of (A7.78) and (A7.79). In short, the three models are identical in terms of accounting. However, this only indicates that the three models are consistent; it does not imply that they do not have practical differences. These differences are summarized in Table A7.1.

A7.7 THE MONOPOLY MODEL IN ECONOMIC THEORY

Table A7.2 summarizes the monopoly model in economic theory. It is often overlooked that economic theory assumes the firm to know its demand, inverse demand, and cost functions. These assumptions do not result in a system that can be solved, since, by definition,

$$\pi = R - C = PQ - C(Q)$$

We still have one equation in two variables: π and Q (P is a function of Q by the inverse function). It is the behavior assumption of profit maximization which imposes a further restriction on the system. The resulting first-order condition for profit maximization (i.e., MR = MC) enables us to have a determinate system, that is, one variable in one equation, so that we may write

$$MR(Q) = MC(Q) \quad \text{or} \quad G(Q) = MR(Q) - MC(Q) = 0$$

$$(A7.80)$$

The solution Q^* of this system is the profit-maximizing (equilibrium) quantity, corresponding to Q^* in Figures 7.4 and 7.5 in the short run and to Q^* in Figures 7.7 and 7.8 in the long run.

It is important to note that the equilibrium condition (A7.80) is an implicit function of Q. Although MR can be written in an alternative way, that is, in terms of P and e (the price elasticity of demand) as in (A7.12) this does not make any difference in general, since P and e are, in general, functions of Q. The equilibrium condition is still an implicit function of Q. However, in the special case where both MC and price elasticity of demand are constant, the price can be computed directly from the equilibrium condition (A7.80) and (A7.12), that is, without computing

TABLE A7.2

Decision variable	Information available to the firm	Behavior assumption
Q	$Q = D(P)$ or $P = D^{-1}(Q)$ and $C = f(Q)$	Profit maximization

Q, by the following formula:

$$P = \frac{\overline{M}}{1 - 1/\overline{e}} \tag{A7.81}$$

where $\overline{M}$ denotes the constant MC and $\overline{e}$ the constant price elasticity of demand. On the other hand, this does not mean that (A7.81) cannot be used to compute the price P when MC and e are not constant. In general, (A7.81) should be written

$$P(Q) = \frac{M(Q)}{1 - 1/e(Q)} \tag{A7.82}$$

where $P(Q)$, $M(Q)$, and $e(Q)$ indicate that the price, MC, and price elasticity of demand are functions of Q. There is no dispute, we believe, about the statement that P and MC are functions of Q. In order to illustrate that e is also a function of Q, we shall use the linear demand function (A7.21):

$$Q = A/B - (1/B)P \tag{A7.21}$$

Thus,

$$dQ/dP = -1/B$$

By definition,

$$e = -(dQ/dP)P/Q \tag{A7.11}$$

Through substitution, we obtain

$$e = A/BQ - 1$$

Thus, when Q approaches zero, e approaches infinity, whereas when $P = 0$, $Q = A/B$ and hence $e = 0$. (Students may wish to try to determine why $e = 1$ at the midpoint of the demand curve.) Since all of the terms on the right side of (A7.11) are functions of Q (dQ/dP is a function of P, which, in turn, is a function of Q), e is also a function of Q.

The important thing to realize in terms of mathematics is that, except for the special case where both MC and e are constant, both (A7.80) and (A7.82) are implicit functions of Q, the solution of both being the equilibrium quantity Q^*. One cannot solve for price directly from (A7.82) because $M(Q)$ and $e(Q)$ are not known before Q is known. However, when Q is known to be Q^*, the corresponding price P^* can be computed by using either (A7.82) or the inverse demand function (A7.4b). In fact, using the latter is easier than using the former, and, in this respect, (A7.82) is rather confusing.

The above conceptual clarification is important in theory, particularly with respect to mark-up pricing. Most microeconomic textbooks that cover the topic of mark-up pricing use (A7.82) to show the consistency between economic theory and mark-up pricing practice in business. Unfortunately, some authors have made misleading statements to the effect that this consistency holds only in the special case where MC and price elasticity of demand are constant. We shall show in Section A7.8 that economic theory in imperfect competition (i.e., the traditional monopoly model) and mark-up pricing in business are theoretically equivalent not only in the special case, but also in general.

A7.8 MATHEMATICAL PROOF OF THE THEORETICAL EQUIVALENCE BETWEEN MARK-UP PRICING MODELS AND THE TRADITIONAL MONOPOLY MODEL OF ECONOMIC THEORY

The mathematical proof of Theorem 7.2 amounts to showing that there exists a mark-up parameter a^* that will result in a profit-maximizing price P^* for a given v^*, which is the AVC corresponding to the profit-maximizing quantity Q^*. The price P^* will be identical to the profit-maximizing price of the monopoly.

The proof of Theorem 7.2 makes use of the results that we have developed in previous sections of this appendix. In order to make the proof more explicit, we shall use a more-detailed notation than before.

The demand function (A7.3) is now written in the equivalent form (see, e.g., Samuelson, 1965)

$$Q = D(P, a_1, a_2, ..., a_n) \tag{A7.83}$$

where a_i, $i = 1, 2, ..., n$, are the parameters of the demand function. For different demand functions, we may have a different number of parameters, that is, the index number n may be different for different functions. For example, the linear demand function (A7.21) has two parameters: A and B; thus, $n = 2$ in this special case (A and B correspond to a_1 and a_2, respectively). The constant elasticity demand function (A7.38) also has two parameters, but this is just a coincidence. In general, two different demand functions may have different numbers of parameters. For example, the demand function (A7.38') has only one parameter if we ignore the constant 1.

The inverse demand function (A7.4b) can be written

$$P = D^{-1}(Q, a_1, a_2, ..., a_n) \tag{A7.84}$$

where a_i, $i = 1, 2, ..., a_n$, are the same as in (A7.83). However, D^{-1} is different from D, that is, the two functions involve the same number of parameters, but in a different way. This is indicated by (A7.21) and (A7.22); the former corresponds to (A7.83) and the latter to (A7.84).

Similarly, the cost function (A7.14) can be written

$$C = f(Q, b_1, b_2, ..., b_m) \tag{A7.85}$$

where b_i, $i = 1, 2, ..., m$, are the m parameters in the cost function. The AVC and MC functions can be written

$$v = v(Q, b_1, b_2, ..., b_m) \tag{A7.86}$$

and

$$MC = M(Q, b_1, b_2, ..., b_m) \tag{A7.87}$$

The bs in (A7.85)–(A7.87) are the same, but the functions v and M may involve a different number of parameters than the function f; that is, there may be fewer parameters in (A7.86) and (A7.87) than in (A7.85). For example, the TC function (A7.32) involves three parameters, whereas the MC function (A7.31) involves only two. This implies that some parameters in (A7.86) and (A7.87) may equal zero.

The equilibrium condition (A7.18) can be written in implicit form:

$$G(Q, A, B) = 0 \tag{A7.88}$$

For convenience in notation, we define $A \equiv (a_1, a_2, ..., a_n)$ and $B \equiv (b_1, b_2, ..., b_m)$.

The implicit function of the equilibrium condition involves most, if not all, of the parameters of both the demand and the cost function [see, e.g., (A7.26), (A7.33), (A7.44), and (A7.48)]. The solution of (A7.88), if it exists, is an explicit function of Q in terms of the parameters which can be written

$$Q = g(A, B) \tag{A7.89}$$

It should be pointed out that the explicit function g may be single-valued or multivalued, or it may not even exist; that is, Q may not be explicitly expressible in terms of the parameters. For example, (A7.27), (A7.34), and (A7.45) correspond to (A7.89). However, the function g implicit in (A7.48) is a different matter. This example shows that a solution of (A7.88) cannot be taken for granted. Furthermore, there are additional restrictions imposed on the function g in order to make economic sense. For example, for certain sets of the parameters, the function g may assign a negative or even an imaginary number to Q, which makes good sense in terms of mathematics, but not in terms of economics.

Once the implications are understood, it is clear that what we have actually done in the previous sections is to deal only with a class of functions such that the function g not only exists, but also assigns a nonnegative value to Q. This is not always recognized by economists, even though all graphical presentations imply this approach, which actually makes good sense in terms of business operations. Suppose that a monopoly model is based on certain demand and cost functions such that the implicit function (A7.88) cannot be solved for Q in terms of the parameters, that is, the function g does not exist. This means that if a monopoly does face such demand and cost functions, there is no way to find the profit-maximizing quantity. Under these circumstances, economic theory is useless insofar as business operations are concerned. In terms of business operations, it is meaningful to assume that the function g does exist.

Substituting (A7.89) into (A7.84), we obtain

$$P = D^{-1}[g(A, B), A]$$

which can be written

$$P = h(A, B) \tag{A7.90}$$

The point here is that if g exists, then the function h also exists.

Similarly, substituting (A7.89) into (A7.86), we obtain the AVC:

$$v = v[g(A, B), B]$$

which can be written

$$v^* = v^*(A, B) \tag{A7.91}$$

Again, if the function g exists, then the function v^* also exists.

Let us define

$$a \equiv h(A, B)/v^*(A, B) \equiv H(A, B)$$

Thus, whenever the functions h and v^* exist, the function H also exists.

The naive mark-up pricing model defined by

$$P = av \tag{A7.73}$$

is identical to (A7.90), which represents the profit-maximizing price of the monopoly model in economic theory. This proves Theorem 7.2: The naive mark-up pricing method used by business firms in practice is theoretically equivalent to the traditional monopoly model of economic theory.

The AC mark-up pricing model is represented by (A7.74). Recall that, in the notation of this section, at equilibrium, by definition,

$$\text{ZPM} = f[g(A, B), B]/g(A, B)v^*(A, B) \tag{A7.92}$$

$$\pi = g(A, B)h(A, B) - f[g(A, B), B] \tag{A7.93}$$

$$r = [g(A, B)h(A, B) \tag{A7.94}$$

$$- f[g(A, B), B]/g(A, B)h(A, B)$$

or

$$r = 1 - f[g(A, B), B]/g(A, B)h(A, B) \tag{A7.95}$$

and hence,

$$1 - r = f[g(A, B), B]/g(A, B)h(A, B) \tag{A7.96}$$

Substituting (A7.92) and (A7.96) into (A7.74), we obtain a result that is identical to (A7.90), which represents the profit-maximizing price of the monopoly model in economic theory. This proves Theorem 7.3: The AC mark-up pricing method used by business firms in practice is theoretically equivalent to the traditional monopoly model of economic theory.

The target profit mark-up pricing model is represented by (A7.75). In the notation of this section, at equilibrium by definition,

$$F = f[g(A, B)] - g(A, B)v^*(A, B) \qquad (A7.97)$$

Taking (A7.93) into consideration, we have

$$F + \pi = g(A, B)h(A, B) - g(A, B)v^*(A, B) \qquad (A7.98)$$

Thus,

$$(F + \pi)/Q = h(A, B) - v^*(A, B) \qquad (A7.99)$$

Substituting (A7.99) into (A7.75), we obtain a result that is identical to (A7.90), which represents the profit-maximizing price of the monopoly model in economic theory. This proves Theorem 7.4: The target profit mark-up pricing method used by business firms in practice is theoretically equivalent to the traditional monopoly model of economic theory. Thus, we have proven Theorem 7.1.

MONOPOLISTIC COMPETITION

INTRODUCTION

Perfect competition and pure monopoly are economic models that have considerable theoretical importance in that they provide a foundation upon which more realistic models can be constructed. The problem with the simplified models of perfect competition and pure monopoly is that they are far removed from reality. It may be worthwhile to point out once again that the applicability of an economic model is determined by the assumptions with respect to the conditions of the actual economic system upon which it is based. In other words, if the assumptions underlying a model are far removed from reality, then its applicability is questionable, even though it may have considerable importance with respect to the development of a theory. By way of illustration, consider that although the assumption of a homogeneous product (Assumption 6.1) for an industry or market in the perfect competition model seems quite innocent in theory, it turns out to be very restrictive in reality. For example, two identical items sold by two adjacent retailers are not homogeneous products due to the different locations and/or different attitudes of the salespeople. Furthermore, two identical (or almost identical) products with different brand names are obviously not homogeneous. Thus, two gasoline stations that are right next to each other do not sell homogeneous products if one is Gulf and the other is Mobil. These points will be clarified in Section 8.1.

In any treatment of homogeneous products, the important criterion is not whether the products are physically identical, but whether consumers consider them to be identical. Thus, if sellers can make consumers believe that two physically identical items are different, then the items are no longer homogeneous products,

The model of monopolistic competition combines elements of perfect competition and monopoly

and one can be sold at a higher price than the other. Hence, almost all of the commodities that we buy in everday life are not homogeneous or even close to it. The example of a homogeneous product cited most often is that of the shares of a corporation's common stock traded on the stock exchange. In this case, a buyer does not distinguish between various sellers or units, which is a true indication of a homogeneous product. In addition, the purchases (if any) of these items by an average buyer represent a very small part of his or her total expenditure. In short, the model of perfect competition has only limited applicability in real life because the things that we buy everyday are not homogeneous products (although many of them are only slightly differentiated close substitutes). The theory of monopolistic competition, which was developed by the late Professor Edward H. Chamberlin of Harvard University, is an economic model that addresses this situation. This model combines elements of the models of perfect competition and pure monopoly. Chapter 8 is devoted to a discussion of the model of monopolistic competition.

8.1 ASSUMPTIONS

Monopolistic competition is an economic model that, like the models of perfect competition and pure monopoly, is based on four assumptions. Although these assumptions are similar to those underlying the two previously discussed models, they are not identical. Since even a slight variation in one of the assumptions can make an essential difference, a thorough understanding of all the assumptions is necessary in order to grasp the true meaning of the model. The following four assumptions define the model of monopolistic competition.

Assumption 8.1: Differentiated Products That Are Close Substitutes. A monopolistically competitive market consists of a group of sellers or firms that sell differentiated products which are close substitutes.

For example, two shirts of identical color, style, and material but carrying different brand names are *differentiated* (not homogeneous) products because the brand name may communicate a certain prestige and trustworthiness (or the lack of these qualities) to the consumer. As a result, these two shirts may command different prices. On the other hand, these two shirts certainly represent close substitutes. Strictly speaking, two identical shirts that carry the same brand name and are sold by two adjacent retailers may still not be considered as homogeneous products because different salespeople, together with a difference in general atmosphere between the two shops, may cause buyers to prefer one over the other.

Given the importance of Assumption 8.1, we are faced with the
question, in theory, of defining a "close substitute"; that is, how
close is close? Since there is hardly a scientific measure of clo-
seness, the definition of monopolistically competitive industry or
market is not clear-cut. Some economists oppose this model for
just this reason, since in the economic analysis of market behavior
it is traditional to identify the market in terms of the concept of
an industry, which itself can only be theoretically and unambiguously defined in terms of a homogeneous product. When one
introduces the notion of differentiated products, the concept of
an industry becomes ambiguous. However, the same economists
who oppose the model of monopolistic competition on these
grounds usually remain silent on the implication of homogeneity
in connection with market realities.

*Differentiated
products make the
concept of an
industry ambiguous*

As we have mentioned, shirts carrying different brand names
are not homogeneous products even though they may be identical
in all other respects. Moreover, two shirts of the same brand
name, style, and material but different color are definitely not
identical (homogeneous products). Based on this implication of
the meaning of homogeneity, we do not have, for example, a
sports shirt industry (market) nor a dress shirt industry (market).
What we do have are hundreds or even thousands of shirt industries (markets).[1] Similarly, we do not have automobile industries because passenger cars, pick-up trucks, and buses are definitely not homogeneous products. For the same reason, similar
automobile models manufactured by General Motors, Ford,
Chrysler, and American Motors are not homogeneous products.
Moreover, two automobiles of the same model (e.g., the Chrysler
New Yorker®) but having different colors or options are also not
homogeneous products. Thus, applying the homogeneity concept
for defining an industry or market, we do not have a passenger
car industry (market)—virtually each car is an industry (market)
by itself. Therefore, the question arises of how useful, in reality,
is such a concept in connection with the specification of a market
or industry. Thus, we can see that the concept of a group of firms
dealing in differentiated but closely substitutable products is not
any more unrealistic than the traditional industry concept that
deals with a homogeneous product.

As Chamberlin (1947) has indicated, it may be more fruitful in

---

[1] It is interesting to note that many economists will overlook these distinctions
in some cases while recognizing them in others. A good case in point is the
treatment of labor markets as highly fragmented and of labor as a nonhomo-
geneous commodity for which no single, identifiable market can be specified
(and thus the market model is inapplicable). However, the same economists who
make these distinctions will ignore the differentiation in such items as shirts,
stockings, and shoes and treat them as if the market model of perfect competition
were applicable for analysis. Thus, they speak of the market for shirts, shoes,
or stockings as if there were no product differentiation and as if the product was
homogeneous with respect to consumers.

market analysis to abandon the industry concept altogether. Instead, the firm can be considered as the basis of market analysis. Owing to the profound implications of the concept of homogeneity in connection with the classification of industry mentioned above, Chamberlin's approach may be more meaningful than the traditional one. We shall have more to say on this point later.

It should be noted that the assumption of product differentiation with close substitutes (Assumption 8.1) brings a monopoly element into the model because the differentiation of products attaches unique features to the commodity sold by a specific firm. This uniqueness changes the demand curve for a firm from one of perfect elasticity facing a perfectly competitive firm to one of less-than-perfect elasticity, that is, a negatively sloped demand curve.

Assumption 8.2: Relatively Free Entry and Exit. Since this assumption is almost identical to Assumption 6.2 of the perfectly competitive model, no further explanation is necessary.

Assumption 8.3: Many Small Sellers and Buyers. This assumption is also very similar to the corresponding assumption (Assumption 6.3) of the model of perfect competition.

Assumptions 8.2 and 8.3 make the model of monopolistic competition similar (but not identical) to the model of perfect competition.

Assumption 8.4: Perfect Information or Knowledge. This assumption underlies almost all economic models. Since we have explained the meaning of this assumption previously, no further discussion is necessary.

As we have already noted, Assumption 8.1 brings in monopoly elements, whereas Assumptions 8.2 and 8.3 attach competitive features to the model. Thus, since the model is a mixture of the features of both pure monopoly and perfect competition, the name monopolistic competition is quite proper. We shall shortly see that some special features of the short-run and long-run equilibrium of a firm under monopolistic competition are similar to those of a firm under perfect competition, whereas other special features are similar to those of a firm under pure monopoly.

8.2 THE TWO DEMAND CURVES FACING A FIRM UNDER MONOPOLISTIC COMPETITION

In a monopoly market, the monopolist is, by definition, the industry. Consequently, the demand curves facing the monopolist and the industry are identical. In a perfectly competitive market, the demand curve facing a firm is a horizontal straight line, and the industry's demand curve is usually negatively sloped (the only exception being a Giffen good), as shown in Chapters 5 and 6. This difference in the slopes of the demand curves results in different equilibrium conditions (particularly with respect to the second-order condition for profit maximization and long-run profit) for a perfectly competitive firm and for a monopoly. A special feature of a firm under monopolistic competition is that it faces two distinct demand curves: one which shows the price–quantity relationship when the firm varies its price and its competitors do not, and one which shows the price–quantity relationship when all competitors change their prices accordingly.

Traditionally, textbooks present the model of monopolistic competition in terms of a representative firm; that is, it is assumed that all firms in the group have identical demand and cost curves. This assumption renders the model logically inconsistent because, if the products are dissimilar, their demand and cost curves cannot be expected to be identical. The extension of the traditional analysis of a perfectly competitive firm in an industry based on the assumption of identical demand and cost curves is not only incorrect, but is also unnecessary. One can obtain essentially the same result without this restrictive assumption.

The assumption of identical demand and cost curves is inconsistent with monopolistic competition

Instead of a representative firm, we can consider any firm out of a group of firms that exhibit similar (but not identical) demand and cost curves. The two distinct demand curves that we noted above as facing a firm under monopolistic competition can be derived in the following manner.

Consider Figure 8.1, in which P_0 is the current price of the commodity; and the firm can sell quantity Q_0 for a given period of time. Suppose that the firm reduces its price to P_1 and its competitors do not change their prices. Let us say that, as a result, the quantity sold by the firm for the given period of time increases to Q_1. Thus, demand curve d, which contains points E and F, represents the price–quantity relationship for the firm when it alone reduces its price. On the other hand, when its competitors also reduce their prices accordingly, the increase in sales for our firm will be less, for example, to Q_1' instead of Q_1. The reason for this is obvious: When the firm reduces its price without retaliation by its competitors, not only will its usual customers buy more of the commodity (the concept of a negatively

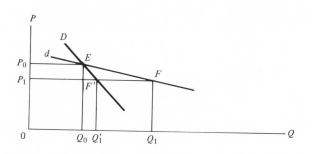

FIGURE 8.1

sloped demand curve), but it will also attract the business of some (but not all) of its competitors' customers. This is the case when one department store sponsors a storewide sale but its competitors do not. In such a case, the store will be very crowded and sales will expand substantially. On the other hand, when all firms in the group reduce their prices accordingly, the quantity sold by the firm will still increase, but by less than before because its competitors' customers will not be diverted. This is similar to the situation where all department stores in a shopping center or mall sponsor a sale. For this reason, Q_1' will be less than Q_1, and F' will be to the left of F. Demand curve D, which contains the points E and F', represents the price–quantity relationship when all firms reduce their price from P_0. Since P_1 can be any price below P_0, all points on D are accordingly to the left of points on d below P_0.

Similarly, when a firm raises its price alone, the quantity that it sells will be reduced more than if all firms in the group raised their prices accordingly. This is true because not only will the usual customers of the firm buy less due to the higher price, but also some (but not all) of its usual customers will patronize its competitors. Thus, d is to the left of D above P_0. It should be pointed out that both d and D are not usually straight lines. Nevertheless, whatever their shapes may be, the relationship between d and D is definite: d is to the right of D below and to the left of D above the current price P_0. We draw both d and D as straight lines for the sake of convenience.

It should be noted that contrary to many textbook presentations, when a firm reduces or raises its price, it is not necessary for its competitors to reduce or raise their prices by the same amount in order to have the price–quantity relationship indicated by demand curve D. In the first place, the product is differentiated and, as a result, different firms can charge different prices for essentially the same product, (e.g., two different brand-name shirts that are essentially the same can be sold at different prices by adjacent retailers). Some identical products can be sold at different prices due to a difference in packaging (e.g., a breakfast cereal in a 10-ounce box will be sold at a different price than the same cereal in a 12-ounce box, but the variation in price may not be strictly proportional to the actual contents). Thus, it is not necessary that the firm's competitors vary their prices by the same amount in order for the price–quantity relationship indicated by demand curve D to exist or be derived. For mathematical convenience (and as we shall show in the appendix to this chapter), it can be assumed that demand curve D represents the price–quantity relationship when all firms in the group vary their prices proportionally. In reality, competitors even do not need to vary their prices proportionally. Thus, two stores sponsoring sales would both have more customers than usual even if their reduction in prices were not proportional. Moreover, the increase in the number of customers in each of the two stores may not be directly proportional to their relative degree of price reduction. However, it is true that a firm usually has more customers when it alone sponsors a sale.

8.3 ADVERTISING AND QUALITY VARIATION

Traditionally, economists consider the demand of a monopolist or a perfectly competitive industry from the firm's point of view. As we have shown in Chapters 4 and 5, the demand for a commodity is derived from the consumer's preference in conjunction with income constraints. The determinants of demand rest on the consumer side, not on the seller side. According to this approach, sellers cannot change the demand; they have to face a given demand, which is determined by consumers collectively, in order to make a proper decision.

Under monopolistic competition the firm can shift the demand curve

One innovation introduced by the late Professor Edward H. Chamberlin in his theory of monopolistic competition is the recognition of a firm's ability to shift the demand curve to the right by advertising. Thus, the firm does have some control over the demand curve. Although advertising can shift demand and is therefore advantageous, it also incurs added costs. The incorporation of advertising into the analysis presents no difficulties in the theory once its effects on the proper shift of the demand and cost curves are taken into consideration.

Another innovation that Chamberlin introduced into economic theory was the recognition of competition in quality or "product differentiation" by monopolistically competitive firms. Again, quality or simply "product" competition, just like advertising has the effect of shifting the demand and cost curves. Theoretically, there is no difficulty in taking this factor into consideration in the analysis, it only makes the model more complicated. In Sections 8.8 and 8.9, we shall discuss the topics of advertising and quality competition in greater detail.[2]

8.4 THE EQUILIBRIUM OF A FIRM IN THE SHORT RUN UNDER PRICE COMPETITION

As we have mentioned above, economists have traditionally considered the quantity of a product as the decision variable of a firm, whereas the quality of the product was not subject to choice. This approach is perfectly acceptable under the conditions of the perfect competition and pure monopoly models, since the assumed homogeneity of the product implies that its quality is given

---

[2] The serious reader is advised to carefully read Chamberlin (1947).

and cannot be changed. If a firm does change the quality, then, by definition, it becomes a different product. For example, in the Chicago Commodity Exchange, a certain grade of wheat is considered to be a homogeneous product. In a technical sense, if farmers improve their product to a higher grade next year, they are dealing with a different product (i.e., a different market) in the Chicago Commodity Exchange. Thus, under the homogeneity assumption in economic theory, there is no room for a firm to vary the quality of its product.

Firms under monopolistic competition have a wider choice of decision variables

Under monopolistic competition, we have an entirely different story because product differentiation is assumed. In this case, in order to maximize profits, the choice of the quality of a product by a monopolistic competitor can be of equal (if not greater) importance to the choice of a price. For the sake of simplicity in analysis, in this section we shall assume that the optimal choice of quality has already been made, that is, the analysis is based on a given quality. The choice of quality will be reconsidered in Section 8.5.

Traditional economic analysis also does not discuss the topic of advertising. Some economists consider advertising to be useless and thus not worthy of discussion. It is true that, in a perfectly competitive market, advertising is a waste for sellers, since they can sell as many units of their product as they wish at the market price without it. However, in any other market model, such as monopolistic competition, oligopoly, and monopoly, the demand facing a firm is not a horizontal straight line, and thus the promotion of sales by means of advertising as Chamberlin (1947) pointed out, can be just as important as the choice of quantity or, equivalently, the proper choice of price (but not both) in fulfilling the goal of profit maximization. Again for the sake of simplicity, in this section we shall also assume that the choice of advertising expenditure has already been made and hence is a constant.

Another assumption that we shall make for the sake of simplicity is that the number of firms in the product group (market) is optimal. This assumption renders the shift of demand curve D unnecessary in the adjustment process. The omission of this assumption would cause the adjustment process to become more complicated in terms of a graphical representation without adding to the understanding of the argument. Once the basic rationale is understood, one should have no difficulty in dealing with the more-complicated case. Thus, this assumption is justified.

Under the above-noted three assumptions and the assumption of perfect information or knowledge (Assumption 8.4), we can draw the demand (average revenue—AR) curve, the associated marginal revenue (MR) curves, and the relevant cost curves for a firm. Traditionally, this firm is called a typical firm, and the corresponding curves of all other firms in the product group (in-

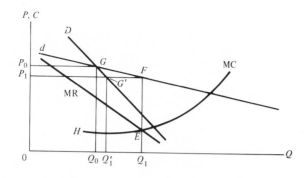

FIGURE 8.2

dustry) are considered identical to those of the typical firm. This approach is valid for the model of perfect competition under the assumption of homogeneous products and homogeneous inputs (Assumption 6.1). However, under the assumption of differentiated products (Assumption 8.1) of monopolistic competition, identical demand and cost curves for different firms in the same product group cannot be realistic. Actually, it is not necessary to assume that the firm under discussion is typical in the sense that the demand and cost curves of all other firms in the product group are identical to its curves. It is sufficient to assume that the *essential characteristics* of the various curves of all other firms are similar to those of the curves of the firm under discussion, that is, the demand curve is negatively sloped instead of horizontal and the marginal cost (MC) and average variable cost (AVC) curves in the short run are smooth, U-shaped, or else horizontal in the relevant range. When the curves of all firms in the product group have a similar shape, the essential nature of the results of the analysis for any firm will be theoretically applicable to all firms, even though the quantity and price may not be identical for different firms. This modification of the model eliminates the grounds upon which it is frequently criticized.

In order to demonstrate the short-run adjustment process of a firm, we start with a situation where the firm under discussion is not in short-run equilibrium. Consider Figure 8.2, which contains the given demand curves D and d (for the meaning of the two different demand curves, see Section 8.3); the firm is currently charging the price P_0, and buyers purchase the quantity Q_0 at this price. By the nature of D and d, they intersect at point G, which corresponds to P_0 and Q_0. The marginal cost of the firm is represented by MC, which intersects MR at point E.[3] If the firm believes that d is its demand curve and thus MR its marginal

---

[3] Note that in this case the MR curve corresponds to the demand curve d, since by assumption the firm is only a small part of the market and a change in its price will not have a perceptible effect on the demand of its competitors. In short, this assumes no retaliation by competitors to the firm's price adjustments.

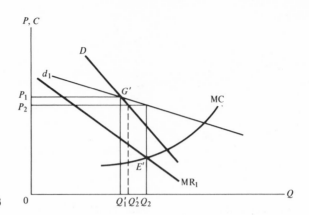

FIGURE 8.3

*The profit-
maximizing price is
conditional on the
relevant demand
curve*

revenue curve, then P_0 is certainly not the profit-maximizing price. (Anyone who has doubt concerning this statement would benefit from review of the discussion in Chapter 7 on the conditions of maximum profit for a monopolist.) Instead, P_1 is the profit-maximizing price for the firm. If all other firms in the market do not change their prices, the quantity sold by the firm at a price of P_1 will be Q_1, and its profit will be maximum.

Although we do not assume that the demand and cost curves of other firms are identical to those of the firm under discussion, we do assume that all other firms, like the one under discussion, are not at short-run equilibrium; that is, they are also charging a price higher than the profit-maximizing price. Thus, all firms will reduce their prices accordingly (although not necessarily by the same amount—see Section 8.2). As a result, the quantity sold by the firm under discussion will not be Q_1 at a price of P_1, but Q_1', which is determined by the intersection of P_1 and D, not P_1 and d. This result comes about by a "sliding down" of d along D (due to competitors' actions) to a new intersection at the new price P_1. This is so because, by assumption, the number of firms in the market does not change and hence D does not shift. Furthermore, the new demand curve (say, d_1) must intersect the given demand curve D at the price P_1, since d_1 shows the new price–quantity relationship for the firm if the other firms' prices remain constant at the newly conceived profit-maximizing prices. This situation is shown in Figure 8.3, in which D, MC, P_1, and Q_1' are the same as in Figure 8.2, but d has shifted to the new position d_1; d_1 intersects D at G', which corresponds to the price P_1 and quantity Q_1'. When d shifts, the corresponding marginal revenue curve also shifts, and the new marginal revenue curve is MR_1, which intersects the given curve MC at E'. For similar reasons as before, P_1 is no longer the profit-maximizing price; instead, the profit-maximizing price is now P_2—if d_1 is the relevant demand curve.

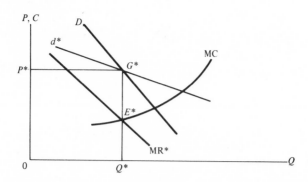

FIGURE 8.4

If the firm again adjusts its price to P_2, but its competitors do not further adjust their prices, the firm can sell the quantity Q_2, and its profit will be maximum. However, for the same reasons as stated in the previous paragraph, all competitor firms will also adjust their prices accordingly. Hence, the relevant demand curve is D, not d, and the actual quantity sold will be Q'_2, not Q_2. Again, the demand curve d_1 shifts to intersect D at the new price P_2, and the process goes on.

This adjustment process will come to an end only if the firm has no reason to change its price. In other words, the short-run equilibrium of a monopolistically competitive firm will be reached when the situation shown in Figure 8.4 obtains, that is, where MR* and MC intersect at E^* and D and d^* intersect at G^*. If the firm charges a price P^*, buyers will purchase the quantity Q^*. It can easily be verified that the firm has no incentive to change its price from P^*. Since the marginal revenue curve MR* based on demand curve d^* intersects the marginal cost curve MC at E^*, which in conjunction with D and d^* determines a profit-maximizing price P^*, the firm will not gain by charging any other price than P^*. Of course, the firm (as well as all other firms) may not earn an economic (excess) profit in the short run. However, as long as P^* exceeds the firm's AVC at Q^*, the firm will continue to produce in the short run.

It is interesting to note that Figure 8.4 does not explicitly show whether the firm is making a positive, zero, or negative economic profit in short-run equilibrium. An easy way to show the profit position of the firm is to draw its average total cost (ATC) curve. If the ATC curve is below G^* at Q^*, then the firm is making positive economic profit; if it is equal to G^* at Q^*, then the firm is making zero economic profit; and if it is above G^* at Q^*, then the firm is making negative economic profit. Remember that in economics the ATC includes a normal return to capital. In order to test their understanding, students would do well to draw graphs that illustrate the various possible situations mentioned above.

It should be pointed out that there is no time element involved in the above adjustment process. Although we have made step-by-step adjustments from disequilibrium to equilibrium for the purpose of illustration, in the nature of comparative statics, the adjustment should be instantaneous. At any rate, no time element is involved, which would be important in dynamic analysis.

8.5 CONSTANT AVC, MARK-UP PRICING, AND SHORT-RUN EQUILIBRIUM

The short-run equilibrium analysis of a monopolistically competitive firm is conventional in two aspects: (1) The MC curve is smooth and U-shaped and (2) no mention is made of the business practice of mark-up pricing. In this section we shall show that the analysis can be carried out equally well (if not better) in terms of constant AVC and/or mark-up pricing.

8.5.1 Constant AVC and Short-Run Equilibrium

As we have already noted in Chapter 7, everyday experience and empirical studies show that in most (if not all) cases the AVC is constant in the relevant range. However, constant AVC is inconsistent with short-run equilibrium analysis for a perfectly competitive firm because a perfectly competitive firm faces a horizontal demand curve, that is, a constant market price and MR. Hence, if it also faces a constant AVC and the corresponding constant MC, then it must equate two constants—MR and MC—in order to maximize profit, which cannot be done. However, many economists ignore or even go so far as to attack the existence of the common phenomenon of constant AVC. This is certainly due to misunderstanding. Granted that constant AVC is inconsistent with the short-run equilibrium analysis of a perfectly competitive firm; however, since perfect competition is the simplest economic model, we cannot leave out a common phenomenon that is inconsistent with it without losing sight of the true purpose of the simple model and hence impeding progress in the development and use of economic theory.

Constant AVC is consistent with short-run equilibrium under monopolistic competition

In this section we shall show that the phenomenon of constant AVC and the short-run equilibrium analysis of a monopolistically competitive firm are mutually consistent. Since monopolistic competition and constant AVC are both common phenomena in everyday life, this extension of traditional economic analysis may help to bring economic theory closer to reality.

Compare Figure 8.2 with Figure 8.5. The only difference between them is the shape of the MC curves. In the former, we have the conventional smooth, U-shaped MC curve, whereas the AVC is constant—and thus MC = AVC—in the latter. Since the intersections of the respective MR and MC curves in both figures do not correspond to the current price P_0, we therefore do not

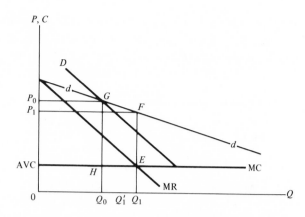

FIGURE 8.5

have a profit-maximizing price. As we have argued in Section 8.4, the firm will reduce its price to P_1 and an adjustment process will take place until short-run equilibrium is reached.

In the conventional approach, the short-run equilibrium is indicated by Figure 8.4. In order to eliminate unnecessary details, we have omitted the intermediate steps of the adjustment process (e.g., Figure 8.3) and the arguments corresponding to them. The short-run equilibrium of a monopolistically competitive firm in the constant-AVC case is shown in Figure 8.6, where the intersection between MC = AVC and MR* is E^*, which corresponds precisely to E^* in Figure 8.4. The equilibrium price P^* and quantity Q^* in both figures correspond to each other. It can easily be checked that the first- and second-order conditions for profit maximization at the price P^* are satisfied in both figures. This demonstrates that constant AVC (and thus constant MC) is consistent with the short-run equilibrium analysis of a monopolistically competitive firm in which profit maximization is concerned. Therefore, there is no problem in applying marginal analysis to a firm's short-run behavior under conditions of monopolistic competition even when the AVC and MC are constant and equal. This result extends the traditional monopolistic competition model to the commonly experienced case of constant AVC.

FIGURE 8.6

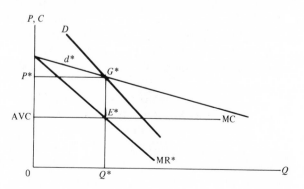

8.5.2 Mark-Up Pricing and Monopolistic Competition

As we have argued in Chapter 7, most (if not all) firms practice mark-up pricing in one way or another. We have shown that the business practice of mark-up pricing and the monopoly model in economic theory are theoretically equivalent. In a similar manner, it can easily be shown that the business practice of mark-up pricing and the monopolistic competition model are theoretically equivalent.

Recall that we have defined two models (which may be quite different in appearance) as being theoretically equivalent if they lead to the same result under identical conditions. The theoretical equivalence of the monopolistic competition model in economics and the business practice of mark-up pricing is proved by showing that the arguments in Sections 8.4 and 8.5.1 are equally valid when presented in terms of mark-up pricing and that identical conclusions will be reached under the same set of assumptions.

Given perfect information, mark-up pricing and the monopolistic competition model are equivalent

In terms of mark-up pricing, the firm's mark-up on marginal cost $\overline{HQ_0}$ is $\overline{GH}$ in both Figures 8.2 and 8.5. In reference to the naive mark-up pricing model of Chapter 7, the mark-up parameter a is $\overline{GQ_0}/\overline{HQ_0}$ in both figures. According to the cost and revenue conditions in the figures, the mark-up price P_0 will not result in maximum profit. It is P_1, a mark-up of $\overline{EF}$ on marginal cost $\overline{EQ_1}$, that will result in maximum profit, provided that the relevant demand curve d and the associated MR curve do not shift. Using the same arguments as in the previous sections, we can note that since all firms are not in a profit-maximizing position, but all of them are profit maximizers, they will adjust their mark-up price downward. However, the quantity sold at P_1 will not be Q_1, but Q_1'. This leads to further adjustment of the mark-up price for a profit maximizer.

This adjustment process goes on until the firm reaches the position represented by either Figure 8.4 or Figure 8.6 (depending on the shape of the MC curve). The adjustment process will not stop until it reaches a mark-up price of P^*, because any other mark-up will not result in maximum profit. In addition, the adjustment process will terminate at the mark-up price P^* because any further ajustment will result in reduced profit. Thus, we reach identical conclusions in both cases—mark-up pricing and traditional monopolistic competition. This proves that they are theoretically equivalent.

The above arguments are based on the important assumption that the firms know precisely the shape and location of their demand, revenue, and cost curves. In reality, a firm does not actually know the shape and location of its demand and associated revenue curves. Hence, although mark-up pricing and marginal analysis in monopolistic competition are theoretically equivalent, the application of marginal analysis in mark-up pricing is definitely handicapped by a lack of reliable information on the shape and position of the demand and revenue curves.

8.6 LONG-RUN EQUILIBRIUM OF A FIRM UNDER MONOPOLISTIC COMPETITION

Just as under perfect competition and pure monopoly, the long-run adjustment of a firm is essentially different from the short-run adjustment under monopolistic competition. The short-run adjustment of a firm in any economic model involves a change in the quantity of the commodity produced for a given plant size. On the other hand, the long-run adjustment of a firm is essentially a change in plant size. In addition, for the industry or sellers in a product group, the number of firms is assumed to be constant in the short run, whereas in the long run the number of firms is subject to change (except for a monopoly, where, by definition, there is only one seller). Hence, whereas we can assume that the demand curve D for a firm under monopolistic competition will be given in the short run, this assumption has to be eliminated in the long run. In order to eliminate unnecessary details, we shall first state the long-run equilibrium conditions of a firm under monopolistic competition and then illustrate why other situations cannot be considered as long-run equilibrium.

Figure 8.7 illustrates the long-run equilibrium situation of a firm under monopolistic competition; P^* is the long-run equilibrium price, and Q^* is the quantity bought by the firm's customers for a given period of time. Curve AC is the long-run average cost curve, which is the envelope of a family of short-run ATC curves (see Chapter 3). The special features of the long-run equilibrium of the firm are (1) the demand curve d is tangent to the long-run average cost curve AC at point E (and, by implication, d is also tangent to a short-run ATC curve at E) and (2) the demand curve D intersects, but is not tangent to, both AC and d at point E. These conditions imply that the profit of this and all other firms under monopolistic competition is zero in long-run equilibrium because, for the price P^*, the quantity bought by buyers is Q^*, and at Q^* both the long-run and the short-run AC are equal to AR, that is, the price P^*. Furthermore, the zero profit is also the maximum profit. This is indicated by the relationship between d and AC in Figure 8.7. If the firm either raises its price above P^*

Unlike monopoly, under monopolistic competition the firm cannot earn positive profit in long-run equilibrium

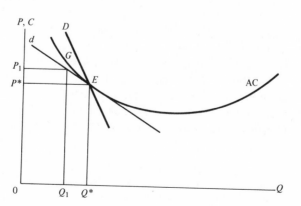

FIGURE 8.7

or reduces its price below P^*, and other firms do not follow (since we are assuming that the market is in long-run equilibrium, there is no reason for the other firms to do anything), the firm's long-run and short-run profits will become negative, as indicated by the fact that either an upward or a downward movement along d will result in a price below AC for the quantity that can be sold at the corresponding price. For example, if the firm charges a higher price than P^* (e.g., P_1) and other firms make no change, the quantity sold will be reduced to Q_1. It can be seen from Figure 8.7 that the long-run average cost $\overline{GQ_1}$ is higher than the price P_1 at quantity Q_1. Hence, the profit is negative at P_1. It can also be appreciated that the short-run ATC (not shown in the figure) at the optimal plant size for producing output Q^* is higher than AC at Q_1. Thus, the short-run profit is less than the long-run profit at price P_1 and quantity Q_1,[4] so that a larger negative profit would be experienced in the short run. Similarly, if the firm reduces its price below P^*, profit will also become negative. Consequently, profit will be maximized at price P^* when Q^* of the product is produced (sold).

The above arguments also imply that the MR curve corresponding to demand curve d in Figure 8.7 intersects both the long-run and the short-run MC curve at a point on the vertical straight line $\overline{EQ^*}$ (for the sake of simplicity, these curves are not drawn in the figure). As explained in Chapters 6 and 7, the necessary condition for profit maximization requires that MR = MC; moreover, for long-run equilibrium to exist, the firm must also be in short-run equilibrium. The latter condition becomes obvious if we recognize that if a short-run adjustment for a given plant size can increase profit, then a long-run adjustment can result in *at least* as good a profit.

Figure 8.7 also shows that if all firms raise their prices accordingly (not necessarily by the same amount, as explained in Section 8.2), then their profit can be increased from zero to positive, as indicated by the fact that D is above AC for a price above P^*. Thus, if all the sellers in the market are controlled by a single firm (essentially a monopoly without competition), then the profit-maximizing price will be higher than P^*. However, under the assumption of price competition among many sellers of a differentiated but close substitute product (e.g., Assumptions 8.1 and 8.3), this cannot be done; hence, the equilibrium price in the long run is P^*, and the profit is zero for each and every firm.

Another way to show why Figure 8.7 characterizes long-run equilibrium is to start with an opposite situation and then prove that such a situation cannot be a long-run equilibrium condition. Consider Figure 8.8, in which D and d intersect at F, the firm

---

[4] To verify this condition, the student should refer back to Chapter 3, where we show the derivation of the long-run envelope AC curve from the smooth, U-shaped short-run ATC curves.

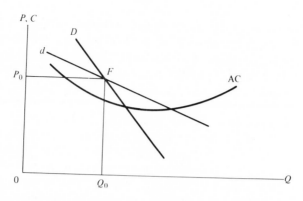

FIGURE 8.8

charges a price P_0, and buyers purchase a quantity Q_0. This firm (and all other firms in the market) are making a positive economic profit. Hence, this cannot be a long run equilibrium condition for the market because new firms will enter under our assumption of relatively free entry into the industry (Assumption 8.2). Consequently, we can conclude that the situation depicted in Figure 8.8 cannot be a long-run equilibrium condition for the market.

When new entry takes place, the demand curves D and d of all existing firms, as well as of the firm represented in Figure 8.8, will shift to the left. Suppose that the new situation depicted in Figure 8.9 is reached after the shifting of the demand curves. Both D and d intersect AC, but neither is tangent to AC at point F. The firm charges a price P_0 and its customers buy a quantity Q_0. For this price–quantity combination, the firm is making zero profit. This may seem to be a long-run equilibrium condition for the product group (market) because there is no incentive for new firms to enter (nor is there reason for existing firms to exit). However, this situation cannot be long-run equilibrium because there exists an opportunity for the firm to make a positive profit by reducing its price (provided that other firms in the same market do not reduce their prices). For example, if the firm reduces its price to P_1 and the other firms take no action, then the quantity that it sells will increase to Q_1 (a movement along d). It can easily be seen that the profit of the firm will become positive, as illus-

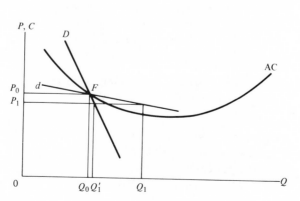

FIGURE 8.9

trated in the figure. However, this condition cannot be expected to occur because as we have argued in our discussions of the short-run adjustment process in previous sections, all firms will take similar action, that is, reduce their prices. The relevant demand curve is D, not d, and the quantity sold at P_1 is Q_1', not Q_1. Therefore, it cannot be a long-run equilibrium condition for the market because when individual firms adjust their prices, the market price also tends to change.

Zero profit for all firms is not a sufficient condition for long-run equilibrium

The above discussion demonstrates that the market cannot be in long-run equilibrium under monopolistic competition if a firm makes a positive economic profit. Furthermore, zero profit for all firms in the market is not a sufficient condition for long-run equilibrium. A market under monopolistic competition is in long-run equilibrium if and only if the demand curve d is tangent to AC and the demand curve D intersects d and AC at the point of tangency (point E in Figure 8.7).

8.7 INCREASING RETURNS TO SCALE AND LONG-RUN EQUILIBRIUM UNDER MONOPOLISTIC COMPETITION

In Chapter 6, we showed that increasing returns to scale (but not the phenomenon of a decreasing-cost industry) is inconsistent with perfect competition because increasing returns to scale implies decreasing long-run AC, which, in turn, implies that there does not exist a minimum of the firm's long-run AC curve. A firm under perfect competition faces a horizontal, straight-line demand curve, and, in long-run equilibrium, the demand curve must be tangent to the AC curve at the minimum of the latter. When a minimum of the AC curve does not exist, the horizontal demand curve cannot be tangent to it. Therefore, a long-run equilibrium condition for the firm and the industry cannot exist under perfect competition when increasing returns to scale prevails.

The situation is different under conditions of monopolistic competition. Since the demand curve d is negatively sloped, the tangency between d and the AC curve must occur at a point where the AC curve is negatively sloped, not at the minimum of the AC curve. For this reason, it can be concluded that increasing returns to scale and monopolistic competition are mutually consistent (in contrast to the inconsistency between increasing returns to scale and perfect competition).

8.8 PRODUCT DIFFERENTIATION AND LONG-RUN EQUILIBRIUM OF THE FIRM

Traditionally, economic theory deals with the situation of a homogeneous product in the market. As a consequence, the problem of product differentiation and quality competition among the sellers does not exist. One important characteristic of Chamberlin's (1947) monopolistic competition model is the existence of a differentiated product in the market. As a result, both quality and price can be considered decision variables. In reality, most business firms use quality competition more frequently than price competition.

According to Chamberlin (1947), product differentiation can take different forms, for example, trademark, location, service, and quality. Due to the lack of a better term, we use *quality* to represent all of the forms (including those listed above) of product differentiation. The important point as far as economic analysis is concerned is that product differentiation has the dual effect of increasing both the cost and the revenue for a commodity. Profit maximization then becomes a case of obtaining the proper balance between cost and revenue through the choice of price and quality.

Product differentiation increases both costs and revenues

In traditional economic theory, the firm's sole choice variable under perfect competition is quantity, whereas under monopoly it is quantity or price (but not both). In partial analysis, under the assumption of other things being equal, a two-dimensional graphical representation will have quantity plotted on the horizontal axis and price, revenue, and cost on the vertical axis. Since both revenue and cost are considered functions of quantity, revenue and cost curves can be drawn on the same graph. In keeping with this tradition, Chamberlin (1947) and others still use the same type of graph to analyze the implication of product differentiation (choice of quality). In this approach, a change in quality will result in a shift of both the revenue and cost curves. To simplify matters further, Chamberlin's graphical analysis proceeds under the assumption that an optimal price and advertising expenditures have been chosen. As a result, product differentiation only shifts the cost curve, not the revenue curve.

A symmetric and, in our opinion, better way of dealing with this situation is to treat price, quality, and advertising as choice (independent) variables, revenue and cost being the dependent variables. Since the demand function is the link between price and quantity, a change in either quality or advertising activity (expenditure) will shift both the demand (and thus revenue) and the cost curves in the traditional graphical presentation. The distinction between shifts of curves and movements along curves in graphical analysis is the result of using two-dimensional graphs to represent the situation of more than one independent variable. If multidimensional graphs could be drawn, one axis for each variable, then the distinction between shifts of curves and movement along curves would disappear. This is the advantage of mathematical representation in economic analysis: Regardless of how many variables an equation system may have, there is no need to make the distinction between shifts of curves and movements along curves. Based on this mathematical principle, if we drew graphs using the horizontal axis to represent quality instead of quantity, then a change in quality would no longer result in a shift of the cost and revenue curves.

The measurement of quality in reality presents a problem. In many cases, quality is multidimensional. For example, an automobile can be produced by using different grades of steel and tires, different materials and standards of work on the engine, and even a different degree of quality control on the assembly line. With respect to the latter, even in the case of the most-expensive automobiles, only a certain percentage of them are inspected after they come off the assembly line. Automobiles that are inspected one-by-one after being assembled command a higher price. The quality of almost all commodities can be made different by using different materials and a different quantity and quality of labor. Therefore, it is difficult to talk about a single measure of quality. However, it is possible to construct an index that will serve as a measure of quality for a certain commodity. For the sake of simplicity, we shall assume that such an index does exist.

As we have mentioned above, higher quality will shift the demand curve of a commodity to the right (i.e., a higher price for the same quantity or a larger quantity for the same price). If this were not the case, higher quality would not have economic meaning, since high quality usually involves higher cost. This implies that total revenue (TR) is an increasing function of quality. The rate of increase in TR as a function of quality can be either constant, decreasing, or increasing. This rate of change in TR with respect to a change in quality can be considered the marginal revenue (MR). However, in economics, the term marginal revenue is traditionally defined as the ratio of a change in TR to a small change in quantity. In order to avoid confusion, we shall name the rate of change in TR with respect to a change in quality the *marginal revenue with respect to quality* MR(G), where G denotes quality.

Quality as the decision variable implies that TR and TC are increasing functions of quality

Similarly, the total cost (TC) must be an increasing function of quality, since otherwise the quality would not be a meaningful factor in economic analysis, and the choice problem with respect to quality would not exist because, in this case, highest quality would always be the best choice. The rate of increase in TC for an increase in quality can also be constant, decreasing, or increasing. Thus, the rate of change in TC with respect to a change in quality can similarly be defined as the *marginal cost with respect to quality* MC(G).

Once MR(G) and MC(G) are defined, the traditional marginal analysis of the profit maximization of a firm can be applied. The only difference between the analysis here and that of the previous sections is that now quality rather than quantity (or, alternatively, price) is considered to be the choice (independent) variable.

Theoretically, there are three possibilities concerning the behavior of MR(G) and MC(G): They can be either constant, increasing, or decreasing functions of G. (Of course, they may also be increasing functions in a certain range of the value of G, decreasing functions in a different range, and constant functions in some other range.[5]) The shape of MR(G) is essentially determined by market conditions (demand), whereas the shape of MC(G) is conditioned by technical factors. Different markets will usually have MR curves of different shapes. Theoretically, we cannot exclude any of the possibilities in our analysis, although certain shapes may be more meaningful than others. We shall now proceed to analyze the implications of the shapes of the various curves.

The necessary and sufficient conditions for profit maximization of a firm are identical to those stated in Chapter 7 for a monopoly, except that the relevant MR and MC curves are MR(G) and MC(G), that is, functions of quality instead of quantity. In the appendix to this chapter we shall prove that the first- (necessary) and second-order (sufficient) conditions for profit maximization of a firm under monopolistic competition are as follows:

First-order (necessary)

$$MR(G) = MC(G)$$

Second-order (sufficient)

MC(G) increases at a faster rate than MR(G), or

MC(G) decreases at a slower rate than MR(G).

Although the above results will be proven mathematically in the appendix to this chapter, here we shall use the graphical method to demonstrate the rationale behind them. Let us denote quality by G, total revenue by R, and total cost by C. For simplicity in exposition, we assume that the MR(G) and MC(G) curves are both straight lines. It can easily be seen that if both MR(G) and MC(G) are constants, then we cannot derive a meaningful result. Consequently, we have the three possible cases depicted in Figure 8.10. In part (a), the additional revenue from any improvement in quality is always higher than the corresponding additional cost. In this case, an improvement in quality always adds to net profit and, for profit maximization, quality should be raised to the highest possible level. Thus, no choice problem exists here so far as quality is concerned.

A unique profit-maximization quality is not possible if both MR(G) and MC(G) are constant

Part (b) represents the opposite situation, where the additional cost for any improvement in quality exceeds the additional revenue. In this case, the quality should be kept at the lowest possible level.

Part (c) shows the case where the additional revenue and ad-

---

[5] MC(G) is analogous to our treatment of cost as a function of output (quantity) in Chapter 3.

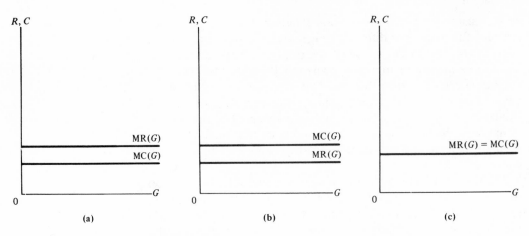

FIGURE 8.10

ditional cost are the same for any improvement in quality. Hence, the seller cannot benefit from quality improvement; that is, one quality is just as good as any other. In all three cases, there does not exist an optimal quality so far as profit maximization is concerned. Thus, they do not present great interest in economic analysis.

When MR(G) is constant, the second-order condition for profit maximization requires an increasing MC(G). Similarly, when MC(G) is constant, MR(G) must be decreasing in order to satisfy the second-order condition for profit maximization. Otherwise, profit maximization requires the highest possible quality. Figure 8.11 shows the profit-maximizing quality G^* for the two aforementioned conditions. In both graphs, if the quality is below G^*, the additional revenue from quality improvement exceeds the additional cost; that is, any improvement in quality will result in more net profit. Therefore, profit cannot be a maximum. On the

FIGURE 8.11

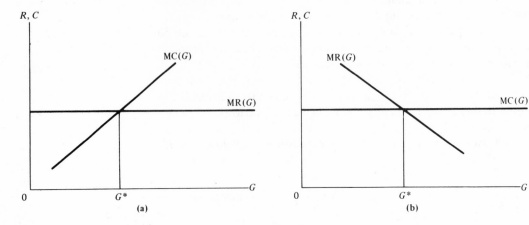

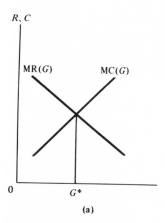
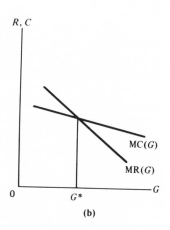
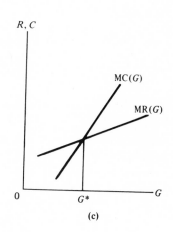

FIGURE 8.12

other hand, if the quality exceeds G^*, the additional cost of quality improvement exceeds the additional revenue, and thus any improvement in quality will result in a net loss in profit. To put it another way, by reducing quality back toward G^*, the firm will increase its profit. In short, profit cannot be a maximum if quality either exceeds or falls below G^*. Hence, G^* is the profit-maximizing quality.

Students may wish to convince themselves, using similar reasoning, that if the MC(G) and MR(G) curves were to change their positions in both graphs, G^* would then result in minimum profit.

We shall now state, without a detailed explanation, the other cases for which optimal quality exists. When either the MR(G) or the MC(G) curve increases and the other decreases, the second-order condition for profit maximization requires a rising MC(G) curve and a declining MR(G) curve, as indicated by part (a) of Figure 8.12. Otherwise, the intersection of the curves would result in a minimum profit, that is, the higher the quality, the higher the profit without bound. When both curves decrease, the second-order condition requires that MC(G) decrease more slowly than MR(G), as shown in part (b); if both curves increase, MC(G) must increase faster than MR(G) for maximum profit to occur in part (c). Otherwise, the intersection of the curves would result in a minimum profit, and the profit-maximizing quality would be infinite in both part (b) and part (c). By the aforementioned reasoning, it can be seen that G^* results in a maximum profit in all three cases depicted in Figure 8.12.

Although the above arguments are based on the simplified assumption of straight-line MR(G) and MC(G) curves, it can be demonstrated that the rationale behind the arguments will hold equally well even if the curves are not straight lines. Thus, our arguments are quite general, and their validity does not depend on the assumption of straight-line curves.

Firms with different MR(G) curves but the same MC(G) curves can coexist in one market

The above demonstration shows that under certain assumptions concerning the behavior of the MR(G) and MC(G) curves, there exists an optimal quality that maximizes the firm's profit. It follows that a firm in a market involving a differentiated product can choose a quality that maximizes its profit. Since MR(G) is functionally related to the demand curve of a firm, the optimal quality is indirectly related to demand. This explains why two stores in the same shopping center which sell essentially the same kind of merchandise can both prosper even though one specializes in high-quality goods and the other in low-quality goods. The reason for this phenomenon is that the firms face a different group of customers who, in turn, form different demand functions. This will result in different MR(G) curves for the firms. Even if both firms have the same MC(G) curve, their profit-maximizing qualities will be different. Consequently, our theory explains the diversity of quality in the same market.

Although the above marginal analysis provides the profit-maximizing quality, the graphs by themselves do not show whether the maximum profit is positive, negative, or zero. In order to show the magnitude of the profit, either a set of TR and TC curves or, alternatively, a set of AR and AC curves must be drawn in each case. Since very little is known about revenue and cost behavior when quality is the independent variable, any conclusion with respect to the measure of profit based on certain shapes of the revenue and cost curves would be pure conjecture. However, it is useful to point out that the above results are consistent with the long-run equilibrium condition under monopolistic competition, that is, zero maximum profit with respect to the choice of quality.

In Figure 8.13, we illustrate the cases depicted in Figure 8.11 in terms of TR and TC curves. The constant MR(G) and rising MC(G) curves in part (a) of Figure 8.11 imply a straight-line TR

FIGURE 8.13

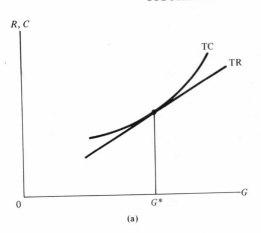

(a)

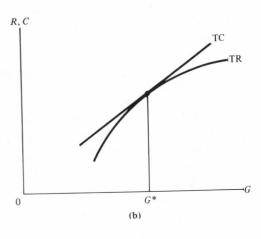

(b)

curve and a concave (from above) TC curve, the point of tangency between them being above G^*. Similarly, the constant MC(G) and decreasing MR(G) curves in part (b) of Figure 8.11 imply a straight-line TC curve, a convex (from above) TR curve, and a point of tangency between them that is directly above G^*. These two cases are shown in parts (a) and (b) of Figure 8.13, respectively.

It can be seen that the curvatures of the TC and TR curves in Figure 8.13 are consistent with the curvatures of the MC(G) and MR(G) curves in the corresponding graphs of Figure 8.11 and that the former show zero long-run maximum profit at G^* in both cases. It can similarly be shown that the cases depicted in Figure 8.12 are also consistent with zero long-run maximum profit. This conclusion is the result of competition among many small sellers, which is one of the basic assumptions of the model (Assumption 8.3).

8.9 ADVERTISING AND OTHER SALES EXPENSES

Advertising and other sales expenses have no place in traditional economic analysis. This is justified in the analysis of perfect competition, since any seller can sell any quantity that he or she wishes at the market price. As we noted earlier, additional expenses would be an unnecessary waste. Since supply and demand analysis deals essentially with perfect competition, it is no wonder that many economists completely ignore advertising and other sales expenses in their analysis.

In reality, advertising and other sales efforts are as important a part of business operations as price and quality decisions. For the sake of simplicity, we shall use the symbol A to represent both advertising and other sales efforts. Like improved quality, intensive advertising and other sales efforts will increase both cost and, at the same time, revenue through the rightward shift of the demand curve. In a manner similar to that in the Section 8.8, the rate of increase in cost and revenue concomitant with increased sales activity can be defined as the *marginal cost and marginal revenue with respect to A*, denoted by MC(A) and MR(A), respectively. The analysis of optimal choice in A can be carried out in the same manner as in Section 8.8.

Firms under monopolistic competition, unlike perfect competition, benefit from advertising

The three possible shapes for the MC(A) and MR(A) curves are identical to those of the MC(G) and MR(G) curves of Section 8.8, that is, they can be constants, decreasing, or increasing functions of A. [Of course just as for the MC(G) and MR(G) curves in Section 8.8, they may also be decreasing functions in a certain range of the value of A, increasing functions in a different range and constant functions in another range.] Although certain shapes of the curves are more meaningful than others, we cannot theoretically rule out any of the possibilities.

The first- and second-order conditions for profit maximization with respect to a choice of A are identical to those with respect to a choice of G in Section 8.8. As a result, the graphical analysis with respect to an optimal choice of A is also identical to that with respect to an optimal choice of G. Hence, Figures 8.10–8.12 can be made to apply equally as well to the analysis with respect to a choice of A by simply changing the horizontal axis from G to A and the MR(G) and MC(G) curves to MR(A) and MC(A) curves. Thus, the G*s will be A*s—the profit-maximizing level of advertising and other sales efforts. Since the model of monopolistic competition assumes competition among many sellers (Assumption 8.3), the maximum profit in long-run equilibrium will also be zero with respect to advertising and other sales efforts.

8.10 GRAPHICAL PRESENTATION AND THE SIMULTANEOUS SOLUTION FOR PRICE, QUALITY, AND ADVERTISING

In Sections 8.7–8.9, we have considered the choice of optimal price, quality, and advertising (which includes other sales efforts) separately. It was implicitly assumed that the optimal choices of quality and advertising level had already been made in the determination of the profit-maximizing price. Similarly, it was implicitly assumed that the optimal choices of price and advertising level had already been made in the determination of the profit-maximizing quality (and so on). In other words, when we analyze the determination of the optimal value of one choice variable, it is assumed that the optimal values of all the other choice variables have been determined. This may appear to be circular reasoning, since one could certainly ask where we start. Actually, circular reasoning is not a problem. Mathematically, the determination of price, quality, and advertising level is based on the simultaneous solution of a system of equations that is, they are determined simultaneously (as will be shown in the appendix to this chapter). Thus, theoretically, the problem of circular reasoning does not arise.

In two-dimensional graphical analysis, only two variables—one dependent and one independent—can be dealt with at a time. In the present case, the analysis involves three independent variables—price (or quantity), quality, and advertising level—all of which are interrelated. In the context of the familiar quantity–cost–revenue graph, we have, for each different quality, a different cost curve and a different revenue curve, which is the result of shifts in the demand and cost curves for changing quality. Corresponding to each level of quality, we have a set of cost and revenue curves which, taken together, determine a profit-maximizing quantity and a corresponding price for a given demand. If quality is a continuous variable, then the locus of these equilibrium points constitutes a curve, and the equilibrium point E

in Figure 8.7 will be only one point on this curve. For the sake of simplicity, when we analyze the determination of price or quantity, we assume that quality and advertising level have been determined. Thus, only one set of cost and revenue curves is relevant. This also applies to the graphs of Section 8.8. It is hoped that this brief explanation will eliminate any possible confusion encountered by the thoughtful student.

8.11 COMPARISON WITH PERFECT COMPETITION AND PURE MONOPOLY

Economists often compare the long-run equilibria of perfect competition, pure monopoly, and monopolistic competition and make certain statements concerning the advantages and disadvantages of these various market models. Most of these comparisons, in particular, those concerned with the advantages or disadvantages of each model, have some flaws. Therefore, students should be exposed to the pros and cons of these arguments in order to intelligently judge the applicability of these models in problem analysis.

The most common comparison (which is quite popular among economists) is based on the differences in quantity and price in the long-run equilibrium of firms under perfect competition and monopolistic competition with similar cost curves. In Chapter 6, we concluded that, in long-run equilibrium under perfect competition, the market price must be equal to the minimum long-run AC of a typical firm with a smooth, U-shaped AC curve. On the other hand, under monopolistic competition, the price will be higher (and, consequently, the quantity lower) in long-run equilibrium for a firm with identical cost curves due to the different shapes of the demand curves that firms face. Parts (a) and (b) of Figure 8.14 depict the long-run equilibrium of firms under perfect competition and monopolistic competition, respectively.

FIGURE 8.14

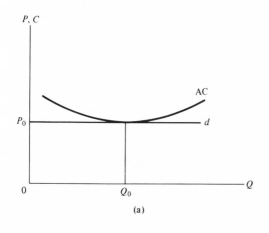

(a)

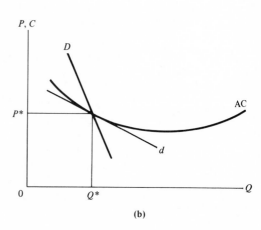

(b)

Without qualifying assumptions, one cannot state that perfect competition is superior to monopolistic competition

If the long-run average cost curves AC in parts (a) and (b) are identical, then it is obvious that P_0 in (a) is lower than P^* in (b) and that Q_0 in (a) is larger than Q^* in (b), even though profit is zero in both cases. The differences in price and quantity in the two cases are due to the difference in the shapes of the demand curves. Based on this, many economists make three general statements:

1. The firm under monopolistic competition produces less and charges a higher price than the firm under perfect competition.
2. Firms under monopolistic competition tend to be less efficient than firms under perfect competition (economists consider most-efficient production to be commensurate with the minimum long-run AC).
3. The firm under monopolistic competition possesses excess capacity. This refers to the fact that its size is less than optimal when minimum short-run ATC, which corresponds to its equilibrium point on long-run AC, is compared to the minimum point in the long-run AC. Thus, the firm produces less than the "ideal output" when taken in the context of the minimum long-run AC in long-term equilibrium of an identical firm under perfect competition.

Based on the above, some economists have gone so far as to conclude that consumers pay a higher price for a smaller quantity under monopolistic competition than under perfect competition. By the economist's yardstick, this implies that economic welfare for consumers, as a whole, is lower under monopolistic competition than under perfect competition.

The problem with these comparisons is that they ignore the important fact that all firms under perfect competition are providing homogeneous products, whereas firms under monopolistic competition provide differentiated products, that is, consumers can have a variety of choices. Some economists argue that since consumers have diversified preferences, the wide range of choice under monopolistic competition provides a certain degree of satisfaction to consumers which may more than offset the higher prices that they pay. The following example will serve as a good illustration of this point.

In the United States, the clothing market certainly deals with differentiated products. It is extremely rare to see any two people in a group wearing identical clothes. In many cases, garments are abandoned not because they are worn out, but because they are out of fashion. A few years ago street scenes of Peking, China, appeared on television. One quite noticeable difference from any comparable scene in the United States was that all men, women, boys, and girls wore the same color and same style of garments.

Thus, it would seem that the same product market can be organized to deal with either homogeneous or differentiated products under different systems. If a dictator in the United States issued an order to the effect that all men, women, boys, and girls must wear garments of the same color, style, and material (i.e., a homogeneous product), the savings on garments in the United States would total billions of dollars each year. From a theoretical or welfare point of view, the critical question is as follows: Would Americans be happier with the homogeneous product and less cost or with the colorful and varied-style garments at a higher cost? If the answer is yes to the former, then the economist's traditional arguments against monopolistic competition are valid. However, if the answer to the latter is yes, the validity of the traditional arguments is in doubt. Students can make up their own minds on this matter.

The comparison between pure monopoly and monopolistic competition is less controversial. If a market under monopolistic competition is converted to one under pure monopoly (this is possible if all of the small firms in a monopolistically competitive market are placed under a single management, such as has been done in Communist countries), then the profit-maximizing price will be higher and the quantity lower under monopoly. Moreover, the long-run profit of the monopoly will be positive, in contrast to the zero-profit situation under monopolistic competition. This is clearly indicated by Figure 8.7, in which the long-run equilibrium price is P^* for quantity Q^* under monopolistic competition, and the profit of the firm is zero. Although the price and quantity of other firms in the monopolistically competitive industry may not be identical to those shown in Figure 8.7 because of differences in quality and advertising levels, the essential characteristics will be the same, that is, d will be tangent to AC and D will intersect d at the point of tangency.

Price may be lower and quantity higher under monopolistic competition than under monopoly

The above result is a consequence of the fact that, under monopolistic competition, the firm can only make decisions according to d, not D. However, if all firms are under a monopoly management, then and only then will D be the relevant demand curve, since the monopoly can change the prices of all the firms simultaneously if it is beneficial to do so. As a result, the monopoly can raise its profit from zero to positive by raising the prices of all the firms. We can easily see that in such a case (see Figure 8.7) the demand curve D is above AC for a price higher than P^*. Thus, we may conclude that competition, even with certain monopoly elements such as under monopolistic competition, can indeed result in a lower price and a higher quantity of product sold than under monopoly given the same commodity. In fact, under monopoly, even though no product differentation might be offered the price could still be higher and output lower than under monopolistic competition.

SUMMARY

In this chapter we showed that the model of monopolistic competition shares some of the features of both perfect competition and monopoly. The assumptions of perfect information, of many small sellers and buyers, and of relatively free entry and exit are features that the model shares with perfect competition, whereas the assumption of differentiated products with close substitutes gives the model an element of monopoly. Because of the latter assumption, it was shown that monopolistically competitive firms face two distinct demand curves: one price–quantity relationship for a firm that changes its price but whose competitors do not, and one for the situation in which all firms in the industry change their price simultaneously. We explained that in a short run analysis monopoly theory can be applied. This is, however, primarily a long run theory, and, as in perfect competition, in long-run equilibrium zero profit is earned by the monopolistically competitive firm. However, unlike in the long-run case with perfect competition, the price under monopolistic competition will be higher than the long-run MC and minimum AC of the firm. We noted that this condition has been used by some economists to argue that, in comparison with perfect competition, monopolistic competition engenders a loss in economic welfare to society. On the other hand, Professor Edward H. Chamberlin, who first advanced the systematic theory of monopolistic competition, believed that the gain in variety under monopolistic competition more than offsets the disadvantage of a higher price and a reduction in quantity. The validity of either of these two arguments is, of course, difficult, if not impossible, to prove.

Because the features of the theory of monopolistic competition come closer to conditions that prevail in the real world, we examined the consistency of the model with the prevalent business practice of mark-up pricing. Not only did we demonstrate that mark-up pricing is consistent with the theory of monopolistic competition, but we also showed that the model of monopolistic competition is consistent with the conditions of a constant AVC, a decreasing long-run AC, and increasing returns to scale, all of which are supported by empirical studies.

We further showed that because of the role which product differentiation plays in monopolistic competition, quality competition and advertising can be analyzed within the construct of economic theory by treating them as independent variables in the same manner as quantity is used in the traditional approach. Thus, the cost and revenue functions, and the concepts of MR and MC, can be defined in terms of quality and advertising outlays, and with this modification traditional marginal analysis can be used to evaluate the profit-maximization behavior of a firm. This, we argued, brings economic theory closer to reality and current business practice.

EXERCISES AND QUESTIONS FOR CHAPTER 8 ON MONOPOLISTIC COMPETITION

1. What are the special features of the demand curve that is assumed to be faced by a firm under conditions of monopolistic competition? Why is it different from that faced by a perfectly competitive firm? Explain. Use the graphical method to illustrate your answer.

2. What are the special features of the long-run equilibrium of a firm under conditions of monopolistic competition? What are the differences between this case and that of a perfectly competitive firm? Explain.

3. Describe how long-run equilibrium is reached under conditions of monopolistic competition. Start from the point where all firms are making excess profits.

4. Use a simple model to demonstrate the differences in quantity and price in long-run equilibrium under conditions of perfect competition and monopolistic competition. From this result, can you make any statement concerning the advantages and disadvantages of the two systems? Why or why not?

5. What are the characteristics of the long-run equilibrium of a monopolistically competitive firm under *price* competition? Is the firm represented by Figure E8.1 in long-run equilibrium? Why or why not?

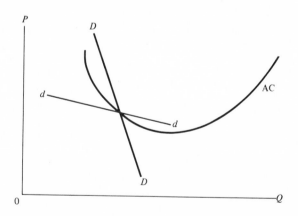

FIGURE E8.1

6. Some economists consider advertising as wasteful. Comment on both sides of the argument.

7. How can advertising be brought into meaningful economic analysis? Explain.

8. How can the quality of goods and services be brought into meaningful economic analysis? Explain.

9. Is perfect competition or monopolistic competition a closer approximation to the world that we experience in everyday life? Explain.

10. Is the business practice of mark-up pricing theoretically consistent with the model of monopolistic competition as developed by Chamberlin? Explain.

11. Empirical studies indicate that in most (if not all) cases, the short-run AVC of a firm is constant. Is this phenomenon consistent with the model of monopolistic competition for profit maximization? Explain.

A MATHEMATICAL NOTE
ON MONOPOLISTIC COMPETITION

The demand function is a special feature of the monopolistic competition model. Since each firm under monopolistic competition has certain monopoly power with respect to its own differentiated product, the demand curve for its product, as a function of price, is negatively sloped (in contrast to a firm under perfect competition, whose demand curve is a horizontal straight line). The demand curve of a monopoly is different from the demand curve of a firm under monopolistic competition in that the monopoly demand is identical to the market demand because a monopoly is, by definition, the only seller in the market. However, under the model of monopolistic competition as developed by Chamberlin (1947), the firm faces two demand curves: one indicates the price–quantity relationship when the firm changes its price alone, whereas the other indicates the price–quantity relationship when all firms in the same market change their prices accordingly (but not necessarily by the same amount). In the text, these two demand curves are denoted by d and D, respectively.

In a conventional, two-dimensional price–quantity graph (price being plotted on the vertical axis and quantity on the horizontal axis), the demand curve D has a steeper slope than d. In the text, we explained this situation in commonsense terms. Chamberlin did not develop the D–d relationship mathematically, and to our knowledge nobody else has deliberated on this matter. We shall first present the mathematics of the D–d relationship; we shall then consider the mathematical relationship between quantity, on the one hand, and price, quality, and advertising level, on the other hand, in connection with both demand and cost; finally, we shall obtain the simultaneous solution for the optimal price, quality, advertising, and sales effort of a firm.

A8.1 THE TWO DEMAND FUNCTIONS FOR A FIRM UNDER MONOPOLISTIC COMPETITION

In the graphical presentation of the text, the two demand curves d and D show the different price–quantity relationships when a price change takes place under monopolistic competition. The two demand curves d and D always intersect at the current market price P_0. This implies that, at the current market price P_0, the quantity sold can be found by using either d or D. In other words, the quantity corresponding to P_0 on d is identical to that corresponding to P_0 on D. Only when the price is different from P_0 will the quantity on d be different from that on D.

Mathematically, the firm faces only one demand function under monopolistic competition. The difference between d and D is that, for the former, all but one of the independent variables are held constant, whereas none of the independent variables is held constant for the latter. In particular, when the independent variables are assumed to be governed by a definite relationship, we have two distinct functional relationships under the two different behavior assumptions for the same function. This will become more clear in our discussion of (A8.1) and (A8.2) below (see also Section 8.2).

For the purpose of illustration, we start with a simple example. Suppose that there are only three firms and that the demand for each firm's commodity is a function of only the prices they charge. For the sake of simplicity, we further assume that the demand functions are linear with respect to price. Let us denote the prices charged by firms 1, 2, and 3 as P_1, P_2, and P_3, respectively. Similarly, let Q_1, Q_2, and Q_3 denote the quantities sold by the respective firms. Under our simplified assumptions, the demand function for firm 1 can be written

$$Q_1 = A + a_1 P_1 + a_2 P_2 + a_3 P_3 \tag{A8.1}$$

where A, a_1, a_2, and a_3 are constants. In general, the quantity demanded is inversely related to its own price, which implies that $a_1 < 0$. Since the model implies that both Q_2 and Q_3 are close substitutes of Q_1, we have $a_2, a_3 > 0$.

In the original Chamberlin model, it is assumed that the prices are identical. Since the demand function (A8.1) satisfies both d and D in the graphical presentation of the text, for the current market price P_0 that is, $P_{02} = P_{03} = P_0$, the quantity sold by firm 1 is

$$Q_0 = A + (a_1 + a_2 + a_3)P_0 \tag{A8.2}$$

Hence, d and D intersect at the point $\langle Q_{01}, P_{01} \rangle$ in quantity–price space.

The difference between d and D is the result of the behavior assumption. For d, it is assumed that both P_2 and P_3 are constant at $P_{02} = P_{03} = P_0$. Hence, the demand curve d is represented by

$$Q_1 = [A + (a_2 + a_3)P_0] + a_1P_1 \qquad \text{(A8.1a)}$$

where P_0 is a constant and P_1 is the independent variable. The slope of d is

$$\partial Q_1 / \partial P_1 = a_1 < 0 \qquad \text{(A8.3)}$$

The original Chamberlin model assumes that demand curve D represents the price–quantity relationship when the prices of different firms change by the same amount. When combined with the simplified assumption of an identical price for all of the firms, this implies that demand curve D is represented by[1]

$$Q_1 = A + (a_1 + a_2 + a_3)P \qquad \text{(A8.1b)}$$

Since $P_1 = P_2 = P_3 = P$ by assumption, the slope of D is

$$dQ_1 / dP = a_1 + a_2 + a_3 > a_1 \qquad \text{for} \quad a_2, a_3 > 0 \qquad \text{(A8.4)}$$

It is also implicitly assumed that $-a_1 > a_2 + a_3$; thus, $a_1 + a_2 + a_3 < 0$, and demand curve D is negatively sloped. When both a_1 and $a_1 + a_2 + a_3$ are negative, $a_1 + a_2 + a_3 > a_1$ implies that $a_1 + a_2 + a_3$ is smaller in absolute value than a_1, which, in turn, implies that the slope of D is flatter than the slope of d. This conclusion is based on a graph where quantity Q_1 is plotted on the vertical axis and price P is plotted on the horizontal axis. The graphs in the text, as most similar graphs in economics, are just the opposite; that is, quantity is plotted on the horizontal axis and price on the vertical axis. Taking this difference between the graphical presentation and the mathematical representation into consideration, the above result implies the d–D relationship cited in the text, that is, demand curve D has a steeper slope than demand curve d.

As we have stated in the text, the restrictive assumption of the original Chamberlin model that the prices and their changes for different firms in the same market are identical is not necessary. For example, two kinds of breakfast cereal (e.g., two different brand names of corn flakes) can be packaged in different size boxes. Although it is natural to expect that a larger box will command a higher price, this price does not necessarily have to be proportionally larger. Thus, a 16-ounce box may command a price that is less than double the price of an 8-ounce box. These two different kinds of cereal must be considered in the same product group in the Chamberlin model. In order to account for this situation, which is a very common phenomenon in monop-

---

[1] Here we use P, as distinct from P_0, as a general expression.

olistic competition, a proportional rather than identical price assumption seems more practical and reasonable.

We modify the original Chamberlin model by introducing the following assumption:

$$P_1 = b_2 P_2 = b_3 P_3 \qquad\qquad (A8.5)$$

If $P_2 > P_1$, then $0 < b_2 < 1$ and vice versa (i.e., if $b_2 > 1$, it implies that $P_1 > P_2$). Similarly, the value of b_3 indicates the relationship between P_1 and P_3. The relationship between P_2 and P_3 is also implied by (A8.5), that is, $P_2 = (b_3/b_2)P_3$. Since (A8.5) implies that $P_2 = (1/b_2)P_1$ and $P_3 = (1/b_3)P_1$, we can, by substitution, write the demand function (A8.1) as

$$Q_1 = A + a_1 P_1 + (a_2/b_2)P_1 + (a_3/b_3)P_1 \qquad\qquad (A8.6)$$

For the current price P_{01} both d and D satisfy the expression

$$Q_{01} = A + a_1 P_{01} + (a_2/b_2)P_{01} + (a_3/b_3)P_{01} \qquad\qquad (A8.6')$$

Hence, both d and D pass through the point $\langle Q_{01}, P_{01} \rangle$. This is also the point of their intersection.

Under our behavior assumption, demand curve d is the demand function when both P_2 and P_3 are held constant at $(1/b_2)P_{01}$, and $(1/b_3)P_{01}$, respectively. Therefore, d is represented by the demand function

$$Q_1 = A + (a_2/b_2)P_{01} + (a_3/b_3)P_{01} + a_1 P_1 \qquad\qquad (A8.6a)$$

Since P_{01} is a constant, the sum of the first three terms on the right side is also a constant, and the slope of demand curve d is again

$$\partial Q_1/\partial P_1 = a_1 < 0 \qquad\qquad (A8.3)$$

In this case, the demand curve D can be defined as the price–quantity relationship when all of the prices change proportionally; that is, $dP_1 = b_2 dP_2 = b_3 dP_3$, which implies that $dP_2 = dP_1/b_2$ and $dP_3 = dP_1/b_3$.

From (A8.1), we have

$$dQ_1 = a_1 dP_1 + a_2 dP_2 + a_3 dp_3 \qquad\qquad (A8.7)$$

By substitution, (A8.7) becomes

$$dQ_1 = a_1 dP_1 + a_2 dP_1/b_2 + a_3 dP_1/b_3 \qquad\qquad (A8.8)$$

Hence, the slope of the demand curve D is

$$dQ_1/dP_1 = a_1 + a_2/b_2 + a_3/b_3 > a_1 \qquad\qquad (A8.9)$$

since $a_2, b_2, a_3, b_3 > 0$. As before, in the conventional price–quantity graph, where quantity is plotted on the horizontal axis and price on the vertical axis, demand curve D has a steeper slope than d.

In the general case, suppose that there are n firms in the market and that each firm sells a homogeneous product which is differentiated from, but a close substitute for, the products of the other firms. Each firm charges a price that can be identical to or different from the prices of the other firms. Let us denote the prices charged by the n firms by $P_1, P_2, \ldots, P_n$ such that

$$P_1 = b_2 P_2 = b_3 P_3 = \cdots = b_n P_n \tag{A8.10}$$

The demand for the product of firm 1 is assumed to be a function of the prices of all the other firms; this can be written

$$Q_1 = D_1(P_1, P_2, \ldots, P_n) \tag{A8.11}$$

Let us denote the partial derivatives of the demand function by the following compact notation:

$$D_{1i} = \partial D_1 / \partial P_i, \qquad i = 1, 2, \ldots, n \tag{A8.12}$$

Taking the differential of both sides of (A8.11), we obtain

$$dQ_1 = D_{11} dP_1 + D_{12} dP_2 + \cdots + D_{1n} dP_n = \sum_{i=1}^{n} D_{1i} dP_i \tag{A8.13}$$

In (A8.13), the demand law requires that

$$D_{11} < 0 \tag{A8.14}$$

Since $Q_2, Q_3, \ldots, Q_n$ are close substitutes of Q_1, we have

$$D_{1i} > 0, \qquad i = 2, 3, \ldots, n \tag{A8.15}$$

By the behavior assumption, the slope of demand curve d is

$$\partial D_1 / \partial P_1 = D_{11} < 0 \tag{A8.16}$$

If the prices change proportionally such that

$$dP_1 = b_2 dP_2 = b_3 dP_3 = \cdots = b_n dP_n \tag{A8.17}$$

then we have

$$dP_i = dP_1 / b_i, \qquad i = 2, 3, \ldots, n \tag{A8.18}$$

By substitution, (A8.13) becomes

$$dQ_1 = \sum_{i=1}^{n} D_{1i} dP_1 / b_i \tag{A8.19}$$

Hence, the slope of demand curve D is

$$dQ_1 / dP_1 = \sum_{i=1}^{n} D_{1i} / b_i > D_{11} \tag{A8.20}$$

since $D_{1i}, b_i > 0$ for $i = 2, 3, \ldots, n$.

For the current market prices $P_{01}, P_{02}, \ldots, P_{0n}$, demand curves

d and D intersect at the point $\langle Q_{01}, P_{01} \rangle$ in the two-dimensional price–quantity graph. At the point of intersection, the slope of d is D_{11} and the slope of D is

$$\sum_{i=1}^{n} D_{1i} b_i > D_{11}$$

in a graph where Q is plotted on the vertical and P on the horizontal axis (as explained above). This implies that the slope of D is steeper than the slope of d at the point of intersection in a conventional graph, that is, where P is plotted on the vertical axis and Q on the horizontal axis. This result not only agrees with the Chamberlin model, but also shows that the restrictive Chamberlin assumption of identical prices and changes of prices is not necessary.

A8.2 SHORT-RUN AND LONG-RUN EQUILIBRIUM OF THE FIRM AND MARKET

A8.2.1 Short-Run Equilibrium

For our purposes, the short run can be defined as that period of time in which the number of firms in the market for the product group is fixed and the plant size is fixed for each firm, but each firm may vary its output by changing its use of one or all of the variable inputs. By this definition, the analysis can proceed under the assumption that the number of firms in the market N is constant.

It is assumed that the goal of a firm is to maximize its profit, which is defined as the difference between its TR and TC. Let us denote the profit of firm i by π_i. We have

$$\pi_i = Q_i P_i - C_i(Q_i), \qquad i = 1, 2, ..., n \tag{A8.21}$$

Assuming that the second-order conditions are satisfied, the first-order conditions for profit maximization are

$$\partial \pi_i / \partial Q_i = P_i + Q_i \partial P_i / \partial Q_i - \partial C_i(Q_i) / \partial Q_i$$
$$= 0, \qquad i = 1, 2, ..., n \tag{A8.22}$$

From the demand function (A8.11), it can be seen that, in terms of the inverse function of D_i, P_i is a function of Q_i and all the prices of the other firms, which, in turn, are functions of the quantities. In other words, the implicit function (A8.22) for the ith firm involves all of the N quantities. Thus, we have N equations and the same number of variables in the Q_is in the system of equations (A8.22), which can, in principle, be solved. The solution of this system of simultaneous equations yields the equilibrium quantities for all of the N firms. Note that the optimal quantity for each firm is not independent of the quantities of the other firms.

The above first-order condition is none other than the familiar MR = MC. Since both MR and MC are expressed in terms of the output quantity, the profit-maximizing solution is conveniently and traditionally also expressed in terms of quantity. However, price and quantity are related by the demand function, which is assumed to be single-valued. Therefore, one and only one price corresponds to the optimal quantity, and this can certainly be considered the theoretical profit-maximizing mark-up price. Thus, theoretically, mark-up pricing and traditional marginal analysis are mutually consistent.

A8.2.2 Long-Run Equilibrium

In the long run, the essential adjustment of the firm is with respect to its size, whereas the adjustment of the market for the product group is with respect to the number of firms that comprise it. Since the number of firms is assumed to be fixed (i.e., constant) in the short run, we have not explicitly written the number of firms N on the right side of demand function (A8.11), although the demand for Q_1 is definitely a function of the number of firms as well as all the prices. In a sense, the demand function (A8.11) is useful only for short-run analysis. For the purpose of long-run analysis, the demand function for the ith firm must be written

$$Q_1 = D(P_1, P_2, ..., P_i, ..., N) \tag{A8.23}$$

Note that we have not written out P_n in the above expression. Since N is now a variable, the number of independent variables itself is a variable; hence, the noncommittal form given in (A8.23) may be better. However, Q_1 is a function of $N + 1$ variables for any N.

The assumption of competition among many relatively small firms (Assumption 8.3) implies that the long-run profit of each and every firm must be zero (or virtually zero). This imposes the following conditions:

$$\pi_i = Q_i P_i - C_i(Q_i) \geq 0 \quad \text{for all } i = 1, 2, ..., N \tag{A8.24}$$

$$\sum_{i=1}^{N^*} Q_i P_i - \sum_{i=1}^{N^*} C_i(Q_i) \geq 0 \quad \text{for } N^* \tag{A8.25}$$

$$\pi_i = Q_i P_i - C_i(Q_i) \leq 0 \quad \text{for } N^* + 1 \tag{A8.26}$$

$$\sum_{i=1}^{N^*+1} Q_i P_i - \sum_{i=1}^{N^*+1} C_i(Q_i) < 0 \tag{A8.27}$$

The traditional approach is to consider equalities as being valid in the $N + 1$ system of equations (A8.24) and (A8.25). However, these expressions are essentially functions of N (the number of firms), which is necessarily an integer. Although both the revenue and cost functions for each and every firm are continuous, theoretically, the equilibrium number of firms N^* that results in an equality for all the expressions (A8.24) and (A8.25) may not exist. If it does exist, it can be only coincidental or as a result of more-restrictive assumptions. This is often overlooked by economists. In our specification, for given demand and cost functions for all of the firms, N^* will always exist. This is why we used the phrase "or virtually zero" earlier.

Although we have used the same notation $C_i(Q_i)$ in both (A8.21) and (A8.24)–(A8.27) to denote the TC for firm i, there is an essential difference: In the former this notation represents the short-run TC, whereas in the latter it represents the long-run TC. Since a firm can be in long-run equilibrium only if it is also in short-run equilibrium (a firm in short-run equilibrium may or may not be in long-run equilibrium), in addition to (A8.24)–(A8.27), the short-run first-order condition for profit maximization (A8.22) must also be satisfied. We have a system that consists of N equations and $2N + 2$ inequalities in only $N + 1$ variables: N Qs and N itself. This is not a simple system of simultaneous equations. However, it can be solved by a programming technique. Here we shall only point out that a solution of the system of equations (A8.22) which also satisfies the constraints (A8.24)–(A8.27) is consistent with the Chamberlin tangency solution for the long-run equilibrium condition of a firm under monopolistic competition. However, our system implies more than this. Theoretically, for the given demand and cost functions of all firms in the product market, there may not exist an integer N (number of firms) such that each and every firm's demand will be precisely tangent to its long-run AC. Although economists have not paid attention to this theoretical problem, it is indeed a question that must be answered before the theory can be considered complete. Our formulation "plugs" the theoretical hole.

A8.3 QUALITY, ADVERTISING, AND SALES COMPETITION

In Section A8.2, for the sake of simplicity, we have assumed (as do most economists) that the demand for the commodity of a firm is a function of the price(s). This is perfectly acceptable under the assumption that the optimal quality and advertising and sales strategies have been chosen. In reality, the elements of price, quality, advertising, and sales effort are interrelated and must be chosen simultaneously. We now deal with this problem by means of a system of simultaneous equations.

For the sake of simplicity, we assume that quality can be represented by a variable G, (a grade or some index of quality), whereas advertising and sales effort can be represented by a variable A. The demand is now not only a function of price, but also of quality, advertising, and sales effort. Also for the sake of simplicity, we omit both the prices of the other firms and the subscript for the firm (since it can be any firm in the market) in the demand function. Thus, we have

$$Q = D(P, G, A) \tag{A8.28}$$

Again, the TC of the firm is, not only a function of the quantity, but also of the quality, advertising, and sales effort. Thus, the TC function can be written

$$C = C(Q, G, A) \tag{A8.29}$$

By definition, the profit π of the firm is equal to the TR minus the TC; that is,

$$\pi = QP - C(Q, G, A) \tag{A8.30}$$

It is assumed that the inverse function of (A8.28) exists; hence, we have

$$P = D^{-1}(Q, G, A) \tag{A8.31}$$

Thus, (A8.30) can be written

$$\pi = QD^{-1}(Q, G, A) - C(Q, G, A) \tag{A8.30'}$$

The profit of the firm is a function of Q, G, and A. If it is assumed that the second-order conditions are satisfied, then the first-order conditions for profit maximization are

$$\frac{\partial \pi}{\partial Q} = P + Q\frac{\partial P}{\partial Q} - \frac{\partial C}{\partial Q} = 0$$

$$\frac{\partial \pi}{\partial G} = P\frac{\partial Q}{\partial G} + Q\frac{\partial P}{\partial G} - \frac{\partial C}{\partial G} = 0 \tag{A8.32}$$

$$\frac{\partial \pi}{\partial A} = P\frac{\partial Q}{\partial A} + Q\frac{\partial P}{\partial A} - \frac{\partial C}{\partial A} = 0$$

We have three equations in the three variables Q, G, and A [according to (A8.31), P is not an independent variable but a function of the other variables]. Assuming that the second-order conditions are satisfied, the solution of the system of simultaneous equations yields the profit-maximizing values for Q, G, and A. In the text, we have stated that, in theory, there is no circular reasoning involved in finding the optimal values of Q, G, and A. This result substantiates our statement.

Let us denote the solution of the system of equations (A8.32) by Q^*, G^*, and A^*. The profit-maximizing mark-up price is

$$P^* = D^{-1}(Q^*, G^*, A^*) \tag{A8.33}$$

and the maximum profit is

$$\pi^* = Q^*P^* - C(Q^*, G^*, A^*) \tag{A8.34}$$

Although π^* is the maximum profit, it can be either positive, zero, or negative in the short run, depending on both the demand function D and the cost function C (over which the firm has little control). On the other hand, the π^* given by (A8.34) must be nonnegative in the long run. If it were negative in the long run, the firm would obviously go out of business. It is generally stated by almost all economists that π^* must be zero in the long run due to the assumption of competition among many relatively small sellers (Assumption 8.3). However, as we have stated in Section A8.2, since the number of firms N is an integer, in a given market, the equilibrium N^* may not exist for all firms for π^* equal to zero. On the other hand, it is always possible that competition may make π^* virtually, but not precisely, zero in the long run, and hence no new firm will get into the market. This situation can certainly be considered as long-run equilibrium. Thus, our model requires less-restrictive assumptions than the traditional zero long-run profit model. According to the principle of "Occam's Razor" (see Chapter 4), our model is superior.

9

OLIGOPOLY THEORY

INTRODUCTION

In Chapters 6–8, we have discussed three different market models: perfect competition, pure monopoly, and monopolistic competition. Each of these models is based on four fundamental assumptions, a variation in one or more of which will result in a different model. Although the models are quite different in many respects, they do have one thing in common: Each leads to a logical and indisputable conclusion. For example, the profit of a perfectly competitive firm will be maximized when $MR = MC$ and MC is increasing. From these conditions, it is inferred that the short-run supply curve of a perfectly competitive firm is that portion of the rising MC curve which is above the minimum AVC. On the other hand, in the long run, the maximum profit of a perfectly competitive firm is zero, and production always takes place at the quantity that corresponds to the minimum of the long-run AC curve. In the case of a monopoly, we have a different situation. Although the MC curve is no longer the short-run supply curve, the quantity and price can be uniquely determined by the first- and second-order conditions for profit maximization for given demand and cost curves. In long-run equilibrium, the monopolist can make either positive (very likely) or (by coincidence) zero profit. It is very unlikely that a monopolist will produce at the point of minimum long-run AC. Finally, under monopolistic competition, the long-run profit of a firm is zero, but, in equilibrium, production takes place at a point higher than the minimum long-run AC. These are the commonly recognized results for the three models that we have discussed.

Oligopoly represents yet another situation. Even though the oligopoly model is also based on four fundamental assumptions,

Oligopoly is characterized by interdependence of firms and the reactions of competitors

it does not lead to a unique, logical result. It will soon become obvious that the same oligopoly model may result in different equilibrium quantity and price conditions. The reason for this is that one of the important characteristics of an oligopoly is the interdependence of the firms. The final results of one firm's pricing policy depends on the reactions of its competitors. A given policy of one firm can lead to different results if its competitors react differently. For example, if an oligopolist raises his or her price, the quantity sold will change, but the magnitude of the change will depend on whether the competitors raise their prices accordingly or keep them unchanged. It is hard to tell a priori what the reactions of competitors will be. Different assumptions concerning the reactions of competitors will lead to different results. We shall demonstrate this point in more detail later. The important thing that the student should realize is that oligopoly theory is more complicated than the economic models that we have dealt with previously. We do not have a single oligopoly theory; in fact, we have a multitude of oligopoly theories.

9.1 ASSUMPTIONS

Similar to the other three economic models that we have discussed, the oligopoly model is based on four fundamental assumptions, which, as we have seen, are different in their form or essence with respect to each economic model. In the case of oligopoly, the assumptions are as follows.

Assumption 9.1: Either a Homogeneous or Differentiated Product. Under perfect competition, a homogeneous product is an essential feature, whereas a differentiated product is an essential feature of monopolistic competition. However, in an oligopoly market, firms can sell either a homogeneous product or a differentiated product.

In theory, it is easier to deal with an oligopoly model for a homogeneous product. However, in practice, most oligopoly industries (e.g., the automobile and steel industries) involve differentiated products. As long as the differentiated products are close substitutes (e.g., an Impala® by General Motors and a Galaxie® by Ford), they can be considered one commodity for analytical purposes.

Assumption 9.2: Limited Entry. The situation presented by Assumption 9.2 is distinct from both perfect competition, where entry is free, and monopolistic competition, where entry is relatively free. However, unlike monopoly, where entry is largely governed by an exclusive franchise (or full control of a resource), entry under oligopoly is conditioned by a host of factors, the most important being technology and cost.

For example, there is no legal barrier to entry into either the automobile or the steel industry. However, to reach an economically operational level in either industry requires considerable initial investment. Many people are probably capable and willing to run a business in either industry, but very few have the financial backing to start such an operation. Furthermore, even if many enterprising businesspeople start firms in the early stages of the development of an industry, if the cost behavior of a firm and the market demand for the industry are not conducive to many small firms, the number of firms will be reduced by market forces. The automobile industry is one example of this condition.

High initial investment often limits entry into an industry

We shall not trace the history of the automobile industry. Still, one can note from exhibitions of antique cars in Pittsburgh that at one time many different automobiles were produced by firms in that city. However, no assembly plant, let alone automobile firm, now exists in Pittsburgh. The many small auto makers that were established during the early stages of the industry have disappeared, the latest victim being Studebaker. Moreover, the smallest of the four survivors—American Motors—is continually shrinking. Only time will tell whether it can survive. More recently, the survival of the Chrysler Corporation in the automobile industry has been questioned by some market analysts.

The above examples show that the cost behavior of a firm together with the extent of the market of an industry constitute the main determinants of oligopoly. As a result of these economic conditions, some industries are destined for oligopoly whether we like it or not. The job of economists is to analyze the implications of this type of market and describe the economic behavior of oligopolistic firms under different economic conditions.

Assumption 9.3: Few Sellers and Many Buyers. There are a few firms in the industry and each firm holds such a substantial portion of the market that the action of one cannot be ignored by its competitors, since one firm's policy will have a large effect on the sales volume of its competitors.

Assumption 9.3 essentially distinguishes oligopoly from the other economic models that we have discussed. By definition, under monopoly there is only one firm in the industry; that is, competitors do not exist. Therefore, a competitor's reaction in response to a policy decision is not a problem. In the markets of perfect competition and monopolistic competition, there are many competitors and each one is too small for its actions to have a perceptible effect on the others. Thus, the reaction of the competitors is not an essential factor in the policy decisions of a firm under perfect competition, monopoly, or monopolistic competition. On the other hand, in an oligopoly market, each firm's policy decision (e.g., a change in the price it charges) will have a considerable effect on the business of its competitors. This effect cannot be ignored by sensible competitors, since it could lead to a reduction in their profits. As a result, profit maximizers must (at least in theory) take proper countermeasures in order to maintain their maximum-profit position.

The above discussion raises the following question: How few firms must comprise the market in order to generate the hypothesized results or actions? In general, most economists agree that an oligopoly market must consist of at least two firms. This is the special case of *duopoly*, which we shall discuss in more detail later in this chapter. Alternatively, there is no absolute upper limit on the number of firms required for an oligopoly to exist. Most economists agree that an oligopoly exists when the number of firms in an industry is such that, if a firm contemplates a policy measure (e.g., a change in the price it charges), then its competitors' possible reactions must be taken into consideration.

There is no magical number dividing oligopoly from monopolistic competition

However, when the number of competitors becomes sufficiently large so that one firm's actions do not trigger any reactions by its competitors, the market can be considered either one of perfect competition or one of monopolistic competition. There is no single number (of firms) that divides oligopoly and monopolistic competition; however, in the United States, the automobile, steel, electrical equipment, and metal-can industries are obvious examples of oligopolies.

In Chapter 7 we stated that not all monopoly firms are necessarily large; analogously, not all oligopoly firms are necessarily large. Hence, although two grocery stores in an isolated community may be quite small compared with stores in big cities, they are nevertheless oligopolists (in fact, duopolists).

Assumption 9.4: Perfect Information or Knowledge. Assumption 9.4 is common to all four economic models that we have discussed. Since we have explained the implications of Assumption 9.4 previously, further discussion is not required.

9.2 DUOPOLY: A SPECIAL CASE OF OLIGOPOLY

Assumption 9.3 implies that duopoly is a special case of oligopoly. Since the early 19th century, mathematical economists have constructed various duopoly models. Although the models are very simple and cannot be considered realistic, they serve an important illustrative purpose in explaining the interdependence of firms.

Moreover, they have considerable theoretical importance. We shall discuss the classical Cournot model and the modified Chamberlin model in great detail. The Edgeworth model will be covered in less detail because of its more-restrictive assumptions.

In the text, only the graphical method will be used. However, a full exposition of the mathematical models will be presented in the appendix to this chapter. It will be seen that, mathematically, the result of the Cournot model is the quite straightforward solution of a system of simultaneous equations. On the other hand, the graphical presentation can be easily misinterpreted if the characteristics of comparative statics are not fully taken into consideration. We shall have more to say on this point later.

Attention is called to the fact that we shall construct a simple mathematical duopoly model that is very similar, if not identical, to the original Cournot model. Our model will explicitly show that the difference between the Cournot and Chamberlin models rests on the different behavior assumptions with respect to the interdependence of the duopolists. Our model will also show to be incorrect the commonly held view that the difference between the Cournot and Edgeworth models is due to the fact that the Cournot model treats the quantity of the competitor of a duopolist as a constant whereas the Edgeworth model treats the price as constant. The instability of the Edgeworth duopoly model is the result of the restrictive assumption that the capacity of each duopolist is constant and less than a given number; it is not due to the fact that a duopolist considers his or her competitor's price to be constant. As we have explained earlier, both quantity and price can be equivalently treated as decision variables. The duopoly model bears out our view of the differences between the Cournot and Edgeworth models.

9.2.1 The Cournot Model

The earliest duopoly model was developed early in the 19th century by the French economist Augustin Cournot [see Cournot, 1927 (originally published in 1838)] who assumed a homogeneous product with a straight-line demand curve. In the Cournot model, cost is assumed to be zero, which is not as unrealistic as it may sound. For example, if the commodity is mineral water and buyers bring their own containers, then the cost to the seller is zero.

Since this is a duopoly model, there are two sellers in the market. The analysis usually proceeds by assuming that one of the sellers is originally a monopolist who is confronted by another seller entering into the market. Consequently, a series of adjustments takes place until a new equilibrium is reached. The new equilibrium is the *Cournot duopoly solution*.

Consider Figure 9.1, in which $\overline{DD'}$ is the demand curve. If A

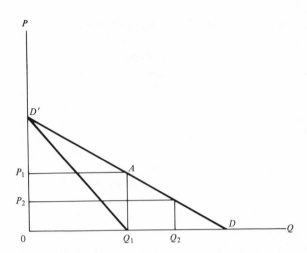

FIGURE 9.1

is the only seller in the market, then A's profit-maximizing quantity is Q_1, where MR = MC = 0 and the price is P_1. (The student should review Chapter 7 on monopoly theory for an explanation of why Q_1 maximizes profit.) Note that $\overline{0Q_1} = \overline{Q_1 D}$. When the seller B enters into the market and notices that the market opportunity left open is represented by the segment $\overline{AD}$ of the demand curve, the best B can do is to sell $\overline{Q_1 Q_2} = \overline{Q_1 D}/2$ in order to maximize profit, since $\overline{AD}$ is considered as B's demand curve. Since the product is homogeneous, there can be only one market price. When the quantity in the market is

$$\overline{0Q_1} + \overline{Q_1 Q_2} = \overline{0Q_2}$$

the price will be P_2.

In the Cournot model quantity is the decision variable

The Cournot model assumes that duopolists consider their competitor's quantity a parameter or a constant. In other words, at any given moment, when duopolists try to make a decision, they look at their competitor's quantity and the market demand, and then choose the quantity that maximizes their profits. Duopolists always try their best under the circumstances. Based on this behavior assumption, it can easily be seen that the profit-maximizing quantity for A, after B enters into the market, is

$$\overline{0Q_2}/2 = (\overline{0D} - \overline{Q_1 Q_2})/2$$

which is less than $\overline{0Q_1} = \overline{0D}/2$. When A's quantity is $\overline{0Q_2}/2$, B's profit-maximizing quantity is

$$\frac{\overline{0D} - \overline{0Q_2}/2}{2} = \frac{5\overline{Q_1 Q_2}}{4} = \overline{Q_1 Q_2} + \frac{\overline{Q_1 Q_2}}{4}$$

In turn, A's profit-maximizing quantity will be further lowered.

It can be shown that the end result of the adjustment process of A's profit-maximizing quantity takes the form of the following infinite series[1]:

$$[\tfrac{1}{2} - \tfrac{1}{8} - 1/8\cdot(\tfrac{1}{4}) - 1/8\cdot(\tfrac{1}{4})^2 - \cdots - 1/8\cdot(\tfrac{1}{4})^n]\overline{0D} = \overline{0D}/3$$

Similarly, the end result of the adjustment process of B's profit-maximizing quantity takes the form of a different infinite series[2]:

$$[\tfrac{1}{4} + (\tfrac{1}{4})^2 + (\tfrac{1}{4})^3 + \cdots + (\tfrac{1}{4})^n]\overline{0D} = \overline{0D}/3$$

This is expected because we have a symmetric system, and in long-run equilibrium Q_1 must be equal to Q_2. The equilibrium market quantity is

$$Q^* = Q_1 + Q_2 = \tfrac{2}{3}\overline{0D}$$

With this quantity, the market price is $\overline{0D}/3$.

The above result is illustrated by Figure 9.2, in which the demand curve $\overline{DD'}$ is identical to that of Figure 9.1. The equilibrium quantity Q^* is equal to $\tfrac{2}{3}\overline{0D}$, and the corresponding equilibrium price P^* is equal to $\overline{0D'}/3$. The duopolists share the market equally; thus, each duopolist sells $Q^*/2$, that is, $\overline{0D}/3$, at the same price P^*.

---

[1] The value of the infinite series in the brackets is $\tfrac{1}{3}$. This can be derived as follows. The series can also be written

$$\tfrac{1}{2} - \tfrac{1}{8}[1 + \tfrac{1}{4} + (\tfrac{1}{4})^2 + \cdots + (\tfrac{1}{4})^n]$$

Let

$$S = 1 + \tfrac{1}{4} + (\tfrac{1}{4})^2 + \cdots + (\tfrac{1}{4})^n$$

Multiplying both sides by $\tfrac{1}{4}$, we obtain

$$S/4 = \tfrac{1}{4} + (\tfrac{1}{4})^2 + (\tfrac{1}{4})^3 + \cdots + (\tfrac{1}{4})^n + (\tfrac{1}{4})^{n+1}$$

Subtracting the second equation from the first, we obtain

$$S - S/4 = 1 - (\tfrac{1}{4})^{n+1}$$

Since $(\tfrac{1}{4})^{n+1} \to 0$ when $n \to \infty$, $3S/4 = 1$ or $S = \tfrac{4}{3}$. Substituting back, we have

$$\tfrac{1}{2} - (\tfrac{1}{8})(\tfrac{4}{3}) = \tfrac{1}{3}$$

[2] Let

$$S = \tfrac{1}{4} + (\tfrac{1}{4})^2 + \cdots + (\tfrac{1}{4})^n$$

Multiplying both sides by $\tfrac{1}{4}$, we obtain

$$S/4 = (\tfrac{1}{4})^2 + \cdots + (\tfrac{1}{4})^n + (\tfrac{1}{4})^{n+1}$$

Subtracting the second equation from the first, we obtain

$$S - S/4 = \tfrac{1}{4} - (\tfrac{1}{4})^{n+1}$$

Since $(\tfrac{1}{4})^{n+1} \to 0$ when $n \to \infty$, $3S/4 = \tfrac{1}{4}$; therefore, $S = \tfrac{1}{3}$.

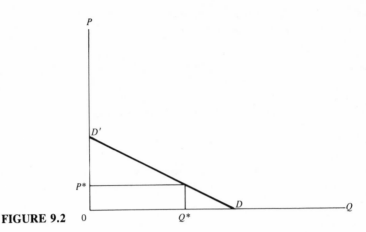

FIGURE 9.2

9.2.2 The Chamberlin Model

Except for the assumed behavior of the duopolists, the Chamberlin model is very similar to the Cournot model. This slight difference in assumptions results in a different equilibrium solution.

It is usually argued that the Cournot model implies that duopolists never learn from experience. In other words, the graphical presentation indicates that when duopolists make a decision, they consider their competitor's quantity to be given, even though after each of their own adjustments, their competitors adjust their quantities accordingly. This kind of behavior seems to indicate that the model is too naive. The Chamberlin model assumes that the duopolists learn from experience, that is, finally conclude that their best interests will be served if they act to maximize their joint profits.

As we have mentioned in Section 9.2.1, our graphical presentation does indicate that the equilibrium quantities for the duopolists are the final results of two infinite series, each representing an infinite series of steps of adjustment and readjustment that shows the interaction between the duopolists. This infinite series of defined adjustments is only designed to illustrate the mathematical result of the Cournot model; it should not be interpreted as an actual adjustment process. In particular, it would be misleading to interpret each step of the adjustment as involving a time period. The important thing to remember is that we are dealing with comparative statics, not dynamics. In statics, the adjustment from one equilibrium to another (or from a situation of disequilibrium to one of equilibrium) is supposed to be instantaneous. At any rate, there is no time period involved in the adjustment process. Thus, any step-by-step adjustment process can only be considered as being designed for illustrative purposes.

It cannot be interpreted as the actual adjustment steps of the model. Thus, the criticism of the Cournot model as being naive is not well founded.

It will be shown in the appendix to this chapter that if duopolists treat their competitor's quantity as a parameter or constant for the purpose of choosing their own profit-maximizing quantities, then we have the Cournot result. On the other hand, if each duopolist considers that the competitor's quantity will change in a consistently matching fashion, then we have the Chamberlin result. The latter behavior assumption seems more reasonable because, under the assumption of homogeneity of the product, both duopolists are in the same boat, so to speak. They face the same demand and the same cost. Therefore, if it is to the advantage of one of them to adjust quantity, then it must also be to the advantage of the other to make the same adjustment. It is not surprising that duopolists will act in unison without collusion once they recognize that their interests are identical. The solution of the Chamberlin duopoly model is identical to that of monopoly. In the appendix to this chapter it is shown that if the duopolists realize that each of them will always share the market equally and acts accordingly, then the result is also the Chamberlin solution. As we have explained above, based on the assumption of a homogeneous product and the fact that costs are identical for both duopolists, there is no reason why they should not be expected to share the market equally.

The Cournot and Chamberlin models differ in the duopolists' assumed behavior

The Chamberlin solution is illustrated by Figure 9.3, in which the equilibrium quantity $Q^* = \overline{0D}/2$, and the corresponding equilibrium price $P^* = \overline{0D'}/2$. The duopolists share the market equally. Thus, each duopolist sells one-half of Q^*, that is, $\overline{0D}/4$, and earns a profit of $Q^*P^*/2$. The Chamberlin solution for the market quantity and price of the duopoly model is identical to the monopoly solution.

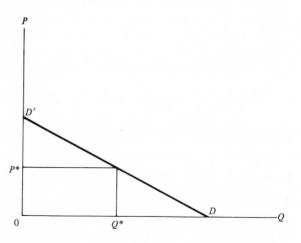

FIGURE 9.3

9.2.3 The Edgeworth Model

Almost 70 years after the publication of Cournot's work, F. Y. Edgeworth (1925) accepted Joseph Bertrand's criticism of Cournot, who treated quantity as the decision variable. It was suggested that, if the decision variable was price instead of quantity, an entirely different result might be obtained. Edgeworth constructed a model similar to the Cournot model, but price was considered as the decision variable.

The Edgeworth model, like that of Cournot, assumes the existence of two sellers of a homogeneous product with zero cost. Since the product is homogeneous, the demand curves facing the sellers are identical. In addition, the Edgeworth model assumes that each seller has a limited capacity which is less than the quantity that could be sold if the price were zero. This model is illustrated by Figure 9.4, in which $\overline{DD}$ is the demand curve for seller 1 and $\overline{DD'}$ is the demand curve for seller 2. In Figure 9.4, 0 is the origin, the vertical axis represents price, and the horizontal axis represents quantity. It should be noted that a positive quantity occurs both to the right and to the left of the origin: To the right, we have the quantity for seller 1, whereas to the left, we have the quantity for seller 2. Seller 1's capacity is $\overline{0C_1}$ and that of seller 2 is $\overline{0C_2}$. Finally, A and B are the midpoints of $\overline{DD}$ and $\overline{DD'}$, respectively, whereas Q_1 and Q_2 are the midpoints of $\overline{0D}$ and $\overline{0D'}$, respectively.

If there is only one seller in the market, a price P^* will be charged in order to maximize profit. (Students who doubt the above statement should review Chapter 7 with respect to the conditions of monopoly profit maximization.) With zero cost, the seller's profit will be $0P^*AQ_1$ or $0P^*BQ_2$, depending on who is in the market. By construction, $0P^*AQ_1$ is equal to $0P^*BQ_2$. However, the second seller entering into the market and assuming that the original seller's price will remain constant, will be best served by charging a price a little bit lower than P^*. In this way,

FIGURE 9.4

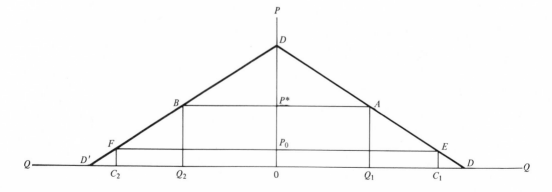

according to Edgeworth, all of the second seller's goods will be sold that is, $0C_1$ or $0C_2$ (depending on who enters the market second), because, with a homogeneous product at a lower price, the competitor's market will also be gained. It is implicitly assumed that $\overline{AB}$ is greater than $\overline{0C_1} = \overline{0C_2}$; otherwise the second seller could not expect to sell $\overline{0C_1}$ or $\overline{0C_2}$ by lowering price by a small amount.

An equilibrium price cannot exist in the Edgeworth model

The second seller's pricing policy drastically reduces the profit of the first seller, whose best interest will, in turn, be served by charging a price a little bit lower than that of the second seller and selling the capacity quantity. The second seller will then react by further price reductions which, in turn, will cause the first seller's price to be reduced again, and so on. The price war will finally reduce the price to P_0, at which both sellers can sell their capacity quantities.

However, P_0 is not the equilibrium price because one of the sellers will notice that the competitor is selling at capacity and cannot, therefore, increase sales even if the other raises the price. Hence, one seller will raise the price to P^*, and, according to the demand, obtain sales of $\overline{0Q_1}$ or $\overline{0Q_2}$ (depending on who takes the last step). Provided that

$$0P^*AQ_1 = 0P^*BQ_2 > 0P_0EC_1 = 0P_0FC_2$$

the price will go back to P^* after it reaches P_0. As we have explained above, P^* is not the equilibrium price either, since it will go down bit by bit until it reaches P_0 (at which time the price starts to climb again). Hence, the price will continually fluctuate between P^* and P_0. Thus, the duopoly system, according to Edgeworth, is indeterminate.

The observant student will have noticed that the Edgeworth model requires more assumptions than the Cournot model. In the first place, it assumes a limited capacity for both duopolists; otherwise, the arguments of the model would not follow. In the second place, there is inconsistency with respect to demand. Both duopolists should face the market demand, which is the one and only demand. It is logically inconsistent to assume that one of them faces the demand curve $\overline{DD}$ and the other the demand curve $\overline{DD'}$.

The logical inconsistency of the Edgeworth model can easily be eliminated by a slight modification of the argument. It is generally argued (as we have done above) that the one who enters into the market first as the only seller will charge a price P^* and earn a profit $0P^*AQ_1$ or $0P^*BQ_2$. This is based on the assumption that one duopolist faces the demand curve $\overline{DD}$, whereas the other faces the demand curve $\overline{DD'}$. This argument can be modified by assuming that both duopolists face the market demand. In this case, the graph has to be modified.

Consider Figure 9.5, which corresponds precisely to the tra-

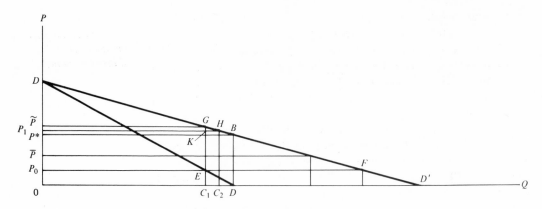

FIGURE 9.5

ditional graphs in terms of the demand and revenue curves. Demand curve $\overline{DD}$ is the same as in Figure 9.4. However, the sum of $\overline{DD}$ and $\overline{DD'}$ in Figure 9.4 is represented by $\overline{DD'}$ in Figure 9.5. For example, $\overline{P*B}$ in the latter is equal to $\overline{AB}$ in the former, whereas $\overline{OD'}$ in the latter is equal to $\overline{DD'}$ in the former; $\overline{OC_1}$ has the same meaning in both graphs, but $\overline{OC_2}$ in the latter is equal to $\overline{C_2C_1}$ in the former.

With this modification, when only one of the duopolists is in the market, that one will not charge $P*$ because the quantity demanded is $\overline{P*B} = \overline{OD}$, which is greater than the capacity $\overline{OC_1}$. Furthermore, this duopolist can increase profit at a higher price that exactly equates demand with capacity. With the limited capacity $\overline{OC_1}$, the duopolist's total profit at price $P*$ is only $0C_1KP*$, but can be increased to $0C_1G\widetilde{P}$ by raising the price to $\widetilde{P}$ in the absence of competition. The second duopolist has two choices in entering the market: (1) charge the same price $\widetilde{P}$ and share half the market of $\overline{OC_1}$ with a profit of one-half of $0C_1G\widetilde{P}$, or (2) charge a price $P_1 = \widetilde{P} - \epsilon$ and earn a profit of $(\widetilde{P} - \epsilon) \times \overline{OC_1}$, since $\overline{OC_1} = \overline{C_1C_2}$ (provided that the competitor's price does not change). The Edgeworth model assumes that the competitor will stick to price $\widetilde{P}$; thus, these two alternatives are available to the latecomer.

The latecomer compares the profit of one-half of $0C_1G\widetilde{P}$ with that of $(\widetilde{P} - \epsilon)0C_1$ and chooses the alternative giving the higher profit. Since ϵ is very small, the latter profit is larger than the former. Thus, the second duopolist will charge a price $P_1 = \widetilde{P} - \epsilon$.

When the price is $P_1 < \widetilde{P}$, the quantity demanded in the market will be greater than $\overline{OC_1}$, say $\overline{OC_1} + \delta$, where δ is a function of ϵ and the market demand function. However, when ϵ is small, δ will also be small.

The duopolist who is first in the market and charges a price $\widetilde{P}$

has two alternatives: (1) stick to price $\tilde{P}$ and sell a quantity[3] less than δ for a total profit less than $P\delta$, or (2) lower the price to P_2, which is a little bit less than P_1 (say, $P_1 - \epsilon = \tilde{P} - 2\epsilon$), and earn a total profit of

$$P_2 C_1 = (\tilde{P} - 2\epsilon)\overline{0C}_1$$

(provided that the competitor sticks to a price of P_1, which is assumed by the Edgeworth model).[4] Since both ϵ and δ are small, alternative 2 results in a higher profit. The price war will go on until price P_0 is reached, where the total quantity sold is $C_1 + C_2$, and both duopolists are sold up to capacity and each earns a total profit of $0C_1EP_0$ or C_1EFC_2.

However, P_0 is not the equilibrium price under certain circumstances. For example, when both duopolists are selling at capacity, one will discover that $\overline{GD'}$ can be considered as the demand curve. If $\overline{C_1C_2} > \overline{C_1D'}/2$, profit will not be maximized at price P_0. Therefore, this oligopolist will raise the price to $\overline{P}$.

Since $0C_1EP_0 < \overline{P} \cdot \overline{C_1D'}/2$, seller 2, by increasing the price, can still sell at capacity and increase profits even when increasing the price. Thus seller 2 will raise the price, staying just short of $\overline{P}$. However, seller 1, in turn, can also sell at capacity by slightly undercutting the competition. Thus, the price war starts all over again, and the price will fluctuate somewhere between $\overline{P}$ and P_0. Hence, the unrealistic assumption of separate demand functions for the duopolists is not necessary in order to achieve the Edgeworth result. However, the Edgeworth result cannot be obtained without the assumption of the limited capacity of the duopolists. Unfortunately, such an assumption may not be warranted even in the short run, since capacity is often not strictly fixed in the real world.

The assumption of separate demand functions is not essential to the Edgeworth result

It is also interesting to note the following. Assume the duopolists realize that, since the product is homogeneous, they will share the market equally if they charge the same price, whereas if one charges a different price, the other will take proper counter action. In this case, the logical solution will again be the Chamberlin result.

Although we have devoted considerable space to the three different theoretical models of duopoly, it is not because we consider them to be realistic and useful in real life, but rather because

---

[3] If the market price were $\tilde{P} - \epsilon$, the quantity sold in the market would be $C_1 + \delta$. Thus, the quantity sold by the first duopolist would be $C_1 + \delta - C_1 = \delta$. However, now there are two prices—P_1 and $\tilde{P}$—and the total quantity sold is less than $C_1 + \delta$. Hence, the duopolist who charges $\tilde{P}$ can only sell a quantity less than δ. Similarly, the total quantity sold is greater than C_1 with the dual prices. Therefore, the quantity sold of the higher-priced duopolist is not zero.

[4] For the sake of simplicity, P_2, which is a bit lower than P_1, is not shown in Figure 9.5.

they are classical models and well known. Furthermore, they fully illustrate the difficulties in the theory of duopoly and its extension—the theory of oligopoly. Under essentially the same circumstances, one may obtain entirely different results with different behavior assumptions concerning the participants. In general, these comments apply equally well to oligopoly theory. For our purposes, it will only be necessary to cover a few well-known models of oligopoly.

9.3 A FEW WELL-KNOWN OLIGOPOLY MODELS

The multitude of oligopoly models greatly exceeds the number of duopoly models. Thus, a thorough analysis of the various oligopoly models is relatively complicated, although the application of game theory does seem to represent a promising approach. However, a full discussion of game theory would require a level of mathematical involvement beyond that of this book. Hence, rather than providing an explicit mathematical formulation of the relationship between game theory and oligopoly, we shall use some very simple examples to illustrate the basic rationale behind our models. Since some of the models can be illustrated by the graphical method, we shall employ it liberally. At this point it should be noted that some oligopoly models deal with a differentiated product, some with a homogeneous product, and some with both (see Assumption 9.1). Although many textbooks do not always make these distinctions, we shall specify which of the three possibilities is applicable to each model.

9.3.1 The Kinked Demand Curve and Stability of Oligopoly Price

It has long been noted by economists that the price is quite stable in oligopoly industries. Even when there is a change in cost (e.g., a sizable adjustment in wages), the price of the product may not change. According to economic theory, profit maximization requires that MR = MC. Thus, if MC changes owing to sizable adjustment in wages (other things being equal), then we should expect profit maximizers to adjust the prices of their products accordingly. However, experience indicates that oligopolists do not usually act in this way and this fact has led some economists to conclude that oligopolists are not profit maximizers. The well-known model of an oligopolist facing a kinked demand curve provides an explanation of this phenomenon and maintains the profit-maximizing behavior.

Given a kinked demand curve, stable prices and profit maximization are consistent

This oligopoly model is based on the following fundamental assumption concerning the behavior of oligopolists.

Assumption 9.5. When an oligopolist raises price competitors will not raise their prices in the hope of attracting additional customers; on the other hand, when an oligopolist reduces price, competitors will do the same in order to prevent the loss of their customers.

Assumption 9.5 results in a kink in the demand curve at the current price and quantity, which, in turn, results in a discontinuity of the MR curve at the current quantity. Moreover, Assumption 9.5 implies a stable price in the event of a change in cost, even for a profit maximizer. This theoretical development can be illustrated graphically.

The kink in the demand curve can easily be understood if we recall the meaning of the two demand curves faced by a firm under monopolistic competition. In Chapter 8, we explained that a firm under monopolistic competition faces the two demand curves $\overline{DD'}$ and $\overline{dd'}$. The former represents the price–quantity relationship facing a firm when all firms raise or reduce their prices accordingly, whereas the latter indicates the price–quantity relationship facing a firm when it alone raises or reduces its price. These two demand curves always intersect at the current price. Consider Figure 9.6, in which the two demand curves $\overline{DD'}$ and $\overline{dd'}$ intersect at point E. The current profit-maximizing price and quantity for the firm are P_0 and Q_0, respectively. By Assumption 9.5, when the firm raises its price above P_0, its competitors will not raise their prices; hence, the effective demand curve for prices above P_0 is $\overline{dd'}$ (or, more accurately, segment dE of $\overline{dd'}$). On the other hand, when the firm reduces its price below P_0, its competitors will do the same (by Assumption 9.5). Therefore, the effective demand curve for prices below P_0 is $\overline{DD'}$ (or, more accurately, segment $\overline{ED}$ of $\overline{DD'}$). Thus, given Assumption 9.5, the actual demand curve facing the firm is $\widehat{dED}$, which clearly manifests a kink at point E.

In Figure 9.6, MR_1 is the marginal revenue curve corresponding to $\overline{dd'}$ and MR_2 is that corresponding to $\overline{DD'}$. Since $\overline{dE}$ is the effective demand curve to the left of Q_0, MR_1 is relevant only to

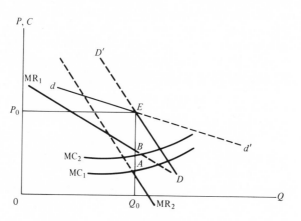

FIGURE 9.6

the left of Q_0. Similarly, MR_2 is relevant only to the right of Q_0. Hence, it follows that the marginal revenue curve corresponding to demand curve dED is represented by the solid segments of MR_1 and MR_2, which means that there is a gap (discontinuity) at Q_0.

Given a kinked demand curve, a change in MC may leave price undisturbed

The implication of a discontinuity in the MR curve due to a kink in the demand curve is a stable price, even for a profit maximizer. Suppose that we have marginal cost curve MC_1, which, at the profit-maximizing quantity Q_0, falls in the gap of the marginal revenue curve. The profit-maximizing price is P_0. Mark-up pricing (see Chapter 7) is applicable here. The profit-maximizing mark-up on marginal cost is $\overline{AE}$. Even if an increase in wages leads to an increase in marginal cost such that MC_2 rather than MC_1 is the relevant marginal cost curve, a profit-maximizing firm will continue to charge price P_0 because MC_2 still falls in the gap of the marginal revenue curve at Q_0. In this case, the mark-up has to be reduced from $\overline{AE}$ to $\overline{BE}$. For the same reason, as long as the marginal cost at the profit-maximizing quantity fluctuates within the gap of the marginal revenue curve, the profit-maximizing firm will not change its price. It only changes its mark-up according to the fluctuation in marginal cost. This explains why profit-maximizing oligopolists may not adjust their prices in reaction to a change in cost.

The kinked demand curve model was developed by Paul Sweezy (see Sweezy, 1939). Since this model explained the phenomenon of "sticky" prices in an oligopoly market, it became very popular at one point, and some economists even considered it a general theory of oligopoly. However, this model starts with a given profit-maximizing price and quantity for a firm at the kink in the demand curve, that is, it neither explains how this price is achieved nor why some other price is not achieved. A complete oligopoly theory must provide adequate answers to these questions. For this reason, most economists no longer take the kinked demand curve model seriously. However, since it does provide an answer to a commonly recognized question in oligopoly, it is worth knowing.

The kinked demand curve model is consistent only with differentiated product markets. In markets where the product is homogeneous, the demand curve $\overline{dd'}$ for a firm will be a horizontal straight line, since the quantity demanded will be zero if it charges a price higher than the market price.

9.3.2 Price Leadership

The phenomenon of *price leadership* is often observed in an oligopoly, that is, when one firm in an industry raises or reduces its price, the other firms follow suit. It is commonly recognized that the markets for steel, newsprint, agricultural implements, and tires, as well as even the grocery industry, are characterized by price leadership. In this section, we shall discuss two types of price leadership: *dominant firm* and *low-cost firm*.

Dominant Firm Price Leadership

Dominant firm price leadership prevails when there is one dominant firm and many small firms in an industry. Although it is more convenient to deal with a homogeneous product, this model is also consistent for a differentiated product.

The small firms are treated as perfect competitors. In Chapter 6, we noted that the rising portion of the MC curve which is above the minimum AVC is the supply curve of the firm in a perfectly competitive market. In the absence of externality and given constant input prices, the horizontal sum of the supply curves of the firms is the supply curve of the industry. For a given market demand, the demand for the dominant firm is the difference between the market demand and the supply of the small firms in the industry. Let us examine this concept in more detail.

Consider Figure 9.7, in which D is the market demand curve and S is the supply curve of the small firms. If the price is P_1, the market demand is equal to the supply of the small firms; hence, the quantity demanded is zero for the dominant firm. However, when the price is reduced to P_2, the quantity demanded by the market is $\overline{P_2 A}$ whereas the quantity supplied by the small firms is $\overline{P_2 B}$. Therefore, the excess quantity demanded $\overline{AB}$ is left to the dominant firm. Let $\overline{P_2 G} = \overline{AB}$; then the demand curve for the dominant firm goes through G. The demand curve for the dominant firm $P_1 d$ is constructed in a similar fashion for each and every price. Thus, the horizontal distance between $\overline{P_1 d}$ and the vertical axis is the same as the horizontal distance between S and D for each and every price.

In Figure 9.7, MR is the marginal revenue curve for the dominant firm corresponding to the demand curve $\overline{P_1 d}$, whereas MC

Under price leadership, low-cost firms generally set the price

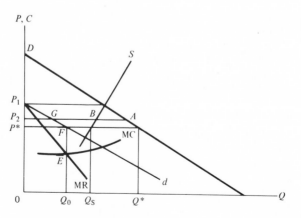

P, C

FIGURE 9.7

is the marginal cost curve for the dominant firm. The profit of
the dominant firm will be maximized if it marks up by the amount
$\overline{EF}$ on its marginal cost and sets its price at P^*. At this price, the
small firms as a group will sell the quantity Q_s, whereas the
dominant firm sells Q_0. It can easily be seen that $Q_0 + Q_s = Q^*$
(the quantity demanded for the market) at price P^*, since $\overline{P_1d}$ is
so constructed.

This model can still be applied even if there are a few dominant
firms. In this case, the MC curve will be the horizontal sum of
the MC curves of the dominant firms, and $\overline{P_1d}$ will be their demand curve.

Low-Cost Firm Price Leadership

Low-cost firm price leadership can easily be demonstrated by
assuming a homogeneous product, which, in turn, implies that
the demand curves of the oligopolists are identical. Consider Figure 9.8, in which d is the demand curve for an oligopolist (or,
more generally, the demand curve for each and every oligopolist);
MR is the corresponding marginal revenue curve. If an oligopolist
has the marginal cost curve MC_1, the profit-maximizing mark-up
price is P_1. On the other hand, a low-cost oligopolist with the
marginal cost curve MC_2 has a profit-maximizing mark-up price
P^*. As a profit maximizer, the low-cost oligopolist will not charge
a price higher than P^*. Since we are assuming a homogeneous
product, if the high-cost oligopolist charges a price higher than
P^*, the quantity sold at the higher price will be zero. Assuming
that P^* is higher than the average cost of the high-cost oligopolist,
a price of P^* will be necessary to sell the product.

FIGURE 9.8

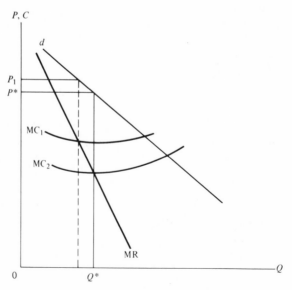

Admittedly, this is a very simple model. However, it does explain a common phenomenon: Although in some markets the costs of the various firms are quite different, the firms nevertheless coexist. In the case of a differentiated product, their prices may be quite close but, on the other hand, their profit levels may be quite different. Under these circumstances, the low-cost firm usually sets the tune, so to speak, and the high-cost firms have to manage or perish.

9.3.3 Cartels and Collusion

All of the oligopoly models discussed thus far have one thing in common: Each oligopolist acts according to his or her own best interest; that is, there is no collusion among the oligopolists. Even the Chamberlin model, which provides an identical solution to the monopoly model, does not assume or consider the possibility of collusion. Realistically, we should recognize that the small number of firms in oligopolistic industries are quite aware of their interdependence. Hence, their best interests can be better served by cooperation rather than competition. Cooperation in the marketplace by a group of sellers who deal with buyers is called *collusion*.

Collusion takes many different forms. In a broad sense, the professional organizations (e.g., those of lawyers and physicians), that set minimum fee schedules, as well as trade associations, which frequently set prices in by means of unwritten agreements, are instruments of collusion. Although this informal practice of collusion does usually manifest various degrees of effectiveness, it is often not at all effective. On the other hand, the *cartel* represents a very effective form of collusion.

Definition: Cartel. A group of sellers who agree upon certain rules concerning the price and/or allocation of the market according to some geographical or other characteristic.

A cartel can consist of several firms from one country or of several firms from different countries. The former type of cartel is very common in Europe (in particular, Germany, where the word is *Kartelle*). On the other hand, the latter type is found almost everywhere and can even be formed by the governments of different countries, an obvious example being the international cartel known as OPEC (Organization of Petroleum Exporting Countries).

A common feature of cartels is price setting and the sharing of profits

Cartels are illegal in the United States by virtue of the Sherman Antitrust Act, which dates back to 1890. However, secret collusion is not uncommon in the history of U.S. commerce. As we have already mentioned, in many ways some professional orga-

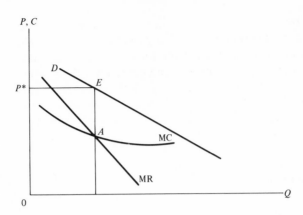

FIGURE 9.9

nizations and trade associations act as cartels. Therefore, it is useful to devote some space to this topic.

If a cartel contains all of the sellers of a homogeneous product, it is, in fact, a monopoly with multiple plants. If the goal of the cartel is to maximize the profit of the sellers as a whole, then under certain conditions it can consider the market demand curve to be its demand curve and the combined MC curve (i.e., the horizontal sum of the MC curves of the individual firms) to be its MC curve. Furthermore, the cartel can use the mark-up pricing method to set a market price that maximizes the profit of the sellers as a whole, each seller sharing in the profit in accordance with their individual sales (which are based on allocated shares of the market) and their cost behavior. A graphical illustration will be helpful in understanding this form of market collusion.

Consider Figure 9.9, in which D is the market demand curve and MR the corresponding marginal revenue curve. If the combined marginal cost curve of all the oligopolists is MC, then a mark-up on MC by the amount $\overline{AE}$ will produce a market price P^*, which will maximize the profits of the oligopolists as a whole. The cartel not only sets the price of the commodity, but also distributes the quantity to be produced or sold among its members in order to maximize profit. A necessary condition for profit maximization in the distribution of the quantity is that the MC of all firms according to their relative share of the market must be equal. Otherwise, the cartel could increase its profit by reducing the production of high-MC firms and, at the same time, increasing the production of low-MC firms by the same amount, since the same revenue with lower cost results in higher profit. In fact, under certain conditions, the existence of a cartel can actually lead to firms with zero production sharing in the profits. This is especially true when the production by high-MC firms if permitted, would act as a depressant on the market price.

The so-called ideal allocation of the product market among the firms is unlikely to be achieved in practice. There is evidence to indicate that, in reality, allocation is often determined by the level of past sales or the existing capacity at the time of the cartel's formation. In some cases, a cartel divides its market geographically; that is, each firm is given specific regions or countries in which to market its product. In general, the allocation of the market is a political process that is settled by negotiation. For this and other reasons (which will be explained later), cartels are inherently unstable.

9.4 GAME THEORY AND OLIGOPOLY THEORY

Shortly after the publication of Von Neumann's and Morgenstern's (1953) remarkable book, *The Theory of Games and Economic Behavior*, economists had high hopes that game theory might be the answer to the difficult problems presented by oligopoly theory. Although game theory could not be applied as successfully as had been hoped, it nevertheless represents a unique approach to the analysis of oligopoly behavior, particularly with respect to the interaction of the participants. We shall now proceed to use some simple examples to illustrate the basic principles of game theory as applied to an oligopoly.

The most fully developed game theory is the *two-person zero-sum game*, in which one player's loss is equal to the other player's gain. This is a special case[5] of a *constant-sum game*, in which the players' gain or loss is a constant. Although the situation in oligopoly theory is usually more complicated than the simple models of game theory, under common circumstances a constant-sum game can be considered a good approximation of an oligopoly market. For example, if the demand is very inelastic, the business (profit) gained by one oligopolist will be equal to the business (profit) lost by others. This is precisely a constant-sum game. Since a constant-sum game can be transformed into a zero-sum game by a change of origin, we shall discuss the latter in great detail. However, we shall also briefly discuss a famous nonzero-sum game—*the Prisoner's Dilemma*. This particular nonzero-sum game has the most relevance with respect to oligopoly theory.

9.4.1 Zero- and Constant-Sum Games:
The Maximin–Minimax Principle

A simple zero- or constant-sum game can be completely specified by a payoff matrix. For the purpose of illustration, we shall discuss a two-person zero-sum game. Since one player's gain is equal to the other player's loss in a two-person zero-sum game,

Zero-sum games are normally noncooperative games

---

[5] This will become clear later when we illustrate a nonzero-sum game. See also Section A9.2 in the appendix to this chapter.

TABLE 9.1. Payoff Matrix to A

		B		
A	B_1	B_2	B_3	B_4
A_1	4	0	3	4
A_2	8	-1	-4	-4
A_3	-3	-2	4	4

the payoff matrix for this kind of game is greatly simplified. Consider the payoff matrix of Table 9.1, in which the payoffs are to A from B (i.e., positive numbers indicate payments from B to A, whereas negative numbers indicate payments from A to B). In game theory, the term *strategy* usually refers to a sequence of moves (such as in chess, bridge, and poker). However, in the simple game now under discussion, a strategy is limited to a single move; that is, it consists of the specification of a particular move for one of the participants. In this sense, the payoff matrix of Table 9.1 indicates that A has three available strategies (A_1, A_2, and A_3), whereas B has four (B_1, B_2, B_3, and B_4).

Player A is free to employ any one of the three strategies A_1, A_2, and A_3. However, the payoff to A not only depends on A's strategy, but also on B's. Table 9.1 completely describes the outcome of the game for all possible combinations of the two players' strategies. For example, if A employs strategy A_1 and B employs B_1, the latter pays the former \$4 (or \$4 million, if one wishes). Clearly, the strategy that will be most advantageous depends on the opponent's strategy. The problem is that a player is not supposed to know what the opponent will do.

One fundamental assumption in a *noncooperative game* such as the one under discussion is that each player takes *only* his or her own interest into consideration when making a move. This assumption implies the Dominance Principle, which we state as follows.

Definition: Dominance Principle. If a strategy is *dominated* by another strategy, then the former will never be employed by a rational player. Thus, a dominated strategy can be ignored for the purpose of analysis. One strategy is dominated by another if (1) the payoff of the former is no greater than that of the latter regardless of what the opponent does and (2) the payoff of the former is less than that of the latter for at least one of the opponent's strategies.

The data in Table 9.1 can be used to illustrate the above principle. For example, player B will be neutral between B_3 and B_4 with respect to A_2 or A_3 because in either case the same gain and the same loss will result. However, if player A employs strategy

TABLE 9.2. Payoff Matrix to A

		B		
A	B_1	B_2	B_3	Row minima
A_1	4	0	3	0
A_2	8	-1	-4	-4
A_3	-3	-2	4	-3
Column maxima	8	0	4	—

A_1, B pays only \$3 if B_3 is employed and \$4 if B_4 is employed. Thus, B_3 dominates B_4 and B_4 can be ignored for the purpose of analysis.

Table 9.2 is derived from Table 9.1 by eliminating B_4 from the latter. It can easily be seen that the two payoff matrices result in the same solution for the game. Since Table 9.2 is simpler than Table 9.1, the dominance principle does make good sense.

In Table 9.2, we have added a column of *row minima* (i.e., we enter the minimum payoff of each row) and a row of *column maxima* (i.e., we enter the maximum payoff of each column). Thus, 0 is the minimum payoff of row A_1, -4 is the minimum payoff of row A_2, and -3 is the minimum payoff of row A_3. Similarly, 8 is the maximum payoff of column B_1, 0 is the maximum payoff of column B_2, and 4 is the maximum payoff of column B_3.

The Maximin–Minimax Principle

The *maximin–minimax principle* requires that each player attempt to maximize the minimum gain and minimize the maximum loss (hence, the terms maximin and minimax). This principle is very conservative in that it requires that the players always guard against the worst and states that each gains the most or loses the least by assuming the worst will occur. The data in Table 9.2 can be used to illustrate the maximin–minimax principle.

The last column of Table 9.2 shows the minimum gain that A can get using each available strategy. For example, if A employs A_1, the minimum possible gain is 0. However, employing A_2 (A_3), A's minimum gain is -4 (-3)—a loss of \$4 (\$3). According to the maximin–minimax principle, A will employ the strategy that results in the maximization of minimum gains, in this case 0; thus, strategy A_1 will be employed.

Since this is a zero-sum game, the values in Table 9.2 represent not only A's payoff, but also B's losses. The last row of the table shows the maximum possible losses for B with respect to each possible strategy. For example, if strategy B_1 is employed, the loss is \$8, whereas with B_2 it is 0 and with B_3 it is \$4. According to the maximin–minimax principle B will employ the strategy that

The maximin–minimax principle requires guarding against the worst possible occurrence

results in minimalization of maximum losses, in this case 0; thus, strategy B_2 will be employed.

There is an interesting phenomenon in our example: A's maximum gain among the minima, 0, is equal to B's minimum loss among the maxima. Hence, in adopting strategy A_1 to maximize the minimum gain, A chooses a course of action that matches B's loss-minimizing choice of strategy (i.e., B_2). In short, we have a unique solution—a *pure strategy*. Is this always the case? The answer is no. However, when this is the case, we say that there is a solution for the game, and the value that equates the maximin to the minimax is called the *value of the game*. In our example, the value of the game is 0. (It should be pointed out that the value of a zero-sum game is not necessarily 0.)

A pure strategy does not always yield a solution

The concept of a *saddle point* is related to the zero-sum game.

Definition: Saddle Point. The pair of strategies for a two-player game such that neither could be improved even if each player were to know the other's choice.

In our example of Table 9.2, the saddle point is $\langle A_1, B_2 \rangle$. If A knows that B's choice is B_2, then he or she can do no better than choose A_1, and vice versa. Therefore, we can state that a saddle point represents a *stable solution* of the game. However, not all games have a saddle point, and some require additional information before a solution can be found.

Consider Table 9.3, which is identical to Table 9.2 except that now the cell corresponding to $\langle A_3, B_2 \rangle$ holds the value 1 instead of -2. Although the last row, which represents the column maxima, has changed, according to the maximin–minimax principle, A's choice is still A_1 and B's choice is still B_2. However, this case is different from the previous one in that A's maximin value of 0 is not equal to B's minimax value of 1. Hence, a saddle point (i.e., a solution) does not exist in this case. Let us see why.

That $\langle A_1, B_2 \rangle$ is no longer a saddle point can be seen from the following reasoning. According to the maximin–minimax principle, B's optimal strategy is B_2. However, if A knows that B will employ B_2, then A's best choice will be A_3, not A_1 as before. In turn, if B knows that A's choice is A_3, then B's best choice will

TABLE 9.3. Payoff Matrix to A

A	B_1	B_2	B_3	Row minima
A_1	4	0	3	0
A_2	8	−1	−4	−4
A_3	−3	1	4	−3
Column maxima	8	1	4	—

be B_1. Now, A's best choice is A_2, and, in turn, B's best choice becomes B_3, in which case A's best choice is A_3, and so forth. In this case, we say that a solution to the game represented by Table 9.3 does not exist for pure strategies.

Strategies A_1–A_3 and B_1–B_3 are all pure strategies. On the other hand, if A assigns specific probabilities to A_1, A_2, and A_3, such that their sum is equal to 1, then we have a *mixed strategy*. Similarly, B can assign probabilities (whose sum again must equal 1) to his or her available pure strategies in order to form mixed strategies. Von Neumann and Morgenstern (1953) have proved that a saddle point (i.e., a solution) for a two-person zero-sum game always exists with mixed strategies. However, whereas the use of probabilities and mixed strategies may have considerable theoretical value, their practical significance has not been convincingly demonstrated. Consequently, we shall not discuss it further.

The Distinction Between Zero-Sum and Constant-Sum Games

One topic that deserves further discussion is the relationship between a zero-sum game and a constant-sum game. Table 9.2 provides a good example of a zero-sum game because A wins with certain combinations of both players' strategies and loses with other combinations. In an oligopoly game, it is usually not just a matter of gains exactly canceling out the losses, but a case of greater gain or less gain for each oligopolist. Thus, although one oligopolist's gain may be equal to another oligopolist's loss, their total gain (e.g., combined profit) is usually positive, not zero. Thus, a constant-sum game makes more sense than a zero-sum game insofar as oligopoly theory is concerned.

In oligopoly, gains may equal losses but total gain may still be positive

Since the theory of zero-sum games has been more fully developed than the theory of constant-sum games, most examples such as our own are conveniently given in that form. However, the results can be interpreted in terms of constant-sum games by a proper transformation. For example, if we add 4 to the values of all the cells of Table 9.2, we obtain the payoff matrix of Table 9.4. Comparing the last row and the last column of Table 9.2 with those of Table 9.4, it can be seen that the values in the latter just

TABLE 9.4. Payoff Matrix to A

A	B_1	B_2	B_3	Row minima
		B		
A_1	8	4	7	4
A_2	12	3	0	0
A_3	1	2	8	1
Column maxima	12	4	8	—

represent an addition of 4 to the corresponding values in the former. According to the maximin–minimax principle, $\langle A_1, B_2 \rangle$ is still the saddle point, and we have a solution to the game as before. However, in the former case the value of the game was 0, whereas now it is 4, the value of the latter again being the value of the former plus 4. Thus, the addition or subtraction of a constant to all elements of a payoff matrix does not change the essential characteristics or the solution of the game, but merely changes the value of the outcome.

The data in Table 9.4 can be interpreted as an oligopoly game for two sellers in which the maximum possible total profit for the whole market is $12 million and each one's share of the profits depends not only on one's own strategy, but also on the opponent's strategy. By employing strategy A_1, A is assured a minimum profit of $4 million (and possibly more if B does not employ an optimal strategy). On the other hand, by employing strategy B_2, B can hold A's profit down to a maximum of $4 million (and possibly less if A makes a mistake). Hence, B is assured a minimum profit of $12 million − $4 million = $8 million by employing B_2.

For the sake of simplicity, we have not explained what the strategies of A and B actually are. In terms of oligopoly, a strategy may involve a certain pricing policy, advertising expenditure, and/or sales crew. A different strategy involves a different combination of these factors. Thus, a high price combined with low expenditures in the advertising and sales departments may not result in a high profit. Similarly, a low price combined with high expenditures on advertising and sales also may not result in a high profit. Hence, the proper combination of these factors is the key to high profits. However, the proper combination for one oligopolist depends not only on the demand, but also on the opponent's strategy. The payoff matrix is constructed by taking all of these complicated factors and interactions into consideration. The student should appreciate that the development of strategies for operational use can quickly become a quite involved and complex process. Nor, as we shall explain later, does game theory provide the basis of a theory of oligopoly or enable quick and ready solutions to problems arising in an oligopoly model.

9.4.2 The Prisoner's Dilemma and Economic Behavior

Given certain strategies, both players can gain (lose)

The Prisoner's Dilemma is a famous example of a different kind of game than those considered previously that has important implications with respect to economic behavior in particular and social behavior in general. In Section 9.4.1, we discussed two-person zero-sum (constant-sum) games, in which one player's gain *always* equals the other player's loss. However, in everyday life, we encounter games that often involve gains for *both* players for certain combinations of strategies and losses for *both* players for other combinations. This situation is illustrated by the following example.

Suppose that two persons, say A and B, are picked up by the police and accused of bank robbery. The District Attorney is quite sure that they are indeed bank robbers, but there is insufficient evidence to convict them. Hence, the District Attorney talks to them separately, making the following statement to each:

> I am pretty sure that you are the bank robbers. If you confess and your partner does not, you can turn State's evidence, your partner will be sent to prison for 30 years, and you will be freed immediately (and vice versa). If you both confess, then both of you will be sent to prison for 20 years. On the other hand, if neither of you confess, I have evidence to convict both of you for a minor crime, and you will be sent to jail for 1 year.

Assuming that the District Attorney is 100% right, then the payoff matrix (more accurately, the negative payoff matrix) for A and B is as shown in Table 9.5, in which the top number in each cell is A's prison term and the bottom number is B's.

Table 9.5 clearly shows that the best strategy for either A or B is to confess, provided that the other does not confess. Since the situation is symmetric, it can hardly be expected that one partner will make a sacrifice for the other's benefit. Thus, neither of the two "confess–do not confess" combinations would seem to be a reasonable solution, and they can hence be eliminated. Of the two remaining possibilities, the "do not confess–do not confess" combination is the better alternative, since both A and B will get only a 1-year sentence rather than the 20-year sentence each would get if they both confessed. By this logic, the "do not confess–do not confess" combination would seem to be a good compromise solution for the game (provided that both A and B are sure that the other will not confess). However, the District Attorney's office certainly will not give A and B the opportunity to work out an agreement. In the absence of such reliable assurance, both will confess in court, and each will get a 20-year term in prison.

This result may sound strange, but it agrees with our previously mentioned dominance principle. It can be seen that the "confess"

TABLE 9.5. Negative Payoff Matrix for A and B

A	B Confess	Do not confess
Confess	A: 20 years B: 20 years	A: 0 years B: 30 years
Do not confess	A: 30 years B: 0 years	A: 1 year B: 1 year

strategy actually dominates the "do not confess" strategy for both A and B. From A's point of view, it is better to confess regardless of what B does. For example, if B confesses, A is better off confessing because this way he or she gets only 20 years instead of the 30 years that would result from the "do not confess" strategy. If B does not confess, A is still better off confessing because this strategy results in immediate freedom, whereas not confessing would result in 1 year in prison. Therefore, A is better off confessing regardless of what B does (and similarly for B). Thus, the "confess" strategy dominates the "do not confess" strategy for both participants. According to the dominance principle, the "do not confess" strategy should be eliminated, and hence the only advantageous strategy for both would be to confess. On the other hand, from Table 9.5 it is seen that both participants will be better off if they do not confess. From the "participants as a whole" point of view, the "do not confess–do not confess" combination actually dominates the "confess–confess" strategy. In Chapter 13 (Welfare Economics) it will be shown that the "do not confess–do not confess" combination is Pareto superior to the "confess–confess" alternative. Thus, the dominance principle results in a solution that is Pareto inferior, which brings into doubt its value in theory as well as in practice. Although the dominance principle seems very sound in theory and is quite appealing in commonsense terms, the above simple example does shed some doubt on its validity. This is not the place to engage in a lengthy and esoteric discussion of this topic; however, it does deserve more attention by game theorists.

In the Prisoner's Dilemma the dominant principle may prove elusive

The above simple example also illustrates the difference between a cooperative and a noncooperative game. The conventional "confess–confess" solution of the Prisoner's Dilemma applies to a noncooperative game. Although most games are noncooperative, on special occasions it is useful to talk about cooperative games. If our example were a cooperative game, then the solution would be the "do not confess–do not confess" combination.

As we have argued, if both prisoners take only their own interests into consideration and deem their partner to be untrustworthy, then the "confess" strategy is the best alternative for both. On the other hand, if both prisoners are part of a large organization that has the power to enforce its own rules (e.g., if each knows perfectly well that a confession would not only mean freedom from jail, but also certain death at the hands of the organization), then the solution of the game will be "do not confess–do not confess."

Hence, in a sense, death threats by underworld organizations represent a means of converting a noncooperative game into a cooperative game. Analogously, a merger between two duopolists to form a monopoly or the formation of cartels also represent conversions of a noncooperative game into a cooperative game. These two examples suggest that cooperative games *may* be socially undesirable. However, this is not necessarily so, that is, one cannot make generalized statements as to whether noncooperative games are socially more desirable than cooperative games—it all depends on the situation. Underworld organizations benefit criminals, not their victims, whereas monopolies and cartels benefit sellers, but buyers are very likely to suffer. Thus, the benefits to the players of these cooperative games are contrary to the best interests of society as a whole. However, there are cases where both the players and society as a whole benefit if, under the same circumstances, a cooperative game rather than a noncooperative game is played. For example, if there is a conflict of interest between a husband and wife, and the alternatives of one yielding to the other are ruled out, then the two remaining alternatives are as follows: (1) Each remains adamant and they fight to the very end or (2) the two have a sincere talk and try to reach a compromise. Alternative 2—cooperative game—is obviously superior to alternative 1—a noncooperative game—because choosing alternative 2 does not eliminate the option of later returning to alternative 1, whereas the converse is not true. Unfortunately, many husbands and wives do play a noncooperative game, which results in unnecessary suffering for both. The same argument applies to games between employers and employees, landlords and tenants, and even between neighbors or countries. In a sense, the laws and regulations of a civilized society are devised to convert the noncooperative game of the jungle into a cooperative game of orderly activities.

Not all cooperative games are socially undesirable

Most economists are obsessed with competition rather than cooperation. Thus, in most cases they usually prefer to employ the word collusion rather than cooperation. This is particularly justified in the analysis of economic activities, since it is neither feasible nor necessary for buyers and sellers to play a cooperative game in order to benefit both sides in the market. On the surface, exchange seems to be a zero-sum game because one's financial gain is equal to the other's financial loss. Actually, exchange is not even a constant-sum game in terms of utilities. It will be shown in Chapter 12 that if two people are not on the contract curve (which will be defined in Chapter 12), there exist trading possibilities such that both will gain from trade. Consequently, in the marketplace, self-interest and noncooperative games may result in mutual benefit to both sides. Although a cooperative game may benefit all participants, in many cases the enforcement of the rules of the game may constitute a problem. If there are no "teeth" in the enforcement of the rules of a cooperative game, cheaters can usually benefit at the expense of noncheaters. For example, in the Prisoner's Dilemma game, the cheater (i.e., the confessor) could obtain immediate freedom at the expense of the partner who sticks to the "do not confess" strategy. This illustrates the inherent instability of cartels (which are not legal in the United States), as we have mentioned at the end of Section 9.3.3. It also explains why many economists are highly skeptical about the durability of a cartel that does not have effective and enforceable rules. A few years ago, a well-known economist predicted that the international oil cartel (OPEC) would not exist at the end of one year's time. Although this prediction was obviously wrong, the economist's mistake was not one of principle, but rather in his choice of the time it would take for the cartel to disintegrate. There are many variables involved in determining the incidence of any economic event; thus, any definite prediction regarding such an event, particularly with respect to its time of occurrence, is a risky business. Hence, strictly doctrinaire predictions of economic events may not be the best policy. A conditional statement, such as "if such and such takes place, then the given result is likely to follow," will usually be a better prediction or forecast.

9.4.3 Limitations of Game Theory with Respect to Oligopoly

Although game theory has been of help in the development and refinement of economic theory (not only with respect to oligopoly, but also with respect to other areas of advanced theory), the high hopes that economists once had for it have not materialized. In fact, game theory has been severely criticized on several grounds.

The main criticism of game theory relates to the maximin–minimax principle, which is fundamental to the theory. According to this principle, a player always must guard against the worst. Many economists consider this view to be so unnecessarily pessimistic that it cannot be realistic or provide a decision criterion either for business or even for people in matters of everyday life. For example, it is commonly recognized that one function of entrepreneurs is to bear the risk of a venture.

*The maximin–
minimax principle is
probably not
compatible with
innovation and risk
taking*

Thus, the pessimistic approach of game theory may not be conducive to the adventurous spirit of the business world. Although game theory (and the decision criteria that are an explicit part of it) may be useful in developing the military strategy of large-scale operations, it is hardly applicable to day-to-day decisions in business and dealing with everyday problems. It is a psychologically fascinating exercise that can, at times, even provide a useful method for problem analysis; however, the method provided is not one that can be used with frequency.

On theoretical grounds, game theory is not sophisticated enough to deal with the complicated situation of oligopoly in a realistic fashion. The examples that we have cited are one-move games; however, even the more complicated games that use mixed strategies (these games will be discussed in the appendix to this chapter) are still one-move games. In real life, a game usually involves a sequence of moves (such as in chess, bridge, and poker), and one's optimal move at each stage of the game depends on his or her opponent's next move, which is unknown and can be any of numerous possibilities. Game theory must enumerate each and every possible move of every opponent at each stage of the game if the maximin–minimax principle is to be applied in order to select a single move. Hence, the solution of the game involves a complete description of all possible moves for all players involved under every contingency at all possible stages of the game. Consequently, most games are too complicated for game theory to handle. Thus, bridge and poker, which involve more than two players, are too complicated for game theory. Even chess, which involves only two players, is too complicated for game theory, given the current state of the art. When considered as games, duopoly and oligopoly are probably more complicated than chess; therefore, they are unlikely to be amenable to the application of game theory for the derivation of solutions to decision problems. No wonder that the usefulness of game theory is quite limited in the development of the oligopoly theory.

Despite its limitations, game theory is a useful addition to the economist's toolbox. It provides insight into the modus operandi of oligopolists and is suggestive of probable outcomes in the analysis of complicated oligopoly situations. As game theory advances, it may become more helpful in the development of oligopoly theory. For the moment, it is more a learning or pedagogical tool than a decision tool.

SUMMARY

We dealt in this chapter with oligopoly, the most difficult market model in economic theory owing to the interdependence that exists between oligopolists. Thus, because different assumptions concerning the reaction of competitors lead to different solutions for the same set of data, we found that instead of one model we have a multitude of oligopoly models. For example, models of duopoly, a special form of oligopoly, by Cournot, Chamberlin, and Edgeworth were shown to yield different solutions because of the different assumptions in each model concerning the behavior of duopolists. The Cournot model (which is generally considered the classical forerunner of oligopoly theory) assumes price to be the basis on which duopolists compete, a straight line demand curve, and zero cost; in this case a determinate solution is obtained in which the equilibrium price is higher and the quantity is lower than under perfect competition. On the other hand, the Edgeworth model assumes that quantity instead of price is the basis on which the duopolists compete; the result of the slightly different set of assumptions is indeterminancy in price and quantity. Although the Cournot model yields an equilibrium price that is two-thirds of the monopoly price and a quantity one-third greater than under monopoly, Chamberlin was able by slightly modifying the behavior assumption of the Cournot model to develop a duopoly model in which the price–quantity solution is identical to that in a monopoly.

We then described other models of oligopoly that have been developed to bring theory closer to reality. We first looked at several price leadership models, after which we directed attention to the cartel and the case of a kinked demand curve as special variants of oligopoly. We noted that a cartel is characterized by collusion rather than cooperation and that its success depends on favorable market conditions. Hence, it is because of a favorable market for oils that the Organization of Petroleum Exporting Countries (OPEC) has been able to survive when other cartels have failed.

We concluded our discussion of oligopoly with a brief excursion into zero-sum and constant-sum game theory. We saw that, so long as relatively simple strategies are involved, game theory is able to provide a new dimension to the analysis of oligopoly behavior. However, the application of game theory to determining the outcome of the complex strategies more often used in business becomes exceedingly difficult, if not impossible. For this reason the early expectations of game theory have not been realized.

EXERCISES AND QUESTIONS FOR CHAPTER 9 ON OLIGOPOLY THEORY

1. Describe the assumption underlying the kinked demand curve said to be faced by firms under conditions of oligopoly. Of what use is the kinked demand curve in explaining price stability in oligopoly markets? Explain.

2. Why is the oligopoly market more difficult to analyze than the competitive and monopoly markets? Why are there so many different oligopoly models in microeconomic theory? Explain.

3. What are the essential differences between the Cournot and Chamberlin duopoly models? Explain.

4. What are the essential differences between the Cournot and Edgeworth models in duopoly? Explain.

5. Use a simple model to demonstrate the differences in quantity and price in long-run equilibrium under perfect competition, monopoly, and duopoly. From this result, can you make any statement about the advantages and disadvantages of the various market systems? Why or why not?

6. Why do economists generally consider a cartel organized by a group of oligopolists to be inherently unstable? Explain.

7. What are the essential features of the price leadership model of oligopoly theory? Which industry in the United States can be approximated by this model? Explain.

8. What can be learned from the simple model of the Prisoner's Dilemma in game theory? Explain.

9. Empirical studies indicate that in most (if not all) cases, the short-run AVC of a firm is constant. Is this phenomenon consistent with the various models of oligopoly? Explain.

10. Is mark-up pricing as practiced by most business firms consistent with the various models of oligopoly? Explain.

11. Based on your understanding of oligopoly theory, do you think that the OPEC oil cartel will survive? Explain. What elements of stability and instability can you identify?

A MATHEMATICAL NOTE ON OLIGOPOLY

A9.1 DUOPOLY MODELS

A9.1.1 The Cournot Model

Let us assume the demand function to be linear, that is,

$$P = A - aQ \tag{A9.1}$$

where P and Q are the market price and quantity demanded, respectively, and A, $a > 0$ are constants. Let Q_1 and Q_2 denote the quantities sold by sellers 1 and 2, respectively. By definition,

$$Q = Q_1 + Q_2 \tag{A9.2}$$

By substitution, the demand function can be written

$$P = A - a(Q_1 + Q_2) \tag{A9.1'}$$

By definition, the total revenue R_1 for seller 1 is equal to the price multipled by the quantity Q_1; this can be written

$$R_1 = PQ_1 = AQ_1 - aQ_1^2 - aQ_1Q_2 \tag{A9.3}$$

Similarly, the total revenue R_2 for seller 2 is

$$R_2 = PQ_2 = AQ_2 - aQ_2^2 - aQ_1Q_2 \tag{A9.4}$$

It is assumed that the cost is zero for both sellers. Thus, the profit and total revenue are identical. Denoting the profit for sellers 1 and 2 by π_1 and π_2, respectively, we have

$$\pi_1 = AQ_1 - aQ_1^2 - aQ_1Q_2 \tag{A9.5}$$

$$\pi_2 = AQ_2 - aQ_2^2 - aQ_1Q_2 \tag{A9.6}$$

The equilibrium quantities for the sellers are obtained by solving the system of simultaneous equations consisting of the first-order conditions for profit maximization, which are

$$\partial\pi_1/\partial Q_1 = A - 2aQ_1 - aQ_2 = 0 \tag{A9.7}$$

$$\partial\pi_2/\partial Q_2 = A - 2aQ_2 - aQ_1 = 0 \tag{A9.8}$$

Equations (A9.7) and (A9.8) can alternatively be written

$$2aQ_1 + aQ_2 = A \quad \text{or} \quad Q_1 = A/2a - \tfrac{1}{2}Q_2 \tag{A9.9}$$

$$2aQ_2 + aQ_1 = A \quad \text{or} \quad Q_2 = A/2a - \tfrac{1}{2}Q_1 \tag{A9.10}$$

Equations (A9.9) and (A9.10) are called *reaction functions*. By using Cramer's rule or by substitution, we obtain

$$Q_1 = A/3a \tag{A9.11}$$

$$Q_2 = A/3a \tag{A9.12}$$

The result that $Q_1 = Q_2$ is expected because the product is homogeneous and costs are identical; that is, we have a symmetric system. Therefore, the equilibrium prices and quantities for the duopolists must be identical.

The second-order conditions for maximum profit are satisfied, since

$$\partial\pi_1^2/\partial Q_1^2 = -2a < 0 \tag{A9.13}$$

$$\partial\pi_2^2/\partial Q_2^2 = -2a < 0 \tag{A9.14}$$

Thus, we are sure that solution (A9.11), (A9.12) signifies maximum profit for both firms.

The equilibrium price can be computed by substituting (A9.11) and (A9.12) into (A9.1'):

$$P^* = A/3 \tag{A9.15}$$

In terms of the figures in Section 9.2 of the text, the constant A in (A9.1) is equal to $\overline{0D'}$, whereas $\overline{0D}$ is equal to A/a. It can easily be seen that the mathematical solution is consistent with the graphical solution. The simultaneous solution of the mathematical model is straightforward in that it avoids the confusing step-by-step adjustment process. Theoretically, in comparative statics the adjustment process is supposed to take place instantaneously and not period-by-period as in a dynamic system. This distinction seems to have confused some economists, leading them frequently to make unjustified unfavorable comments concerning the Cournot model.

One good feature of the Cournot model is that it can be generalized to any number of sellers. For example, in the case of a monopoly, where the number of sellers is 1, it can easily be seen that the equilibrium quantity and price, respectively, are

$$Q^* = A/2a \tag{A9.16}$$

$$P^* = A/2 \tag{A9.17}$$

When there are three sellers, we shall have three equations similar to (A9.5) and (A9.6). Consequently, there will also be three equations of the types (A9.7) and (A9.8), as well as three reaction functions of the types (A9.9) and (A9.10). The solution of the three-equation system will yield

$$Q_1 = Q_2 = Q_3 = A/4a \tag{A9.18}$$

As a result, the equilibrium price in the three-firm case will be

$$P^* = A/4 \tag{A9.19}$$

In general, when the number of sellers is n, the Cournot model yields the following equilibrium quantity and price:

$$Q_i^* = A/(n + 1)a, \quad i = 1, 2, ..., n \tag{A9.20}$$

$$P^* = A/(n + 1) \tag{A9.21}$$

It has been shown that we have the special case of monopoly when $n = 1$ and the special case of duopoly when $n = 2$. When n becomes very large, we have the special case of perfect competition. Since A is a constant, it can easily be seen from (A9.21) that $P \to 0$ when $n \to \infty$. With zero cost, this is consistent with the model of perfect competition.

A9.1.2 The Chamberlin Model

The solution of the Chamberlin duopoly model is identical to the Cournot monopoly solution (A9.16) and (A9.17). Thus, from (A9.16) it can be seen that, if two sellers share the market equally, we obtain

$$Q_1 = Q_2 = A/4a \tag{A9.22}$$

The corresponding price is indicated by (A9.17).

The above result can be derived in two alternative ways. By the first method, we recognize the fact that $Q_1 = Q_2$ for an identical price because of the homogeneity of the product. Denoting this quantity by Q_i, the demand function (A9.1') can be written

$$P = A - 2aQ_i \tag{A9.23}$$

Since the price, quantity, and cost are identical for both duopolists, their total revenue and profit functions are also identical. The analysis can proceed for one seller only; the profit function is

$$\pi = Q_iP = AQ_i - 2aQ_i^2 \tag{A9.24}$$

The first-order condition for profit maximization is

$$d\pi/dQ_i = A - 4aQ_i = 0 \qquad \text{(A9.25)}$$

which yields the solution

$$Q_i = A/4a \qquad \text{(A9.26)}$$

The second-order condition for profit maximization is also satisfied, since

$$d^2\pi/dQ_i^2 = -4a < 0 \qquad \text{(A9.27)}$$

Thus, (A9.26) is the solution for maximum profit.

The quantity Q_i given by (A9.26) is for one duopolist only. The market quantity is twice the quantity Q_i. Hence, the equilibrium quantity for the market is

$$Q^* = 2Q_i = A/2a \qquad \text{(A9.28)}$$

and the equilibrium price for the market is

$$P^* = A/2 \qquad \text{(A9.29)}$$

This result is identical to the Cournot monopoly solution (A9.16) and (A9.17).

Another way of deriving this result is to proceed as with the Cournot model. However, the first-order conditions for profit maximization in the present case will be different from those of the Cournot model, which sets the partial derivatives of the profit functions equal to zero [see (A9.7) and (A9.8)]. The Chamberlin model sets the total derivatives of the profit functions equal to zero. Since the profit functions in the present case are identical to those of the Cournot model, we can take the derivatives of (A9.5) and (A9.6):

$$d\pi_1/dQ_1 = A - 2aQ_1 - aQ_2 - aQ_1 dQ_2/dQ_1 = 0 \qquad \text{(A9.30)}$$

$$d\pi_2/dQ_2 = A - 2aQ_2 - aQ_1 - aQ_2 dQ_1/dQ_2 = 0 \qquad \text{(A9.31)}$$

The Chamberlin result is derived if we let

$$dQ_1 = dQ_2 \qquad \text{(A9.32)}$$

With this behavior assumption, (A9.30) and (A9.31) respectively become

$$A = 3aQ_1 + aQ_2 \qquad \text{(A9.33)}$$

$$A = aQ_1 + 3aQ_2 \qquad \text{(A9.34)}$$

The solution of this two-equation system is

$$Q_1 = Q_2 = A/4a \quad \text{and} \quad Q^* = Q_1 + Q_2 = A/2a \qquad \text{(A9.35)}$$

The above two equations are identical to (A9.26) and the Cournot monopoly solution (A9.16), respectively.

A9.1.3 The Difficulties in Price Competition

Traditionally, economists consider the quantity, not the price, as the decision variable of the firm. Under perfect competition, firms are price takers, and quantity is the only possible decision variable. However, the situation under monopoly and monopolistic competition is different: Either quantity or price—but not both—can be considered the decision variable (the latter being the mark-up price, as we have shown in Chapters 7 and 8). The Cournot and Chamberlin duopoly models are based on the traditional approach in that the decision variable of the duopolists is quantity. The Cournot model has been criticized for this reason, the critics stating that price, not quantity, should be the decision variable. For the sake of simplicity, we could assume the demand functions to be linear, in which case they would be written

$$Q_1 = B_1 - b_{11}P_1 + b_{12}P_2$$
$$Q_2 = B_2 + b_{21}P_1 - b_{22}P_2$$
$$(A9.36)$$

where B_1, B_2, b_{11}, b_{12}, b_{21}, and b_{22} are positive constants. The inverse functions of (A9.36) can easily be derived by solving for P_1 and P_2 in terms of Q_1 and Q_2, respectively, and the parameters. However, this kind of mathematical operation is misleading, since the fact that the product is homogeneous makes the demand functions more complicated than (A9.36).

Since the product is homogeneous, the demand for Q_1 will be the market demand when $P_1 < P_2$ and zero when $P_1 > P_2$. Similarly, the demand for Q_2 will be the market demand when $P_2 < P_1$ and zero when $P_2 > P_1$. Only when $P_1 = P_2$ will the market demand be $Q = Q_1 + Q_2$. Using the above notation, the market demand is

$$Q = Q_1 = B_1 - b_{11}P_1, \quad Q_2 = 0 \qquad \text{for} \quad P_1 < P_2$$
$$Q = Q_2 = B_2 - b_{22}P_2, \quad Q_1 = 0 \qquad \text{for} \quad P_2 < P_1 \qquad (A9.37)$$
$$Q = Q_1 + Q_2 = B_3 - b_3P \qquad \qquad \text{for} \quad P_1 = P_2$$

The Cournot model considers only one of the above three possible market demand functions, namely, the last expression in (A9.37). Since the demand is the inverse function in the Cournot model, it can easily be seen that the parameters of (A9.1) and the third equation of (A9.37) have the following correspondence:

$$A = B_3/b_3 \qquad \text{and} \qquad a = 1/b_3 \qquad (A9.38)$$

It should be pointed out that the three expressions in (A9.37) are conditional; that is, only one of them holds under given conditions. In a static model, the demand for the same product must be the same; hence, the three expressions in (A9.37) must be identical, notwithstanding the different notation.

The above result shows that a duopoly model that deals with

a homogeneous product may generate different results when price instead of quantity is considered to be the decision variable. Since the demand function is more complicated when price is considered to be the decision variable, a result derived when quantity is considered as such may not be sophisticated enough.

Although the Edgeworth model does result in an unstable situation, the price fluctuation will have an upper and lower limit provided that we additionally assume a limited capacity for both duopolists. Without the limited-capacity assumption, the long-run equilibrium price of a homogeneous product under price competition of the Edgeworth type will be zero for zero cost. However, with the assumption of perfect information or knowledge (Assumption 9.4), a logical conclusion would be the Chamberlin solution. Collusion is not necessary for duopolists to arrive at a mutually beneficial position—each one must only know how to get there. However, the existence of perfect information or knowledge is essential to this conclusion.

A9.1.4 The Stackelberg Leadership–Followership Model

The model formulated by the German economist Heinrich von Stackelberg (1952) represents a variation of the Cournot and Chamberlin models. This model permits the duopolists to consider all possible alternatives and then choose the one that results in maximum profit. The alternatives are presented in terms of "*leadership*" and "*followership*." When there are two sellers, say A and B, in the market, there are four possible outcomes:

1. A is a leader and B is a follower.
2. B is a leader and A is a follower.
3. Both A and B are followers.
4. Both A and B are leaders.

The activities of both sellers are consistent in cases 1 and 2: One seller acts as a leader and the other acts as a follower. Hence, there is no conflict in the market insofar as the sellers are concerned, and the solution is stable. In case 3, both sellers take a defensive position, and it is likely that the solution is also stable. In fact, according to the Stackelberg definition, case 3 is precisely the Cournot solution. In a sense, the Cournot model is a special case of the Stackelberg model.

Case 4 results in an unstable situation. Each seller strives to be a leader, and hence optimal choice with respect to quantity may not be consistent with market demand. This conflict of interest can result in a price war. Stackelberg thought that the last case should be the common outcome of duopoly.

Stackelberg defines a follower as one who obeys the reaction function [see (A9.9) and (A9.10)] and then, given the quantity decision of the competitor, who is assumed to be a leader, adjusts the output level so as to maximize profit. A leader assumes that a competitor acts as a follower and, given the competitor's reaction function, adjusts output so as to maximize profit. Thus, in case 4, each duopolist calculates maximum profit on the basis of assumed leadership while assuming the competitor to be a follower. If leadership results in a higher profit than followership, then the seller chooses to be a leader regardless of what the competitor does. Otherwise, the seller chooses to be a follower.

Using the example of Section A9.1.1, the leadership profit function for A is obtained by substituting B's reaction function (A9.10) into A's profit equation (A9.5):

$$\pi_A = AQ_1 - aQ_1^2 - aQ_1(A/2 - Q_1/2)$$

$$= AQ_1/2 - aQ_1^2/2 \tag{A9.39}$$

The first-order condition for profit maximization is

$$d\pi_A/dQ_1 = A/2 - aQ_1 = 0 \tag{A9.40}$$

which yields

$$Q_1' = A/2a \tag{A9.41}$$

It can easily be seen that the second-order condition for profit maximization is satisfied, since, by assumption, $a > 0$. Substituting (A9.41) into (A9.39), the maximum leadership profit for A is

$$\pi_A' = A^2/8a \tag{A9.42}$$

Since the system is symmetric, it can easily be shown that the profit-maximizing quantity and the maximum leadership profit for B are the same as those for A. Thus, we have

$$Q_2' = A/2a \tag{A9.43}$$

$$\pi_B' = A^2/8a \tag{A9.44}$$

According to Stackelberg, the followership profit for A is obtained by first substituting B's leadership quantity into A's reaction function in order to compute A's optimal followership quantity and then substituting this quantity and B's leadership quantity into A's profit equation.

The optimal followership quantity for A is computed by substituting (A9.43) into (A9.9):

$$Q_1^f = A/4a \tag{A9.45}$$

Comparing (A9.45) with (A9.41), we see that in our case the optimal followership quantity is one-half the optimal leadership quantity.

Substituting (A9.43) and (A9.45) into A's profit function (A9.5), we obtain the following maximum profit for A:

$$\pi_A^f = A(A/4a) - a(A/4a)^2 - a(A/4a)(A/2a)$$
$$= A^2/16a \tag{A9.46}$$

By symmetry, we also have B's optimal followership quantity and maximum profit:

$$Q_2^f = A/4a \tag{A9.47}$$

$$\pi_B^f = A^2/16a \tag{A9.48}$$

Comparing (A9.46) with (A9.42) and (A9.48) with (A9.44), it can be seen that the leadership profit is twice the followership profit for both A and B. As a result, both A and B want to be leaders. However, if this were the case, their profits could not be maximum; instead, they would be minimum. Substituting (A9.41) and (A9.43), that is, the leadership quantities for A and B, respectively, into demand function (A9.1), we obtain the market price:

$$P = 0 \tag{A9.49}$$

This indicates that the profit for both duopolists will be zero, which can hardly be considered a stable solution.

Thus, an example that results in a stable solution under the Cournot assumption has become a Stackelberg disequilibrium owing to an alteration of the basic behavior assumptions. These results fully illustrate the difficulties in oligopoly theory which we mentioned earlier in this chapter. The result generated by an oligopoly model is very sensitive to the assumptions made concerning the behavior of the participants. Since nobody knows how real oligopolists actually react (most likely, different oligopolists react differently under different circumstances), it is rather risky to attempt to formalize the oligopoly market. What we would need is a family of assumptions and given conditions, each producing a specific outcome. In short, we would have many theories of oligopoly.

A9.2 ELEMENTARY GAME THEORY

A game usually consists of a sequence of *moves* (such as in chess, bridge, and poker). At each stage of the game, there are many possible moves that a player may make. A specific sequence of successive moves is called a *strategy*. A simple game may involve only a single move on the part of each of its participants. In a single-move game, the strategy and move are identical.

Games can be categorized with respect to the number of players; thus, we have one-person, two-person, three-person, and, in the general case, n-person games. Monopoly can be considered a one-person game, which, in general, is not very interesting. On the other hand, a game that involves more than two persons is extremely complicated. At the elementary level, it is two-person games that are discussed most extensively.

Games can also be categorized with respect to the payoffs; on this basis, we have *constant-sum games* and *nonconstant-sum games*. A constant-sum game involves a constant payoff to all of the participants. An oligopoly market with perfectly inelastic demand is an example of a constant-sum game. Any gain in an oligopolist's share of the market must come at the expense of at least one competitor. A *zero-sum game*, in which the sum of the gains of all the players is zero, is a special case of a constant-sum game. Many games that people play for money (e.g., poker) are zero-sum games. However, many casino games are not zero-sum games insofar as the players are concerned, since after the casino takes its cut, the sum of the gains of the players as a whole is negative. In the market, many games are of the nonconstant-sum type because the demand is not perfectly inelastic. In fact, external economies and diseconomies usually prevail with respect to advertising and other market activities. In many cases, one oligopolist's gain may not come at the expense of any of his or her competitors. Actually, some advertising can have the side effect of benefiting a competitor. Thus, nonconstant-sum games are more common in economics. The Prisoner's Dilemma, which was discussed in the text, is an example of a nonconstant-sum game.

Finally, games can also be categorized with respect to the rules by which they are played; thus, we make a distinction between *cooperative games* and *noncooperative games*. A cooperative game permits the players to work out agreements among themselves. In particular, they are allowed to exchange information freely. On the other hand, a noncooperative game does not allow players free exchange of information nor the contracting of an agreement.

In this section, we shall only discuss the simple case of a two-person, zero-sum, single-move, noncooperative game. Since in our game one player's gain is the other player's loss (negative gain), only one payoff matrix will be necessary.

A *payoff matrix* specifies all of the possible outcomes of a game. Suppose that player A has m possible strategies and that player B has n possible strategies. Let us denote the payoff to A (the negative payoff to B) when A takes strategy i and B takes strategy j by a_{ij}; the total of $m \times n$ of the a_{ij}s will constitute the payoff matrix:

$$\begin{bmatrix} a_{11} & a_{12} & \cdots & a_{1n} \\ a_{21} & a_{22} & \cdots & a_{2n} \\ & & \vdots & \\ a_{m1} & a_{m2} & \cdots & a_{mn} \end{bmatrix}$$

The payoff matrix of Table 9.1 indicates that $m = 3$ and $n = 4$. On the other hand, Table 9.2 indicates that $m = 3$ and $n = 3$. From the numerical examples in the text, it is obvious that some of the a_{ij}s are positive and others negative. This must be the case; otherwise, only one player would be willing to play such a game because no one wants to enter a game that they are sure to lose. It is understood that none of the strategies is dominated by any other strategy for both A and B. (See the text for the statement of the dominance principle.)

The interdependence of the players is indicated by the payoff matrix, in which we see that the gain or loss not only depends on a player's own strategy, but also on that of the opponent. Each player always tries to get the highest gain or the lowest loss; however, his or her opponent's counteraction may convert the highest possible gain to the highest possible loss, since the highest gain is usually associated with a high loss for a certain strategy. Otherwise, the highest-gain strategy would dominate all other strategies (which would be eliminated in the first place by the dominance principle). Thus, the selection of the best strategy is a problem.

The maximin–minimax principle of von Neumann and Morgenstern, as stated in the text, is to guard against the worst. Therefore, when selecting the ith strategy, A only considers the minimum gain for this strategy as the anticipated gain. Thus, A's anticipated gain from the employment of the ith strategy is

$$\min_{j} a_{ij}$$

In this way, A's gain can be more, but never less, than that anticipated from each and every strategy. Hence, player A is conservative, but still desires a large gain. Therefore, A selects the strategy i for which

$$\min_{j} a_{ij}$$

is largest. It is for this reason that we obtain the term maximin, which denotes that one always maximizes the minimum gain. Player A's expected outcome of the game is

$$\max_{i} \min_{j} a_{ij}$$

that is, A's gain from the game cannot be smaller than this, but it can possibly be larger.

Since A's gain is B's loss, B wants to hold down A's gain as much as possible. According to the maximin–minimax principle, B also tries to guard against the worst. The anticipated loss for whatever strategy B takes (e.g., the jth), is considered to be the maximum gain by A. Consequently, the anticipated loss for B from employing the jth strategy is the maximum of the a_{ij}s in the column, that is,

$$\max_i a_{ij}$$

The maximin–minimax principle requires player B to select the strategy j that minimizes the column maximum, that is,

$$\min_j \max_i a_{ij}$$

If we have a game in which

$$\max_i \min_j a_{ij} = \min_j \max_i a_{ij} \tag{A9.50}$$

then the combination of the ith strategy of A and the jth strategy of B is called a *saddle point*. Thus, we have a solution to the game, and (A9.50) is called the *value of the game*. The example in the text indicated by Table 9.2 corresponds to $i = 1$ and $j = 2$; the value of the game is zero.

As we have mentioned in the text, a saddle point may not exist in a game involving *pure strategies* (such as those indicated above). In other words, more often than not we may have

$$\max_i \min_j a_{ij} \neq \min_j \max_i a_{ij} \tag{A9.51}$$

(see Table 9.3). If this is the case, then a solution for the game does not exist if only pure strategies are considered. However, it has been proved by von Neumann and Morgenstern (1953) that if *mixed strategies* are permitted for two-person zero-sum games, then a saddle point and, thus, a solution always exists.

As we have mentioned, the payoff matrix is constructed for pure strategies. The above example assumed that A has m pure strategies and that B has n pure strategies. Each row of the matrix indicates the payoff to A when employing a given pure strategy for B's possible pure strategies. A mixed strategy for A is to assign a given set of nonnegative probabilities (one probability for each strategy), the sum of the probabilities being equal to one. If A assigns probability p_1 to pure strategy 1, p_2 to pure strategy 2, and p_m to pure strategy m, then we have

$$0 \le p_i \le 1 \quad \text{and} \quad \sum_{i=1}^{m} p_i = 1 \tag{A9.52}$$

Similarly if B assigns probability q_j to pure strategy j, we have

$$0 \le q_j \le 1 \quad \text{and} \quad \sum_{j=1}^{n} q_j = 1 \tag{A9.53}$$

A pure strategy is a special case of a mixed strategy. For example, if $q_j = 1$ and $q_i = 0$ for $i \neq j$, then this particular mixed strategy corresponds to the jth pure strategy.

It should be noted that a mixed strategy does not mean that one mixes the pure strategies in each play of the game. In fact, only one pure strategy is employed in each game. Mixed strategy only means that each and every pure strategy is given a chance, according to its designated probability, to be employed in each game. (Remember that we are discussing only single-move games.) For example, an oligopolist may have only two strategies: (1) high price and high advertising expenditure or (2) low price and low advertising expenditure. A 50%–50% mixed strategy means that the oligopolist will flip a coin: A head will entail the choice of strategy 1 and a tail the choice of strategy 2, but only strategy 1 or 2 will be employed depending on whether a head or a tail appears. It does not mean that the oligopolist will employ strategy 1 half of the game and strategy 2 half of the game.

The selection of the probabilities is the most important aspect of mixed strategies. A different set of probabilities for the pure strategies will result in a different payoff to the player. Since we are dealing with a noncooperative game, each player only considers his or her own best interest and is assumed to select the probabilities that will either maximize the expected gain or minimize the expected loss in terms of mathematical expectation. The expected gain for A if B employs strategy j is

$$\sum_{i=1}^{m} a_{ij} p_i \tag{A9.54}$$

The value of this mathematical expectation depends on both A's selection of the p_is and B's selection of his or her strategy. However, the only thing over which A has complete control is the selection of the p_is. The optimal selection of the p_is by A is defined as

$$\sum_{i=1}^{m} a_{ij} p_i \geq V, \qquad j = 1, 2, \ldots, n \tag{A9.55}$$

where V is defined as the value of the game. Similarly, the expected loss for B if A employs strategy i is

$$\sum_{j=1}^{n} a_{ij} q_j \tag{A9.56}$$

B tries to hold down A's gain as much as possible, and therefore selects the q_js such that (A9.56) is minimized. The optimal selection of the q_js by B is defined as

$$\sum_{j=1}^{n} a_{ij} q_j \leq V, \qquad i = 1, 2, \ldots, m \tag{A9.57}$$

The relations (A9.55) state that A's expected gain is at least as large as V whatever pure strategy B employs. Similarly, the relations (A9.57) state that B's expected loss cannot be larger than V whatever pure strategy A may employ. Von Neumann and Morgenstern (1953) have proved the following theorem.

Theorem A9.1. *There always exists a set of probabilities p_i for A and a set of probabilities q_j for B such that both (A9.55) and (A9.57) are satisfied and V is unique.*

The proof of Theorem A9.1 is as follows. If both players select their strategies on a probabilistic basis, the A's expected gain E_A can be computed from (A9.55):

$$E_A = \sum_{j=1}^{n} q_j \left(\sum_{i=1}^{m} a_{ij} p_i \right) \geq \sum_{j=1}^{n} q_j V \qquad (A9.58a)$$

or

$$E_A = \sum_{j=1}^{n} \sum_{i=1}^{m} a_{ij} p_i q_j \geq V \qquad (A9.58b)$$

since

$$\sum q_j V = V(\sum q_j) = V$$

and

$$\sum q_j = 1$$

by (A9.53).

Similarly, B's expected gain (i.e., loss) E_B can be computed from (A9.57):

$$E_B = \sum_{i=1}^{m} p_i \left(\sum_{j=1}^{n} a_{ij} q_j \right) \leq \sum_{i=1}^{m} p_i V \qquad (A9.59a)$$

or

$$E_B = \sum_{j=1}^{n} \sum_{i=1}^{m} a_{ij} p_i q_j \leq V \qquad (A9.59b)$$

The middle terms in (A9.58b) and (A9.59b) are identical, which implies that A's expected gain equals B's expected loss. Combining (A9.58b) and (A9.59b), we obtain

$$V \leq E_A = E_B \leq V \qquad (A9.60)$$

which proves that

$$E_A = E_B = V \qquad (A9.61)$$

This result implies that a saddle point (solution) of a two-person zero-sum game always exists if mixed strategies are permitted.

Although we have proven that there exist optimal sets of probabilities for both A and B such that the maximum expected gain for one player is equal to the minimum expected loss of the other player, it should be pointed out that the computation of the p_is and q_js may not be a simple matter when m and n are large. However, linear programming can be used to compute the optimal p_is and q_js once the payoff matrix is known. Since we shall not discuss linear programming in this book, our discussion of this topic ends here.

INCOME DISTRIBUTION THEORY
AND THE PRICING OF
FACTORS OF PRODUCTION

Income distribution is an important topic in economic theory. Regardless of what political system a country has, not only must it manage to produce the commodities and services that it needs, but it must also allocate them to the people in some way. Different political and economic systems have different methods of allocating their products. In primitive societies, custom usually settles the allocation problem: The amount that each person receives is determined by his or her traditionally established status in the society. In a socialist country, the government performs an important function in the allocation of commodities and services to the final users. ''To each according to one's needs'' is the ideal goal of a Communist system. However, in a private ownership (capitalist) system, it is the market, through a system of prices, that allocates the commodities and services produced to the final users. In the marketplace, only those who are willing and *able* to pay can obtain the things they want. Thus, since income determines the ability to pay, income distribution and the allocation of the final products are closely related.

There are at least two approaches to a discussion of income distribution. One sensible approach is to look at the income of individuals or families. We see that some are rich, some are poor, and others are in the middle. Methods can be developed to measure the equality or inequality of income distribution in an economy, and comparisons between regions and/or countries can be made. This is the approach employed to analyze personal income distribution, the *Lorenz curve* and *Gini coefficient* often being used to measure the equality or inequality of income distribution.

The other approach to the discussion of income distribution involves the use of functional analysis. In this approach, we view income as being distributed in accordance with the economic function that people perform in the economy. In economics, income distribution theory concerns itself essentially with the question of functional income distribution.

In economics, *labor, land, capital,* and *entrepreneurship* are considered to be the four productive factors. The income to labor is called *wages*, whereas the incomes to land, capital, and entrepreneurship are called *rent, interest,* and *profit,* respectively. In the capitalist system, wages, rent, interest, and profit are determined in the marketplace. In a perfectly competitive market, supply and demand together determine the price in both the factor and product markets.[1] The demand for and the supply of productive factors constitute the main body of income distribution theory, and it is to these topics that Chapters 10 and 11 are directed.

Some economists treat factor markets in the same manner as product markets. As a result, income distribution no longer exists as a separate theory. Since the demand for productive factors is a derived demand, which is essentially different from the demand for a product for final use, and since the determination of the supply of productive factors does have certain special features, it is more meaningful to discuss factor markets separately from product markets.

To simplify the exposition and promote a better understanding of the subject, we shall discuss the demand for productive factors in Chapter 10, whereas the special features of supply and the determination of price will be considered in Chapter 11. As we have stressed in our dicussion of product markets in Part III, demand is very important in all types of markets, but supply is meaningful only under perfect competition. Thus, we have shown it to be cost, rather than supply, that is relevant in the determination of price under imperfect product markets. Cost may not be as important in factor markets as it is in product markets. However, government participation in factor markets, such as the determination of interest rates and minimum wage rates, are not only more active and decisive, but also commonly recognized. Consequently, government activities in factor markets and their consequences will be discussed to a proportionally greater extent than government activities in product markets.

---

[1] Price determination in product markets was covered in Chapter 6.

MARGINAL PRODUCTIVITY THEORY AND THE DEMAND FOR FACTORS OF PRODUCTION

INTRODUCTION

Most productive factors are purchased on a contractual basis by business for the purpose of making a profit. Although a small part of labor (e.g., chauffeurs for private cars and domestics) as well as a small part of land and capital (e.g., residential land and housing) are contracted for direct consumption, the latter is less important in terms of capital expenditures than investment in nonresidential expenditures.[1] Thus, it is reasonable to develop the demand theory for productive factors on the basis of business behavior with respect to profit maximization. Moreover, since market forces are largely conditioned by business behavior, the pricing of all productive factors can be said to be pretty much determined by the desire of business to maximize profits.

Profit maximization and business behavior largely govern the demand for productive factors

10.1 PROFIT MAXIMIZATION AND THE DERIVED DEMAND FOR ONE VARIABLE PRODUCTIVE FACTOR UNDER PERFECTLY COMPETITIVE MARKETS

In Chapter 6, we developed the necessary and sufficient conditions for profit maximization under perfect competition; the quantity of the product was considered to be the decision (independent) variable. For our present purposes, the variable input (instead of the output) is considered to be the decision (independent) variable. For this reason, when we talk about profit, we

---

[1] On a *national income accounts* basis, for example, residential fixed investment comprises, on average, about one-third of gross private domestic investment. If we added government investment in land, buildings, and capital works, residential expenditures would be closer to one-fourth of the total.

shall use the cost equation of Chapter 2 rather than the cost function of Chapter 3. When there is only one variable input, for example, labor L with wage w, the total cost C can be written

$$C = C_0 + wL \tag{10.1}$$

where C_0 is the total fixed cost (TFC), which is a constant. We can observe that the total output is a function of labor only because all other inputs are fixed. The production function can be written

$$Q = f(L) \tag{10.2}$$

where Q denotes the quantity of output, and f denotes the production function, the characteristics of which are determined by technology. By definition, the total revenue that a firm can obtain is equal to the market price of the product multiplied by the quantity that a firm produces and sells under the assumption of zero inventory. Hence, we have

$$R = PQ = Pf(L) \tag{10.3}$$

where R denotes the total revenue, and P denotes the market price of the product. By definition, the total profit is equal to the total revenue minus the total cost:

$$\pi = Pf(L) - C_0 - wL \tag{10.4}$$

where π denotes the total profit. It should be noted that this total profit function is different from the total profit function that we used in Part III: In Part III, profit was considered a function of output, but now profit is being considered a function of the variable input.

The assumption of perfect competition in both the output and the input market implies that both P and w in (10.4) are constants, since the firm is a price taker in both the output and the input market. The only variable that is under the control of the firm in (10.4) is labor L. In other words, the firm faces given market prices of both output and input, a predetermined fixed cost, and a production function that is determined by technology. The only choice that the firm has in our simple model is to hire either more or less labor in order to accomplish its goal. However, the quantity of output and the variable input are not independent—they are functionally related by the production function. It is also understandable why the total profit of the firm depends on the quantity of labor that it hires. In order to determine the relationship between total profit and the amount of labor, we start with the relationship between a small change in the amount of labor and the corresponding change in profit. From (10.4) we have

The relationship between profit and labor demand depends on cost and the production function

$$d\pi = Pdf(L) - wdL \tag{10.5}$$

where d denotes change. Equation (10.5) says that when labor changes (e.g., increases) by a small amount dL, cost changes (increases) by wdL. The corresponding change (increase) in quantity of output due to the small change in labor is dQ or $df(L)$, whereas the corresponding change (increase) in total revenue is $Pdf(L)$. Therefore, the corresponding change in profit is given by (10.5). It should be noted that (10.5) is valid only under the assumption of perfect competition in both the input and the output market. Otherwise, P and/or w will no longer be constants, and the situation will become more complicated. We shall deal with the more-complex model in a later section.

When labor increases, cost increases at a constant rate, namely, w, the wage rate. This simply says that the firm pays the same additional cost, according to the going wage rate for each additional worker, regardless of how many workers it hires (i.e., the firm is a price taker). In an imperfect input market, a firm must raise the wage rate in order to induce more workers to seek employment. Thus, under imperfect input markets, the wage rate can no longer be treated as a constant. Returning to Equation (10.5), we see that when labor increases by a small amount dL, the corresponding increase in output is $df(L)$. Consequently, the corresponding increase in total revenue is $Pdf(L)$. Hence, the corresponding change in profit is the difference between the increase in total revenue and the increase in total cost.

Note that when labor increases, both total revenue and total cost will increase. However, the profit may either increase or decrease, depending on whether the increase in revenue will exceed the increase in cost. Usually, the increase in total revenue at first exceeds the increase in cost for a small increase in labor input, so that total profit increases and the change in profit is positive, that is, $d\pi > 0$. As long as profit increases for a small increase in labor input, the firm will continue to hire more labor. However, as more workers are hired, a stage will eventually be reached such that the increase in profit will become smaller with each additional unit of labor (the law of diminishing returns). This must be the case, since otherwise the firm could expand without bound, and perfect competition would break down. Finally, the firm will reach a stage where, for the discrete case, the last unit of labor hired results in either a positive or a zero increase in profit, and any further increase in the amount of labor hired will result in a negative additional profit, that is, a decrease in total profit. The firm must stop hiring at this point because it is where the profit will be maximum.

The law of diminishing returns prevents firms from profitably adding the variable input without limit

The above reasoning implies that an amount of labor input L^* will result in maximum profit if and only if

$$d\pi = Pdf(L) - wdL \geq 0 \quad \text{for} \quad L^*$$
$$d\pi = Pdf(L) - wdL < 0 \quad \text{for} \quad L^* + 1$$

(10.6)

In the continuous case, there exists an L^* such that

$$d\pi = Pdf(L) - wdL = 0$$

(10.7)

This is the first-order condition for profit maximization. The second-order (sufficient) condition for profit maximization requires that the change in profit $d\pi$ must be decreasing in the neighborhood of L^*.

It should be pointed out that (10.7) is a special case of (10.6): The latter applies to both the discrete and continuous cases, whereas the former can only be applied to the continuous case, because, in the discrete case, the L^* for which (10.7) holds may not exist. Hence, expression (10.6) is more general. However, in textbooks, and in economics literature in general, (10.7) is most often discussed and (10.6) omitted.

If we divide (10.6) and (10.7) by dL, omit the far left-hand parts, and rearrange the terms, we obtain the following expressions, respectively:

$$Pdf(L)/dL \geq w \qquad\qquad\qquad (10.8)$$

and

$$Pdf(L)/dL = w \qquad\qquad\qquad (10.9)$$

The right sides of (10.8) and (10.9) are the wage rate, whereas the left side is the product of two terms: the market price of the output P and the ratio of the change in output for a small change in labor $df(L)/dL$. In Chapter 1, we defined $df(L)/dL$ as the marginal product (MP) of labor. For the sake of convenience, we provide the following definition.

Definition: Value of the Marginal Product. The value of the marginal product (VMP) of an input is defined as the product of the market price of the output and the marginal product of the input.

With the above definition, we can state the condition for profit maximization when the variable input is considered as the decision variable in the form of the following proposition.

Proposition 10.1 The profit of a firm will be maximized when it hires workers to the extent that the last worker hired results in a positive or zero additional profit, but any additional worker will result in negative additional profit for the discrete case. On the other hand, for the continuous case, the profit will be maximized only if the firm hires workers to the point where the additional profit is zero (provided that the additional profit is decreasing).

The above arguments can be illustrated by means of a numerical example. In Table 10.1, the first column gives the labor input and the second column gives the corresponding output; these two columns constitute the production schedule (production func-

TABLE 10.1

(1) L	(2) Q	(3) P	(4) R	(5) w	(6) wL	(7) C_0	(8) $C = C_0 + wL$	(9) π	(10) MP	(11) VMP	(12) $d\pi$
1	4	3	12	5	5	5	10	2	4	12	2
2	10	3	30	5	10	5	15	15	6	18	13
3	15	3	45	5	15	5	20	25	5	15	10
4	18	3	54	5	20	5	25	29	3	9	4
5*	20	3	60	5	25	5	30	30*	2	6*	1
6	21	3	63	5	30	5	35	28	1	3	-2

tion). The third column gives the market price of the product, which is a constant owing to the assumption of perfect competition in the output market. The fourth column gives the total revenue, that is, the product of the second and third columns. The fifth column gives the wage rate, which is a constant because of the assumption of perfect competition in the labor market. The sixth column gives the total wage cost, that is, the product of the first and fifth columns. The seventh column gives the total fixed cost, which is a constant. The eighth column gives the total cost, that is, the sum of the sixth and seventh columns. The ninth column gives the total profit, that is, the fourth column minus the eighth column. (Note the behavior of total profit with respect to our explanation above.) The tenth column gives the marginal product of labor, which is computed by dividing the successive differences of the second column by the corresponding differences of the first column. (It might help the student to review those portions of Chapter 1 concerned with the marginal product.) The eleventh column gives the value of the marginal product, which is computed by multiplying the third column by the tenth column. The last column shows the change in profit when labor increases. The values in the last column increase at first, then decrease, and finally become negative. This implies that total profit at first increases at an increasing rate when labor increases, then increases at a decreasing rate, and finally begins to decrease.

Under perfect competition the value of MP depends on factor productivity

Column 11 of Table 10.1 corresponds to the left-hand terms of (10.8) and (10.9), whereas column 5 corresponds to the right-hand terms. It is interesting to observe that as long as the values in column 11 exceed those in column 5, total profit increases as labor increases, which is shown by the data in column 9. For the fifth unit of labor, (10.8) holds; that is, the corresponding value in column 11 is greater than that in column 5. However, for the sixth unit of labor, (10.8) is violated. Taking expressions (10.6) into consideration, 5 is the value that corresponds to $L*$.[2] Column 9 shows that this is precisely the case: Profit is maximized for 5

---

[2] The asterisks in the table denote the profit-maximizing level of labor.

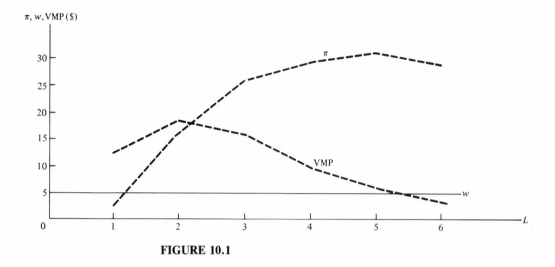

FIGURE 10.1

units of labor. The values in the last column of Table 10.1 show the rationale behind expressions (10.6). The last unit of labor which shows a positive change in profit (in our case, the fifth unit) corresponds to the profit-maximizing input. This shows that (10.6) and (10.8) are equivalent, as are (10.7) and (10.9) in the special, continuous case.

The data in Table 10.1 can also be plotted on a graph, the independent variable labor being plotted on the horizontal axis. For the sake of simplicity, in Figure 10.1 we only plot the total profit, value of the marginal product, and wage rate on the vertical axis. For the discrete case, both the total profit and VMP have only six isolated points each. Although we have used dots to connect the points, it should be noted that these dotted curves are meaningful only in the continuous case, that is, under the assumption of divisibility (Assumption 1.2).

It should be noted that, when moving to the right, the last point on the dotted VMP curve which is above w corresponds to the maximum profit. This is precisely the meaning of the equivalence of (10.6) and (10.8).

Before we proceed to make use of the above result to derive the demand for an input, two points should be made. First, although we have drawn the VMP curve in such a way that it first increases and then decreases, only the decreasing part has analytical significance. This is a result of the fact that production can only economically take place in stage II (see Chapter 1), which corresponds to a decreasing MP. With market price constant, a decreasing MP implies a decreasing VMP. Second, for a given production function and the associated VMP function corresponding to each input price w, there is a unique profit function. Students may convince themselves of this condition by computing the profit figures for various values of w by using the method of

Given a production function, and the associated VMP for each w, the profit function is unique

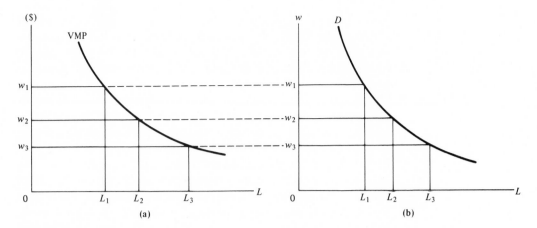

FIGURE 10.2

Table 10.1. It can easily be seen that, if $w = 2$, then profit will reach its maximum at $L = 6$. On the other hand, if $w = 7$, profit will reach its maximum at $L = 4$. Similarly, if $w = 10$, profit will reach its maximum at $L = 3$ and so forth.

The second point is very significant with respect to the demand for a productive factor. Once this is fully understood, it immediately follows that, for the continuous case and the simple one-variable-input model, the VMP curve is actually the demand curve for the variable input of the firm.

Consider Figure 10.2. In part (a), with the given VMP curve, if the wage rate is w_1, then, in the continuous case, profit will be maximum if amount L_1 of labor is used. Since the firm is assumed to choose the L that maximizes profit, it can be concluded that, if the wage is w_1, then the firm will hire amount L_1 of labor. Similarly, if the wage goes down to w_2 (w_3), L_2 (L_3) amount of labor will be hired. If we transfer this information to part (b), we obtain a relationship between the market wage rate and the quantity of labor that a firm will hire. According to the definition of demand, this wage–quantity relationship is precisely the demand function for labor. Thus, we have proved the following proposition.

Proposition 10.2. Under perfect competition in both the product and the factor market, when there is only one variable input, the negatively sloped portion of the value of the marginal product (VMP) curve is the demand curve for the variable input.

It is important to observe that the VMP of a variable input is the product of the price of a unit of output and the MP of the input. For a given technology and, thus, MP, the VMP curve shifts to the right for a higher product price and to the left for a lower product price. Similarly, given the market price of the product, the VMP curve will shift to the right for an improvement in technology which raises MP (i.e., causes the MP curve to shift to the right). Since the demand curve for the variable input depends on the conditions of the product market, the demand for the productive factor is referred to as a *derived demand*, that is, it depends on the market demand for the product. However, the student should recognize that here we have been examining the demand for labor by the individual firm, in which case the price of the product is given and the firm's demand curve for labor depends exclusively on the marginal *physical* product of the labor hired. Later on, we shall describe the derivation of the market demand curve for a factor of production such as labor. For the moment, it is only important to recognize the distinction.

10.2 THE DEMAND FOR SEVERAL VARIABLE INPUTS UNDER PERFECTLY COMPETITIVE MARKETS

Although we have shown that the demand curve for an input is identical to the negatively sloped portion of the VMP curve when there is only one variable input, this is not the case when more than one variable input is involved. In other words, the VMP curve for an input is not the demand curve for the input when there are two or more variable inputs. However, the demand curve will still be negatively sloped, as we shall show in the appendix to this chapter.

The VMP for one input among two or more is not its demand curve

The reason that the VMP curve is no longer the demand curve when two or more variable inputs are involved is that the VMP curves for all of the variable inputs are interrelated. In technical terms, the VMP for any variable input is a function of all of the variable inputs. When the amount of one input used changes because of a change in its price, the VMP for all of the inputs will change. This will result in a change in the quantity of all other inputs, which, in turn, will result in a shift of the VMP curve for the input whose quantity has changed in the first place. In mathematical terms, the demand functions of the variable inputs are derived as a solution of a system of simultaneous equations, not just as the equality of the input price of a variable input to its VMP in isolation. Graphically, a change in the quantity of one variable input will result in a shift of its own VMP curve due to the interaction between all of the variable inputs. Thus, a change in the price of one variable input will result in a shift of its VMP curve, which can no longer be considered as its demand curve.

We shall use the two-variable-input case of labor L and capital K to illustrate briefly what is meant by the demand functions of the variable inputs being derived as a solution of a system of simultaneous equations. We shall first state without proof (this fact will be proved in the appendix to this chapter) that the first-order condition for profit maximization in the continuous case requires that

$$PMP_L = w \quad \text{and} \quad PMP_K = r \tag{10.10}$$

where P is the price of the output, w and r are the input prices, and MP_L and MP_K are the marginal products of labor and capital, respectively. Expressions (10.10) represent two equations in two variables, namely, L and K. This is so because both MP_L and MP_K are functions of L and K, whereas the prices of the output and the inputs are constants, not variables. The solution of this system of equations can be written

$$L = D_1(w, r, P) \quad \text{and} \quad K = D_2(w, r, P) \tag{10.11}$$

These are the demand functions of labor and capital, respectively. In general, the individual demands for labor and capital are functions of all of the prices, that is, those of inputs as well as those of outputs. It should be noted that D_1 is usually quite different from D_2.

The difference in the demands for the one-variable-input case and the more-than-one-variable-input case can be demonstrated by a simple example. If labor is the *only* variable input, the first equation in (10.10) constitutes the demand function of labor. On the other hand, when capital is the *only* variable input, the second equation in (10.10) constitutes the demand function of capital. This implies that the VMP curve of an input is its demand curve. However, when two or more variable inputs are involved, the equality of the VMP and the price of one factor of production in isolation no longer constitutes the demand for the input because the two equations are interrelated. This is why the VMP curve for an input cannot be considered the demand curve for the input when more than one variable input is involved.

With more than one variable input, price-induced shifts in the VMP curve are likely

This situation can also be briefly illustrated by the graphical method. Consider Figure 10.3 in which the initial wage rate is w_1

FIGURE 10.3

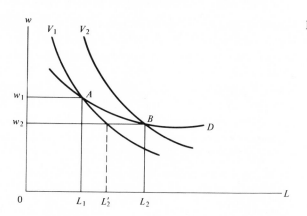

and the corresponding VMP is V_1. From our earlier discussion, we can see that the firm will hire L_1 amount of labor in order to maximize profit. However, we now find that when the wage rate goes down to w_2, the prices of the other inputs being constant, labor becomes relatively cheaper than the other inputs. Thus, the firm will substitute labor for other inputs. Since the MP and, concurrently, the VMP of labor depends on both the amount of labor and the amounts of other inputs used, the decrease in other inputs due to substitution will shift the VMP curve for labor. Theoretically, a decrease in the wage rate may result in either a rightward shift or a leftward shift of the VMP curve for labor.[3] For the sake of simplicity, if the net result of a decrease in the wage rate is a rightward shift of the VMP curve for labor (as shown in Figure 10.3) from V_1 to V_2, then the amount of labor hired by the firm will be L_2 because profit maximization requires the equality between the wage rate and VMP in the continuous case. Note that if the VMP curve did not shift, the profit-maximizing quantity of labor would have been L_2'. When the wage rate changes continuously, the VMP curve for labor shifts accordingly, and the points of intersection (e.g., A and B) will generate a curve that represents their locus, that is, the demand curve for labor. The demand curves for capital and all other productive factors can be similarly derived.

In the graphical method, we cannot make the assertion that the demand functions of productive factors are negatively sloped when two or more variable inputs are involved. However, in the appendix of this chapter we shall show that the second-order conditions for profit maximization will guarantee that the demand curve is negatively sloped. Thus, students will have to take our word on the validity of this conclusion if they lack the mathematical background to comprehend the appendix.

10.3 THE DEMAND FOR ONE VARIABLE INPUT UNDER IMPERFECT COMPETITION IN THE PRODUCT MARKET

Expressions (10.1)–(10.4) in Section 10.1 are valid for either perfectly competitive or imperfect markets. However, all expressions from (10.5) on are valid only for perfectly competitive markets. Since this section deals with imperfect competition in the product market, the latter expressions will have to be modified.

---

[3] Although it is tempting to use the substitution and output effects to explain the change in the demand for labor when the wage rate changes as many economists and textbooks have done, actually it is not proper to do so. The reason for this is that the substitution and output effects are meaningful only for a given cost, as we have demonstrated in Chapter 2. In this chapter, we have not assumed that the cost is constant. In fact, when the wage rate goes down, the total expenditure of a firm on production will be more likely to change than to stay constant.

As we have mentioned earlier, under perfect competition in the product market, the price P is a constant to the firm. Hence, the change in total revenue is equal to the change in the quantity of output multiplied by the market price. However, in an imperfect market, when the quantity of output changes, price also changes. Thus, the change in total revenue will be more than just the product of price and the change in quantity. However, it is still true that

Under imperfect competition the change in total revenue exceeds price times output change

$$d\pi = dR - wdL \qquad (10.12)$$

Since, by definition,

$$MR = dR/dQ$$

(see Chapter 5), we have

$$dR = MRdQ \qquad (10.13)$$

By substitution, we can rewrite (10.12) as

$$d\pi = MRdQ - wdL \qquad (10.14)$$

In the one-variable-input, continuous case, in which

$$MP = dQ/dL$$

the first-order condition for profit maximization which corresponds to (10.9) can be written as follows for the imperfect product market:

$$MR \cdot MP = w \qquad (10.15)$$

It can easily be seen that (10.9) is a special case of (10.15), since, under perfect competition in the product market, $P = MR$. Therefore, (10.15) is nothing more than a reformulation of (10.9) to make it applicable to imperfect competition.

We have defined the VMP as PMP, which, in general, is different from $MR \cdot MP$. Accordingly, we need a new term to cover the distinctive feature of this difference. By common usage, it has been named *marginal revenue product* (MRP).

Definition: Marginal Revenue Product of an Input. The ratio of the change in total revenue to the change in the variable input. In the discrete case, MRP can be considered the change in total revenue due to an increase of 1 unit in the variable input. Equivalently, MRP is also equal to the product of the MR of the output and the MP of the input.

The equivalence part of the above definition can be proved in the following way. By our definition,

$$MRP = dR/dL \qquad (10.16)$$

and since

$$MP = dQ/dL$$

TABLE 10.2

(1)	(2)	(3)	(4)	(5) MRP =	(6)	(7)	(8) MRP =	(9)
L	Q	P	R	dR/dL	MR	MP	MR · MP	w
1	4	7	28	28	7	4	28	5
2	10	6	60	32	$\frac{32}{6}$	6	32	5
3	15	5	75	15	3	5	15	5
4	18	4	72	− 3	− 1	3	− 3	5
5	20	3	60	− 12	− 6	2	− 12	5
6	21	2	42	− 18	− 18	1	− 18	5

by substituting (10.13) into (10.16) we can obtain

$$\text{MRP} = \text{MR} \cdot \text{MP} \qquad (10.17)$$

With the above definition, the first-order condition for profit maximization of a firm under imperfect competition, which is embodied in (10.15), can be written

$$\text{MRP} = w \qquad (10.18)$$

We shall use a numerical example to illustrate the above arguments. Consider Table 10.2. The first two columns of Table 10.2 and Table 10.1 are identical. This implies that we are using the same production function in both examples. As was to be expected, the MP columns in both tables are also identical. The essential difference between the two tables rests in the values of the P (the price of the output) column. In Table 10.1, the price is a constant—$3 for all quantities of the output—which implies that the firm faces a perfectly competitive market for its output. On the other hand, in Table 10.2, the price decreases as the quantity of the output increases, which indicates a negatively sloped demand curve and the fact that the firm operates under an imperfect market. This is the essential difference between the two models.

Column 4 of Table 10.2 gives the total revenue, which is the product of columns 2 and 3. Column 5 gives the MRP computed by our definition, that is, the change in total revenue divided by the change in labor input. On the other hand, column 8 gives the MRP computed by the alternative—but equivalent—formula (10.17). These two columns demonstrate the fact that the two methods for computing the MRP are indeed equivalent.

Given the same production function, MRP will decrease faster than VMP

Comparing the VMP of Table 10.1 and the MRP of Table 10.2 we see that although both of them decrease when the labor input increases after the second unit of labor, the MRP decreases faster. This is easy to understand once one realizes that

$$\text{VMP} = w\text{MP}$$

whereas

$$\text{MRP} = \text{MR} \cdot \text{MP} \qquad (10.17)$$

In the former, the wage rate w is a constant; thus, the decrease in VMP is entirely due to the decrease in MP. From column 6 of Table 10.2, it can be seen that MR is not constant, but rather increases at first and then decreases when additional units of labor are hired. Moreover, since MRP is the product of MR and MP, the decrease in MRP is the result of decreases in both MR and MP. For the same production function, MRP must decrease at a faster rate than VMP.

Since perfect competition in input markets is still assumed, in both models the firm faces a constant wage rate. In the previous case, given a wage rate of $5, it was shown that the firm's profit was maximized with a labor input of 5 units, which satisfies expression (10.8). In the present case, if the wage rate is $5, the first-order condition for profit maximization is satisfied for 3— not 5—units of labor. [In the discrete case, the first-order condition for profit maximization (10.18) should be modified to MRP $\geq w$.] As in the previous case, for the same production function and output price, a higher wage rate will result in fewer workers being hired, whereas at a lower wage rate more workers will be employed.

We have previously explained that, in the continuous case, the decreasing portion of the VMP curve is the firm's demand curve for labor. By a similar argument, it can be shown that the decreasing portion of the MRP curve is the demand curve for the variable input under the condition of imperfect product markets.

Under imperfect competition and for one variable input the MRP curve is the demand curve

By way of illustration, consider Figure 10.4, in which, in the continuous case, MRP is the marginal revenue product curve for labor [shown in part (a)]. If the wage rate is w_1, the firm's profit will be maximum if L_1 amount of labor is hired. Since the firm's goal is to maximize its profit, point A on MRP is also on the firm's demand curve. Similarly, B, and C, and infinitely many other points on MRP are also on the firm's demand curve for labor. If

FIGURE 10.4

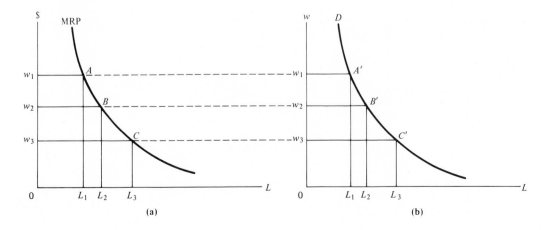

(a)   (b)

A, B, C, and all other points on the decreasing portion of MRP in part (a) are transferred to part (b), then A', B', C', and all other points precisely describe the price–quantity relationship (i.e., the demand curve) for labor, and, therefore, the curves in parts (a) and (b) are identical. The above arguments can be summarized in the form of the following proposition.

Proposition 10.3. Under imperfect competition in the output market, in the special case when there is only one variable input, the decreasing portion of the MRP curve is the firm's demand curve for the variable input.

10.4 THE DEMAND FOR TWO OR MORE VARIABLE INPUTS UNDER IMPERFECT COMPETITION IN THE PRODUCT MARKET

Given only one variable input the decreasing portion of the MRP curve is the firm's demand curve; however, once two or more inputs can vary simultaneously, the MRP curve is no longer the demand curve for an input. The reason for this is similar to our explanation in Section 10.2. The MRP curve of the given input shifts when the quantity of another input changes. Because a change in price of the given input will cause the relative price of other inputs to change, it generates a chain reaction, which may cause all of the MRP curves to shift. Thus, none of the MRP curves can be considered the demand curve.

As a simple example, suppose that there are only the two variable inputs labor L and capital K. Figure 10.5 shows the demand for labor. We initially assume that the wage rate is w_1 and that the corresponding marginal revenue curve is $\mathrm{MRP_1}$ for a given capital input. Under these circumstances, the firm's profit is maximized if the firm hires L_1 amount of labor. The reason for this result is identical to that discussed in the Section 10.3: The

FIGURE 10.5

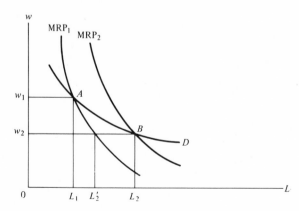

profit of a firm is maximized only if it hires workers to the extent that the market wage rate is equal to MRP in the continuous case.

Suppose that, because of market conditions, the wage rate falls to w_2. Since the firm is a price taker in the input market, it can only adjust the quantity of labor in order to maximize its profit under the new circumstances. If the MRP curve does not shift, then the firm will hire more workers according to MRP_1, that is, L_2'. However, when the wage rate decreases while the price of capital remains constant, labor becomes relatively cheaper. From Chapter 2, we know that in production the optimal combination of the inputs requires the substitution of labor for capital [except in the special case of a fixed input ratio (rectangular isoquants)]. When labor increases, the optimal quantity of capital to be combined with labor may also increase. There is a certain similarity between this case and the substitution and output effects mentioned in Chapter 2; however, the present situation is more complicated than that in Chapter 2, where the substitution and output effects were only defined for a given cost. In this chapter, profit maximization does not require constant cost. In fact, when the wage rate changes, the profit-maximizing total expenditure of a firm will be more likely to change than to remain constant. Therefore, the unmodified application of the substitution and output effects in the present case as practiced by many economists and textbooks is not theoretically proper (see footnote 3). On the other hand, these ideas do help to explain the likelihood of a shift of the MRP curve for an input when the price of the input undergoes change.

Without going into great detail, it should be pointed out that the effect of a change in the price of an input with respect to a shift of its MRP curve is quite complex. A decrease in the wage rate may shift the MRP curve for labor either to the left or to the right (or it may not shift it at all). The existence and direction of this shift are essentially determined by the characteristics of the production function. Without knowing the precise properties of the production function, no general statement concerning the precise shift of the MRP curve is possible given the change in the price of an input. For the purpose of illustration it was assumed in Figure 10.5 that the MRP curve for labor shifts to the right—from MRP_1 to MRP_2—when the wage rate is reduced from w_1 to w_2. When the firm faces a market wage rate of w_2 and a marginal revenue product curve of MRP_2, its profit will be maximized only if L_2—instead of L_2'—units of labor are hired. Thus, A, B, and many other similar points on the MRP curve are also on the firm's demand curve for labor. When the change in the wage rate and the shift in the MRP curve are continuous, an infinite number of points like A and B will be generated, and the locus of these points—as denoted by curve D in Figure 10.5— will be the firm's demand curve for labor.

The production function characterizes the shift in the MRP curve due to a price change

Another way of explaining the above rationale is based on the fact that the firm's profit is maximized only if it equates the price and MRP of each and every input. In short, we have

$$\text{MRP}_i = r_i, \qquad i = 1, 2, \ldots, n \qquad\qquad (10.19)$$

where r_i denotes the price, and MRP_i the marginal revenue product, of input i. Given a total of n inputs, the MRP of each input is not only a function of all of the inputs, but also of the parameters of the production function and the demand function of the output. If one is given n input prices r_i as parameters, then there are n equations in n variables, namely, the quantities of the inputs. The solution of the system of equations yields the n demand functions of the inputs in terms of the n input prices and the price of the output. These demand functions take the interaction, substitution, or complementarity of the inputs into consideration. Hence, one equation in isolation does not yield the demand for the input.

In the special case where only one variable input is involved, the equality of the input price and its MRP yields the demand for the input. This implies that, in this special case, the MRP curve is the demand curve for the input. When two or more variable inputs are involved, the demand for any input depends not only on the equality of its MRP to its price, but also on similar equations for all of the other inputs. Consequently, the MRP curve of one input by itself is no longer the demand curve for the input. The interrelationship of the inputs makes a big difference when two or more variable inputs are involved.

As we have explained in Section 10.2, the demand curve for two or more variable inputs is negatively sloped in the case of perfect competition in output markets. When there is imperfection in the output market, the firm's demand curve for the product is negatively sloped; as a result, the MRP curve has a steeper slope than the corresponding VMP curve for the same production function. Other things being equal, the demand curve for an input under imperfect competition in the output market will have a steeper slope than the demand curve under perfect competition. Therefore, the firm's demand curve for inputs must be negatively sloped.

10.5 THE MARKET DEMAND FOR FACTORS OF PRODUCTION

The market demand for a productive factor, just like the market demand for a product in Chapter 5, is the aggregate of the constituent individual demands. We have shown that the market demand curve for a product is the horizontal sum of all of the individual consumer demand curves under Assumptions 1.4 and 1.5 (the absence of externalities). However, the derivation of the market demand for a productive factor is more complicated owing to the fact that the demand of each individual firm for a productive factor is not only a function of the prices of all of the inputs, but also of the price of the output. When the price of an input changes, the profit-maximizing behavior of a firm usually dictates that it adjust its output. When all firms adjust their outputs, the market price of the output will change, which, in turn, will shift the firm's demand curve for the input. Thus, any change in the price of an input will usually result in a shift of the firm's demand curve for that input. Thus, we do not have given firm demand curves to add together for various prices. In fact, for different prices of the input, the MRP curves for that input will usually be different even in the same firm. The market demand curve must take the shifts of the individual demand curves into consideration.

The market demand curve cannot always be derived by simply summing up the individual firm demands

Without knowing the properties of the demand and production functions of the output, it is impossible to tell how the firm's demand curve for a productive factor will shift when the market price of the input changes. Therefore, since a graphical illustration of the derivation of the market demand for a productive factor can only be speculative, we shall not provide one. Students who are interested in obtaining greater detail can do the derivation themselves as an exercise. The important thing to remember is that for each given market price of the input each firm has a given demand for the input. For this price, add up the corresponding quantities of the inputs for all of the firms. The price–quantity combination so obtained is one point on the market demand curve. For a different price, each firm will have a different demand curve, which can be either to the right or to the left of the first curve, depending on the properties of the market demand for, and the production function of, the product produced. This new price and the corresponding demand determine the quantity of the input that the firm will purchase. The sum of the purchased quantities of all the firms is the market quantity for the new price. This price–quantity combination constitutes another point on the market demand curve for the input. When the price changes continuously, an infinite number of such points showing the price–quantity combination for the factor can be traced out. The locus of such points is the market demand curve for the factor of production (labor in our example).

Although it has not been theoretically proven that the market demand curve of productive factors must be negatively sloped in general, in the special case where the market demand curve is the horizontal sum of the demand curves of individual firms, the market demand curve is indeed negatively sloped, since all the demand curves of individual firms are negatively sloped. As we have shown in the previous sections, the sum of negatively sloped demand curves must be negatively sloped. The thoughtful student may be disturbed by the lack of a proof that the market demand curve for productive factors is necessarily negatively sloped. There is no reason to be overly concerned. Recall that

Negatively sloped firm demand curves assure a negatively sloped market demand curve

the individual consumer demand curves for the final product can be either negatively or positively sloped according to the Slutsky equation (which we discussed in Chapter 4). Thus, theoretically, the market demand curve for a final product can have either a negative or a positive slope. The well-known Giffen good is a special case of a positively sloped demand curve. Nevertheless, in economics, price theory is essentially based on the demand curve being negatively sloped. We may conclude that, even though we cannot theoretically rule out the possibility that the demand curve for a productive factor may have a positive slope, for practical purposes it is negatively sloped.

The properties of the demand function of productive factors which we have derived apply not only to labor and capital, but also to all other productive factors. The marginal productivity theory as developed above to explain the demand for productive factors is quite general.

10.6 DETERMINANTS OF THE DEMAND FOR A PRODUCTIVE FACTOR

In terms of a graphical exposition, two aspects of the demand curve are relevant: its curvature and its location. The curvature of a demand curve is related to the following question: How sensitive is the response in quantity demanded to a given change in the market price? In Chapter 5, we defined the price elasticity of demand as a quantitative measure of the responsiveness of demand to a given change in price. This concept can be applied equally well here. Knowing the determinants of price elasticity of demand helps one to understand the characteristics of demand. In distinction to the curvature of the demand curve, its location is related to a different question: For a given price in the input, what determines the quantity that will be purchased? In other words, what determines whether a demand curve is either far to the right or relatively close to the vertical axis. A good understanding of these two aspects of the demand curve will also help one gain an in-depth understanding of the nature of the demand for an input. The remainder of this chapter is devoted to a detailed discussion of these two aspects of the demand curve.

10.6.1 Determinants of the Price Elasticity of Demand for an Input

Price elasticity measures the sensitivity of demand for an input to price change

As we have pointed out in Chapter 5 with respect to the final product, for some commodities the quantity demanded is very sensitive to price changes, whereas in the case of other commodities it is quite insensitive. In other words, the price elasticity of demand is quite high for some commodities, whereas for others it is quite low. The determinants of the price elasticity of demand for a productive factor can, in general, be summarized with reference to the following three items.

1. The more easily other inputs can be substituted for a certain input, the higher the price elasticity of demand for the input. The substitutability of inputs is determined by technology, which is embodied in the production function. Thus, the shape of the demand curve for an input is partially determined by the property of the production function. In commonsense terms, if the technological conditions of production are such that an input can easily be substituted by other inputs, then an increase in the price of the input will most likely result in a substantial decrease in its use. On the other hand, if firms cannot substitute other inputs readily for the given input, a large increase in the price of the input may result in only a small decrease in its use.

2. The higher the price elasticity of demand for the product of which an input is a part in its production, the higher the price elasticity of demand for the input. This agrees with our earlier statement that the demand for a productive factor is closely related to the demand for the product of which the input is a part (e.g., a component in an assembled product) or whose production the input accommodates (e.g., labor, land, or capital). In other words, the demand for an input is a derived demand, as we have mentioned repeatedly. In Part III, we explained that for a given demand, when cost increases, market price will increase and quantity will decrease. For a given increase in cost, the increase in market price—and the corresponding decrease in quantity—is closely related to the price elasticity of demand for the product. Consequently, when the input price increases, the cost of production increases, and, for a given demand, the equilibrium quantity of the product will change; thus, the quantity of the input used will also change. The extent to which the quantities will change is closely related to the price elasticity of demand for the product. In short, the higher the price elasticity of the product, the higher the price elasticity of demand for the input (other things being equal).[4]

3. The price elasticity of demand for an input is usually higher in the long run than in the short run. We specify inputs in particular as compared to final products because substitution of inputs usually takes time. For example, if the wage rate

---

[4] From the above discussion it can also be deduced that if the input were to constitute a very small portion of the cost of the product, a change in the price of the input would not materially affect the total cost or price of the product; hence, other things being equal, the demand for the input would tend to be relatively insensitive to price changes.

goes up, it may not be possible for most plants to reduce the quantity of labor for a given output in the short run, since plants are built for a relatively fixed input ratio. However, in the long run, firms can build new plants to reduce the utilization of labor and more capital, thereby facilitating the substitution of cheaper inputs for those that are expensive.[5]

10.6.2 Determinants of the Location of the Demand Curve for a Productive Factor

In economics, when we say that the demand for a commodity or a productive factor is high, we mean that the demand curve is high and to the right when compared with a demand curve that is close to the vertical axis (in which case the demand is low). Consider Figure 10.6, in which D_1 represents a higher demand than D_2. The point is that a higher demand represents a higher quantity demanded for each and every price. Thus, we consider the whole curve, not just one point on the curve. The following five factors are important determinants of the location of the demand curve for a productive factor.

Other things equal, the higher a factor's MP the higher its demand

1. The greater the quantity of cooperating productive factors employed (other things being equal), the higher the demand for the variable input in question. The reason for this is that the demand for a productive factor is closely related to its MP. The higher the MP of an input (other things being equal), the higher the demand for it. In the single-variable-input case, this is obvious, since the demand for the input is the product of its MP and either the price of the output or the MR, depending

FIGURE 10.6

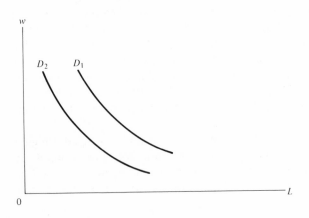

[5] The student should be careful not to draw an improper conclusion from this statement. The terms "cheaper" and "expensive" must be interpreted in terms of relative prices. When the wage rate goes up and other prices are constant (due to the "other things being equal" assumption), labor becomes more expensive and other factors cheaper. Thus, substitution may take place.

on whether or not the output market is under perfect competition. We can readily appreciate that a higher MP will result in a larger product in either case (i.e., PMP or MP $\cdot$ MR) and thus in a larger demand. In Chapter 2, we demonstrated that in stage II the MP of the variable input will be high for a large quantity of the fixed input; hence our statement that the greater the quantity of cooperating factors employed, the higher the demand for the variable input.

2. The higher the demand for the output for which the input is used in production, the higher the demand for the input (other things being equal). The reasoning here is similar to that in paragraph 1. Thus, when the demand for the output is high, its price and MR will be high (other things being equal), and, in turn, the higher price or MR of the output results in a higher demand for the input. The student may wish to attempt to demonstrate the validity of this statement, Remember that if the price or MR is high, the product PMP or MP $\cdot$ MR will also be high.

3. The demand for an input is inversely related to the quantity of the input currently in use. In other words, the more of the input currently in use (other things being equal), the lower the demand for it, and vice versa. This is due to a diminishing MP of the input and to the fact that the demand for an input is directly related to its MP, as was explained above.

4. The demand for an input depends on technology. It was shown in Chapter 2 that the shape of the isoquants is determined by technology. For given prices of the inputs and a given cost, the quantity of an input used depends on the shape of the isoquants. Therefore, technology is an important determinant of the demand for an input.

5. Finally, the number of firms is relevant with respect to the market demand for an input. The more firms that use the input (other things being equal), the higher the demand for it. This is obvious, since the market demand is an aggregate of the demands for the productive factor by all firms employing it.

In this chapter, we have primarily employed labor as the variable input for short-run analysis. However, the same reasoning would apply if we had instead used capital as the variable input. In the long run, all factors are variable; consequently, it is important that the student recognize the nature of complementarity of inputs, on the one hand, and substitutability of inputs, on the other hand. Both of these factors normally operate in production, and, therefore, an awareness of their impact on the demand for an input is essential in order to avoid drawing improper conclusions. Thus, labor and capital are both complementary and substitute factors of production; however, at any given time their complementarity may outweigh their substitutability or vice versa.

SUMMARY

In this chapter we showed that factor markets differ from product markets owing to differences in the forces governing factor supply and demand. Thus, whereas the demand for products is determined by consumer preference and income, the demand for a factor of production is determined by the profit-maximizing behavior of the producer of the product (i.e., the firm). On the supply side, the supply of the product is closely tied to the profit-maximizing behavior of the producer, but the supply of the factors of production is primarily determined by owner preferences for leisure or consumption. We also noted that factor markets deserve treatment distinct from that of commodity or product markets, since factor prices and quantities are important in determining the functional distribution of income.

We explained, assuming the goal of profit maximization for producers of a product, that the marginal productivity of labor plays an important role in the derivation of the demand curve for labor. Using the simple one-variable-input model, we first showed that the demand for labor under perfect competition in the product market is identical to the value of the marginal product (VMP) of labor. In this context, we noted that, since production can take place economically only in stage II (see Chapter 1), in which MP is decreasing, and since the firm faces a horizontal demand curve for its product, it follows that for a product with decreasing MP and constant price the VMP or labor demand curve will be negatively sloped. We then demonstrated that in an imperfect market for the product a firm faces a negatively sloped demand curve for its product, which means that price falls continuously as more is produced, thus causing the demand curve for labor to fall faster than the MP curve. We defined this new curve as the marginal revenue product (MRP) curve and explained that it is the relevant demand curve for labor under imperfect competition. Students were therefore advised to recognize the distinction between the demand for labor derived under perfect competition and that derived under imperfect markets for the products produced by labor.

To lend more realism to our discussion of factor demand, we then introduced the notion of two or more variable inputs in order to show that the demand curve for the factors of production can no longer be considered identical with the VMP or MRP curves and that, instead, the demand for the factors of production will depend on the simultaneous solution of a system of equations involving all of the inputs. We concluded by noting that factor demand is conditioned by (1) the substitutability of inputs, (2) the price elasticity and level of demand for the products produced by the factor, (3) the quantity and quality of cooperating factors, (4) the state of technology, (5) the amount of the factor currently in use, and (6) the number of firms using the factor.

EXERCISES AND QUESTIONS FOR CHAPTER 10 ON THE DEMAND FOR FACTORS OF PRODUCTION

1. Given the state of technology and the market price of the product produced by labor, use both tabular and graphical methods to show the derivation of an individual firm's demand curve for labor. Assume perfect competition in product markets and labor as the only variable input.

2. Prove that the demand curve for labor which you derived in question 1 provides a profit-maximizing level of labor input to be used for a given supply (price) of labor. Explain why the use of more or less labor than that defined by the intersection of the demand curve for labor and the supply curve of labor would not be profit maximizing to the individual firm under conditions of perfect competition.

3. From your work in question 1, derive the industry demand curve for labor assuming that four identical firms comprise the industry. What can you say about the price elasticity of demand for labor in the industry as opposed to that of the firm?

4. Using the graphical method, show how an individual firm's demand curve for labor under conditions of imperfect competition will differ from that of a firm under perfect competition. Does this suggest anything to you with respect to the relative levels of employment that would obtain under perfect and imperfect competition? Why is it difficult to develop a definitive answer to this question? Explain.

5. Why is the VMP curve for an input such as labor not its demand curve when the production process involves more than one variable input? You may wish to employ graphical analysis to show the substitution and output effects in order to reinforce your explanation.

6. Assume oligopoly in both the product and the labor supply market. Also assume that labor is the only variable input. Show that an equilibrium level of quantity and price cannot always be specified.

7. If one uses two inputs to produce an output, the following conditions are necessary for profit maximization:

$$Pf_1 = r_1 \qquad \text{and} \qquad Pf_2 = r_2$$

where P is the price of the output, f_1 and f_2 are the marginal productivities of inputs 1 and 2, respectively, and r_1 and r_2 are the prices of inputs 1 and 2, respectively. In your own words, explain why the above equations are the profit-maximizing conditions.

For questions 8–11: In the text, it is concluded that, for the simple one-variable-input case, the condition of the equality between the VMP of the variable input and its market price results in the demand function of the input. In the case of two or more variable inputs, the equality between the VMP and the market price of the corresponding input for all of the inputs results in the demand functions for them. The following questions are designed to give the student a better understanding of the meaning of the above-mentioned propositions by means of algebra.

8. Suppose that labor L is the only variable input. We have the following production function:

$$Q = A + aL - bL^2 \qquad (E10.1)$$

where Q is the quantity of the output and A, a, and b are positive constants. The marginal product of labor corresponding to production function (E10.1) is

$$MP = a - 2bL \qquad (E10.2)$$

By definition, the value of the marginal product (VMP) is equal to

$$VMP = PMP = aP - 2bLP \qquad (E10.3)$$

where P is the market price of the product. Let us denote the price of labor by w. The condition of the VMP of labor being equal to its price implies the following equation:

$$aP - 2bLP = w \qquad (E10.4)$$

Show that the demand function for labor is

$$L = a/2b - w/2bP \qquad (E10.5)$$

Also show that the demand for labor is a decreasing function of the wage rate w (i.e., that at a higher wage rate, less labor is hired and vice versa). Finally, show that the demand for labor is an increasing function of the product price P, other things being equal.

9. If the production function in question 8 was of the form

$$Q = AL^a \qquad (E10.6)$$

(which is a variety of the well-known Cobb–Douglas production function), then the corresponding marginal product would be

$$MP = aAL^{a-1} \qquad (E10.7)$$

and the value of the marginal product would be

$$VMP = aAL^{a-1}P. \qquad (E10.8)$$

Show that the demand function for labor is

$$L = (aAP)^{1/(1-a)} w^{-1/(1-a)} \qquad (E10.9)$$

Also show that the demand for labor is a decreasing function of w and an increasing function of P provided that $a < 1$ (which is actually the second-order condition for profit maximization).

10. Suppose that in the two-variable-input case, with labor and capital as the inputs, the production function is

$$Q = A + aLK - bL^2 - cK^2 \qquad (E10.10)$$

where Q, L, and K denote the quantities of output, labor, and capital, respectively, and A, a, b, and c are constants. The corresponding marginal products of labor and capital, respectively, are

$$MP_L = aK - 2bL$$
$$\qquad\qquad\qquad\qquad (E10.11)$$
$$MP_K = aL - 2cK$$

and the values of the marginal products of labor and capital, respectively, are

$$VMP_L = (aK - 2bL)P$$

$$VMP_K = (aL - 2cK)P$$

(E10.12)

Denote the prices of labor and capital, respectively, w and r. Show that the demand functions for labor and capital, respectively, are

$$L = -ar/(4bc - a^2)P - [2c/(4bc - a^2)P]w$$

$$K = -aw/(4bc - a^2)P - [2b/(4bc - a^2)P]r$$

(E10.13)

Also show that the demand for labor is a decreasing function of the wage rate w (other things being equal) and that the demand for capital is a decreasing function of the price of capital r (other things being equal) provided that $4bc > a^2$ (which is the second-order condition for profit maximization. If the last condition is not satisfied, the solutions (E10.13) will result in minimum profit, and thus they cannot be the demand functions.

11. If the production function for a two-variable-input case is of the Cobb–Douglas type:

$$Q = AL^aK^b$$

(E10.14)

then the corresponding marginal products, respectively, are

$$MP_L = aAL^{a-1}K^b$$

$$MP_K = bAL^aK^{b-1}$$

(E10.15)

and the corresponding values of the marginal products, respectively, are

$$VMP_L = aAL^{a-1}K^bP$$

$$VMP_K = bAL^aK^{b-1}P$$

(E10.16)

Equating the values of the marginal products for labor and capital to their corresponding prices w and r, and solving for L and K simultaneously, show that the resulting demand functions for labor and capital, respectively, are as follows:

$$L = (a^{1-b}b^bAPr^{-b})^{1/c}w^{-(1-b)/c}$$

$$K = (a^ab^{1-a}APw^{-a})^{1/c}r^{-(1-a)/c}$$

(E10.17)

where $c = 1 - a - b$. Also show that the demand functions for both labor and capital are decreasing functions of their own prices (other things being equal) only if $c = 1 - a - b > 0$ or $1 > a + b$ for $a, b > 0$. The last condition is the second-order condition for profit maximization.

APPENDIX TO CHAPTER 10

A MATHEMATICAL NOTE
ON FACTOR DEMAND

As we have explained in the text, the demand function of an input can only be derived explicitly if we know the production function under the assumption of perfect competition in product markets. When the product market is imperfect, the precise form of the demand for the output has to be known in order to derive an explicit demand function of an input. For the purpose of illustration, we shall use the Cobb–Douglas production function as well as a constant elasticity of demand function (when necessary).

A10.1 THE DEMAND FUNCTION OF PRODUCTIVE FACTORS UNDER A PERFECTLY COMPETITIVE PRODUCT MARKET

The demand function of a productive factor is derived from the first-order conditions of profit maximization, where the inputs are considered to be the independent variables, provided that the second-order conditions of profit maximization are satisfied. The satisfaction of the second-order conditions is important because, if they are not satisfied, the first-order conditions may indicate a minimum profit.

A10.1.1 The Demand Function of Productive Factors in the One-Variable-Input Case, Including the Special Case of the Cobb–Douglas Production Function

In the one-variable-input case, output is a function of the variable input only. Thus, the production function can be written

$$Q = f(L) \tag{A10.1}$$

where Q denotes the quantity of the output, L denotes the quantity of the variable input (in our case, labor), and f denotes the production function.

The total revenue that a firm derives from producing and selling the product is given by

$$R = PQ = Pf(L) \tag{A10.2}$$

where R denotes the total revenue and P denotes the price of the output.

The total cost of the inputs is

$$C = C_0 + wL \tag{A10.3}$$

where C denotes the total cost, C_0 denotes the TFC, which is determined by the quantity (quantities) and price(s) of the fixed input(s), and w denotes the wage rate. The alert student will realize that we are using the cost equation of Chapter 2, not the cost function of Chapter 3.

By definition, the total profit π is equal to the total revenue minus the total cost:

$$\pi = R - C = Pf(L) - C_0 - wL \tag{A10.4}$$

The first-order condition for profit maximization is

$$d\pi/dL = Pdf(L)/dL - w = 0 \tag{A10.5}$$

Since we are assuming perfect competition in the product market, P is a constant. By definition, we have

$$MP = df(L)/dL \tag{A10.6}$$

where MP is the marginal physical product of labor in the one-variable-input case. Thus, substituting (A10.6) into (A10.5), we can write the first-order condition for profit maximization in the form

$$w = PMP \tag{A10.7}$$

The equivalence of (A10.7) to (A10.9) constitutes the proof of the arguments we presented in the text. Since w and P are constants under the assumption of perfect competition in both the output and the input market, and since MP is a function of the variable input L, (A10.7) comprises one equation in one variable, which can, in principle, be solved for L in terms of w and P. We write the solution to (A10.7) in the form

$$L = D(w, P) \tag{A10.8}$$

which is the demand function of L. Since the properties of D depend on the properties of the production function f, we can state the second-order condition for profit maximization as

$$d^2\pi/dL^2 = Pd^2f(L)/dL^2 < 0 \tag{A10.9}$$

where $d^2f(L)/dL^2$ is the slope of the MP of L. Since $P > 0$, the second-order condition for profit maximization requires that $d^2f(L)/dL^2 < 0$, which implies diminishing returns. Moreover, since diminishing returns prevail in stage II of production, the statement in the text that only the decreasing portion of the VMP curve has analytical significance is consistent with the result noted here.

In order to illustrate the meaning of (A10.8), we shall now use the Cobb–Douglas production function

$$Q = AL^\alpha K^\beta \qquad (A10.10)$$

in place of (A10.1).

In the short run, capital K is fixed (we shall denote fixed capital K_0). Thus, in the one-variable-input case, we can write

$$Q = BL^\alpha \qquad (A10.11)$$

where $B = K_0^\beta A$ is a positive constant. From (A10.11), we obtain

$$dQ/dL = \alpha BL^{\alpha-1} \qquad (A10.12)$$

Therefore, the expression corresponding to (A10.7) in this special case is

$$w = \alpha BPL^{\alpha-1} \qquad (A10.13)$$

The solution to (A10.13), that is, the demand function of labor, can be written

$$L = (\alpha BP/w)^{1/(1-\alpha)} \qquad (A10.14)$$

The second-order condition for profit maximization requires that

$$Pd^2f(L)/dL^2 = (\alpha - 1)\alpha BPL^{\alpha-2} < 0 \qquad (A10.15)$$

which, in turn, implies that

$$\alpha - 1 < 0 \quad \text{or} \quad 0 < \alpha < 1 \qquad (A10.16)$$

The demand function of labor (A10.14) is negatively sloped, since

$$\frac{dL}{dw} = -\frac{1}{1-\alpha}\left(\frac{\alpha BP}{w}\right)^{1/(1-\alpha)}\frac{1}{w} < 0 \qquad \text{for} \quad \alpha < 1 \qquad (A10.17)$$

It is also interesting to point out that the demand for labor is an increasing function of the price of the output P. In other words, the higher the market price of the output, the higher the demand for labor (other things being equal), since

$$\frac{\partial L}{\partial P} = \frac{1}{1-\alpha}\left(\frac{\alpha B}{w}\right)^{1/(1-\alpha)} P^{\alpha/(1-\alpha)} > 0 \qquad \text{for} \quad \alpha < 1 \qquad (A10.18)$$

A10.1.2 The Demand Function of Productive Factors in the *n*-Variable-Input Case, Including the Special Case of the Cobb–Douglas Production Function for Two Inputs

When there are n variable inputs $x_1, x_2, ..., x_n$, the production function can be written

$$Q = f(x_1, x_2, ..., x_n) \qquad\qquad (A10.19)$$

The cost equation is

$$C = C_0 + \sum_{i=1}^{n} r_i x_i \qquad\qquad (A10.20)$$

where r_i denotes the price of input i.

The profit function can be written

$$\pi = Pf(x_1, x_2, ..., x_n) - C_0 - \sum_{i=1}^{n} r_i x_i \qquad\qquad (A10.21)$$

The first-order conditions for profit maximization are

$$\partial \pi / \partial x_1 = Pf_i - r_i = 0, \qquad i = 1, 2, ..., n \qquad\qquad (A10.22)$$

where f_i denotes the partial derivative of the production function with respect to input x_i, that is, $f_i = \partial f / \partial x_i$, which is precisely the MP of input x_i.

System (A10.22) comprises a total of n equations in the n variables $x_1, x_2, ..., x_n$ (all of the f_is, $i = 1, 2, ..., n$, are functions of the inputs, whereas the prices P and $r_1, r_2, ..., r_n$ are constants—not variables—due to the assumption of perfect competition in both the output and the input market). The system of n equations in n variables (A10.22) can, in principle, be solved explicitly in terms of the prices and written

$$x_1 = D_1(r_1, r_2, ..., r_n, P)$$

$$x_2 = D_2(r_1, r_2, ..., r_n, P) \qquad\qquad (A10.23)$$

$$\vdots$$

$$x_n = D_n(r_1, r_2, ..., r_n, P)$$

Expressions (A10.23) represent the n demand functions of the inputs. In general, the demand for each and every input is a function of the prices of all the inputs and the output. In addition, the properties of the demand functions depend on the properties of the production function. Without knowing the production function, it is impossible to derive the precise demand functions for the inputs. However, it can be shown that the second-order conditions for profit maximization imply that each and every demand function is negatively sloped in a two-dimensional graph.

For the sake of simplicity in notation, we define

$$f_{ij} \equiv \partial^2 f / \partial x_j \partial x_i, \qquad i, j = 1, 2, ..., n \qquad\qquad (A10.24)$$

The second-order conditions for profit maximization are

$$Pf_{11} < 0$$

$$\begin{vmatrix} Pf_{11} & Pf_{12} \\ Pf_{21} & Pf_{22} \end{vmatrix} > 0$$

$$\begin{vmatrix} Pf_{11} & Pf_{12} & Pf_{13} \\ Pf_{21} & Pf_{22} & Pf_{23} \\ Pf_{31} & Pf_{32} & Pf_{33} \end{vmatrix} < 0 \qquad\qquad (A10.25)$$

$$\vdots$$

$$(-1)^n \begin{vmatrix} Pf_{11} & Pf_{12} & \ldots & Pf_{1n} \\ Pf_{21} & Pf_{22} & \ldots & Pf_{2n} \\ & & \vdots & \\ Pf_{n1} & Pf_{n2} & \ldots & Pf_{nn} \end{vmatrix} > 0$$

Expressions (A10.25) are called the *Hessian determinants* of the second partial derivatives of the profit function. For maximum profit, the Hessian determinants must alternate in sign (starting with a negative).

Differentiating the first-order conditions for profit maximization (A10.22) totally and rearranging the terms, we obtain

$$Pf_{11} dx_1 + Pf_{12} dx_2 + \cdots + Pf_{1n} dx_n = -f_1 dP + dr_1$$

$$Pf_{21} dx_1 + Pf_{22} dx_2 + \cdots + Pf_{2n} dx_n = -f_2 dP + dr_2$$

$$\vdots$$

$$Pf_{n1} dx_1 + Pf_{n2} dx_2 + \cdots + Pf_{nn} dx_n = -f_n dP + dr_n$$

$$(A10.26)$$

Let us denote the determinant of the $n \times n$ matrix in (A10.25) by D and the cofactor of the element in the ith row and jth column by D_{ij}. Considering the dx_is as variables, the system of equations (A10.26) yields

$$dx_j = \sum_i [(-f_i dP + dr_i) D_{ij}]/D, \qquad j = 1, 2, \ldots, n \qquad (A10.27)$$

Dividing both sides of the jth equation by dr_j, and setting $dr_i = dP = 0$ for $i \neq j$, we obtain

$$\partial x_j / \partial r_j = D_{jj}/D < 0 \qquad\qquad (A10.28)$$

Since j can be any number from 1 to n, it can be $n - 1$. By the second-order conditions, D_{jj} and D must have opposite signs, that is, one must be negative and the other positive. Hence, their ratio must be negative. Since (A10.28) precisely presents the slope of the demand function (curve) in a two-dimensional graph, this proves our assertion (see Section 10.2) that, based on the assumption of profit maximization, the demand function (curve) for productive factors is negatively sloped.

To illustrate this point, we shall use the Cobb–Douglas production function to derive the demand functions for two variable inputs. We again write the Cobb–Douglas production function:

$$Q = AL^\alpha K^\beta \tag{A10.29}$$

The profit function can be written

$$\pi = PAL^\alpha K^\beta - C_0 - wL - rK \tag{A10.30}$$

where, as before, A, α, and β are positive constants, w and r are the prices of labor and capital, respectively, and P is the price of the output.

The first-order conditions for profit maximization are

$$\partial\pi/\partial L = \alpha PAL^{\alpha-1}K^\beta - w = 0$$
$$\partial\pi/\partial K = \beta PAL^\alpha K^{\beta-1} - r = 0 \tag{A10.31}$$

The second-order conditions for profit maximization are

$$\partial^2\pi/\partial L^2 = \alpha(\alpha - 1)PAL^{\alpha-2}K^\beta < 0$$

$$\partial^2\pi/\partial K^2 = \beta(\beta - 1)PAL^\beta K^{\beta-2} < 0$$

$$\begin{vmatrix} \alpha(\alpha - 1)PAL^{\alpha-2}K^\beta & \alpha\beta PAL^{\alpha-1}L^{\beta-1} \\ \alpha\beta PAL^{\alpha-1}K^{\beta-1} & \beta(\beta - 1)PAL^\alpha K^{\beta-2} \end{vmatrix} > 0 \tag{A10.32}$$

The solution of the two-equation system (A10.31) yields the following demand functions of labor and capital, respectively:

$$L = (\alpha/w)^{(1-\beta)/a}(\beta/r)^{\beta/a}(PA)^{1/a} \tag{A10.33}$$

$$K = (\beta/r)^{(1-\alpha)/a}(\alpha/w)^{\alpha/a}(PA)^{1/a} \tag{A10.34}$$

where $a = 1 - \alpha - \beta$.

The slopes of the demand functions are indicated by the signs of the partial derivatives:

$$\frac{\partial L}{\partial w} = -\frac{1 - \beta}{a}\left(\frac{\alpha}{w}\right)^{(1-\beta)/a}\left(\frac{\beta}{r}\right)^{\beta/a}(PA)^{1/a}\frac{1}{w} < 0 \tag{A10.35}$$

$$\frac{\partial K}{\partial r} = -\frac{1 - \alpha}{a}\left(\frac{\beta}{r}\right)^{(1-\alpha)/a}\left(\frac{\alpha}{w}\right)^{\alpha/a}(PA)^{1/a}\frac{1}{r} < 0 \tag{A10.36}$$

Since the first two expressions of (A10.32) imply that $1 - \alpha > 0$ and $1 - \beta > 0$, the last expression implies that $1 - \alpha - \beta = a > 0$. Thus, the demand functions of the variable inputs derived from the Cobb–Douglas production function are negatively sloped, provided that the second-order conditions for profit maximization are satisfied.

It can also be observed that $\partial L/\partial P > 0$ and $\partial K/\partial P > 0$. This implies that the demand functions of both labor and capital are increasing functions of the market price of the product. In other words, when the market price of the product increases (other things being equal), the demand curves for labor and capital shift to the right. All of the above properties are quite reasonable for a derived demand function of a productive factor.

A10.2 THE DEMAND FUNCTION OF PRODUCTIVE FACTORS UNDER AN IMPERFECT PRODUCT MARKET, INCLUDING THE SPECIAL CASE OF A CONSTANT ELASTICITY OF DEMAND FUNCTION AND THE COBB–DOUGLAS PRODUCTION FUNCTION

The results of the previous sections are based on the assumption that both the input and the output market are perfectly competitive, so that the prices of both the inputs and the outputs are treated as constants (parameters). When the output market is not under perfect competition, the price of the output can no longer be treated as a constant, and the situation becomes more complicated. We shall omit the one-variable-input case and only demonstrate the case for two or more variable inputs.

The profit function in this case is identical to (A10.21). However, the first-order conditions for profit maximization are different from (A10.22). Instead, we have the following first-order conditions for profit maximization:

$$\partial\pi/\partial x_i = f_i P + Q(dP/dQ)f_i - r_i$$
$$= 0, \qquad i = 1, 2, ..., n \tag{A10.37}$$

Note that (A10.22) implies the following conditions:

$$Pf_i = r_i \tag{A10.38}$$

where Pf_i is called the value of the marginal product (VMP) of input i. On the other hand, (A10.37) implies the conditions

$$\left(P + Q\frac{dP}{dQ}\right)f_i = r_i, \qquad i = 1, 2, ..., n \tag{A10.39}$$

where f_i is the MP of input i and the expression in parentheses on the left side is the MR. By definition, MR $= dR/dQ$. However, since $R = PQ$,

$$dR/dQ = P + QdP/dQ.$$

In the text, the product of MR and MP is defined as the marginal revenue product (MRP). It can be seen that dP/dQ is the slope of the demand function (curve). In the special case of perfect competition, the firm faces a horizontal, straight-line demand function (curve). Therefore, $dP/dQ = 0$, and hence (A10.38) and (A10.39) are equivalent. Since the demand function usually has a negative slope, we have MR $\leq P$.

The derivation of explicit demand functions for two or more variable inputs can be quite complicated for certain demand functions of the output and the Cobb–Douglas production function. In some cases, explicit expressions for the demand functions for the inputs may be very hard—if not impossible—to obtain. Due to its simplicity, a linear demand function is very often used for the purpose of illustration. However, the use of a linear demand function together with the Cobb–Douglas production function can make the derivation of the explicit demand functions considerably difficult even in the two-variable-input case. On the other hand, the combination of a constant elasticity of demand function and the Cobb–Douglas production function is quite easy to handle. We shall use this case to illustrate the derivation of explicit demand functions of labor and capital under the condition of an imperfect product market.

In Chapter 5, we discussed the class of constant elasticity of demand functions which can be written

$$Q = BP^{-1/c} \tag{A10.40}$$

where c is a constant, and the price elasticity of demand is $1/c$. The inverse of the demand function (A10.40) is

$$P = B^c Q^{-c} \tag{A10.40'}$$

Given the Cobb–Douglas production function (A10.29), we can, by substitution, write the inverse demand function as

$$P = B^c(AL^\alpha K^\beta)^{-c} = B^c A^{-c} L^{-\alpha c} K^{-\beta c} \tag{A10.40''}$$

The profit function can be written

$$\pi = A^{-c} B^c L^{-\alpha c} K^{-\beta c} \cdot AL^\alpha K^\beta - C_0 - wL - rK \tag{A10.41}$$

or

$$\pi = EL^a K^b - C_0 - wL - rK$$

where $E = A^{1-c} B^c$, $a = \alpha(1 - c)$, and $b = \beta(1 - c)$. Comparing (A10.41) with (A10.30), we can see that they are very similar. The difference is that (A10.30) involves the market price of the product, whereas (A10.41) involves the parameters of the demand function of the product.

The first-order conditions for profit maximization are

$$\partial\pi/\partial L = aEL^{a-1}K^b - w = 0$$
$$\partial\pi/\partial K = bEL^a K^{b-1} - r = 0 \tag{A10.42}$$

Note that expressions (A10.42) and (A10.31) are strikingly similar.

It can also be shown that the second-order conditions for profit maximization require that $a < 1$, $b < 1$, and $a + b < 1$. These conditions impose considerable restrictions on both the demand function and the production function of the product.

It can be shown that the demand functions of labor and capital, respectively, are

$$L = \left(\frac{a}{w}\right)^{(1-b)/(1-a-b)} \left(\frac{b}{r}\right)^{b/(1-a-b)} E^{1/(1-a-b)}$$ (A10.43)

$$K = \left(\frac{b}{r}\right)^{(1-a)/(1-a-b)} \left(\frac{a}{w}\right)^{a/(1-a-b)} E^{1/(1-a-b)}$$

Taking the second-order conditions for profit maximization into consideration, we observe that the demand functions (curves) for both labor and capital are negatively sloped in a traditional price–quantity two-dimensional graph.

Although the demand functions do not involve the output price, they do involve the parameter B in the demand function for the product because E is a function of B. In addition, $\partial L/\partial B > 0$ and $\partial K/\partial B > 0$, which implies that the higher the demand for the product, the higher the demand for the inputs (and vice versa). In other words, a rightward shift of the demand curve for the product will result in a rightward shift of the demand curves for the inputs. These properties are again quite reasonable for derived demand functions of the inputs.

The parameters a, b, and E must be positive in order that the demand functions (A10.43) make sense. Parameter E is definitely positive, since both A and B are positive. According to the definition of a and b, they can be positive only if $c < 1$, since both α and β are positive. Recall that the price elasticity of demand for the product is $1/c$ for the demand function that we are using. Hence, $c < 1$ implies an elastic demand for the product. This restriction agrees with the theory developed in Chapter 7, where it was shown that monopolists will never sell their products at a price for which the demand is inelastic, because an inelastic demand implies a negative MR. [Recall the expression MR $= P(1 - 1/e) < 0$ for $e < 1$, where e is the price elasticity of demand as defined in Chapter 5.]

The sole purpose of the above illustrations is to give students a feeling for the nature of the derived demand for the inputs, that is, the close relationship between the demand and production functions of the product, on the one hand, and the demand function of the inputs, on the other hand. Although the Cobb–Douglas production function and the constant elasticity of demand function are widely used in theoretical as well as empirical work (and, therefore, possess certain desirable properties), the real market is probably much more complicated than can be represented by these functions. Nevertheless, they do serve our illustrative purposes very well.

FACTOR SUPPLY AND FACTOR PRICES

INTRODUCTION

In Part III, we explained that, in a perfectly competitive market, the market price of a product is determined by supply and demand. However, under conditions of monopoly, monopolistic competition, and oligopoly, the concept of market supply does not have much meaning. Instead, demand and cost determine the market price of a product. In certain respects, the situation in factor markets is similar to that in product markets, but, in other respects, it is different.

The market price is determined by supply and demand under conditions of perfect competition. This applies to both factor and product markets. We have derived the demand functions for productive factors in Chapter 10. We now must examine the supply functions in order to discuss the determination of the market price for the factors of production. Although the supply curve for the product of a firm is the rising portion of the marginal cost (MC) curve which is above the minimum of the average variable cost (AVC) curve (as was shown in Chapter 6), the derivation of the supply curve for a productive factor is more complicated because the sellers of productive factors in the market are not solely concerned with maximizing profit. In fact, the profit derived from the selling of a productive factor may not be well defined in many cases. For example, how would one define the profit derived by a worker from selling his or her own labor? Because of this difference in circumstances, the approach used in the derivation of the supply curves for productive factors is entirely different from that used in the derivation of the supply curves for commodities. This difference will be clarified shortly.

Sellers of productive factors are not solely concerned with maximizing profits

As we have explained, the concept of supply in commodity markets is not quite meaningful under conditions of imperfect competition. This also applies in factor markets; that is, the intersection of the supply and demand curves no longer determines the market price of a productive factor under either monopoly or *monopsony* (the latter refers to the case where there is only one buyer in the market). We shall have more to say on this topic later in the chapter.

This chapter will be devoted to a discussion of labor, land, and capital markets, in that order. We shall show that the various supply functions of the different productive factors have their own unique characteristics as a result of the different circumstances that apply to their provision. Thus, unlike the demand functions of all productive factors (which are derived from one fundamental principle—marginal productivity) or the supply functions of all produced commodities under perfect competition (which is identified as that rising portion of the MC curve which is above the minimum AVC), the supply functions of all productive factors are determined subject to the special conditions or features that apply in factor markets. It is perhaps these special features that have caused economists traditionally to discuss factor markets apart from commodity markets and to treat the theory of factor markets as part of income distribution theory. On the other hand, some textbooks include a consideration of factor markets as part of their discussion of commodity markets, thereby eliminating the discussion of traditional income distribution theory. However, since demand and supply in factor markets both have special features that are distinct from those in commodity markets, the traditional approach has virtue.

11.1 THE SUPPLY OF LABOR OF AN INDIVIDUAL WORKER: AN APPLICATION OF UTILITY ANALYSIS

In Chapter 4, we developed the utility theory of consumer behavior, from which we then derived the individual demand function of a commodity under the assumption that the goal of consumers is to maximize their satisfaction (utility) for a given level of income. This same theoretical tool can be used to derive the supply of labor of an individual worker. It is recommended that the student review Chapter 4 before reading this section.

Although the theoretical tools used in this section are essentially the same as those used in Chapter 4, some details differ. For example, in Chapter 4, we assumed that the consumer had a given income—the budget. We now assume that, analogous to this given income, the consumer has a given amount of time—*exactly* 24 hours a day—that can be allocated to different endeavors. Thus, whereas in Chapter 4 a consumer chose between commodities for given prices, here a consumer chooses between

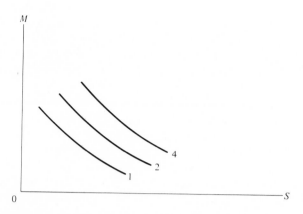

FIGURE 11.1

leisure and work, that is, between leisure and income from work for a given wage rate. Although the details differ, we can—under the assumption of maximization of satisfaction (utility) by the consumer—use the utility function or an indifference map and the budget constraint in both cases. Let us examine the application of these concepts (tools) for analyzing factor supply, in particular, labor supply.

Consider Figure 11.1, in which the horizontal axis is leisure S and the vertical axis is money income from work M. Since both money and leisure are desirable, they can be considered commodities. The indifference curves have the usual shape—negatively sloped and convex toward the origin. As we have previously noted, the indifference curves cannot intersect, and a curve that lies to the right and above another curve represents a higher level of satisfaction (utility). Thus, all bundles on indifference curve 2 represent a higher level of satisfaction (utility) than do bundles on indifference curve 1, whereas all bundles on indifference curve 4 represent a higher level of satisfaction (utility) than do those on indifference curve 2. Recall that since we are employing ordinal utility, the absolute magnitudes of the numbers used to label the indifference curves are irrelevant—it is the order that really counts. Thus, we could have just as well used 1, 200, and 201 instead of 1, 2, and 4 to label the indifference curves. As before, there are an infinite number of indifference curves, only three of which are drawn in Figure 11.1. In short, indifference curve 2 represents a higher-preference combination of money (work) and leisure than does indifference curve 1, whereas indifference curve 4 represents a higher-preference combination than does indifference curve 2.

As in Chapter 4, the budget constraint in the present case is again a negatively sloped straight line (see Figure 11.2) that starts from the horizontal axis, where all of the available time is used for leisure and thus the income from work is zero. This line ends at a point on the vertical axis, where all of the available time is

Indifference curves represent the worker's choice between leisure and work (income)

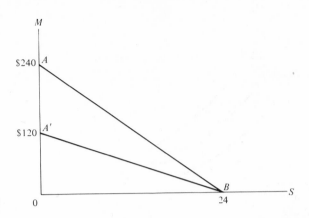

FIGURE 11.2

used for work and hence there is zero leisure time. The height of the point of intersection between the vertical axis and the budget line depends on the wage rate: The higher the wage rate, the higher the intersection point on the vertical axis.

Let us consider Figure 11.2. As noted earlier, we assume that the time period under discussion is exactly 1 day, that is, the total amount of time available is 24 hours, which is represented by point B. All budget lines must start from point B, since if all of a worker's available time is used for leisure, his or her income from wages must be zero, regardless of the wage rate. The budget line $\overline{AB}$ represents a wage rate of $10 per hour. This is clearly shown by point A, which indicates zero leisure time, that is, 24 hours of work, and an income from work of $240, thus giving a wage rate of $10 per hour. Similarly, the budget line $\overline{A'B}$ indicates a wage rate of $5 per hour. Hence, the slope of the budget line is determined by the wage rate: The higher the wage rate, the steeper the slope of the budget line. When the wage rate changes continuously, it will generate an infinite number of budget lines, each of which corresponds to a unique wage rate and all of which start from point B.

The equilibrium of a consumer is achieved when the time between work and leisure is allocated such that the consumer's level of satisfaction (utility) is a maximum. Note that we are assuming a perfectly competitive labor market, in which the worker is a price taker and thus seeks to maximize his or her satisfaction (utility) at the given market wage rate. This implies that a worker faces a given budget and chooses a point on the budget line which is on the highest indifference curve. We illustrate this condition in Figure 11.3, in which $\overline{AB}$ is the budget line for a given wage rate. Our worker could choose high income M_1, but the leisure time would be only $\overline{0S_1}$, as indicated by point F on the budget line. Figure 11.3 shows that this choice results in a satisfaction (utility) of level 1. In this case, the worker can increase the level of satisfaction (utility) by increasing the leisure

The tangency of the budget line to an indifference curve represents maximum satisfaction

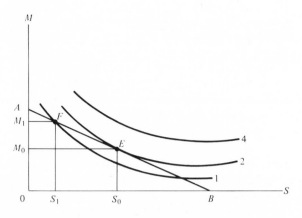

FIGURE 11.3

time and, at the same time, reducing the money income by moving down along the budget line from point F to, for example, point E. The worker's satisfaction (utility) level has been increased from 1 to 2 as a consequence of this move. Of course, the worker would like to achieve a satisfaction (utility) level of 4, but indifference curve 4 is out of reach for the given wage rate. Figure 11.3 also shows that if the worker moves further down along the budget line from point E so as to increase leisure time and reduce money income, then his or her satisfaction (utility) will decrease. Hence, point E, with leisure time S_0 and money income M_0, represents the consumer equilibrium.

If one remembers the condition of consumer equilibrium in the commodity market as developed in Chapter 4, then the situation described above will be very familiar. The consumers' equilibrium is denoted by the point of tangency between the budget line and an indifference curve. In the case of two commodities, the tangency is characterized by the equality of the price ratio of the commodities and the marginal rate of substitution between them. In the case of leisure and work, that is, leisure and money from work, the price ratio corresponds to the ratio between the wage rate and the price of money.

What is the price of money? It is 1; that is, $1 is worth $1, no more and no less, regardless of the general price level. In the literature of economics, the term *numeraire* is used to designate a commodity whose price is set equal to 1. Although, in theory, any commodity can be used as the numeraire, in practice, money is the numeraire. For our purposes, it is sufficient to know that the price of money is 1. Hence, the price ratio between leisure and money income is $w/1 = w$, where w denotes the wage rate.

This can also be shown by writing down the budget constraint

$$M = wL \qquad (11.1)$$

where M denotes the amount of money derived from work, and L denotes the number of hours of work. By definition, the number of hours of work performed is equal to the total time available minus the leisure time:

$$L = T - S \tag{11.2}$$

where T denotes the total amount of time available (24 hours a day), and S denotes the number of hours for leisure.

Substituting (11.2) into (11.1), we obtain

$$M = wT - wS \tag{11.3}$$

Since both T and w are constants, whereas M and S are the variables, (11.3) defines a straight line. In terms of Figure 11.3, wT is the vertical intercept $\overline{0A}$, whereas $-w$ is the slope of $\overline{AB}$. This further strengthens our arguments (indicated by Figure 11.2) that the higher the wage rate, the steeper the slope of the budget line.

As defined in Chapter 4, the negative slope of an indifference curve is the marginal rate of substitution (MRS), which, in the present case, is equal to the ratio of the marginal utility of leisure MU_S to the marginal utility of money MU_M:

$$MRS = MU_S/MU_M \tag{11.4}$$

At the point of consumer equilibrium (point E in Figure 11.3), the slope of indifference curve 2 is equal to the slope of the budget line. Thus, we have

$$dM/dS = -w \tag{11.5}$$

Since the MRS is defined as the negative slope of an indifference curve, we have the usually employed consumer equilibrium condition, which in the present case can be written

$$MRS = MU_S/MU_M = -dM/dS = -(-w) = w \tag{11.6}$$

In the case of cardinal utility, where the concept of marginal utility is meaningful, equilibrium condition (11.6) can be written in the following alternative form:

$$MU_S/w = MU_M \tag{11.7}$$

When $MU_S/w = MU_M$ no satisfaction is gained from changing the leisure–work mix

The commonsense interpretation of (11.7) is that a consumer's satisfaction (utility) will be maximized only at that point where the last dollar's worth of leisure provides a satisfaction (utility) equal to that obtainable from $1, provided that MU_S is decreasing. This can be illustrated by means of a simple example. Assume that (11.7) does not hold. Let $MU_S = 8$ utils and $w = \$4$ per hour. In this case, the value of the left side of (11.7) will be 8/4 = 2, which implies that our worker derives 2 utils of satisfaction (utility) from 15 minutes of leisure time at the margin. In other words, since the worker derives 8 utils at a wage rate of $4 per hour, he or she therefore derives 2 utils at a cost of $1. Hence, the consumer (worker) can forego $1 by cutting working time by

15 minutes and, in so doing, can gain 2 utils of satisfaction (utility) from the resulting 15 minutes of leisure time. Since the cost of the 15 minutes of leisure time is $1, we wish to know how many utils this $1 is worth. The answer is that it depends on the marginal utility of money MU_M. Suppose that the MU of $1 is 1 util; then the value of the right side of (11.7) is 1, which is smaller than that of the left side. Thus, $1's leisure time is worth 2 utils, whereas $1 by itself is worth only 1 util. Apparently, our consumer can derive a net gain in satisfaction (utility) by purchasing more leisure time or, equivalently, cutting work time. In terms of Figure 11.3, this condition is represented by point F, and any downward movement along the budget line will result in a higher level of satisfaction (utility). Conversely, if the value of the right side of (11.7) is greater than that of the left side, then the satisfaction (utility) derived by a consumer can be increased by doing more work and earning more money at the expense of leisure time.

The commonsense interpretation of (11.6), which is equivalent to (11.7), is similar. The right side (i.e., the wage rate) represents the market opportunity facing the consumer. The consumer can either work 1 hour in order to earn wage w or enjoy his or her leisure time. If the consumer chooses the latter, he or she must forego w amount of money. In general, the left side of (11.6), that is, MRS, represents the consumer's subjective view. However, in our particular example it represents the ratio of the satisfaction (utility) that the consumer derives from 1 hour of leisure time to that derived from $1. Based on our assumption concerning consumer behavior (of marginal utility diminishing as more of a commodity is consumed), we can state that this ratio decreases when more leisure time is enjoyed and, at the same time, less money is earned. This is the phenomenon of a decreasing MRS. However, since the market wage rate is a constant to an individual worker, we can see that when (11.6) does not hold, the consumer (worker) can freely substitute leisure for money (work)—or vice versa—in order to increase his or her satisfaction. However, when (11.6) does hold, the consumer's subjective view is in agreement with the market opportunity; that is, the consumer has taken full advantage of the market opportunity and no further action can improve his or her situation. In other words, the consumer is at equilibrium.

Because it is of importance in the derivation of a worker's supply of labor, we have explained in considerable detail that, for a given wage rate, a worker (consumer) is at equilibrium when the budget line is tangent to one of the indifference curves. Since the amount of time that a worker has available for a combination of work and leisure is a constant for a day, or a week, once the worker makes a decision with respect to the amount of leisure time, the amount of hours that he or she will work is automatically determined. Given the preference pattern of a worker and a mar-

Worker supply curves show the satisfaction-maximizing leisure–work mix changes as the wage rate changes

ket wage rate, the conditions for maximum satisfaction (utility) will determine a unique leisure time and, thus, a unique work time. However, given the same preference pattern when the market wage rate changes, a different leisure time (and, hence, a different work time) will result in maximum worker satisfaction (utility). This wage rate–work time relationship is actually the supply function of labor for the individual worker.

Consider Figure 11.4. In part (a), $\overline{AB}$ is the budget line for wage rate w_0. The consumer (worker) is at equilibrium at point E, which represents an amount $\overline{0S_0}$ of desired leisure time. Since $\overline{0B}$ represents the total amount of time available, the number of hours that the consumer devotes to work is $\overline{S_0B}$ for wage rate w_0. In part (b), we show the number of hours of work on the horizontal axis and the wage rate on the vertical axis. Let $\overline{0L_0}$ in part (b) equal $\overline{S_0B}$ in part (a); thus, point (E) in part (b) corresponds to point E in part (a). For wage rate w_0, the worker chooses to work $\overline{S_0B} = \overline{0L_0}$ hours. When the wage rate decreases to w_1, the budget line shifts from $\overline{AB}$ to $\overline{A'B}$. For the given preference pattern, the worker chooses to have more leisure time than before and thus work fewer hours in order to maximize his or her satisfaction (utility). The work time corresponding to w_1 is $\overline{S_1B}$. Let $\overline{0L_1} = \overline{S_1B}$; then point ($E_1$) in part (b) corresponds to point E_1 in part (a). If the wage rate decreases continuously below w_0, then there will be an infinite number of equilibrium points, the locus of which constitutes the curve $\overset{\frown}{EE_1}$ in part (a). Curve EE_1 corresponds to curve (E)(E_1) in part (b). The latter curve shows the relationship between wages and hours worked, which is precisely the supply curve of labor for the individual worker. We can see that, over a given range, the curve is positively sloped, which indicates that the higher the wage rate, the more hours per day the worker is induced to work.

When the wage rate increases above w_0, the budget line shifts from $\overline{AB}$ to $\overline{A''B}$, and the new equilibrium point is E_2. The consumer (worker) now wants more leisure time, that is, less work time, at a higher wage rate. Let $\overline{0L_2}$ and point (E_2) in part (b) correspond to $\overline{S_2B}$ and point E_2 in part (a). If the wage rate increases continuously above w_0, the locus of equilibrium points constitutes a curve such as $\overset{\frown}{EE_2}$. If the corresponding points are plotted in part (b), we obtain curve ($\overset{\frown}{E})(E_2)$ for a wage rate above w_0. Curve ($\overset{\frown}{E})(E_2)$ is also part of the labor supply curve, but it bends back somewhere above w_0. This backward-bending labor supply curve has been noted by economists for a long time, and its rationale can be best explained by the substitution and income effects developed in Chapter 4, which we shall briefly recap in the following paragraphs.

When the wage rate goes up, the worker's income increases for the same number of hours worked. With a higher income, the worker consumes more of every normal good (for the definition

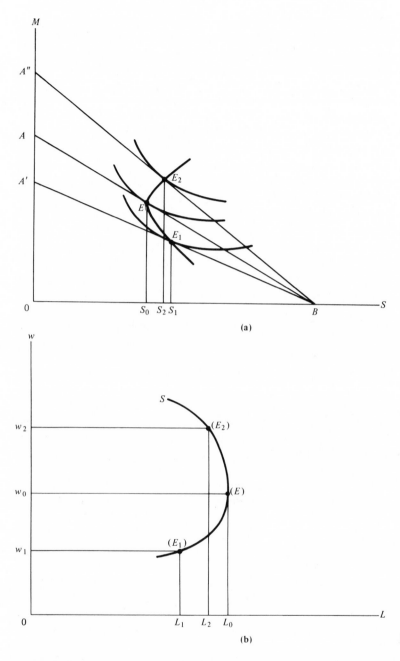

FIGURE 11.4

of this term, see Chapter 4). In general, leisure is considered to be a normal good. Hence, a higher wage rate will result in the worker opting for more leisure time and less work time solely on the basis of the income effect.

However, as we have explained earlier, the cost of leisure is the wage that the worker foregoes. Consequently, with a higher wage rate, the cost of leisure is also higher. Hence, all other prices being constant, leisure becomes relatively more expensive than other goods. Given his or her preference pattern, the worker will substitute other goods and/or services (in our case, money from work) for leisure. Thus, an increase in the wage rate will result in less leisure and more work solely on the basis of the substitution effect.

As far as leisure and work time are concerned, the substitution and income effects work in opposite directions when the wage rate undergoes change. In particular, when the wage rate increases, the substitution effect results in less leisure (i.e., more work) because leisure becomes more expensive and work becomes more valuable. On the other hand, the income effect results in more leisure and less work because the worker can afford more enjoyment in leisure and less suffering from work. The net effect of these opposing forces cannot be foretold. It all depends on which force is dominant at a particular time for a given wage rate.

The net result of the substitution and income effects on labor supply cannot be foretold

It is argued that when the wage rate (and thus income) is low, leisure may not be a very attractive good and the substitution effect will dominate. Hence, given a low initial wage, an increase in the wage rate will result in more work and less leisure. Therefore, over a range of low wage rates, the supply of labor is positively sloped. However, when the wage rate is high, all necessities are met, leisure becomes more attractive, and hence the income effect will be dominant. Consequently, a further increase in the wage rate may result in more leisure and less work, and the labor supply of an individual worker will be negatively sloped. This justifies the shape of the supply curve in part (b) of Figure 11.4.

The above arguments do have certain merits, as can be seen from the fact that wage earners in this country spend a considerable amount of time playing golf and other expensive sports, whereas in poor countries, most wage earners must work a long day in order to make a living. Furthermore, during the off-season, agricultural workers in these poor countries migrate to cities or industrial centers to seek work instead of enjoying their leisure time. Although this does not prove the existence of the backward-bending labor supply curve, it does indicate that leisure is more attractive to people with high incomes than to people with low incomes.

It should be pointed out that an implicit assumption underlying the derivation of the labor supply curve is that workers can decide on the number of hours per day that they are willing to work. In reality, institutional factors deny workers a freedom of choice in the number of hours they can work in a day or week. In a majority of cases, workers can only choose to either work 8 hours a day or remain idle. This and other institutional factors impose certain limitations on the applicability of general supply analysis. Never-

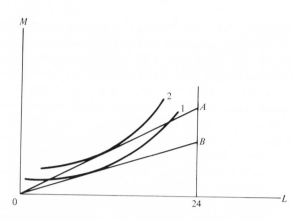

FIGURE 11.5

theless, the theoretical development does provide a useful tool for the analysis of the labor market and permits the establishment and testing of certain hypotheses regarding the operation of different labor markets as well as the effects of different manpower policies.

As we mentioned in Chapter 4, the indifference map of a worker can also be drawn in terms of money and work, treating the former as a desirable good and the latter as an undesirable good. However, in this case, the shape and slope of the indifference curves will be entirely different from those of the usual indifference curves. Furthermore, the budget line will be different from the one noted in Figure 11.2. The derivation of the supply of labor from this graph will be identical to that from Figure 11.4, but with necessary modifications. Figure 11.5 shows a family of indifference curves and budget lines; indifference curve 2 represents a higher level of satisfaction (utility) than indifference curve 1, whereas budget line $\overline{0A}$ represents a higher wage rate than budget line $\overline{0B}$. The horizontal axis plots the quantity of work, and the vertical axis plots money income. As an exercise, the student should try to determine why the indifference curves and budget lines have the shapes shown in Figure 11.5.

11.2 THE MARKET SUPPLY OF LABOR AND THE DETERMINATION OF THE MARKET WAGE RATE UNDER PERFECT COMPETITION

The market supply curve for labor can be considered the horizontal sum of the individual workers' supply curves under the assumption that each worker's supply is independent of those of other workers. This is quite reasonable, since, as noted in Chapter 4, our utility theory implicitly assumes the absence of externality. The graphical and numerical examples used in the derivation of the market demand from the individual consumer demands in Chapter 5 can be applied to the derivation of the market supply

The market supply of labor may be positively or negatively sloped

of labor. Since the two derivations are identical with respect to methodology, it is not necessary that we repeat the details here. We merely emphasize that, since the individual worker's supply curve is usually positively sloped at a low wage rate and may be negatively sloped at a higher wage rate, the market (aggregate) supply curve for labor is positively sloped at low wage rates, but may be either positively or negatively sloped in the range of high wage rates. Also, it should be noted that the slope of the supply curve will have some bearing on the stability and uniqueness of the market equilibrium, as was demonstrated in Chapter 6.

In Chapter 10, we derived the demand curves for productive factors and demonstrated that they are negatively sloped, regardless of whether the product market is perfectly competitive or monopolistic. Since we are dealing with a perfectly competitive labor market, the market wage rate is determined by the supply of and demand for labor.

As a simple example, consider Figure 11.6, in which the supply and demand curves intersect at point E. Although the supply curve for labor is backward bending, the market equilibrium is unique and stable. (For an explanation of the uniqueness and stability of market equilibrium, see Chapter 6.) The market wage rate is w_0 and total employment is L_0. Given perfect competition in the market, at the market wage rate w_0 the individual worker faces a horizontal demand curve and the individual employer faces a horizontal supply curve. Since the market (aggregate) supply curve is the horizontal sum of the individual supply curves, and since the demand is derived by allowing all of the employers (see Chapter 10) to make all necessary production adjustments to the specific price, the aggregate of individual decisions of the workers and employers will be consistent with the market quantity L_0 at wage rate w_0. With this wage rate and employment level, all workers' satisfactions (utilities) and all employers' profits will be maximized. If there is no external disturbance, then

FIGURE 11.6

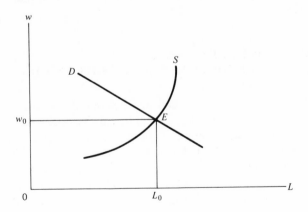

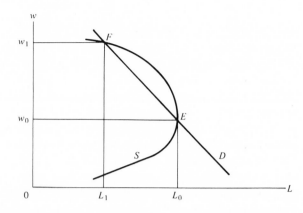

FIGURE 11.7

there is no tendency to change. A unique and stable market equilibrium exists.

Because of the backward-bending supply curve, equilibrium in the labor market may neither be unique nor stable. Consider Figure 11.7, in which the supply and demand curves intersect at the two points E and F. In this case, the uniqueness of equilibrium is violated. Furthermore, according to the arguments presented in Chapter 6, the equilibrium at point E is stable, whereas at point F it is unstable.

Point F can be interpreted as a situation where the wage rate is so high that workers can make a comfortable living by working very few hours per day. The workers and employers are both happy, and there will be no tendency toward change in the absence of an external disturbance. However, should some external factor produce a wage rate higher than w_1, then the quantity of labor demanded would exceed the quantity supplied. As a result, employers would bid up the wage rate. We can see that at a higher wage rate, more leisure and less work would simply push up the wage rate still further and increase the disparity between supply and demand. According to Figure 11.7, there is no built-in force in the market mechanism which would reestablish equilibrium. Consequently, each upward adjustment in wages would merely increase the disparity between supply and demand, and the system would eventually break down. Empirically, this kind of situation can hardly be observed, since, in comparative statics, the adjustment from disequilibrium to equilibrium is assumed to be instantaneous. Hence, only the equilibrium itself can be observed. What is significant here is that the existing system cannot be taken for granted: The possibility of an unstable equilibrium suggests that certain market systems may not be long-lasting. In this respect, the backward-bending labor supply curve can be illuminating, especially with respect to the markets for certain factors of production.

11.3 MONOPSONY AND MARKET WAGE RATE

Monopsony (in contrast to monopoly) is the situation of having only a single buyer in the market. Monopsony is quite common in the labor market. Company towns, in which a single firm is the sole employer of the labor force, are classic examples. A special feature of monopsony is that the monopsonist faces a positively sloped supply curve, whereas in a perfectly competitive labor market the firm faces a horizontal straight-line supply curve. One implication of the positively sloped supply curve is that a monopsony has to pay a higher wage rate in order to attract more workers. Since no wage discrimination is allowed, the higher wage rate must be applied to all workers, not just the additional worker. Consequently, the additional cost to the employer for each additional worker (except for the first one) is higher than the wage rate. A numerical example will serve to illustrate this point. The data in the first and second columns of Table 11.1 define a positively sloped labor supply curve; that is, a higher wage rate is associated with a higher quantity of labor. The third column shows the total cost of labor, which is the product of the first two columns. Finally, the fourth column gives the marginal expenditure on labor, which is defined as the ratio of a change in the total cost or total expenditure to a small change in the amount of labor purchased. For practical purposes, the marginal expenditure can be considered the change in total expenditure resulting from the purchase of one additional unit of labor. Thus, the marginal expenditures listed in the fourth column are computed by dividing the successive differences of the third column by the corresponding differences of the first column. For example, assuming that the total labor cost is zero for zero units of labor, the first marginal expenditure value is $(10 - 0)/(1 - 0) = 10$; the second value is $(22 - 10)/(2 - 1) = 12$, and so forth.

Comparing the second and fourth columns, it can be seen that (except for the first unit of labor) the marginal expenditure for successive units of labor is higher than the wage rate. The reason for this situation can be explained in terms of common sense. When one worker is hired, a wage rate of $10 is sufficient. However, in order to attract an additional (second) worker, the wage rate offered must be increased to $11. Since no wage discrimi-

Marginal expenditures increase faster than the wage rate for a monopsonist

TABLE 11.1

L	w	Total cost	Marginal expenditure
1	10	10	10
2	11	22	12
3	12	36	14
4	13	52	16
5	14	70	18

nation is allowed, the first worker must also be paid a wage rate of $11. Thus, the additional cost for the second worker is the wage rate of $11 plus the $1 added to the wage rate of the first worker, that is, $11 + $1 = $12; similarly, the additional cost for the third worker is the new wage rate of $12 plus $1 for each of the first two workers, that is, $12 + $2 = $14 (and so forth).

The data in Table 11.1 can be plotted in a graph. For our purposes, we do not need the third column; only the information in the first and second columns and the first and fourth columns is needed to develop the supply (S) and marginal expenditure (ME) curves, respectively. The data are summarized in Figure 11.8, in which labor is plotted on the horizontal axis, whereas the wage rate and marginal expenditure are plotted on the vertical axis. For the sake of simplicity, the supply and marginal expenditure curves are both drawn as straight lines.

For the purpose of illustration, assume that labor is the only variable input. In this special case, the value of the marginal product (VMP) curve or the marginal revenue product (MRP) curve—depending on whether the *output market* is perfectly competitive or monopolistic, respectively—is the firm's demand curve for labor (see Chapter 10). In Figure 11.8, DR is such a curve. In the absence of monopsony, and given DR as the market demand curve for labor, the intersection of S and DR—point F— would determine the market wage rate and employment level. However, since monopsony prevails in the labor market, F is not the point of market equilibrium. Instead, G determines L_0 as the amount of labor to be purchased.

In Chapter 10, it was shown that, in the continuous (discrete) case, the profit of a firm is maximized when the additional revenue derived from hiring one additional worker is equal to (greater than or equal to) the additional cost of the worker. Either VMP or MRP precisely represents the additional revenue derived from an additional worker, whereas the marginal expenditure of labor precisely represents the additional cost to the monopsonist for

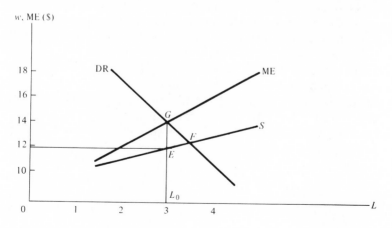

FIGURE 11.8

the additional worker. Hence, the first-order condition for profit maximization by the monopsonist in the discrete and continuous cases is as follows:

$$VMP \geq ME \quad \text{or} \quad MRP \geq ME \tag{11.8}$$

in the discrete case

$$VMP = ME \quad \text{or} \quad MRP = ME \tag{11.9}$$

in the continuous case.[1]

In the continuous case condition (11.9) determines the quantity—not the price—of labor. In Figure 11.8, point G satisfies (11.9). Since the goal of the firm is assumed to be profit maximization, the monopsonist will hire $L_0 = 3$ units of labor. However, the monopsonist does not pay a wage rate of \$14 (indicated by point G) in order to attract the three workers needed. In fact, the supply of labor clearly shows that a wage rate of \$12 is sufficient to attract L_0 workers. Hence, as a profit maximizer, the monopsonist will pay only \$12 for each of the three workers. This market price–quantity combination is represented by point E in Figure 11.8.

Our illustration makes two points that merit special comment. First of all, neither the price nor the quantity is determined by the intersection of the supply and demand curves. In fact, it is doubtful whether the concept of demand is meaningful under monopsony (just as supply is not very meaningful under monopoly, as explained in Chapter 7). This indicates that the usefulness of elementary supply and demand analysis is quite limited when we depart from conditions of perfect competition.

Under monopsony, the market wage rate is below the competitive wage rate

Secondly, the first-order condition for profit maximization determines only the quantity of labor to be hired—it does not determine the price of labor. In fact, the market wage rate is not only below the VMP or MRP, but it is also below the competitive wage rate (determined by point F in Figure 11.8) in the absence of monopsony. Many economists refer to the phenomenon of a lower wage rate under monopsony as *exploitation*. This kind of argument shows that perfect competition results in a higher wage rate and more employment than does monopsony. However, circumstances (such as those that *could possibly* exist in a company town) may not readily support the accommodation of more than one company and hence are not conducive to perfect competition. Therefore, when all aspects of the different markets are taken into consideration, the comparison may turn out to be meaningless. We shall not devote any more space to this topic, since it would be best handled in a separate monograph on labor market studies.

---

[1] A mathematical proof of (11.9) will be presented in the appendix to this chapter.

The above graphical illustration is based on the simplified assumption that labor is the only variable input. When two or more variable inputs are involved, the situation is more complicated. However, in the appendix to this chapter, it will be shown that, in the continuous case, the first-order (necessary) condition for monopsony profit maximization must be satisfied for each of the n variable inputs, that is,

$$VMP_i = ME_i \quad \text{or} \quad MRP_i = ME_i, \quad i = 1, 2, ..., n \quad (11.10)$$

where the i refers to the ith variable input of the monopsonist.

As was shown in Chapter 10, since under perfect competition the price of a product is equal to the marginal revenue, we can write

$$MRP = MP_i \cdot MR \quad \text{and} \quad VMP = MP_i \cdot P = MP_i \cdot MR$$

Thus, the first-order conditions for monopsony profit maximization can be written

$$MP_i/ME_i = MP_j/ME_j, \quad i, j = 1, 2, ..., n \quad (11.11)$$

When input markets are under perfect competition, $r_i = ME_i$ for all $i = 1, 2, ..., n$, where r_i denotes the price of input i. In this case, (11.11) and the conditions, developed in Chapter 2, for maximum output at a given cost or for minimum cost at a given output are identical.

11.4 LABOR UNIONS, COLLECTIVE BARGAINING, AND BILATERAL MONOPOLY

The above models (i.e., perfect competition and monopsony) demonstrate the theoretical determination of the wage rate and employment level under different market conditions if organized intervention in the market is absent. In reality, in many cases, labor is organized and the wage rate is more often than not determined by union officials and management representatives at the bargaining table. In this case, the market wage rate is no longer entirely determined by impersonal market forces. How can economic theory explain this situation? The answer to this question is by the use of a *bilateral monopoly model.*

Bilateral monopoly prevails when there is only one buyer and one seller in the market. Although the one-buyer case is generally called monopsony (as defined in the Section 11.3), bilateral monopoly is the term generally used when a monopolist encounters a monopsonist in the market. One major characteristic of bilateral monopoly is the indeterminacy of both price and quantity in theory. Hence, a system that is not solely based on market forces is required for determining the market price. *Collective bargaining* is one such system.

The bilateral monopoly model combines the application of sup-

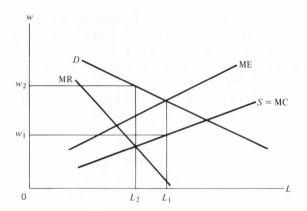

FIGURE 11.9

ply and demand analysis with monopoly/monopsony theory. Suppose that there is perfect competition in the market; then the intersection of the demand and supply curves determines both the equilibrium price and the equilibrium quantity of the commodity (e.g., labor) that is purchased. As we have previously noted, the demand curve faced by a monopolist is the market demand curve D, which is negatively sloped.[2] As was shown in Chapter 7, the MR curve corresponding to a negatively sloped demand curve is both negatively sloped and below D, as indicated by MR in Figure 11.9. If S is the MC curve of the monopolist, then (from Chapter 7) the profit-maximizing quantity is L_2. When

Given bilateral monopoly, theory cannot ascertain the specific price–quantity outcome

the monopoly decides to put L_2 amount of commodity in the market, the demand determines a wage rate of w_2. Thus, if the buyer were one of many in a perfectly competitive market, the wage rate and employment level would be w_2 and L_2, respectively. However, the buyer is not a perfect competitor. As we have shown, a monopsonist's profit will be maximized when the amount of labor L_1—determined by the intersection of ME and D—is hired. Under the assumption that the seller is only one of many competitors, the buyer expects to pay w_1 for amount of labor L_1.[3] Thus, we see that, under the assumption that the buyer is a small competitor, the monopolist as a seller expects to sell L_2 at w_2, whereas, under the assumption that the seller is a small competitor, the monopsonist as a buyer expects to buy L_1 at a wage rate of w_1.

Actually, neither the seller nor the buyer is a small competitor: One is a monopoly and the other is a monopsony. As a result,

---

[2] This is true because the monopolist is the only seller of the commodity.

[3] This follows because, as explained in Chapter 6, the rising portion of the MC curve is the supply curve of a perfectly competitive firm. As we have shown in Table 11.1, the monopsonist's ME rises faster than the increase in the wage rate as more workers are hired. In Figure 11.4, $S = $ MC is the labor supply curve of the monopolist, who in our case is the labor union.

neither one's expectation can be realized. If both the seller and the buyer persist, then there is no solution for either the price or the quantity in the market. Thus, we have the characteristic of theoretical indeterminacy mentioned earlier. This does not mean that no exchange can take place, but only implies that market forces by themselves cannot determine a consistent solution. As noted earlier, we require a system that is not solely based on market forces in order to obtain a solution.

In those industries where strong labor unions exist and a few large companies act together as a unit (e.g., the automobile, steel, and coal industries), the actual labor market closely approximates the bilateral monopoly model. In such cases, collective bargaining between union officials and management representatives determines the wage rate, provided that the bargaining is successful. If the bargaining does not succeed, a strike or arbitration will be the result. (In some rare cases, a company has gone out of business after a long strike.) Economic theory cannot ascertain what specific labor market will result from each of the possible outcomes, even if the supply and demand functions are known. Furthermore, even if we assume that the bargaining will be successful, economic theory still cannot specify what wage rate will result from the settlement. It all depends on the mood of the union members and the executives of the industry, the respective bargaining skills of their representatives, and the willpower of union and industry officials. In some cases, the result may even depend on public opinion. In a given situation, most (if not all) of these noneconomic and nonmarket factors will play an important role in the determination of the wage rate. Thus, the determination of the actual wage rate cannot be described by economic theory. However, in terms of Figure 11.9, economic theory does tell us that, given rational behavior, a collective bargaining settlement will result in a wage rate between w_1 and w_2.

11.5 THE FIXED SUPPLY OF AND RENT ON LAND

As we have mentioned earlier, one special feature of factor markets is that the supply of productive factors is different from the supply of a produced commodity in that the rising portion of the MC curve which lies above the minimum of the AVC curve is the supply curve under perfect competition in product markets but not in factor markets. Furthermore, the supply curve of each factor may have its own unique characteristic. To illustrate this point, let us consider the supply curve for land as an example.

Traditionally, economists consider the supply of land as fixed, since the size of the earth is a constant. However, some economists argue that this is not strictly true because land can be created by drainage, whereas the fertility of land can be either depleted by overutilization or enhanced through adding soil nu-

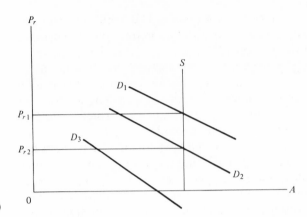

FIGURE 11.10

trients. Although this argument is valid for farm land or any other specific category of land, overall, land, as a whole, is indeed fixed.

When the supply of land is fixed (or perfectly inelastic above zero price), the price of land will be determined by demand alone. Consider Figure 11.10, in which A denotes acreage (i.e., the quantity of land), and P_r is the price for the right to use (i.e., rent), rather than for the ownership of, the land. As the representation of the fixed supply of land, S is a line that is perpendicular to the horizontal axis for all prices above and coincides with the horizontal axis at zero price. Thus, the amount of land available does not change (i.e., increase or decrease) at any price above zero. If the demand is D_1, the market price is P_{r1} whereas if the demand is D_2, the market price is P_{r2}. When the demand is as low as D_3, the price is zero. There are numerous examples of the last case. Even in the United States, land located in remote areas or in the Nevada desert does not command a positive price because of low demand.

In economic literature, the amount of money paid to buy the right to use an acre of land (commonly called *rent*) rather than the amount of money paid to buy ownership is considered to be the price of land. The economic concept of rent coincides with the commonsense usage of the term; that is, when one buys the right to use, for example, a house, apartment, car, or truck for a given period of time, he or she pays a rent. Although the concept of rent is distinct from that of ownership, theoretically, the price for ownership of an object and the price for the right to use (i.e., rent) the same object are closely related. Thus, one could conceivably use either as the price when analyzing the land market. However, for the sake of convenience, we shall follow the traditional approach and consider rent as the price of land. Hence, our use of the term "price" in the following discussion will be somewhat different from its common usage in commodity markets, where price, in general, refers to the amount of money paid to buy ownership of a commodity. On the other hand, rent as the price of land is consistent with the price concept in factor markets. For example, the wage rate is not the money paid to buy the ownership of labor (slavery is illegal in almost all countries in the modern world), but rather, analogously to rent, is the money paid for the right to use labor for a given period of time. Although the consideration of the wage rate as the price of labor does not produce any confusion, the same is not true when the rental concept is applied to the price of land. The confusion results from the fact that, in common usage, the price of land means the price for ownership, whereas, in economics, the price of land denotes the price for the right to use (i.e., rent) the land. For this reason, we consider it advisable to explain in greater detail the implications of the two different concepts of the price of land.

We have defined the fixed supply of land as being represented by two straight-line segments: a straight line perpendicular to the horizontal axis and that portion of the horizontal axis from the origin to the vertical straight line. This definition prevents the possible invalid inference of negative rent. Most textbooks define the fixed land supply as being represented by a vertical straight line, but neglect to specify that this vertical line will never extend below the horizontal axis. Hence, whereas this definition of fixed supply does not theoretically exclude the possibility of negative rent, our definition does.

Economic rent is earned by factors for which supply is fixed

Our analysis of the supply of and demand for land shown in Figure 11.10 was fairly simple, and students having only a limited background in economics would probably accept the result without question. However, the analysis itself may puzzle some (if not all) of the more-knowledgeable students.

In early 19th century England, corn was a staple food for the populace. When the price of corn went up, the public blamed the high price on the high price of land and the related high rent. Thus, landlords were accused of being responsible for the high price of corn by virtue of the high rent on land. However, in 1815, the famous classical British economist David Ricardo explained the situation in the following terms:

> It is not really true that the price of corn is high because the price of cornland is high. Actually, the reverse is more nearly the truth; the price of cornland is high because the price of corn is high. Land's total supply being inelastic, it will always work for whatever is given to it by competition. Thus the value of the land is completely derived from the value of the product, and not vice versa.

In short, Ricardo was explaining the situation as the result of the inelasticity of supply. In light of our own analysis of the supply of and demand for land with respect to Figure 11.10, the logic of Ricardo's arguments is not difficult to understand. However, the absence of this analysis would make it quite difficult to sort out his arguments. Therefore, we shall extend our discussion on rent, using some examples that are familiar to students.

11.6 ECONOMIC RENT AND QUASI-RENT

As we have already pointed out, the outstanding feature of the land market is that the supply of land is fixed. However, this phenomenon is by no means unique to land. For example, the special talents and abilities that certain people naturally possess and that cannot be acquired through training or education are similar to land in that their supply is fixed. Hence, economists extend the concept of rent to all those factors for which the supply is fixed. Let us consider a few examples of these factors.

Although anyone can be trained to play the quarterback position in football, only a few specially talented people will ever be good enough to play on a professional team. Similarly, anyone can be trained to be a pitcher in baseball, but only a few of them will have the talent to become outstanding players in the major leagues. In fact, a special talent, far exceeding the skill that can be obtained from just training and practice, is needed in order to be an outstanding player at any position in football, baseball, and all other sports.

It is often publicized that certain football players have signed contracts for a million or more dollars over a given period of time or that certain baseball players are paid six-digit salaries for a single season. These salaries are far above the annual earnings that the average new college graduate can achieve. However, in terms of economic analysis, only part of the earnings of these highly paid players is considered salary—the rest is considered to be *economic rent*.

As an example, suppose that a quarterback is paid an annual salary of $200,000. Let us also assume that the highest annual salary that our quarterback could earn in any other field is $20,000. In this case, economists would only consider $20,000 of the $200,000 to be salary—the rest, namely, $180,000, would be considered economic rent. This economic rent, just like the rent on land, is essentially determined by demand. The reason that football and baseball players can earn such a high salary in this country is not only because they have such special talent, but also because the fans are willing to pay a high price for tickets to watch them. Although there is probably a great number of equally talented (or even more talented) people playing football or baseball in other parts of the world, they do not earn as high a salary as players in the United States because the demand for these sports is low. Thus, in other countries, no economic rent is paid for such talents.

In economics, economic rent is defined as follows.

Definition: Economic Rent. The payment to any productive factor which is above what is required to bring forth the services of that factor.

In other words, economic rent is the payment to any productive factor in fixed supply which is above the best earnings that the factor could achieve when employed in any other way. With this definition, economic rent actually represents a broader concept than does rent alone. Rent on land is a special case of economic rent.

Capital goods represent a situation that is both similar to and different from the example discussed above. In the short run, the amount of capital goods is given; thus, the short-run supply of capital goods can be considered perfectly inelastic. However, in the long run, capital goods can be produced or, alternatively, used up without replacement. Therefore, the long-run supply of capital goods is not fixed. Since any existing capital goods have been paid for by the owner, their possible earnings are determined by demand, not by the original cost. Consequently, the payment to capital goods is "water under the bridge," so to speak, and is dependent on current and future earnings. For this reason, a rational owner of capital goods would, in the short run, hire out the services that flow from them for whatever could be obtained, so long as it was above zero.

As we have demonstrated in Part III, producers who own the capital goods that they use will stay in business in the short run as long as their total earnings are above the TVC. This implies that the services of capital goods will be offered as long as the payment to capital is greater than or equal to zero in the short run. However, in the long run, we have a different situation. If the earnings of a capital good are below its replacement cost, it will not be replaced when it wears out. Therefore, the earnings of capital goods in the long run must, at a minimum, cover the AC of capital. Due to this special situation, 19th century economists began to call the positive earnings of capital goods in the short run *quasi-rent*. Thus, quasi-rent can be defined as follows.

Quasi-rent is largely a short-run phenomenon

Definition: Quasi-Rent. The payment to any input in temporarily fixed supply or, more formally, the earnings of a productive factor which are economic rent in the short run, but which are converted into necessary payments required to bring forth the services of the factor in the long run.

Economists generally use a graph to illustrate quasi-rent. Consider Figure 11.11, in which the horizontal axis plots the quantity of output, the vertical axis plots the price and cost, AVC is the average variable cost curve, ATC is the average total cost curve, and MC is the marginal cost curve. Under perfect competition, if the price is P_1, then the conditions for profit maximization will specify an output of Q_1. (For the reasoning behind this statement, see Chapter 6.) The TVC for Q_1 is given by rectangle $BC0Q_1$, whereas the TR is given by rectangle AP_10Q_1. Thus, the quasi-rent is given by rectangle $ABCP_1$: The amount earned by the firm which is above the necessary payment to variable factors of pro-

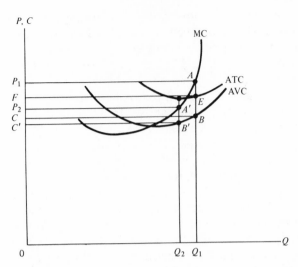

FIGURE 11.11

duction. In the present case, the quasi-rent can be divided into two parts: TFC (given by rectangle $BCFE$) and economic profit (given by rectangle $AEFP_1$). Needless to say, the quasi-rent does not have to exceed the TFC, nor does the economic profit have to be positive in the short run.

If the market price is P_2, then the profit-maximizing quantity is Q_2. In this case, the TVC is given by rectangle $B'C'0Q_2$, whereas the TR is given by rectangle $A'P_20Q_2$. The quasi-rent is given by rectangle $A'B'C'P_2$ and is hence less than the TFC. One can observe that if the price is P_2 (or any price less than the minimum ATC), then the quasi-rent will be less than the TFC, and thus we shall have negative economic profit.

11.7 THE PRICE (COST) OF CAPITAL: A CONTROVERSY

In economics, wages, rent, and interest are traditionally considered the prices for labor, land and capital, respectively. We have discussed the determination of wages and rent in terms of supply and demand analysis under perfect competition as well as the implications of labor unions and monopsony in the labor market. These are logically consistent and generally recognized theories. There is also a logically consistent and technically deliberate theory of capital that allows the determination of the market rate of interest starting with the concept of a consumer's time preference and the notion of savings as a function of interest rate on the supply side and extending to the discounted present value of an income stream and capital investment as a function of the interest rate on the demand side. As in the case of the prices of labor and land, the intersection of the supply and demand curves determines the price (market interest rate) of capital. Underlying the theory of the determination of the interest rate is the assumption of either perfect knowledge of future events or the existence of future

A logically consistent theory of the price of capital requires heroic assumptions

markets (see Fisher, 1930; Lutz and Lutz, 1951; Henderson and Quandt, 1971, Chapter 8; and Quirk, 1976, Chapter 11).

There are two important omissions in the theory of the determination of the interest rate: The first concerns the important roles played by such financial intermediaries as banks or savings and loan associations, whereas the second concerns the implication of corporations investing their own savings or undistributed earnings. The power of the banks in the capital market can hardly be overstated. Capital rationing is a well-known fact in reality, but the significance of perfect competition in the operation of capital markets is not easy to evaluate.

The availability of different means of finance (namely, debt and equity) and the increasing importance of corporate investment through the use of internal funds have created a theoretical controversy as regards how to evaluate the cost of capital when risk or uncertainty are involved. Many theories and methods for measuring the cost of capital have been advanced, but a simple solution to this problem has not been found.[4]

The traditional theory assumes perfect information or knowledge (Assumption 6.4, 7.4, 8.4, and 9.4) with respect to the future as well as certainty and perfect competition in the capital market. A complicated theoretical construct and logical deduction leads to the natural conclusion that the price or cost of capital is the interest rate. In reality, the situation is much more complicated. In particular, a corporation has at least two ways of financing a given capital investment: It can use debt finance by issuing bonds or borrowing money from financial institutions or it can use equity finance by issuing stocks or retaining undistributed earnings. Although it might seem a simple matter to estimate the cost of debt finance because the payment of interest is obviously the cost, even in this case we are still faced with the question of why some financial institutions pay a higher interest rate than others. The common answer to this question is the risk factor. However, an objective measure of risk has not been developed.

The determination of the cost of equity is an even more-complicated problem. The dividend cannot represent the cost of equity capital, since the fact that many corporations do not pay dividends would imply zero cost according to the above arguments. Furthermore, Durand (1952) has demonstrated that neither the current rate of return to equity or the total investment represents the cost of capital. (Note that the rate of return to equity is different from the rate of return to total investment when the rates of return to debt and to total investment are different.)

---

[4] For the origin of this question see, Durand (1952). For an attempted simple solution to the problem, see Modigliani and Miller (1958). For problems with the Modigliani–Miller arguments, see Durand (1959) and Sher (1968). For an alternative answer to the cost of capital question, see Baumol and Malkiel (1967) and Sher (1973).

*An objective measure
of the cost of
capital is
complicated by risk*

The central problem in formulating a method for measuring the cost of capital is that an objective measure of risk in terms of money has not been successfully developed. The return on an investment is always dependent on a future that is neither known nor certain. The situation is further complicated by the availability of alternative ways of financing a given physical investment. However, regardless of what happens in the future, the return on a given *physical* investment will be the same whether it is financed by debt or by equity. However, if it is financed by debt, the investor's obligation consists in meeting the fixed periodical interest and principal payments. If the investment is successful in that the returns are sufficient (or more than sufficient) to pay the obligations, and there is sufficient equity to ensure the payments in case of failure, then default on the payment of interest and principal can be avoided and risk reduced. Since no undertaking is assured of being 100% successful, pure debt finance is not feasible in reality. Legally, the debt holder has a priority claim on the investment returns, whereas the equity holder has a claim only on the residual. Hence, in an uncertain world, the equity holder assumes most of the risk of an investment. However, by bearing this risk, the equity holder will most probably be rewarded with a higher rate of return than the debt holder.

Another problem in measuring the cost of capital is that neither a monetary measure for business failure nor a futures market for stocks and bonds exists. Hence, the cost of capital for the optimal combination of debt and equity financing is not independent of subjective judgment. The attempt by Modigliani and Miller (1958) to find a simple solution to this complex problem has fallen short of total success, although the Baumol–Malkiel theorem (see Baumal and Malkiel, 1967) convincingly establishes the existence of an optimal capital structure in theory. Thus, we observe that the cost of capital in debt financing may be different from that in equity financing for certain combinations of the two; however, an objective measure of the cost has not been established. At our level of presentation, it seems sufficient simply to alert the student to the inherent difficulties of developing a theory of the cost of capital. Since the benefits of a detailed presentation of the controversy would not justify the time and space needed, we shall forgo a full exposition. However, interested students can refer to the books and articles cited in this section.

11.8 INTEREST AS THE COST OF CAPITAL UNDER THE CONDITION OF CERTAINTY

Although capital theory is more complex than the analysis of other factor markets, we can simplify the analysis by limiting it to a special case. When only consumers (i.e., not business) save, and when there is perfect competition in both the loan and capital

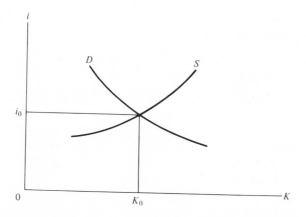

FIGURE 11.12

goods markets, perfect and certain knowledge of the future, and no government or central bank intervention (or no financial intermediary such as banks), it can be shown (see the appendix to this chapter) that the demand curve for capital, as a function of the interest rate, will be negatively sloped, whereas the supply curve for capital will be positively sloped within the relevant range. The resulting intersection of the demand and supply curves will determine the equilibrium interest rate and quantity of capital in the market.

Consider Figure 11.12, in which the vertical axis plots the interest rate i, the horizontal axis plots the quantity of capital goods K in terms of money (not in terms of physical units), D is the demand curve (rather, the inverse demand curve), and S is the (inverse) supply curve. With this demand and supply, the equilibrium market rate of interest is i_0, and the total new capital investment is K_0.

It should be pointed out that, under the assumption of perfect competition, which implies homogeneity and the absence of uncertainty, there is one and only one market rate of interest. In the real world, the various interest rates that actually exist are a combination of interest and payments on risk. The risk factor causes the interest rates that are actually charged to different individuals to deviate from the true interest rate i_0.

In a perfectly competitive market only one rate of interest can prevail

In a perfectly competitive capital market, individual investors can borrow as much as they wish or lend as much as they wish at the going interest rate. Under these circumstances, if investors make an investment using borrowed capital, then the cost of the investment is the going market rate of interest. On the other hand, if investors use their own funds to make the investment, then they must forgo the interest that they would have obtained if the investment were not made. (Recall the concept of opportunity or alternative cost, mentioned in Chapter 3.) Thus, in either case, the cost of capital is the market rate of interest. Hence, under perfect competition, which implies perfect information, lack of uncertainty, and consequently, no risk, the cost of capital is the market rate of interest.

11.9 IMPERFECT CAPITAL MARKETS AND INFORMAL CAPITAL RATIONING BY FINANCIAL INSTITUTIONS

Up to this point we have assumed perfect competition in the capital market and the absence of such financial institutions as banks or savings and loan associations. These two assumptions are interrelated. One of the functions of financial institutions is to accumulate small amounts of individual savings, which cannot be economically loaned out to productive investors, into larger sums that can be channeled to producers. The accumulation of large sums of money by financial institutions destroys the possibility of perfect competition because the assumption of many small sellers is violated.

The power of financial institutions makes applying the perfectly competitive model inappropriate

Financial institutions specialize in the capital market. They not only have large sums of funds to accommodate large borrowers, but they also possess more-reliable information about prospective borrowers and the market in general, which gives them a distinct advantage in the capital market. It is obvious that individual savers cannot effectively compete against the large financial institutions. Hence, from the concentration of power in the financial institutions, it follows that the results derived from the perfectly competitive model are inappropriate in defining and explaining the operation of the capital market. Small sellers (savers) cannot sell their commodity (savings) at the market price (equilibrium interest rate) nor they can buy (borrow) at the market price directly from sellers. Since they must deal with the financial institutions, they must also meet the terms set by the latter.

On the other hand, investors are usually large borrowers, and one might think that bilateral monopoly would exist when a large borrower encounters a large lender. (This, of course, would result in the type of indeterminacy described earlier in the chapter.) Actually, not only must large borrowers deal with a financial institution on its terms, but they must also be satisfied with the amount that it is willing to lend. In many cases, the informal rationing of funds by banks is a reality, and, in such cases, the market rate of interest becomes irrelevant and the cost of capital is conditional on funds being obtained or made available. Moreover, interest is not the only cost of borrowing. Service charges and many other disguised costs may in some cases outweigh the total amount of interest.

Despite the market imperfections and institutional implications, consumer behavior with regard to savings and the resultant supply of capital, on the one hand, and the returns to business and resultant demand for capital, on the other hand, still play an important role in the determination of the market rate of interest.

However, the determination of the market rate of interest is far more complicated than can be explained by static supply and demand analysis of the capital market. This is understandable, since the market rate of interest is also closely related to the money supply, which is determined by the monetary authorities. Because the money supply has been increasingly used by the monetary authorities to influence the price level, it has reduced the importance of microeconomic theory in predicting and explaining the determination of the market rate of interest. Consequently, in order to understand how the capital market works, a knowledge of the effects of monetary policy on the market rate of interest is necessary. It is to this question that we now turn.

11.10 FEDERAL MONETARY POLICY AND THE DETERMINATION OF THE MARKET RATE OF INTEREST

We have already noted that microeconomic theory can be usefully employed to explain the determination of the market rate of interest in a free and perfectly competitive market. In the real world, however, the activities of the Federal Reserve System in the United States and of the central banks in other countries have a most important effect on the determination of the market rate of interest. Although it is the study of macroeconomics which usually considers this topic in detail, a brief discussion of the role that the Federal Reserve System plays in the determination of the market rate of interest is essential to bringing theory closer to reality. Therefore, a brief review of the impact of money market policy and the operations of the Federal Reserve System appears in order.

As established at present, the law permits the Federal Reserve System in the United States (and the central banks in other countries) to control the market rate of interest in order to accomplish certain economic and/or political goals that have been decided upon through the political process. Thus, the market rate of interest is, in reality, not only determined by economic factors, but also by political considerations. A discussion of these public policy implications is beyond the scope of our present purpose. Therefore, we shall only discuss the ways and means by which the Federal Reserve seeks to control the market rate of interest.

It should be noted that the Federal Government in the United States ordinarily does not regulate the interest rate by direct order, although there are federal and state regulations that govern the maximum rate of interest that financial institutions can charge to their borrowers or, alternatively, that they can pay to their depositors. In general, the market rate of interest is allowed to fluctuate within a certain range according to market conditions. However, the Federal Reserve usually keeps a close watch on the interest rate and will often intervene in the market whenever the movement of the market rate of interest is considered not to be in harmony with federal policy measures or Federal Reserve objectives.

For the sake of brevity, we shall discuss the two tools that the Federal Reserve System primarily (and often) uses to effectively control the market rate of interest: the rediscount rate and open market operations.

The *rediscount rate* is the interest rate that the Federal Reserve banks charge to the member banks when the latter borrow money from them. In their economic principles classes, students have undoubtedly learned that the Federal Reserve banks are banker's banks; that is, they accommodate the needs of the banking community in servicing the financial requirements of business and industry. When commercial banks are short of money, they can borrow from a Federal Reserve bank, and the interest that they pay is called the rediscount rate. Obviously, the rediscount rate is the cost of borrowing to the commercial banks. Usually, the market rate of interest is higher than the rediscount rate. If the gap is large, then commercial banks can make money by borrowing from the Federal Reserve banks and making loans at the market rate (as a result, the market rate tends to go down). If the gap is narrow, then commercial banks will tend to ration credit, causing the market rate to rise. Normally, the gap between the rediscount rate and the market rate of interest is quite stable, and the market rate fluctuates with the rediscount rate. Thus, under certain circumstances, the rediscount rate is an effective tool that the Federal Reserve System has at its disposal to control the market rate of interest.

Open market operations is the term used to designate the activities of the Federal Reserve in selling or purchasing Federal Government bonds in the financial market. Why is this an effective tool for controlling the market rate of interest? First of all, as we have mentioned earlier, the various market rates of interest that borrowers actually pay are a combination of the true interest rate, which is free of risk charges, and the payments for risk. Since the probability of default on federal bonds is very low (but not zero, since a revolution could render them worthless), they can be considered practically free of risk. Hence, the interest rate on federal bonds can be considered the true interest rate (sometimes called the *pure rate of interest*).

Secondly, the nature of bonds, both government and private, must be understood in order to appreciate how open market operations affect the interest rate. First of all, a bond is a debt instrument that is characterized by at least three factors: (1) the face value of the bond, (2) the annual interest rate, and (3) the date of maturity.

A bond is a document that can have a face value of $100, $1000, $10,000, or more. The interest rate (called the *coupon rate*) of the

Central banks attempt to control interest rates by controlling commercial banks' ability to lend

bond, which is also specified on the document, is fixed for the life of the bond, regardless of the fluctuation of the market rate of interest. The face value and the specified interest rate together determine the fixed amount of annual payments from the issuer of the bond to its holder until the maturity of the bond, at which time the bondholder receives the face value of the bond and the last annual interest installment. Before the date of maturity, the bond issuer is not obliged to pay the principal, but only to meet the annual interest payments on time. For example, if the face value of a bond is $100 and the interest rate is 5%, then the annual payment from the issuer to the bondholder is $5 per year until the date of maturity. If there were a default, the bond might become worthless, but default is one of the risks that a bondholder has to bear. Although the bondholders have a first claim to the assets of a company, they will, at best, realize only a fraction of their investment through the sale of such assets.

Open market purchases and sales of government securities give central banks control over interest rates

At any given time, a bondholder may need cash before the maturity date of the bond, in which case the bond is sold on the market for whatever price it will bring. Similarly, an investor wishing to enter into the bond market at some given time does not have to wait for new issues, but can purchase existing issues in the bond market. (To keep our exposition simple, we shall ignore capital gains or losses, assuming that an investor purchases a bond only for the interest payments.) For an old bond, it is the future stream of interest earnings, when considered in relation to the market rate of interest, that determines its market value. The higher the market rate of interest, the lower the market value that a given bond can command and vice versa.

For example, on a bond with a face value of $100 and 5% interest, the bondholder would receive $5 per year in the absence of default. Suppose that the market rate of interest for an investment with the same risk is 10%. What is the maximum amount that an investor would be willing to pay for the bond according to its earning power? The answer is $50 for a simple reason. The owner of the $50 can earn $5 per year either by lending the money out at a 10% interest rate or by purchasing a new bond with a face value of $50 which bears 10% interest. In other words, any bond that pays interest in the amount of $5 annually does not command a market value of more than $50 when the market rate of interest is 10%. However, if the market rate of interest decreases to 2.5%, then someone would be willing to pay $200 for the bond because of its relative earning power. Hence, the market rate of interest and bond prices are inversely related.

Since the Federal Reserve banks are the biggest holders of federal bonds, the demand for and the supply of bonds to them are not perfectly elastic. When the Federal Reserve System decides to sell a large volume of government bonds, it tends to suppress the bond price and thus raise the true interest rate.

Conversely, when the Federal Reserve System decides to buy large quantities of government bonds in the market, it tends to raise the price of the bonds and thus suppress the true interest rate. Hence, the Federal Reserve System can, to a certain extent, control the market rate of interest through the sale or purchase of government bonds. This is one aspect of open market operations.

In macroeconomics, the effects of open market operations on the money supply are often stressed. When the Federal Reserve banks sell government bonds, the reserves that commercial banks must maintain against their deposits will be reduced, and their ability (taken together as a system) to make loans will be reduced by a multiple of the reduction of their reserves due to the fractional reserve requirements imposed on bank deposits. This reaction will, in turn, put pressure on the market rate of interest. Conversely, when the Federal Reserve banks purchase government bonds in the open market, it tends to reduce the market rate of interest by increasing the reserves and lending ability of commercial banks.

It should be noted that the sale of government bonds by the Federal Reserve banks works on the market rate of interest in two different ways. On the one hand, large amounts of bond sales suppress bond prices, thus raising interest rates. This effect is direct. On the other hand, the sale of bonds will also reduce the money supply and the ability of the commercial banks to make loans, which again will put pressure on market rate of interest. Although this effect is indirect, it is nonetheless effective.

In the last few decades, monetary policy has become an increasingly important instrument of central governments in their attempt to influence, if not control, not only the price level, but also the level of income. Some economists have gone so far as to argue that both the price level and the income level of an economy are essentially determined by the money supply. For this reason, these economists are often labeled as *monetarists*. Regardless of one's belief, the fact is that the market rate of interest is under the tight control (if not strict regulation) of the Federal Reserve System in the United States (and of the central banks of other countries). However, there is a considerable body of literature that questions how effective the Federal Reserve actually is in controlling interest rates. In fact, some economists feel that the Federal Reserve actually follows rather than leads the market and, therefore, that its effective control is doubtful. Such observations notwithstanding, the power to induce expansions and contractions in the money supply does constitute an intervention in the market with which static demand–supply analysis cannot adequately deal, particularly as it applies to the determination of the market rate of interest. Therefore, more complex models of interest rate determination are necessary.

Such models are beyond the scope of this book and are reserved for special courses in advanced analysis.

SUMMARY

In this chapter we examined the different supply conditions that are applicable to labor, land, and capital and showed how the price–quantity relationships for the factors of production are determined by the market condition that prevails. We showed that the labor supplied by individual workers is determined by their preference for leisure as opposed to money income, and that the individual worker's supply curve can be derived from the locus of equilibrium points on the worker's indifference map. It was explained that the supply curve for labor, while usually positively sloped in the lower wage range, may bend backward and become negatively sloped at higher wage rates. We then showed that, if each worker's labor supply is independent of those of other workers, the market supply curve for labor can be secured by a horizontal summing of the supply curves of the individual workers, and that the market supply curve may then exhibit a backward bend at high wage rates. In such a case, the equilibrium wage rate given by the intersection of the demand and supply curves may not be unique, but rather stable at the lower wage rates and unstable at high wage rates.

We proceeded to distinguish between the price–quantity equilibrium conditions for labor in perfect competition and in imperfect markets. It was demonstrated that, whereas the equilibrium wage and quantity under perfect competition is given by the intersection of the supply and demand curves for labor, this is not the case under monopsony. Instead, the monopsonist's marginal expenditure (ME) curve is above the corresponding positively sloped supply curve of labor and, therefore, the profit-maximization objective of the monopsonist requires equality between ME and VMP if the product market is one of perfect competition, and between ME and MRP if the product market is one of imperfect competition (i.e., monopoly, oligopoly, or monopolistic competition). We also showed that, since the supply curve for labor under monopsony is below the ME curve, the market price (wage rate) will be lower than ME and, according to the type of product market, either VMP or MRP.

It was explained that a monopsonist in the labor market may sometimes face a strong union with monopoly power on the supply side. When that is the case, a condition of bilateral monopoly is said to exist and the wage rate and quantity are theoretically indeterminant. Hence, the final wage and quantity under bilateral monopoly will depend on the relative strength of the two protagonists.

In contrast to that of labor, the supply of land was described as fixed and, as a result, the market price of land (usually called rent) depends on demand alone. Thus, the higher the level of demand, the higher the rent. We also explained that the concept of rent can be extended to those factors that exhibit unique or special characteristics, such as works of art or sports and cinema celebrities. In such cases, the high prices paid for the talent or special characteristics of the object sold are considered as a payment over and above what the resource could earn in an alternative use. We defined this differential as economic or quasi-rent and indicated that it is, as in the case of land, demand determined.

Finally, we directed attention to the price of capital (the interest rate), which in traditional capital theory is based on the time-preference and savings habits of consumers on the supply side and the present value of the income stream of invested capital on the demand side. We explained that under perfect competition and perfect foresight the interest rate is the price of capital, but that, in reality, the financial market is far removed from perfect competition. We noted that instead capital rationing by large institutions, together with the significant role the Federal government plays in capital markets, precludes any meaningful exposition of traditional capital theory. We then described how the use of the rediscount rate and open market operations by the Federal Reserve influences the market rate of interest and the price of bonds in the market.

EXERCISES AND QUESTIONS FOR CHAPTER 11 ON FACTOR SUPPLY AND FACTOR PRICES

1. The owner of a tract of land in downtown Minneapolis claims that he is perfectly free to set his price at any level whatsoever because the supply of that particular kind of land is perfectly inelastic. Is he correct? Explain. (Clearly state the assumptions that are implicit in your response.)

2. In your own words, explain in terms of substitution and income effects why the supply curve for labor may be negatively sloped in the range of high wage rates?

3. Many professional basketball, football, and baseball players in the United States earn an annual income of hundreds of thousands of dollars for less than one-half year's work. On the other hand, athletes in many other countries (in particular, poor countries) whose skills in the same sports are equal (if not superior) to those of the professionals in the United States do not earn nearly as much. How can economic theory explain this apparent paradox? Explain.

4. What do we mean by economic rent? Can a productive factor other than land earn an economic rent? Explain.

5. What are the essential differences between the supply of a produced good and that of a productive factor in a perfectly competitive market? Explain.

6. What are the conceptual differences between the demand for a consumption good and the demand for a productive factor? Explain.

7. In your opinion, how are market interest rates determined? Explain.

8. Why do banks charge their most-favored customers a lower interest rate (the prime rate) and other customers a higher rate? Explain.

9. If perfect competition prevailed in the money market, everyone would be able to borrow a reasonable amount of funds at the going market interest rate. Can you borrow a few thousand dollars even if you are willing to pay a little higher interest rate than the market rate? In particular, do you think you can borrow a reasonable amount of funds to start a profitable business after your graduation? Give reasons for your response.

10. In your own words, explain why higher land rent cannot cause a higher price for corn, but a higher price for corn may cause higher land rent.

11. Explain why wage rates under bilateral monopoly are indeterminate.

APPENDIX TO CHAPTER 11

A MATHEMATICAL NOTE ON FACTOR SUPPLY AND FACTOR PRICES

A11.1 THE SUPPLY OF LABOR

For the exposition at hand, we can state that the satisfaction (utility) workers derive depends on their income from work and the amount of leisure time at their disposal. Thus, the utility function for an individual worker can be written

$$U = U(S, M) \tag{A11.1}$$

where S (as in the text) denotes leisure time, and M denotes the amount of money earned from work.

If we use T to denote the total amount of time at the worker's disposal and L to denote the work time, then we have

$$T = S + L \tag{A11.2}$$

Suppose that we are talking about 1 day and that the unit of measure for time is 1 hour; then $T = 24$. If the worker works 8 hours, then $L = 8$ and $S = 16$, since, by definition, the time that is not used in work is considered to be leisure time.

By definition, money income is equal to the wage rate multiplied by the hours of work:

$$M = wL \tag{A11.3}$$

where w is the wage rate.

Consider work as the decision variable. By substitution, the worker's satisfaction (utility) becomes a function of work alone, which can be expressed mathematically as

$$U = U(T - L, wL) \tag{A11.4}$$

where T and w are constants, and L (work time) is variable.

The first-order condition for utility maximization is

$$dU/dL = -U_S + U_M w = 0 \tag{A11.5}$$

where U_S is defined as $\partial U/\partial S$ and U_M is defined as $\partial U/\partial M$.
From (A11.5), we have

$$U_S/U_M = w \tag{A11.6}$$

Expression (A11.6) is equivalent to (11.6) in the text. The left side of (A11.6) is the marginal rate of substitution between leisure and money, whereas the right side is the wage rate, which is, theoretically, the price ratio, since the price of leisure is the wage rate that the worker must forgo and the price of money (which is omitted) is equal to one. Hence, the first-order conditions for utility maximization in the labor market and the commodity market are technically identical.

Since both U_S and U_M are functions of L, T, and w, and L is the only variable, we see that, in principle, (A11.6) can be solved for L in terms of T and w. Assuming that an explicit solution exists, we can write the solution in the following form:

$$L = S(w) \tag{A11.7}$$

which is the supply function of labor. Since T is a constant, it is omitted in (A11.7).

The second-order condition for utility maximization requires that

$$d^2U/dL^2 = U_{SS} - 2wU_{SM} + w^2 U_{MM} < 0 \tag{A11.8}$$

where

$$U_{SS} = \partial^2 U/\partial S^2$$

$$U_{SM} = \partial^2 U/\partial M \partial S = \partial^2 U/\partial S \partial M = U_{MS}$$

$$U_{MM} = \partial^2 U/\partial M^2$$

are all second-order partial derivatives of the utility function.

For the purpose of illustration, assume that the utility function is

$$U = M^a S^b \tag{A11.9}$$

Then the labor supply of an individual will be

$$L = aT/(a + b)^1 \tag{A11.10}$$

---

[1] Since

$$U_S = bM^a S^{b-1} \quad \text{and} \quad U_M = aM^{a-1}S^b$$

we have

$$bM/aS = w$$

(Footnote continues on next page)

The labor supply is not a function of the wage rate, but only depends on the parameters of the utility function. This is the result of the specific utility function that has been postulated. A different utility function will result in a different labor supply function, which shows that the supply of labor depends on the preference pattern of the worker, since the utility function represents the worker's preference. For example, if the utility function is

$$U = MS + S \tag{A11.9'}$$

then

$$U_M = S \quad \text{and} \quad U_S = M + 1$$

Corresponding to the expression

$$U_S/U_M = w \tag{A11.6}$$

(the first-order condition for utility maximization), we have

$$(1 + M)/S = w$$

which by substitution yields

$$(1 + wL)/(T - L) = w$$

(It is easily seen that the second-order condition for utility maximization is satisfied.) Solving for L, we obtain the labor supply function of an individual worker:

$$L = T/2 - 1/2w^2 \tag{A11.10'}$$

Thus, the supply of labor is a function of the wage rate w. The upper limit of working hours is $T/2$. When the wage rate approaches infinity, the worker works 12 hours per day. When the wage rate decreases, the work time will decrease accordingly. The supply of labor is an increasing function of the wage rate, since we have

$$dL/dw = 1/2w^2 > 0$$

A11.2 THE DETERMINATION OF FACTOR PRICE (WAGE RATE) UNDER CONDITIONS OF MONOPOLY AND MONOPSONY

For the sake of simplicity, suppose that labor is the only variable input and that monopsony prevails in the labor market, whereas monopoly prevails in the product market. Consider labor as an

---

(Footnote 1 continued)   corresponding to

$$U_S/U_M = w$$

Substituting (A11.2) and (A11.3) into the above expression, we obtain

$$bwL/a(T - L) = w$$

Expression (A11.10) follows.

independent variable. Then the profit function can be written

$$\pi = f(L)D[f(L)] - C_0 - LS(L) \tag{A11.11}$$

Expression (A11.11) is based on the definition that profit is equal to total revenue minus total cost. The production function is

$$Q = f(L) \tag{A11.12}$$

where Q denotes the quantity of the output. Since monopoly prevails in the product market, the price of the product P is a function of Q. We can state the demand (rather, the inverse demand) function of the output as

$$P = D(Q) \tag{A11.13}$$

By substitution, the total revenue is

$$R = f(L)D[f(L)]$$

Since monopsony prevails in the labor market, the wage rate w is a function of the quantity of labor L (along the labor supply curve):

$$w = S(L) \tag{A11.14}$$

Since C_0 is the total fixed cost, the total cost is

$$C = C_0 + LS(L).$$

If we switch the notation to variables from functions, then the first-order condition for profit maximization can be written

$$\frac{d\pi}{dL} = \left(P + Q\frac{dP}{dQ}\right)\frac{dQ}{dL} - w - L\frac{dw}{dL} = 0 \tag{A11.15}$$

or

$$\left(P + Q\frac{dP}{dQ}\right)\frac{dQ}{dL} = w + L\frac{dw}{dL} \tag{A11.15'}$$

The left side of (A11.15′) is the marginal revenue product (MRP), whereas the right side is the marginal expenditure (ME). When perfect competition prevails in the output market, $dP/dQ = 0$, and the left side of (A11.15′) becomes the value of the marginal product (VMP). When perfect competition prevails in the labor market, $dw/dL = 0$, and the marginal expenditure becomes the wage rate. With a positively sloped supply curve for labor, $dw/dL > 0$; thus, ME $> w$ for $L > 0$. This proves the relationship between S and ME as given in Figure 11.8. Assuming that the second-order condition for profit maximization is satisfied, the equilibrium quantity of labor can be obtained from (A11.15′).

It may seem that one would be able to directly solve (A11.15′) for the monopsony wage rate w by simple subtraction of the second term on the right from the left side. However, this is not correct, since Q, P, and the derivatives are all functions of L.

What we have is an expression of the wage rate as a function of the quantity of labor, not a solution for the equilibrium wage rate in the monopsony market. Some economists make a similar mistake in their treatment of a monopoly market by using the expression for marginal revenue,

$$MR = P(1 - 1/e)$$

where e is the price elasticity of demand, in solving for the monopoly price under the condition of constant AVC. With this assumption, MC equals AVC V_0, and since the first-order condition for profit maximization requires that $MR = MC$, it is concluded that the profit-maximizing price for the monopoly is

$$P^* = V_0/(1 - 1/e)$$

In general, this is not correct, since the price elasticity of demand e is a function of the quantity Q. This expression shows implicitly that P is a function of Q, not a solution for P^*. (For details on this point, see Chapter 7.)

The correct way to make use of (A11.15') is to solve for the equilibrium quantity of labor. Since P, Q, and all of the derivatives are functions of L, so is the wage rate w [according to (A11.14)], and the equation actually involves only one variable: L. If we assume that (A11.15') can be solved explicit for L in terms of the parameters of the production function, the demand function of the product, and the supply function of labor, then the solution corresponds to L_0 in Figure 11.8. The equilibrium wage rate in the monopsony market is derived by substituting L_0 into the labor supply function (A11.14). The wage rate corresponds to w_0 in Figure 11.8.

It should be pointed out that, in general, an explicit expression for labor L in terms of the parameters of (A11.15') may not exist, and that even if it does exist, the solution may not be unique (for the latter case, see, e.g., p. 241 in Henderson and Quandt, 1971). When we assume that an explicit and unique solution for L exists in (A11.15'), we are in fact dealing with a small class of many possible production and demand functions of the product and the supply function of labor.

When there is more than one variable input, the mathematics for the input markets is more complicated but still manageable. In this case, the revenue part of the profit function is identical to that in the previous simple one-variable-input case, except that the production function will involve all of the variable inputs. On the other hand, the cost part of the profit function will involve all of the quantities and supply functions of the inputs. Suppose that there are n inputs with quantities $X_1, X_2, ..., X_n$ and prices $r_1, r_2, ..., r_n$, respectively, and that monopsony exists in all n input markets (i.e., their supplies will be functions of all of the input prices. The inverse supply functions can be written

$$r_1 = S_1(X_1, X_2, ..., X_n)$$
$$r_2 = S_2(X_1, X_2, ..., X_n)$$

$$\vdots$$

$$r_n = S_n(X_1, X_2, ..., X_n)$$

(A11.16)

and the profit function can be written

$$\pi = f(X_1, X_2, ..., X_n)D[f(X_1, X_2, ..., X_n)]$$
$$- C_0 - \sum_{i=1}^{n} X_i S_i(X_1, X_2, ..., X_n)$$

(A11.17)

For short-run analysis, $C_0 > 0$, and for long-run analysis, $C_0 = 0$, since fixed cost is zero in the long run. The first-order conditions for profit maximization are

$$\partial\pi/\partial X_i = (P + QdP/dQ)\partial Q/\partial X_i - r_i$$
$$- \sum_{j=1}^{n} X_j \partial r_j/\partial X_i = 0, \qquad i = 1, 2, ..., n$$

(A11.18)

or

$$(P + QdP/dQ)\partial Q/\partial X_i = r_i + \sum_{j=1}^{n} X_j \partial r_j/\partial X_i, \qquad i = 1, 2, ..., n$$

(A11.18′)

Assuming that the second-order conditions for profit maximization are satisfied, the solution of the n equations (A11.18′) in the n variables $X_1, X_2, ..., X_n$ yields the equilibrium quantities of the n inputs $X_1^*, X_2^*, ..., X_n^*$. Substituting these values into the supply functions (A11.16), we obtain the equilibrium input prices $r_1^*, r_2^*, ..., r_n^*$. These arguments are again based on the implicit assumption that the Xs can be solved for in the system of equations (A11.18′) and that the solution is both nonnegative and unique. We are actually dealing with a small class of the many possible production and demand functions of the output and the supply functions of the inputs.

The left side of the ith equation in (A11.18′) is the MRP of input X_i and the right side is the ME of X_i. Furthermore, the term $P + QdP/dQ$ is the MR of the output, which is identical for all inputs, and the term $\partial Q/\partial X_i$ is the MP of input X_i. If the ith equation in (A11.18′) is divided by the jth equation, then the term $P + QdP/dQ$ cancels out. Rearranging terms, we obtain (11.11) in the text. This proves our assertion made in the text that Equation (11.11) is identical to the conditions for maximum output at a given cost or minimum cost for a given output.

The difficulty of graphically deriving the equilibrium quantity and price when two or more variable inputs are involved can easily be seen from the first-order conditions of profit maximization and the supply functions of the inputs. Each of the n equations in (A11.18') involves all of the n inputs, not just the one concerned, because all the quantities of the inputs are interrelated. Furthermore, the supply price of the ith input is also a function of all the inputs. In terms of two-dimensional graphs, when the quantity of the jth input changes, the supply curve for the ith input shifts and vice versa. This is true because the supply curve for the ith input is obtained for given values of the quantity of all of the other inputs. Hence, with a different value for even one quantity of the other inputs, we obtain a different supply curve for the ith input. Since the equilibrium quantities of the other inputs are not known before that of the ith input is known, the supply curve of the ith input is not known before its quantity is known. Without knowing the supply curve of the ith input, there is no way to determine its equilibrium quantity. In mathematics, we do not encounter this difficulty, since all the Xs are solved for simultaneously. Thus, the interrelationship between them is taken into account. This is one of the advantages of mathematics (and, correspondingly, one of the disadvantages of the graphical method) in economics.

A11.3 COMPOUND INTEREST AND DISCOUNTED PRESENT VALUE OF FUTURE INCOME

Suppose that the annual interest rate on money deposited in a financial institution is 5%. Then $100 deposited today will be worth $105 one year from now. If the $105 is left in the account, 5% interest is paid on that amount for the second year, that is, $5.25, and so the investment grows to $110.25 at the end of the second year (and so forth). The question is: Can we obtain a simple expression for the compound interest after t years at an annual interest rate i? The answer is yes.

If an amount A_0 is deposited in a bank at an annual interest rate i compounded annually, then at the end of the first year A_0 becomes the sum of the principal A_0 plus the interest payment iA_0. If we denote this value by A_1, we then have

$$A_1 = A_0 + iA_0 = A_0(1 + i) \qquad \text{(A11.19)}$$

At the end of the second year, A_1 becomes the sum of the principal A_1 plus the interest on A_1 that is, iA_1. Denoting the value of the investment at the end of the second year by A_2, we obtain

$$A_2 = A_1 + iA_1 = A_1(1 + i) = A_0(1 + i)^2 \qquad \text{(A11.20)}$$

where we have substituted (A11.19) into (A11.20) in the second step of the above algebra. Similarly, the value of the investment at the end of the third year becomes A_3, which can be written in the equivalent form

$$A_3 = A_2 + iA_2 = A_2(1 + i) = A_0(1 + i)^3 \qquad \text{(A11.21)}$$

It can easily be seen that, by successive substitution, the total value of the investment at the end of year t is

$$A_t = A_0(1 + i)^t \qquad \text{(A11.22)}$$

Using our numerical example, after 10 years ($t = 10$), the $100 will become $100(1 + 0.05)^{10} = \$162.89$. (It should be noted that a 5% interest rate is written 0.05 not 5.) There are compound interest tables that give values of the term $(1 + i)^t$ for various combinations of i and t. Such tables are very convenient to use; however, even if such a table is not available, the computation of compound interest is a rather easy matter when logarithms are used.

The compound interest formula (A11.22) is only applicable in the simple case where the interest is compounded annually. If the interest is compounded quarterly, then the quarterly interest rate is $i/4$ for an annual interest rate i. Using the above method, for an initial deposit of A_0, the total value of the investment at the end of the first year is

$$A_1 = A_0(1 + i/4)^4 \qquad \text{(A11.23)}$$

The value of A_1 in (A11.19) is smaller than that in (A11.23) because, in the latter, the principal starts to earn interest at the beginning of the second quarter. Using our numerical example, we obtain that $A_1 = \$105$ by (A11.19), whereas $A_1 = \$105.09$ by (A11.23). For quarterly compounded interest, the total value of an initial investment A_0 at the end of year t is

$$A_t = A_0(1 + i/4)^{4t} \qquad \text{(A11.24)}$$

It can easily be shown that with continuous (instantaneous) compounding the formula becomes

$$A_t = A_0 e^{ti} \qquad \text{(A11.25)}$$

where $e = 2.71828$ is the base for the system of natural logarithms. For example, with $t = 1$ and $i = 0.05$, $e^{0.05} = 1.0512$ (approximately). This implies that an annual interest rate of 5% compounded on a continuous basis is effectively equal to an annual interest rate of approximately 5.12%.

To discount income received at some future date into present value, we reverse the process of compounding interest. As a simple example, suppose that a student was given $105 in the form of a one-year note (not cash) by a rich relative as a reward for receiving good grades. Since the student's relative is the president of the local bank, the credit rating of the note is not in question; that is, after 1 year, the note is just as good as cash. However, assume that the student is impatient and wants to spend the money now. How much can the student get from the bank for the note? The answer is that it depends on the interest rate. With this risk-free note, the bank will give the student X dollars, which, with the interest payment on the X dollars, is equal to $105 at the end of one year. If the interest rate is 5%, then the interest on X dollars is $0.05X$. Thus, we have

$$X + 0.05X = 105$$

or

$$X = 105/(1 + 0.05) = \$100$$

We can see that the bank is willing to do this because, to the bank, it is equivalent to making a risk-free loan. When the bank advances $100 today on the student's note, it will get back $105 one year later. Thus, it can be observed that there is no difference between this transaction and a loan of $100 for one year, provided that, as in this case, there is no risk involved.

In our numerical example, the $100 is called the *discounted present value* of $105 received one year hence at an interest rate of 5%. In general, we can state that the present value of a given amount of income received at some future date is the amount of money required to accumulate a sum of funds (principal plus interest) that is equal to the future income. Thus, the present value of a given income received at some future date depends on the interest rate and the length of time intervening before the income will be realized. If the future income (or revenue received one year from now) is R_1 and the interest rate is i, then we can obtain the present value of that income if we designate the present value by X and set X according to (A11.19) to satisfy

$$X(1 + i) = R_1$$

This will yield the solution

$$X = R_1/(1 + i)$$

Similarly, if a future income or revenue received two years from now is R_2, then the present value X of R_2 must satisfy

$$X(1 + i)^2 = R_2$$

which yields the solution

$$X = R_2/(1 + i)^2$$

If we denote the discounted present value by V and the future income n years from now by R_n, then at an interest rate i we have the following discounted present value formula for R_n,[2]

$$V = R_n/(1 + i)^n \qquad\qquad (A11.26)$$

In economics, capital theory usually must consider the situation of a future income stream as opposed to a one-time-only payment at some future date. For example, if one buys a truck to engage in the moving business, and it is known that the income from the operation for the first year will be R_1, the second year R_2, and the third year R_3, then we might wish to know the present value of this income stream. According to (A11.26), the discounted present value is

$$V_1 = R_1/(1 + i)$$

for R_1,

$$V_2 = R_2/(1 + i)^2$$

for R_2, and

$$V_3 = R_3/(1 + i)^3$$

for R_3. The discounted present value of the income stream is the sum of the discounted present values for the individual future incomes. If we denote the discounted present value of the income stream by V, we have, for our example,

$$V = R_1/(1 + i) + R_2/(1 + i)^2 + R_3/(1 + i)^3 \qquad (A11.27)$$

In general, if the income stream involves n years, R_1, R_2, ..., R_n denote the annual incomes, and we are given the interest rate i, the discounted present value V of these incomes is

$$V = R_1/(1 + i) + R_2/(1 + i)^2 + \cdots + R_n/(1 + i)^n \qquad (A11.28)$$

Formula (A11.28) may look simple, but the computation of V is not an easy matter even with log tables when the income is not

---

[2] The student should be careful to note that so far we have been considering a given payment at the end of n years. We shall in a moment see that this is different from receiving payments of money at periodic intervals over n years. The latter can be treated as an annuity, in which case the receipts of each individual payment is discounted back to the present and the discounted values then summed up. Thus, an income stream of $60 per year for 5 years can be discounted into present value at a market rate of interest of 8% as follows:

$$\frac{\$60}{(1 + 0.08)} + \frac{\$60}{(1 + 0.08)^2} + \frac{\$60}{(1 + 0.08)^3} + \frac{\$60}{(1 + 0.08)^4} + \frac{\$60}{(1 + 0.08)^5}$$

This is different from discounting $300 received 5 years hence into present value. In this case, we would have $\$300/(1 + 0.08)^5$. Thus, an income stream of $60 per year (or a total of $300) for 5 years yields a present value different from a single payment of $300 at the end of 5 years.

a constant; that is, $R_i \neq R_j$ for $i \neq j$. Furthermore, we cannot reduce the large number of terms on the right into a compact expression with few terms. However, a simple formula relating V, on the one hand, and the interest rate and income, on the other hand, can be obtained for the special case where the income stream is a constant, that is, $R_1 = R_2 = \cdots = R_n$. Denoting the constant income stream by R, we have

$$V = R/(1 + i) + R/(1 + i)^2 + \cdots + R/(1 + i)^n \qquad (A11.29)$$

When n is infinitely large, (A11.29) becomes an infinite series. In this special case, (A11.29) can be reduced to a simple expression. The mathematical manipulation begins by multiplying both sides of (A11.29) by $1/(1 + i)$, so that the equality still holds:

$$V/(1 + i) = R/(1 + i)^2 + R/(1 + i)^3$$
$$+ \cdots + R/(1 + i)^n + R/(1 + i)^{n+1} \qquad (A11.30)$$

The right side of (A11.30) has the same number of terms as does that of (A11.29). Furthermore, $n - 1$ of the terms are identical in the two series, namely,

$$R/(1 + i)^2 + \cdots + R/(1 + i)^n$$

and the sum of these $n - 1$ terms is present in both series. On the other hand, each series has an extra term that the other does not have: The term $R/(1 + i)$ is present in (A11.29) but not in (A11.30), whereas the term $R/(1 + i)^{n+1}$ is present in (A11.30) but not in (A11.29). This phenomenon makes it possible to reduce this infinite series into a finite number of terms.

Subtracting (A11.30) from (A11.29) on both sides of the equality sign, we can see that the equality still holds. This operation eliminates all of the terms common to both series on the right side, leaving only the extra terms. Thus, we have

$$V - V/(1 + i) = R/(1 + i) - R/(1 + i)^{n+1}$$

Since $i > 0$, $1 + i > 1$, and $(1 + i)^{n+1}$ becomes infinitely large when $n \to \infty$. For a finite R, $R/(1 + i)^{n+1} \to 0$ as $n \to \infty$. Therefore, this term can be ignored for large n. The left side can also be simplified by simple algebraic operations. The above expression can be written

$$Vi/(1 + i) = R/(1 + i)$$

Multiplying both sides by $(1 + i)/i$, we obtain

$$V = R/i \qquad (A11.31)$$

which is the familiar expression for the present value of an infinite, constant income stream R with interest rate i. The following should be pointed out: (1) Expression (A11.31) is only applicable for a constant income stream and (2) (A11.31) is a poor approximation when the income stream does not cover a large number of periods.

Formula (A11.31) is useful in the study or analysis of capital markets. For example, if a bond pays $8 per year forever, its present value is $100 at an 8% interest rate and $200 at a 4% interest rate, regardless of the face value of the bond. If the market value and discounted present value of the income stream from a bond are closely related, then, as we have explained in the text, the market value of the bond will change in the opposite direction of the change in the interest rate.

Formula (A11.31) has considerable theoretical importance in capital theory. For example, if one buys a truck to engage in the moving business, rational behavior implies that the truck will be purchased only if the discounted present value of the income stream is greater than (or at least equal to) the price of the truck. Competition and perfect information imply that the price of the truck must be equal to the present value of the income stream at equilibrium. Therefore, the price of capital goods and, thus, total investment will be a function of the interest rate for a given income stream, and the first derivative of this function will be negative. It follows that, other things being equal, a higher interest rate results in less investment, whereas a lower interest rate induces more investment. This is precisely the demand function of capital, which, in conjunction with the supply of capital in a competitive market, determines the equilibrium interest rate in theory.

As we have explained in the text, the market rate of interest is, to a great extent, controlled by the Federal Reserve System in the United States and central banks in other countries; therefore, the capital market far from represents perfect competition. This means that the importance of traditional demand and supply analysis of the capital market is severely limited. For this reason, we have not devoted space to the deliberate derivation of the supply of capital based on the notion of choice between consumption today and consumption in the future. This is also why we only briefly explained the derivation of the demand for capital. However, we feel that the concepts of compound interest, the discounted value of income received at some future date, and the discounted present value of a future income stream are important in their own right to economists as well as to those who may engage in business. Therefore, we have devoted considerable space to the rationale of these topics. Students who desire a more-detailed discussion of these topics should consult any good text on the theory and practice of finance.

GENERAL EQUILIBRIUM
AND WELFARE ECONOMICS

In Parts III and IV, we discussed commodity and factor markets under various degrees of competition. Under perfect competition, market equilibrium was characterized by a single market price that equated demand and supply. Under imperfect competition (e.g., monopoly), we noted that the concept of supply was no longer meaningful in the product market. However, we stated that market demand, in conjunction with cost, could still determine a unique market price and quantity. It was implied that all participants in the market are satisfied at equilibrium; that is, the satisfaction (utility) of all consumers and the profits of all producers are maximized under the given circumstances. Thus, market equilibrium implies certain optimality conditions.

Another assumption that has been present up to now in our analysis of the behavior in a specific market is that all of the other markets were already in equilibrium. Furthermore, it was implied that all of the other markets would remain in equilibrium even if the market under analysis underwent a certain change. In other words, the interrelationship between markets was ignored in our previous analyses. This method of study is called *partial analysis,* in contrast to *general equilibrium analysis*. The concept of partial analysis was inherent to our treatment of the demand function in Chapter 6, where it was shown that the market demand for a commodity is, in general, a function of the price of all of the commodities as well as of the income and population of an economy [see (5.1)]. Under the "other things being equal" assumption, the prices of all the commodities other than the one under consideration, as well as the income and population, were assumed to be constant. Consequently, the demand for a commodity was considered only as a function of its own price, as indicated by (5.2). Similarly, our treatment of the supply function under

Partial analysis ignores interrelationships between markets. General equilibrium analysis treats all relevant variables simultaneously

perfect competition was subject to the same type of limiting assumption.

One of the problems with partial analysis is that it can only be considered as giving a first approximation of the outcome resulting from a change in conditions. A more-realistic approach is provided by general equilibrium analysis, in which all of the relevant variables are taken into consideration simultaneously. As a result, the interrelationship between markets is fully taken into account in the analysis. On the other hand, since there are so many relevant variables involved in the analysis of all of the markets on a simultaneous basis, the graphical method is for the most part useless. Even with the help of advanced mathematics, general equilibrium analysis is still a very difficult topic. Although considerable progress has been made in the advanced theory of this method in the last few decades, many problems remain unsolved. This is one area of economics which requires more research and effort. Given the intended level of this book, we shall be forced to use only the simplest examples to illustrate the essentials of the more-general approach.

Welfare economics (which has nothing to do with government welfare programs) is a topic that is related to the general equilibrium approach. The objective of welfare economics is to develop a theoretical framework and criteria for evaluating the desirability of economic alternatives with respect to resource allocation and the distribution of the rewards from economic activity. The evaluation of alternative forms of resource allocation and the different methods of distributing the commodities and services of an economy can only be carried out in a general equilibrium setting. This is why we, as well as many other economists, group general equilibrium analysis and welfare economics together.

The theoretical development of welfare economics largely involves a level of advanced mathematics which is beyond the scope of this book. Thus, we can only acquaint the student with the fundamental ideas and important theorems in welfare economics. In most cases, we shall not attempt to prove the theorems formally but only to provide an explanation of their meaning and economic significance. Chapter 12 is devoted to a discussion of general equilibrium, and Chapter 13 covers the topic of welfare economics.

GENERAL EQUILIBRIUM IN PERFECTLY COMPETITIVE MARKETS

INTRODUCTION

The development of general equilibrium analysis was pioneered by the French economist Leon Walras (see Walras, 1874). He developed the model which showed that general equilibrium is consistent with an economic system in which perfect competition prevails in each and every market. That is to say, if all buyers and sellers were price takers, then it would be possible to have a set of prices (one price for each market) such that all markets would *clear* (i.e., demand would equal supply in every market) and all participants would realize their greatest satisfaction (utility) under the given circumstances.

Walras showed the perfect competition model to be consistent with general equilibrium

Although Walras' result was quite an accomplishment at the time, he left many important questions unanswered. First of all, he had only shown that it was possible to solve for a set of prices from a system of equations—he had not shown that an explicit solution for the prices would always exist. In technical terms, he had shown a necessary but not sufficient condition for the existence of general equilibrium. Although the necessary and sufficient conditions would guarantee that such a set of prices could be achieved in the market, the necessary condition alone is not enough. Secondly, even if it is ensured that a set of prices can be mathematically solved for from a system of equations, it is possible that some of the prices and/or the equilibrium quantities in the solution may be negative, imaginary, or complex numbers. In order to make economic sense, all of the prices and quantities must be real and nonnegative. Finally, the third problem is that for each market there may be more than one price and/or quantity consistent with the system of equations. Recent advanced work (mostly mathematical) has been directed at solving these delicate problems.

As we noted earlier, in the text we shall use only simple examples to illustrate the rationale—but not the theoretical details—of the general equilibrium model. Moreover, we shall avoid advanced mathematics even in the appendix. In Section 12.1, we shall use a two-person–two-commodity model to illustrate the concept of general equilibrium in pure exchange without production. In Section 12.2, we shall use a two-input–two-output model to illustrate the existence of general equilibrium in production. In Section 12.3, a general equilibrium model of exchange and production for the simple two-input–two-output–two producer case will be demonstrated. In Section 12.4, the condition for general equilibrium will be discussed. The Walras model, together with some of the new developments in general equilibrium analysis, will be briefly discussed in Section 12.5. Section 12.6 and 12.7 are devoted to a brief description of the Leontief input–output model and its use for analyzing interdependencies in the economy.

12.1 PURE EXCHANGE: THE TWO-PERSON–TWO COMMODITY CASE; CONTRACT AND OFFER CURVES

Our simple model assumes the absence of production; that is, we have a given amount of commodity X and a given amount of commodity Y, which are owned by A and B. We further assume that the preference patterns of A and B satisfy the assumptions concerning the behavior of a rational consumer which were explained in Chapter 4. Consequently, there exists a set of indifference maps for A and B which possess the desirable properties: decreasing MRS, continuous and smooth indifference curves, and so forth. In addition, both A and B are utility maximizers, and we assume the absence of externalities. Our goal is to determine the conditions under which exchange between A and B will result in maximum satisfaction (utility) for both. Since the analysis in this section is essentially an application of the theory of consumer behavior as developed in Chapter 4, it might be beneficial for students to review that chapter before proceeding.

In exchange the possibility exists for an increase in satisfaction to both consumers

Suppose that A originally has X_A^0 of X and Y_A^0 of Y. This status quo bundle of commodities is represented by point S on indifference curve 2A in Figure 12.1. We have also drawn indifference curves 3A and 4A, which represent higher levels of satisfaction (utility) than indifference curve 2A.

In the absence of exchange, A is stuck with satisfaction (utility) level 2A, that is, no improvement is possible. However, once exchange between X and Y is introduced, there exists the possibility that the satisfaction (utility) level of A may be raised. Whether this is possible depends on the exchange ratio or the relative prices of X and Y.

It was shown in Chapter 4 that a consumer's satisfaction (util-

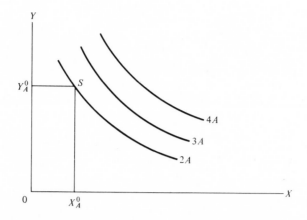

FIGURE 12.1

ity) is maximized for a given budget and an interior solution if his or her budget line is tangent to an indifference curve. This condition was referred to as a *consumer's equilibrium*. Thus, in order to determine A's equilibrium, we must know A's budget.

Since our model is that of a barter system, no money is involved. However, since the budget in Chapter 4 was given in terms of a fixed money income, we shall, for the reader's convenience, imagine that there is such a thing called money. Although this is not essential to our argument, it will facilitate the student's understanding; that is, we shall introduce the concepts of prices and money because students are more familiar and comfortable with such a presentation.

We begin our discussion of the construct of an *offer curve* (this term will be defined later on) by noting that the market value of the bundle of commodities (in our case, X_A^0 and Y_A^0) obviously depends on the respective market prices of the two commodities. If the prices for X and Y are P_X^0 and P_Y^0, respectively, then the market value of the bundle can be expressed as

$$M^0 = X_A^0 P_X^0 + Y_A^0 P_Y^0 \qquad (12.1)$$

where M^0 can be considered A's income or budget. On the other hand, if the prices for the two commodities are P_X^1 and P_Y^1, respectively, then the market value of the same bundle (and thus A's income or budget) is

$$M^1 = X_A^0 P_X^1 + Y_A^0 P_Y^1 \qquad (12.2)$$

where M^1 may be either greater or less than M^0. Actually, this is irrelevant to our analysis. The important thing to understand is how these two budget lines are related.

From Chapter 4, it can be seen that the budget line (equation) for the set of prices P_X^0 and P_Y^0 can be written

$$Y_A = M^0/P_Y^0 - (P_X^0/P_Y^0)X_A \qquad (12.3)$$

By substituting (12.1) into (12.3) and simplifying, (12.3) can be written in the equivalent form

$$Y_A = Y_A^0 - (P_X^0/P_Y^0)(X_A - X_A^0) \tag{12.4}$$

Expression (12.4) implies that $Y_A = Y_A^0$ when $X_A = X_A^0$ (i.e., the status quo) and that the slope of the budget line is $-(P_X^0/P_Y^0)$.

Similarly, when the prices are P_X^1 and P_Y^1, the equation of the budget line can be written

$$Y_A = Y_A^0 - (P_X^1/P_Y^1)(X_A - X_A^0) \tag{12.5}$$

Again, the status quo bundle $\{X_A^0, Y_A^0\}$ is on the new budget line. However, the slope of the new budget line will be P_X^1/P_Y^1, and the new budget line will be flatter (steeper) than the old one if the absolute value of P_X^1/P_Y^1 is less (greater) than that of P_X^0/P_Y^0.

What we have developed is that (1) all of A's budget lines pass through the status quo bundle $\{X_A^0, Y_A^0\}$ and (2) for different relative prices of X and Y, the slopes of the budget lines will be different: The higher (lower) the relative price of X to that of Y, the steeper (flatter) will be the slope of the budget line. It is important to note that the slope of the budget line is related to the relative—not absolute—prices. If both of the prices were doubled or halved, the slope of the budget line would remain the same. In Figure 12.2, we have drawn two of the infinite number of possible budget lines. The relative price of X to that of Y is higher for the budget line $\overline{SA}$ than for the budget line $\overline{SB}$. When the relative price of X to that of Y decreases continuously, the budget line will rotate counterclockwise continuously (S being the fulcrum about which it will rotate).

The slope of the budget line represents relative, not absolute, prices

It should be noted that the characteristics of the budget lines do not depend on the existence of money, since M^0 and M^1 in (12.1) and (12.2) do not have to be interpreted as money income—they can simply be considered mathematical symbols. Whatever they represent, we still obtain (12.4) and (12.5) by substitution. A further indication of the irrelevance of the existence of money

FIGURE 12.2

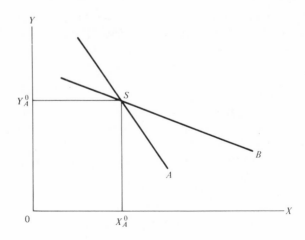

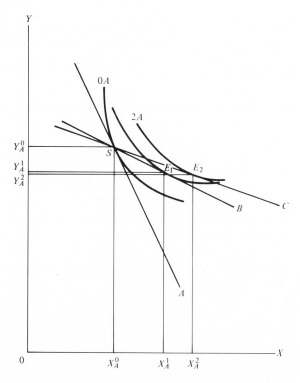

FIGURE 12.3

to the analysis is that it is the relative prices of X and Y—not the absolute prices—that are important to our theory. (Students may wish to refer to our earlier discussion of this point in Chapter 4.)

As was shown in Chapter 4, neither the indifference curves nor the budget lines can indicate the equilibrium of the consumer when considered in isolation. Only when the two sets of information are brought together will the conditions of maximum satisfaction (utility) for a given income be shown. We shall now proceed to do just this.

Consider Figure 12.3, in which the status quo bundle $\{X_A^0, Y_A^0\}$ is on the indifference curve 0_A. If the budget line is $\overline{SA}$, which is tangent to 0_A at point S, then the status quo is A's equilibrium. With the relative prices represented by the budget line $\overline{SA}$, A does not wish to make any exchange even if such an opportunity exists; that is, any exchange would leave A in a worse rather than better position. On the other hand, if the relative price of X with respect to Y goes down, so that the budget line rotates from $\overline{SA}$ to $\overline{SB}$, then we see that $\overline{SB}$ is not tangent to indifference curve 0_A, but instead intersects it at point S. However, we also note that $\overline{SB}$ is tangent to a higher indifference curve—$1A$—at point E_1. If there is any opportunity for trade between X and Y, A will certainly be glad to give up $\overline{Y_A^0 Y_A^1}$ of Y for $\overline{X_A^0 X_A^1}$ of X because he or she will obtain a higher level of satisfaction (utility) from bundle $\{X_A^1, Y_A^1\}$ at point E_1 than from bundle $\{X_A^0, Y_A^0\}$ at point S. Similarly, if the relative price of X with respect to Y goes down further, so that the budget line rotates from $\overline{SB}$ to $\overline{SC}$, then A will give up $\overline{Y_A^1 Y_A^2}$ of Y for $\overline{X_A^1 X_A^2}$ of X, since E_2 is on a higher indifference curve than E_1.

By the above argument, when the relative price of X with respect to Y decreases continuously, the budget line will rotate counterclockwise continuously. Each budget line will be tangent to an indifference curve, such as evidenced by points S, E_1, and E_2 in Figure 12.3. The locus of the infinite number of points of tangency will form a curve, such as SE_1E_2 in Figure 12.3. This curve shows the amount of Y that A is willing to offer in exchange for a certain amount of X when the relative price of X with respect to Y decreases and is hence usually called A's *offer curve*. It should be noted that A's offer curve for Y can also be considered the demand curve for X in a barter system. The important thing to remember is that an offer curve is the locus of different equilibrium points for the consumer.

It can easily be shown that when the relative price of X to that of Y is higher than that represented by the budget line $\overline{SA}$, the point of tangency between the new budget line and an indifference curve will be above the point S and to the right of indifference curve 0_A, since A can be better off only if he or she reaches a higher indifference curve, that is, one to the right of 0_A. From this, it can be inferred that the offer curve is tangent to 0_A at S and that it intersects all other indifference curves. Furthermore, the offer curve has a slope that is not as steep as that of any indifference curve at a point of intersection between the offer curve and the indifference curve which is below S, and whereas the slope of the offer curve is steeper than the slope of any indifference curve at points of intersection above S. In Figure 12.4, 0_A is the indifference curve and OC is the offer curve; both of which pass through S. This relationship between the offer curve and the indifference curves is valid not only for A but also for B. This fact will soon be used in our analysis.

An offer curve represents a consumer's willingness to trade as relative prices change

FIGURE 12.4

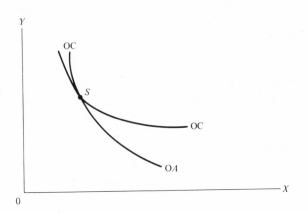

Before we make use of the above result, we must first develop another tool that is very useful for illustrating the logic or essence of both the theory of exchange and the theory of welfare economics: the Edgeworth box.[1] The Edgeworth box is especially useful for illustrating the possible gains that two individuals can attain by trading. Since we are dealing with pure exchange (i.e., no production), the quantity of the commodities can be considered fixed.

Suppose that we have fixed amounts X^0 and Y^0 of the two commodities X and Y which are possessed by the two individuals A and B. Let X_A^0 and Y_A^0 denote the quantities of X and Y originally owned by A. Similarly, let X_B^0 and Y_B^0 denote the quantities of X and Y originally owned by B. By assumption,

$$X^0 = X_A^0 + X_B^0 \quad \text{and} \quad Y^0 = Y_A^0 + Y_B^0$$

This information can be represented in the form of two graphs (one for A and one for B), such as, for example, those given by parts (a) and (b) of Figure 12.5. In part (a), the point $S_A = (X_A^0, Y_A^0)$ represents the status quo for A. Three indifference curves are drawn, and the graph indicates that A is at satisfaction (utility) level $4A$, indifference curve $8A$ representing a higher level of satisfaction (utility), whereas indifference curve $1A$ represents a lower level of satisfaction (utility). However, with the original quantities of the two commodities possessed by A, attainment of a higher level of satisfaction (utility) is impossible. [It should be noted that the numbers used to label the indifference curves only indicate ordering, not absolute magnitudes of satisfaction (utility). For example, bundles on $8A$ represent a higher level of satisfaction (utility) than bundles on $4A$, but not necessarily twice as

The gains from trade depend on the initial amount of commodities held and relative prices

FIGURE 12.5

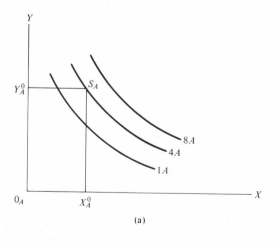

(a)

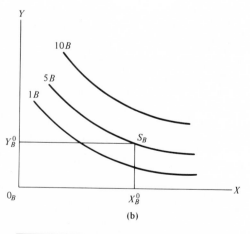

(b)

[1] The first use of this diagram is generally attributed to the English economist Francis Edgeworth.

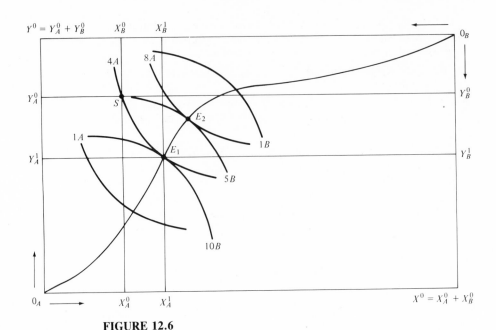

FIGURE 12.6

much. This was explained in detail in Chapter 4.] Similarly, S_B in part (b) of Figure 12.5 represents the status quo for B, and the same observations apply as in the case of part (a) for A.

The Edgeworth box is constructed by rotating B's indifference map by 180°, moving it opposite to A's indifference map, and letting S_A and S_B coincide as in Figure 12.6. What we have done is combine parts (a) and (b) of Figure 12.5 into one graph without any loss of information.

Inasmuch as we shall be making extensive use of the Edgeworth box for the analysis in the following pages, a more-complete description of this tool may be of help to the student. As is obvious from Figure 12.6, an Edgeworth box is rectangular in shape with points of origin for the commodities (in our case, X and Y) represented by the lower-left and upper-right corners. In the case of Figure 12.6, 0_A represents the origin for commodities X and Y possessed by A, whereas 0_B represents the origin for the same commodities possessed by B. For A, the quantity of X is given by the horizontal distance between 0_A and any point to the right (as indicated by the arrow), whereas the quantity of Y is given by the vertical distance between 0_A and any point upward along the left side of the rectangle. For B, the quantity of X is indicated by a leftward movement from 0_B along the top of the rectangle, whereas the quantity of Y is represented by a downward movement from 0_B along the right side of the rectangle. An important feature of Edgeworth box that must be remembered is that the total amount of commodity X is given by the length of the horizontal side (labeled X^0 in Figure 12.6) of the rectangle, whereas the total amount of commodity Y is given by the length of the vertical side (labeled Y^0 in Figure 12.6) of the rectangle. Thus, in our case,

$$X^0 = X_A^0 + X_B^0 \qquad \text{and} \qquad Y^0 = Y_A^0 + Y_B^0$$

where X_A^0 and Y_A^0 represent the amounts possessed by A, and X_A^0 and Y_B^0 represent the amounts possessed by B. In short, the width of the Edgeworth box is determined by the total amount of X possessed by A and B combined, whereas the height of the box is determined by the combined amount of Y possessed by them.

As we noted earlier, the indifference curves for A in Figure 12.6 are identical to those in part (a) of Figure 12.5. Thus, an indifference curve to the right and above another curve represents a higher level of satisfaction (utility). However, B's indifference curves are the opposite of A's; that is, to B a higher level of satisfaction (utility) is represented by a movement to the left and down from one indifference curve to another. Thus, movement from indifference curve $1A$ to indifference curve $4A$ in Figure 12.6 represents a change to a higher level of satisfaction (utility) for A, whereas movement from indifference curve $1B$ to indifference curve $5B$ represents a change to a higher level of satisfaction (utility) for B. Therefore, we can see that a movement from a given point in the box to the right and/or up will result in a higher level of satisfaction (utility) for A, but a lower level of satisfaction (utility) for B. Hence, there is a conflict of interest between A and B. The question is: Do opportunities exist such that trade between A and B may result in benefits to both? The answer is yes—provided that certain conditions exist. Figure 12.6 can be used to validate and illustrate this point.

It can be seen from Figure 12.6 that the status quo position— point S—is on indifference curves $4A$ of A and $5B$ of B. The graph also indicates that indifference curve $4A$ is tangent to indifference curve $10B$ at point E_1, whereas indifference curve $5B$ is tangent to indifference curve $8A$ at point E_2. With this situation, it can easily be seen that if B can trade $\overline{X_B^0 X_B^1}$ of X for $\overline{Y_B^0 Y_B^1}$ of Y, which is the same as A trading $\overline{Y_A^0 Y_A^1} = \overline{Y_B^0 Y_B^1}$ of Y for $\overline{X_A^0 X_A^1} = \overline{X_B^0 X_B^1}$ of X (a movement from the status quo position S to E_1), then, although A will be just as well off as before (since both S and E_1 are on the same indifference curve, that is, $4A$), B's satisfaction (utility) will be increased from $5B$ to $10B$. Consequently, this trade results in a net gain of satisfaction (utility) for B without any loss in satisfaction (utility) for A. Another trading possibility is a movement from S to E_2, which puts B and A on indifference curves $5B$ and $8A$, respectively. By reasoning similar to that above, it can be shown that this trade will result in a net gain of satisfaction (utility) for A without any loss of satisfaction (utility) for B. Between these two extreme cases, there are infinitely many

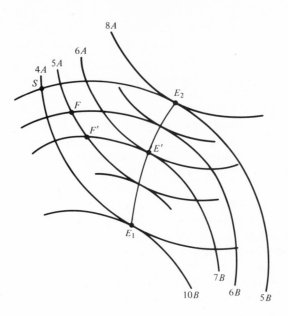

FIGURE 12.7

other possible trades that would benefit both A and B. In order to illustrate this point, let us magnify the area between indifference curves $4A$ and $8A$ of A and $5B$ and $10B$ of B (in particular, the area between indifference curves $4A$ and $5B$) from Figure 12.6.

Consider Figure 12.7, in which the points S, E_1, and E_2 as well as the indifference curves $4A$, $8A$, $5B$, and $10B$ are the same as in Figure 12.6. In addition, we have drawn indifference curves $5A$ and $6B$ of A and B, respectively, such that they intersect at point F. By reasoning similar to that above, if A trades Y for X and B trades X for Y, a movement from S to F will occur, and A's satisfaction (utility) will be raised from $4A$ to $5A$, whereas B's satisfaction (utility) will be raised from $5B$ and $6B$. In contrast to our earlier example, where only one individual benefited (but the other did not lose anything), Figure 12.7 shows that this trade is a good move for both A and B. However, further observation will show that point F, although superior to the status quo S, cannot be considered the end result of trading between A and B. This is true because, starting from point F, there exist such other trading possibilities as F' (which represents an intersection of yet higher imaginary indifference curves) that will benefit both A and B even more. In turn F' cannot be the end result of trading because there are infinitely many other possible trades that could yield a still higher benefit to both A and B. In short, as long as a point is at an intersection of the indifference curves of A and B, there exist other possible trades that will produce a gain in satisfaction (utility) for one or both traders without loss to the other. However, when a point such as E' is reached, where indifference curve $6A$ of A is tangent to indifference curve $7B$ of

B, it is impossible to benefit one individual through further trade without reducing the satisfaction (utility) of the other. This observation will be very important in our discussion of welfare economics in Chapter 13. For the moment, we simply mention in passing that the set of points of tangency between the two individuals' indifference curves is called Pareto optimal. This condition will be fully explained in Chapter 13.

Returning to our discussion on trade, it is important to realize that any trade will end at a point of tangency between the indifference curves of the two individuals because without the tangency condition there exist mutually beneficial trading possibilities. In Chapter 4 on consumer behavior, we indicated that indifference curves pass through each and every point of an indifference map. This implies that there is an infinite number of tangency points such as E' between E_1 and E_2 in both Figure 12.6 and Figure 12.7. The locus of the tangency points constitutes a curve such as $\widehat{E_1E'E_2}$ in Figure 12.7 and $\widehat{0_AE_1E_20_B}$ in Figure 12.6. Since a mutually acceptable trade exists at these tangency points, their loci are generally called *contract curves*. Thus, a contract curve in an Edgeworth box is the locus of tangency points between the two individuals' indifference curves. It extends from the origin for one individual to the origin for the other (in our case, 0_A and 0_B). The shape of the contract curve depends on the preference patterns of the individuals concerned.

A contract curve is the locus of tangency points between two consumers' indifference curves

The above analysis suggests that the situation represented by Figure 12.6, in which the status quo point is S, will result in trade between A and B. However, any trade that ends at a point below and to the left of E_1 on the contract curve will not be feasible, since, although B will be better off from trade, A will be worse off. For similar reasons, trade will not be feasible on the contract curve to the right and above point E_2 because B will be worse off.[2] Hence, trade is only feasible on segment $\widehat{E_1E_2}$ of the contract curve. However, since there are infinitely many points on $\widehat{E_1E_2}$, one is tempted to ask whether we have a theory that asserts where trade will end on $\widehat{E_1E_2}$. The offer curves of A and B that were developed in the earlier part of this section provide us with an answer. Let us reexamine the nature of this problem.

In Figure 12.4 we have shown that, given a conventional indifference map, the offer curve of an individual will always go through the status quo point and lie between the two individual's indifference curves in the region between E_1 and E_2. Figure 12.8 is based on the same set of information as Figure 12.6 and takes into account our discussion of the offer curve in Figure 12.4.

---

[2] Students who wish to reinforce their learning experience should attempt to validate the aforementioned conclusions by means of the indifference curve approach.

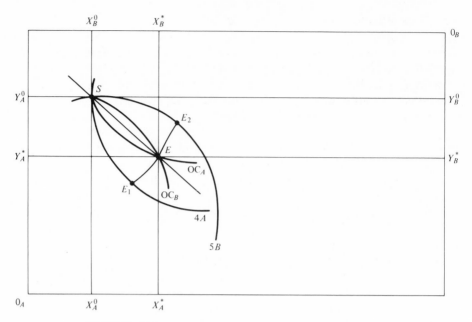

FIGURE 12.8

However, only two indifference curves 4A and 5B, one for each
individual and both passing through point S, are drawn. In Figure
12.8, A's offer curve OC$_A$ is above and to the right of indifference
curve 4A. Since B's indifference map has been rotated 180°, B's
offer curve OC$_B$ is below and to the left of indifference curve 5B.
It should be observed that both OC$_A$ and OC$_B$ lie between the two
indifference curves 4A and 5B, which not only pass through point
S, but are also bounded by the contract curve and S. Recall that
OC$_A$ is the locus of points of tangency between A's indifference
curves and rotating budget lines, where S is the center of rotation.
Similarly, OC$_B$ is the locus of tangency points between B's indifference curves and rotating budget lines, S again being the
center of rotation. This implies that OC$_A$ and OC$_B$ must intersect
at some point on the contract curve (say point E) because, by the
definition of OC$_A$ and OC$_B$, one of A's indifference curves must
be tangent to the budget line $\overline{SE}$ at E and, alternatively, one of
B's indifference curves must be tangent to $\overline{SE}$ at point E. Thus,
the corresponding indifference curves of A and B must be tangent
to each other at E, since they have the same slope at the point
that defines a tangency. By the definition of an offer curve, if
trade takes place at all, each individual will move along his or
her own offer curve because that is where the individual's satisfaction (utility) will be maximized for different price ratios of
the commodities in question. However, it should be noted that
although any point on OC$_A$ in Figure 12.8 indicates maximum
satisfaction (utility) from trade for A at a given price ratio, it will

not necessarily provide maximum satisfaction (utility) for B. Similarly, although any point on OC_B indicates maximum satisfaction (utility) from trade for B at a given price ratio, it does not necessarily mean the same for A. However, there will be some point on both OC_A and OC_B which will indicate maximum satisfaction (utility) for both individuals from trade at a given price ratio, provided that the two offer curves intersect. In Figure 12.8, E is such a point of equilibrium. For the given incomes and preference patterns of the individuals, A's satisfaction (utility) will be maximized when he or she trades $\overline{Y_A^0 Y_A^*}$ of Y for $\overline{X_A^0 X_A^*}$ of X, which is the same as saying B's satisfaction (utility) is maximized by trading $\overline{X_B^0 X_B^*} = \overline{X_A^0 X_A^*}$ of X for $\overline{Y_B^0 Y_B^*} = \overline{Y_A^0 Y_A^*}$ of Y.

The offer curves of two consumers must intersect at some point on the contract curve

We can summarize the results of the above analysis on pure exchange as follows:

1. If the indifference curves of the two individuals intersect but are not tangent at the status quo point S, then trade will result in a higher level of satisfaction (utility) for both.
2. Trade will take place at the point of intersection of the two offer curves, which is also a point on the contract curve.
3. At the point of equilibrium, the marginal rates of substitution between X and Y for both A and B are equal to the common price ratio (i.e., the indifference curves of both are tangent to the budget line at the same point on the budget line and tangent to each other). Consequently, their marginal rates of substitution are equal.
4. It is the relative prices (or the price ratio) and not the absolute prices that are essential for an appropriate evaluation of trade to be made. In terms of symbols, the first-order condition of equilibrium for pure exchange between two individuals for two commodities can be written

$$\text{MRS}_A = \text{MRS}_B = P_X/P_Y \tag{12.6}$$

or

$$\text{MU}_{XA}/\text{MU}_{YA} = \text{MU}_{XB}/\text{MU}_{YB} = P_X/P_Y \tag{12.7}$$

where the MUs are the marginal utilities and thus $\text{MU}_{XA}/\text{MU}_{YA}$ and $\text{MU}_{XB}/\text{MU}_{YB}$ denote the marginal rate of substitution (MRS) for A and B, respectively.

12.2 GENERAL EQUILIBRIUM IN PRODUCTION: THE TWO-INPUT–TWO-OUTPUT MODEL

The analysis in Section 12.1 is essentially an application of the theory of consumer behavior developed in Chapter 4. On the other hand, the analysis in this section is an application of the theory of production with two variable inputs developed in Chapter 2 to the theory of exchange. The Edgeworth box will again

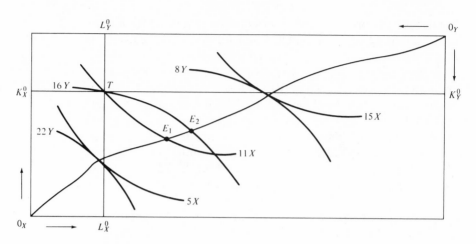

FIGURE 12.9

be used for the purpose of illustration. For the most part, this section is technically similar to Section 12.1, the only difference being one of interpretation.

Assume that we have fixed amounts L^0 and K^0 of labor and capital (i.e., two inputs) which are used to produce the two commodities X and Y. Furthermore, assume that the technologies used in producing the commodities are also given. Thus, we have a given set of isoquant maps for both X and Y. Consider Figure 12.9, in which L_X^0 of labor and K_X^0 of capital are initially used in producing X, whereas L_Y^0 of labor and K_Y^0 of capital are initially used in producing Y.[3] By the logic of the Edgeworth box as described in Section 12.1, we can see from Figure 12.9 that

$$L^0 = L_X^0 + L_Y^0 \quad \text{and} \quad K^0 = K_X^0 + K_Y^0$$

The quantity of labor used in producing X is represented by the horizontal distance between 0_X and any point to the right, whereas the quantity of capital is represented by the distance between 0_X and any point upward along the vertical axis. On the other hand, the quantity of labor used in producing Y is represented by the distance between 0_Y and any point to the left, whereas the quantity of capital is represented by the distance between 0_Y and any point below it. These four conditions are indicated by the directional arrows.

We have also drawn three isoquants for X and three isoquants for Y in Figure 12.9. The essential difference between this figure and those in Section 12.1 is that the relative magnitudes of the numerical labels for the isoquants are meaningful; for example,

---

[3] In Figure 12.9, the horizontal axis represents the amount of labor, whereas the vertical axis represents the amount of capital. Furthermore, 0_X is the origin for commodity X and 0_Y is the origin for commodity Y.

15X indicates an output three times that of 5X, whereas 16Y indicates an output twice that of 8Y. As we have explained before, the numerical labels for the indifference curves in an indifference map indicate only an ordering of magnitude. On the other hand, the numerical labels for the isoquants are on a cardinal scale, that is, they not only indicate ordering, but also relative magnitude. Once this distinction is made, the analysis in this section is very similar to that in Section 12.1.

The status quo in the distribution of labor and capital in the production of the two commodities X and Y is represented by point T. With this allocation of resources, the maximum outputs of X and Y are 11 and 16 units, respectively. This means that the production of each commodity, taken by itself, is operating efficiently for the given technology. However, with respect to society as a whole, there exists the potential for a reallocation of resources which can result in an increase in output of one commodity without a decrease in the output of the other. In fact, it may be possible to increase the outputs of both commodities. This can easily be seen by an application of the arguments detailed in Section 12.1.

Production processes may be efficient, but a reallocation of resources may increase total output

Using the concept of the contract curve as developed in Section 12.1, the locus of the tangent points between the isoquants of X and Y can be drawn, that is, $\overset{\frown}{0_X E_1 E_2 0_Y}$, which intersects 11$X$ at point E_1 and 16Y at point E_2. A reallocation of resources between the commodities which produces a movement from T to E_2 not only results in more labor and less capital for X and more capital and less labor for Y than the status quo, but also generates more output of X without any sacrifice in the level of output of Y. This is true because E_2 is still on the 16Y isoquant, but X is now represented by a higher isoquant. Similarly, a reallocation of resources which produces a movement from T to E_1 will result in an increase in the output of Y without any decrease in the output of X. Figure 12.9 also shows that any reallocation of labor and capital which results in a movement from T to a point between E_1 and E_2 will produce an increase in the outputs of both X and Y. As long as the allocation of resources is on the curve $\overset{\frown}{E_1 E_2}$, it will be optimal in the sense that any further reallocation of resources, although resulting in an increase in one output, will also produce a decrease in the other. This is a characteristic of the contract curve.

The above arguments show that the status quo allocation of resources at point T is not optimal. However, there are infinitely many ways in which a reallocation of resources will result in an increase of both outputs (or at least an increase in one output without a reduction in the other). The question is whether we have a theoretical tool that enables us to obtain a unique solution to the problem. Again, the answer is yes.

The solution to the problem depends, in part, on the social and

Under perfect competition, unique and economically efficient solutions to trade and production can be obtained

political system. Under a dictatorship or central planning, the ruling authority may make a decision according to the dictator's preference or some kind of social and/or political criteria. In such a case, any reallocation of resources resulting in a movement from T to a point on $\widehat{E_1E_2}$ would be considered a sound decision insofar as economic efficiency is concerned since it would involve more output of one commodity without loss of the other. As a matter of fact, even a reallocation of resources that is represented by a point not on $\widehat{E_1E_2}$ could still be considered a sound decision as long as final production takes place at a point on the contract curve. What we wish to emphasize here is that economic analysis does not provide a unique solution to the problem on pure theoretical grounds alone. Additional information is necessary in order to obtain a unique solution. However, our analysis is still helpful in making a judgment as to whether a decision is economically efficient. With free-enterprise systems operating under perfect competition, unique and economically efficient solutions to the trade and production problems can be obtained. Let us see why this is so.

Recall that in Section 12.1 the offer curve under pure exchange was defined as the locus of tangent points between a consumer's indifference curves and rotating budget lines for various price ratios of the commodities. These tangent points indicated maximum consumer satisfaction (utility) for different prices. Thus, market equilibrium was given at the point where the two consumer's offer curves intersected. In production, we have a similar situation. In Chapter 2, we proved the proposition that the output of a firm would be maximized for a given cost if its isocost curve was tangent to an isoquant. In the present case, when the relative prices of labor and capital change, the isocost curve for the industry producing commodity X will rotate around T. When the relative price of labor with respect to capital increases, the isocost curve corresponding to the given resources L_X^0 and K_X^0 for the industry producing commodity X will rotate clockwise, that is, its slope will become steeper. Conversely, when the relative price of labor with respect to capital decreases, the isocost curve for the industry producing commodity X will rotate counterclockwise, and, consequently, its slope will become flatter. When the relative prices (remember, relative, not absolute, prices are relevant here) change continuously, each isocost curve will, under certain regularity assumptions of the isoquants, be tangent to a different isoquant. The locus of these points of tangency constitutes the offer curve for the industry producing commodity X. In Figure 12.10, OC_X is such an offer curve.

Although there is 180° rotation of the isoquant map for the industry producing commodity Y, once the relative price of labor with respect to the price of capital increases, the isocost curve for this industry corresponding to the initial endowment of re-

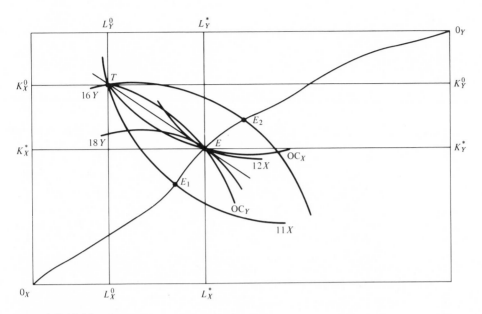

FIGURE 12.10

sources L_Y^0 (labor) and K_Y^0 (capital) will still rotate clockwise around T. As the relative prices of the inputs change continuously, the locus of the points of tangency between the various isocost curves and the corresponding isoquants will generate an offer curve for the industry producing commodity Y. In Figure 12.10, OC_Y is such an offer curve.

From Figure 12.10, it can be observed that E is the point of intersection of OC_X and OC_Y. This point represents equilibrium in the production of X and Y for the relative input prices represented by the slope of $\overline{TE}$. Equilibrium in production occurs when (1) the outputs of commodities X and Y are both maximized, (2) the demands for both labor and capital are equal to their supplies, and (3) any other price ratios of labor with respect to capital will result in an inequality of demand and supply in factor (input) markets. Conditions 1 and 2 actually constitute the definition of equilibrium in production, whereas condition 3 indicates that the equilibrium is unique.

By way of proof, it can be seen that point E indicates maximum output of both X and Y because E is on both offer curve OC_X and offer curve OC_Y, which are, by definition, the loci of maximum production for the given costs of X and Y, respectively. It should be noted that point E is on a higher isoquant than point T (the status quo) for both X and Y. This proves condition 1. With the relative prices of labor and capital represented by the slope of $\overline{TE}$, the supply of labor is $\overline{L_Y^0 L_Y^*}$, which is equal to the demand for labor $\overline{L_X^0 L_X^*}$. and the supply of capital $\overline{K_X^0 K_X^*}$ is equal to the demand for capital $\overline{K_Y^0 K_Y^*}$ (as indicated by Figure 12.10). This

The production equilibrium condition is like that for maximizing consumer satisfaction through trade

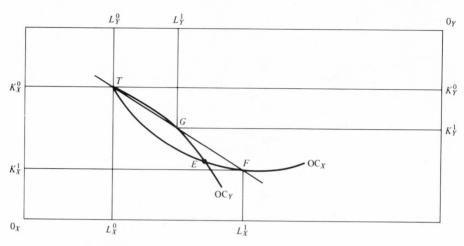

FIGURE 12.11

proves condition 2. For the proof of condition 3, suppose that the relative price of labor with respect to capital is represented by the slope of a budget line other than $\overline{TE}$, for example, $\overline{TF}$ (see Figure 12.11), which is flatter than $\overline{TE}$. (For the sake of simplicity, we have only shown OC_X, OC_Y, and $\overline{TF}$ in Figure 12.11.) Budget line $\overline{TF}$ intersects OC_X at F and OC_Y at G. According to the meaning of the offer curves, the output of X will be maximized for the input prices if L_X^1 of labor and K_X^1 of capital are used. This is in accord with the best interest of the industry producing commodity X, which calls for a supply of capital of $\overline{K_X^0 K_X^1}$ and a demand for labor of $\overline{L_X^0 L_X^1}$. On the other hand, the output of Y will be maximized for the same input prices if L_Y^1 of labor and K_Y^1 of capital are used. However, the best interest of the industry producing commodity Y dictates that the supply of labor be $\overline{L_Y^0 L_Y^1}$ and the demand for capital be $\overline{K_Y^0 K_Y^1}$. Consequently, for the given relative input prices, the supply of capital exceeds the demand for capital, whereas the supply of labor is less than the demand for labor. Since this relative input price (i.e., represented by the slope of $\overline{TF}$) is different from the one represented by the slope of $\overline{TE}$, we can conclude that any relative price other than the one represented by the slope of $\overline{TE}$ will likewise not result in factor (input) market equilibrium. It should be noted that this result also encompasses the case where the slope of $\overline{TF}$ is steeper than that of $\overline{TE}$. In this case, not only will the demand for capital exceed the supply of capital, but now the supply of labor will also exceed the demand for labor. However, market disequilibrium will nevertheless persist.

The above conditions with respect to general equilibrium in production for the special case of the two-input–two-output model can be summarized as follows:

1. If the isoquants of the two industries that produce commodities X and Y, respectively, intersect (i.e., are not tangent) at the status quo point T, then a reallocation of resources will result in higher outputs for both.

2. The free-enterprise system, when combined with perfect competition, will result in a reallocation of resources at a point of intersection of the two offer curves on the contract curve such that the outputs of both industries will be increased.

3. At the point of equilibrium, the marginal rate of technical substitution (MRTS) of both industries will be equal to the common input price ratio (i.e., the isoquants of X and Y are tangent to the budget line at the same point). Consequently, their MRTSs will be equal at equilibrium.

4. It is the relative factor (input) prices (or the price ratio of the productive factors) and not the absolute prices that are essential in our analysis. In terms of symbols, the first-order condition of general equilibrium in production for the special case of the two-input–two-output model can be written

General equilibrium in production requires the MRTSs for commodities to be equal

$$\text{MRTS}_X = \text{MRTS}_Y = w/r \tag{12.8}$$

or

$$\text{MP}_{LX}/\text{MP}_{KX} = \text{MP}_{LY}/\text{MP}_{KY} = w/r \tag{12.9}$$

where MRTS_X and MRTS_Y denote the marginal rates of technical substitution in X and Y, respectively; MP_{LX}, MP_{KX}, MP_{LY}, and MP_{KY} are the marginal products of labor and capital for X and Y, respectively; and w and r are the prices of labor and capital, respectively.

12.3 THE PRODUCTION POSSIBILITY (TRANSFORMATION) CURVE

Although we have analyzed pure exchange and production equilibria, we must develop a new tool before we can put exchange and production together in order to demonstrate a condition of general equilibrium for an economy. This tool is the *production possibility (transformation) curve* (PPC), which is usually introduced but not derived in textbooks on economic principles. We believe that illustrating the derivation of a PPC will help the student to gain more insight into its meaning and significance. We shall employ the graphical method to derive a PPC.

In general, the graphical method can only be used to demonstrate the simple case of two outputs. For the two-product case, a PPC is defined as the locus of maximum output of a commodity for a given quantity of another under the assumption of a fixed quantity of inputs and a given technology. Since the contract curve for production in an Edgeworth box from Section 12.2

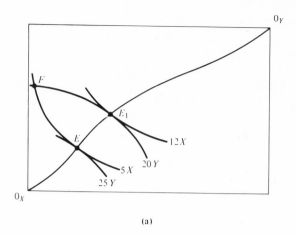
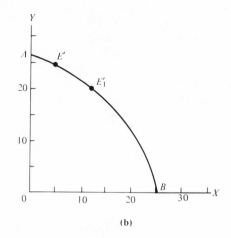

(a)   (b)

FIGURE 12.12

satisfies precisely these requirements, it follows that the contract curve and the PPC must be closely related. In fact, a PPC can be derived from the corresponding contract curve. It is a simple transfer of the same set of information from one type of graph to another. Let us see why.

Consider Figure 12.12, in which part (a) shows an Edgeworth box with the contract curve $0_x EE_1 0_y$. The fact that the contract curve shows the locus of the maximum quantity of one output for a given amount of the other is obvious. For example, if 5 units of X are produced, then the maximum amount of Y that can be produced with the allocation of resources represented by point E (a point on the contract curve) is 25 units. If the resources are instead allocated between the commodities according to point F rather than point E, then the output of X is the same—5 units—but the output of Y will be lower (reduced from 25 to 20 units). In fact, for any other allocation of the resources on the isoquant $5X$ other than that represented by point E, the output of X will be the same, but the output of Y will be less than 25 units. Similarly, we can see that if 20 units of Y are produced, then the maximum output of X that can be produced with the allocation of resources, represented by point E_1, is 12 units. Any other allocation of the resources along the isoquant $20Y$ will result in a lower output of X. Since E_1, like E, is on the contract curve, we have established the fact that the contract curve is indeed the locus of maximum output of one commodity for a given quantity of the other.

In part (b) of Figure 12.12, the horizontal axis gives the output of X, whereas the vertical axis gives the output of Y. Point E in part (a) shows that the maximum amount of Y is 25 units for 5 units of X, which is the same as saying that the maximum amount of X is 5 units for 25 units of Y. Point E' in panel (b) represents this condition. Analogously, we can see that point E'_1 in part (b) corresponds to point E_1 in part (a). In general, for each and every point on the contract curve of part (a), there is one and only one corresponding point in part (b). Therefore, corresponding to the contract curve in part (a), we have the continuous curve $\overarc{AE'E'_1B}$ in part (b), which is the production possibility curve derived from the contract curve $\overarc{0_X EE_1 0_Y}$. As per our usual practice, we have drawn a smooth PPC that is concave toward the origin. However, it should be noted that the shape of the PPC is determined by technology, just as were the shapes of the isoquants and contract curve in part (a). Nevertheless, there are good reasons for believing that this particular shape of the PPC is most common, although other shapes (such as a straight line) cannot be ruled out. However, it is important to understand that the PPC in part (b) indicates a case of increasing cost, whereas a straight-line PPC would indicate constant cost. Since this condition is usually explained in textbooks on economic principles, we shall not consider it further at this point.

The shape of the PPC curve is determined by technology

It is worthwhile to point out that for a given amount and quality of resources and state of technology, there is only one PPC for an economy. When the quantity of one or more of the resources increases and/or the quality of the resources and/or technology improves, the PPC will shift upward and to the right. Without the occurrence of any one or a combination of the above, it is impossible to increase the output of one commodity without reducing that of the other. Thus, change in the quantity of resources and/or in the quality of resources and/or technology will bring about a shift in the PPC, whereas a reallocation of resources between two points on the contract curve generates movement along the PPC. When movement along a given PPC takes place, the rate at which one commodity has to be forgone for a small increase in the other has some significance in economic analysis. Economists usually call this ratio the *marginal rate of product transformation* (MRPT), which we shall define as follows for the sake of convenience.

Definition: Marginal Rate of Product Transformation Between Two Commodities. The rate at which one commodity must be forgone to obtain a small increase of the other commodity for a given amount of resources and a given state of technology.

For practical purposes, the MRPT can be considered the quantity of one commodity which has to be forgone to secure one additional unit of the other commodity. In mathematical terms, the MRPT is the negative slope of the PPC (transformation curve) at a given point on the curve.

12.4 THE EQUALITY OF MRPT AND MRS: THE CONDITION FOR GENERAL EQUILIBRIUM

In Section 12.1, we proved that, in pure exchange, mutually beneficial trade between consumers will end at a point on the contract curve regardless of the initial incomes possessed by each. We also demonstrated that since the contract curve is the locus of tangency points between the consumers' indifference curves, equilibrium in trade implies the equality of the MRSs of the two consumers. In other words, if the MRSs of two consumers for two commodities (e.g., X and Y) are not equal, then there exist possible trades such that both will be better off. On the other hand, when the MRSs are equal, if further trade benefits one consumer, then it will necessarily make the other worse off. Although we have shown this result by the graphical method only in the special two-persons–two-commodity case, it is valid for any number of consumers and commodities so far as pure exchange is concerned. This can be illustrated by means of the following simple example.

Suppose that we pick any two consumers among many (e.g., A and B) and any two commodities among many (e.g., X and Y). In addition, assume that A's MRS is higher than B's. For the sake of simplicity, further assume that A is willing to give up 3 units of Y for 1 unit of X, whereas B is willing to give up 2 units of Y for 1 unit of X. This implies that $MRS_A = 3$ for A and $MRS_B = 2$ for B, as well as that B is equally willing to give up 1 unit of X for 2 units of Y. Now suppose that A gives up $2\frac{1}{2}$ units of Y to B for 1 unit of X. We can see that A is better off because he (or she) gives up less of Y for the unit of X than he was actually willing to give, that is, since A would have been willing to give up 3 units of Y for 1 unit of X, he therefore must be better off if he only has to give up $2\frac{1}{2}$ units of Y. Similarly, B is also better off because he gains one-half more units of Y than he would have actually been satisfied to obtain. This shows that when the MRSs of two consumers are not equal, there always exists an opportunity for mutually beneficial trade. On the other hand, similar examples will show that if the MRSs of two consumers are equal, then such an opportunity does not exist. Inasmuch as we have picked any two consumers and any two commodities among many, we can state that since this proposition is true for any pair of consumers and commodities, it is also applicable to any number of consumers and any number of commodities. For example, if $MRS_A = MRS_B$ for A and B at equilibrium, and $MRS_A = MRS_C$ for A and C at equilibrium, then our proposition implies that $MRS_B = MRS_C$ at equilibrium. This principle or condition can be applied to any number of consumers for a specific pair of commodities X and Y. By similar reasoning, it can also be applied to any other pair of commodities, for example, Y and Z. Another way of proving this proposition is by means of the example in

Chapter 4 in which it was shown that a consumer's satisfaction (utility) is maximized for a given income if and only if his or her MRS is equal to the price ratio of the commodities. Since all consumers face the same market prices under perfect competition, it follows that when their satisfaction (utility) is maximized, their MRSs for a given pair of commodities must also be equal. Although we dealt only with partial analysis in Chapter 4, the same result is obtained from general equilibrium analysis.

The equality between any consumer's MRS and the MRPT in production implies optimality

We now proceed to show that a general equilibrium of exchange and production requires the equality between the MRSs of all consumers and the MRPT for a given pair of commodities. Since we have already shown that a necessary condition for consumer equilibrium is the equality of the MRSs of all consumers, to prove our assertion it is only necessary for us to show that the equality between any one consumer's MRS and the MRPT implies general optimality.

A simple numerical example can best illustrate our proof. Suppose that the MRPT = 3. In terms of the two commodities X and Y, let this mean that technical conditions specify that 3 units of Y have to be sacrificed in order to produce one additional unit of X. If the MRS between X and Y is 4 for our consumer, then let us assume this to mean that he or she is willing to give up 4 units of Y for one additional unit of X. This is a case where MRS > MRPT. We want to show that, in this case, the consumer's satisfaction (utility) can be increased with the same given resources and technology by producing more X and, at the same time, less Y. Thus, the economy is not in an optimal state and general equilibrium is not achieved.

Under the circumstances stated above, the satisfaction (utility) of the consumer can be increased with the same resources and technology by producing one more unit of X and sacrificing 3 units of Y. Since, by our assumption, MRS = 4 means that the consumer is willing to give up 4 units of Y for 1 unit of X, it follows that his satisfaction (utility) will be increased if 1 unit of X is gained by giving up only 3 units of Y.

For similar reasons, if the MRPT is greater than the MRS of the consumer, then the consumer's satisfaction (utility) can be increased given the same resources and technology by producing more of Y and less of X. It can be observed that if MRPT = 4 and MRS = 3, then four additional units of Y can be produced at the expense of 1 unit of X. On the other hand, when MRS = 3 we know that the consumer is satisfied with a gain of 3 units of Y for a loss of 1 unit of X. Thus, if the consumer is given 4 units of Y for the price of 1 unit of X, he or she will obviously be happier than before. Hence, when MRPT is either greater than or less than the MRS of the consumer (i.e., MRPT ≠ MRS), some consumer's satisfaction (utility) can be increased with the given resources and technology without any other consumer being

When MRPT ≠ MRS, consumer satisfaction can be increased by a reallocation of resources

worse off. Thus, such a condition cannot be considered optimal or in equilibrium.

When MRPT = MRS, it is impossible to increase the consumer's satisfaction (utility) with the given resources and technology by increasing the production of one commodity and, at the same time, reducing that of the other. For example, MRPT = MRS = 3 means that (technically) 3 units of Y can be produced at the expense of 1 unit of X and, at the same time, that if the consumer is given 3 units of Y at a cost of 1 unit of X, he (or she) is no better or worse off than before. If, for some reason, three more units of Y and one less unit of X are produced, then we note that although the consumer gives up 1 unit of X, he gains 3 units of Y, and since his MRS = 3, he is neither better off nor worse off. Similarly, no improvement of the consumer's satisfaction (utility) can be made by increasing the production of X at the expense of Y. This shows that if consumers in pure exchange are at equilibrium (i.e., on the contract curve), and if the production side of the economy is also at equilibrium (i.e., on the contract curve and thus the PPC), then their satisfaction (utility) will be a maximum for the given resources and technology only if MRPT = MRS. This result actually solves the problem of the distribution of products for a given mix of commodities.

The simple two-commodity–two-person case can be represented in graphical form. Consider Figure 12.13. Suppose it has been decided that point B represents the proper product mix, that is, X_0 of X and Y_0 of Y are considered the optimal product combination. In the two-person case, an Edgeworth box can be constructed by using 0 and B as the origins for the two consumers. Suppose that $\widehat{0EB}$ is the contract curve. The MRPT is represented by the negative slope of the tangent $\overline{AB}$, whereas the MRS of A

FIGURE 12.13

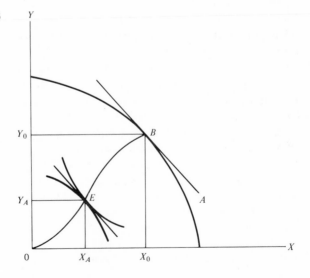

is represented by the negative slope of his or her indifference curve at a given point. We know that the two consumers' MRSs are equal everywhere on the contract curve. Suppose that, at point E, and only point E, the slope of A's indifference curve (and thus also B's) is equal to the slope of the PPC (transformation curve) at point B. Only then will the distribution of the products represented by E satisfy the optimal conditions as developed above. We can see from Figure 12.13 that the given product mix— $\overline{0X_A}$ of X and $\overline{0Y_A}$ of Y for A and $\overline{X_A X_0}$ of X and $\overline{Y_A Y_0}$ of Y for B—will be the solution of the general equilibrium problem for this simple case.

Although we have achieved a solution for the simple two-commodity–two-person case illustrated in Figure 12.13, we have left an important question unanswered: How is the point B, that is, the proper product mix, determined? Although this seems to be an innocent question, obtaining the answer is considerably more difficult. In fact, no definite theoretical answer yet exists. Most economists rely on utility theory, but the difficulty with this approach is that the problem of how to construct a utility function for a group of people (commonly referred to as a *social welfare function*) has to be solved before it can be used. It turns out that under even the most reasonable assumptions a social welfare function cannot be constructed (see Arrow, 1951). When a social welfare function does not exist, the utility approach is certainly not very realistic. However, many textbooks proceed to use it after providing the reader with some kind of warning. We believe that instead of the theoretically unjustified utility approach, an alternative method may be more reasonable. Although we do not claim that our approach is the best, it nevertheless is a reasonable way of solving a difficult theoretical problem.

In our approach the solution depends on the initial endowments of the fixed inputs to the various commodities. We began by observing that for the same fixed amounts of the inputs, we shall have different solutions for different endowments to the various commodities. This can be considered a disadvantage of our model, but, at the same time, it can also be considered an advantage because any solution to any social and/or economic problem must have its roots at a given starting point. A solution that does not depend on the initial conditions may be theoretically superior, but it will still be impractical because even a revolution cannot wipe out everything and enable us to start over again from base zero. In any event, our model results in a determinant solution without begging the difficult and yet unsolved problem of a specification of the social welfare function. In short, our model provides a reasonable alternative to the other models.

The product mix problem is soluble by assuming initial endowments of fixed inputs

Starting with any initial endowments of fixed amounts of two inputs to two commodities, we can observe from Figure 12.12 that if this condition is a point on the contract curve in an Edgeworth box [such as point E in part (a)], then efficiency in production has been achieved, and the equilibrium price ratio between labor and capital is represented by the common negative slope of the isoquants at point E. On the other hand, the equilibrium of the commodity market can be determined by using the result embodied in Figure 12.13. In other words, an Edgeworth box can be drawn in part (b) of Figure 12.12 by using the origin and the point E' as the origins for the two consumers. A contract curve between points 0 and E' can then be drawn. A point on the contract curve can be found such that the common slope of the two individuals' indifference curves is equal to the slope of the PPC (transformation curve) at point E'. This point on the contract curve is the general equilibrium solution. It not only determines the equilibrium shares of the two commodities between the two consumers, but also the price ratio of the two commodities, which is the negative common slope of the indifference curves of the consumers at the equilibrium point. We have a general equilibrium solution of our simple model, since the prices of the inputs and outputs, the efficient shares of the inputs between the commodities, the total output of each commodity, and the shares of the commodities between the consumers have all been determined.

For the purpose of illustration, a more-interesting case is one in which the initial endowments of the inputs to the two commodities are not represented by a point on the contract curve. A graphical analysis of this case is offered below because it will enhance one's understanding of the logic of the preceding discussion.

Consider part (a) of Figure 12.14, in which an Edgeworth box for the simple two-input–two-output case is presented. Point T represents the initial endowments of the inputs to the two commodities, whereas OC_X and OC_Y are the offer curves for X and Y, respectively. The curve between 0_X and 0_Y is the contract

FIGURE 12.14

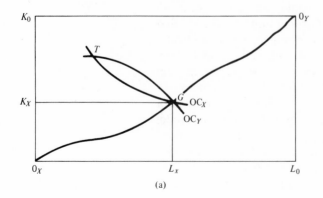

(a)

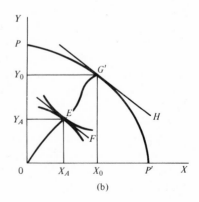

(b)

curve. Since T is not on the contract curve, the outputs of both X and Y can be increased for the fixed inputs by a reallocation of the inputs between the two commodities. Based on the theory developed in Section 12.2, the optimal solution in production is the intersection of the two offer curves, that is, point G, which is on the contract curve. Thus, the optimal allocation of the inputs is L_X of labor and K_X of capital for commodity X and $L_0 - L_X$ of labor and $K_0 - K_X$ of capital for commodity Y, respectively. The relative price of labor and capital is represented by the common negative slope of the isoquants (not drawn for the sake of simplicity; for more detail, see Figure 12.10) of X and Y at point G. The isoquants of X and Y which go through the point G also give us the optimal outputs X_0 and Y_0 of X and Y, respectively. Since the equilibrium prices of the inputs, the optimal allocation of the inputs to the commodities, and the optimal outputs of the commodities are determined by market forces, this is an equilibrium solution in production. Note that the outputs of both commodities are maximized for the given inputs and initial endowments.

> *Given initial endowments and inputs, at equilibrium, the slopes of the consumers' indifference curves and the PPC curve match*

In part (b) of Figure 12.14, the PPC (transformation curve) $\widehat{PP}'$ is constructed from the contract curve $\widehat{0_X 0_Y}$, and the point G' in part (b) corresponds to the point G in part (a). Furthermore, $\overline{0X_0}$ in part (b) corresponds to the isoquant of X which passes through point G in part (a). Similarly, $\overline{0Y_0}$ in part (b) corresponds to the isoquant of Y which passes through G in part (a). The rectangle $0X_0 G' Y_0$ in part (b) is an Edgeworth box. For two individuals A and B, the origin 0 can be considered A's origin, whereas point G' can be considered B's origin. The curve $\widehat{0EG'}$ is the contract curve. Suppose that the common slope of the indifference curves of A and B (i.e., the slope of $\overline{EF}$) is equal to the slope of $\overline{G'H}$, which is tangent to $\widehat{PP}'$ at G'. Then, based on the result indicated by Figure 12.13, point E is the equilibrium solution in the commodity market. The equilibrium relative price of X and Y is represented by the negative slope of $\overline{EF}$, and A's equilibrium shares of X and Y are $\overline{0X_A}$ and $\overline{0Y_A}$, respectively, whereas B's equilibrium shares are $\overline{X_A X_0}$ of X and $\overline{Y_A Y_0}$ of Y. The satisfaction (utility) of either of the consumers is maximized for the given level of satisfaction (utility) of the other. In this sense, the satisfaction (utility) of all of the consumers is maximized and we have equilibrium in both production and exchange. To put it more technically, we have $\text{MRS}_A = \text{MRS}_B = \text{MRPT}$.

12.5 A SIMPLE LEON WALRAS GENERAL EQUILIBRIUM MODEL OF COUNTING EQUATIONS AND VARIABLES

The Walras model uses *excess demand functions* rather than the usual demand and supply functions for determining equilibrium. However, it can easily be seen that there is a direct link between these two approaches. In general, the demand for a given commodity is a function of the prices of all of the commodities in the market, the income level, and the number of consumers [as was shown in (5.1)]. For a given level of income and a given number of consumers, the demand function for any one of the n commodities, for example, the ith, can be written

$$Q_i = D_i(P_1, P_2, ..., P_i, ..., P_n), \qquad i = 1, 2, ..., n \qquad (12.10)$$

In a perfectly competitive market, the supply of each commodity is, in principle, also a function of the prices of all of the commodities. (In Chapter 7, it was explained that the supply function of a commodity is not meaningful in an imperfect market.) For a given number of firms, the supply function for the ith commodity can be written

$$Q_i = S_i(P_1, P_2, ..., P_i, ..., P_n), \qquad i = 1, 2, ..., n \qquad (12.11)$$

The difference between demand and supply for a commodity at various prices determines excess demand

The *excess demand function* for the ith commodity is defined as the difference between demand and supply. If we denote the excess demand of the ith commodity by E_i, then

$$E_i(P_1, P_2, ..., P_i, ..., P_n) = D_i(P_1, P_2, ..., P_i, ..., P_n)$$

$$- S_i(P_1, P_2, ..., P_i, ..., P_n)$$

$$i = 1, 2, ..., n \qquad (12.12)$$

Since both terms on the right side of (12.12) are functions of the n prices, the left side is definitely also a function of the prices.

In terms of a two-dimensional graph, the excess demand curve can be derived from any given set of demand and supply curves. As a simple example, consider Figure 12.15, in which the demand and supply schedules are both represented by straight lines (D and S, respectively). At the price level P_0, where D intersects S,

FIGURE 12.15

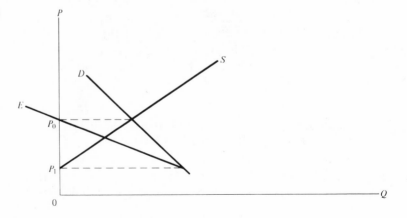

$D(P)$, $= S(P)$, and the excess demand is zero. Thus, the excess demand curve E intersects the vertical axis at P_0. When the price is higher than P_0, the quantity supplied exceeds the quantity demanded; hence, we have negative excess demand. On the other hand, when the price is below P_0, the quantity demanded exceeds the quantity supplied, and thus excess demand is positive. Finally, at the price level P_1, the quantity supplied is zero, and, therefore, excess demand is equal to total demand. It can easily be shown that when demand and supply are linear functions, excess demand is also a linear function. For example, if the demand and supply functions are

$$Q_d = A - aP, \qquad A, a > 0 \tag{12.13}$$

and

$$Q_s = B + bP, \qquad B, b > 0 \tag{12.14}$$

respectively, then the excess demand function is

$$E_Q = (A - B) - (a + b)P \tag{12.15}$$

Curve E in Figure 12.15 represents the inverse of (12.15), which can be written

$$E_P = A' - a'Q \tag{12.16}$$

where

$$A' = (A - B)/(a + b)$$

and

$$a' = 1/(a + b)$$

Equation (12.16) obviously defines a straight line.

Convenience in notation is just one of the reasons for using the excess demand function instead of the demand and supply functions. For example, not only are consumers the owners of the productive factors (i.e., labor, capital, and land), but they are also the users of the final products. Traditionally, the demand for final products is derived from the behavior of consumers (see Chapter 4), whereas the supply of labor is derived from income distribution theory (see Part IV). In terms of excess demand, if supply is considered as negative demand, then the distinction between demand and supply disappears. In the case of labor, the amount of time that a consumer uses for such personal activities as sleep, rest, and entertainment is considered positive demand, whereas the remaining time can be treated as excess demand (which is usually negative). On the other hand, producers may use part of their own products as input (which constitutes positive demand) and treat the rest as negative excess demand. The aggregate excess demand for each commodity is the sum of the individual positive and negative excess demand functions. Con-

In the Walras model the market is in equilibrium when excess demand is zero

sequently, the distinction between factor and product markets disappears.

In the Walras model, the n excess demand functions (12.12) not only include all of the products, but also the productive factors and other commodities traded in the market. In other words, there is a total number of n commodities that are traded in the market: Some of them are productive factors, some are produced commodities, and some could be, for example, antiques.

One condition of market equilibrium is that excess demand be equal to zero. Hence, when all markets are in equilibrium, we have

$$E_i(P_1, P_2, ..., P_i, ..., P_n) = 0, \qquad i = 1, 2, ..., n \qquad (12.17)$$

We have a system of n equations in n commodities. However, not all of the n equations are independent of the others. For an economy as a whole, the total monetary value of purchases is always equal to the total monetary value of sales. Therefore, we have

$$\sum_{i=1}^{n} P_i E_i(P_1, P_2, ..., P_i, ..., P_n) = 0 \qquad (12.18)$$

Identity (12.18) is generally referred to as *Walras' law*. Consequently, whenever $n-1$ of the n markets are in equilibrium the remaining market is necessarily also in equilibrium. This indicates that the maximum number of independent equations in the n-equation system (12.17) is $n-1$.

Theoretically, it is impossible to solve for the n prices from $n-1$ independent equations. However, the number of variables in (12.17) can be reduced by one if one commodity is arbitrarily chosen as the *numeraire*, that is, the commodity whose price is equal to unity. In the Walras model, any commodity can serve as the numeraire. In everyday life, the price of \$1 is identically equal to \$1 of U.S. currency. Thus, the dollar in United States currency—and money in general—can be considered as the numeraire. In this special case, money is also considered a commodity, albeit of a special kind.

A solution in the Walras model involves assigning one commodity as the numeraire

Suppose that commodity 1 is chosen as the numeraire and that all prices are divided by P_1. The system of equations (12.17) can then be written

$$E_i(1, P_2/P_1, P_3/P_1, ..., P_i/P_1, ..., P_n/P_1) = 0 \qquad (12.19)$$

$$i = 1, 2, ..., n$$

As a result of using one commodity as the numeraire, we now have $n-1$ independent equations and $n - 1$ variables in the price ratios. Thus, system (12.19) is consistent with a unique solution for the $n-1$ price ratios. This is as far as the Walras general equilibrium model goes.

We have assumed that the number of producers or firms is given. However, in the long run, the number of firms is an important variable. In this case, each excess demand will be a function of the n prices and the m number of firms, one for each producing industry. Moreover, the total profit of each producing industry will be zero, since the profit of each firm is zero in long-run equilibrium under perfect competition. The condition of zero profit results in m equations, which taken together with the n excess demand functions gives us a total of $n + m$ equations in $n + m$ variables (with n prices and m firms N_j, $j = 1, 2, ..., m$, one for each industry). However, due to Walras' law, there are actually just $n + m - 1$ independent equations. Of course, we should remember that only the relative prices and not the absolute prices can be determined. However, once a numeraire is chosen, all of the other prices can be expressed in terms of it. A more-complete mathematical description of the Walras model will be presented in the appendix of this chapter.

It should be noted that the simple exchange and production models presented in Sections 12.1 and 12.2 are part of the Walras model. The offer curves correspond to negative excess demands. The following can be observed to be true for a consumer: (1) The excess demand is a function of the relative prices and (2) satisfaction (utility) is maximized along the offer (and, thus, excess demand) curve. On the other hand, the following can be shown to be true for a producer: (1) The excess demand is a function of the prices of the inputs and outputs and (2) the profit is maximized along the offer (and, thus, excess demand) curve. The market excess demand of a factor of production or a commodity is defined as the sum of the individual excess demands (some positive and some negative) for all consumers and producers. It has been shown that equilibrium can only take place on a contract curve. This result implies that an equilibrium solution satisfies the following conditions: (1) Every consumer's satisfaction (utility) is maximized, (2) every producer's profit is maximized, and (3) every market is cleared. For long-run equilibrium under perfect competition, one additional condition is satisfied: Every producer earns a zero profit.

If the prices of all of the factors of production and the produced commodities can be explicitly determined from the system of zero excess demand functions, and if all of the prices are nonnegative, then the excess demands of each individual consumer and seller for each factor and/or commodity can be computed from his or her excess demand functions. At the equilibrium prices, some of the excess demands will be positive and others will be negative. However, the sum of the excess demands of all of the consumers and all of the producers for each factor or produced commodity will be zero. Thus, this model is quantitatively meaningful in a general equilibrium setting.

At the equilibrium price some of excess demands will be positive and others negative

It must be noted that the above result is obtained under two crucial assumptions: (1) The prices can be explicitly determined and (2) all of the prices are nonnegative. Anyone who has some knowledge of mathematics will know that a system containing the same number of variables as equations may not have a solution if the equations are not consistent. As a simple example, we have the following two equations in two variables:

$$X + Y = 5 \tag{12.20}$$

$$X + Y = 2 \tag{12.21}$$

then there do not exist an X and a corresponding Y that satisfy both equations, since the two equations are not consistent. When there are a large number of excess demand functions and the same number of variables, the conditions that guarantee the consistency of the equations and, therefore, the existence of a solution are not simple. Furthermore, even if the equations in the system are independent and consistent, an explicit solution for each variable may not be possible. Finally, even if an explicit solution for each variable is possible, the solutions for some variables may not be unique. In fact, some of the solutions may even be negative or result in complex or imaginary numbers, which makes perfect mathematical sense but is meaningless in economics. (As we have mentioned above, the prices must be nonnegative in order to be meaningful in economics.) Hence, the Walras model does not provide a proper solution to these complex problems.

Recent developments in advanced theory have shed some light on the problems of existence and uniqueness. The proofs of the theorems involve the advanced mathematics of topology, which is beyond the scope of this book. However, students who are interested in this topic can consult Allen (1959), Debreu (1959), or Kuenne (1963).

12.6 INPUT–OUTPUT ANALYSIS AS A GENERAL EQUILIBRIUM SYSTEM

Although the notion of an input–output table was first introduced in 1759 by the French economist Francois Quesnay in his *Tableau Economique* (see Blaug, 1962), it was not until Wassily Leontief formulated a complete model of the interindustry workings of the American economy that input–output analysis became recognized and accepted as an integral part of theoretical economics. Leontief's contribution to economics not only provided a theoretical framework for linking all industries together (thus representing a form of general equilibrium analysis), but also introduced a useful tool to business and government for solving practical problems dealing with the allocation of resources and production economics. (See, e.g., Leontief, 1953, 1966; and Chenery and Clark, 1959.) For his pathbreaking efforts in economics, Leontief was awarded the Nobel prize in 1973.

Input–output analysis is essentially a model of production in which we regard the quantity of each output for final use (i.e., consumption, investment, and government) as being given. In this sense, it is not a general equilibrium system for the economy as a whole. However, it is a very useful tool for the purpose of economic planning of an economy as a whole or for use by a large firm in first estimating the total demand for the industry's output and then estimating its annual sales according to its market share of industry sales. The model (as well as the input–output table itself) also provides an especially good tool for empirical research; for this reason, economics and business students should become familiar with it. For our purposes, we only use a simple example to illustrate the basic rationale of the model. A mathematical description of the general model will be presented in the appendix of this chapter.

Input–output analysis enables estimation of demand for an industry's output, given final demand

Input–output analysis starts with an input–output table that gives the total output of each and every industry, the distribution of that output among the various industries as inputs, and the amount that is allocated for final use. The left margin of the table usually lists the producing industries, whereas the top margin lists the purchasing (user) industries of the output of the given industry. Since each industry is, at the same time, both a producer and a user, the table is a square matrix. For the sake of simplicity, we shall assume that the economy consists of only two industries, which can be referred to as *consumer goods* and *investment products* industries (or, alternatively, agriculture and manufacturing). Also for the sake of simplicity, we shall assume that there is only one primary input—labor. Although the figures in an input–output table usually represent monetary value, they can also represent physical units. In the latter case, only the row totals make any sense, since the columns cannot be added (i.e., we would be adding oranges with machinery, an obvious anomoly). In our simple example, we shall use physical units.

Consider Table 12.1. The first row shows that sector I produces a total output of 40 units, of which 20 units are used by themselves as an input, 9 units are used by sector II as an input, and 11 units are left for final consumption. The second row shows that sector II produces a total output of 30 units, of which 12 units are used by sector I as an input, 6 units are used by themselves as an input,

TABLE 12.1

Producing sector	Using sector			
	I	II	Final use	Total output
I	20	9	11	40
II	12	6	12	30
Primary input	20	10	5	35

and 12 units are left for final investment. The last row shows the amount of labor used by each sector (final consumption including such primary inputs as servants and chauffeurs), whereas the last column actually contains the row sums. As we have noted above, the column sums do not make sense in terms of physical units. For example, the first column indicates that 20 units of commodity I, 12 units of commodity II, and 20 units of labor are used as inputs in order to produce the 40 units of commodity I. The sum of 20 units of commodity I, 12 units of commodity II, and 20 units of labor is neither commodity I, commodity II, nor labor in terms of physical units. However, if the data were in terms of monetary value instead of physical units, then the column figures could be added together. In the appendix, monetary value is used for the general model.

The technology matrix assumes that constant returns to scale will prevail

From the above information, a technological matrix can be computed. Under the assumption of constant returns to scale, we can say that if 20 units of commodity I and 12 units of commodity II are required to produce 40 units of commodity I, then 0.5 unit of I and 0.3 unit of II are required to produce 1 unit of commodity I. Similarly, the information in Table 12.1 implies that 0.3 unit of I and 0.2 unit of II are required to produce 1 unit of commodity II. This information can be arranged as shown in Table 12.2, in which final use and total output columns are omitted. Table 12.2 is called the *technology matrix*.

Table 12.2 can be computed from Table 12.1 arithmetically. By dividing the items in the first column by the total output of the first row in Table 12.1, we obtain the first column of Table 12.2. The same operation is then performed for the second column and total output of the second row of Table 12.1 to obtain the second column of Table 12.2. The first column of Table 12.2 shows that 0.5 unit of commodity I, 0.3 unit of commodity II, and 0.5 unit of the primary input are required as inputs in order to produce 1 unit of commodity I. Similarly, column 2 shows that 0.3 unit of commodity I, 0.2 unit of commodity II, and 0.33 unit of the primary input are required as inputs in order to produce 1 unit of commodity II. It should be observed that there is no technological substitution between the inputs for producing any one of the outputs in this model. This implies a zero MRTS and the existence of rectangular isoquants.

TABLE 12.2

Producing sector	Using sector	
	I	II
I	0.5	0.3
II	0.3	0.2
Primary input	0.5	0.33

This model has many uses, the most important of which is for estimating both the total output of each and every industry in an economy as well as the amounts of primary inputs required to produce a certain amount of each commodity for final use. Thus, in principle, the production of each and every commodity for final use requires each and every commodity as an input, which, in turn requires each and every commodity as an input, and so on in a never-ending succession of continuing cycles. The sum of the immediate (direct) and indirect input requirements for each and every commodity, together with the amount required for final use, constitutes the total output requirements for each commodity. For example, the data in Table 12.1 show that the total output of industry I is 40 units, of which 20 units are used by themselves as an input and 9 units are used by industry II as an input, leaving only 11 units for final use. Similarly, for industry II we note that out of 30 units of total output, 18 units are used as inputs and only 12 units are left for final use. Such data as these are obtained from past records. However, since business and government agencies (in particular, planning agencies) are more interested in the future, their problem is usually one of determining the total output requirements to meet a known or assumed final use given the existing technology. The input–output model provides an answer to this question—provided that the technological information is available and reliable.[4] In Section 12.7, by means of iterative method, we shall demonstrate the use of this model in terms of a highly simplified example. The more-general mathematical solution of an input–output model will be presented in the appendix to this chapter.

12.7 THE ITERATIVE METHOD AND THE INVERSE OF THE LEONTIEF MATRIX

In the iterative method, we start by working backward from the final use to a total output requirement that satisfies both intermediate and final demand. The technological matrix is important for accomplishing this. The computational procedure is to start with the final use figures. In our numerical example, the 11 units of commodity I for final use require $11 \times 0.5 = 5.5$ units of commodity I as a direct input. This is true because Table 12.2 tells us that 0.5 unit of commodity I is required as an input in order to produce 1 unit of commodity I. Hence, when 11 units

---

[4] The reliability of the technical information has two facets. First of all, it depends on how carefully the information has been gathered and at what level of industry detail. Secondly, it depends on whether the technology existing at the time that the data were gathered can be assumed to remain relatively fixed over the period of time for which the analysis and projected use of the technical coefficients are applied. (See, e.g., Leontief, 1953, for a good discussion of this problem.)

TABLE 12.3

	Input requirements				Output	
	I	Subtotal	II	Subtotal	I	II
	5.5		3.3		11	
	3.6		2.4			12
Round 1: direct input requirements		9.1		5.7		
	4.6		2.7		9.1	
	1.7		1.1			5.7
Round 2: indirect input requirements		6.3		3.8		
	3.2		1.9		6.3	
	1.1		0.8			3.8
Round 3: indirect inputs		4.3		2.7		
	2.2		1.3		4.3	
	0.8		0.5			2.7
Round 4: indirect inputs		3.0		1.8		
	1.5		0.9		3.0	
	0.5		0.4			1.8
Round 5: indirect inputs		2.0		1.3		
	1.0		0.6		2.0	
	0.4		0.3			1.3
Round 6: indirect inputs		1.4		0.9	1.4	0.9
Total		26.1		16.2	37.1	28.2

of commodity I are produced, 5.5 units of this commodity are required as an input under the assumption of constant returns to scale. Similarly, $11 \times 0.3 = 3.3$ units of commodity II are required as an input for the 11 units of commodity I. Thus, the direct inputs for 11 units of commodity I are 5.5 units of commodity I and 3.3 units of commodity II. These figures are entered into Table 12.3 as input requirements under I and II, respectively. The 11 units of output of commodity I are also recorded in Table 12.3 in the output column under 1. Hence, from the first row of Table 12.3 we can see that in order to obtain 11 units of commodity I, 5.5 units of commodity I and 3.3 units of commodity II are required as inputs. In a similar fashion, the 12 units of commodity II for final use require $12 \times 0.3 = 3.6$ units of commodity I and $12 \times 0.2 = 2.4$ units of commodity II as inputs. These figures are entered into the second row of Table 12.3.

The technology matrix is the basis for estimating direct and indirect commodity inputs

Table 12.3 should be read beginning from the right. Thus, the first row says that, based on the technological information of Table 12.2, the production of 11 units of commodity I will require the direct use of 5.5 units of commodity I and 3.3 units of commodity II as inputs. Similarly, the second row indicates that to produce 12 units of commodity II will require the direct use of 3.6 units of commodity I and 2.4 units of commodity II as inputs. The sum of the first two figures in the input I column (i.e., 9.1) indicates the total *direct* input requirements of commodity I for producing 11 units of commodity I and 12 units of commodity II.

This sum is recorded in the subtotal column for input I. Similarly, the sum of the first two figures in the input II column (i.e., 5.7) indicates the total direct input requirements of commodity II for producing 11 units of commodity I and 12 units of commodity II. These 9.1 units of commodity I and 5.7 units of commodity II must be first produced in order to be used as inputs to produce the commodities for final use. For the sake of convenience, we have noted these initial direct requirements in the last two columns of the table under the heading "output."

The fourth row of Table 12.3 is computed in a fashion similar to that of the first row. Using the information in the first column of the technological matrix (i.e., Table 12.2) we have input requirements of 4.6 units of commodity I and 2.7 units of commodity II for producing 9.1 units of commodity I. Analogously, by using the information in the second column of Table 12.2, we have input requirements of 1.7 units of commodity I and 1.1 units of commodity II for producing 5.7 units of commodity II. The subtotals for commodities I and II—6.3 and 3.8, respectively—are *indirect* inputs for producing 11 units of commodity I and 12 units of commodity II for final use. In turn, these inputs have to be produced before they can be used as inputs. Accordingly, they are recorded in the appropriate output column. The rows that follow are computed in the same manner as above, and they all show the indirect input requirements of the succeeding rounds for the given quantities of the commodities that are needed, in the end, for final use. Theoretically, this iteration can go on for an infinite number of rounds. However, it can easily be seen from Table 12.3 that the input requirements decrease rapidly in each succeeding round. Hence, a reasonable number of rounds would, under the usual circumstances, give a good approximation for the total output figures.

In our simple example, we have computed six rounds. After six rounds of iteration, the bottom row shows that the total outputs of commodities I and II needed to satisfy the final use requirements of these commodities are approximately 37.1 and 28.2 units, respectively. The total direct and indirect input requirements of commodities I and II needed to satisfy the 11 and 12 units (respectively) for their final use are approximately 26.1 and 16.2 units, respectively. These total figures are approximations due to the limited number of iterations. However, we do know that the more rounds of iterations that are carried out, the better the approximations of production requirements. In our specific case, we know that the precise total outputs are 40 and 30 units for commodities I and II, respectively. Hence, after six rounds of iterations, the approximation errors are roughly 5%.

Once the total commodity outputs have been estimated, the total labor requirements can easily be estimated by using the labor coefficients and the already-estimated total outputs. In our ex-

Given the direct and indirect commodity inputs, resource requirements can be easily estimated

ample, we can see from Table 12.2 that the labor coefficient for industry I is 0.5. This is true because to produce 40 units of commodity I, 20 units of labor are required; thus, 0.5 unit of labor is required for the production of 1 unit of commodity I. Similarly, the labor coefficient for industry II is 10/30 = 0.33; that is, 0.33 unit of labor is required for the production of 1 unit of commodity II. In our example, the estimated labor requirement is 0.5 × 37.1 + 0.33 × 28.2 = 27.9. From Table 12.1, we see that the actual labor requirement for the two industries is 30 units. Hence, the error of the estimate for labor is less than 7%.

The iterative method was employed here for the sole purpose of illustrating the rationale of the model. In practice, more-sophisticated mathematical methods are used such that precise quantities and not just estimates can be computed. As we noted earlier, the general input–output model and its mathematical solution are presented in the appendix to this chapter. For the moment, we shall use a simple numerical example to demonstrate the mathematics that are involved.

As we have already mentioned, Table 12.2 is called the technology matrix of the model. If we subtract the diagonal elements (i.e., the first row–first column and second row–second column elements) from one and put a negative sign in front of all of the other elements, we obtain a new matrix:

$$\begin{bmatrix} 0.5 & -0.3 \\ -0.3 & 0.8 \end{bmatrix}$$

This matrix is generally called the *Leontief matrix*. The inverse of the Leontief matrix is not only quite important from a computational point of view, but also has an important economic interpretation. We first illustrate the computational value of the inverse matrix, which is

$$\begin{bmatrix} 2.58 & 0.97 \\ 0.97 & 1.61 \end{bmatrix}$$

Once the final use estimates of commodities I and II are shown, the total outputs can be computed directly from the inverse matrix. In our case, for example, the quantities of commodities I and II for final use are 11 and 12 units, respectively. Using the inverse matrix, we find that the total output of commodity I is the sum of the 11 × 2.58 + 12 × 0.97 = 40.02, whereas the total output of commodity II is the sum of the products 11 × 0.97 + 12 × 1.61 = 29.99. Comparing these figures with Table 12.1, it can be seen that, except for a small error due to rounding, they are precisely the total outputs.

The reason the above computation is correct is that the elements of the inverse matrix indicate the direct *and* indirect inputs that are involved in producing one unit of a commodity for final use, whereas the elements in the technology matrix only indicate the direct—not the indirect—input. By direct input we mean that amount of each commodity required as an input for producing one unit of a commodity for final use. By indirect input we mean that amount of each commodity required as an input for producing the commodities that are subsequently used as direct inputs, plus the amount of each commodity required as an input for producing the indirect inputs, and so forth. For example, in Table 12.3, the direct input requirements are indicated by the round 1 figures, whereas the indirect input requirements are shown by the sums of input figures for round 2, round 3, ..., and round n, where n approaches infinity.

For further clarification, let us go back to the figures in Table 12.2 and the inverse matrix. The number 0.5, that is, the element of the first row and first column in the table, shows that 0.5 unit of commodity I is required as a *direct input* for producing 1 unit of commodity I for final use. In addition, the table also shows that this unit of commodity I also requires 0.3 unit of commodity II as a direct input. These direct inputs, in turn, require both commodities I and II as inputs, which, in turn, require successive amounts of commodities I and II as inputs, and so on without end. The elements in the inverse matrix take both direct and indirect inputs into consideration. For example, the element in the first row and first column of the inverse matrix (i.e., 2.58) indicates that 2.58 units of commodity I are required as direct and indirect inputs in order to produce 1 unit of commodity I for final use. In other words, a total output of 2.58 units of commodity I is necessary in order to produce 1 unit of commodity I for final use. Similary, the element of the first row and second column in Table 12.2, (i.e., 0.3) indicates the direct input of commodity I that is required to produce 1 unit of commodity II for final use. The corresponding element in the inverse matrix (0.97) shows the requirements of commodity I as direct and indirect inputs in order to produce 1 unit of commodity II for final use. Since 2.58 units of commodity I are required as direct and indirect inputs in order to produce 1 unit of commodity I for final use, then if 11 units of commodity I are required for final use, we have 11×2.58 = 28.38 units of commodity I required as total input to satisfy the final use of commodity I. Similary, each unit of commodity II for final use requires 0.97 unit of commodity I as direct and indirect inputs; therefore, when 12 units of commodity II are required for final use, $12 \times 0.97 = 11.64$ units of commodity I are required as direct and indirect inputs. In our simple example of only two commodities in the whole economy, the total output requirement of commodity I is the sum of the above two figures: $28.38 + 11.64 = 40.02$, as we have computed before.

The elements in the second row of Table 12.2 (i.e., 0.3 and 0.2) indicate the requirements of commodity II as a direct input for

Direct and indirect inputs always equal total industry output

producing 1 unit of commodities I and II, respectively. The corresponding elements in the inverse matrix (i.e., 0.97 and 1.61) show the requirements of commodity II as direct and indirect inputs in order to produce 1 unit, respectively, of commodities I and II for final use. Thus, when 11 units of commodity I are required for final use, $11 \times 0.97 = 10.67$ units of commodity II are required as direct and indirect inputs. Similarly, 12 units of commodity II for final use require $12 \times 1.61 = 19.32$ units of commodity II as direct and indirect inputs. Hence, to have 11 units of commodity I and 12 units of commodity II for final use, we require a total output of $10.67 + 19.32 = 29.99$ units of commodity II, as we have computed before.

We have gone into considerable detail in presenting the iterative method and explaining the meaning and use of the inverse of the Leontief matrix. The former illustrates the rationale of the input–output model, whereas the latter demonstrates the practical value of the model in solving certain economic and business problems. It should be pointed out that the construction of a technology matrix and the computation of the inverse of the Leontief matrix are not simple matters when many sectors of an economy are involved. For the U.S. economy, the cost of producing these tables involves millions of dollars of expenditure. Hence, it is not practical for a firm or a private organization to produce them, and, in fact, there is no need to. Leontief has constructed 41 sector tables for the U.S. economy of 1919 and 1929. There are 81 sector tables for the technology matrix, inverse matrix, and dollar flow between the sectors included in his book, *Input–Output Economics* (Leontief, 1966). The United States Bureau of Labor Statistics (BLS) constructed a 96-sector set of tables for 1939 and published them in 1951. The BLS and the Interagency Committee on Input–Output also constructed such tables for 450 industry sectors for 1947 transactions and published them in 1951. The United States Department of Commerce, in cooperation with the Department of Agriculture, Department of Labor, and several other agencies, constructed such tables for the U.S. economy based on the 1958 Census of Manufacturers, which, it was said, incurred a cost of more than $5 million. It was subsequently revised and published in the *Survey of Current Business* in September 1965. Updates to 1963 have been constructed, and work on the production of new input–output tables is taking place continuously. Many other countries, such as Norway, Denmark, The Netherlands, Italy, Britain, Japan, Canada, Australia, France, New Zealand, Mexico, Yugoslavia, and Spain, have constructed such tables for their respective economies.[5] Thus, such infor-

---

[5] In addition, several regional and special-use tables have been prepared for the United States by various agencies of the federal, state, or local government.

mation with respect to the U.S. economy or for use in practical problem solving can be obtained without too much difficulty.

Although the input–output model covers only the production sectors, it does link all of the sectors together. This is done through the integration of expenditures for services and transport into the total expenditures of the producing sectors. Therefore, it can be considered a general equilibrium model. Students who desire a more-complete introduction to input–output analysis should refer to some of the excellent books on the subject (e.g., Chenery and Clark, 1956; Cameron, 1968; Leontief et al., 1953; and Samuelson, Dorfman, and Solow, 1958, provide a thorough and rigorous treatment of the subject). For those who are interested in exploring the practical uses of input–output tables, we suggest that they obtain a bibliography of articles from the U.S. Department of Commerce, Bureau of Economic Analysis, or U.S. Department of Labor, Bureau of Labor Statistics.

SUMMARY

In the previous chapters we analyzed various aspects of consumer and producer behavior under different models of the market. Although the material covered differed from chapter to chapter, partial analysis and its concomitant assumption of "other things being equal" were the basis upon which consumer and producer behavior was examined. In this chapter, this assumption was relaxed in order that the more global method of general equilibrium analysis pioneered by Leon Walras could be employed. We explained that whereas Walras had shown perfect competition to be consistent with the maximization of consumers' satisfaction and the firms' profits under general equilibrium, it was left to later economists to solve the problems of the *existence* and *uniqueness* of general equilibrium under perfect competition.

Leaving the mathematics of general equilibrium analysis for the appendix to this chapter, we used the graphical method to illustrate the main postulates of general equilibrium. We began with a simple two-person–two-commodity model, using the Edgeworth box to demonstrate general equilibrium in pure exchange. We showed that equilibrium of exchange occurs along the contract curve, which is the locus of points of tangency of the indifference curves of the two consumers, and, hence, assures the equality of the marginal rate of substitution (MRS) for the two traded commodities for the two consumers. Thus, a point on the contract curve indicates that the MRS of one commodity for the other is the same for each of two consumers. We then pointed out that under certain assumptions concerning the consumer's behavior a unique equilibrium in exchange will occur at the intersection of the offer curves of the two consumers, which intersection is necessarily a point on the contract curve satisfying the condition of equality of the MRS for the two consumers.

Next we used the two-input–two-output model of production to show that general equilibrium is again represented by a production contract curve that is given by the locus of points of tangency of production isoquants and assures the equality of the marginal rates of technical substitution (MRTS). We described the derivation of the production possibility curve (PPC) from the production contract curve to demonstrate that the PPC is the locus of maximum output of the one commodity for any given amount of the other commodity under the assumption that resources and technology are fixed. It was also noted that since the PPC curve is derived from the production contract curve, the slope of the PPC curve at any point represents the MRPT between the two commodities under the conditions of maximum output for a given level of resources and fixed technology.

Bringing together our separate analyses of equilibrium in exchange and production, we explained that general equilibrium in both exchange and production is achieved when the MRPT in production is equal to the MRS of consumers in exchange between any pair of commodities, and that this condition is valid not only for the simple case but for any number of consumers and commodities, provided perfect competition prevails in all markets. Discussion of the more general n person, m commodity case will be found in the mathematical appendix that follows.

We concluded with a discussion of Walras' concept of excess demand and the Leontief input–output model as different approaches to general equilibrium analysis. It was explained that the Walras model of excess demand can only be used to solve for relative prices, whereas the Leontief model has a more general applicability for determining resource requirements to satisfy final and intermediate demand in an interdependent economy.

EXERCISES AND QUESTIONS FOR CHAPTER 12 ON GENERAL EQUILIBRIUM ANALYSIS

1. What is the essential difference between partial and general equilibrium analysis? Why do you suppose that economics textbooks devote a disproportionate amount of space to partial equilibrium analysis? Explain.

2. What has Leon Walras contributed to general equilibrium analysis? Explain the significance of his contribution.

3. Why is input–output analysis considered a general equilibrium model? Explain.

4. Why is the Edgeworth box an important tool in general equilibrium analysis? Explain.

5. Define an individual's offer curve in pure exchange. Starting from

an initial endowment, how is an offer curve derived? Explain. Use a graph(s) to enhance your explanation.

6. Can pure exchange without production result in a higher level of satisfaction (utility) for all consumers? Explain. A simple two-person–two-commodity economy may be used to illustrate your point.

7. Two producers use labor and capital to produce the two commodities X and Y. Each producer has an initial endowment of a certain quantity of labor and capital. Is it possible that a reallocation of labor and capital will result in an increase in the output of both commodities for the same total amounts of resources? Explain.

8. How can a production possibility (transformation) curve between two products be derived? Use a graph(s) to assist in your explanation.

9. What do we mean by the term *"excess demand function"*? Explain.

10. What kind of problems is the input–output model most useful for solving? Explain.

11. How are the Leontief and technology matrices related? What does an element (say $a_{ij} = 0.3$) of a technology matrix corresponding to industry i for the left margin and industry j for the top margin mean? Explain.

12. What does an element (say $a^{ij} = 1.5$) of the inverse of a Leontief matrix mean? Explain.

13. What does the slope of a production possibility curve (PPC) tell you?

APPENDIX TO CHAPTER 12

A MATHEMATICAL NOTE ON GENERAL EQUILIBRIUM THEORY

A12.1 THE WALRAS GENERAL EQUILIBRIUM MODEL

The Walras general equilibrium model is based on a number of assumptions that are necessary to a general solution for the outputs and prices of the system. First of all, it is assumed that each individual has a certain initial endowment of each of the productive factors (land, labor, and capital); furthermore, the individual can buy and sell (at prevailing market prices) any of the factors or commodities produced using the productive factors. Secondly, it is assumed that, as a consumer, the individual derives satisfaction (utility) from the consumption (use) of the factors or commodities that he or she retains or purchases, whereas, on the other hand, as a producer, the individual will attempt to combine inputs for the production and sale of a product with the objective of maximizing profits. Finally, technology is assumed to be given and specified by a production function that describes the relationship between factor inputs and output.

Given these assumptions, we can state that if the second-order conditions for utility or profit maximization are satisfied, then the solution of a system of simultaneous equations which comprises the first-order conditions for utility or profit maximization will yield the excess demand function (positive or negative) of a consumer or firm. The sum of the excess demands of all consumers and producers for a commodity or productive factor is the market excess demand, which is a function of all of the prices (which, in turn, are considered the independent variables). For the economy, the number of excess market demand functions is equal to the number of variables (i.e., prices); hence, the system is consistent. This is the essential point of the Walras general equilibrium model. We shall now proceed to give a detailed mathematical description of the Walras model.

Suppose that there are a total of n goods, the first m of which are productive factors, whereas the remainder are produced commodities. Let q_i denote the quantity of the ith good; then q_1, $q_2, ..., q_m$ are the quantities of the productive factors, whereas $q_{m+1}, q_{m+2}, ..., q_n$ are the quantities of the produced commodities. Let us denote the prices of the goods by $P_1, P_2, ..., P_n$. Suppose that there are a total of H consumers. The initial endowment of productive factors for the hth consumer can be denoted by $q_{h1}^0, q_{h2}^0, ..., q_{hm}^0$, whereas his or her consumption of the goods can be denoted by $q_{h1}, q_{h2}, ..., q_{hn}$. The hth consumer's excess demand for a productive factor is equal to the quantity consumed minus the initial stock, whereas for a produced commodity it is equal to the quantity consumed. If E_{hj} denotes the excess demand for the jth good by consumer h, then we have

$$E_{hj} = q_{hj} - q_{hj}^0 \gtreqless 0, \quad j = 1, 2, ..., m$$

$$E_{hj} = q_{hj} \geq 0, \qquad j = m + 1, m + 2, ..., n$$

(A12.1)

It is assumed that a consumer's preference can be represented by a utility function, the arguments of which are the quantities of goods consumed. Thus,

$$U_h = U_h(q_{h1}, q_{h2}, ..., q_{hn}) \tag{A12.2}$$

The utility function can also be written in terms of excess demands; by substitution, (A12.2) becomes

$$U_h = U_h(E_{h1} + q_{h1}^0, ..., E_{hm} + q_{hm}^0, E_{hm+1}, ..., E_{hn}) \tag{A12.3}$$

Assume that there are k_i firms in industry i. Let us denote the profit of firm k in industry i by π_{ki} and the proportion of firm k in industry i owned by consumer h by $a_{hki} \geq 0$. The income of consumer h is equal to the monetary value of his or her factor endowment plus his or her profit; this can be written

$$Y_h = \sum_{j=1}^{m} P_j q_{hj}^0 + \sum_{i=m+1}^{n} \sum_{k=1}^{k_i} a_{hki} \pi_{ki} \tag{A12.4}$$

The monetary value of all of the goods that an individual consumer consumes must also be equal to his or her income, that is,

$$Y_h = \sum_{j=1}^{n} P_j q_{hj} \tag{A12.5}$$

By substituting (A12.1) into (A12.4) and (A12.5) and subtracting, the consumer's budget constraint can be written

$$\sum_{j=1}^{n} P_j E_{hj} - \sum_{i=m+1}^{n} \sum_{k=1}^{k_i} a_{hki} \pi_{ki} = 0 \tag{A12.6}$$

The first-order conditions for utility maximization, subject to the consumer's budget constraint, can be derived by using the

Lagrange multiplier technique. We construct the Lagrange function such that

$$L = U_h(E_{h1} + q_{h1}^0, ..., E_{hm} + q_{hm}^0, E_{hm+1}, ..., E_{hn})$$
$$- \lambda(\sum P_j E_{hj} - \sum \sum a_{hki} \pi_{ki}) \tag{A12.7}$$

where λ is the Lagrange multiplier. The first-order conditions for constrained utility maximization require that the partial derivatives of the Lagrange function with respect to E_{hj} and λ be zero. Thus,

$$\partial L/\partial E_{hj} = \partial U_h/\partial E_{hj} - \lambda P_j = 0, \qquad j = 1, 2, ..., n$$
$$\partial L/\partial \lambda = -(\sum P_j E_{hj} - \sum \sum a_{hki} \pi_{ki}) = 0 \tag{A12.8}$$

Eliminating λ from the first n equations of system (A12.8), we have $n-1$ independent equations of the form

$$\frac{\partial U_h/\partial E_{hi}}{\partial U_h/\partial E_{hj}} = \frac{P_i}{P_j}, \qquad i, j = 1, 2, ..., n \tag{A12.9}$$

This implies that the consumer must equate the MRS (marginal rate of substitution) of every pair of goods to their price ratio in order to maximize his or her satisfaction (utility) for a given income.

The $n-1$ equations (A12.9), together with the last equation in (A12.8), constitute n equations. It will be shown below that profits can be expressed as a function of price. Thus, the n equations involve $2n$ variables E_{hj} and P_j, $j = 1, 2, ..., n$. Solving for the E_{hj}s in terms of the prices, the excess demands of consumer h can be expressed as functions of the respective prices. Hence,

$$E_{hj} = E_{hj}(P_1, P_2, ..., P_n), \qquad j = 1, 2, ..., n \tag{A12.10}$$

Since profits are homogeneous of degree one with respect to prices, it can easily be verified that the consumer's excess demand functions are homogeneous of degree zero with respect to the prices of all of the factors and commodities.

In the simple two-commodity–two-person case of pure exchange, a positive excess demand for one commodity by a consumer implies a negative excess demand for the other commodity, that is, the demands are functionally related. As we have already pointed out, the MRS between the two commodities is equal to their price ratio everywhere along an offer curve. The excess demand functions (A12.10) also satisfy this condition. Thus, the excess demand functions derived here correspond to the respective offer curves in Figures 12.3 and 12.4.

The second-order conditions for constrained utility maximization require that the determinants involving the second-order partial derivatives of the utility function and prices should alternate in sign. Let us define

$$U_{ij} \equiv \partial^2 U_h/\partial E_{hj} \partial E_{hi}, \qquad i, j = 1, 2, ..., n$$

We then have

$$\begin{vmatrix} U_{11} & U_{12} & -P_1 \\ U_{21} & U_{22} & -P_2 \\ -P_1 & -P_2 & 0 \end{vmatrix} > 0$$

$$\begin{vmatrix} U_{11} & U_{12} & U_{13} & -P_1 \\ U_{21} & U_{22} & U_{23} & -P_2 \\ U_{31} & U_{32} & U_{33} & -P_3 \\ -P_1 & -P_2 & -P_3 & 0 \end{vmatrix} < 0 \qquad \text{(A12.11)}$$

$$(-1)^n \begin{vmatrix} U_{11} & U_{12} & \cdots & U_{1n} & -P_1 \\ U_{21} & U_{22} & \cdots & U_{2n} & -P_2 \\ & & \vdots & & \\ U_{n1} & U_{n2} & \cdots & U_{nn} & -P_n \\ -P_1 & -P_2 & \cdots & P_n & 0 \end{vmatrix} > 0$$

On the production side, each firm uses productive factors and produced commodities as inputs to produce a commodity. The output for firm k in industry i is denoted by Q_{ki}, and the production function can be written

$$Q_{ki} = F_{ki}(q_{ki1}, q_{ki2}, ..., q_{kin}) \qquad \text{(A12.12)}$$

where q_{kij}, $j = 1, 2, ..., n$, denotes the quantity of factor or commodity j used as inputs by firm k in industry i.

The total profit of the firm is its total revenue minus the total cost of its inputs, which can be written

$$\pi_{ki} = P_i F_{ki}(q_{ki1}, q_{ki2}, ..., q_{kin}) - \sum_{j=1}^{n} P_j q_{kij} \qquad \text{(A12.13)}$$

The first-order conditions for profit maximization require that the partial derivatives of the profit function with respect to each and every input be equal to zero. Therefore, we have

$$\partial \pi_{ki}/\partial q_{kij} = P_i \partial F_{ki}/\partial q_{kij} - P_j = 0, \qquad j = 1, 2, ..., n \quad \text{(A12.14)}$$

which implies that the firm will utilize each input up to a point where the value of its marginal physical product is equal to its price. Expressions (A12.14) represent a system of n equations in $2n$ variables, that is, n prices P_j, $j = 1, 2, ..., n$, and n quantities q_{kij}, $j = 1, 2, ..., n$. If the second-order conditions for profit maximization are satisfied, then we can solve for the n quantities in terms of the n prices. Thus, we have

$$q_{kij} = D_{kij}(P_1, P_2, ..., P_n), \qquad j = 1, 2, ..., n \qquad \text{(A12.15)}$$

which are the demand functions of good $j = 1, 2, ..., n$ for firm k in industry i and are obviously functions of all of the prices.

Substituting the n equations (A12.15) into the production function (A12.12), we obtain

$$Q_{ki} = F_{ki}[D_{ki1}(P_1, P_2, ..., P_n), ..., D_{kin}(P_1, P_2, ..., P_n)]$$

$$\text{(A12.16)}$$

which can also be written

$$Q_{ki} = F_{ki}(P_1, P_2, ..., P_n) \tag{A12.17}$$

Denoting the excess demand function of good j for firm k in industry i by E_{kij}, we have

$$E_{kij} = q_{kij} \qquad \text{for} \qquad i \neq j$$
$$E_{kij} = q_{kij} - Q_{ki} \qquad \text{for} \qquad i = j \tag{A12.18}$$

Taking (A12.15) and (A12.17) into consideration, it is obvious that each and every excess demand is a function of all of the prices. For simplicity in notation, the excess demands can be written

$$E_{kij} = E_{kij}(P_1, P_2, ..., P_n), \qquad j = 1, 2, ..., n \tag{A12.19}$$

The profit function (A12.13) is homogeneous of degree 1 with respect to price. If all of the prices on the right side of (A12.13) are multiplied by a constant t, then the profit is also a multiple of t. This is precisely the definition of a homogeneous function of degree 1. Since the quantities q_{kij} are a function of price as shown in (A12.15), we can, by substitution, express profit in terms of prices, as we have mentioned earlier.

The excess demand functions (A12.19) are homogeneous of degree zero with respect to price because they are solutions of the system of equations (A12.14) and will not change if both P_i and P_j are multiplied by a constant t. Thus,

$$tP_i \partial F_{ki}/\partial q_{kij} - tP_j = 0$$

Factoring out the constant t, we obtain

$$t(P_i \partial F_{ki}/\partial q_{kij} - P_j) = 0$$

or

$$P_i \partial F_{ki}/\partial q_{kij} - P_j = 0$$

which is identical to the right side of (A12.14). This implies that the excess demands (A12.19) are homogeneous of degree zero with respect to price.

The aggregate excess demand of industry i for good j is the sum of the excess demands of all of the firms in the industry. In the special case when all of the firms in the industry are identical, the aggregate demand is equal to the number of firms k_i multiplied by the excess demand of the typical firm; this can be written

$$E_{ij} = k_i E_{kij}(P_1, P_2, ..., P_n), \qquad i = m + 1, m + 2, ..., n$$
$$j = 1, 2, ..., n \tag{A12.20}$$

where E_{ij} is the aggregate excess demand for good j by industry i.

The second-order conditions for profit maximization of a firm require that the principal minors of the relevant Hessian determinant alternate in sign. Therefore, we have

$$f_{11} < 0, \quad \begin{vmatrix} f_{11} f_{12} \\ f_{21} f_{22} \end{vmatrix} > 0, \quad \ldots, \quad (-1)^n \begin{vmatrix} f_{11} & f_{12} & \cdots & f_{1n} \\ f_{21} & f_{22} & \cdots & f_{2n} \\ & & \vdots & \\ f_{n1} & f_{n2} & \cdots & f_{nn} \end{vmatrix} > 0$$

$$(\text{A}12.21)$$

where

$$f_{hj} = \partial Q_{ki} / \partial q_{kij} \partial q_{kih}$$

So far we have derived both the excess demand for good j by consumer h [(A12.10)] from the first-order conditions for utility maximization as well as the excess demand for good j by industry i [(A12.20)] based on the assumption of profit maximization of the firms. We are now ready to derive the aggregate excess demand for good j by all consumers and all producers, that is, the market excess demand for good j.

The market excess demand for a produced commodity and/or a productive factor is the sum of the excess demands of the H consumers in (A12.10) and the $n - m$ industries on an input account in (A12.20); this can be written

$$E_j = \sum_{h=1}^{H} E_{hj}(P_1, P_2, \ldots, P_n)$$

$$+ \sum_{i=m+1}^{n} E_{ij}(P_1, P_2, \ldots, P_n, k_i), \quad j = 1, 2, \ldots, n$$

$$(\text{A}12.22)$$

Excess demand functions (A12.22) can be written in the following more-compact form:

$$E_j = E_j(P_1, P_2, \ldots, P_n, k_{m+1}, \ldots, k_n), \quad j = 1, 2, \ldots, n$$

$$(\text{A}12.23)$$

We can readily observe from (A12.23) that the excess market demand for each good is a function of the n prices and the numbers of firms within the $n - m$ industries.

Long-run equilibrium for perfectly competitive markets requires that all markets be cleared (i.e., all excess demands be zero) and that the profit for each firm (and, thus for each industry) also be zero. Therefore, we have

$$E_j(P_1, P_2, \ldots, P_n, k_{m+1}, \ldots, k_n) = 0$$

$$j = 1, 2, \ldots, n$$

$$\pi_j(P_1, P_2, \ldots, P_n) = 0 \qquad (\text{A}12.24)$$

$$j = m+1, m+2, \ldots, n$$

where π_j is the profit of a typical firm in industry j.

We can see that (A12.24) is a system of $2n - m$ equations in

$2n - m$ variables: n prices and $n - m$ k_is. If all of the $2n - m$ equations are independent, then the n prices and the $n - m$ k_is can, in principle, be successfully solved for, since the number of equations in the system will be equal to the number of variables. However, according to Walras' law, the total monetary value of the excess demands for all consumers and producers is necessarily zero for the economy as a whole. Consequently, there are only $2n - m - 1$ independent equations. This can be shown as follows.

By adding together the budget constraints (A12.6) of all consumers, we obtain

$$\sum_h \sum_j P_j E_{hj} - \sum_h \sum_i \sum_k a_{hki} \pi_{ki} = 0 \tag{A12.25}$$

Substituting the excess demands for producers (A12.18) into the profit function (A12.13), summing over all of the firms in industry i, and rearranging terms, we obtain

$$\sum_k \sum_j P_j E_{kij} + \sum_k \pi_{ki} = 0 \tag{A12.26}$$

If we now sum over all of the industries, we obtain

$$\sum_i \sum_k \sum_j P_j E_{kij} + \sum_i \sum_k \pi_{ki} = 0 \tag{A12.27}$$

The sum of (A12.25) and (A12.27) can conveniently be written

$$\sum_j P_j E_j = 0 \tag{A12.28}$$

Since, for an economy as a whole, the total profit of all producers is equal to the total profit of all consumers, the negative total profit in (A12.25) and the positive total profit in (A12.27) cancel each other out. Thus, the sum of the values of the aggregate excess demand of all consumers and the values of the aggregate excess demand of all producers is equal to the value of aggregate excess demand for the economy as a whole; therefore, (A12.28) follows.

Expression (A12.28) is an identity for any set of prices for the economy as a whole. In particular, it holds for a set of equilibrium prices. Because of this identity, when $n - 1$ of the markets, productive factors, and produced commodities are in equilibrium, the remaining factor and commodity markets are also in equilibrium. Hence, only $n - 1$ of the n excess demand functions are independent.

For n goods in an economy, there can be only a maximum of $n - 1$ independent aggregate excess demand functions. As a result, it is impossible to determine the n absolute prices and $n - m$ numbers of firms in the producing industries. However, a set of $n - 1$ relative prices is consistent with the system.

As we have verified above, the excess demands of each and

every consumer and producer are homogeneous of degree zero with respect to price. Therefore, the aggregate excess demands are also homogeneous of degree zero with respect to price. Thus, if all of the prices change by the same proportion, then the aggregate excess demands will not change. It has also been shown that the profits of such firms are homogeneous of degree one with respect to price. Thus, if all of the prices change by the same proportion, then the input and output levels of the firm will remain the same, as is implied by the zero-degree homogeneity of the excess demands of the firm. However, total revenue, total cost, and hence profit will change by the same proportion. Consequently, if a long-run equilibrium is established for one set of prices, the system will remain in equilibrium if all of the prices change by the same proportion. For example, if all of the prices are doubled, then the excess demands will remain zero, each firm's revenues and costs will be doubled, and profit levels will remain equal to zero. Hence, in accord with our theory of perfect competition, no existing firms will go out of business and no new firms will be induced to enter any industry, that is, the number of firms in each industry will remain constant.

Because of this homogeneity of the excess demands and profits of the firm, the number of variables in (A12.24) can be reduced by one if we divide the n absolute prices by the price of an arbitrarily selected commodity (Walras called it the numeraire). In this context, we can see that the price of the numeraire is equal to one, which is the price of money in the real world. If good n is selected as the numeraire, then (A12.24) can be written

$$E_j(P_1/P_n, P_2/P_n, ..., P_{n-1}/P_n, 1, k_{m+1}, ..., k_n) = 0$$

$$j = 1, 2, ..., n$$

$$\pi_j(P_1/P_n, P_2/P_n, ..., P_{n-1}/P_n, 1) = 0 \tag{A12.29}$$

$$j = m + 1, ..., n$$

The Walras model assumes that this system (A12.29), which contains $2n - m - 1$ independent equations, can be solved for the equilibrium values of the $n - 1$ relative prices and the $n - m$ number of firms (one for each industry). Furthermore, the values of the variables from the solution at equilibrium will all be nonnegative. Once the prices and the number of firms in each industry are determined, the excess demands of every consumer and firm can be computed by substituting their values into the individual excess demand functions (A12.10) or (A12.18) [taking (A12.15) and (A12.17) into consideration in the case of the latter].

The above result implies that a long-run equilibrium solution of the Walras general equilibrium system satisfies the following conditions: (1) The satisfaction (utility) of every consumer is maximized, (2) the profit of every firm is maximized, (3) every market is cleared, and (4) every firm earns a zero profit. These are the four conditions of long-run equilibrium stated in the text.

Walras' contribution to general equilibrium theory is in showing the consistency of a free-enterprise market system under perfect competition with both the satisfaction-maximizing (utility-maximizing) behavior of consumers and the profit-maximizing behavior of firms. After counting the number of equations and the number of variables, it is assumed that the relative prices and the number of firms in each industry can be determined and that the solution of the values of the variables are nonnegative at equilibrium. The conditions under which the solution values of the relative prices are nonnegative and unique have been the subject of extensive research in advanced economic theory for the last few decades (under the topical nomenclature of existence and uniqueness of general equilibrium). As we have noted in the text, there have been some important contributions in this area, but most of these developments involve an advanced level of mathematics which is beyond the scope of this book.

A12.2 THE INPUT–OUTPUT MODEL

Input–output analysis begins with the production of an input–output table, which shows the interindustry flows of commodities and services, usually at producer price. Suppose that there are n industries, one final use sector (e.g., consumption), and one primary input (e.g., labor). In addition, assume that there is no export or import of commodities or services. Finally, suppose that each industry uses all of the commodities and the primary factor as inputs to produce a homogeneous commodity, which, in turn, is used by all of the other industries as inputs, some amount being left over for final consumption. Let us denote the total output of industry i by X_i, the quantity of commodity i used by industry j as inputs by X_{ij}, the quantity of commodity i for final use by F_i, the total primary input by K, and the quantity of K used by industry j by K_j. Given this information (data), an input–output table can be constructed as shown in Table A12.1.

TABLE A12.1. Input–Output Table

Producing sector	Using sector				Final use	Total
	1	2	...	n		
1	X_{11}	X_{12}	...	X_{1n}	F_1	X_1
2	X_{21}	X_{22}	...	X_{2n}	F_2	X_2
$\vdots$	$\vdots$	$\vdots$	$\vdots$	$\vdots$	$\vdots$	$\vdots$
n	X_{n1}	X_{n2}	...	X_{nn}	F_n	X_n
Primary input	K_1	K_2	...	K_n	K_{n+1}	K

By definition, from Table A12.1 we obtain the following $n + 1$ equations:

$$X_{11} + X_{12} + \cdots + X_{1n} + F_1 = X_1$$

$$X_{21} + X_{22} + \cdots + X_{2n} + F_2 = X_2$$

$$\vdots \qquad\qquad\qquad\qquad\qquad\text{(A12.30)}$$

$$X_{n1} + X_{n2} + \cdots + X_{nn} + F_n = X_n$$

$$K_1 + K_2 + \cdots + K_n + K_{n+1} = K$$

where K_{n+1} is the primary factor directly used for final consumption (such as in the case of servants and maids, where labor is used for direct consumption).

A12.2.1 The Production Function, Input Coefficients, and the Technology Matrix

The production function for input–output analysis is assumed to be of the simplest form, that is, constant input coefficients (which implies rectangular isoquants, as explained in Chapter 2). Let us denote the input coefficient of commodity i in the production of commodity j by a_{ij}. Then, by definition, the following holds:

$$a_{ij} = X_{ij}/X_j \qquad \text{or} \qquad X_{ij} = a_{ij}X_j \qquad\text{(A12.31)}$$

In fact, a_{ij} is the quantity of commodity i required as an input in producing one unit of commodity j. The input coefficient of the primary input can be similarly defined as

$$k_j = K_j/X_j \qquad \text{or} \qquad K_j = k_j X_j \qquad\text{(A12.32)}$$

where k_j is the quantity of the primary input required to produce one unit of commodity j.

The input coefficients for the n produced commodities constitute an $n \times n$ square matrix, which we shall denote as A:

$$A = \begin{bmatrix} a_{11} & a_{12} & \cdots & a_{1n} \\ a_{21} & a_{22} & \cdots & a_{2n} \\ & & \vdots & \\ a_{n1} & a_{n2} & \cdots & a_{nn} \end{bmatrix} \qquad\text{(A12.33)}$$

Matrix (A12.33) is usually referred to as the *technology matrix*. By substituting (A12.31) into (A12.30), the first n equations of (A12.30) can be written

$$a_{11}X_1 + a_{12}X_2 + \cdots + a_{1n}X_n + F_1 = X_1$$

$$\vdots \qquad\qquad\qquad\qquad\qquad\text{(A12.34)}$$

$$a_{n1}X_1 + a_{n2}X_2 + \cdots + a_{nn}X_n + F_n = X_n$$

A12.2.2 The Leontief Matrix and the Solution of the System

Using matrix notation, system (A12.34) can be written

$$
\begin{bmatrix} a_{11} & a_{12} & \dots & a_{1n} \\ a_{21} & a_{22} & \dots & a_{2n} \\ & & \vdots & \\ a_{n1} & a_{n2} & \dots & a_{nn} \end{bmatrix}
\begin{bmatrix} X_1 \\ X_2 \\ \vdots \\ X_n \end{bmatrix}
+
\begin{bmatrix} F_1 \\ F_2 \\ \vdots \\ F_n \end{bmatrix}
=
\begin{bmatrix} X_1 \\ X_2 \\ \vdots \\ X_n \end{bmatrix}
\tag{A12.35}
$$

By rearranging terms, (A12.35) can also be written

$$
\begin{bmatrix} 1 & 0 & \dots & 0 \\ 0 & 1 & \dots & 0 \\ & & \vdots & \\ 0 & 0 & \dots & 1 \end{bmatrix}
\begin{bmatrix} X_1 \\ X_2 \\ \vdots \\ X_n \end{bmatrix}
-
\begin{bmatrix} a_{11} & a_{12} & \dots & a_{1n} \\ a_{21} & a_{22} & \dots & a_{2n} \\ & & \vdots & \\ a_{n1} & a_{n2} & \dots & a_{nn} \end{bmatrix}
\begin{bmatrix} X_1 \\ X_2 \\ \vdots \\ X_n \end{bmatrix}
=
\begin{bmatrix} F_1 \\ F_2 \\ \vdots \\ F_n \end{bmatrix}
$$

or   (A12.36)

$$
\begin{bmatrix} 1-a_{11} & -a_{12} & \dots & -a_{1n} \\ -a_{21} & 1-a_{22} & \dots & -a_{2n} \\ & & \vdots & \\ -a_{n1} & -a_{n2} & \dots & 1-a_{nn} \end{bmatrix}
\begin{bmatrix} X_1 \\ X_2 \\ \vdots \\ X_n \end{bmatrix}
=
\begin{bmatrix} F_1 \\ F_2 \\ \vdots \\ F_n \end{bmatrix}
$$

$$\tag{A12.37}$$

The first matrix in (A12.37) is usually called the *Leontief matrix*. Thus, the Leontief matrix is derived by subtracting the technology matrix from a unit matrix.

Since the Leontief matrix contains only constants, if the quantities for final use are known, then the total output requirements of each industry $X_1, X_2, \dots, X_n$ that will satisfy the direct and indirect input requirements as well as leave the required amounts for final use can be computed by means of the inverse of the Leontief matrix:

$$
\begin{bmatrix} X_1 \\ X_2 \\ \vdots \\ X_n \end{bmatrix}
=
\begin{bmatrix} 1-a_{11} & -a_{12} & \dots & -a_{1n} \\ -a_{21} & 1-a_{22} & \dots & -a_{2n} \\ & & \vdots & \\ -a_{n1} & -a_{n2} & \dots & 1-a_{nn} \end{bmatrix}^{-1}
\begin{bmatrix} F_1 \\ F_2 \\ \vdots \\ F_n \end{bmatrix}
\tag{A12.38}
$$

If we denote the element of the ith row and jth column of the inverse matrix by a^{ij}, then the solution for the total outputs of the industries can be written

$$
\begin{bmatrix} X_1 \\ X_2 \\ \vdots \\ X_n \end{bmatrix}
=
\begin{bmatrix} a^{11} & a^{12} & \dots & a^{1n} \\ a^{21} & a^{22} & \dots & a^{2n} \\ & & \vdots & \\ a^{n1} & a^{n2} & \dots & a^{nn} \end{bmatrix}
\begin{bmatrix} F_1 \\ F_2 \\ \vdots \\ F_n \end{bmatrix}
\tag{A12.39}
$$

or

$$X_1 = a^{11}F_1 + a^{12}F_2 + \cdots + a^{1n}F_n$$

$$X_2 = a^{21}F_1 + a^{22}F_2 + \cdots + a^{2n}F_n \qquad \text{(A12.40)}$$

$$\vdots$$

$$X_n = a^{n1}F_1 + a^{n2}F_2 + \cdots + a^{nn}F_n$$

An economic interpretation of the elements of the inverse matrix is meaningful. Recall that a_{ij} in the technology matrix indicates the quantity of commodity i required as direct input in producing one unit of commodity j. In other words, one unit of commodity j for final use requires a_{ij} of commodity i as a direct input, which, in turn, requires every other commodity as an input in order to be produced. The other inputs, in turn, need every commodity (in particular, commodity i) as an input (as shown by the iterative method in the text). The elements in the inverse matrix take both direct and indirect inputs into consideration. In fact, a^{ij} indicates the quantity of commodity i required as both direct and indirect inputs in order to produce one unit of commodity j for final use. Thus, $a^{11}F_1$ is the amount of total output of commodity 1 that is required as direct and indirect inputs in order to produce F_1 units of commodity 1 for final use. Similarly, $a^{12}F_2$ is the quantity of total output of commodity 1 that is required as direct and indirect inputs in order to produce F_2 units of commodity 2 for final use. This explains the rationale of system (A12.40).

Once the total output requirements $X_1, X_2, \ldots, X_n$ are computed, the total primary input requirement can be calculated by the formula

$$K = k_1X_1 + k_2X_2 + \cdots + k_nX_n + K_{n+1} \qquad \text{(A12.41)}$$

The inverse of the Leontief matrix only gives the inverse elements corresponding to the elements of the technology matrix for the produced commodities, that is, it does not give the primary input (or, in the general case, primary inputs). However, the corresponding inverse elements for the primary input can easily be computed once the inverse of the Leontief matrix is available. Let us denote the inverse element of k_j by k^j, which indicates the direct and indirect input requirements of the primary input in order to produce one unit of commodity j for final use. Then

$$k^j = a^{1j}k_1 + a^{2j}k_2 + \cdots + a^{nj}k_n, \qquad j = 1, 2, \ldots, n$$

$$\text{(A12.42)}$$

where k^j indicates the amount of primary input required for direct and indirect input in order to produce one unit of commodity j for final use. Consequently, the total primary input requirement can also be computed directly from the final use figures F_i, i

$= 1, 2, \ldots, n$. Thus, we have

$$K = k^1 F_1 + k^2 F_2 + \cdots + k^n F_n + K_{n+1} \qquad \text{(A12.43)}$$

It can easily be checked that (A12.41) and (A12.43) are equivalent: If one substitutes (A12.40) into (A12.41), the result obtained will be identical to that obtained when (A12.42) is substituted into (A12.43), which proves the equivalence of the expressions. With the k^js known, the primary input requirement can easily be computed once the final use figures are available.

This is a simple input–output model that can easily be extended to include the foreign sector, that is, exports and imports. In this way, international and interregional flows of factors and commodities can be analyzed.

The quantities in Table A12.1 (the input–output table) and (A12.30) can be either in real terms or in terms of nominal monetary value. In reality, they are mostly in terms of nominal monetary values, which are the products of price and quantity. The input–output model can also be used to compute shadow prices of commodities and productive factors. One of the main difficulties with the input–output model is the problem of securing good data. Too often, data are sketchy, which makes the derivation of reliable input coefficients difficult. In addition, the assumption of linearity, which is implicit, raises questions regarding the validity of input usage requirements for different levels of final demand. We shall not cover the extension of the basic model. Interested students can consult *Interindustry Economics* by Chenery and Clark (1965) for an excellent treatment of the input–output model. The student should also refer to *Input–Output Economics* by Leontief (1966).

WELFARE ECONOMICS

INTRODUCTION

Although welfare economics has a long history, some of the technical elements and principles of the modern concept represent comparatively new developments in microeconomic theory. Welfare economics constitutes a special branch of economics which considers the problem of evaluating the relative desirability of economic alternatives with respect to society as a whole from an *ethical* viewpoint; thus, welfare economics involves value judgments. Because it involves ethical (value) judgments, welfare economics is referred to as *normative economics*, which is distinct from *positive (scientific) economics*, where ethical judgments concerning, for example, the use of scarce resources are not involved. Our discussion of production theory in Chapters 1–3 was devoid of ethical considerations and dealt only with objective phenomena.

Up until now, our analysis has been devoted to the interrelationships between economic activities. The implication is that certain phenomena lead to predictable economic results. For example, a change in consumer preference or consumer income would have a certain effect on the demand for a commodity, which, in turn, would have a certain effect on its market price and quantity under given cost conditions. This enables economists to make certain predictions from given economic phenomena. It also enables economists to make policy suggestions for the purpose of achieving certain predetermined economic goals. However, nothing is said with respect to whether or not a given policy is desirable. For example, although economists can predict that an increase in the demand for a commodity will result in both a higher market price and a higher quantity under given cost conditions, as far as economic theory is concerned, nothing can

Welfare economics concerns itself with the desirability of economic alternatives and policy

be said with respect to whether these increases are desirable from the viewpoint of society as a whole. It is in this context that positive (scientific) economics is distinguished from normative (welfare) economics.

We hasten to point out that welfare economics is in no way related to the various government social welfare programs (except as they affect resource allocation), which are based on political and/or humanitarian considerations, not economic efficiency. We also wish to point out that the desirability of commodities and services is essentially subjective. Individuals usually have diverse views on almost everything. Thus, two people having totally different opinions on the same subject is the rule rather than the exception. Hence, it follows that if individual sovereignty is recognized, then the evaluation of two different alternatives may be impossible unless a common denominator between individual subjective views is developed. It turns out that neither economists nor philosophers have been able to develop such a common denominator, and thus some insurmountable difficulty still exists. For example, with given resources, given technology, and full employment, an economy can only produce more of commodity X at the expense of commodity Y. Usually, some people will prefer X to Y whereas others will prefer Y to X. Without a common denominator to measure individual preferences, it is impossible to compare even these two simple alternatives, that is, more of X but less of Y or more of Y but less of X. In spite of these difficulties, economists have developed several criteria, based on which they can make certain assertions concerning the desirability of some (but not all) possible alternatives under certain circumstances. Although it may seem imperfect, this is indeed a remarkable accomplishment.

Evaluating alternatives is impossible without a common denominator to measure individual preference

Since welfare economics is concerned with the society as a whole, the interrelationships between sectors of the economy have to be taken into consideration in the analysis. Therefore, partial analysis is inappropriate to the task, and we must rely on the general equilibrium approach. In fact, the discussions in Chapter 12 will prove very helpful with respect to both our development and the student's understanding of the materials that are covered in this chapter.

In concrete terms, welfare economics is concerned with the level of satisfaction (utility) of all consumers in an economy and the efficient allocation of resources in production. The assumption that more production can lead to higher levels of satisfaction (utility) for some consumers without lowering the levels of satisfaction (utility) of others is implicit to our consideration of welfare economics. Although such an assumption involves value judgments, it is nevertheless a reasonable one upon which a theory can be constructed. To those who disagree with this assumption, welfare economics, as it has been developed, may not make much sense. In this chapter, we shall provide a relatively terse dicussion of the methodology and accepted theorems of modern welfare economics. Although formal proofs of the theorems will not be presented, their commonsense explanations will be discussed. As usual, the mathematical aspects of welfare economics will be developed in the appendix to this chapter.

13.1 CARDINAL UTILITY, ORDINAL UTILITY, INTERPERSONAL COMPARISONS OF UTILITY, AND SOCIAL ECONOMIC WELFARE

At the outset, it should be noted that economists generally regard consumer sovereignty as the cornerstone of economic analysis. It is in this context that one may state, for example, that with respect to a single consumer, alternative A is more desirable than alternative B if the consumer prefers A to B. Similarly, we may state that, for society as a whole, A is more desirable than B if *all* members of society prefer A to B. Although this obviously involves value judgments, most economists would agree that it is an acceptable basis for developing a theory of welfare economics. Of course, we must also realize that if some members of society prefer A to B, whereas, at the same time, other members prefer B to A, then a comparison between A and B becomes complicated; hence, although there may be many possible solutions to the problem, none are entirely satisfactory. It is to the resolution of this type of problem that welfare economics is directed.

One obvious solution to the problem is to count the number of people who prefer A to B and vice versa. Thus, for example, if more members of society prefer A to B than B to A, then A can be judged more desirable than B. (This method precisely represents the democratic system of majority rule, by which political problems are solved using the one-person–one-vote principle.) The conclusion we have arrived at implicitly assumes that there is no difference in the degree of preference. For example, in the one-person–one-vote system, if one person *slightly* prefers A to B, whereas another *intensely* prefers B to A, their preferences will nevertheless cancel each other out in the voting place. By the same logic, in the democratic political system, if one person only slightly prefers A, whereas another intensely hates A, their individual preferences will still cancel each other out in the voting place. Thus, the intensity of preference or hatred does not effect the final result. Obviously, such a system can result in tragedy when it leads to political assassination. We can also appreciate the fact that a system which completely ignores the intensity of individual preference does not seem to be a very satisfactory basis on which to gauge economic welfare.

The one-person–one-vote principle ignores the intensity of individual preference

A second method of solving the problem is to design a measure by which individual preferences (i.e., satisfaction or utility) can not only be compared, but also added together; in technical terms, we must derive an additive cardinal utility function. If it were possible for individual satisfaction (utility) to be measured by some kind of unit scale such as a util (e.g., a pound in weight or a foot in length), then it would be a simple matter to compare the total number of utils that individual members of society would derive from different economic alternatives in order to evaluate their relative desirability with respect to society as a whole. For example, suppose that there are three individuals in a given society. If they derive 5, 6, and 7 utils of satisfaction (utility), respectively, from alternative A, whereas their corresponding levels of satisfaction (utility) for alternative B are 6, 7, and 3 utils, then A can be considered more desirable than B because A offers more *total* satisfaction (utility) to society as a whole than B, since $5 + 6 + 7 = 18$ is greater than $6 + 7 + 3 = 16$. This method of measuring and evaluating satisfaction (utility) is similar to that of measuring and evaluating physical weight. Thus, if three pieces of rock weigh 5, 6, and 7 pounds, respectively, whereas three bales of cotton weigh 6, 7, and 3 pounds, respectively, then it can definitely be said that the first three pieces of material are heavier than the latter, because $5 + 6 + 7 = 18$ pounds is greater than $6 + 7 + 3 = 16$ pounds. This shows that weight is a measure of a physical characteristic such that the weights of individual objects can not only be compared but also added to give comparable sums. Hence, it follows that weight is a comparable and additive cardinal measure. However, it is not always true that cardinal measures are both comparable and additive; in certain cases, they can be comparable, but not additive. As an example of such a case, consider the unit "degree" on a thermometer as a measure of temperature. If the temperature on Sunday was 85° and that on Monday was 80°, then it can generally be agreed that Sunday was warmer than Monday. Therefore, the "degree" is a measure of temperature with which two different dates (or, for that matter, locations) may be compared. However, if the daily temperatures over one week were 85°, 80°, 85°, 70°, 65°, 70°, and 75°, whereas over another week they were 75°, 75°, 65°, 70°, 85°, 80°, and 85°, then it can hardly be agreed that the latter week was warmer than the former, even though the sum of the daily temperatures of the second week was 5° higher than that of the first week. Another example would be if one year had a cool summer and a warm winter, whereas a second year had a hot summer and a cold winter, the total number of degrees of the second year being lower than that of the first. In this case, it can hardly be agreed that the first year was hotter than the second. Moreover, if one day the temperature was 100°, whereas the next day it was 50°, then we would not be likely to agree that the first day was twice as hot as the second. In fact, people would refer to the first day as hot and the second day as chilly. Another reason why 100° cannot be considered twice the temperature of 50° is that 100° in the Fahrenheit scale is about 38° in the Centigrade scale, whereas 50°

Fahrenheit corresponds to 10° Centigrade. Although 100° is exactly two times greater than 50°, 38° is more than three times greater than 10°. Since both systems are considered valid measures of the temperature of a given phenomena, "twice as high" for one system may not be "twice as high" for the other. Thus, this kind of comparison cannot be properly made with respect to temperature.

The above examples show that although certain cardinal measures are both comparable and additive, others have only limited comparability and are not additive. If a measure of satisfaction (utility) having both the property of comparability and the property of additivity (e.g., weight and length) could be devised, then the comparison of economic alternatives would be an easy matter. Unfortunately, although a cardinal utility function having limited comparability can reasonably be constructed, a cardinal utility function that possesses both the property of comparability and the property of additivity is generally considered too restrictive to be realistic. In particular, interpersonal comparisons of satisfaction (utility) are generally considered unrealistic.

Interpersonal comparisons of utility are difficult if not impossible to make

In the cardinal utility approach that played an important role in traditional theory the assumption of diminishing marginal utility was considered important in explaining the law of demand, that is, the existence of a negatively sloped demand curve. Based on the assumption of diminishing marginal utility, some people went on to infer that the marginal utility of a dollar to a rich person should be lower than that to a poor person. In fact, this may be true in most cases, since many rich people do spend their dollars in much the same manner that poor people spend their dimes, nickels, or pennies. However, there are cases where this kind of comparison will not hold. For example, hobos may sometimes spend their dollars—if they have any—more liberally than a miser. Moreover, some rich people seem to value additional dollars more than do some not-so-rich people. Since a good theory must hold under all circumstances, interpersonal comparisons of satisfaction (utility) in the traditional cardinal utility approach were considered questionable. If interpersonal comparisons of satisfaction (utility) are not valid, then the additive property of satisfaction (utility) is out of the question. When this is the case, all of the important theorems in economics must be derived by using an ordinal utility function rather than a cardinal utility function. In addition, it must be recognized that although ordinal utility is inappropriate for such economic problems as the measurement problem in welfare economics for society as a whole, a cardinal utility function, because of its limited comparability, is not helpful either. Since the former requires less-restrictive assumptions than the latter, it follows that (according to the principle of Occam's Razor) ordinal utility theory, in general, is superior to cardinal utility theory. At the same time, however, it does result in considerable difficulty when we come to deal with

Given the inability to make interpersonal comparisions of utility, cardinal measures of utility are out of the question

the measurement problem in welfare economics for society as a whole.

In reality, the market system is, in a sense, a one-dollar–one-vote scheme analogous to the one-person–one-vote political system mentioned earlier. However, since the intensity of a buyer's preference is reflected in the price that he or she is willing to pay for a commodity, the market system, with the help of prices as a manifestation of the cardinal utility of consumers, provides a better way of solving economic problems than does the model of a democratic political system. However, in the marketplace, not only does the *willingness* to pay count, but also the *ability* to pay. It is easily seen that a dollar vote in the marketplace will result in a different product mix for different income distributions. Since the long-run profit of a firm under perfect competition is different from that under, for example, monopoly, and the wage rate and other factor prices may be different under such different market systems as perfect competition, monopoly, and/or monopsony, both the income distribution and product mix will differ under different market systems. Consequently, a theory that can evaluate income distribution and product output conditions under various market systems should be helpful in making policy suggestions that involve value judgments. In spite of all the handicaps of measurement, economists have made considerable progress in welfare economics in the last few decades. Although there is considerable room for improvement, it is worthwhile to describe some of the accomplishments that have so far been made.

13.2 PARETO SUPERIORITY, PARETO OPTIMALITY, AND THE UNANIMITY PRINCIPLE

As we have already stated, welfare economics is concerned with the evaluation of the desirability of various economic alternatives for society as a whole. Each economic alternative, which is generally called a *state of the economy*, involves the economic status of every consumer and firm. In this respect welfare economics is concerned with (1) the amount of each commodity and/or service each consumer receives, as well as the amount of resources that each provides, and (2) the amount of each input used by a firm, as well as the amount of each output produced by it. Thus, the evaluation of the desirability of economic alternatives takes into account the allocation of resources in connection with the level of satisfaction (utility) of all consumers concerned. In this context, however, we should recognize that whereas efficient production is a necessary condition for maximum satisfaction (utility) for society as a whole, it is not a sufficient condition, because different mixes of outputs, although technically efficient with respect to production, may result in different levels of satisfaction (utility) for various consumers. Hence, different allocations of given resources between industries or productive agents, no matter how efficient from a technical perspective, can result in different levels of satisfaction (utility) for some consumers. Given consumer sovereignty, it should be understandable that the ultimate measure of the desirability of an alternative allocation of resources will depend on consumer preference and the level of satisfaction (utility) derived by consumers from that particular allocation.[1]

In a market system the ultimate desirability of alternative allocations of resources depends on consumer preference

A serious problem encountered by economists in welfare economics is the inability to develop a good measure of the level of satisfaction (utility) for society as a whole. As discussed in Section 13.1, a cardinal utility function for consumers which possesses the properties of interpersonal comparability and additivity has not been developed for the reasons stated. If such a utility function were possible, the desirability of different economic alternatives could be easily evaluated by simply adding up the individual utilities for each, and then a comparison of the total utility of each alternative could be used to derive a proper conclusion. Because such a cardinal utility function could not be developed, economists have found it necessary to formulate a theory of consumer behavior based on ordinal utility, with the result that a good measure of the level of satisfaction (utility) for society as a whole cannot be constructed. In technical terms, the determination of the existence of a *social welfare function* is a problem that cannot be satisfactorily solved. This problem led Kenneth Arrow, a Nobel Prize winner in economics, to prove the well-known possibility (or, rather, impossibility) theorem, which implies that, under reasonable assumptions, a social welfare function does not exist (see Arrow, 1951).

Since economists, like other scholars, must work with the tools that are available to them, they have, in the absence of a social welfare function, found it necessary to rely on the *unanimity principle* (commonly referred to as *Pareto optimality*), which was developed by the Italian mathematician and economist Vilfredo Pareto. Although this approach fails to consider many of the noncomparable aspects of different alternatives, it does have the advantage of focusing attention on those particular alternatives

In the absence of a social welfare function, economists must rely on the unanimity principle

[1] As long as we assume the supremacy of consumer sovereignty, the problem of resource allocation becomes one of efficiency in production under perfect competition, since incomes will be distributed according to the contribution of the productive agents, and, in turn, productive agents are free to move into areas where they will best be used. Under imperfect competition, however, income distribution becomes an important issue in welfare economics which, because of a failure on the part of some economists and noneconomists to make proper distinctions, ends up being confused as a shortcoming of the assumption of consumer sovereignty. This is unfortunate, since it can easily lead to improper criticism of the theory and/or an improper evaluation of resource allocation alternatives.

that are at least no worse than any of the others and most distinctively better than some. Inasmuch as Pareto optimality is a very important concept in welfare economics, a formal definition and more-detailed explanation of it is in order. However, before offering a definition of Pareto optimality, it is useful to first define a related concept in order to provide a more-complete basis upon which to evaluate the unanimity principle. Thus, we define *Pareto superiority* as follows.

> **Definition: Pareto Superiority.** A state *A* of the economy is said to be Pareto superior to another state *B* if at least one person is better off in *A* than in *B* but none is worse off.

The concept of Pareto superiority can be illustrated by using an Edgeworth box of the type developed in Figure 12.6 of Chapter 12. Consider Figure 13.1, in which we are given a two-person–two-commodity economy. Suppose that the current state of the economy with respect to income distribution is represented by point *S*, which is on indifference curves 1A and 1B of consumers *A* and *B*, respectively. Points *P* and *Q* on indifference curve 1A also lie on indifference curves 2B and 3B of consumer *B*, respectively. Since *P* is on a higher indifference curve than *S* for *B*, but on the same indifference curve for *A*, it follows that *B* is better off at *P* than at *S*, whereas *A* is no worse off. Therefore, point *P* is said to be Pareto superior to point *S*. For the same reason, *Q* is Pareto superior to both *P* and *S*. Similarly, *F* is Pareto superior to *S*, whereas *G* is Pareto superior to both *F* and *S*. By implication, *H* is Pareto superior to *S* because both *A* and *B* are on higher indifference curves (and are thus better off) at *H* than at *S*. It can also be seen that *H* is Pareto superior to both *F* and *P*, which are both Pareto superior to *S*. This illustrates the following important

FIGURE 13.1

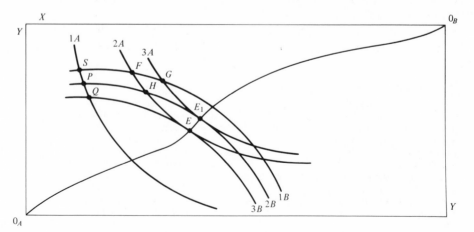

condition: Pareto superiority expresses a transitive relationship. (See Chapter 4 for the meaning of transitivity.) On the other hand, point F is not Pareto superior to point P, nor is point P Pareto superior to point F, because we can see that although A is better off at F than at P, at the same time, B is worse off, whereas although B is better off at P than at F, at the same time, A is worse off. Thus, related to the concept of Pareto superiority we have the concept of Pareto noncomparability.

Definition: Pareto Noncomparability. A state of the economy, say A, is Pareto noncomparable to another state B if neither A is Pareto superior to B nor B is Pareto superior to A.

We are now ready to define the concept of Pareto optimality in a general form that incorporates the concepts of both Pareto superiority and Pareto noncomparability as defined above.

Definition: Pareto Optimality. For a given set of all possible states A, B, ..., E, ... of the economy, if there does not exist a single state that is Pareto superior to E, then E is said to be Pareto optimal for the given set of states.

Figure 13.1 can also be used to illustrate the concept of Pareto optimality. As we have explained above, although F and P are both Pareto superior to S, H is Pareto superior to both F and P. Therefore, F and P cannot be Pareto optimal. Furthermore, although H is Pareto superior to F, P, and S, E is Pareto superior to H; consequently, H cannot be Pareto optimal either. However, there does not exist a point in the Edgeworth box which is Pareto superior to E; thus, E is Pareto optimal. It should be noted that E is a point of tangency between two of the indifference curves of consumers A and B, respectively. When such a point of tangency exists between two indifference curves, it is impossible to find another point on such indifference curves which is Pareto superior to it; hence, in an Edgeworth box, only points of tangency between indifference curves can be Pareto optimal. Furthermore, since it is impossible to find a point that is Pareto superior to such a point of tangency, all points of tangency between indifference curves are Pareto optimal. In Figure 13.1, the curve $\overparen{0_A E E_1 0_B}$ can be seen to represent the locus of tangent points; therefore, it constitutes the Pareto optimal set in the Edgeworth box.

From the above explanation, it is obvious that Pareto optimality can be considered to represent the set of states of an economy such that it is impossible to make a single person better off without making some other person worse off. This is the essence of the unanimity principle. In a sense, the Pareto optimality concept recognizes the veto power of every member of a society. It means

Points of tangency between the indifference curves of two consumers are Pareto optimal

that a change of any kind cannot be considered to be better if it makes *one* person worse off, even if millions of other people are made better off. This is owing to the lack of interpersonal comparability of utility. For this reason, the Pareto optimality approach leaves a lot of room for the noncomparability of alternatives. Since a decrease in income for an individual will, other things being equal, presumably result in a lower level of satisfaction (utility), any redistribution of income cannot be judged as either better or worse by the Pareto approach. Hence, the Pareto approach is of no help in dealing with the problem of income distribution, which should be considered one of its limitations. On the other hand, recognition of the Pareto optimality concept should not be construed as favoring the status quo. Therefore, care must be exercised in the interpretation of the concept in order to avoid misunderstanding and improper inferences with respect to its use in policy analysis. The following anecdote illustrates this point.

A number of years ago, while in graduate school, one of the authors was taking a course in welfare economics. After the professor, who was one of the leading scholars in welfare economics in the country, explained the Pareto optimality concept, a student immediately protested that these kind of arguments were nothing more than an attempt by the "haves" to protect their interest against the "have-nots." Although it is true that, if carried to extremes, use of the Pareto optimality concept as the only standard to judge social or economic desirability could be considered a reactionary argument against the redistribution of income regardless of how inequitable the current situation might be, we must not be trapped into rejecting a concept without regarding the context in which it is employed.[2] On the other hand, if its virtues as well as its limitations are recognized, Pareto optimality can be a useful analytical tool to screen out undesirable alternatives. Hence, it must be understood that nonexistence of a state that is Pareto superior to a state in the Pareto optimal set does not imply that all states in the Pareto optimal set are equally desirable. It only means that from a purely theoretical point of view, economists cannot make a proper evaluation of the relative desirability of the states contained in the Pareto optimal set without introducing more-restrictive assumptions concerning value judgment.

All states in a Pareto optimal set are not necessarily equally desirable

[2] As we shall momentarily point out, Pareto optimality does not mean or imply Pareto superiority. Hence, the value of the concept is that it provides us with yet another tool for evaluating alternatives. It does not say or argue that the current or given distribution of income is Pareto superior; it merely begs the question as to whether a redistribution of income will make someone better off without making someone worse off. In that context, the use of the Pareto optimality concept helps to ensure against undesirable redistribution schemes.

For example, we can note that given a point in an Edgeworth box which is not in the Pareto optimal set, there exists at least one point in the Pareto optimal set which is Pareto superior to it. In this sense, all points that are not in the Pareto optimal set are undesirable because someone can be made better off without making anyone else worse off by moving to a Pareto optimal point. However, this does not say or imply that all points in the Pareto optimal set are equally desirable or even desirable. In fact, our definition of Pareto optimality actually implies this restriction by stating only that there does not exist a state which is Pareto superior to a Pareto optimal state, not that a Pareto optimal state must be Pareto superior to at least one other state of the economy. In reality, a Pareto optimal state may not be Pareto superior to any other state. Points 0_A and 0_B in Figure 13.1 are obvious examples of this. Although these two points are Pareto optimal, they are not Pareto superior to a single point in the Edgeworth box. Hence, Pareto optimality does not imply Pareto superiority. We can make another observation that is closely related to the above. It should be noted that the Pareto optimal set is not usually unique. What this really means is that a *Pareto optimal set is a collection of noncomparable states of the economy after certain undesirable states have been eliminated according to a well-defined criterion, that is, Pareto superiority*. Furthermore, we again emphasize that, due to the unanimity principle, the Pareto optimality approach fails to consider a number of the noncomparable aspects of alternatives. Thus, although the term Pareto optimal seems to imply that each point in the Pareto optimal set is more desirable than any point not in the set, such an interpretation is unfortunate and incorrect. For example, in Figure 13.1, points 0_A and 0_B are Pareto optimal, whereas point G is not Pareto optimal. Since neither 0_A nor 0_B can be said to be Pareto superior to G, according to the Pareto approach, there is nothing that can be said as regards which one of these three states is more desirable than the others. However, if we introduced an additional value judgment, such as equality is better than inequality or that a subsistence level of income must be provided to each individual, then G can be judged more desirable than both 0_A and 0_B because 0_B indicates that A has everything and B has nothing, whereas 0_A indicates that B has everything and A has nothing. On the other hand, the Pareto approach asserts that if all states in the Edgeworth box are attainable, then point G cannot be considered a desirable final solution because there are points in the Pareto optimal set, such as E_1, that are Pareto superior to G. Again, this does not imply that G is inferior to either 0_A or 0_B. On the other hand, if 0_A, G, and 0_B are the *only* possible choices available, G may well be the better choice if survival is considered essential.

As a result of our inability to make interpersonal comparisons of satisfaction (utility), economists are forced to use the Pareto

A point in the Pareto optimal set may not be more desirable than a point not in the set

approach in welfare economics. Again, although the concept of Pareto optimality is very useful in many ways, it has often been misunderstood as favoring the status quo. For this reason, we have devoted more space than usual to the subject in order to provide clarification with respect to the meaning and implications of the concept. The purpose of our book is not to make every student an expert on welfare economics, but to prevent the type of misunderstanding that frequently occurs in the interpretation and use of the Pareto optimality concept. This may be more important than the advanced technical discussions to which students are often exposed without having obtained a basic understanding of the concept.

13.3 PERFECTLY COMPETITIVE EQUILIBRIUM AND PARETO OPTIMALITY

As we have explained above, the Pareto approach is of no help in judging the desirability of different levels of income distribution between individuals for a given total income; however, it can be used to evaluate the various market systems, such as perfect competition, monopoly, monopolistic competition, and oligopoly, that we have discussed in Parts III and IV. Although, as we explained earlier, Pareto optimality may not imply superiority of one system over another, if a system can reach each and every point (not just a few specific points) in the Pareto optimal set, then it should be considered more desirable than another system that can only reach a non-Pareto optimal point, since there exists at least one point in the Pareto optimal set which is Pareto superior (and thus more desirable) than a non-Pareto optimal point. In this sense, a system that is consistent with Pareto optimality should be considered more desirable than a system that is not. It turns out that perfect competition is the best market system in this respect, which further strengthens the economist's belief in the virtue of the perfectly competitive market. However, because the assumptions underlying a theory impose certain limitations on its applicability, a full understanding of their implications is basic to a true understanding of the theory. Before discussing the implications of the assumptions that underlie the theory of Pareto optimality, we shall first state and prove in nontechnical terms the following important theorem.

An economic system consistent with Pareto optimality is preferable to one that is not

Theorem 13.1. *Given certain assumptions, every perfectly competitive equilibrium is Pareto optimal, that is, every perfectly competitive equilibrium occurs at a Pareto optimal state of the economy.*

A formal proof of Theorem 13.1 is beyond the scope of our book. (For a formal proof of Theorem 13.1, see Koopmans, 1957.) However, we can provide a commonsense explanation of the proof which will be illuminating to the student. As we explained in Section 13.2 with regard to the two-person–two-commodity case, Pareto optimality can only occur at a point of tangency between the indifference curves of the two consumers. This result can be extended to any number of consumers by realizing that the tangency of indifference curves also implies the equality of all consumers' marginal rates of substitution (MRSs) between the commodities. (For the meaning of MRS, see Chapter 4.) A commonsense explanation of Theorem 13.1 can be based on first showing that a state of the economy cannot be Pareto optimal if the MRSs of any two individuals are not equal. For example, if the MRSs between X and Y for consumers A and B are 2 and 1, respectively, then A is willing to give up 2 units of Y for 1 unit of X, whereas B is willing to give up 1 unit of X for 1 unit of Y. Under these circumstances, there obviously exist ways of making both A and B better off, or at least of making one better off without making the other worse off. For example, if A gives 1.5 units of Y to B, who in turn gives 1 unit of X to A, then (assuming they are not satiated) both of them will be better off.[3] Similarly, if the MRSs of any two individuals are different in any fashion, then there exist ways to make one of them better off without making anyone else worse off; thus, different MRSs cannot be Pareto optimal. On the other hand, when the MRSs of all individuals are equal, it is impossible to make any one of them better off without making someone else worse off for the given amounts of the commodities. Therefore, a condition of Pareto optimality exists. Hence, in a system of pure exchange, Pareto optimality implies the equality of the MRSs for all consumers between any pair of commodities and vice versa. It also implies that the contract curve is the Pareto optimal set, since the tangency of indifference curves represents the equality of the MRS and points on the contract curve.

Equality of MRSs for all consumers assures Pareto optimality in pure exchange

As we explained in Chapter 6, all buyers face the same market price for each and every commodity in a perfectly competitive market. Hence, all consumers face the same price ratio for any pair of commodities. As was shown in Chapter 4, each consumer's satisfaction (utility) will be maximized for a given income or endowment only if his or her MRS between a pair of commodities is equal to their price ratio. Thus, in a pure exchange, perfectly

---

[3] The student may wish to refer to Chapter 12 for a more-detailed discussion of this point. Simply stated, if A were willing to give up 2 units of Y for 1 unit of X, then it logically follows that he or she would be no worse off in giving up only 1.5 units of Y for 1 unit of X. Obviously, B is better off receiving 1.5 units of Y for 1 unit of X, since he or she would have been willing to surrender 1 unit of X for just 1 unit of Y.

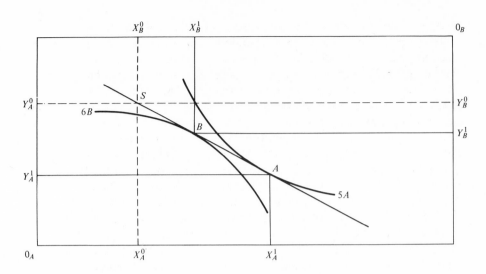

FIGURE 13.2

competitive market, the MRSs between any pair of commodities must be equal for all consumers in equilibrium. This implies that perfectly competitive equilibrium must be Pareto optimal in a pure exchange system. In a two-person–two-commodity case, this is obvious, as can be shown with the use of the Edgeworth box given in Figure 13.2. In this case, we can see that if a budget line is tangent to the two individuals' indifference curves at two different points, then the market cannot be at equilibrium. In Figure 13.2, S represents the status quo. Suppose that the market prices of X and Y result in a price ratio represented by the negative slope of the budget line $\overline{SA}$, which is tangent to A's indifference curve $5A$ at point A and to B's indifference curve $6B$ at point B. With the relative prices as implied by the budget line, A's satisfaction (utility) is maximized if he or she offers $\overline{Y_A^0 Y_A^1}$ of Y in exchange for $\overline{X_A^0 X_A^1}$ of X. On the other hand, B's satisfaction (utility) is maximized if he or she offers $\overline{X_B^0 X_B^1}$ of X in exchange for $\overline{Y_B^0 Y_B^1}$ of Y. Under these circumstances, the quantity demanded for X (i.e., $\overline{X_A^0 X_A^1}$) exceeds the quantity supplied of X, (i.e., $\overline{X_B^0 X_B^1}$), and, at the same time, the quantity supplied of Y (i.e., $\overline{Y_A^0 Y_A^1}$) exceeds the quantity demanded for Y (i.e., $\overline{Y_B^0 Y_B^1}$). This is obviously not a market equilibrium pair of prices. As a consequence of the demand and supply pressures, the market price of X will tend to go up and/or the market price of Y will tend to go down. In any event, the budget line $\overline{SA}$ will rotate clockwise about the center S. This change has the effect of reducing the quantity demanded for and, at the same time, raising the quantity supplied of X. Since A and B both have a fixed amount of X and Y, this is equivalent to a decrease in the quantity supplied of and, simultaneously, an increase in the quantity demanded for Y. An equilibrium can only be achieved when the

prices are such that the budget line is tangent to the indifference
curves of both A and B at a point on the contract curve; this is
precisely a Pareto optimal point. Since this is true for any pair
of commodities and any two individuals, and equality is a transitive relationship, this result applies to any number of commodities and any number of individuals. We may conclude that perfectly competitive equilibrium can only occur at Pareto optimality
in a pure exchange system.

A similar argument can be made in production. Since maximum
output for a given cost of a firm can be achieved only if the ratio
of the input prices is equal to the marginal rate of technical substitution (MRTS) for an interior solution (see Chapter 2 for a
proof of this statement), and since in a perfectly competitive input
market all producers face the same input prices, then for the same
price ratio, the MRTS between any two inputs for any pair of
products must be the same for any number of producers at equilibrium. This implies that perfect competition in input markets
will result in Pareto optimality in production at equilibrium, that
is, production takes place on the contract curve.

*Perfect competition
in input markets
results in Pareto
optimality in
production at
equilibrium*

As we have shown in Chapter 12, the production possibility
(transformation) curve (PPC) in the two-commodity special case
is derived from the contract curve in a corresponding Edgeworth
box. It can easily be seen that actual production on a PPC is a
necessary but not sufficient condition for maximum consumer
satisfaction (utility) for given resources. In order to maximize the
consumer satisfaction (utility), a proper mix of the products must
be achieved. In order to illustrate this point graphically, we shall
use the simple case of two commodities and a single person.

Consider Figure 13.3, in which PP' is the PPC, and 1 and 2
are indifference curves of the consumer which reflect two levels
of satisfaction (utility), 2 representing a higher level than 1. Points
F and G are both on the PPC. However, at point F, the MRS is
greater than the marginal rate of product transformation (MRPT),
whereas at point G, the MRS is less than the MRPT. In either

FIGURE 13.3

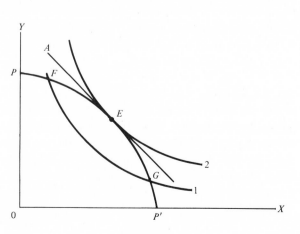

case, the consumer's satisfaction (utility) can be increased by producing a different mix. For example, if the product mix is represented by point F, more production of X and less of Y (a movement down along PP') will result in a higher level of satisfaction (utility) for the consumer. Similarly, if the present product mix is represented by point G, the production of more Y and less X will also result in higher level of satisfaction (utility) for the consumer. Since F and G are any points at which MRS and MRPT are not equal, we may conclude that whenever MRS is not equal to MRPT, the consumer's satisfaction (utility) can be increased by producing a different product mix.

Under perfect competition, since all consumers face one market price, consumer satisfaction is maximized when MRS = price

Point E in Figure 13.3 is the point at which PP' is tangent to indifference curve 2; this implies that MRS = MRPT. A visual inspection indicates that any other product mix will be on a lower indifference curve than 2, thus resulting in a lower level of satisfaction (utility). We have shown that if the MRS between the two commodities for the consumer is not equal to the MRPT for the two commodities, then there exists at least one other product mix that will result in a higher level of satisfaction (utility) for the consumer, and that when MRS = MRPT, the product mix will result in maximum consumer satisfacton (utility) for the given resources. Therefore, we can conclude that for the simple case of one consumer and two commodities, the satisfaction (utility) of the consumer is maximum if and only if MRS = MRPT.

This result can be extended to any number of consumers, any number of commodities, and any number of producers under perfect competition. Since in a perfectly competitive market all consumers face the same market price and each consumer's satisfaction (utility) is maximized only if the MRS between any two commodities is equal to their price ratio, it follows that, at equilibrium, the MRS between any pair of commodities must be the same for all consumers. This implies that any perfectly competitive equilibrium will occur on the contract curve for any number of consumers. As we have explained earlier, the contract curve is identified as the Pareto optimal set. Consequently, perfectly competitive equilibrium can only occur at a Pareto optimal point on the consumption side.

On the production side, the MRPT between any two commodities is always equal to the ratio of the MCs of the commodities. For example, if the MRPT between X and Y is 3 (i.e., one additional unit of X can be produced at the expense of three units of Y), then this means that the production of one unit of X requires, at the margin, three times more resources than does the production of one unit of Y; in other words, the MC of X is three times greater than the MC of Y. From Chapter 6, we know that the profits of perfectly competitive firms are maximized only if their MCs are equal to their MRs. However, in a perfectly competitive market, a firm's MR is equal to the market price (see

Chapter 5). This implies that, at equilibrium, the price ratio between any pair of commodities must be equal to the corresponding MC ratio, which, by implication (as explained above), is equal to the corresponding MRPT. This means that perfectly competitive equilibrium must occur at a point on the PPC (or, what is the same thing, at a point on the contract curve) for any pair of commodities. Hence, we have Pareto optimality on the production side.

What we have shown is that each and every consumer's satisfaction (utility) will be maximized for a given endowment of resources only if the MRS between any pair of commodities is equal to the corresponding price ratio, *and* that the MRS must also be equal to the MRPT for the pair. Furthermore, in production, perfectly competitive equilibrium can take place at a point on the PPC (or, equivalently, at the corresponding point on the contract curve) which represents Pareto optimality. We may conclude that equilibrium in the perfectly competitive market can only take place at a point in a Pareto optimal set. In Figure 13.3, the ratio of the prices of X and Y is represented by the negative slope of the straight line $\overline{AE}$, which is tangent to both the PPC and indifference curve 2 at point E. When there are more than two commodities and more than one consumer, a graphical illustration is rather difficult, if not impossible. Nevertheless, it will still be true that, under perfect competition, the market prices will equate the MRPT between any pair of commodities to the MRS of all consumers, thus ensuring Pareto optimality on the consumption side for the given product mix. At the same time, this implies Pareto optimality on the production side because any point on the PPC corresponds to a point on the contract curve in production. This should convince the student that perfectly competitive equilibrium will occur at a Pareto optimal state of the economy.

There is another well-known theorem in welfare economics which is both closely related to and, at the same time, slightly different from Theorem 13.1. These two theorems combined imply the virtue of perfect competition. Before we explain the combined significance of the two theorems, let us state the second as follows.

Theorem 13.2. *Any Pareto optimal state of the economy can be achieved by means of perfect competition, that is, any Pareto optimal state can be associated with a perfectly competitive equilibrium, given the proper distribution of resources among the individuals and under certain assumptions.*

Although it may seem that Theorems 13.1 and 13.2 are identical, in fact they are not. Theorem 13.1 says that if we have perfectly competitive equilibrium, then it must be Pareto optimal. This

*Perfect competition
may not be
acceptable to
society even if it
is consistent with
Pareto optimality*

might be taken to mean that certain Pareto optimal states of the economy may not be reached by means of perfect competition. For example, in Figure 13.1, all points on the curve $0_A\widehat{EE_1}0_B$ are Pareto optimal. Theorem 13.1 assures us that if we have perfectly competitive equilibrium, then it must be represented by a point on this curve. However, it does not rule out the possibility that perfectly competitive equilibrium might *only* be attained at either 0_A or 0_B. If extreme inequality of income is considered to be undesirable on moral grounds, then perfect competition, although consistent with Pareto optimality, cannot be considered a useful market system from the viewpoint of society as a whole.

On the other hand, Theorem 13.2 says that, in our simple example, any point on the curve $0_A\widehat{EE_1}0_B$ of Figure 13.1 is achievable for some initial distribution of the commodities. This is reassuring because if a certain point on the curve, say E, is considered desirable on other than economic grounds, then the government or some alternative authority can allocate the resources in such a way that the perfectly competitive market will lead to point E at equilibrium. In a sense, the authority can achieve a desirable pattern of consumption that is determined by other than economic factors without actually interfering with efficient production and consumers' free choice. If Pareto optimality is considered to be desirable, then Theorems 13.1 and 13.2 taken together make perfect competition not only desirable, but also useful.

In Section 12.1 of Chapter 12, we established the fact that, in the simple two-person–two-commodity case, pure exchange will lead to an equilibrium at which the offer curves of the two individuals intersect at a Pareto optimal point. For the sake of convenience, the graph is reproduced here as Figure 13.4, in

FIGURE 13.4

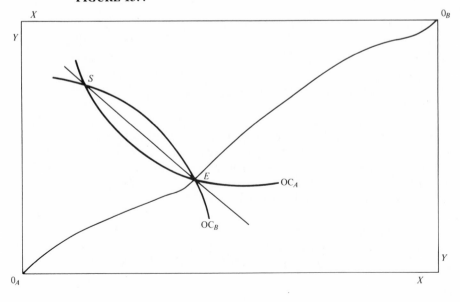

which S represents the status quo, whereas OC_A and OC_B are the offer curves of consumers A and B, respectively. Theorem 13.2 means that, in the simple two-person–two-commodity case, for each point (say E) on the contract curve, there exists at least one point in the Edgeworth box from which the two individuals' offer curves will intersect at the point E. This is quite reasonable, since we know that the straight line $\overline{SE}$ is tangent to both consumers' indifference curves at point E. Moreover, if their indifference curves are smooth, then $\overline{SE}$ is the only straight line that is tangent to them at E, since their common slope is unique at a given point. If we do not know the location of point S, Theorem 13.2 asserts that point S does exist and it is on the straight line $\overline{SE}$. As can be seen, there are probably many points on $\overline{SE}$ from which the two individuals' offer curves will intersect at point E.

Theorem 13.2 is quite reasonable for a point such as E. On the other hand, for points such as 0_A and 0_B, the only point that satisfies the theorem is probably the point itself. Nevertheless even in these extreme cases, Theorem 13.2 still (in a sense) holds.

Theorems 13.1 and 13.2 attribute considerable virtues to perfect competition as a market system. However, the assumptions underlying the theorems impose considerable limitations on their significance. Hence, a good knowledge of the assumptions are necessary in order to avoid misunderstanding. For our purposes, we need only explain the important assumptions in nontechnical terms.

The first assumption underlying Theorems 13.1 and 13.2 is the absence of externalities with respect to both consumption and production. We have explained the meaning of externality in both Chapter 2 (on production) and Chapter 4 (on consumption). Because of their importance in welfare economics, we shall discuss these concepts in detail in Section 13.5. However, we may mention in passing that if consumers buy things for the purpose of keeping up with the Joneses or, alternatively, if the production (or cost of production) of one firm is not independent of the quantity produced by another firm, then our assumption of an absence of externalities is violated. Whenever such conditions prevail, perfect competition may not produce Pareto optimality, nor will a Pareto optimal condition be achievable by means of perfect competition.

If externalities exist in either consumption or production, Pareto optimality may not be achieved

In addition to the assumed absence of externalities, we also assume nonsatiation, the absence of lexicographic ordering, and perfect information or knowledge. Although these are Assumptions 4.5, 4.3, 4.4, and 1.3 we wish to reemphasize them again so as to avoid any misunderstanding. Finally, for Theorem 13.2, but not necessarily Theorem 13.1, perfect divisibility of the commodities is assumed.

The above are the necessary assumptions for a formal proof of Theorems 13.1 and 13.2. Without these assumptions, a formal proof cannot be accomplished. For our purposes, it is sufficient to know that these assumptions imply definite limitations on the theorems and are necessary to give them validity.

In the literature, Theorem 13.1 is referred to as the *efficiency condition of a perfectly competitive system*, which means that whereas perfectly competitive equilibrium is always Pareto optimal, this is not so in the cases of equilibrium in monopoly, oligopoly, and monopolistic competition. The term "condition" means that if Pareto optimality is considered desirable, then the perfectly competitive system is efficient. Theorem 13.2 is generally referred to as a *condition of unbiasedness of the perfectly competitive system*. The market system of perfect competition is considered unbiased because each and every Pareto optimal state can be achieved for a proper distribution of the resources by means of perfect competition.

13.4 MARKET IMPERFECTION, MARGINAL COST PRICING, AND THE THEORY OF SECOND BEST

In Section 13.3 we showed that, in effect, Pareto optimality in the market requires that the MC ratio for all firms must be equal to the MRS for all consumers for any pair of commodities. This may be further explained by the following brief discussion.

It was earlier concluded that Pareto optimality requires the equality between MRPT and MRS for any pair of commodities X and Y. In terms of symbols, we can write the definitions as follows:

$$\text{MRPT} = -dY/dX \qquad \text{along a PPC (transformation curve)}$$

$$\text{MRS} = \text{MU}_X/\text{MU}_Y \qquad \text{along an indifference curve}$$

In order to avoid confusion, it should immediately be pointed out that, in Chapter 4, we also wrote $\text{MRS} = -dY/dX$ as the definition of MRS. Hence, it may seem that MRPT and MRS are identical by definition; however, because we are dealing with different things, this is not so. The expression $-dY/dX$ as a definition of MRPT represents the negative slope of the PPC at a point, whereas the same expression as a definition of MRS represents the negative slope of an indifference curve at a given point. Thus, the expression $-dY/dX$ represents the slopes of two different functions in the same X, Y space. In order to avoid confusion, we shall only use the ratio of the MUs to represent MRS here.

It was also shown in Section 13.3 that, by implication, MRPT is equal to the ratio of the MCs of the two products. In symbols, we can write

$$\text{MC}_X/\text{MC}_Y = \text{MRPT} = -dY/dX$$

We have shown that Pareto optimality requires that

$$\text{MRPT} = \text{MRS}$$

for all consumers and for any pair of commodities. Therefore, this condition for Pareto optimality implies, by substitution, that

$$MC_X/MC_Y = MU_X/MU_Y$$

for all firms that produce either X or Y and for all consumers who consume positive amounts of X and Y.

Under perfect competition in the market for both X and Y, the above condition is satisfied because each firm equates its MC to the market price in order to maximize profit. As shown in Chapter 6, $P_X = MC_X$ and $P_Y = MC_Y$ for all firms that produce either X or Y, whereas, as shown in Chapter 4, all consumers who consume positive amounts of X and Y equate their MRS to the ratio of market prices in order to maximize their satisfaction (utility) for a given income. Since all firms and consumers face the same market prices, in equilibrium, the Pareto optimality condition is satisfied. This is the essence and validation of Theorem 13.1 in Section 13.3.

We shall now show that the situation is different when there is monopoly. As was shown in Chapter 7, the profit of a monopoly firm is maximized if MC = MR. However, since a monopoly firm faces a negatively sloped demand curve, it is implied that MR < P for a positive amount of quantity (see Chapter 5). Therefore, it can be observed that, although, in the market, consumers' equilibrium is still

Pareto optimality is violated under monopoly because $MC_X < P_X$ in production equilibrium

$$P_X/P_Y = MU_X/MU_Y$$

on the production side we no longer have $P_X = MC_X$ and $P_Y = MC_Y$; hence,

$$P_X/P_Y \neq MC_X/MC_Y$$

when monopoly prevails. For example, if industry X is a monopoly and industry Y operates under perfect competition, then $MC_X < P_X$ and $MC_Y = P_Y$ at equilibrium. Thus,

$$MC_X/MC_Y < P_X/P_Y$$

By substitution, we have

$$MC_X/MC_Y < MU_X/MU_Y$$

and the Pareto optimality condition is violated in equilibrium. In terms of Figure 13.3, when industry X is a monopoly and industry Y represents perfect competition, equilibrium takes place at a point such as F instead of E. It can be seen that the commodity produced by the monopoly will be underproduced when compared to the Pareto optimal mix of the two products. For this reason, economists generally consider monopoly and any other market imperfections as resulting in a misallocation of resources, that is, resource allocation is not Pareto optimal. Although not all Pareto optimal allocations of resources are necessarily to be considered desirable, a non-Pareto optimal allocation is certainly not desirable because there exist ways to make someone better off without making anyone else worse off. In this sense, monopoly is undesirable.

If monopoly is an economic reality because cost conditions and the extension of market dictate it, then perfect competition may not be feasible. Under these circumstances, some economists advocate MC pricing in order to correct the misallocation of resources. One of the early advocates of this practice was Harold Hotelling (see Hotelling, 1938). There are many interesting welfare implications in MC pricing. For example, the MC for a vehicle to go over a bridge is zero. Thus, MC cost pricing results in free-of-charge passage. However, the cost of construction of the bridge has to come from somewhere. If it is built using public funds, then this will result in a redistribution of income, which is something that the Pareto approach cannot deal with adequately. Another example is the airline passenger rate. If an airplane is not full, then the MC of an additional passenger is practically zero. According to the MC pricing principle, passenger rates should be near zero as long as airplaines are not filled up to capacity. Since we know that most, if not all, airplanes are not full on an average day, therefore, airplane tickets should have a near-zero price. However, if this were the case, then private business would not exist in passenger airlines. Of course, the long-run MC will not be zero. (See Chapter 3 with regard to the derivation of the long-run MC curve from the short-run MC curves.) Hence, although MC pricing in the long run will not result in zero price for either bridge traffic or airplanes, it is usually not sufficient to cover the long-run AC. As we have mentioned before, natural monopoly occurs in an industry where AC decreases at the intersection of the MC and demand curves. As was shown in Chapter 7 (see Figure 7.10), MC pricing would result in a price below AC. For the sake of convenience, a graph similar to that of Figure 7.10 is drawn below.

Consider Figure 13.5, in which D is the demand curve, MR is

Because MC pricing may involve a subsidy and redistribution of income it cannot be Pareto evaluated

FIGURE 13.5

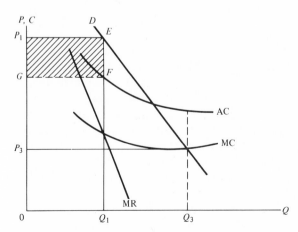

the corresponding marginal revenue curve, and AC and MC are the long-run average cost and marginal cost curves, respectively. The profit-maximizing mark-up price for the monopoly is P_1, the resulting quantity is Q_1, and a positive economic profit is indicated by the shaded area in the graph. On the other hand, MC pricing calls for a price of P_3 and a resulting quantity of Q_3, as determined by the demand. However, since AC exceeds the price at Q_3, it results in a negative long-run economic profit. In this case, there are two possible outcomes from the introduction of MC pricing:

1. The monopoly goes out of business; that is, the industry disappears.
2. The government subsidizes the monopoly in an amount equal to the difference between AC and P_3 for each unit sold.

If the commodity is considered desirable, the second alternative is feasible with MC pricing. However, this results in a redistribution of income, the desirability of which cannot be judged by the Pareto approach. This illustrates that MC pricing is not without its problems in a broader setting.

13.4.1 The Theory of Second Best[4]

As we have already explained, a non-Pareto optimal allocation of resources is undesirable because there exist ways of making someone better off without making anyone else worse off. The following question arises: If there are market imperfections (e.g., perfect competition in some industries, whereas monopoly, oligopoly, and monopolistic competition prevail in others) that result in a non-Pareto optimal allocation of resources, then will public policies that eliminate monopoly and oligopoly, but leave monopolistic competition alone, result in an improvement in economic welfare for society as a whole? According to the *theory of second best*, the answer, in general, is no. In other words, between two states of the economy which are both non-Pareto optimal, if one is not Pareto superior to the other, then there is no yardstick by which to measure their relative desirability. This is understandable, since, as we have already noted, the Pareto approach fails to consider many noncomparable aspects of alternatives. Hence, all states within a Pareto optimal set are noncomparable, and most (but not all) states of the economy are noncomparable in the non-Pareto optimal set.

Although the theory of second best asserts that it is, in general, impossible to judge whether a change from one non-Pareto optimal state to another is for the better, it does not actually say

---

[4] See Lancaster and Lipsey (1956–1957).

that it is impossible to judge this *under all circumstances*. In other words, it does not deny that the criterion of Pareto superior is applicable to the non-Pareto optimal states of the economy, but only says that a change among the non-Pareto optimal states which eliminates certain undesirable factors may not be for the better. For example, in Figure 13.1, a change from F to P (or vice versa) cannot be said to be better, but it by no means denies the possibility that a change from F to G or H is for the better. The implication is that if G and H are non-Pareto optimal, then there exist other (in fact, in the continuous case, infinitely many) states of the economy which, although non-Pareto optimal, may be Pareto superior to them. In a sense, neither G, H, nor some other point that is Pareto superior to them can be called second best, since there can be infinitely many other states, which although better than them, are still not one of the best.

Noncomparability among non-Pareto optimal sets rules out a second best alternative

The above explanation is important because some economists interpret the theory of second best in such a way that any piecemeal attempt to fulfill the Pareto optimality conditions would be in vain. This interpretation seems misleading and overly pessimistic. Since many, if not all, practical attempts to apply the principles of welfare economics are piecemeal attempts of some sort, a good understanding of the true meaning of the theory of second best is very important. The important point to understand is that a non-Pareto optimal state is undesirable because there exists at least one other Pareto optimal state that is Pareto superior to it. On the other hand, if Pareto optimality cannot be achieved due to the prevailing circumstances, then attempts should be made to eliminate the more-undesirable states by the criterion of Pareto superiority. It is expected that one may likely encounter Pareto noncomparability, but this is beside the point. The theory of second best should be interpreted in this manner in order to avoid any unnecessary mistakes.

13.5 EXTERNAL ECONOMIES, EXTERNAL DISECONOMIES, AND PUBLIC GOODS

Theorems 13.1 and 13.2 in Section 13.3 attribute considerable virtues to the perfectly competitive market system. However, as we mentioned earlier, the assumptions underlying these theorems impose certain limitations on their significance and applicability. In this respect, the assumption of the absence of externalities (Assumption 4.5) is particularly important in welfare economics. Although we have discussed this assumption previously (see Chapters 2 and 4) because of its special significance, we shall now offer a more detailed explanation of the concepts of externality and their applicability to welfare economics.

Externality may prevail on either the consumption or the production side, and in both cases there can be either *external econ-*

omy or *external diseconomy*. Although there are different ways of defining these two terms, externality always exists when there is interdependence between economic units (i.e., between consumers or producers). For example, one consumer's level of satisfaction (utility) may depend on the quantity of a commodity consumed by others. Alternatively, the same consumer's consumption of a certain commodity may influence the levels of satisfaction (utility) of other consumers. Similarly, on the production side, the output level or cost of a firm not only depends on the inputs it uses, but also on the inputs used by other firms. Moreover, the amount of inputs used by one firm not only directly determines its own output, but also influences the output of other firms and/or the levels of satisfaction (utility) of some consumers. Thus, we can give the following definitions.

Definition: External Economy in Consumption. External economy on the consumption side exists if satisfaction (utility) is secured not only by the consumer but also by someone else who does not pay for it.

There are many examples of external economy on the consumption side. Thus, if you have a rose garden and your neighbors derive satisfaction (utility) from the roses without paying the cost, then external economy in consumption exists. Similarly, if some residents of a neighborhood hire a private security agency to patrol their streets in order to prevent burglary and robbery, then the residents who do not pay for the service will also obtain the benefits of better security; hence, external economy in consumption would again exist.

Definition: External Diseconomy in Consumption. External diseconomy on the consumption side exists if one's consumption of something gives him or her satisfaction (utility) but causes someone else to suffer dissatisfaction (disutility).

There are many examples of this concept also. Thus, although you may derive satisfaction (utility) from eating garlic because you like the taste, if you go to a class after eating it without first using a good mouthwash, then the person who sits next to you will suffer from the unpleasant smell. Similarly, a drunkard in a public place may be a nuisance to many people as a result of his or her overindulgence. Finally, smoking in a public place can be an irritant to those who do not smoke.

Definition: External Economy in Production. External economy on the production side prevails if the production of one firm helps the production of other firms or increases the satisfaction (utility) derived by someone else without charge or cost.

A classic example of external economy in production is the production of honey by bees. The bees aid in the pollination of fruit trees, which, in turn, aids in the production of honey by providing nectar to the bees. Thus, honey production aids in the production of fruit at no cost to the grower. In this case, fruit production also aids in the production of honey without charge. Although this is a mutually beneficial condition, the economies are nevertheless external. Another well-known example is the training of workers by a firm for its own production purposes; although this training is carried out for the firm's own purposes, it may nevertheless eventually provide skilled workers for other firms without cost to them.

Definition: External Diseconomy in Production. External diseconomy on the production side prevails if the production of one firm results in an additional cost or dissatisfaction to others.

Air and water pollution are obvious examples where production may result in additional cost to both other producers and consumers. Thus, we can see that external diseconomies on the production side are not strictly confined to the sphere of production. Similarly, external economies on the production side are not confined to production alone.

The implication of externality with respect to the optimal allocation of resources is obvious. Since our analysis is based on individual decisions, we examine the maximization of the consumer's own satisfaction (utility) according to the commodities and services that each consumes, not according to those consumed by others. In the same manner, we treat the firm as an agent that maximizes its own profit according to its own cost and revenue, not those of others. However when external economies prevail on the consumption side, the social benefits received by the consumer, as well as those received by others, exceed the individual benefits received by the consumer alone. As a result, individual decisions tend to result in underconsumption in the sense that the MRS for society as a whole will be different from the corresponding price ratio; thus, we have non-Pareto optimality from the point of view of society as a whole. On the other hand, when external diseconomies prevail on the consumption side, the social benefits will be less than the individual consumer's benefits due to the dissatisfaction suffered by others. Again, we see that activity or consumption that is Pareto optimal for the individual consumer results in non-Pareto optimal activity or consumption for society as a whole.

On the production side, external diseconomies may create serious problems for a community in which there is a high concentration or large-scale operation of industries. As noted above, air and water pollution are obvious examples. In the absence of a high concentration or large-scale operation of industries, and where Mother Nature can take care of the effects of pollution by industries, external diseconomy does not create social problems nor does it result in the misallocation of resources. Thus, in less-developed areas, externality is not a very important factor in economic analysis. On the other hand, when industrial development and concentration of industries goes beyond a certain level, the accumulative effects of external diseconomies may create serious social and economic problems. In the United States, these have been grave problems in many localities for some time, although serious attempts to solve them have been undertaken only recently. Regulations requiring industries to install air- and water-pollution control devices are actually measures to internalize externalities. We noted earlier that the enforcement of pollution control regulations may result in the optimal allocation of resources in the Pareto sense because complete internalization of externalities is equivalent to the elimination of external diseconomy. In this case, the market mechanism will lead to Pareto optimality at equilibrium, provided that perfect competition prevails.

Internalization of externalities can lead to Pareto optimal production under perfect competition

In contrast to external diseconomies, external economies on the production side result in higher benefits to society as a whole than to the individual producer. In this case, we find that the firm generates by-products that are valuable to society, but the individual producer cannot collect any revenue from them. Since the individual producers are paid according to the quantity of output directly under their control, they are underpaid and society as a whole obtains valuable products at their expense. Since individual decisions are based on private cost and revenue, and the latter is less than the imputed social benefits, including the value of the by-products, actual production based on an optimal private decision will be less than the level of production for social optimality. Consequently, private business decisions and the market mechanism will result in underproduction for society as a whole. It is commonly recognized that basic research results in considerable external economies. In fact, although many theoretical accomplishments have very little immediate market value, they may develop very high social—as well as commercial—value long after the producer has vanished. In many cases, the producer can collect very little, if any, income from his or her products. For these reasons, economic analysis suggests that basic research will be underproduced without public support.

External economies can result in socially undesirable underutilization of resources

13.5.1 Strong Externality and Public Goods

Many economists are in favor of less government interference in private business operations. Some even consider ''do nothing goverment'' as the best government. This conservative view has its roots in the most liberal idea of laissez-faire, which means to let people do as they please, that is, noninterference of government. According to Theorems 13.1 and 13.2 in Section 13.3, if perfect competition prevails, government interference in business activities is indeed undesirable. However, the existence of externalities renders the theorems meaningless. In particular, when strong externalities exist, the market system and private business may not be capable of dealing with the situation.

In general, private business and the market mechanism are capable of dealing with the distribution of commodities and services when the *exclusion principle* applies; that is, owners can exclude anyone from sharing the benefits of a commodity or service if they wish. Therefore, externality can be viewed as a partial inapplicability of the exclusion principle, and hence when strong externality exists, private business and the market system cannot deal with the situation properly. This is the basis upon which the case for *public goods* is predicated. Defense is an extreme example. If a country is well defended, then all residents of the nation are protected. It is hard, if not impossible, to single out residents (short of expulsion) for exclusion from protection. Thus, defense has to be run by the government, and all residents have to share the cost in some way. This is a public good.

The existence of externalities often justifies public goods

In some cases, the exclusion principle can be applied by certain arrangements, but external economies and cost considerations will generally make it less suitable for private business except under special circumstances. Roads and bridges are good examples. There are toll roads and toll bridges, but the vast majority of roads and bridges are built and maintained by public funds and thus are public goods. If all roads and bridges were built and run by private business, the quantity produced would be much less.[5]

Police and fire protection are mostly provided by the government and paid for out of tax revenues. However, in some cases, the mill rate for tax purposes differentiates between the type of protection, that is, residential versus commercial. Although there are private security agencies and some large business establishments that have their own security arrangement and fire protection equipment, publicly financed and operated services by far predominate.

---

[5] We are, of course, excluding the use of subsidies. However, even when financed and operated by the government, less-traveled roads are, in effect, subsidized by the taxes on fuel which accrue from the use of trunk highways and well-traveled roads. It is possible that under special arrangements, private business could operate a road system by permitting the firm to realize economic rent on well-traveled roads as a price for construction and maintenance of less-traveled roads. Such arrangements would, however, entail high administrative costs and, most likely, complex coordination problems, thereby negating their use. Forms of tie-in arrangements using the exclusion principle are, however, employed in some areas where a public good is involved. Thus, a private business may be given a food concession that provides an exclusive right, but also requires the business to keep the grounds free of debris or waste. To the degree that such a requirement engenders more than simply cleaning up the wastes generated by the food concession, a public service is being provided in which the cost is internalized to the food concessionaire.

The exclusion principle can also be applicable to education. It is the prevailing viewpoint that considerable external economies exist in education. Thus, up to high school, education is considered a public good in the United States, individuals having the option of attending private schools as a substitute. Higher education is partially subsidized by public funds in state institutions, whereas private institutions are subsidized to an even smaller degree by tax exemption arrangements. Some private institutions are run by administrators who are proud of being businesslike and regard the operation of the institution as exemplifying all the elements of private business. Even some economists argue that educational institutions should be run just like private business. Such arguments, however, beg the following question: If the market mechanism can properly deal with the education "industry" in the same manner as the banking or tourist industries provide their services, why should private education institutions enjoy tax exempt status? In fact, it is due to external economies in education that the market mechanism will not result in the optimal allocation of resources in the sphere of education. Consequently, business practice cannot be fully applied to the operation of institutions, even if higher education cannot be strictly treated as a public good.

13.6 MODIFICATIONS OF THE UNANIMITY PRINCIPLE

It has long been recognized that most, if not all, social changes involve gains for some people and, at the same time, losses for others. Although the unanimity principle may have theoretical significance, it has little practical value without some kind of modification. An attempt at such a modification was made in the late 1930s by Nicholas Kaldor (see Kaldor, 1939), who formulated the *compensation criterion* as follows:

> The state of the economy A is considered socially preferable to state B if those who gain from A could compensate the losers and still be better off in A than in B. In other words, if the gainers from a change can bribe the losers to agree with the change, then the change is considered preferable.

This at first seems to be a very reasonable principle. However, it refers to potential rather than actual welfare, since the criterion does not require that compensation be actually paid. Even if a net gain in satisfaction (utility) could result from the given change in the case that actual compensation is made, if the compensation is *not* made, we cannot, in general, conclude that the change results in net gain. A more-serious problem concerning the compensation criterion is that, under certain circumstances, state A may be judged preferable to B and, at the same time, B may be judged preferable to A. The following simple example is due to Tibor Scitovsky (see Scitovsky, 1941–1942).

Compensation of losers by winners is a practical substitute for the unanimity principle under certain conditions

Assume that there are only two commodities X and Y and only two individuals 1 and 2. Also assume that there are only two production possibilities and their associated distributions of the commodities, designated by A and B. Let state A involve the production of 2 units of X and 1 unit of Y, whereas state B involves the production of 1 unit of X and 2 units of Y, which in compact notation can be written $(2, 1)$ and $(1, 2)$, respectively. Using a similar notation, the two individuals' preferences are as follows:

1 prefers $(1, 1)$ to $(2, 0)$ and $(2, 0)$ to $(1, 0)$

2 prefers $(1, 1)$ to $(0, 2)$ and $(0, 2)$ to $(0, 1)$

In other words, individual 1 prefers the bundle of 1 unit of X and 1 unit of Y to the bundle of 2 units of X and zero Y. By the nonsatiation rule, we can state that individual 1 prefers 2 units of X and zero Y to 1 unit of X and zero Y. The same interpretation can be applied to individual 2's preference.

If the distribution of the output in states A and B of the economy is

	1	2	Total production
A	$(2, 0)$	$(0, 1)$	$(2, 1)$
B	$(1, 0)$	$(0, 2)$	$(1, 2)$

Then it can be seen that *both* a change from A to B and a change from B to A are considered preferable according to the compensation criterion.

Suppose that the status quo is A and a change is made to B. Individual 1 loses 1 unit of X and is compensated with 1 unit of Y, whereas individual 2 has precisely the same quantities as before. We thus have the following compensated distribution in state B, which is denoted by B_c:

	1	2	Total production
B_c	$(1, 1)$	$(0, 1)$	$(1, 2)$

By our assumption concerning the individuals' preferences, individual 1 prefers B_c to A, whereas 2 is indifferent between A and B_c. Hence, B_c is socially preferable to A. Thus, a compensated change from A to B is considered preferable.

The situation is similar if the status quo is B and a change is made to A. Individual 2 loses 1 unit of Y and is compensated with 1 unit of X. We thus have the following compensated distribution in state A, which is denoted by A_c:

	1	2	Total production
A_c	$(1, 0)$	$(1, 1)$	$(2, 1)$

Individual 1 is indifferent between B and A_c, but 2 prefers A_c to

B. Therefore, a compensated change from B to A is considered preferable because A_c is socially preferred to B.

The above simple example demonstrates that, logically, the compensation criterion is not a reliable principle to use in judging which of two alternatives is best. In order to avoid this kind of inconsistency, an improved principle is provided by the *Scitovsky criterion*, which can be stated as follows:

> The state of the economy A is considered socially preferable to state B if those who gain from A could bribe the losers into accepting the change to A and, simultaneously, the losers could not bribe the gainers into not making the change.

In other words, the Scitovsky criterion requires a two-way test in order to assert that one state is preferable to another. This criterion does seem more reassuring than the compensation criterion; however, as before, no actual compensation is required. Thus, even if a case does pass the Scitovsky test, it cannot, in general, be said that a change is for the better, since interpersonal comparisons, which involve more theoretical difficulties, are still implied.

We have sketched some of the important theorems and issues in welfare economics. By the necessity of space and thrust of this book, we have only briefly covered some of the salient elements of this topic. Students who are interested in this area can consult the references that we have cited as well as other publications covering welfare economics at various levels.

SUMMARY

In this chapter we dealt with the problem of choice between alternatives in the context of normative, as contrasted with positive, economics. We explained that since welfare economics is concerned with society as a whole, partial analysis does not provide a sufficient basis on which to judge between economic alternatives; hence there is a need for general equilibrium analysis. However, we noted that, given consumer sovereignty and recognizing that interpersonal comparisons of utility are not feasible, we face considerable difficulties in the development of a scientific theory of welfare economics, free of subjective value judgements. We observed that despite these difficulties economists have made progress in formulating a systematic method for evaluating economic alternatives. Thus, the condition of Pareto optimality, which can be defined as a state of an economy in which it is impossible to improve one person's economic welfare without making another person any worse off, can be used to order preferred alternatives.

We proceeded to demonstrate the concept of Pareto optimality by first noting the rules of transitivity that need to be observed in any system of preferred ordering and then illustrating the application of the concept by using the Edgeworth box to derive the contract curve in a two-person–two-commodity example of exchange. We were careful to explain that the concept of Pareto optimality does not necessarily imply that all points in the Pareto optimal set are desirable, only that a non-Pareto optimal is undesirable. This is because there is at least one point in the Pareto optimal set where one person is made better off without another being made worse off. It was further explained that all points in a Pareto optimal set are essentially non-comparable without either a value judgment or additional information. Hence, on purely theoretical grounds, the concept of Pareto optimality requires the intrusion of value judgment in choosing between some economic alternatives.

After describing and illustrating the concept of Pareto optimality, we proceeded to state and prove two important theorems of welfare economics: every competitive equilibrium is Pareto optimal, and any Pareto optimal state of the economy can be reached by perfect competition. It was explained that the economic welfare of society will be maximized in the sense of Pareto optimality when the price of a commodity is equal to MC, and that, whereas such a condition holds under perfect competition, in imperfect markets the profit-maximization behavior of the firm produces a divergence between market price and MC. We then explained that marginal cost pricing can be used to maximize economic welfare; however, government intervention and subsidy payments may then be required, which begs the question as to whether government policy that eliminates certain market imperfection while leaving other imperfections untouched is really an improvement in economic welfare. We also examined the theory of second best.

In concluding our discussion of welfare economics, we noted the importance of external economies and external diseconomies in the development of this branch of economic theory. We explained that some goods or services that involve strong externalities (e.g., highways, education, and defense) become public goods. On the other hand, we find public regulation being used to handle other externalities, such as air and water pollution. In this case, regulation often involves the internalization of cost in the production process, which in turn can entail either a forward shifting of costs onto consumers, a backward shifting of costs onto suppliers, the absorption of costs by producers, or some combination of the three.

**EXERCISES AND QUESTIONS FOR CHAPTER 13
ON WELFARE ECONOMICS**

1.   Why is it difficult to order economic alternatives for society as a whole under a democratic system? Do you anticipate the same difficulty under some kind of dictatorship? Explain.

2. Under what circumstances is a state of the economy considered Pareto superior to another state of the economy? Explain.

3. What do we mean by Pareto optimality? Is the concept of Pareto superiority helpful in defining Pareto optimality? Without using the Pareto superiority concept, how would you define Pareto optimality? Explain.

4. Why is the concept of Pareto optimality so important in welfare economics? What difficulty is involved in relying on the concept of Pareto optimality in welfare economics? Explain.

5. Is any Pareto optimal state of an economy necessarily better than all states of the economy which are non-Pareto optimal? Use a simple example to illustrate your point. If the answer is negative, in what sense is the concept of Pareto optimality useful in welfare economics? Explain.

6. Why is perfect competition considered highly desirable according to the Pareto optimality approach in welfare economics? Explain.

7. Explain the use of the Edgeworth box as an analytical tool in welfare economics.

8. What problems are usually encountered in MC pricing under monopoly? Is the political situation under democracy compatible with MC pricing? Explain.

9. What is the theory of second best? Is there really such a thing as second best according to the theory? Explain.

10. Use your own words to define external economy and external diseconomy. Give examples where externalities prevail on the consumption side and/or on the production side.

11. Why are externalities important in welfare economics? Are public goods closely related with externalities? Explain.

12. What modifications implied by the concept of Pareto optimality can be made to the unanimity principle? What difficulty may one encounter in an attempt at a modification of the unanimity principle? Explain.

APPENDIX TO CHAPTER 13

A MATHEMATICAL NOTE
ON WELFARE ECONOMICS

A13.1 THE CONTRACT CURVE IS PARETO OPTIMAL
IN PURE EXCHANGE

We shall show that the contract curve in pure exchange is identical to the Pareto optimal set. Since the equations describing production are essentially similar to those obtained in the theory of consumption the identity of the contract curve and the Pareto optimal set in production can easily be shown in a similar fashion.

Pareto optimality exists in pure exchange or consumption if any reallocation of commodities and services which increases the satisfaction (utility) of one or more consumers results in a reduction of satisfaction (utility) for at least one consumer. Mathematically, the conditions of Pareto optimality in pure exchange can be derived by maximizing one consumer's satisfaction (utility) subject to given levels of satisfaction (utility) for all of the other consumers and given amounts of the commodities.

Assume that there are n consumers and m commodities in the economy and that there is no production. Each consumer may have an initial endowment of every commodity, but the amount consumed may be different from this endowment. We shall use the following notation:

q_{ij}^0 initial endowment of commodity j for consumer i

q_{ij} quantity of commodity j consumed by individual i

In the absence of production, the total consumption of each commodity for all of the consumers must be equal to the total initial endowments of the consumers for the commodity. Thus, the following equality must hold identically:

$$\sum_{i=1}^{n} q_{ij}^{0} = \sum_{i=1}^{n} q_{ij}, \qquad j = 1, 2, ..., m \qquad (A13.1)$$

In the absence of externalities on the consumption side, the satisfaction (utility) of a consumer is a function of the quantity of the commodities consumed by that consumer, but not those consumed by others. The utility function of consumer i can be written

$$U_i = U_i(q_{i1}, q_{i2}, ..., q_{im}), \qquad i = 1, 2, ..., n \qquad (A13.2)$$

Pareto optimality will be achieved if, given the satisfaction (utility) levels of all of the other consumers, the satisfaction (utility) of each consumer is at a maximum subject to constraint (A13.1). Using the Lagrange multiplier technique, consider the maximization of the satisfaction (utility) of consumer 1 for the given satisfaction (utility) levels of all of the other consumers subject to constraint (A13.1). Form the Lagrange function as follows:

$$L = U_1(q_{11}, q_{12}, ..., q_{1m}) + \sum_{i=2}^{n} \lambda_i [U_i(q_{i1}, q_{i2}, ..., q_{im}) - U_i^0]$$

$$+ \sum_{j=1}^{m} \mu_j \left(\sum_{i=1}^{n} q_{ij}^{0} - \sum_{i=1}^{n} q_{ij} \right) \qquad (A13.3)$$

where λ_i, $i = 2, 3, ..., n$, and μ_j, $j = 1, 2, ..., m$, are Lagrange multipliers, of which there are a total of $n + m - 1$. Partially differentiating (A13.3) with respect to q_{ij} for all $i = 1, 2, ..., n$ and all $j = 1, 2, ..., m$, and setting the partial derivatives equal to zero, we obtain

$$\partial L/\partial q_{1j} = \partial U_1/\partial q_{1j} - \mu_j = 0, \qquad j = 1, 2, ..., m \qquad (A13.4)$$

$$\partial L/\partial q_{ij} = \lambda_i \partial U_i/\partial q_{ij} - \mu_j = 0, \qquad i = 2, 3, ..., n$$
$$j = 1, 2, ..., m \qquad (A13.5)$$

From (A13.4), for consumer 1 we have

$$\frac{\partial U_1/\partial q_{1j}}{\partial U_1/\partial q_{1k}} = \frac{\mu_j}{\mu_k}, \qquad j, k = 1, 2, ..., m \qquad (A13.6)$$

From (A13.5), for each and every consumer i we have

$$\frac{\partial U_i/\partial q_{ij}}{\partial U_i/\partial q_{ik}} = \frac{\mu_j}{\mu_k}, \qquad j, k = 1, 2, ..., m, \quad i = 2, 3, ..., n$$
$$(A13.7)$$

since λ_i cancels out on the left side. Assuming that the second-order condition for utility maximization is satisfied, (A13.6) and

(A13.7) give us the conditions for Pareto optimality in the case of pure exchange. Combining (A13.6) and (A13.7), we obtain the conditions for Pareto optimality in pure exchange:

$$\frac{\partial U_i / \partial q_{ij}}{\partial U_i / \partial q_{ik}} = \frac{\partial U_h / \partial q_{hj}}{\partial U_h / \partial q_{hk}}, \qquad i, h = 1, 2, ..., n$$

$$j, k = 1, 2, ..., m \qquad \text{(A13.8)}$$

Expression (A13.8) says that Pareto optimality in the case of pure exchange requires that the MRSs between any pair of commodities be equal for all consumers. It should be noted that (A13.4) and (A13.5) hold for any possible *initial* endowments and consumption pattern. In particular, the Pareto optimality condition (A13.8) holds even if the initial endowment is concentrated in one individual, that is, even if some consumers have nothing. In terms of a graphical representation of the simple two-person–two-commodity case, (A13.8) corresponds to the contract curve, and the points 0_A (where B has all and A has nothing) and 0_B (where A has all and B has nothing) are included in the Pareto optimal set.

It may be helpful to again emphasize that the utility function (A13.2) implies the absence of externalities. If externalities on the consumption side do exist, then the satisfaction (utility) of consumer i is not only a function of the quantity of the commodities he or she consumes, but also of the quantity of the commodities consumed by others. In general, if the assumption of the absence of externalities is not made, the utility function of the ith consumer must be written

$$U_i = U_i(q_{11}, q_{12}, ..., q_{1m}, ..., q_{i1}, q_{i2}, ...,$$

$$q_{im}, ..., q_{n1}, q_{n2}, ..., q_{nm}) \qquad \text{(A13.2')}$$

in which case (A13.4) and (A13.5) will be much more complicated and (A13.8) may not be achieved. In terms of a graphical representation of the simple two-person–two-commodity case, when the distribution (and thus consumption) of the commodities between the individuals changes, their indifference curves for them will shift. Therefore, a unique contract curve does not exist, and the situation becomes much more complicated.

A13.2 PARETO OPTIMALITY IN PRODUCTION

Under the assumptions of nonsatiation of consumers and the absence of externalities, an increase in the output of one consumer good, given all other outputs constant, will result in a higher level of satisfaction (utility) for at least one consumer without reducing the level of satisfaction (utility) for any others. For the sake of simplicity, assume that all commodities are consumer goods.[1] In such a case, Pareto optimality in production requires that the level of each output must be at a maximum for given levels of all other commodities. Suppose that there are m commodities as before. Furthermore, assume that there are m producers who each produce a single commodity by using G inputs. We shall use the following notation:

q_j $\qquad$ quantity of commodity j produced by producer j

X_g^0 $\qquad$ fixed amount of input g

x_{jg} $\qquad$ quantity of input g used by producer j

Since we are assuming that all inputs will be used up in production, we have

$$X_g^0 = \sum_{j=1}^{m} x_{jg}, \qquad g = 1, 2, ..., G \tag{A13.9}$$

The production function of producer j can be written

$$q_j = f_j(x_{j1}, x_{j2}, ..., x_{jG}), \qquad j = 1, 2, ..., m \tag{A13.10}$$

The conditions of Pareto optimality in production are found by calculating of the first-order conditions for output maximization for a given level of other outputs subject to constraint (A13.9) and assuming that the second-order conditions are satisfied. For the purpose of illustration, we shall maximize commodity 1 subject to the necessary constraints. Construct the Lagrange function:

$$L = f_1(x_{11}, x_{12}, ..., x_{1G}) + \sum_{j=2}^{m} \alpha_j [f_j(x_{j1}, x_{j2}, ..., x_{jG}) - q_j^0]$$

$$+ \sum_{g=1}^{G} \beta_g \left(X_g^0 - \sum_{j=1}^{m} x_{jg} \right) \tag{A13.11}$$

where α_j, $j = 2, 3, ..., m$, and β_g, $g = 1, 2, ..., G$, are Lagrange multipliers, of which there is a total of $G + m - 1$. Partially differentiating (A13.11) with respect to x_{jg} for all $j = 1, 2, ..., m$ and $g = 1, 2, ..., G$, and setting the partial derivatives equal to zero, we obtain

$$\partial L / \partial x_{1g} = \partial f_1 / \partial x_{1g} - \beta_g = 0, \qquad g = 1, 2, ..., G \tag{A13.12}$$

$$\partial L / \partial x_{jg} = \alpha_j \partial f_j / \partial x_{jg} - \beta_g = 0, \qquad j = 2, 3, ..., m$$
$$g = 1, 2, ..., G \tag{A13.13}$$

---

[1] *Consumer goods* are here defined as those which enter directly into consumption, as distinct from *capital goods*, which are used to produce other goods (including consumer goods).

From (A13.12), we have

$$\frac{\partial f_1/\partial x_{1g}}{\partial f_1/\partial x_{1p}} = \frac{\beta_g}{\beta_p}, \qquad g, p = 1, 2, ..., G \tag{A13.14}$$

From (A13.13), for each and every producer j we have

$$\frac{\partial f_i/\partial x_{jg}}{\partial f_j/\partial x_{jp}} = \frac{\beta_g}{\beta_p}, \qquad j = 2, 3, ..., m, \quad g, p = 1, 2, ..., G$$

$$\tag{A13.15}$$

Finally, from (A13.14) and (A13.15) taken together we have

$$\frac{\partial f_j/\partial x_{jg}}{\partial f_j/\partial x_{jp}} = \frac{\partial f_k/\partial x_{kg}}{\partial f_k/\partial x_{kp}}, \qquad j, k = 1, 2, ..., m$$

$$g, p = 1, 2, ..., G \tag{A13.16}$$

Expression (A13.16) says that Pareto optimality in production requires that the marginal rates of technical substitution (MRTSs) between any pair of inputs be equal for all of the commodities produced. The contract curve in an Edgeworth box for the simple case of the two-input–two-output model satisfies condition (A13.16). Thus, the contract curve of an Edgeworth box for production is identical to the Pareto optimal set.

A13.3 PARETO OPTIMALITY IN GENERAL: PRODUCTION AND EXCHANGE

The conditions for Pareto optimality in pure exchange (consumption) and production which were derived separately above can be combined for the general case of an economy as a whole. As before, suppose that there are n consumers and m commodities that are produced by P producers who use the commodities and G primary resources as inputs. We shall use the following notation:

Y_{ij} the quantity of commodity j consumed by individual i

X_{ig}^0 the initial endowment of resource factor g for individual i

X_{ig}^* the quantity of resource factor g supplied to producers by individual i

q_{pj} the quantity of commodity j produced by firm p

X_{pg} the quantity of resource factor g used by firm p

$X_{ig}^0 - X_{ig}^*$ the quantity of resource factor g consumed directly by individual i

The utility function for individual i can be written

$$U_i = U_i(Y_{i1}, Y_{i2}, ..., Y_{im}, X_{i1}^0 - X_{i1}^*, ..., X_{iG}^0 - X_{iG}^*)$$

$$i = 1, 2, ..., n \tag{A13.17}$$

The production function for firm p can be written in the following implicit form:

$$F_p(q_{p1}, q_{p2}, ..., q_{pm}, X_{p1}, X_{p2}, ..., X_{pG}) = 0,$$

$$p = 1, 2, ..., P \tag{A13.18}$$

For the economy as a whole, the total amount of each primary resource factor supplied by all individuals must be equal to the total amount used by all of the producers. Therefore, the following equality holds as an identity for each factor:

$$\sum_{i=1}^{n} X_{ig}^* = \sum_{p=1}^{P} X_{pg}, \qquad g = 1, 2, ..., G \tag{A13.19}$$

In addition, for the economy as a whole, total consumption by all consumers for each commodity must be equal to the total production of the commodity by all of the producers. Hence, we also have the following identity:

$$\sum_{i=1}^{n} Y_{ij} = \sum_{p=1}^{P} q_{pj}, \qquad j = 1, 2, ..., m. \tag{A13.20}$$

The conditions for Pareto optimality can be derived by maximizing the satisfaction (utility) of each consumer for the given satisfaction (utility) levels of all of the other consumers subject to the constraints (A13.18)–(20). For the sake of simplicity, we assume the maximization of the satisfaction (utility) of consumer 1 for given levels of satisfaction (utility) for the other $n - 1$ consumers subject to the said constraints. In order to make use of the Lagrange multiplier method, construct the Lagrange function:

$$
\begin{aligned}
L = \; & U_1(Y_{11}, Y_{12}, ..., Y_{1m}, ..., X_{1G}^0 - X_{1G}^*) \\
& + \sum_{i=2}^{n} \lambda_i[U_i(Y_{i1}, ..., Y_{im}, ..., X_{iG}^0 - X_{iG}^*) - U_i^0] \\
& + \sum_{p=1}^{P} \mu_p F_p(q_{p1}, ..., q_{pm}, ..., X_{pG}) \\
& + \sum_{g=1}^{G} \alpha_g \left(\sum_{i=1}^{n} X_{ig}^* - \sum_{p=1}^{P} X_{pg} \right) \\
& + \sum_{j=1}^{m} \beta_j \left(\sum_{i=1}^{n} Y_{ij} - \sum_{p=1}^{P} q_{pj} \right)
\end{aligned}
\tag{A13.21}
$$

where λ_i, $i = 2, 3, ..., n$, μ_p, $p = 1, 2, ..., P$, α_g, $g = 1, 2, ..., G$, and β_j, $j = 1, 2, ..., m$, are Lagrange multipliers, of which there is a total of $n + P + G + m - 1$. If we assume that the second-order conditions are satisfied, then the first-order conditions for maximum L [(A13.21)] yield the necessary conditions for Pareto optimality of the economy as a whole. Setting the partial derivatives of L with respect to Y_{ij}, q_{pj}, X^*_{ig}, and X_{pg} equal to zero, we obtain

$$\frac{\partial L}{\partial Y_{1j}} = \frac{\partial U_1}{\partial Y_{1j}} + \beta_j = 0$$

$$\frac{\partial L}{\partial Y_{ij}} = \lambda_i \frac{\partial U_i}{\partial Y_{ij}} + \beta_j = 0$$

$$\frac{\partial L}{\partial X^*_{1g}} = -\frac{\partial U_1}{\partial (X^0_{1g} - X^*_{1g})} + \alpha_g = 0$$

$$\frac{\partial L}{\partial X^*_{ij}} = -\lambda_i \frac{\partial U_i}{\partial (X^0_{ig} - X^*_{ig})} + \alpha_g = 0 \qquad \text{(A13.22)}$$

$$\frac{\partial L}{\partial q_{pj}} = \mu_p \frac{\partial F_p}{\partial q_{pj}} - \beta_j = 0,$$

$$\frac{\partial L}{\partial X_{pg}} = \mu_p \frac{\partial F_p}{\partial X_{pg}} - \alpha_g = 0$$

where $i = 2, 3, ..., n$, $j = 1, 2, ..., m$, $p = 1, 2, ..., P$, and $g = 1, 2, ..., G$. From the first equation in (A13.22), the MRS between commodities j and k for consumer 1 can be written

$$\frac{\partial U_1/\partial Y_{1j}}{\partial U_1/\partial Y_{1k}} = \frac{\beta_j}{\beta_k}, \qquad j, k = 1, 2, ..., m \qquad \text{(A13.23)}$$

From the second equation in (A13.22), the MRS between commodities j and k for consumer i can be written

$$\frac{\partial U_i/\partial Y_{ij}}{\partial U_i/\partial Y_{ik}} = \frac{\beta_j}{\beta_k}, \qquad i = 2, 3, ..., n, \quad j, k = 1, 2, ..., m$$

$$\text{(13.24)}$$

Although we may not know the precise values of the Lagrange multipliers β_j and β_k, we do know that $\beta_j/\beta_k = \beta_j/\beta_k$ must hold regardless of their values. This is the beauty of the Lagrange method. From (A13.23) and (A13.24), we have

$$\frac{\partial U_i/\partial Y_{ij}}{\partial U_i/\partial Y_{ik}} = \frac{\partial U_h/\partial Y_{hj}}{\partial U_h/\partial Y_{hk}}, \qquad i, h = 1, 2, ..., n$$

$$\text{(A13.25)}$$

$$j, k = 1, 2, ..., m$$

Expression (A13.25) is precisely equivalent to (A13.8), which was derived in Section A13.1 for the special case of pure exchange. It is also identical to the contract curve in an Edgeworth box, which was described with respect to the graphical method in the text. Thus, our general model is consistent with our simple model in pure exchange.

From the last equation in (A13.22), for each producer p, the

MRTS between resource factors g and h can be written

$$\frac{\partial F_p / \partial X_{pg}}{\partial F_p / \partial X_{ph}} = \frac{\alpha_g}{\alpha_h}, \qquad g, h = 1, 2, ..., G, \quad p = 1, 2, ..., P$$

$$(A13.26)$$

Since condition (A13.26) holds for all producers, we have

$$\frac{\partial F_p / \partial X_{pg}}{\partial F_p / \partial X_{ph}} = \frac{\partial F_s / \partial X_{sg}}{\partial F_s / \partial X_{sh}}, \qquad p, s = 1, 2, ..., P$$

$$(A13.27)$$

$$g, h = 1, 2, ..., G$$

Expression (A13.27) is equivalent to (A13.16), which was derived in Section A13.2 for the special case of production. Thus, our general model is also consistent with our simple model in production. However, our general model not only shows that the Pareto optimal conditions in both pure exchange (consumption) and production are satisfied simultaneously, but also something that cannot be shown by the simple models. From (A13.22), for each producer p we have

$$\frac{\partial F_p / \partial q_{pj}}{\partial F_p / \partial q_{pk}} = \frac{\beta_j}{\beta_k}, \qquad j, k = 1, 2, ..., m, \quad p = 1, 2, ..., P$$

$$(A13.28)$$

which is the marginal rate of production transformation (MRPT) between commodities j and k for producer p. Since condition (A13.28) holds for all producers, we have

$$\frac{\partial F_p / \partial q_{pj}}{\partial F_p / \partial q_{pk}} = \frac{\partial F_s / \partial q_{sj}}{\partial F_s / \partial q_{sk}}, \qquad p, s = 1, 2, ..., P$$

$$(A13.29)$$

$$j, k = 1, 2, ..., m$$

From (A13.23), (A13.24), and (A13.28), we also have

$$\frac{\partial U_i / \partial Y_{ij}}{\partial U_i / \partial Y_{ik}} = \frac{\partial F_p / \partial q_{pj}}{\partial F_p / \partial q_{pk}}, \qquad i = 1, 2, ..., n$$

$$p = 1, 2, ..., P \qquad (A13.30)$$

$$j, k = 1, 2, ..., m$$

which says that the MRSs for all consumers between any two commodities j and k must be equal to the MRPTs for all producers for the corresponding pair of commodities. This is the condition for Pareto optimality in the case of both consumption and production in the text, where only a commonsense explanation and simple numerical examples were employed to justify our assertion. This constitutes a formal proof of the proposition in the text.

From (A13.22), we also have

$$\frac{-\partial U_i/\partial Y_{ij}}{\partial U_i/\partial (X_{ig}^0 - X_{ig}^*)} = \frac{\beta_j}{\alpha_g} = \frac{\partial F_p/\partial q_{pj}}{\partial F_p/\partial X_{pg}} \tag{A13.31}$$

for every consumer $i = 1, 2, ..., n$, every producer $p = 1, 2, ..., P$, all commodities $j = 1, 2, ..., m$, and all resource factors $g = 1, 2, ..., G$. Thus, we have a relationship that connects the substitution between a commodity and a resource for a consumer, on the one hand, and the transformation from inputs to commodities for a producer, on the other hand. This means that Pareto optimality requires that the MRS between a commodity and a resource factor for every consumer must be equal to the marginal product (MP) of the corresponding factor for the corresponding commodity.

A13.4 PERFECT COMPETITION AND PARETO OPTIMALITY

There are different ways of proving the two theorems (Theorems 13.1 and 13.2) concerning Pareto optimality and perfect competition that were explained in the text. As mentioned in the text, those who are interested in a formal proof of the theorems can consult Koopmans, 1957. For our purpose, we only wish to show that the conditions for Pareto optimality derived in Section A13.3 are consistent with perfect competition. Although this is not a proof of either of the two theorems in the text, it does indicate their rationale.

In Chapter 4, it was shown that a consumer's satisfaction (utility) is maximized for a given income if his or her MRS between any pair of commodities is equal to the corresponding price ratio; that is, for any consumer i we have

$$\frac{\partial U_i/\partial q_j}{\partial U_i/\partial q_k} = \frac{P_j}{P_k} \tag{A13.32}$$

where q_j and q_k denote the quantities and P_j and P_k the prices of commodities j and k, respectively. In a perfectly competitive market, all consumers face the same prices for the commodities. Hence, we have

$$\frac{\partial U_i/\partial q_{ij}}{\partial U_i/\partial q_{ik}} = \frac{P_j}{P_k} = \frac{\partial U_h/\partial q_{hj}}{\partial U_h/\partial q_{hk}}, \qquad i, h = 1, 2, ..., n$$

$$j, k = 1, 2, ..., m \tag{A13.33}$$

which is precisely equivalent to condition (A13.25) of Section A13.3. Thus, conditions of consumer equilibrium for a given income are consistent with the conditions for Pareto optimality provided that (1) the second-order conditions for consumer equilibrium are satisfied and (2) we have an interior solution, which implies that each consumer consumes a positive amount of each commodity. In the general case, this is not very realistic since each consumer may not consume each and every commodity. However, only minor modifications of the expressions will be required to permit corner solutions, namely, changing the equalities to weak inequalities, that is, equal to or greater than. The second-order condition for consumer equilibrium requires a decreasing MRS. Otherwise, the solution from the first-order condition will result in minimum rather than maximum satisfaction (utility).

In a sense, the Lagrange multipliers β_j, $j = 1, 2, ..., m$, can be interpreted as efficient commodity prices. They are efficient prices because if they performed the function of prices in the market, they would lead the economy to Pareto optimality. However, if they are considered as prices, then the set of prices is not unique. For example, if a set of multipliers β_1, β_2, ..., β_m is such that $P_j = \beta_j$ is satisfactory, then any other set of multipliers β_1^*, β_2^*, ..., β_m^*, where $\beta_j^* = a\beta_j$ for $a > 0$ and thus $P_j^* = \beta_j^*$, is equally satisfactory. Hence, the Lagrange multipliers β_j, $j = 1, 2, ..., m$, can, at most, only be considered as relative prices of the commodities.

Similarly, for producers in perfectly competitive input markets, a necessary condition for profit maximization is the equality between the MRTS and the corresponding input price ratio. This is equivalent to the condition shown in Chapter 2 for points along an expansion path and similar to the condition of the equality between values of the marginal product (VMP) of an input and its price for profit maximization as shown in Chapter 10. Let us denote the price of a resource factor g by r_g. Then efficiency in production requires that

$$\frac{\partial F_p / \partial X_{pg}}{\partial F_p / \partial X_{ph}} = \frac{r_g}{r_h}, \qquad p = 1, 2, ..., P, \quad g, h = 1, 2, ..., G$$

$$(A13.34)$$

When perfect competition prevails in the input markets, all producers face the same input price for each resource factor, and the Pareto optimality condition (A13.27) is satisfied. Therefore, perfect competition in the input market is consistent with Pareto optimality with respect to production.

So far, the above arguments seem to imply that as long as price discrimination is absent in both the commodity market and the input market, the market system will lead to Pareto optimality, and that perfect competition and monopoly are both consistent with Pareto optimality. In fact, this is not the case. For example, when there is monopsony in input markets, the input prices will no longer be parameters to the producers. As shown in Chapter 11, the first-order condition for profit maximization requires the equality between the VMP and marginal expenditure (ME) instead of the input price. (See, e.g., Figure 11.9.) Thus, condition (A13.34) may not be satisfied. Similarly, if there are imperfections in the commodity markets, then the commodity prices may no longer be considered parameters by consumers, and the first-order condition for utility maximization for a given income requires the equality between MRS and the ME ratio instead of the price ratio. Therefore, the condition for Pareto optimality may not be satisfied when consumers are at equilibrium in imperfect markets. This situation will be more obvious when both consumption and production are taken into consideration simultaneously.

The concept of the MRPT between two commodities for a producer can only make sense when joint products are considered, that is, one producer produces more than one commodity. We have not dealt with this topic in either production or cost theory. However, it can easily be shown that the MRPT between commodities is actually equal to the MC ratio of the commodities (see, e.g., Henderson and Quandt, 1971, p. 90). Profit maximization requires that $MR = MC$. Under perfect competition in the commodity markets, $MR = P$, where P denotes the price of the commodity. Hence, equilibrium of the firm or of a producer requires the equality between the MRPT and the price ratio of the corresponding commodities:

$$\frac{\partial F_p / \partial q_{pj}}{\partial F_p / \partial q_{pk}} = \frac{P_j}{P_k}, \qquad p = 1, 2, ..., P, \quad j, k = 1, 2, ..., m$$

$$(A13.35)$$

Equations (A13.33) and (A13.35) taken together imply that

$$\frac{\partial U_i / \partial q_{ij}}{\partial U_i / \partial q_{ik}} = \frac{\partial F_p / \partial q_{pj}}{\partial F_p / \partial q_{pk}}, \qquad i = 1, 2, ..., n$$

$$p = 1, 2, ..., P \qquad (A13.36)$$

$$j, k = 1, 2, ..., m$$

which is precisely equivalent to the condition for Pareto optimality (A13.30) when both consumption and production are taken into consideration simultaneously. This shows that the perfectly competitive market system is consistent with Pareto optimality for the economy as a whole.

It should be pointed out that when there are monopoly elements in commodity markets, the demand curve for the product will be negatively sloped, and the price of a commodity will be greater than the corresponding MR for some positive quantity demanded, that is, $P_j > MR_j$ for $Q_j > 0$. For the sake of simplicity, assume that the jth market is a monopoly, whereas perfect competition prevails in the kth market. Then $P_j > MR_j$ and $P_k = MR_k$. If the consumers are still price takers, then the condition for consumer equilibrium is the same as before, that is,

$$\frac{\partial U_i/\partial q_{ij}}{\partial U_i/\partial q_{ik}} = \frac{P_j}{P_k}, \qquad j, k = 1, 2, ..., m \tag{A13.37}$$

On the other hand, profit maximization for a producer requires that MR = MC for each commodity, which implies that

$$\frac{\partial F_p/\partial q_{pj}}{\partial F_p/\partial q_{pk}} = \frac{MR_j}{MR_k} < \frac{P_j}{P_k} \tag{A13.38}$$

Equations (A13.37) and (A13.38) taken together imply that the necessary condition for Pareto optimality (A13.30) is violated if one market is monopolistic and the other markets are perfectly competitive.

It may seem that if all markets are monopolistic, then the condition for Pareto optimality may be satisfied. This is certainly true. However, a price system that meets the Pareto optimality condition under monopolistic markets can only be coincidental, and any change in one market without a corresponding change in the other markets will result in a violation of the Pareto optimality condition. Only when perfect competition prevails in all markets—commodity as well as input—will optimal behavior of all economic units—consumers and producers alike—be consistent with the conditions of Pareto optimality. This is why economists rate perfect competition highly.

In order to avoid misunderstanding, two final observations are in order. Firstly, the above results are valid under the assumption of the absence of externalities, that is, external economies as well as diseconomies, on both the consumption and the production sides. In the real world, externalities are usually present.

Secondly, economists strive to avoid value judgments in developing the theory of welfare economics. The popularity of the principle of Pareto optimality, which may involve fewer ethical evaluations than other approaches, is a result of this effort. We stress, however, that the very acceptance of the concept of Pareto optimality is a value judgment.

MICROECONOMICS
AND ECONOMIC POLICY

Although it has received less attention than macroeconomics over the past three decades, microeconomics is still an important branch of economics for policy analysis. Moreover, given the increased attention that efficiency in resource use will receive in the future, there is every reason to believe that microeconomics will exert a greater influence on policy formulation. Students with only limited exposure to the application of microeconomics to policy formulation should be aware that microanalysis has had a long and useful history in two key areas of policy and analysis. The first is antitrust policy. Here the economic models of perfect competition and monopoly have been employed extensively to establish the value of a policy directed toward the preservation of competition in the market place. Second, microanalysis has been widely used in analyzing tax policy, particularly in the study of the shifting and incidence of different types of taxes.

Other areas where microeconomics has contributed heavily to policy formulation are (1) public utility regulation (especially rate making), (2) the financing of public services such as education and highways, and (3) the development of agricultural price support programs. In more recent years, microeconomics has increasingly been used in the assessment of manpower and income maintenance programs, the study of capital markets and enterprise financing, and the evaluation of water resource development.

One area where microanalysis has not been widely used is the evaluation of monetary and fiscal policy dealing with the dual problem of inflation and unemployment. Chapter 14 examines this problem of the 1970s in the context of our model of mark-up pricing. We hope that our treatment will convince the student that microeconomics is a viable tool for policy analysis beyond the traditional applications. Because of a rebirth of interest in tax policy, we have also devoted considerable space to an analysis of the shifting and incidence of taxes. Students will recognize that, far from being resolved or a closed case, this study remains a complicated problem with far-reaching ramifications in the area of welfare economics.

For two reasons, we have purposely omitted several other policy applications of microeconomic theory. First, their discussion would have added to an already lengthy book whose primary purpose is a complete and rigorous presentation of classical and modern theory. Second, we feel that many of the applications of microanalysis are best treated in specialized monographs, in which adequate space and treatment of the subject is assured. Thus, although we briefly examined marginal cost pricing (see Chapter 7), those who are interested in further study of the topic are best advised to consult books that specifically deal with its application. A similar caveat applies to the microanalysis of man-power programs. Hence, Chapter 14 is meant more as an introduction to than as a primer on the policy applications of micro-economic theory.

14

APPLICATION OF MICROECONOMIC
THEORY TO PUBLIC POLICY ANALYSIS

14.1 MACRO- AND MICROECONOMIC ANALYSIS
OF MONETARY AND FISCAL POLICY

One of the most critical and vexatious problems facing any nation
is that of price inflation. However, considerable disagreement
exists, both in and outside the economics profession, as to the
causes of and cures for inflation. Over the past few decades, the
discussion of a national policy for dealing with the problem of
inflation has included the presumed relationship between inflation
and unemployment. Moreover, this discussion has been almost
completely monopolized by macroeconomic analysis on the sup-
position that traditional microeconomic analysis is inadequate to
the task because its approach is one of partial equilibrium analysis
and, hence, its conclusions are not valid in a general equilibrium
setting. Although there is a certain degree of truth in such an
argument, it must also be recognized that the macroeconomic
approach has been found wanting and can lead to misplaced emphasis or faith in monetary and fiscal policy for controlling inflation. In addressing this question, we shall first provide a brief
review of the macroeconomic approach to the inflation–
unemployment problem and then proceed to a discussion of
mark-up pricing and microanalysis as a possible explanation
for the so-called "stagflation" problem of the 1970s.

14.1.1 Monetary Policy and Mark-Up Stagflation

*The Macroeconomic Approach to the Inflation–
Unemployment Problem*

The macroeconomic approach to the inflation–unemployment
problem is essentially demand oriented, taking cost and supply

*Macroeconomic
analysis considers
the inflation–
unemployment
problem primarily in
the context of
aggregate demand*

as granted. In its simplest form, the macroeconomic approach assumes that as long as there is sufficient purchasing power (aggregate demand) in the economy, commodities and services will be produced to accommodate demand. This condition is represented by the famous intersection of the aggregate demand curve and the 45° line in a graphical representation of national income analysis. In this same context, it is argued that as long as the level of unemployment is high, an increase in aggregate demand will only result in an increase in production and employment (thus, a decrease in unemployment), with no effect on the price level. Only when full employment is approached will an increase in aggregate demand result in upward pressure on the price level, and once full employment is reached, further increases in aggregate demand will be purely inflationary.[1] In short, the macro model implies that the key to both the inflation problem and the unemployment problem is to be found in the behavior of aggregate demand.

An important extension to the simplified macro model of aggregate demand inflation is the development of the so-called *Phillips curve*, which is an attempt to predict the changes in the rate of price inflation on the basis of changes in the unemployment rate. First advanced by the British economist A. W. Phillips (see Phillips, 1958) in terms of an inverse relationship between changes in money wage rates and the level of unemployment, it was subsequently reformulated into a price–unemployment model in which the rate of unemployment became a proxy for the level of aggregate demand, whereas the GNP deflator became the proxy for prices.[2] The theory of a trade-off between inflation and un-

---

[1] In the classic textbook version, an inflationary gap exists when Y_f, which represents national income at the full employment level, is less than Y, the actual income in current dollars. Thus, the inflationary gap is $Y - Y_f$, and prices must rise by a relative magnitude of $(Y - Y_f)/Y_f$ for the market to clear, so to speak. Introductory textbooks generally offer a solution to the inflation problem in terms of either a reduction in government spending, a reduction in consumer spending, or both through a combination of fiscal and monetary policies. Many economists, such as Milton Friedman of the University of Chicago, further argue that the real culprit in our inflation pervasive economy is Federal government deficit spending and the unwarranted expansion in the money supply that it generates, both of which prime the engine of inflation.

[2] Phillips first propounded the notion of an inverse relationship between changes in money wages and unemployment in a journal article in 1958 (see Phillips, 1958). Subsequent studies by others attempted to refine and extend the analysis by using alternative indicators of labor market conditions as proxies for aggregate demand pressures and changes in either earnings adjusted for productivity or the GNP deflator as proxies for price changes. Thus, George Perry adjusted the unemployment rate for changes in the composition of the labor force, whereas Norman Simler and Alfred Tella used the notion of a "labor reserve" to measure changes in the intensity of demand pressures on the economy. More recently, Christopher Green has shown that the employment ratio provides a better proxy for measuring aggregate demand pressure than the unemployment rate. In all of these studies, the inflation problem is analyzed as an essentially aggregate demand problem.

employment found wide acceptance by both economists and non-economists in the 1960s. Not only did the theory fit the emphasis on the aggregate demand approach to inflation of the simple macro model, but it gave rise to a pessimistic outlook regarding the attainment of full employment because, as the theorists argued, full employment could only be bought at the price of inflation. Conversely, it implied that price stability could only be achieved at relatively high (or at least higher than previously thought) un-employment rates. Some research findings even suggested a con-tinued rightward shift in the Phillips curve, thus adding to the pessimistic outlook for reducing unemployment rates without re-sultant spiraling inflation.

The Phillips curve is essentially based on aggregate demand behavior

The evolution of concomitant high rates of unemployment and inflation in the 1970s caused many economists and policymakers to challenge the validity of the Phillips curve, and faith in the trade-off theory on inflation and unemployment has waned. More-over, macroeconomic policies that seemed appropriate under the special circumstances of high unemployment in the 1930s and strong demand pressures of the earlier post-World War II years became clearly suspect for dealing with the inflationary problems of the 1970s, since the so-called "stagflation" of the past decade seemed immune to the macro prescriptions for "fine tuning" the economy. This was particularly true for attempts to bring inflation under control through monetary policy. Obviously, the economic system was not behaving in accord with the assumptions implicit in the macro model. Let us see why.

In our opinion, the problem with macroeconomics is not in its theoretical structure or logic, but in its implicit assumptions of perfect information or knowledge and perfect competition, which implies that producers are price takers and that they are satisfied with a normal return to capital. From these assumptions, it fol-lows that as long as unemployed resources exist, there is no tendency under the market mechanism for the price of resources, nor the products produced by these resources, to rise. Hence, the macroeconomic model of Keynes takes prices as given and deals with output and employment in real terms because it does not have a built-in mechanism to determine prices. Therefore, any policy suggestions concerning inflation which are based on the model involve pure conjecture in accordance with elementary microeconomic principles, that is, a high level of demand results in a high price and a low level of demand in a low price. Although such a conjecture is valid for a given cost or supply, in the general market we know that price is not determined by demand alone. This is true even in a perfectly competitive market, where, as we have shown in Chapter 6, supply is equally (if not more) impor-tant. Again, as we have demonstrated in Chapters 7–9, demand and cost taken together determine market prices under the as-sumption of profit maximization in imperfect markets.

The fact that most (if not all) firms practice mark-up pricing without reliable information or knowledge of the demand for their products further complicates the determination of market price. However, since firms usually have reliable information on costs, it should come as no surprise that their pricing decisions rest mainly on cost instead of demand.[3] Consequently, when there is an exogenous increase in cost (in particular, an increase in interest cost), the mark-up price will increase accordingly.[4] As we have explained in Chapter 7, the increase in the mark-up price is also likely to be more than the profit-maximizing mark-up due to the lack of reliable information on demand and a misconception or lack of knowledge about the inelasticity of demand. We can observe the implied pricing policy of the San Francisco waterworks as illustrative of the latter case.

On June 29, 1977, a national television network carried a news item which indicated that because of a water shortage in the early spring of that year, people had gotten into the habit of using less water. However, as water became more plentiful, people still continued to refrain from using more water. Meanwhile, the management of the waterworks made the assertion that, if residents of San Francisco continued to use less water than before, the price of water would go up by at least 20%. Clearly, what such a pronouncement indicates is that we have a leftward shift of the demand schedule for a given cost, resulting in a higher price based on mark-up pricing.

More recently, an article appeared in the St. Paul Dispatch (October 30, 1978) which reported that a spokesman for the Northern States Power Company had confirmed that the utility was studying the possibility of assessing special charges against customers who cut their natural gas use through conservation or alternative energy sources. This proposal came on the heels of action taken by a Washington, D. C., utility to gain the right to charge its customers more for using less natural gas. The comment by the Northern States Power Company spokesman was that the entire industry was beginning to look at the problem of reduced demand "... because as people begin to conserve, we have to realistically look at our revenues ... to stay financially sound ... ." Thus, we have another indication that costs, together with demand and mark-up pricing, are the keystone of pricing policy by business.[5]

---

[3] As we noted in Chapter 7, businesspeople, as distinct from economists, do not include a normal return to their own capital as cost. Rather, the return to their capital is considered profit, which is consistent with the definition of cost for tax purposes.

[4] It is generally recognized that both wages and prices are flexible upward, but inflexible downward.

[5] We have already shown in Chapter 7 that Westinghouse and General Motors practice mark-up pricing and that General Motor's mark-up is predicated on 70–80% of capacity.

It is an undeniable fact that many business decisions are based on exactly the same philosophy as that of the cases referred to above. This is especially true of oligopolistic or monopolistic enterprises, which, when they cut back on their production, will maintain a standard mark-up on production costs. Since, in many cases, these enterprises have elongated, negatively sloped cost curves, it means that at less-than-capacity operation their output costs rise, and, given a policy of mark-up pricing, higher prices are unavoidable. Hence, policy measures that ignore such enterprise practices cannot be expected to always work. Therefore, analysis that takes both demand and cost behavior into consideration is superior to that which ignores the cost factor and mark-up pricing practice.

Mark-up pricing based on cost explains why prices rise in spite of reduced demand

The equal importance of both cost and demand in the determination of market prices, either in a perfectly competitive or a monopolistic setting, is fully demonstrated by the microeconomic models that we have covered in Chapters 6–9. In Chapter 6, we showed that although technically a commodity can easily be produced, the possibility of a zero amount of production will take place in a perfectly competitive market in equilibrium when cost is too high compared with effective demand. In Chapter 7, we argued that an industry characterized by monopoly will disappear from the market if the cost and demand conditions do not permit a positive (or at least zero) profit to be earned in the long run. Since the mark-up price of a commodity is intended to cover at least the average cost (including a normal return on the firm's capital investment), it is understandable that the mark-up pricing practice of business is consistent with the theory of economics of the firm. It also follows that, because of the uncertainty of demand, the quantity that can be sold is unknown until the end of a given time period, and, therefore, the intended mark-up price may end up producing a loss rather than a profit. When this happens, the business can either raise the price or reduce its cost by lowering the quality of the product on the assumption that production efficiency already exists. If the demand and cost conditions do not permit a higher profit-maximizing price or the lowering of quality, then the only remedy is bankruptcy. Obviously, if all firms in the industry are in the same situation, then the industry will be in serious trouble, and if all industries face the same conditions, then the whole economy is in trouble. Certainly, macroeconomic models do not have the mechanism to analyze this possibility.

Given the above arguments, we can see that demand essentially determines the quantity to be produced and, thus, employment, but that cost conditions determine the price level. When cost increases due to such exogenous factors as a politically determined oil embargo or an arbitrary (i.e., not economically induced) increase in oil prices, prices will go up as a result of mark-up pricing by business firms based on cost. In such an environment,

*Monetary and fiscal
policy aimed at
aggregate demand
ignores the cost-
induced rise in
mark-up prices*

fiscal and monetary policies aimed at reducing aggregate demand
can only lead to a reduction in both output and employment, with
little or no effect on inflation. It is in this framework that we shall
examine the model of mark-up pricing and its implications relative
to the use of monetary policy for controlling inflation.

Monetary Policy and the Mark-Up Pricing Model

In addressing monetary policy to the problem of inflation, economists too often base their arguments on the IS and LL curves
of John R. Hicks (see Hicks, 1937). They argue that, provided
the system is not in a liquidity trap, a tight money policy will
engender a leftward shift of the LL curve and, therefore, higher
interest rates and a lower level of aggregate demand. The lower
level of aggregate demand will, in turn, release the pressure on
prices, thereby curbing inflation, albeit at the expense of higher
levels of unemployment. As we have already noted, however,
the tight money policies of the 1970s, instead of curbing inflation,
seemed only to produce high rates of inflation. Moreover the
higher interest rates that resulted from tight money policies appeared to move in unison with the higher rates of inflation. Consequently, it may be useful to analyze the effects of money policy
on inflation and employment in the context of the theory of the
firm, which involves a reexamination of cost behavior and pricing
practices as described in Chapters 7–9. We shall restrict our
analysis to the use of the mark-up model of the firm and a consideration of interest as a cost.[6] However, the implications of the
analysis can be extended to a more-general evaluation of the
inflation problem.

At the outset, we reiterate the fact that empirical studies show
that most, if not all, firms practice mark-up pricing (see, e.g.,
Blair, 1972; Hall and Hitch, 1939; and Lanzillotti, 1958). Furthermore, as we have explained in Chapter 7, under the assumptions of certainty and perfect information or knowledge, mark-
up pricing practice and the profit-maximization hypothesis of the
firm are mutually consistent with the economic theory of imperfect competition. Since imperfect competition and mark-up pricing are the rule rather than the exception in our economic system,
the mark-up pricing model has direct relevance to both the inflation problem and the use of monetary policy to resolve it.

---

[6] In the more-familiar analysis of cost-push inflation, the wage rate is considered
the main cost factor. The presumption is that businesses simply pass the wage
increases on to the consumer and that only productivity increases and the elasticity of demand for the firm's product will act to moderate the increase in prices.
Most cost-push inflation theories implicitly assume that businesses know the
price elasticities of demand for their products. As we have explained in Chapter
7, such an assumption is unwarranted.

For the reasons noted in Chapter 7, supply under imperfect competition does not have the same clear meaning that it has under perfect competition. Therefore, it is not meaningful to speak of a supply function or supply curve when discussing the operation of an imperfectly competitive market. Instead, we employ the concept of a cost function as the important factor in the determination of the equilibrium price and quantity under conditions of imperfect competition.

If we begin by assuming that the firm is out to maximize its profits, then given certainty and perfect information or knowledge, we find that the first-order condition for the firm's equilibrium will be met when

$$MR = MC \tag{14.1}$$

where MR and MC denote marginal revenue and marginal cost, respectively. The fact that the firm faces a negatively sloped demand function under imperfect competition also implies that the MR curve is negatively sloped. If the MC is either a constant or an increasing function of the quantity produced, then the second-order condition for the firm's equilibrium is also satisfied. In Chapter 7, we demonstrated that even if the MC is a decreasing function of the quantity produced, the second-order condition may still be satisfied, provided that the MC decreases more slowly than the MR in the neighborhood of the intersection of their respective curves. Under these circumstances, it can easily be shown that an increase in the interest rate will result in an increase in cost, which, in turn, will result in both an increase in the profit-maximizing price and a decrease in the quantity produced.

An increase in the interest rate increases cost and the profit-maximizing mark-up price

Consider Figure 14.1, in which parts (a)–(c) have been drawn to show the different MC conditions noted above. In part (a), we have a negatively sloped demand curve, the corresponding neg-

FIGURE 14.1

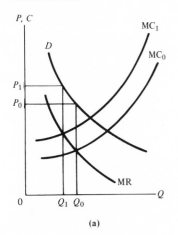

(a)

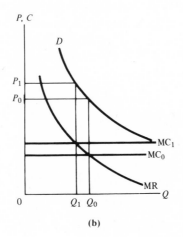

(b)

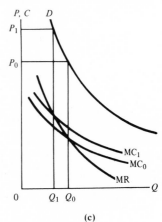

(c)

atively sloped MR curve, and two positively sloped MC curves. Given the original marginal cost curve MC_0, we have the equilibrium price P_0 and equilibrium quantity Q_0. When the marginal cost increases from MC_0 to MC_1, the equilibrium price will rise to P_1, whereas the equilibrium quantity will fall to Q_1. It can be seen that a similar, although not proportional, result occurs with a constant MC [part (b)] and a decreasing MC [part (c)]. Thus, any policy measure that results in an increase in cost, other things being equal (this assumption will be relaxed later), will result in both inflation and unemployment. This result can be shown explicitly by using a simple model of a linear demand function and the Cobb–Douglas production function.

Let us assume that, in the short run, there are two variable inputs—capital and labor—that are combined with some fixed input(s). Denoting capital and labor by the symbols K and L, respectively, the Cobb–Douglas production function can be written

$$Q = AL^\alpha K^\beta \tag{14.2}$$

where A, α, and β are constants. The fixed input(s) can be considered as being taken care of in the scale constant A. The cost equation can then be written

$$C = C_0 + wL + rK \tag{14.3}$$

where C_0 is the total cost for the fixed inputs, and w and r are the prices of labor and capital, respectively.

Using the first-order condition for constrained ouput maximization (the expansion path function) together with (14.2) and (14.3), we can derive the cost function by solving for C in terms of Q, and eliminating L and K. (See the Appendix to Chapter 3 for further explanation.) Thus, we have

$$C = C_0 + Bw^a r^b Q^c \tag{14.4}$$

where

$$B = (\alpha + \beta)(1/A\alpha^\alpha \beta^\beta)^{1/(\alpha + \beta)}$$

$$a = \alpha/(\alpha + \beta)$$

$$b = \beta/(\alpha + \beta)$$

$$c = 1/(\alpha + \beta)$$

the MC becomes

$$MC = cBw^a r^b Q^{c-1} \tag{14.5}$$

and the slope of the MC curve is

$$d^2C/dQ^2 = c(c - 1)Bw^a r^b Q^{c-2} \gtrless 0$$
$$\text{for} \quad c \gtrless 1 \quad \text{or} \quad \alpha + \beta \gtrless 1 \tag{14.6}$$

We can see that the MC derived from the Cobb–Douglas production function can be either a constant, an increasing function of the output, or a decreasing function of the output. On the other hand, from (14.5) it can be seen that, in all cases, MC is definitely an increasing function of the interest rate r, since we have

$$\partial(MC)/\partial r = bcBw^a r^{b-1} Q^{c-1} > 0 \qquad (14.7)$$

When the MC increases, given negatively sloped demand and MR functions, the profit-maximizing price will necessarily increase, as shown in parts (a)–(c) of Figure 14.1. In order to get an idea of the relative magnitudes of an increase in the interest rate r and the corresponding increase in the price P, we may, for the sake of simplicity, use linear functions for both the demand and MC curves.

Suppose that we have the demand function

$$Q = A - BP \qquad (14.8)$$

the inverse of which is

$$P = A/B - (1/B)Q \qquad (14.9)$$

The corresponding MR function is

$$MR = A/B - (2/B)Q \qquad (14.10)$$

Furthermore, suppose that we have an MC function of the form

$$MC = a + bQ \qquad (14.11)$$

Hence, the corresponding profit-maximizing price P_0 is as follows:

$$P_0 = [aB + A(1 + bB)]/B(2 + bB) \qquad (14.12)$$

For this simple example, a change in the MC can be considered a parallel shift of the MC curve. The effect of such a change on the profit-maximizing price can be inferred from the sign of the partial derivative of P with respect to the shifting parameter of the MC function, that is, a change in the value of a.

From (14.12), we have

$$\partial P/\partial a = 1/(2 + bB) \qquad (14.13)$$

Hence, the effect of an upward shift of the MC curve is closely related to the slopes of both the demand curve and the MC curve. From (14.8), it is obvious that B is, in general, positive. However, from (14.11), we can see that b can be either positive, zero, or negative, depending on whether the MC curve is positively sloped, horizontal, or negatively sloped, respectively. It has been shown above that, based on the widely used Cobb–Douglas production function, the MC curve can reasonably be either positively sloped, horizontal, or negatively sloped. Therefore, we must examine all three possibilities.

The demand and supply curves' slopes influence the effect of an upward shift in the MC curve

The simplest case is that of a horizontal MC curve. In this special case, where $b = 0$, we can see from (14.13) that the profit-maximizing price will always increase by one-half of the increase in the MC, regardless of the slope of the demand curve, provided that the demand is neither perfectly elastic nor perfectly inelastic. This may seem a little surprising, but it should be noted that this result holds only if the demand function is linear.

When the MC curve is positively sloped in the neighborhood of its intersection with the MR curve, (14.13) is unambiguously positive, which implies that an upward shift of the MC curve will result in an increase in the profit-maximizing price. However, since both b and B are positive in this case,

$$2 + bB > 2 \quad \text{and} \quad 1/(2 + bB) < \tfrac{1}{2}$$

Therefore, the increase in the profit-maximizing price will be less than one-half of the increase in the MC. Although common sense may lead us to different conclusions, it should be kept in mind that our conclusion depends on the assumptions of linear demand and MC functions.

When the MC curve is negatively sloped, $b < 0$. In this case, whether the absolute value of bB is greater than, less than, or equal to 2 is important. Mathematically, when $|bB| > 2$, (14.13) will be negative. This implies that an increase in the MC will result in a decrease in the profit-maximizing price, which is unreasonable. Further analysis shows that we have the case where the second-order condition for profit maximization is violated; thus, the intersection of the MR and MC curves results in minimum rather than maximum profit. Consequently, this case is ruled out under our profit-maximization hypothesis.[7] When $|bB| = 2$, we have the case in which the MC and MR curves have the same slope; hence, they will either coincide or never intersect (i.e., are parallel), and again the second-order condition for profit maximization is not satisfied. In this case, the quantity and price are indeterminate, and equilibrium is not well defined. This case must also be ruled out. Hence, if $b < 0$, the second-order condition for profit maximization requires that $|bB| < 2$, in which case (14.13) has to be positive and greater than $\tfrac{1}{2}$. This means that the value of (14.13) can be anywhere between $\tfrac{1}{2}$ and positive infinity—at least in theory. When $b \to 0$, we have the case of a horizontal MC curve. If $b \to -2/B$, we have the case in which the MR and MC curves either coincide or are parallel, which must be ruled out owing to the second-order condition for profit

---

[7] $2 + bB < 0$ implies that $2/B < -B$, where $-2/B$ is the slope of the MR curve and $b < 0$ is the slope of the MC curve. Therefore, MC decreases faster than MR in the neighborhood of the intersection of their respective curves. Under these circumstances, either an increase or a decrease in quantity would result in more profits or less losses.

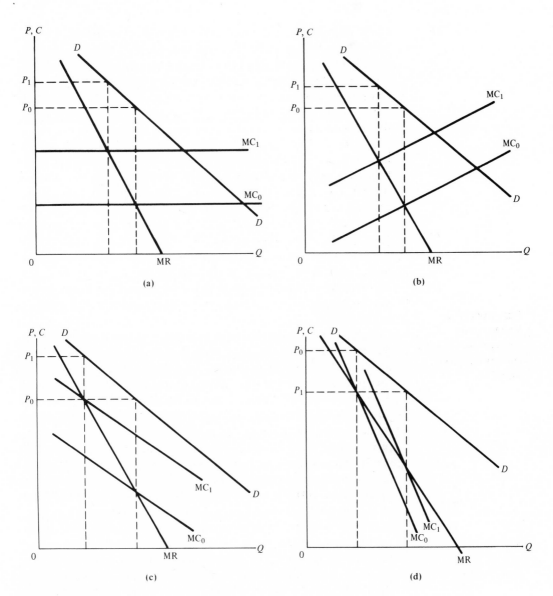

FIGURE 14.2
(a) $b = 0$; (b) $b > 0$; (c) $b < 0$ and $|bB| < 2$; (d) $b < 0$ and $|bB| > 2$.

maximization. It is interesting to note that when $b = -1/B$, then, from (14.13). $\partial P/\partial a = 1$, which implies that the profit-maximizing price will increase by an amount equal to the increase in MC.

Furthermore, since $-1/B$ is the slope of the demand curve, we have the special case in which the MC curve has the same slope as the demand curve. In the linear case, the magnitude of the change in the profit-maximizing price will be equal to the magnitude of the change in the MC.

Parts (a)–(d) in Figure 14.2 have been drawn to illustrate each of the aforementioned conditions with respect to the slope of the MC curve, increases in MC, and the effect of the cost increase on the profit-maximizing price. In part (a), with a horizontal MC curve having a slope $b = 0$, we can observe that the increase in price is roughly one-half of the increase in MC. When the MC curve is positively sloped [part (b)], the increase in the profit-maximizing price is less than one-half of the increase in MC. In part (c), we have the case of a negatively sloped MC curve; however, as we have explained earlier, the second-order condition for profit maximization is still satisfied, since the slope of the MC curve is not as steep as that of the MR curve and, in the context of (14.13), $|bB| < 2$. Here again, the price will increase as a result of the increase in MC. Finally, in part (d) we have the case in which the slope of the MC curve is steeper than that of the MR curve; hence, the second-order condition for profit maximization will be violated. In the context of (14.13), $|bB| > 2$, and an increase in the MC would result in a decrease in the profit-maximizing price, which is clearly not in accord with either reason or theory.

Price rises by at least the cost increase when the MC curve is negatively sloped

Casual observation indicates that many businesspeople believe that when cost goes up, price should go up by at least the amount of the added cost. From the above analysis, it can be seen that this is consistent with the assumed profit-maximizing behavior only when the MC curve is negatively sloped. Since many empirical studies (see, e.g., Eitman, 1960) show that the MC curve is, in general, horizontal, the price should only increase by approximately one-half of the increase in the MC for maximum profit. This observation should certainly have important implications in the case of high inflation and unemployment, since the oil embargo, periodic increases in crude oil prices by OPEC countries, raw material shortages, and rigorous environmental regulation enforcement have all resulted in higher costs.

The above model is also consistent with the mark-up pricing practice of business. However, the effects of mark-up pricing practices on inflation and unemployment may be much worse than indicated by the profit-maximizing model that we have described above. It is well documented (see, e.g., Blair, 1972; Hall and Hitch, 1939; Lanzillotti, 1958; and Section 7.2.3 of Chapter 7) that target profit mark-up pricing is generally practiced by big companies. As we have noted, because of a lack of information regarding demand in actual practice firms do not pay much attention to the concept of the demand function as defined by economists. However, they do need to have some idea of the quantity of output to be produced and sold in order to compute their mark-up price. In general, the quantity that they use is a point estimate—about 70–80% of capacity—which is not considered a function of price. In terms of economics, such a business concept of demand is tantamount to perfectly inelastic demand. On the other hand, business does have reliable information on cost, which—although different from the cost concept in economics in that cost in economics includes a normal profit on investment—does provide a basis for decision making not unlike that in theory. However, since the cost figures in business records do not include profit, the information on quantity and cost alone does not enable business firms to compute a price. Therefore, they need another figure—profit—before they can arrive at a price. In the absence of a knowledge of demand, there is obviously no way that they can compute the *maximum* profit or *profit-maximizing* price. Hence, the resort to a subjectively determined reasonable rate of profit for computing a target profit. This target profit is equal to the product of the predetermined rate of profit and the capital investment on which profit is based. The above model can be formulated in symbols as follows:

Without a knowledge of demand, the mark-up price can exceed the profit-maximizing price

$$P = (F + C_0 + V)/Q \qquad (14.14)$$

where P is the mark-up price, F is the target profit, C_0 is the total fixed cost, V is the total variable cost, and Q is the quantity. It should again be noted that both F and Q are determined subjectively by management. Generally, firms treat average variable cost as a constant. Thus, we have

$$V = vQ \qquad (14.15)$$

where v is the average variable cost. Hence, (14.14) can be written

$$P = v + (F + C_0)/Q \qquad (14.16)$$

This simple equation has important implications. First of all, the interest rate may reasonably enter into both v and C_0, which should be increasing functions of the interest rate. Since the target profit F is an increasing function of both the profit rate and the investment, and since the profit rate is determined subjectively, whereas investment is fixed in the short run, it is conceivable that F may also be an increasing function of the interest rate. Hence, for a given Q, the price P will be an increasing function of the interest rate, which is consistent with our profit-maximizing model presented above. Secondly, as mentioned above, the quantity Q is also determined in a subjective manner, it generally being considered as 70–80% of capacity. Certainly, the quantity to be produced will also be predicated on current market conditions and the market outlook, it presumably being high during prosperity and low during recession. Equation (14.16) clearly shows that the price P is a decreasing function of Q. Thus, business practice will result in lower mark-up prices during prosperity (i.e., higher aggregate demand) and higher prices during recession (i.e., a lower level of employment and lower aggregate demand). This result is just the opposite of that derived from national income analysis and is certainly not consistent with economic theory. However, the actual operations of the market are probably more closely related to business practices than to theoretical inferences or conjecture. This may be an explanation of the so-called "stag-flation" problem. It should be noted that this model is more relevant with respect to cost-push inflation than with respect to demand-pull inflation. Since the "stagflation" problem began with the oil embargo and was reinforced by raw material short-ages, the mark-up pricing model is applicable.

It should be pointed out that both the profit-maximizing model and the business practice (i.e., mark-up pricing) model have ig-nored a shift in demand in a general equilibrium sense (as men-tioned above). With higher prices and lower output, employment and real income will go down. In economic theory, a decrease in income will result in a leftward shift of the demand function of a normal good, which, according to theory, will tend to lower the price. Thus, we can see that a higher interest rate which results from a tight money policy will generate two opposing forces that have an impact on price. First of all, higher interest rates result in a higher cost, which tends to raise prices. Secondly, higher interest rates, through both higher prices and lower in-vestment, also result in lower output, lower employment, and lower real income, which, in turn, tend to suppress prices due to lower aggregate demand. Partial analysis in microeconomics stresses the former effect, whereas macroeconomic analysis stresses the latter effect. However, a complete general equilib-rium analysis should take both effects into consideration. In such a case, the impact of a tight money policy on inflation is theo-retically uncertain. On the other hand, in both micro- and ma-croeconomic analysis its impact on employment is quite certain: higher unemployment.

The net effect of higher interest rates depends on the shifts in the demand and cost curves

It is interesting to point out that there may be an asymmetry with respect to expansionary and contractionary monetary poli-cies. It is probably true that expansionary monetary policy, which macroeconomic analysis has dealt with extensively, would have a considerable effect on inflation, but that contractionary mon-etary policy may not have much effect on curbing inflation. It is well known that wages and prices are generally flexible upward, but inflexible downward. Our analysis may shed more light on the causes of both inflation and high unemployment.

Concluding Remarks on Monetary Policy and the Inflation–Unemployment Problem

Most fiscal and monetary policy measures are based on macro-economic analysis, which has served the post-depression and post-war years quite well. However, the aggregate demand analysis in macroeconomics cannot come up with a good answer to the causes of "stagflation," let alone a solution to it. The traditional tight monetary policy, which is considered by both the classical quantity and Keynesian theorists as a good policy instrument for curbing inflation, has not only had very little effect on inflation but has actually tended to worsen unemployment. Therefore, it seems appropriate to examine business behavior and its effects on inflation and unemployment when there is an exogenous change in cost. Although the business practice of mark-up pricing may not be very rational according to economic theory, it should be considered in the light of the fact that businesspeople do not usually have information on the demand function and that the future is neither certain nor known. Nevertheless, businesspeople must set the prices of their products before they are put on the market. Mark-up pricing is a way that businesspeople can carry out this otherwise impossible task. Regardless of whether their behavior is rational or not, it is certainly not irrelevant in any analysis of the inflation–unemployment problem. Economists have traditionally ignored this business practice in their analyses; however, failure to incorporate this practice or behavior into the analysis will, sooner or later, get us into trouble. It is to be hoped that more economists will come to realize the importance of this business practice, particularly in connection with the inflation–unemployment problem, so that policy measures derived from economic analysis may be more relevant to the problems of the real world.

14.1.2 Fiscal Policy, Inflation, and Unemployment

As we have already noted in Section 14.1.1, in dealing with the problems of inflation and unemployment, it is implicitly assumed that excess aggregate demand is the cause of rising prices, whereas inadequate demand is the cause of rising unemployment. Therefore, traditional macroeconomic policy formulations call for an increase in government spending and/or a reduction in taxes to stimulate an expansion in output and employment, on the one hand, and a reduction in government spending and/or an increase in taxes to combat inflation, on the other hand.

It is generally conceded that an increase in government spending will raise employment (and thus reduce unemployment) because government purchases will—directly or indirectly—require more resources to produce the additional commodities and services demanded. However, as we have previously observed, there is no guarantee that the price level will remain constant (unless the unemployment rate is exceptionally high). Nevertheless, a sufficient expansion in government spending can reduce unemployment, albeit with some lag and depending on the expansion in the labor force that is induced by improved employment conditions. Similarly, a reduction in taxes can stimulate an expansion in output and employment through an increase in disposable income and consumer spending, a reduction in the cost of business, an inducement to investment, or some combination of all of these actions.

One of the problems that macroeconomic policies for reducing

The symmetry of government spending on output, employment, and inflation does not apply to taxes

unemployment must face is creeping inflation when an expansion in output and employment is promoted. In this regard, it is important to recognize that although government spending can be considered symmetrical with respect to its effect on aggregate demand, unemployment, and inflation, the same cannot be said for taxes. Thus, whereas it is conceivable that a sufficient reduction in government spending can reduce the purchases of commodities and services to the extent that inflationary pressures are arrested or eliminated (albeit at the probable expense of higher unemployment), an increase in taxes has a dual effect on aggregate demand and cost which negates its effectiveness. As we have shown in Chapter 7, business firms usually practice mark-up pricing; therefore, any increase in cost resulting from an increase in taxes will, in turn, result in higher prices and more, rather than less, inflation. Let us examine this problem more closely.

We shall first observe that the application of fiscal policy to combat inflation is essentially the exclusive responsibility of the Federal government because individual state and local governments are too small to individually influence aggregate demand. Moreover, state and local governments do not normally have either the legal or the moral responsibility to exercise fiscal policy to combat inflation or deflation. Therefore, we must look to the major Federal taxes in order to properly assess the effects of fiscal remedies on the inflation problem. To put things in the proper perspective, it should be noted that in 1978 over 43% of Federal revenues came from personal income taxes, more than 32% from payroll taxes, and slightly over 14% from corporate income taxes; in sum, almost 90% of Federal revenues came from these three sources.

It should also be noted that in terms of sources of national income, over 75% of the total is comprised of wages and salaries, slightly less than 10% is made up of corporate profits, and the remainder is in the form of rent, interest, and proprietorship income. This, together with tax sources, indicates that for any Federal tax policy to be effective in changing the level of aggregate demand it must be directed primarily at the personal and corporate income taxes and payroll taxes. We shall argue that the net effect of any increase in these taxes is more likely to be inflationary than deflationary. Although we present a fairly complete argument for this conclusion in this section, students are well advised to also read Sections 14.2.2 and 14.2.3 before reaching any conclusions of their own.

Economists generally argue that the personal income tax cannot be shifted by workers to employers or to the producers of the commodities and services that they buy. Thus, the incidence of the personal income tax is assumed to be on the workers. If this were true, we would expect an increase in the personal income tax to have the effect of reducing prices. This is consistent

with microeconomic analysis and our discussions on demand theory in Chapters 4 and 5, where we explained that both individual
demand and aggregate demand are a function of income. Hence,
for a normal good, it was shown that the demand curve shifts to
the right with a higher income and to the left with a lower income.
Therefore, a decrease in disposable income due to an increase
in the personal income tax, other things being equal, will cause
a leftward shift of the demand curve for each and every normal
good, which, in turn, *for a given supply under perfect competition
or a given cost under imperfect competition*, will cause a decrease
in the prices of all normal goods. Moreover, since normal goods
are predominant in the marketplace, an increase in the personal
income tax, other things being equal, should have a deflationary
effect.

From a policy point of view, one of the criticisms of traditional
microeconomic theory is its dependency on partial analysis. At
the same time, one of the heralded advantages of macroeconomic
theory is its general equilibrium analysis approach. Although it
is true that general equilibrium analysis is generally superior to
partial analysis because the former takes interaction between sectors of the economy into consideration, the simple macroeconomic model that is often employed in policy analysis is implicitly
a representation of a one-sector economy with no interaction
between sectors. Moreover, many important factors that condition the workings of the economy are lost when spending and
income activity are brought together during the process of ag-
gregation. The effect of the income tax on the price level is one
example. It is for this reason that microeconomic analysis can
prove to be especially useful.

Returning to our earlier statement that simple microeconomic
analysis justifies the macro aggregate demand argument with respect to the effect of an increase in the income tax on the price
level for a given supply or cost, we offer the additional observation that cost is not, however, independent of the personal
income tax. Unions, for example, not only want a higher wage
rate for their membership, but also higher take-home pay. Consequently, a higher income tax becomes a good basis or cause
for claiming a higher wage rate at the bargaining table. This higher
wage rate must not only leave take-home pay no lower than before
the tax, but usually also involves additional adjustments. Therefore, it is difficult to argue that the personal income tax is independent of the labor cost to producers,[8] since this would require
the hardly realistic assumption that both the unions and employers are stupid as regards their immediate welfare. In reality, a

*Arguments that the
personal income tax
cannot be shifted
ignore the cost
effect*

---

[8] See Sections 14.2.2 and 14.2.3 for a theoretical analysis of the shifting and
incidence of personal and corporate income taxes.

higher income tax can be expected to result in a higher cost, the possibility (as we shall see) of a higher price, and, very definitely, a lower output or quantity.

Under perfect competition, the higher cost induced by the tax will involve a leftward or upward shift of the firm's supply curve, which is equivalent to a decrease in supply, since the firm's supply curve is the rising portion of the MC curve which is above the minimum AVC (see Chapter 6 for further explanation). Because all firms face the same situation under perfect competition, the market supply curve will also shift to the left. Thus, for a *given demand*, a leftward shift in the supply curve will engender a higher price and a lower quantity sold.

If we combine the arguments of the preceding paragraphs, we can conclude that an increase in the personal income tax under conditions of perfect competition in the market will produce a leftward shift in *both* the demand curve and the supply curve. The result will be a decrease in the equilibrium quantity sold and either a lower or a higher market price, depending upon the relative shifts in the demand and supply curves and their respective elasticities. We should, of course, note that the above arguments are essentially for short-run analysis. In the long run, the result is more conclusive. As we showed in Chapter 6, in long-run equilibrium, the market price must be equal to the minimum long-run AC of each and every firm under conditions of perfect competition. Moreover, since the costs of all firms in an industry must be identical under the assumption of homogeneity of inputs (Assumption 1.5) and technology, a cost increase that results from an increase in wages caused by the personal income tax means that the market price must rise in long-run equilibrium due to a higher minimum AC.

The demand and supply curve shifts and elasticities influence the effect of the personal income tax

Where the market is characterized by monopoly, a decrease in demand will result in a shift of the MR curve to the left. Unlike the situation in a perfectly competitive market, where a decrease in the demand for a given supply or cost will unambiguously result in a lower price, under monopoly, a decrease in demand for a given cost may result in a higher price.

Consider Figure 14.3, in which D_0 is the original demand curve and MR_0 is the corresponding marginal revenue curve. For the given marginal cost curve MC, the profit-maximizing price is P_0 and the corresponding quantity is Q_0 (for further details, see Chapter 7). When demand decreases to give curve D_1, and the corresponding marginal revenue curve shifts to MR_1, we can see that, for a given marginal cost curve MC, the profit-maximizing price rises to P_1 and the corresponding quantity falls to Q_1. If the MC curve were to simultaneously shift upward, then the intersection of the higher MC curve with MR_1 would result in a price even higher than P_1 and a corresponding quantity even lower than Q_1.

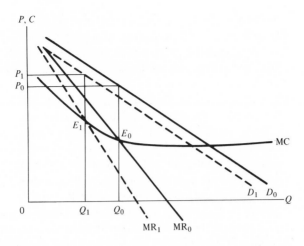

FIGURE 14.3

We have noted earlier (Chapter 8) that in a market characterized by monopolistic competition, a decrease in market demand, when combined with an increase in cost, will likely result in an increase in market price and a decrease in the equilibrium quantity. We also explained that the theory of monopolistic competition is essentially a long-run analysis, whereas, in the short-run, monopoly theory applies to monopolistic competition. We saw that, in long-run equilibrium, a firm's profit under monopolistic competition, just like that of a firm under perfect competition, is zero. One important characteristic of long-run equilibrium for a firm under monopolistic competition is that the demand curve d is tangent to the AC curve at the point where the demand curve D intersects the latter (see Chapter 8 for an explanation of this condition).

In Figure 14.4, we have plotted the original demand curves d_0 and D_0, the average cost curve AC, the equilibrium price P_0, and the equilibrium quantity Q_0. When the market demand decreases,

FIGURE 14.4

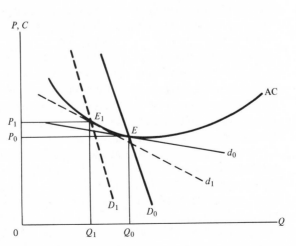

D_0 shifts to the left, and the intersection of the new demand curve D_1 and the AC curve occurs at a point to the left and higher on the latter than the initial equilibrium point E. The result is a higher price and a lower quantity, as denoted by P_1 and Q_1.

The above conclusion is based on the implicit assumption that the *number of firms* that make up the industry is fixed or constant. Otherwise, if the market demand shifted to the left and the number of firms was sufficiently reduced as a result of the decreased demand, then the firm's demand curve D could theoretically shift back to the right, since it is a representation of the market share demand, which is determined by both the market demand and the number of firms in the market (industry). In this context, we can observe that although a decrease in the market demand will likely cause the number of firms to also decline, it is not likely that this decrease in the number of firms will be so extensive as to shift the demand curve D to the right of its original position. Hence, even if we take into consideration the long-run adjustment in the number of firms, we can still expect the demand curve for the firm to shift to the left and the concomitant rise in price to occur as a result of a decrease in market demand, as shown in Figure 14.4.

The result described above is based on partial analysis in its simplest form. However, even in this case one must take into consideration the effects of a personal income tax on both the demand and the cost (or supply). As we have argued, an increase in the personal income tax will result in a leftward shift of *both* the demand curve and the supply curve, whereas the market price in such a situation can be either higher or lower, depending on the circumstances to which we referred earlier. In any event, the market quantity will definitely decline. For these reasons, the use of the personal income tax as a tool to combat inflation, as advanced by macroeconomic analysis, is highly questionable. In fact, such a policy may result in the undesirable combination of more inflation and higher unemployment, that is, "stagflation."

The effects of using the payroll tax to combat inflation are more obvious than those of the personal income tax. First of all, the payroll tax (Social Security tax in our case) is shared equally by employers and employees. Thus, the effect of an increase in payroll taxes on cost is more direct and obvious than that of an increase in personal income taxes. The combined effect of a decrease in demand and an increase in cost on inflation becomes, at best, unpredictable, and, at its worst, more inflationary.

Payroll taxes effect cost more directly than the personal income tax

The effect of an increase in the corporate income tax depends on the shifting and incidence of the tax. If the corporation cannot shift the tax either forward onto the buyers of its products through higher prices or backward onto the suppliers of inputs through lower purchase prices, then a higher corporate tax will cut into corporate profits. When this is the case, the higher corporate income tax will discourage investment, thus reducing aggregate demand and inflationary pressure. Although some economists argue that the corporate income tax cannot be shifted, others argue that shifting of the tax is not only possible but also plausible (see, e.g., Harberger, 1962, and Krzyzaniak and Musgrave, 1963). The fact that most, if not all, corporations practice mark-up pricing and consider the corporate income tax as a part of cost makes it hard to argue that the corporate tax is entirely born by corporations and that a higher tax will not induce higher prices.[9]

We have shown that Federal fiscal policy, which has been primarily based on macroeconomic analysis, is an unreliable tool for combatting inflation and may actually produce unwanted results. In this regard, the "stagflation" that was evidenced through much of the 1970s may at least partially have been the result of misguided fiscal policy. We believe that sound microeconomic analysis can substantially contribute to an improvement in fiscal policy by alerting the policymakers to the likelihood of higher prices and increased unemployment as a result of higher income and payroll taxes.

14.2 THE SHIFTING AND INCIDENCE OF SELECTED TAXES

In the sections that follow, we shall be discussing the shifting and incidence of sales taxes and both personal and corporate income taxes. Each tax will be discussed in the context of both perfect and imperfect markets. As we shall see, the shifting and incidence of these taxes will depend on the assumptions that are made with respect to the shapes of the demand and supply curves, as well as on the particular circumstances that are applicable at a given time.

It is not our purpose to provide an exhaustive treatment of the shifting and incidence of sales and income taxes, since such coverage would require a book by itself. However, we feel that, as in the case of our discussion of monetary policy and the inflation problem, the student will gain a greater appreciation and understanding of the theoretical framework and purpose of microeconomics which we developed in the previous chapters if we devote some space to the shifting and incidence of taxes. Obviously, students should realize that there are many arguments pro and con regarding the shifting and incidence of taxes, and that economists often disagree on the incidence and impact of specific taxes. Our objective is not to take sides in such arguments, but only to show how the theory can help us in making reasoned assessments of the shifting and incidence of selected taxes.

In Section 14.2.1, we discuss the shifting and incidence of sales taxes, albeit in the more-restricted context of a sales tax per unit

---

[9] For a more-complete discussion of the shifting and incidence of the corporate income tax, see Section 14.2.3. The conclusions of that section also apply here.

of product. However, the logic and results are equally applicable to sales taxes based on a percentage of value. The personal and corporate income taxes are treated separately in order to keep the exposition clear and concise. Thus, Section 14.2.2 examines the shifting and incidence of the personal income tax, whereas Section 14.2.3 treats the same problems with respect to the corporate income tax.

14.2.1 The Shifting and Incidence of Sales Taxes Under Perfect and Imperfect Markets

The shifting of a sales tax depends on the shapes of the demand and supply (cost) curves

A sales tax (such as a value-added tax in many countries other than the United States), may nominally be paid by a seller who, in turn, may be able to partially shift the burden of the tax to buyers of the commodity by raising the price; this is generally called a *forward shifting* of the tax. On the other hand, the seller may partially shift the tax to suppliers of such productive factors as labor, capital, and raw material by lowering the prices of the items purchased; this is generally called a *backward shifting* of the tax. Alternatively, a sales tax may nominally be paid by buyers of a commodity (such as in this country), but the buyer may either be able to shift the tax backward to the sellers of the commodity through a reduction in demand, which results in a lower market price for a given supply in a perfectly competitive market, or they may be able to shift the tax forward to their employers by raising wages and salaries. The final burden of a tax is called the *incidence of the tax*. One can see that the shifting and incidence of a tax are closely related. If a tax cannot be shifted, then its incidence will be on the one who nominally pays the tax. On the other hand, if a tax can easily be shifted, then its incidence may at least partially be on somebody other than the one who nominally pays the tax. It is well known that certain kinds of tax can easily be shifted, whereas others cannot.

Economists generally agree that a sales tax can be partially shifted. However, to what extent a sales tax can be shifted will depend on the shapes of the demand and supply curves in a perfectly competitive market and on the shapes of the demand and MC curves in an imperfect market. We shall use the graphical method to explain the theoretical arguments that are involved.

For the sake of convenience, we assume that a unit sales tax is imposed; that is, the tax on each unit of the commodity sold is a fixed amount and does not depend on the price of the commodity. In the United States, the sales tax is, in general, a percentage tax on the monetary value of the total bill of sales. In 1979, it was 6% in Pennsylvania and 4% in Minnesota.[10] Although

---

[10] Only five states (Alaska, Delaware, Montana, New Hampshire, and Oregon) in the United States did not have a sales tax in 1978.

our theory can be applied to both kinds of tax, a unit tax is easier to graphically demonstrate. However, it should be remembered that the logic is essentially the same for both cases.

We shall also assume that sellers pay the sales tax out of their revenues; thus the tax is included in the market price of the commodity (e.g., the tax on a gallon of gasoline). Although this also makes the graphical presentation easier to understand, it should be noted that in most cases the market price does not include the sales tax. However, theoretically, it does not make any difference whether the tax is included in the market price or is added onto it.

Consider Figure 14.5. In a perfectly competitive market, D and S_0 are the demand and supply curves, respectively, before a sales tax is introduced. The market price and quantity are P_0 and Q_0, respectively. Suppose that a \$1 sales tax per unit of the commodity is imposed. Since, by assumption, sellers are required to pay the tax, it is considered a part of cost; therefore, each unit costs the seller one more dollar in tax. Consequently, the MC curve is shifted upward by the amount of the tax (\$1 in this case). Recall that the supply curve of a firm is identical to the rising portion of the MC curve which is above the minimum AVC (as shown in Chapter 6) and that the market supply curve is the horizontal sum of the supply curves of individual firms. When the supply curves of all firms shift upward by \$1, the market supply curve will also shift upward by *exactly* \$1. Hence, the market supply curve is S_1 after the tax, and the vertical distance between S_1 and S_0 is \$1 for each and every quantity produced or supplied. With the given demand, we can see that the market price after the tax is P_1, which is determined by the intersection of the demand and supply curves. The new price is higher than the original price P_0, but not by as much as the tax. This is true because, by construction, $\overline{EA}$ is equal to the tax, whereas $\overline{EB}$ is the increase in market price.

From Figure 14.5, we see that the market price goes up by $\overline{P_0P_1}$ due to the tax. Thus, consumers share the tax by the amount

FIGURE 14.5

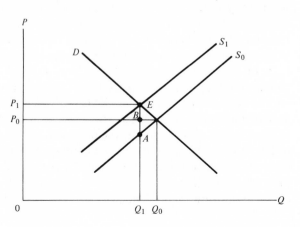

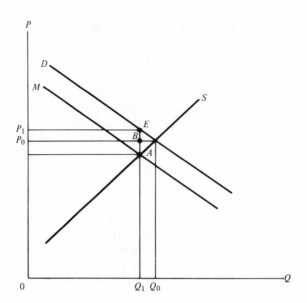

FIGURE 14.6   0 Q_1 Q_0

$\overline{P_0 P_1}$ for each unit of the commodity. However, since $\overline{P_0 P_1}$ is less than the sales tax $\overline{EA}$, we can observe that although a consumer pays a price $\overline{0P_1}$ for the commodity after the tax is imposed, a seller's net revenue per unit after a tax of \$1 per unit is paid to the government is only $\overline{Q_1 A}$, that is, $\overline{0P_1} - \overline{EA}$. Before the tax was imposed, sellers received a net revenue per unit of $\overline{0P_0} = \overline{Q_1 B}$, but after the tax their revenue per unit is reduced by $\overline{AB}$. Thus, a seller's share of the tax is $\overline{AB}$. It can be seen that a buyer's share $\overline{BE}$ plus the seller's share $\overline{AB}$ is precisely the \$1 tax.

An equivalent graphical representation of the sales tax problem can be based on a consideration of the revenue side for the seller rather than the cost side. Under perfect competition, the market price is also the firm's MR. Without a sales tax, the market price (whatever its value) is again the firm's MR. However, with a tax of \$1, the MR of a firm is \$1 less than the market price. Recall from Chapter 6 that a firm's profit is maximized under perfect competition when (1) MR = MC and (2) MC is rising. Consider Figure 14.6, in which, without the tax, profit maximization results in an equilibrium market quantity of Q_0 and an equilibrium market price of P_0. However, once a tax of \$1 is imposed, the MR of the firm is equal to the market price minus the tax. In a sense, M can be considered the MR curve. From this, it follows that profit-maximizing behavior will result in an equilibrium market quantity of Q_1, which is determined by the intersection of S, corresponding to firm's MC, and M, the corresponding MR curve. The vertical distance between the given demand D curve and the MR curve M is the per-unit tax (in this case, \$1). For the given demand curve D and the market quantity Q_1, the market price is P_1. It should be noted that the P_1 and Q_1 in Figure 14.6 will be identical to the P_1 and Q_1 in Figure 14.5, respectively, for identical demand and supply curves in the two graphs. Similarly, the consumer's share of the tax $\overline{BE}$ and seller's share $\overline{AB}$ will also be identical in the two figures. Some economists favor the first approach, whereas others favor the second; therefore, since the two approaches result in the same conclusion, it is useful to be acquainted with both of them.

Although it is obvious that a sales tax is shared by both buyers and sellers for negatively sloped demand and positively sloped supply curves, it is not clear how the relative shares of the tax are determined. It can easily be shown that the relative share of the tax is determined by the price elasticities of both demand and supply.

We first show the relevance of the price elasticity of demand with repect to the relative sharing of a sales tax between buyers and sellers. Consider Figure 14.7. If the demand curve is D_1, then, as shown previously, a buyer's share of the tax is $\overline{BE}$ and a seller's share is $\overline{AB}$. On the other hand, if the demand curve is D_2, the buyer's share of the tax is $\overline{HF}$, which is less than $\overline{BE}$, and the seller's share is $\overline{GH}$, which is more than $\overline{AB}$. From the graph, it can be seen that D_1 has a steeper slope than D_2. Although the slope of a demand curve alone does not determine the price elasticity of demand, it is true that if two demand curves intersect, the demand curve with the flatter slope at the point of intersection has a higher price elasticity than the one with a steeper slope. This statement can easily be proved by an examination of the definition of price elasticity. Thus, D_2 is more elastic than D_1 in the neighborhood of the equilibrium point. The graph shows that the buyer's share of a sales tax is greater (and hence the seller's share is less) when the demand is less elastic for a given supply, which is equivalent to saying that the buyer's share of a sales tax is less (and hence the seller's share is greater) when

The price elasticities of demand and supply will determine the incidence of sales taxes

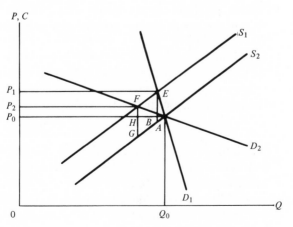

FIGURE 14.7

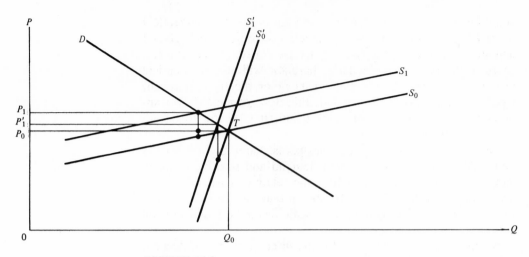

FIGURE 14.8

demand is more elastic for a given supply. This turns out to be true in general, because D_1 and D_2 can be any two demand curves with different elasticities.

We now turn to the case where, for a given demand, the relative sharing of a sales tax depends on the price elasticity of supply. Consider Figure 14.8. The two different supply curves S_0 and S_0' intersect at point T, which is also their point of intersection with demand curve D. It can be seen that the buyer's share of the sales tax is greater with supply curve S_0 than with supply curve S_0'. Again, two supply curves that have different slopes at a point of intersection will have different price elasticities, and the one with a flatter slope has a higher elasticity than the one with the steeper slope. Thus, in the neighborhood of point T, S_0 is more elastic than S_0'. Figure 14.8 shows that buyers share more of the tax, (and thus sellers less) with the more-elastic supply curve S_0 than with the less-elastic supply curve S_0', for a given demand. This turns out to be true in general, because S_0 and S_0' can be any two supply curves with different elasticities.

The above result can be summarized as follows.

Proposition 14.1. For a given supply, the higher the price elasticity of demand, the less will be the consumers' share of a sales tax and the greater will be the sellers' share. Conversely, the more inelastic the demand, the greater will be the buyers' share of the tax and the less will be the sellers' share.

Proposition 14.2. For a given demand, the higher the price elasticity of supply, the less will be the sellers' share of a sales tax and the greater will be the buyers' share. Conversely, the more inelastic the supply, the greater will be the sellers' share of the tax and the less will be the buyers' share.

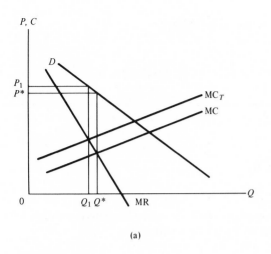

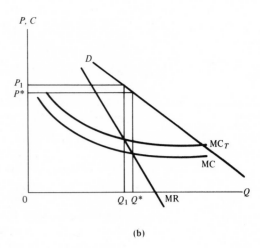

(a)   (b)

FIGURE 14.9

In a perfectly competitive market, unless the demand and/or supply are perfectly elastic or perfectly inelastic, a sales tax will be shared by both sellers and buyers. Under monopoly, however, monopolists may not bear the burden of a sales tax, and, in special cases, they may even benefit from it. Because the monopolist is the industry, the burden of a sales tax is determined by the shapes of the demand and cost (not supply) curves. We shall first demonstrate this graphically and then provide an algebraic proof of the price behavior due to a sales tax.

Consider Figure 14.9, in which part (a) shows a rising MC, whereas part (b) shows a decreasing MC. It can be seen that with the same demand and corresponding MR curves, the price will increase less in the case of a rising MC than in the case of a decreasing MC for a given sales tax. In the latter case, the increase in price may actually be greater than the tax, thereby benefitting the monopolist.

Under monopoly, with MC decreasing price may rise by more than the tax

For the special case of straight-line demand and MC curves, it is possible to make more specific statements. In such a case, if the MC curve is positively sloped in the relevant range, then the steeper the slope of the MC curve, the less the increase in price for a given demand and tax. In any event, the increase in price will be less than half of the tax. On the other hand, when the MC curve is negatively sloped, then the steeper the slope of the MC curve, the greater will be the increase in price for a given demand and tax. If the MC curve has the same slope as the demand curve, then the increase in price will be precisely the amount of the tax. However, if the MC curve has a steeper slope than the demand curve, then the increase in price will be greater than the tax. The above statements can be proved using the following algebra.

A linear demand function can be written

$$P = A - aQ \qquad\qquad (14.17)$$

where, as usual, P and Q denote the price and quantity of the commodity, respectively, and A and a are positive constants.

By definition, the total revenue R is equal to price multiplied by quantity. With the demand function (14.17), R is

$$R = AQ - aQ^2 \qquad\qquad (14.18)$$

The marginal revenue MR is

$$MR = A - 2aQ \qquad\qquad (14.19)$$

The MR function has a negative slope of $-2a$, which indicates that it is twice as steep as the demand function.

A straight-line MC curve can be written

$$MC = B + bQ \qquad\qquad (14.20)$$

where B and b are constants; furthermore, b is the slope of the MC curve ($b > 0$ for a positively sloped MC curve and $b < 0$ for a negatively sloped MC curve).

Without a tax, the first-order condition for profit maximization requires that $MR = MC$. Equating (19.19) and (14.20) and solving for Q, we obtain the equilibrium quantity:

$$Q^* = (A - B)/(2a + b) \qquad\qquad (14.21)$$

Substituting the equilibrium quantity (14.21) into the demand function (14.17), we see that the equilibrium price is

$$P^* = (aA + bA + aB)/(2a + b) \qquad\qquad (14.22)$$

A unit sales tax can be considered an increase in the MC. Thus, with a unit tax T, the after-tax MC can be written

$$MC_T = (B + T) + bQ \qquad\qquad (14.23)$$

The after-tax equilibrium quantity Q_T is derived by equating (14.19) and (14.23) and solving for Q. We have

$$Q_T^* = (A - B - T)/(2a + b) \qquad\qquad (14.24)$$

From (14.21) and (14.24), it can be seen that the equilibrium quantity after the tax is less than it was before the tax and that the decrease in quantity due to the tax depends on the amount of the tax, the slope of the demand curve, and the slope of the MC curve. Equations (14.21) and (14.24) yield

$$\Delta Q = Q^* - Q_T^* = T/(2a + b) \qquad\qquad (14.25)$$

Thus, the higher the tax, the larger the change in quantity Q.

The equilibrium price after the tax can be derived by substituting (14.24) into the demand function (14.17). Therefore, the after-tax equilibrium price P_T^* is

$$P_T^* = (aA + bA + aB + aT)/2(a + b) \qquad (14.26)$$

which can also be written

$$P_T^* = P^* + aT/(2a + b) \qquad (14.27)$$

The change in price due to the tax ΔP is

$$\Delta P = P_T^* - P^* = aT/(2a + b) \qquad (14.28)$$

Thus, the higher the tax, the larger the change in price P.

It is immediately clear that if the MC curve is positively sloped, then $b > 0$, and, for a given a, slope of demand function, and tax T, the larger the b (i.e., the steeper the MC curve), the smaller the increase in price due to the tax. When $b > 0$, $a/(2a + b) < \frac{1}{2}$; hence, the increase in price cannot be as much as half of the tax.

When $b < 0$, the larger the absolute value of b, the smaller the value of $2a + b$ and thus the larger the value of $a/(2a + b)$. When the MC curve has the same slope as the demand curve, $|b| = a$. As a result, $a/(2a + b) = 1$, that is, the increase in price is precisely the amount of the tax. When $|b| > a$, $2a + b < a$; hence, $a/(2a + b) > 1$. As a result, the increase in price due to the tax will be greater than the tax. This proves the statements made earlier.

Given equally sloped demand and supply curves, price will rise by the amount of the tax

It may seem that if $|b| > 2a$ and $b < 0$, then the change in price will be negative for positive T; that is, the tax may result in a lower monopoly price. However, when this is the case, the second-order condition for profit maximization is violated, and the equality of MC and MR results in minimum rather than maximum profit. Thus, it cannot be considered as equilibrium.

In summary, we see that the shifting and incidence of a sales tax not only depends on the shapes of the demand and supply curves, but that under conditions of imperfect competition (in our illustration, monopoly), the slope of the MC curve (not supply curve) becomes a relevant factor. One of the problems that should be obvious to the student by now—and to which we have alluded before (see especially Chapter 7)—is that we do not have very good information about the price elasticity of the market demand curve for different commodities. Although a number of econometric studies have been carried out in order to establish the price elasticity for selected commodities or classes of commodities, they are based on data that may be time biased and/or limited over a given range. Similarly, supply curves, with the cost information that is available, are susceptible to misspecification. Consequently, the amount of sharing of the sales tax, together with the price impact of such a tax, does not lend itself to tidy measurement. Nevertheless, knowledge of the role that the shapes of the demand, supply, and cost curves play in the shifting and incidence of a sales tax is helpful in arriving at reasoned assessments regarding the efficacy of such taxes.

14.2.2 The Shifting and Incidence of the Personal Income Tax

Economists generally agree that any kind of income tax is more difficult to shift than a sales tax. However, their agreement ends at this point. Thus, whereas some economists argue that the income tax cannot be shifted and the burden rests on those who pay it, others argue that the tax can at least partially be shifted, either forward, backward, or both. Because a complete theory of the shifting and incidence of income taxes would demand more space than can be given to the subject in this book, we shall limit our discussion to a theoretical treatment that is connected with the material covered in the preceding chapters.

The shifting and incidence of the personal income tax can be examined in the context of either imperfect labor markets with strong unions or under conditions of perfect competition. In the former case, wage rates are primarily determined at the bargaining table. If there is bilateral monopoly (i.e., a strong union on one side and a monopoly employer on the other), we have shown (see Section 11.4) that the wage rate will be theoretically indeterminate. Under such circumstances, a theoretical discussion of the shifting and incidence of the personal income tax would be fruitless. However, one can, with reason, argue that the wage settlement will likely be at a higher level with a personal income tax than in its absence. This is because union officials will be under strong pressure from the membership to insist on a wage rate that will leave their take-home pay at least as high after the tax as it was before the tax. Moreover, realism will dictate that the management of the firm or the group of employers avoid a long and disasterous strike, particularly if stockholders and bondholders are concerned about the current returns on their investment.

In the environment just described, there will be a likelihood of a backward shift of the personal income tax onto employers, who, in turn, may be able to shift the burden (at least partially) onto buyers of the product through a price increase. Employers may also be able to shift the burden onto suppliers of inputs other than labor by a reduction in purchase prices. At any rate, it seems reasonable to assume that the incidence of the personal income tax will not fall exclusively on the one who pays it. Other things being equal, we should expect that, with strong labor unions, the collective bargaining process will produce at least a partial shifting of the personal income tax. The incidence of this tax on others (employers, consumers, and suppliers of inputs) will depend on

Strong unions can produce a backward shifting of the personal income tax

the price elasticity of demand for and/or supply of the product(s) in question.

If perfect competition prevails in the labor market, the shifting of the personal income tax will depend on whether the wage rate will rise due to the tax: An increase in the wage rate will imply that the tax is shifted, whereas no change in the wage rate will imply that the tax is not shifted. We have already shown that, in a perfectly competitive market, the wage rate can change only if either the demand or the supply (or both) shift (see Chapter 11). In the absence of a shift of either, the market price will not change. Therefore, we shall consider the effect of a personal income tax in the context of perfectly competitive labor markets by examining the possible shifts in the demand and supply curves which may be engendered by the tax.

In Chapter 10, we showed that the demand for labor is given by the value of the marginal product (VMP) or marginal revenue product (MRP) curve for labor when labor is the only variable input. If more than one variable input is involved, the analysis becomes more complicated; however, the demand for labor is still determined by the MP of labor, but in combination with the MPs of the other variable inputs and the MRPs that they produce. Theoretically, the personal income tax does not enter into the production function of a commodity as an independent variable. This implies that the MP of the productive factors is not a function of the tax. Similarly, the price or MR of the product is not directly related to the personal income tax. Thus, we can conclude that the tax may not produce a shift in the demand curve for labor.

Although the personal income tax is not likely to produce a shift in the demand curve for labor under conditions of perfect competition in the labor market, the same cannot be said for the supply curve. Given a consumer's preference pattern, the supply curve will shift because the budget of the consumer, who is also a worker, is based on his or her take-home pay (i.e., after-tax net wage rate). Thus, that portion of wages which goes to pay the income tax is not available to the worker for spending. Consequently, given the worker's preference pattern, the imposition of an income tax will result in a shift in the supply curve for labor. This can be illustrated with reference to Figure 11.4, which is reproduced here as Figure 14.10.

In a competitive labor market an income tax shifts the labor supply curve leftward

Recall that in Chapter 11 we derived the supply curve for labor in part (b) of Figure 11.4 from infinitely many equilibrium points such as E and E_1 when the wage rate underwent continuous change, as represented by the changes in the budget line in part (a). From part (a) in Figure 14.10, which is identical to part (a) of Figure 11.4, we can see that the budget line $\overline{A'B}$ represents a lower wage rate than budget line $\overline{AB}$ and that more leisure ($\overline{0S_1}$ compared to $\overline{0S_0}$) and less labor ($\overline{S_1B}$ compared to $\overline{S_0B}$) will

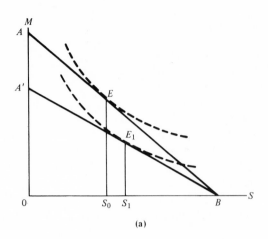 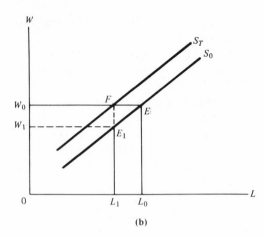

(a)   (b)

FIGURE 14.10

result from the lower wage rate.[11] Hence, points E_1 and E on the positively sloped supply curve S_0 in part (b) are derived from and correspond to points E_1 and E in part (a). Moreover, $\overline{0L_0}$ and $\overline{0L_1}$ in part (b) correspond, respectively, to $\overline{S_0B}$ and $\overline{S_1B}$ in part (a). Finally, in part (b), w_0 is the equilibrium wage rate that corresponds to budget line $\overline{AB}$, whereas w_1 is the equilibrium wage rate that corresponds to budget line $\overline{A'B'}$.

Given the above construct, imagine that the wage rate before the tax is w_0, but that when a personal income tax is imposed on wages, the after-tax net wage rate is $w_1 < w_0$ (or, in essence, a budget of $\overline{A'B}$, which represents a lower take-home wage rate than before the tax). To put it another way, we can see that for the wage rate w_0 before the imposition of the tax, the supply of labor is $\overline{S_0B} = \overline{0L_0}$, but that with the tax the supply of labor becomes $\overline{S_1B} = \overline{0L_1}$. Therefore, we may note that for the wage rate w_0, point E in part (b) is on the supply curve S_0 without the tax, whereas point F will be on a different supply curve—S_T—with the tax. Point F is directly above point E_1 because the supply of labor is now $\overline{0L_1}$ for a wage rate w_1 without the tax and the same for an after-tax net wage rate (again w_1) for the nominal wage rate w_0. This shows that when the supply curve of labor is positively sloped, a personal income tax will result in a leftward shift of the supply curve, as shown by S_T in part (b) of Figure 14.10.

In Chapter 11, we noted that economists recognize the possible phenomenon of the labor supply curve bending backward when the wage rate rises above a certain level (see Figure 11.4). It is important to note for our immediate purpose that the labor supply

---

[11] Students may wish to refresh their understanding of the construct of Figure 14.10 by referring to Section 11.1.

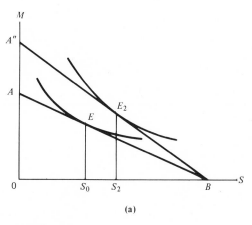

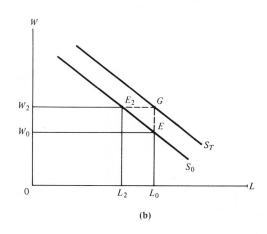

(a)   (b)

FIGURE 14.11

curve under such circumstances will not shift to the left as a result
of the imposition of an income tax. This condition holds because,
in the relevant range, the labor supply curve is negatively sloped.
However, a shift of the supply curve to the right is possible. This
is illustrated in Figure 14.11, in which parts (a) and (b) correspond
to the upper portions of parts (a) and (b) of Figure 11.4 (and thus
Figure 14.10).

From part (a) of Figure 14.11, we can see that the budget line
$\overline{A''B}$ corresponds to the wage rage w_2 in part (b) and that the
labor supply $\overline{S_2B}$ in part (a) corresponds to $\overline{0L_2}$ in part (b), that
is, $\overline{S_2B} = \overline{0L_2}$. For the lower wage rate w_0, the corresponding
labor supply is larger: $\overline{S_0B} = \overline{0L_0}$. Thus within the relevant range,
the supply curve for labor is negatively sloped.

Again, let us imagine that a personal income tax is imposed
such that the after-tax net wage rate is w_0. In part (a), the budget
line AB, by construction, corresponds to the after-tax net wage
rate w_0 in part (b). In addition, point E in part (a) corresponds
to point E in part (b) without the income tax. Finally, points E
and E_2 are on the same supply curve [S_0 in part (b)] for different
wage rates without the tax. Now consider the budget lines
$A''B$ and AB for the nominal wage rate w_2 (the former before the
tax and the latter after the tax). Then point G in part (b), which
corresponds to point E in part (a), and point E_2 in part (b), which
corresponds to point E_2 in part (a), will be on different supply
curves for the same nominal wage rate w_2. Note that point G in
part (b) will lie directly to the right of point E_2 and directly above
point E. Since the relationship between G and E_2 in part (b) is
valid for any negatively sloped labor supply curve, we may conclude that the utility-maximizing behavior of workers implies a
rightward shift of the labor supply curve (in our case, from S_0 to
S_T) due to the imposition of a personal income tax when the labor
supply curve is negatively sloped.

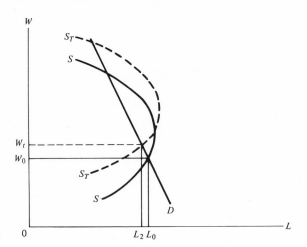

FIGURE 14.12

*An income tax will
likely raise the
market wage rate
whatever the labor
supply curve's slope*

The arguments of the preceding paragraphs imply the relationship between the backward bending labor supply curves before and after a personal income tax is imposed shown in Figure 14.12, in which $\widehat{SS}$ is the labor supply curve before the tax is imposed and $\widehat{S_T S_T}$ is the labor supply curve after the tax is imposed. Since this relationship holds for each and every worker, it must also hold for the market (aggregate) supply. For the sake of simplicity, we can refer to $\widehat{SS}$ and $\widehat{S_T S_T}$ as the market labor supply curves before and after the tax, respectively. Hence, we can conclude that, with a negatively sloped demand curve for labor, the wage rate will go up and, at the same time, the level of employment will go down when a personal income tax is imposed under conditions of either a positively or a negatively sloped supply curve (see Figure 14.12). However, it should be noted that the equilibrium is stable in the Walrasian sense only when the labor supply curve is positively sloped (see Chapters 6 and 11), whereas it will not be stable in the case of a negatively sloped labor supply curve.

In summary, we can conclude from the above graphical analysis that the personal income tax is likely to be partially shifted to employers. It can also be shown that when the disposable income of consumers decreases as a result of the income tax (due to a lower take-home pay and lower employment in spite of a higher nominal wage rate), the demand curve for consumer goods will shift to the left for a normal good (other things being equal), which, in turn, will result in a lower price on the commodities in question. Thus, we have the likelihood of a partial shift of the tax to producers of consumer goods. However, this part of the tax shift is not certain due to the cost-raising effect of the tax. In any event, our analysis shows that it is presumptuous to argue that the personal income tax cannot be shifted. However, because of the complexity of the possible shifting of the tax, its incidence is difficult to ascertain.

14.2.3 The Shifting and Incidence of the Corporate Income Tax and Mark-Up Pricing

As in the case of the personal income tax, the shifting and incidence of the corporate income tax is a complicated problem. Even experts in the field of public finance do not agree on whether or not the tax can be shifted. For example, Richard Musgrave (see Krzyzaniak and Musgrave, 1963) holds the view that the tax can be shifted, whereas Arnold Harberger (see Harberger, 1962) insists that the incidence of the tax is on the corporation. The work of Musgrave and Krzyzaniak is essentially empirical, whereas that of Harberger is theoretical. However, the Harberger model, which is a two-sector (one corporate, the other unincorporated) general equilibrium model, involves some very stringent assumptions and, as a result, can hardly be considered a representation of the real world. One of the authors (see Sher, 1967) has done research on this topic and is more inclined to agree with the conclusions of Musgrave and Krzyzaniak.

Although not all corporations are big, almost all big business firms are corporations. In 1973, unincorporated (proprietorships and partnerships) business comprised 86% and corporations only 14% of all businesses in the United States. However, in terms of volume of sales, corporations far exceed all other forms of business. This coincides pretty much with the public's impression that corporations, in general, are large businesses. In addition, we can observe that very few corporations are price takers, that is, most (if not all) of them operate under conditions of either monopolistic competition, oligopoly, or monopoly and generally practice mark-up pricing. Furthermore, as we have shown in Chapters 7–9, mark-up pricing and the marginal analysis of traditional microeconomic theory are mutually consistent under the assumptions of perfect information or knowledge (see Assumptions 6.4, 7.4, 8.4, and 9.4).

In Section 7.2.2, we presented an AC mark-up pricing model. It was shown that the computation of a mark-up price by firms actually takes the corporate income tax explicitly into consideration. Consequently, other things being equal, the higher the rate of corporate income tax, the higher the price. To demonstrate this result, we repeat the relevant portion of the derivation of that model.

Let ATC denote the average total cost (excluding the return to capital), P the price, and r the rate of profit. With the pricing formula (7.9) actually used by many business firms (see Section 7.2.2), the following relationship between market price and the corporate income tax rate T is implied:

The AC mark-up pricing model explicitly takes the corporate income tax into consideration

$$P = \frac{\text{ATC}}{1 - r/(1 - T)} \tag{14.29}$$

Formula 14.29 is derived in the following manner. Let the rate of profit r be defined as the after-tax return. Then the after-tax profit per unit (*income after tax*) can be denoted IAT and computed as

$$\text{IAT} = rP \qquad\qquad (14.30)$$

On the other hand, the after-tax profit is equal to the profit before tax IBT minus the corporate income tax $T(\text{IBT})$. Hence, we have the relationship

$$\text{IAT} = \text{IBT} - T(\text{IBT}) = (1 - T)\text{IBT}.$$

By substitution, we have

$$\text{IBT} = rP/(1 - T) \qquad\qquad (14.31)$$

Let the mark-up price be defined as ATC + IBT. This implies the following equation:

$$P = \text{ATC} + rP/(1 - T) \qquad\qquad (14.32)$$

It can be seen that pricing equation (14.29) follows immediately from (14.32) and that the mark-up price in (14.29) is an increasing function of the corporate income tax. To illustrate, assuming ATC = 1 and $r = 0.1$, we have derived the following figures to show the corresponding price for a given tax rate:

T	P	%ΔP due to tax
0.5	1.25	13%
0.4	1.20	8%
0.3	1.16	5%
0.0	1.11	0%

The above figures show that, given a unitary ATC (which excludes a return to equity capital in accord with the business concept of cost, in contrast to the economist's concept, which includes a normal return to owner capital) and a 10% return on gross recepts, the price will be 1.11 without the corporate income tax, 1.16 with a 30% tax, 1.20 with a 40% tax, and 1.25 with a 50% corporate income tax. We also show the percentage increase in price due to the different rates of corporate income tax by using the zero tax price as the base. Thus, we can see that, if the rate of return to the corporation is maintained at 10%, then after imposition of a 50% tax on corporate income, the asking price for its product will rise by 13%. It is also interesting to note that even if the demand for the product is perfectly inelastic (i.e., the quantity that can be sold at a higher price is the same as that which can be sold at a lower price) and the rate of return is maintained at 10%, a 50% corporate income tax rate can only cause an increase in price of 13%, a figure not even close to 50%.

It should be noted that the above calculations are based on the assumption that the corporation can maintain its rate of return after imposition of the tax and that its volume of sales will not be cut by higher prices (i.e., it enjoys a perfectly inelastic demand). In this case, the corporate income tax can be shifted 100%, that is, the corporation will not bear any of the tax. However, such a condition is unlikely because the demand for the commodity, even in the case of a monopoly, is seldom perfectly inelastic. Since the elasticities of demand for products of different industries are usually different, it would be impractical to illustrate the possible shift of the tax for demand curves of many differing shapes and elasticities. However, it is useful to show how the rate of return to corporations will be influenced by a 50% corporate income tax if the corporation cannot raise the price of the product after the tax. This is the extreme case of a perfectly elastic demand, where the tax cannot be shifted. Hence, the incidence of the tax is on the corporation.

Using the same example as before, suppose that the price is 1.11 both before and after the imposition of the corporate income tax (recall that with a perfectly elastic demand, the corporation cannot raise the price). Given the same unitary ATC as before, the rate of return r will be lower. By examining to what extent the rate of return must be reduced for a 50% tax rate in the face of a perfectly elastic demand, we may be able to indicate whether or not the incidence of the tax will be entirely on the corporation (i.e., cannot be shifted). In this case, the rate of return due to the tax can be computed by using Equation (14.29).

Since we know that the after-tax price is 1.11, ATC = 1, and the tax rate is 0.5, we obtain the following expression by substituting these figures into (14.29):

$$1.11 = \frac{1}{1 - r/0.5}$$

We have one equation in one variable (namely, r), and solving for r we obtain $r = 0.0495$. Since the rate of return before the tax was 0.10, we can see that it has been approximately halved by imposition of the 50% corporate income tax. Thus, if the corporation cannot raise its price due to a perfectly elastic demand, the result of the tax is to lower the rate of return to owner capital.

Shifts in corporate income tax can be evaluated in context of historical rates of return

We have used the above two extreme cases (a perfectly inelastic demand and a perfectly elastic demand) to illustrate the complete shifting of the corporate income tax, on the one hand, and a zero shifting of the tax, on the other hand. The determination of which case more closely approximates reality is not a matter of theory, but one of empirical study. However, observation may provide some indication of the likelihood of a shift in the tax. For example, if the corporation is now earning a rate of return of 5% with the corporate income tax, it would earn 10% in the absence of the tax if shifting were not possible (as some economists have argued). Analogously, it can be computed from our example that if the present rate of return is 10% with a 50% tax rate, then it would be 20% in the absence of the tax, again assuming the tax cannot be shifted. A study of corporate returns over a period of time would indicate that it is doubtful that the approximately 50% tax rate has actually cut the corporate rate of return by half. This is why we are inclined to argue that the corporate income tax can at least partially be shifted.

This concludes our treatment of some of the policy questions that can be addressed by using microeconomic theory and our coverage of some of the special topics (especially mark-up pricing) that form a synthesis of the classical and modern approaches. Obviously, many other topics (e.g., marginal cost pricing in theory and practice, returns to education, and the economics of manpower training programs) lend themselves to analysis using the microeconomic approach. However, space limitations preclude their treatment. Those students who are interested in further extending the use of microeconomic theory to problem analysis should refer to the bibliography which follows.

SUMMARY

In this chapter we explained that the problem of simultaneous high rates of inflation and unemployment has created theoretical difficulties for simple-minded macroeconomic analysis, notably for the Phillips curve approach to the trade-off between inflation and unemployment. Granted that the high level of unemployment in the 1930s was essentially due to a deficiency in aggregate demand and that the high rate of inflation immediately following World War II was caused by excess aggregate demand, the inflation and unemployment problem of more recent years cannot be explained by macroanalysis alone. Hence, there is a need for other approaches to the problem. It is in this context that we considered microeconomic analysis and the prevalence of mark-up pricing as offering an explanation to the stagflation of the 1970s. In particular, we argued that inflation may be caused by an exogenous increase in cost that, when combined with the general business practice of mark-up pricing, produces cost-induced inflation, which in turn generates a reduction in effective demand and higher unemployment. Thus, if any exogenous source, such as an increase in oil prices by OPEC, causes an increase in costs that exerts continuous pressure on the economy, the result will be concurrent higher rates of inflation and unemployment.

Against this backdrop of the inflation–unemployment problem, we showed that traditional tight money policy to combat inflation may, in fact, worsen the problem because, given the general practice of mark-up pricing, higher interest rates while causing a decrease in investment and aggregate demand will simultaneously generate higher costs and prices. The problem with macroanalysis is that it focuses attention only on the reduction in aggregate demand while totally ignoring the impact that higher interest rates have on costs and, through mark-up pricing, on prices.

It was also shown that a similar argument can be employed to raise serious doubt about the effectiveness of fiscal policy, especially the use of higher taxes to curb inflation. We argued that although an increase in taxes, in particular income taxes, are regarded as reducing inflationary pressures by a reduction in aggregate demand, macroanalysis fails to consider that an increase in taxes can directly or indirectly increase cost, an increase that, because of the practice of mark-up pricing, simply exacerbates the inflation problem. It is with reference to the cost-increasing potential of taxes that we then examined the shifting and incidence of sales and income taxes in order to show that it is theoretically logical to regard the use of higher taxes to combat inflation as self-defeating in certain circumstances. In conclusion we argued that policy analysis that ignores the cost-based pricing practice of business and the shifting and incidence of taxes is bound to err in addressing the problems of inflation and unemployment.

EXERCISES AND QUESTIONS FOR CHAPTER 14 ON THE APPLICATION OF MICROECONOMIC THEORY TO PUBLIC POLICY ANALYSIS

1. Using partial analysis of the market under conditions of perfect competition, monopoly, monopolistic competition, and oligopoly, show what factors may result in inflation and what factors may result in unemployment. Are the results different for a market under perfect competition as compared to an imperfect market? Explain. Use the graphical method to reinforce your arguments.

2. What kind of changes in the market may cause inflation but reduce unemployment? What kind of changes in the market may cause unemployment but lower prices? What kind of changes in the market may cause *both* inflation *and* unemployment? Is the commonly recognized trade-off between inflation and unemployment in macroeconomics (e.g., the Phillip's curve argument) consistent with all of the above cases? Explain. State the assumption(s) that are involved in your response.

3. In your opinion, what are the main causes for the inflation and high unemployment phenomenon (the so-called "stagflation") of the 1970s? Is the mark-up pricing practice of business firms related in any way to the situation? Explain.

4. Why are the problems of shifting and incidence of a tax important in economic analysis? Explain. (It is a good idea to explain the meaning of the terms "shifting" and "incidence" first.)

5. In your own words, explain how a sales tax paid by consumers can be shifted either to the sellers and/or to employers? Use the knowledge acquired from this book.

6. In your own words, explain whether an income tax on a worker can be shifted? A simple yes or no answer is not sufficient—the reasoning behind your answer is essential. Use the knowledge acquired from this book.

7. Why is the concept of the elasticity of demand important in analyzing the shifting and incidence of the sales tax? Explain.

8. A value-added tax will be paid by producers and/or sellers according to the monetary value added to a commodity or service at each stage of production or marketing until finally purchased by consumers. If producers and/or sellers simply add the tax to the selling price they charge to their customers, does this mean that the producers and/or sellers will not bear the burden of the value-added tax? Explain.

9. The corporate income tax is imposed on the net income of a corporation. Experts do not agree as to whether or not the tax can be shifted. What is your opinion? A simple yes or no answer is not sufficient.

REFERENCES

Allen, R. G. D. (1936). Professor Slutsky's theory of consumer choice, *Rev. Econ. Stud.* **3:** 120–129.

Allen, R. G. D. (1959). *Mathematical Economics,* Macmillan, London.

Andrews, P. S. W. (1949). *Manufacturing Business,* Macmillan, London.

Arrow, K. J. (1951). *Social Choice and Individual Values,* Wiley, New York.

Baumol, W. J., and Malkiel, B. G. (1967). The firm's optimal debt–equity combination and the cost of capital, *Quart. J. Econ.* **81:** 547–578.

Blair, J. M. (1972). *Economic Concentration: Structure, Behavior, and Public Policy,* Harcourt-Brace-Jovanovich, New York.

Blaug, M. (1962). *Economic Theory in Retrospect,* Richard D. Irwin, Homewood, Ill.

Boulding, K. E. (1966). *The Impact of the Social Sciences,* Rutgers University Press, New Brunswick, N.J.

Cameron, Burgess (1968). *Input–Output Analysis and Resource Allocation,* Cambridge University Press, London.

Chamberlin, E. H. (1947). *The Theory of Monopolistic Competition: A Reorientation of the Theory of Value,* Harvard University Press, Cambridge, Mass.

Chenery, H. B., and Clark, P. G. (1965). *Interindustry Economics,* 4th printing, Wiley, New York.

Cournot, A. (1927). *Researches into the Mathematical Principle of the Theory of Wealth,* translated by Nathaniel Bacon, Macmillan, New York, 1927.

Debreu, G. (1954). Representation of preference ordering by a numerical function, in *Decision Processes,* edited by R. M. Thrall, C. H. Coombs, and R. L. Davis, Wiley, New York.

Debreu, G. (1959). *The Theory of Value: An Axiomatic Analysis of Economic Equilibrium,* Yale University Press, New Haven, Conn.

Durand, D. (1952). *The Cost of Debt and Equity Funds for Business: Trends and Problems of Measurement,* National Bureau of Economic Research, New York.

Durand, D. (1959). The cost of capital in an imperfect market: a reply to Modigliani and Miller, *Am. Econ. Rev.* **49**: 639–654.

Edgeworth, F. Y. (1925). The pure theory of monopoly, in his *Papers Relating to Political Economy,* Macmillan, London.

Eitman, W. J. (1960). *Price Determination in Oligopolistic and Monopolistic Situations,* Michigan Business Report No. 33, Bureau of Business Research, School of Business Administration, University of Michigan, Ann Arbor, Mich.

Fisher, I. (1930). *The Theory of Interest as Determined by the Impatience to Spend Income and Opportunity to Invest It,* Macmillan, New York.

Hall, R. L., and Hitch, C. J. (1939). Price theory and business behavior, *Oxford Economic Papers,* No. 2 (May), 12–45.

Harberger, A. C. (1962). The incidence of the corporation income tax, *J. Polit. Econ.* **70**: 215–240.

Henderson, J. M., and Quandt, R. E. (1971). *Microeconomic Theory: A Mathematical Approach,* 2nd ed., McGraw-Hill, New York.

Hicks, J. R. (1937). Mr. Keynes and the classics; a suggested interpretation, *Econometrica* **5**: 147–159.

Hicks, J. R. (1946). *Value and Capital: An Inquiry into Some Fundamental Principles of Economic Theory,* Clarenden, London.

Horngren, C. T. (1972). *Cost Accounting: A Managerial Emphasis,* 3rd ed., Prentice-Hall, Englewood Cliffs, N.J.

Hotelling, H. T. (1938). The general welfare in relation to problems of taxation and railway and utility rates, *Econometrica* **6**: 242–269.

Kaldor, N. (1939). Welfare propositions in economics and interpersonal comparisons of utility, *Econ. J.* **49**: 549–552.

Keynes, J. M. (1935). *The General Theory of Employment, Interest, and Money,* Harcourt-Brace, New York.

Koopmans, T. C. (1957). *Three Essays on the State of Economic Science,* McGraw-Hill, New York.

Koutsoyiannis, A. (1975). *Modern Microeconomics,* Wiley, New York.

Krzyzaniak, M., and Musgrave, R. A. (1963). *The Shifting of the Corporate Income Tax,* John Hopkins Press, Baltimore, Md.

Kuenne, R. E. (1963). *The Theory of General Economic Equilibrium,* Princeton University Press, Princeton, N.J.

Lancaster, K. (1966). A new approach to consumer theory, *J. Polit. Econ.* **74**: 132–157.

Lancaster, K. (1971). *Consumer Demand: A New Approach,* Columbia University Press, New York.

Lancaster, K., and Lipsey, R. G. (1956–1957). The general theory of second best, *Rev. Econ. Stud.* **24**: 11–32.

Lancaster, K. (1974). *Introduction to Modern Microeconomics,* Rand-McNally, Chicago, Ill.

Lanzillotti, R. (1958). Pricing objectives in large companies, *Am. Econ. Rev.* **48**: 921–940.

Leontief, W. (1953). *The Structure of the American Economy, 1919–1939,* 2nd ed., Oxford University Press, New York.

Leontief, W. (1966). *Input–Output Economics,* Oxford University Press, New York.

Lutz, F., and Lutz, V. (1951). *The Theory of Investment of the Firm,* Princeton University Press, Princeton, N.J.

Modigliani, F., and Miller, M. H. (1958). The cost of capital, corporation finance, and the theory of investment, *Am. Econ. Rev.* **48**: 261–297.

Nelson, J. R. (1964). *Marginal Cost Pricing in Practice*, Prentice-Hall, New York.

Phillips, A. W. (1958). The relationship between unemployment and the rate of change of money wage rates in the United Kingdom, 1862–1957, *Economica* **25** (November): 283–299.

Quirk, J. P. (1976). *Intermediate Microeconomics*, Science Research Associates, Chicago, Ill.

Samuelson, P. A. (1965). *Foundations of Economic Analysis*, Harvard University Press, Cambridge, Mass.

Scitovsky, T. (1941). A note on welfare propositions in economics, *Rev. Econ. Stud.* **9**: 77–78.

Sher, W. (1967). *The Burden of Capital and the Shifting of the Corporate Income Tax*, Research Studies in Business, University of Alberta, Edmonton, Alta.

Sher, W. (1968). *The Cost of Capital and Corporation Finance Involving Risk*, paper presented at the Annual Convention of the Econometric Society, December 1968.

Sher, W. (1973). An alternative proof of the M–M theorem on the existence of the firm's optimal capital structure, *Quart. J. Econ.* **87**: 474–481.

Slutsky, E. (1952). On the theory of the budget of the consumer, translated by Olga Ragusa, in *Readings in Price Theory*, Richard D. Irwin, Homewood, Ill.

Smith, Adam (1937). *An Inquiry into the Nature and Causes of the Wealth of Nations*, edited by Edwin Cannan based on the 5th edition of Smith's work, Modern Library, New York.

Sweezy, P. (1939). Demand under conditions of oligopoly, *J. Polit. Econ.* **47**: 568–573.

Von Neumann, J., and Morgenstern, O. (1953). *The Theory of Games and Economic Behavior*, Princeton University Press, Princeton, N.J.

Von Stackelberg, H. (1952). *The Theory of Market Behavior*, translated by Alan T. Peacock, Oxford University Press, New York.

Walras, L. (1954). *Elements of Pure Economics*, translated by William Jaffe, Allen and Unwin, London.

INDEX

A

AC, *see* Average cost
Activity analysis, 119, 121
Additivity assumption, 53
Advertising, 427, 428, 445−446, 460−462, 504
Aggregate demand, *see* Demand, market
AMS, *see* Average marginal cost
Antitrust policy, 699
AP, *see* Average product
AR, *see* Average revenue
Arrow, Kenneth, 189, 659
Assumptions
  in consumer choice, 204
  in market equilbrium, 313−319
  in monopolistic competition, 422−424
  in monopoly, 351−352
  in oligopoly, 464−466
  in perfect competition, 294−296
  in production alternatives, 41−43
  and theory, 9, 11−13, 189, 293
  in theory of firm, 23−24
  in utility theory, 189−193, 196
  in welfare economics, 654
AVC, *see* Average variable cost
Average versus marginal relation, 31−32
Average cost, 129−130, 171−174
  decreasing long-run, 155−158
  fixed, 130
  marginal, 132
  mark-up, 376−380, 384, 386−387, 393−394, 414
  pricing, 369
  variable, 130, 133, 302, 331−336
Average product, 30−31
Average product curve, 34−38
Average revenue, 265−268
Average revenue curve, 249
Average total cost, 130, 133, 735−737
Average variable cost, 130, 133, 302, 331−336
  constant, 138−143, 155−162, 176−181, 432−433

B

Barter, 599
Baseball batting average, 31−32
Baumol−Malkiel theorem, 572
Bilateral monopoly, 563−565
Bonds, 576−578, 593
Break-even chart, 140−141, 332−334, 348−350
Break-even point, 140, 308
Budget constraint, 202−203, 223
  in exchange model, 600−602
  in labor supply, 549−550
Budget equation, 202
Budget line, *see* Budget constraint
Buyer, 183−184, *see also* Consumer

C

Capital, *see also* Money
  and labor and demand, 520−522
  and labor substitution, 83−86
  price of, 551, 570−579, 588−593
Cardinal utility, 188−189, 239, 552
  additive, 656
Cartel, 481−483, 492
Ceiling price, 412−413
CES, *see* Constant elasticity of substitution
Chamberlin, Edward H., 422−424, 427, 428, 439, 453, 455
  model, 470−471, 481, 498−501
  solution, 471, 475
Characteristic approach, 226−229, 245−247
Circularity in preference, 191
Close substitute, 422−424, 457, 464
Cobb−Douglas production function, 39, 43, 96−101, 105−106, 108, 111−114, 118, 127, 169−171, 174, 538−546, 708
Cobweb model, 316
Collective bargaining, *see* Labor, Unions
Collusion, 481−483, 491

Comparable measure, 656−657
Compensated demand, 243
Compensation criterion, 681−683
Competition
    imperfect, *see* Imperfect competition
    monopolistic, 421−451
    in oligopoly, 465−466
    perfect, *see* Perfect competition
    pure, 295−296
Complement, 243
    gross, 244
Compound interest, 588−589
Constant average variable cost, 138−143, 155−162,
    176−181, 432−433
Constant-cost industry, 323, 325
Constant-elasticity demand curve, 263−265, 282−283
Constant elasticity of substitution, 119
Constant marginal utility, 187−188
Constant price elasticity of demand, 406−408
Constant returns to scale, 48, 53, 153−155
Constant-sum game, 483, 487−488, 504
Consumer behavior
    characteristic approach, 226−229, 245−247
    versus production theory, 222−226
    theory, 7−8
Consumer equilibrium, 205−209, 550−553, 599
Consumer preference, 185−186, 233
    circularity in, 191
    and cost, 197, 206−207, 214−216
    degree of, 655−656
    and homogeneous products, 294
    and interpersonal comparison, 655−658, 663
Consumer sovereignty, 655, 659
Contract curve, 607−616, 665, 686−688
Cooperative game, 490−491, 504
Corner solution, 78−80, 208
Cost, *see also* Price
    alternative, 123
    average, 129−130, 155−158, 171−174
    average fixed, 130
    average marginal, 132
    average total, 130, 133
    average variable, 130, 133, 302, 331−336
    change and output level, 115
    and consumer preference, 197, 206−207, 214−216
    direct, 377
    in economics versus cost to business, 124−125
    equation, 69, 100, 126, 165
    explicit, 124
    fixed, 125
    function, 69, 126, 165−166
    implicit, 124
    minimum, 109−111, 119−121, 125
    overhead, 377, 379
    private, 122−123
    schedule, 129
    social, 122−123
    sunk, 100
    total, 124, 126−129
    total fixed, 100, 126−127, 300−301
    total variable, 127, 129, 300−301
Coupon rate, 576

Cournot
    duopoly solution, 467
    model, 467−469, 496−498, 500
Cramer's rule, 102, 104, 114, 238, 240, 497
Cross elasticity of demand, 254−255, 259−260

D

Debreau, Gerald, 189
Debt financing, 571−572
Decision-making, sequential, 304
Decision variable, 10, 428
Decreasing-cost industry, 324, 329−330
Decreasing returns to scale, 100, 154
Demand, 248−278
    compensated, 243
    constant elasticity, 263−265, 282−283
    curve
        for competitive firm, 272−273
        for factors of production, 529−534
        for individuals, 216, 248−253, 279−280
        kinked, 476−478
        for market, 184, 249−253, 279−280
        under monopolistic competition, 424−427,
            453−458
        under monopoly, 353−354, 400−402
    derived, 520
    excess, 346−347
    elasticity, *see* Elasticity of demand
    function, 235−237
    inelastic, 259
    law, 215, 242−243
    and mark-up pricing, 704−705
    market, 184, 249−253, 279−280
        for factors of production, 528−532
    multiple-variable-input
        under imperfect competition, 526−528, 544−546
        under perfect competition, 520−522, 541−543
    one-variable-input
        under imperfect competition, 522−526, 544−546
        under perfect competition, 513−520, 538−540
    unitary elastic, 259, 263
Determinant, 102−104
Differentiation, product, 422−424, 427, 428, 438−439,
    448, 464
Diminishing returns, 32−33, 48, 99, 143, 515
Direct cost, 377
Divisibility, 23, 33, 41, 53
Decreasing returns to scale, 49, 65
Deductive reasoning, 12
Derived demand, 520
Discounted present value, 590−592
Dominance principle, 484, 489−490
Dominant firm price leadership, 479−480
Duopoly, 466−476, 496−503

E

Econometrics, 275
Economic models, 288, 290, 292
Economic rent, 125, 568−569

Economics
    classical, 8
    definition of, 7
    normative, 653−654
    positive, 653−654
    welfare, 596, 653−697
Edgeworth box, 19, 603−610, 616, 622, 660, 663,
    666
Edgeworth model, 472−476, 501
Elasticity of demand, 259, 280−286
    cross, 254−255, 259−260, 280
    determinants of, 262−263
    income, 254−255, 280−281
    price, 253−254, 256−263, 271−272, 280−281,
        283−286, 725−726
    and substitution, 530−532
Elasticity of price, 262
Elasticity of substitution, 88−89, 117−119
Employment, see also Labor
    full, 334, 702, 703
    unemployment, 701−706, 715
Engel curve, 212−213, 225
Envelope of a curve, 149, 151, 155, 158, 162, 166−168
Equilibrium, see also General equilibrium analysis,
        Optimality
    consumer, 205−209
    in duopoly, 469−470, 472−473
    of firm and industry, 319
    long-run
        of the market, 319−323, 330, 343−345
        and monopolistic competition, 435−445, 459−460
        and monopoly, 363−365
    and Pareto optimality, 664−672
    partial, analysis, 82, 595−596, 717
    price, 312, 317−318
    production, 73−74, 307−309, 613−615
    short-run
        of the market, 311−319, 341−343
        and monopolistic competition, 427−434, 458−459
        and monopoly, 355−361
    stability of, 317−319, 346−348, 559
    uniqueness of, 315−316, 345−346, 559
Equity financing, 571−572
Equivalency of mark-up models, 389−395, 417−420
Ethics, 653−654
Excess demand, 346−347, 623−628, 644−647
Excess profit, 321, 325−326
Exchange model, 598−609
    indifference curve in, 599−609
Exclusion principle, 680
Expansion path, 80−81, 106, 146, 149, 225, 708
Explicit cost, 124
Extensive margin, 39
External diseconomy
    in consumption, 677
    in production, 123, 678−679
External economy
    in consumption, 677
    in production, 123, 329, 677−678
Externalities
    absence of, 23−24
    and consumer preference, 192−193, 233

    and Pareto optimality, 671
    and public goods, 679−681

F

Factor of production, 512
    supply and demand for, 547−548
Federal Reserve System, 575−579
Firm
    definition of, 21−24
    interdependence of, 464
    numbers of
        in industry, 297−298, 323−324, 720
        for oligopoly, 466
First-degree price discrimination, 366
Fixed cost, 125
Fixed input, 26, 28−29
    and intensive/extensive margin, 39
Free disposal, 23, 41
Free enterprise, 612, 615
Free good, 314−315, 343

G

Game theory, 483−493, 503−509
    and cooperative versus noncooperative game, 490
General equilibrium analysis, 595−652, 717
    input−output analysis, 628−631, 648−652
    iterative method, 631−634
    in production, 609−615
    Walras model, 623−628
General Motors, 380−381
Giffen good, 216−221, 243, 252
Gini coefficient, 511
Good
    free, 314−315, 343
    Giffen, 216−221, 243, 252
    inferior, 210−211, 213
    normal, 210−211, 213
Goods, public, 679−681
Government
    intervention, 318−319, 679−680
        in natural monopoly, 368−370
    spending, 715−716
    subsidy, 369−370, 675, 680n
Greed, 191
Gross complement, 244, 259
Gross substitute, 244, 259

H

Hessian determinant, 109, 110, 236, 542
Hicks, John R., 24n, 189, 217, 706
Homogeneity
    degree of, 49
    of inputs, 24, 41−42
    in production function, 89−91, 98−99, 421−424,
        464
Homotheticity, 90−91, 99
Hotelling, Harold, 674
Hurwicz, Leonid, 189

I

ICC, *see* Income consumption curve
Imperfect competition, 21, 273, 291, *see also* Monopoly
and demand
    one-variable, 522−526, 544−546
    multiple-variable, 526−528, 544−546
    and interest rate, 574−575
Implicit cost, 124
Income
    change and consumption, 209−214, 216−221
    consumption curve, 212, 215, 225
    distribution, 183, 511−512, 662
    effect, 217−221, 555
    elasticity of demand, 254−255
    after tax, 736
    term, 242
Increasing-cost industry, 323, 327
Increasing returns to scale, 49−50, 65, 100, 153−155,
    330−331, 438
Independence
    of processes, 53
    of production cost, 310−311
Independent commodity, 243−244, 259
Indifference
    in production decision, 305
    in utility, 190−191
Indifference curve, 193−197, 222
    in exchange model, 599−609
    in labor analysis, 549
    and marginal rate of substitution, 197−198, 200
Indifference map, 193, 222
Inductive reasoning, 12
Industry, 288
    constant-cost, 323, 325
    decreasing-cost, 324, 329−330
    and differentiated products, 423
Industry supply curve, 297−298
    short-run, 310−311
Inelasticity
    of demand, 259
    perfect, 12, 17
    of supply, 567
Inferior factor of production, 84
Inferior good, 210−211, 213
Inflation, 701−706, 714−716
Inflection point, 37−38
Input
    definition of, 24−25
    direct, 632, 635
    fixed, 26, 28−29, 621−623
    graphing of, 33
    homogeneity of, 24, 41−42
    indirect, 633, 635
    substitution between, 58−62
    two variable, 45−94
    variable, 26, 28−29
Input−output analysis, 628−631, 648−652
Input−output table, 629−630, 648
Intensive margin, 39
Interdependence of firms, 464
Interest
    compound, 588−589

rate, 572−579, 706
    and bond prices, 576−578
    determination of, 570−571, 575−579
    pure, 576
Interior solution, 79−80, 207
Interpersonal comparisons, 655−658, 663
Investment financing, 571−572
Isocline, 81
Isocost curve, 70−72, 75, 78−80, 146−147, 612
Isoquant, 55−65, 71−72, 75, 78−80, 86, 147, 610−611
Isoquant map, 65−66, 144, 222
Isoquant smooth curve, 55−56, 76

J

Jevons, W. Stanley, 186

K

Kaldor, Nicholas, 681
Keynes, John M., 334, 703
Koopmans, Tjalling, 189

L

Labor, *see also* Employment, Unions
    backward-bending supply curve of, 315−316, 554−555,
        558−559, 732, 734
    and capital and demand, 520−522
    and capital substitution, 83−86
    cost and profit, 514−515, 527
    exploitation of, 562
    supply of
        and income tax, 731
        of an individual, 548−557, 582−584
        market, 557−559
Lagrange multiplier, 105, 107−108, 111, 236, 642, 691
Land, 12, 17, 183, 565−570
    price of, 566−570
Law of diminishing marginal utility, 187−188
Law of diminishing returns, 32−33, 48, 99, 143, 515
Law of variable proportions, 32−33, 143
Leadership, dominant firm price, 479−480
Leadership−followership duopoly, 501−503
Least squares method, 275−276
Leisure, 549−557
Leontief, Wassily, 19, 57, 628
    matrix, 634−636, 650−652
Lexicographic ordering, 192
Linear demand function, 403−404
Linear marginal cost, 405−406, 408
Linear programming, 78, 119, 121
Long-run, 26, 45−46
    cost curve, 153−162, 169−171
    cost function, 143−162
    definition of, 125, 297
    equilibrium, 319−323, 330, 343−345
        and monopolistic competition, 435−445, 459−460
        and monopoly, 363−365
    firm analysis, 319−323
    industry analysis, 319−330
    industry supply curve, 323−330

Lorenz curve, 511
Loss minimization, 300−302
Low-cost firm price leadership, 480

M

Macroeconomics
  definition of, 8−9
  and inflation/unemployment, 701−704, 714
Magic, 1−2
Margin
  extensive, 39
  intensive, 39
Marginal analysis
  application of, 4−6
  versus average, 31−32
  and profit maximization, 302−306, 357−360
Marginal cost, 5, 131−134
  long-run curve, 153−162, 173−174
  and mark-up pricing, 707−712
  pricing, 674−675
  with respect to quality, 440
  short-run curve, 151−152, 171−173
  and varying output, 137
Marginal product, 31, 95
  decreasing, 32−33, 38, 99
Marginal product curve, 34−38
Marginal rate of product transformation, 617−620
Marginal rate of substitution, 197−201, 235, 609, 618−621
  and Pareto optimality, 665−666
Marginal rate of technical substitution, 58−62, 98−99
  decreasing, 60−62
  and Pareto optimality, 667−669, 693
  and technology, 60
Marginal revenue, 265−268
  curve, derivation of, 269−270
  and price elasticity of demand, 271−272
  product, 523−528, 561−563
  with respect to quality, 440
Marginal utility, 186−188, 234
  constant, 187−188
  diminishing, 187−188
  ratio of, 199−200, 235
Mark-up parameter, 373, 374, 376, 378
Mark-up pricing, 10, 703−704
  and marginal cost, 707−712
  models, 372−387, 413−414
  and monetary policy, 706−721
  and monopolistic competition, 434
  and monopoly, 387−395
  naive, 372−376, 384, 386, 392−393
Market, 287−288
  demand, 183−184
    curve of, 249−253, 312
    in macroeconomics, 702−703
  entry, 325−326, 464−465
  equilibrium
    long-run, 319−323, 330, 343−345
    short-run, 311−319, 341−343
  interrelationship of, 595−596
  opportunity, 73
  period, 297

power, 291−292
price determination of, 311
research, 273, 275
Marketing new product, 226−229
Marshall, Alfred, 186, 346−347
Matrix
  payoff, 483−489, 504−506
  square, 102−104
  two-way, 66−67
Maximin−Minimax principle, 485−486, 492, 505−506
MC, *see* Marginal cost
Measurement
  comparable, 656−657
  elasticity of, 253−255
Microeconomics
  definition of, 8−9
  relevance of, 13−14
Monetarist, 578
Monetary policy, 575−579, 701−721, *see also* Money
Money, *see also* Capital
  and consumer preference, 197
  and federal monetary policy, 575−579
  marginal utility of, 187−188
  price of, 551, 570−579, 588−593
  tight, 706, 714
Monopolistic competition
  assumptions about, 422−424
  demand curve for, 424−427, 453−458
  versus monopoly, 449
  versus perfect competition, 447−449
  pricing and, 434
Monopoly, *see also* Imperfect competition
  bilateral, 563−565
  and consumer welfare, 365
  demand under, 353−354, 400−402
  long-run equilibrium of, 363−365
  versus monopolistic competition, 449
  natural, 154, 331, 368−370
  versus oligopoly, 371
  and Pareto optimality, 673−675
  and price discrimination, 366−368
  profit maximization under, 402−409
  short-run equilibrium of, 355−361
  supply under, 361−363
  theory of pure, 351−352, 392, 395, 415−420
Monopsony, 548
  and wage rate, 560−563, 584−588
MP, *see* Marginal product
MR, *see* Marginal revenue
MRP, *see* Marginal revenue product
MRPT, *see* Marginal rate of product transformation
MRS, *see* Marginal rate of substitution
MRTS, *see* Marginal rate of technical substitution
MU, *see* Marginal utility

N

Naive mark-up pricing, 372−376, 384, 386, 392−393, 413−414
Natural monopoly, 331
Net income, 377
New product markets, 226

Noncooperative game, 484, 490–491, 504
Nonsatiation, 191
Nonzero-sum game, 483, 488–493, 504
Normal factor of production, 84
Normal good, 210–211, 213, 717
Northern States Power Company, 704
Numeraire, 551, 626

O

Occam's razor, 189, 239, 293
Offer curve, 599, 602, 608–609
Oligopoly, 371, 463–509
    and collusion, 481–483
    and game theory, 483–493, 503–509
    and price leadership, 478–481, 501–503
    and price stability, 476–478
OPEC, 481, 492
Open market operations, 576–578
Opportunity cost, *see* Cost, alternative
Optimality
    in input combinations, 67–68, 71–75, 100, 104, 113
    of firm size, 319–320
    Pareto, *see* Pareto optimality
    of plant size, 144–151, 155–162, 363–364
Ordinal utility, 189–190, 192–193, 239, 549, 657
Organization of Petroleum Exporting Countries, 481, 492
Output
    and cost, 126–129
    definition of, 24–25
    effect, 84, 116
    efficiency
        economic, 63
        technical, 63–64
    graphing of, 33
    input–output table, 629–630, 648
    maximum, 26, 42–43, 107–109
    and plant size, 144–151
    and production processes, 46–48
Overhead cost, 377, 379
Overshot, 328

P

Pairwise comparison, 50–51
Parameter, 127
Pareto noncomparability, 661, 676
Pareto optimality, 19, 659–676
    and contract curve, 665, 686–688
    and equilibrium, 664–672
    and monopoly, 673–675
    and perfect competition, 694–697
    and production, 667–669, 688–690
Pareto superiority, 660–661
Partial analysis, 82, 595–596, 717
Payoff matrix, 483–489, 504–506
Payroll tax, 720
PCC, *see* Price consumptive curve
Perfect competition, 10–11, 21, 288–290, 294–296, 338–350
    breakdown of, 330–334
    demand for one variable input, 513–520
    demand for multiple variable inputs, 520–522

efficiency conditions of, 672
    versus monopolistic competition, 447–449
    and Pareto optimality 664–672, 694–697
    unbiasedness condition of, 672
Perfect information, *see* Perfect knowledge
Perfect knowledge, 23, 41, 295–296, 352
Perfect substitute, 200–201
Phillips curve, 702–703
Planning horizon, 144
Plant size, 144–151, 155–162, 363–364
    and underutilization, 42
Point of bliss, 8, 196
Point of inflection, 37–38
PPC, *see* Production possibility curve
Preference, consumer, *see* Consumer preference
Price
    of capital, 570–579, 588–593
    ceiling, 412–413
    change and equilibrium, 214–216, 239–243
    consumption curve, 215–216, 225, 248
    discrimination, 366–368, 410–412
        and regulation, 370
    effect of taxes on, 729
    elasticity of demand, 253–254, 256–263, 271–272, 280–281, 283–286, 725–726
        and marginal revenue, 271–272
        for productive factor, 530–532
    equilibrium, 312, 317–318
    of land, 566–570
    leadership, 478–481
    maker, 288, 291
    profit-maximizing, 713
    ratio and consumer equilbrium, 206–207
    rise in, 712–713
    taker, 288, 290
    –unemployment model, 702–703
    variation curve, 255
    war, 473, 475, 501
Pricing, *see also* Cost
    average cost mark-up, 376–380, 384, 386–387, 393–394, 414
    comparison of models, 383–395
    marginal cost, 674–675
    and monopolistic competition, 434, 454–458
    naive mark-up, 373–376, 384, 386, 392–393, 413–414
    in oligopoly, 476–478
    target profit, 380–384, 387, 394–395, 414, 713
Prisoner's dilemma, 488–493, 504
Product differentiation, 422–424, 427, 428, 438–439, 448, 464
Product mix, 621, 658, 667, 668
Production
    alternatives, 41, 58, 654
    curve, 25–26, 29, 33–38
    definition of, 25
    efficiency, 50–58
        graphing of, 52
    equilibrium, 73–74, 307–309, 613–615
    expansion path, 80–81
    function, 29, 95, 514
        homogenous, 89–91, 98–99
        homothetic, 90–91, 99
    and general equilibrium analysis, 609–615

inferior factor of, 84
normal factor of, 84
with one variable input, 28−44
and Pareto optimality, 667−669, 688−690
possibility curve, 615−617
process, 46−48
    definition of, 46
schedule, 25−26, 29−30
stages of, 38−39, 64−65
theory versus consumption theory, 222−226
Productive factor, *see* Factor of production
Profit
    in business versus economics, 372
    excess, 321
    margin, 130, 372
    maximization
        as a goal, 21−23
        and labor cost, 514−520
        and marginal analysis, 5, 41, 302−306, 357−360
        under monopoly, 402−409
        in oligopoly, 476−478
        proof, 304−306
        and quality, 439−446
        total revenue−total cost approach, 299−302,
            305−306, 355−357
Public goods, 680
Public utility, 331
Pure competition, 295−296
Pure exchange, 598−609, 666−667, 690
Pure monopoly, 351−352
Pure rate of interest, 576

Q

Quality
    competition and, 439
    of product, 427−428, 439−446, 460−462
Quasi-rent, 18, 569−570

R

Reaction function, 372, 497, 501−502
Reality and theory, 9
Reallocation of resources, 611−612, 615
Record industry, 273−274
Rediscount rate, 576
Religion, 1
Rent, 566−570
    economic, 568−569
Reserve capacity, 42
Resources
    allocation alternatives for, 658
    reallocation of, 611−612, 615
Returns to scale, 48−50, 99
Ricardo, David, 11, 18, 567
Risk, 572−573

S

Saddle point, 486, 506, 508
Sales
    competition, 445−446, 460−462
    events, 426−427

tax, 721−730
Satisfaction, *see* Utility
Science, 2
Scitovsky criterion, 683
Second best, theory of, 675−676
Second-degree price discrimination, 366
Seller, 183
Sherman Antitrust Act, 481
Shifting of taxes, 722−739
Short-run, 26, 43, 45−46
    cost curve, 134−140
    cost function, 126−140, 166−169
    definition of, 125, 297
    excess profits, 325−326
    marginal cost curve, 151
    equilibrium, 311−319, 341−343
        under competition, 427−434, 458−459
        under monopoly, 355−360
    market analysis, 298−319, 338−341
    supply curve, 307−311
Shutdown point, 309
Size, optimal
    of firm, 319−320
    of plant, 144−151, 155−162, 363−364
Slutsky, Eugene, 189
    equation, 216−217, 221, 239−243, 252, 530
Slutsky−Hicks theory, 217−219
Social
    cost, 122−123
    science, 6−7
    welfare function, 621
Spill-over effect, 23
Square matrix, 102−104
Stability
    of equilibrium, 317−319, 346−348
    of market, 316−317
Stackelberg model, 501−503
Stages of production, 38−39, 64−65
Stagflation, 703, 714
Strategy, game, 503, 506−507
Subsidy, government, 369−370, 675, 680n
Substitute, 243
    close, 422−424, 457, 464
    gross, 244
    perfect, 200−201
Substitution, 82−88, 116
    constant elasticity of, 119
    effect of, 217, 219, 221, 555−556
    elasticity of, 88−89, 117−119
    and elasticity of demand, 530−532
    and elasticity of price, 262
    marginal rate of, 197−201, 235, 609, 618−621
    rate of, *see* Marginal rate of technical substitution
    sensitivity of, 86−88, 121
    term for, 241−243
Sunk cost, 100
Supply, 307
    in factor market, 547−548
    fixed, 566−568
Supply curve
    under monopoly, 361−363
    short-run, 307−310
    short-run industry, 310−311

Supply function, 307
Supply schedule, 307
Survey of Current Business, 636
Sweezy, Paul, 478

T

Tangency condition, 78, 102
Target profit pricing, 380–384, 387, 394–395, 414, 713
Tax
    backward shifting of, 722
    corporate income, 720, 735–739
    forward shifting of, 722
    incidence of, 722
    increase in, 715–716
    payroll, 720
    personal income, 716–718, 730–734
    policy and, 699–700
    sales, 721–730
TC, *see* Total cost
Technology
    matrix of, 630–632, 634, 636, 649
    and production processes, 46–48
Theorem
    definition of, 9, 11
    proving, 12–13
Theory
    and assumptions, 9, 11–13
    definition of, 9, 11
    formulation of, 12
    and reality, 9
Third-degree price discrimination, 366
Three input model, 116
Total cost, 124, 126–129
Total fixed cost, 100, 126–127, 300–301
Total product curve, 33, 35–38
Total revenue, 265–268
Total revenue curve, 249, 263–264
Total revenue–total cost approach, 299–302, 305–306, 355–357
Total variable cost, 127, 129, 300–301
TP curve, *see* Total product curve
TR, *see* Total revenue
Trading, *see* Exchange
TVC, *see* Total variable cost
Two-variable-input model, 45–94
Two-way matrix, 66–67

U

Unanimity principle, *see* Pareto optimality
Unemployment, 701–706, 715
    and inflation rate, 702–703

Unions, labor, 563–565
    and income tax, 717, 730
Unique equilibrium, 315–316, 345–346, 559
Unitary elastic demand, 259, 263
U.S. Bureau of Labor Statistics, 636
Util, 186
Utility, 186
    cardinal, 188–189, 239, 552
        additive, 656
    in exchange model, 598–601, 609, 619–621, 623
    interpersonal comparison of, 655–658, 663
    marginal, 186–188, 234
    maximizing, 204–205, 235–237
        and labor, 548–557, 582–584
    ordinal, 189–190, 192–193, 239, 549, 657
    public, 331
    societal, 655–659

V

Value of marginal product, 516–525, 561–563
Variable input, 26, 28–29
    production stage, 38
Vector notation, 66–67
VMP, *see* Value of marginal product

W

Wage rate
    determination, 557–559, 563–565, 584–588
    increase in, 83–87, 553–556, 717
    and monopsony, 560–563, 584–588
Walras, Leon, 18–19, 186, 346–347
    law, 626, 646
    model, 597, 623–628, 640–648
Welfare economics, 596, 653–677
    definition of, 653
Westinghouse generators, 376
Work, *see also* Employment
    and leisure choice, 549–557

Z

Zero profit multiplier, 377–380
Zero sum game, 273, 483–488, 504, *see also* Nonzero sum game, Game theory
ZPM, *see* Zero profit multiplier